More Fool Me

More Fool Me

STEPHEN FRY

MICHAEL JOSEPH
an imprint of
PENGUIN BOOKS

MICHAEL JOSEPH

Published by the Penguin Group
Penguin Books Ltd, 80 Strand, London WC2R 0RL, England
Penguin Group (USA) Inc., 375 Hudson Street, New York, New York 10014, USA
Penguin Group (Canada), 90 Eglinton Avenue East, Suite 700, Toronto, Ontario, Canada M4P 2Y3
(a division of Pearson Penguin Canada Inc.)
Penguin Ireland, 25 St Stephen's Green, Dublin 2, Ireland (a division of Penguin Books Ltd)
Penguin Group (Australia), 707 Collins Street, Melbourne,
Victoria 3008, Australia (a division of Pearson Australia Group Pty Ltd)
Penguin Books India Pvt Ltd, 11 Community Centre,
Panchsheel Park, New Delhi – 110 017, India
Penguin Group (NZ), 67 Apollo Drive, Rosedale, Auckland 0632, New Zealand
(a division of Pearson New Zealand Ltd)
Penguin Books (South Africa) (Pty) Ltd, Block D, Rosebank Office Park,
181 Jan Smuts Avenue, Parktown North, Gauteng 2193, South Africa

Penguin Books Ltd, Registered Offices: 80 Strand, London WC2R 0RL, England

www.penguin.com

First published 2014
001

Typeset in 13.75/16.25 pt Garamond MT Std by Palimpsest Book Production Ltd, Falkirk, Stirlingshire

Printed in Great Britain by Clays Ltd, St Ives plc

A CIP catalogue record for this book is available from the British Library

HARDBACK ISBN: 978–0–718–17978–6
TRADE PAPERBACK ISBN: 978–0–718–17979–3

www.greenpenguin.co.uk

Dedicated to Jo, my Personal AsSister and subject of 'simply the best decision I ever made in my entire life'. In grateful thanks and with profuse apologies for all the extra work that this will bring . . .

The fool doth think he is wise, yet it is the wise man that knows himself to be the fool

As You Like It, Act 5, Scene 1

The past won't sit still for a moment

Jonathan Meades, 2014

Contents

More Fool Me

Chapter One

There is nothing very appealing about showbusiness memoirs. A linear chronology of successes, failures and blind ventures into new fields is dull enough. And then there is the problem of how to approach descriptions of collaborators and contemporaries:

'She was *adorable* to work with, *incredibly* funny and always intensely cheerful and considerate. To know her was to *worship* her.'

'I was captivated by his talent, how *marvellously* he shone in everything he did. There was a luminosity, a kind of transcendence.'

'She always had time for her fans, no matter how persistent they were.'

'What a *perfect* marriage they had, and what *ideal* parents they were. A golden couple.'

I could there be describing actors, TV show presenters or producers with total accuracy, leaving out only their serial polygamies, chronic domestic abuse, violent orgiastic fetishes and breathtaking assaults on the bottle, the powders and the pills.

Is it right of me to be searingly, bruisingly honest about the lives of others? I am quite prepared to be searingly, bruisingly honest about my own, but I just don't have it in me to reveal to the world that, for example, producer Ariadne Bristowe is an aggressively vile, treacherous bitch who regularly fires innocent assistants just for looking at her the wrong way; or that Mike G. Wilbraham has to give a blow-job to the boom operator while finger-banging the assistant cameraman before he is prepared so much as to think about preparing for a scene. All these things are true, of course, but fortunately Ariadne Bristowe doesn't exist and neither does Mike G. Wilbraham. *OR DO THEY?*

The actor Rupert Everett in his autobiographical writings manages to be caustic in what you might call a Two Species manner: bitchy and catty. The results are hilarious, but I am far too afraid of how people view me to be able to write like that. Very happy to recommend both his volumes of autobiography/memoir to you, however: *Red Carpets and Other Banana Skins* and *The Vanished Years*. Ideal holiday or Christmas reading.

So I now must consider how to present to you this third edition of my life. It must be confessed that this book is an act as vain and narcissistic as can be imagined: the *third* volume of my life story? There are plenty of wholly serviceable single-volume lives of Napoleon, Socrates, Jesus Christ, Churchill and even Katie Price. So by what panty-dribbling right do I present a weary public with yet another stream of anecdote, autobiography and confessional? The first I wrote was a memoir

4

of childhood, the second a chronicle of university and the lucky concatenation of circumstances that led to my being able to pursue a career in performing, writing and broadcasting. Between the end of that second book and this very minute, the minute now that I am using to type this sentence, lies over a quarter of a century of my milling about on television, in films, on radio, writing here and there, getting myself into trouble one way or another, becoming a representative of madness, Twitter, homosexuality, atheism, annoying ubiquity and whatever other kinds of activity you might choose to associate with me.

I am making the assumption that in picking up this book you know more or less who I am. I am keenly aware – how could I not be? – that if one is in the public eye then people will have some sort of view. There are those who thoroughly loathe me. Even though I don't read newspapers or receive violent abuse in the street, I know well enough that there are many members of the British public, and I daresay the publics of other countries, who think me smug, attention-seeking, false, complacent, self-regarding, pseudo-intellectual and unbearably irritating: diabolical. I can quite see why they would. There are others who embarrass me charmingly by their wild enthusiasm; they shower me with praise and attribute qualities to me that seem almost to verge on the divine.

I don't want this book to be riddled with too much self-consciousness. There is a lot to say about the end of the 1980s and early 1990s, and you may find the way I go about it to be meandering. I hope a chronology of sorts will emerge as I bounce from theme to theme. There will inevitably be anecdotes of one kind or another, but it is not my business to tell you about the private lives of others, only of my own. I consider myself incompetent when it comes to the business of living life. Maybe that is why I am committing the inexcusable hubris of offering the world a third written autobiography. Maybe here is where I will *find* my life, in this thicket of words, in a way that I never seem to be able to do outside the bubble I am in now as I write. Me, a keyboard, a mouse, a screen and nothing else. Just loo breaks, black coffees and an occasional glance at my Twitter and email accounts. I can do this for hours all on my own. So on my own that if I have to use the phone my voice is often hoarse and croaky because days will have passed without me speaking to a single soul.

So where do we go from here?

Let's find out.

Catch-up

I have a recurring dream. The doorbell sounds at three in the morning. I struggle out of bed and press the entry-phone button.

'Police, sir. May we come in?'

'Of course, of course.' I buzz them in. A series of charges that I cannot quite make out are chanted at me like psalms. I am arrested and cuffed. It is all very hurried and sudden but entirely good-natured. One of the police-men asks for a photograph with me.

We cut, as dreams so cinematically do, to a courtroom, where a much less sympathetic judge sentences me to six months' imprisonment with hard labour. He is disgusted that someone who should know so much better could have committed so foolish a crime and present so ignoble an example to the young, impressionable people who might errantly look up to him. The judge wishes the sentence could be longer but he must abide by the guide-lines laid down by statute.

To the sound of mingled cheers and jeers I am con-ducted down to the police cells and into the back of a van, which is delightfully decorated and exquisitely supplied with crystal, ice buckets and an amazing array of alcoholic drinks.

'Might as well get lashed, Stephen. Last drinks you're going to have for some while.'

I'm at the prison. All the convicts have turned out to greet me. Their welcome is deafening and not in the least threatening.

A vast dining hall. I sit to eat in a huge wide shot like Cody Jarrett as played by James Cagney in *White Heat*. And then we see me in mid-shot, as cool and unruffled as Tim Robbins's ageless Andy Dufresne, taking my tray to the table.

It is clear that I am not in the joint for some appalling sexual or financial misdemeanour that will cause me to be beaten and tormented by my fellow convicts. I have done something that is wrong, that is disapproved of by 'society' yet which is tolerated with amusement by criminals and even police officers.

Nobody lets me see the newspapers. They will only upset me, I am told. It is all very strange.

Friends visit me. Always staying the other side of the bars. Hugh and Jo Laurie. Kim Harris, my first lover. My literary agent Anthony and my theatrical agent Christian. My sister and PA Jo. There is something they are not telling me, but I am comfortable in prison and feel sorry for them, having to leave and return to the world of bustle and business.

I am in the corridor cleaning the floor with an electric

polisher. It has two rotating discs with gently abrasive pads press-studded to the base, and I enjoy holding it like a pneumatic drill, feeling its power under me, how I have to keep it from flying free of my grip as it pulls like an eager dog at the leash. The floor comes up in a glossy shine. This is the life.

An old lag walks up to me, coughing on his tightly rolled-up cigarette, which wags up and down as he speaks. He has seen a letter in the governor's office, which he Pledges and tidies daily. My sentence is to be extended. I will never leave.

I take the news well. Very well.

I wake up, or the dream peters out or merges into something strange and silly and different.

It is easy to attempt a little oneiromancy here. My real life is a prison, so a real prison would be an escape. That would be the one-line pitch, as they say in Hollywood. I am one who, like so many Britons of a certain class and era, was born to institutions. School houses merge into Oxbridge colleges which merge into Inns of Court or the BBC as it was or into regiments or ships of the line or into one of the two Houses of Parliament or into the Royal Palaces or into Albany or the clubs of Pall Mall and St James's. All very male, all very Anglo-Saxon (a few Jews allowed from time to time – it is vulgar to be racially obsessed), all very cosy, absurd and out of date. If you really want to have a look at this world in its last hurrah just before I was born then you should read the first eight or nine chapters of *Moonraker*, a Bond novel, but with an opening that is simultaneously hilarious, fantastically observed, drool-worthily aspirational and skin-pricklingly suspenseful.

I observed of myself in my second book of memoirs, *The Fry Chronicles*, and earlier in my first, *Moab is My Washpot*, that I seem always to be obsessed with belonging. Half of me, I wrote in *Moab*, yearns to be part of the tribe; the other half yearns to be apart *from* the tribe. All the clubs I belong to – six so-called gentleman's clubs and goodness knows how many more Soho-style media watering-holes – are vivid testament to a soul searching for his place in British society. Maybe prison is the ultimate club for people like me.

'That's institootionalized,' as Morgan Freeman's Red puts it in *The Shawshank Redemption*, the world's favourite film.

I am wary of interpretations. I refuse to interpret my life and its motives because I am not qualified. You may choose to do so. You may find me and my history repugnant, fascinating, indicative of an age now long gone, typical of a breed whose time is up. There are all kinds of ways of looking at me and my story.

If you want to bore someone, tell them your dreams. I seem to have got off on the wrong foot. I plead forgiveness for, while I would not claim that there is anything experimental about this memoir, I would ask you to be ready for a flitting backwards and forwards in time. The experience of writing about this period in my life has had some of the qualities of a dream: unexpected, freakish, disgusting, frightening, incredible and at one and the same time crystal clear and maddeningly occluded. It is my job, I suppose in this far from divine comedy, to be Virgil to your Dante, guiding you as straightforwardly and tenderly as I can through the circles of my particular hell, purgatory and heaven. In the following pages I will try to be as truthful as I can; I will leave interpretation and, generally speaking, motivation, to you.

Very Naughty, but . . . in the Right Spirit

Aside from anything else, there is the problem of plunging in as if you already know my past. . .

Bertie Wooster, the hero and first-person narrator of P. G. Wodehouse's Jeeves stories, used to say to his readers at the beginning of each new book something along the lines of 'If you're one of the old faithfuls familiar with previous episodes of my life as given to the world in the volumes *Moab is My Washpot* and *The Fry Chronicles*, now would be a good time to get on with a few odd jobs around the house – go for a walk, wash the cat, get on top of the backlog in your email inbox and so forth – while I fill in newcomers with the story so far . . .' only, of course, he would be referring not to *Moab* or *The Chronicles*, but to *The Code of the Woosters*, say, or *Right Ho, Jeeves*. And it is most unlikely that he would make any reference to inboxes. But you see the point.

There is a faint chance that you might have come across the two predecessors of the memoir you are now holding in your hands, in which case I can imagine you tapping your foot with impatience when it comes to my ushering the uninitiated down old and well-trodden pathways. 'Yes, yes, we know all that, get *on* with it, man,' I seem to hear you mutter from far away. 'Let's come to the new stuff. The juicy bits. Scandal. Showbiz. Drugs. Suicide. Gossip.'

On several occasions, as I meet someone in that embarrassed wine-sipping huddle that always occurs before a dinner party, for example, they might tell me how much they thoroughly enjoyed such and such a book of mine. All fine and charming, if a little embarrassing: 'One never knows what to *say*,' as Agatha Christie's alter ego, the popular author Ariadne Oliver (so splendidly played by Zoë Wanamaker in the television adaptations), often remarks. Anyway, an hour or so in, internally warmed by vinous glassfuls, I might tell, as one does around the dinner table, a story of some kind. I will notice the very person who confessed to admiring my book laughing heartily and whooping in surprise at the punchline. As they wipe the tears of infatuated merriment from their eyes, I will think to myself, '*Hang on!* That *exact* story is told, word for word, in the book they just assured me they liked so much!' Either, therefore, they were lying about having read the book in the first place, which, let's face it, we've all done – so much easier *not* to read books, especially the books of one's friends – *or*, which is in fact quite as likely if not more so, they *have* read it and simply forgotten just about every detail.

What remains, as one ages, of a book, is a smell, a flavour, a fleeting parade of sense-images and characters, pleasing or otherwise. So I have learned not to be offended. One does not write expecting every sentence to be permanently branded into the memory of the reader.

Far from being a curse, such memory leakages are actually rather a blessing. We all become, as readers, a little like the Guy Pearce character in the film *Memento*, only without the attendant physical jeopardies. Every day a new adventure. Every rereading a first reading. That is true at least of *recently* read books. I can recount almost word for word the Sherlock Holmes, Wodehouse, Wilde and Waugh that were the infatuations of my childhood (not to mention the Biggles, Enid Blyton and Georgette Heyer), but don't ask me to repeat the plot of the last novel I read. And it was a really good one too, *The Finkler Question*, by Howard Jacobson, which won a Booker Prize. I should have read it two or three years ago when it came out, but I am hopelessly behind with contemporary fiction. Almost everything I read these days is history, biography or popular science. I laid *The Finkler Question* down, finished from end to end about three months ago, thoroughly satisfied. I remember laughing a lot, there was a (racist?) mugging and a lot of very clever and compelling writing about anti-Semitism and all kinds of other delicious and wildly intelligent prose. But apart from the name Finkler and that incident I honestly don't think I could tell you what happened in the book, only that I loved it. I am way past the age when stories and even exact phrases and speeches stick.

There are seventeen steps up from pavement level to

Holmes and Watson's 221B Baker Street rooms; the Edict of Nantes was revoked in 1685; and the Battle of Crécy was fought on 26 August 1346 (the precise day isn't that hard to fix in my brain as it is my father's birthday). These and all *kinds* of irrelevant nonsenses I can reel off without recourse to Wikipedia. Exact phrases from Holmes, Jeeves, Mr Micawber and Gimlet (Biggles's commando equivalent) come pouring back to me, especially French Canadian Private 'Trapper' Troublay's habit of hissing *sapristi!* whenever he was perturbed.

I actually have a collection at home still of most of the works of Captain W. E. Johns, creator of Biggles and Gimlet (and of their female equivalent, the hearty and heroic 'Worrals of the WAAF'). In a satisfactory row (on my shelf at least, if not in publishing order), three of the Gimlet books are *Gimlet Lends a Hand, Gimlet Bores In* and *Gimlet Mops Up*. Gay innuendo simply rocks. Even Monty Python couldn't do better than that, although their *Biggles Flies Undone* parody made me laugh so much when I first read it in one of the Python books it gave me a serious asthma attack. True. It was the fact that they had so clearly read the books themselves with exactly the same attention to style and mannerism that I had that made me rock backwards, kicking my legs in the air in delight and wheezing like a dying emphysemiac. The point I suppose I am trying to make is that I will have the enormous pleasure of reading Howard Jacobson's book again in a year or so as a fresh and new surprise.

A friend of mine pointed out recently how absurd it was that people reread so little: do you only listen to a piece of music that you love once? Anyway, shush. You're distracting me. The whole point of this opening section is to fill in the newcomers on the subject of *La Vie Fryesque*. And if you are reading this and have also read my previous stabs at autobiography you have been warned: there will be repetition, and possibly even self-contradiction. What I remember now may differ from what I remembered five or ten years ago. But if you feel you know my life up until the ending of *The Fry Chronicles* and have no yearning for a redux reduction, you may happily jump from black arrow to black arrow or pop off and get on with your little tasks about the home, maybe settle into that TV box-set you've always meant to get around to because everyone else seems to have watched it but yourself. Let me try meanwhile to run by the relevant earlier history of my life as briskly as I can.

There is always the opportunity, I might add, for you to put this book down right this very minute and immediately download or buy in hard copy *Moab is My Washpot* and *The Fry Chronicles*, consume them in that order and save both of us all this repetition, but I wouldn't like to come over as greedy for sales. We're all above that kind of unpleasant mercantilism.

So where do I pick the story up from? From whence do I pick up the story? Whence do I pick up the story? Alistair Cooke, the British journalist best known for his broadcasts from America for the BBC, once told me that when he was a very young man contributing material for the legendary C. P. Scott of the *Manchester Guardian* he had submitted a piece of copy which included the phrase 'from whence'.

'Tell me, laddie,' Scott had asked, tapping an angry pair of fingers on the offending phrase, 'what does the word "whence" mean?'

'Er . . . "from where"?'

'Exactly! So you've just written "from from where" – tautology: go and correct it.'

Cooke was foolish enough to stand up for himself. 'Shakespeare and Fielding both frequently used "from whence".'

'Well, they wouldn't have done if they'd written for the *Manchester* fucking *Guardian*,' said Scott.

So. While the others are still at their chores, let me pick the story up for the new arrivals. The others can pick it up whence I dropped it. Doesn't sound right to me, but there we are, Scott must have known what he was talking about.

Our hero, after multiple scholastic expulsions (this is me I'm referring to now, not Alistair Cooke or C. P. Scott – I'm attempting a paragraph of that Christopher Isherwood/Salman Rushdie kind, where I refer to myself in the third person: it won't last long, I promise), after an adolescence steeped in folly, misery, heart-shredding mooncalf romance and a short lifetime of wayward self-delusion and multiple crookedness, a sly, cocky, guileful and self-fantasizing fool, found himself imprisoned for credit-card fraud and – still a teenager – on the brink of a life of permanent failure, incarceration, familial exile and squalid ignominy. He managed somehow to extricate himself from all this and acquire academic qualifications and a scholarship to Cambridge University. Well, he did not 'manage somehow', but broke through thanks to the combined wonders of flawlessly kind parents and his own late discovery that he enjoyed academic work very, very much and could not bear the idea of missing out on a real education, especially amongst the stones and towers and courts of Cambridge, where heroes like E. M. Forster, Bertrand Russell, G. E. Moore, Ludwig Wittgenstein, Alfred Tennyson and William Wordsworth had pursued their silly games, rigorous work, lyrical sodalities, sentimental friendships and semi-serious *sacra conversazione* – reading earnest and intellectually powerful papers from hearthrugs while nibbling anchovies or sardines on toast and being touched up by dons recruiting for MI6 or the KGB.

That Jonathan Miller and Peter Cook of *Beyond the Fringe* and John Cleese, Graham Chapman and Eric Idle of *Monty Python* and Tim Brooke-Taylor, Graeme Garden and Bill Oddie of *The Goodies*, let alone Germaine

Greer, Clive James, Douglas Adams, Derek Jacobi, Ian McKellen, Peter Hall, Richard Eyre, Nicholas Hytner and so on, had also been at that same university, eating up the stage generations before me, was a less self-conscious inducement, although I suppose if I am honest, a small part inside of me did somewhere dream of fame and recognition in an as yet inchoate form.

You do not, I believe, grow up, even if you are Stanislavsky, Brando or Olivier, knowing that you are a great actor. Much less do you grow up believing that you have it in you to make *any* kind of a career out of performance on stage or screen. Everyone has always known that it's 'an overcrowded profession'. We are most of us these days I suppose familiar with the tenets of Malcolm Gladwell's *Outliers: The Story of Success*, which quite cogently argues that no one ever made a success of themselves without having put in at least 10,000 hours of practice before breaking through. No one, not Mozart, not Dickens, not Bill Gates, not The Beatles. Most of us have instead put in 10,000 hours of wishing, and certainly as far as acting was concerned I had long thought I would *like* to take a stab at it but hadn't gone much further than that. I think my first print review, 'Young Stephen Fry as Mrs Higgins would grace any Belgravia drawing-room', went to my head when I was about eleven years old.

'Oooh,' whistling intakes of breath. 'Nine hundred and ninety-nine actors unemployed for every one with a job, young fellow.' How often would I hear this at drinks parties when I was a boy, such remarks always accompanied by the merest flash of a look acutely designed to assure me that with a face and string-bean body like mine I would never make a handsome leading man and should perhaps think of some other career.

'Being a barrister is a little like being an actor,' became my beaming mother's comforting and hopeful mantra. For a while I went along with this and between the ages of twelve and fifteen would tell the Norfolk landowners and their wives to whose parties we came and went that I was all set to make it to the Bar. Norman Birkett's *Six Great Advocates* was now my constant companion, and with all the repulsive self-confidence of the lonely geek I would bore my family with stories of the great forensic triumphs of Marshall Hall (my especial hero) and Rufus Isaacs, a great role model for any Jewish boy, since he rose to become Marquess of Reading and Viceroy of India. From a fruit market in Spitalfields to being curtseyed and bowed at and called Your Highness in the viceregal Palace of New Delhi. Imagine! And unlike Disraeli, a *practising* Jew. Not that I was ever that; nor were any of my mother's immediate family. We were, in Jonathan Miller's immortal words, not Jews, just Jew-*ish*. Not the whole hog. But then, as the Nazis showed, you don't have to practise (even for 10,000 hours) at being Jewish to be beaten, exiled, tortured, enslaved or killed for it, so one might as well embrace the identity with pride. The rituals, genital mutilations and avoidance of oysters and bacon can go hang, as can the behaviour of any given Israeli government, but otherwise consider me a proud Jew.

My background and upbringing in rural Norfolk seem, from a twenty-first-century perspective, a bizarre throwback. I think our way of life was in fact old-fashioned even in its own time. A fish man every Wednesday clopping in by horse and cart, coal trucks, butcher's, grocer's and bread vans arriving to deliver whatever provender that wasn't brought up to the back door by the gardeners for the cook, whose sister-in-law scrubbed floors on her knees three times a week. No central heating, no mains water, just coal or wood fires and a Victorian pump-house to draw up water, one source being a cistern reliant on soft rainwater which filled the tank that fed all the baths and wash basins with soft but rusty-brown bathwater, the other source drawn up from a groundwater aquifer which supplied the house's single drinking-water tap, fixed low down over a wooden bucket in a vast Victorian kitchen warmed only by a coke-fed Aga. There was a china-pantry, a food-pantry, larders, sculleries and an outer-scullery with a huge butler's sink that could only be filled from a grand brass hand pump. Outside the china-pantry, just by the door to the cellar stairs, hung a long rope which ended in a bulging red, white and blue sally. If any of us children were out in the garden and were needed, the rope would be pulled. The clang of the bell could be heard half a mile away at the local pig farm, where I sometimes liked to spend my time ogling piglets. Every time I heard that bell, my stomach seemed to fill with lead, for unless it was lunch or supper time it nearly always meant Trouble. It clanged the news that somehow I had been Found Out and was required to stand on the carpet in front of the desk in my father's study and Explain Myself.

Back inside again, on the wall next to the sally, was the predictable bell panel, which would have told servants from a previous era into which room to scuttle, bow and bob for instructions. Instead of the pulled-by-wire shaking bells so familiar from today's country house films or television series, ours – being an in-its-day modern Victorian house – took the form of a wooden framed box. Each room's name was printed beneath a red star in a white circle which oscillated when an electric bell was pressed. It was said that my parents' house was one of the first in its part of Norfolk to be thoroughly 'on the electric'. I am sure the circuitry was never upgraded from the time of its building in the 1880s until my mother and father finally sold the place nearly a century and a half later. The ceramic fuse boxes, the solid bakelite and brass three- or two-pin plugs were at least eighty years old when I was a boy in the 1960s and I was always astonished by the eye-achingly dazzling white three-pin plugs I saw in friends' houses, just as I was astonished by, and more than passingly envious of, the wall-to-wall carpeting, colour televisions and warm radiators that my friends took for granted. Not to mention their easy access to cinemas, shops and coffee bars. Such ordinary, modern households as theirs may not have had trained plum and pear trees stapled to the gable-ends of their outbuildings, nor could they boast built-in hand-carved linenfold cupboards that a contemporary antiquarian would orgasm over, but they were, to my restless rusticated brain, as *exciting* as my life and household were *dull*.

We move along, as an estate agent would say, from the pantries and cellar door, past the bell panel and rope and encounter an always closed studded baize door which leads through to the house proper. There, hallways, dining room, drawing room, great front stairs and my father's study could be found. Forbidden territory. Next to the baize door were the *back* stairs, which led to our domain.

On the third floor of the house my brother and I each occupied a huge bedroom, leaving the others (one of which was already divided into two rooms) for furniture overspill, spare rooms and attic space. These unfeasibly proportioned rooms, a little William Morris wallpaper still showing through in one of them, had originally been designed as dormitories for servants. Whitwell Elwin, the architect who built the house, had made the mistake earlier, when building his own Victorian rectory in the same village, of providing small individual rooms for his staff. It seems that in these narrow rooms they had suffered acutely from homesickness and loneliness and thus, given a second chance at domestic architecture, Elwin had created in our house enormous servant chambers in which the maids and footmen (in their ruthlessly segregated dorms, naturally) could chatter and console each other through the night.

Elwin's finest work of architecture was neither the rectory nor our house, but the village church. Booton church is worth travelling *miles* to see. 'The cathedral of the villages' it has been called. Sir Nikolaus Pevsner, the great master registrar of Britain's architecture, who visited every county and chronicled any building of worth in the United Kingdom, gave this chapter of my book its subheading when he described St Michael the Archangel's in Booton as 'very naughty, but built in the right spirit'. I remember quoting this observation of Pevsner's to John Betjeman when he came down to the church with a camera crew and some of his Victorian Society friends during one of my school holidays or rustication (temporary punishment suspension) periods. I had been given the exciting job of escorting this distinguished party around, the self-appointed local expert, and telling them about the Bath stone, the knapped flint, the crocketed pinnacles, chamfering and idiomatic Gothic influences and any other such pretentious guff as my mind (stuffed as it then was with prized Banister Fletcher jargonese) could come up with: 'note the influence of the Cluniac revival' – that sort of gobshite, as if they didn't know all that without the cocky pipings of a twelve-year-old who behaved as if he was the Professor of Architecture at the Courtauld. The great Poet Laureate (or were those years still ahead of him?) was very friendly and patient about all this, but it was only years later that I learned that Betjeman and Pevsner were not on the most cordial of terms, despite each of them so valuing, and indeed so *raising* the value of, architecture in Britain; perhaps therefore my quoting of Sir Nikolaus had been injudicious. I spent the rest of the day, I remember, as a guest of the Victorian Society's formidably knowledgeable and likeable Hermione Hobhouse, diving in on unsuspecting Pugin and Gilbert Scott mini-masterpieces around the county.

Whitwell Elwin may have created an astonishing church, but his major interest (outside, one presumes, his fifty-one-year ministry at Booton) was his editorship of the *Quarterly Review*, his querulous correspondence with fellow Victorian greats like Darwin and Gladstone and his somewhat 'inappropriate' relationships with a series of young girls, the most prominent of whom was his 'blessed girl', Lady Emily Bulwer-Lytton, a viceroy's daughter who later went on to marry the truly great architect Edwin Lutyens, best known for his creation of colonial New Delhi and his collaborations with the horticulturalist Gertrude Jekyll. Lutyens also designed Booton Manor, an 'averagely fine' example of his work. After building Booton church and its rectory (envious of Lutyens' superior talent as well as jealous of his snaffling the beloved Emily, one supposes), Whitwell Elwin built our house as a thank you to the spinster sisters who had bankrolled his magnificent ecclesiastical folly.

Just to drive home to you how preposterously old-fashioned a dwelling ours was, I should tell you that the lavatories were the boxed-in kind with a high up cistern. Instead of the later decorated china 'pull me' chain, there had originally been a handle next to the bowl which you pulled *up* to flush. The wash basin in the lavatory's ante-room didn't have a plughole. You pulled on a sprung tap to fill it, washed and rinsed your hands, tipped up a lip in the basin which also served as the overflow slit, and the bowl pivoted to empty its water underneath before swinging back to its original position. You probably can't picture it, and I am dissatisfied with my ability to convey its workings succinctly and clearly. Never mind. Similarly, the bathtub upstairs, with its great lion's claw feet, had a long cylindrical ceramic pole that you twisted and let down to seal the plug hole. It was also one of the few bathrooms I have ever known to possess a fireplace.

My brother and I were only ever allowed to have a fire lit in our bedrooms if we were ill. I cannot overstate the pleasure of waking on a dark winter's morning and seeing the embers still glowing in the grate. Otherwise in winter, one relied for warmth on a mountain of eiderdowns and blankets or the company in bed of a cat or two. I had never even heard of a duvet or quilt.

I once found a thin Dimplex electric radiator in an attic and brought it into my room. When my father discovered

I had kept it, dialled up to maximum heat for three days in a row (the breath steaming from my mouth and nostrils was nonetheless visible), he made me sit down and work out, given the price of kilowatt hours, how much my profligacy had cost him. This was an arithmetical problem, of course, wildly beyond my competence. The radiator disappeared, and my fear of mathematics grew that much greater.

Outside, the gardeners provided what the grocer, butcher, bread man and fish man could not supply with their weekly van visits. Apples, pears and potatoes were stored in outhouses over the winter; jams, pickles and chutneys were prepared in the autumn by the cook, Mrs Riseborough. Lettuces, tomatoes, cucumbers, scarlet runner beans, broad beans, peas, marrows, asparagus in raised beds, figs, damsons, plums, cherries, greengages, strawberries, rhubarb, raspberry and blackcurrant canes and the whole rich bounty of the garden supplied us all. Milk was delivered daily in wax cartons which, when dried, we used as kindling for the fireplaces; a local farm provided eggs and dark-yellow butter patted with carved wooden paddles and wrapped in greaseproof paper. I had never heard of or been into a supermarket before I was . . . I can't even guess what age. If we needed brambles for one of Mrs Riseborough's blackberry and apple pies, I would take my baby sister Jo in her pushchair along a bridle path and pick the fruit by hand. The October mixing of the Christmas puddings and the pouring of the apple jelly . . . I am sure that plenty of people still do this every year – more than *ever* before perhaps, thanks to all the Take-offs of the Bake-offs and Cake-offs that now take up most of our television schedules. Cream of tartar and crystallized angelica have never had it so good. Men and women the length of the land still grow vegetables, apples, pears and soft fruits too; I am not, I hope, over-misting my own childhood idyll. Not that for me it was anything close to idyllic, much as it might and ought to appear to have been from this great distance in time and manners.

A grass tennis court and even a badminton lawn were at our disposal; for whatever reason we didn't use them much, only when American cousins visited.

Behind the stable-block was a cottage and separate garden, where a couple who worked for my father lived, and next to that a paddock filled with noisy geese. I used to brave these hissingly aggressive birds to get to a walnut tree around which they honked and flapped as if it were a sacred temple being vandalized by heathens. Despite growing up in the country, I have never been fully at ease with wild animals.

In the garden's overgrown old pigsty and hidden in a hedged area filled with broken sundials and choked ponds my sister Jo and I found, tamed and finally domesticated feral cats and kittens which had been let loose from the almost incredibly eccentric rector of the village church, who didn't, of course, as a high religionist, believe that animals possessed souls, and so they could therefore happily be thrown away like so much litter. Horses we did not have, for over the way my father had converted the monumentally solid stable block into a laboratory. He was a kind of designer, physicist and electronics engineer, impossible exactly to categorize. The stable mangers were filled with tools, the stalls with lathes, mills and other machinery; the vast upper rooms where the grooms might have slept housed oscilloscopes, ammeters and circuitry of the most curious and impenetrable kind. After ten or twenty years of his work there, the smell of solder, Swarfega and freon finally overcame decades of dung, straw and saddle soap.

Reepham, the nearest village to have proper shops and pubs, was over three miles away, and the inhabitants thought of my father, on the very rare occasions they caught sight of him, as the Mad Inventor. If for some reason he had to go in for a supply of tobacco – my mother having succumbed perhaps to a rare bout of influenza – he would stand in the post office, forlornly holding out money in the palm of his hand like a foreign tourist, allowing the correct amount to be picked out. I think he frightened the villagers a little and that Wordsworth's real world of 'getting and spending' frightened him too.

Nothing like as much as he frightened me, however. In my mind he was a compound of Mr Murdstone and Sherlock Holmes, with an element of *The Famous Five*'s Uncle Quentin thrown in. Certainly he had the sinister saturnine features and snarling intolerance of children that marked out the latter and the almost inhuman brilliance and pipe-smoking gauntness of the great detective. It was Holmes himself who observed that genius was an infinite capacity for taking pains and, awestruck and often filled with rage and hatred against him as I was, there was never a time that I didn't think my father an authentic genius. I still do. Between the ages of seven and nineteen, however, I am not sure I was ever able to look him in the eye, or to hear his disgruntled snorts and growls and sighs, without wanting to wet myself or to fly from him in tears of humiliation and misery. Now in his eighties, he is building, from scratch, to his own design, a 3D printer. I know him enough to be absolutely certain that when he has finished it will be more reliable and more elegantly designed than any other that currently exists on the market.

My mother was and remains the warmest and kindest person you could know. Her first love and duty, however, was, and will always be, to my father. And *vice versa*. Which is as it should be. Their marriage always seemed to me to be so ideal that I often wonder if it completely spoiled my chances of achieving a relationship anything like as perfect. Which must be nonsense, since my brother and sister are both blissfully married. We will come to the squashier bogs, the more mephitically foul marshes of my useless and repulsive private life later in this book if you have the patience. Meanwhile, it is still catch-up time.

*

One marvellous favour J. K. Rowling has done all English writers of a certain generation is to clarify this business of being sent off to school. No Hogwarts Express for the seven-year-old Stephen, of course, no Butter Beers or magical chocolate frogs, but all in all a really very similar affair otherwise. Boaters at the school end of the train were crammed on the heads or waved airily by impossibly mature-looking twelve-year-olds; we new boys braced like mules and clutched on to our mothers as the prospect of months of separation in the company of these frightening-looking seniors approached. 'They'll think I look stupid.' 'They'll think I look weedy.' 'They'll think I look common.' All kinds of immature waves of inadequacy rolled over me. I am not even sure that I knew what 'common' meant. It was two years later, reading Nancy Mitford's indispensable *Noblesse Oblige*, that I discovered it turned out to be a word only ever used by 'common' people in the first place, which is rather a lowering thought.

Before Paddington station was finally cleaned, rejigged and renovated ten or so years ago, complete with the statue of its famous and noble bear, I could never go near the place without my bowels turning to water.

Everybody else new you ever meet, and this continues throughout life, is stronger than you are, knows the system better and sees right through to the back of your brain and finds what they see there to be wholly inadequate. Everyone you encounter carries, as it were, a huge club behind their back, while all you hold behind yours is a weedy cotton-bud. I think I may have written this before, or possibly stolen it from someone else: it is, in any case, hardly a fresh observation, and I should be very surprised if it does not strike home with you. The rest of the world was at That Lesson, the one we missed because of a toothache or diarrhoea, the one where *they* – the rest of the school – were told how the world works and how to comport themselves with confidence and ease. *We* all missed it and have felt insecure ever since. *Other people* know some secret thing, and no other people know more than children who are just a few years older than you are.

To go to a prep school 200 miles away at the age of seven seems, like the fish-cart, the 1880s servants' bells or the cook receiving vegetables from cap-doffing garden-ers, madly silly, English, grand and old-fashioned.

You should know, then, before I go any further, that, contrary to the implication of all that has gone before, we were *poor*. Not dirt poor, not peasant poor obviously, just poor compared to all the kinds of people who sent their sons to the same kinds of schools, poor compared to the kinds of people my parents had to dinner parties. Yes, dinner parties where the men wore black tie and the women 'withdrew' from the dining room to the drawing room after the cheese to allow the men time for strong talk, cigars and port. My mother confided in me her prob-ably accurate opinion that this old and now defunct ritual (defunct even in Royal Palaces I am able to tell you – more of that later too) was in fact a way of allowing women to go to bathrooms together without drawing to the attention of their men that the sweet creatures possessed such things as bladders which needed voiding just as much as any man's or horse's did.

We were poor in that my mother drove an ancient Austin A35 with flicky-uppy indicators and my father an Austin 1800 from the heyday of British motoring incompetence (after he had driven an old Rover 90 into desuetude). We never went on holidays, and every time my mother and I went into a shoe or clothing shop throughout my childhood and adolescence I remember squirming and writhing with embarrassment as she complained (very loudly to my ears) that such and such a pair of shoes were 'shatteringly expensive' and that she 'couldn't *possibly* afford' those trousers. I did grow very fast, of course, and she had a small budget from which to buy anything. The school fees themselves (somehow we found ourselves, my brother and I, going to two not wildly grand private schools that were nonetheless just about the most expensive of any in England) were paid for, I am certain, by my mother's father, the beloved Jewish immigrant who died when I was about ten and whom I wish, greatly wish, I had known better. But I grew up with a quite illusory – 'entitled', as we would now say – sense of aggrieved deprivation. To confess this is deeply embarrassing; how could I possibly feel deprived? Just how cheap must I have been to think a country house with servants and grand rooms was horrible and that a modern house with colour televisions, gas ovens, freezer-cabinets, carpets and central heating was a lost dream of luxury?

There we are, then. Off to a prep school in Gloucestershire, far from Norfolk, but beautiful too in its own way. I wrote in *The Fry Chronicles* about my insatiable appetite for sweets. I devoted pagefuls of panegyrics to the tuck shop and provided pagefuls too of self-reproach for the thieving and sly manipulations that my addiction to all things sugary led me to. I suppose they themselves derived from this sense of being hard done by, wherever the hell that came from. Maybe sugar stood in for a parental love or the domestic prosperity that I felt deprived of. Perhaps I was born with one of those narcissistic fantasy minds. The kind that believes they are really the abandoned son of a duke, or that a solicitor's letter will one day arrive informing them of an unknown cousin's fabulous will, of which they are to be sole benefactor. The crown courts are daily full of such sad people. I happen to be that rare thing – rarer than a straight man in a Hollister T-shirt – a fantasist whose fantasies came true, it would seem. A lot of celeb haters would say that most celebs are narcissists. It could be that they are right. Counterintuitively, self-hatred is one of the leading symptoms of clinical narcissism. Only by telling yourself and the world how much you hate yourself can you receive the reliable shower of praise and admiration in response that you feel you deserve . . . or so at least the theory runs.

I survived prep school – *just*. Stout's Hill School, now a holiday resort, was a marvellous mid-eighteenth-century Strawberry Hill Gothic Revival rococo (if you can have such a mixture) castellated fantasy, complete with cata-combs and crenellations, a butler (Mr Dealey) and entirely strange characters, such as a Mr Sawdon, whose hands shook uncontrollably and whom we imitated without mercy.

It was only in my last year that one of the masters told me that Sawdon had been a brilliant youth, an authentic war hero, his mind shattered by shell shock in the trenches of Flanders, an experience from which he had never recovered. If I think now of the ho-ho number of times I would creep behind him, imitating his flicking, quiver-ing hands, his slack jaw, his drivelling mutters, his drooling and his weaving, dipping gait, him all unaware, the boys in front watching me over his shoulder and squealing with laughter . . . if I think of that now I want to stick a pen through my throat in shame. What made it all the worse was the memory I have that his face would light up whenever he saw laughter. He believed, I suppose, that he was looking at affection and pleasure, and some distant image stirred in him of a happy life of laughter and friendship before the bone-splintering, mind-ravaging war that destroyed everything he had been. Just about 99 per cent of the times that he saw a smiling face, he wasn't looking at the smiles of friends, he was peering unawares at the mocking grins of young fiends who thought him

36

weird and retarded and worthy of nothing but contempt. All the time I was there he was deliberately tormented, impersonated and cruelly teased almost daily. It is no use my apologizing now. He would be 120 were he still alive, I expect, but I weep as I write this. Weep at my own callous, ignorant and ostentatious viciousness, and weep for the hundreds and thousands of Sawdons who didn't even have the shelter of a school folded in the soft green wolds of Gloucestershire to give them a home.

Mr Sawdon was, I think, somehow related by marriage to the founder and headmaster of the school, Robert Angus. Angus had three daughters, each of whom was more or less nutty about horses, especially Jane, the youngest. Our star alumnus had been Mark Phillips, already in training for the Mexico Olympics as an equestrian and later to marry Princess Anne. Riding at Stout's Hill was not an 'extra' like bassoon lessons or fencing, but part of the everyday curriculum. One would descend from a double Latin class to the stables for an equally serious (and to me much duller) lesson in the arcana of equestrianism. I can still recite the pommels, martingales, snaffles, pelhams, gags, Kimblewick and Liverpool bits (even something called a Chifney anti-rearing bit, if I recall correctly), girth-straps and curry-combs whose every detail and proper use we had to master before we were ever allowed so much as to mount a pony. The smell of saddle soap and dubbin, rarely encountered by me these days, is as intense and evocative as the smell of creosote, cloves or candyfloss. I think of myself – despite an assumption amongst some that I am intellectual, rationalist and almost coldly logical – as an emotional, sensual being, led far more by the heart and other organs than by the brain. Smell, as we all know, evokes the past more immediately than any of the other four senses. Where the aroma of saddle soap takes me, your grandmother's lily-of-the-valley hand lotion or the sweat-and-mud reek of the school changing rooms might take you.

In 2009 I swore, not in the sense of using foul language (although I had muttered plenty of that off-camera), that the day I was nearly thrown by a skittering Tennessee walking horse would be the last time anyone would ever, *ever* see me on top of a horse until my dying day. This incident had taken place while filming a documentary series in which I visited each state of the American union.

The humiliation of arranging the title sequence of *Blackadder Goes Forth* had already more or less determined me never to sit atop an equine again. We had shot the sequence down at the Royal Anglian Regiment's HQ in Colchester, and the idea was I, as the blithering General Melchett, would bestride my mount and take salute while the band led by Captain Blackadder and attended by poor old Private Baldrick, along with Hugh Laurie's nobly asinine Lieutenant George and Tim McInnerny's twitchy Captain Darling, marched past, eyes right, to the stirring march 'The British Grenadiers', which then morphed into Howard Goodall's *Blackadder* theme tune. For practice I got my foot into the stirrup of the colonel's mount, whose name I think was – and this should have warned me – Thunderbolt, swung into the saddle and walked experimentally forwards, clucking and tchitching in a way that would have built up confidence and amiability in a tyrannosaurus who had just heard bad news from his bank. I had walked about the whole parade ground feeling more or less confident, cooing Thunderbolt's name, stroking his muzzle, softly patting his flanks and giving him the news that he was safe and that I loved him.

Thunderbolt and I now stood peacefully awaiting the moment. Cameras, action and . . . cue music. The moment the first blare of the trumpet sounded Thunderbolt reared, neighed like a banshee, pawed the air and galloped around the parade ground as if stung by a gadfly. None of this was helped by Hugh all but falling to the ground heaving with such uncontrollable laughter that he could scarcely breathe. I was eight and a half feet at least from solid concrete, holding on for dear life, and my friend thought it was the funniest thing he had ever seen in his life. Men.

So you may well imagine that twenty years later in the Southern states of America the prospect of heaving my carcass on a Tennessee walking horse was causing me a little perturbation. It was Georgia we were investigating at this stage of our documentary series on the fifty states, and we were the guests of a very kind family who lived in a plantation house that didn't seem to have changed since the days of Scarlett O'Hara. It was clear that my discomfort in the presence of horses transmitted itself.

'Now don't you go worrying about her,' my amiable hostess had reassured me with a delicious high-class Southern drawl. 'There never was born a horse so docile ...' that last word pronounced, of course, in the American way, as if to rhyme with 'fossil' or that turdine melodic songbird, the throstle. Yes, isn't turdine a splendid word? Anyway, back to that docile animal.

'That's all very well,' I remember gasping, as I tried to heave my bulk on to its back, 'but horses and I never get on, which is why I never get on horses. They know that I don't like them and they always panic.' Even at my initial gentle, reasonable, unhurried, clucking, apple-offering, muzzle-nuzzling approach the beast's ears had instantly drawn back, the flanks had pricked and twitched, and the hooves had stamped as if it had detected Satan in me.

'Not this one, hun ...' came the complacent, murmured reply.

Five minutes later, just in time for the camera to catch my humiliation, the 'walking horse' freaked out at the horror of having me astride it or possibly (like every fucking horse ever fucking born) became utterly spooked by the astounding existence of such wholly unexpected and terrifying phenomena as wind, trees, sky, a bird gliding in the distance, a chicken, a hedge, a leaf whirling in the wind, a butterfly – you name it – and galloped off, bursting through the corral fence, while I screamed and juddered in the saddle, incompetently trying to operate the brakes.

'Well, I declare she's never done that in her *life* . . .'

You would think a prep school laid out in idyllic countryside, with a lake, woods, spinneys and rolling parkland, and where the riding of biddable and patient ponies was compulsory, might have prepared me for at least normal human competence on horseback. The school achieved this for me no more than it prepared me for normal human competence at life. Just as I can't and never could ride horses, I can't and never could live. At least, I have never felt I could.

So (this is still for the new subscribers, I should warn) I survived six years of prep school and moved at the age of thirteen to Uppingham, an old-fashioned public school set in the glorious county of Rutland. It was here that, to contradict Philip Larkin, love fell on me like an enormous No. Most of my life since has been a response to that. Fortunately, however, there had been books.

I will leap backwards a little to Booton and myself at an earlier age just to explain the effect that books had had on me by the time I arrived at Big School. I relish all things digital, but if I had been born twenty-five years later I dread to think of how little I would know about the written word.

I am not so foolish as to join myself with those heralds of doom who claim that the internet and social networking will inevitably spell the death of literacy, literature, focus, concentration span or 'real' human interaction. When moving-type printing was invented it was damned as a technology that would rot the mind. No longer would a scholar have to know everything, they could just 'look it up'. When the novel arrived it was damned as destructive, escapist, shallow and detrimental to morals. The same howls of protest were screeched at popular theatre, music hall, cinema, then television, video-gaming and now social networking. Human teenagers in particular are tougher than their elders will ever believe. The bullying, abuse and trolling is, of course, horrific, but believe me, a teenager has a better life of it now than he or she ever did a hundred years ago, when physical punishment, cruel sadistic beatings and sexual abuse went unquestioned in schools and in the home.

As it was, my father, who was from the radio (or wireless as it was then called) generation, thought televisions were perhaps permissible for showing events like Churchill's funeral, moon-landings or serious news stories, but otherwise our little black-and-white set at home was relegated to the corner of the kitchen, its aerial being just a wire poked in the rear antenna socket and Blu-Tacked to the wall. My mother pasted a cutout newspaper cartoon on the television's side: a housewife is explaining to her friend, 'Oh, we had one of the very first colour sets, but the colours have faded now.'

Insomnia, especially on hot nights, was one of the chief miseries of my childhood and youth. The only answer therefore was to read, which in itself presented an absurd problem. If I opened the windows to cool the room it would soon fill with huge moths, May-bugs, June-bugs and all kinds of simply terrifying arthropods peculiar to Norfolk which, like crazed winged lobsters, would carom and careen straight to my bedside lamp and flicker, bang and buzz about inside the shade. I happen to be horribly afraid of moths – an utterly irrational fear, I am quite aware, but agonizingly real.

Somehow I managed, despite these abhorred fluttering distractions, to get through hundreds of books a year. My parents had many of their own, most of which I had soon consumed more than once. I further supplemented my reading matter at first from a large grey mobile library which arrived every other Thursday at the corner of two lanes not far from the house. I am not sure such services still operate; it seems doubtful – councils these days seem disobliged so much as to resurface a road, educate a child or empty a dustbin.

One Sunday afternoon, aged twelve, while my father was safely at work in the stable block 'over the way', I watched on the little television Anthony Asquith's film version of *The Importance of Being Earnest*. I vividly recall sitting on an uncushioned wooden kitchen chair, face flushed, mouth half-open, simply astonished at what I was watching and, most especially, *hearing*. I had had simply no idea that language could do this. That it could dance and trip and tickle, cavort, swirl, beguile and seduce, that its rhythms, subclauses, repetitions, *clausulae* and colours could excite quite as much as music.

When Algernon says to Cecily, 'I hope, Cecily, I shall not offend you if I state quite frankly and openly that you seem to me to be in every way the visible personification of absolute perfection?' I wriggled and giggled and repeated the phrase to myself in disbelieving bliss. Enough times to commit it to memory there and then. I would repeat it solemnly to the (faintly bewildered) Mrs Riseborough.

'Oh, you do go on with your nonsense. How that drives Nanny crazy.'

By this time Mrs Riseborough had been promoted to the role of nanny to my sister, something she considered a great advancement (although she still cooked, ironed and performed innumerable other jobs around the house), and thenceforth would much rather be called Nanny Riseborough than Mrs Riseborough. Her Christian name, Dolly, was used only by her immediate family, although her husband Tom, who had after all given her the name, preferred to call her in Janeite, Dickensian fashion 'Mrs Riseborough'. She died only last year, aged almost a hundred. I had visited her a few times over the years but deeply regret missing her funeral. I am not sure that such combinations of independence, strength and unquestioning service still exist. Her son Peter came to own a very successful and popular Norfolk gastropub called The Ratcatchers. Rather than sitting at a table and enjoying a little sip or a well-earned bowl of soup, his mother would insist on washing up in the kitchen behind the bar, right through into her nineties.

That day years before, my repeatedly telling her that I hoped I would not offend her if I stated quite frankly and openly that she seemed to me to be in every way the visible personification of absolute perfection might have flustered her a little, but she was used to my behaviour, which was at times so frantic, fanciful and foolish that it would today quite certainly be diagnosed as Attention Deficit Hyperactivity Disorder.

Wilde's phrase, and many others from the film – 'Cecily, you will read your Political Economy in my absence. The chapter on the Fall of the Rupee you may omit. It is somewhat too sensational' – took hold of me completely. In an age before video recording, the best I could do was imagine myself inside the world of this extraordinary motion picture, which turned out, my mother told me (after of course patiently enduring the matter of her too being the visible personification of absolute perfection), to have been based on a play, a copy of which she was sorry to say was not in the house.

The following Thursday I stood then, the only customer (lender? user? what was the word then?), fretfully at the corner of the lanes, waiting for the battleship-grey mobile library to hove into view. The driver lurched the van, of the kind that I think used to be called a pantechnicon, to a halt, came round to open the door and lower the steps and tousled my hair and patted my bum as I ascended (as adults were quite rightly allowed to do in those days without being hauled up before the courts and having their houses set fire to). The librarian, a be-cardiganed, multi-beaded old dear, was also apt to ruffle my hair. She often told me that I read so many books I would soon grow into one. For a child to read books, especially in the summer, was looked on as very peculiar and, of course, unhealthy, something I had always been used to being considered on account of my loathing of all forms of organized games and sports.

'Have you,' I asked her breathlessly, 'ever heard of a play called *The Importance of Being Earnest*?'

'Why yes, my love, that's just up there, I think.'

It was far from the largest drama section you have ever seen in a library. A smattering of Shaw, Priestley and Shakespeare, but also – marvellously – the collected comedies of Oscar Wilde. She stamped the book out with that splendid springing, spanking sound that will never be heard on these shores again. It had last been lent, the previous stamp showed me, in 1959. I thanked her, dismounted in a bound, flew up the lane, round the rear of the house, up the back stairs and into my bedroom.

Lady Windermere's Fan, A Woman of No Importance, An Ideal Husband, The Importance of Being Earnest. I read them all again and again and again until a fortnight later, when I found myself once more restlessly pacing the corner of the two lanes.

46

'Have you anything else by Oscar Wilde?'

'Well, now, I aren't rightly sure . . .' she lifted her reading glasses from the delicately linked silver chain that hung round her neck, pushed them to her nose and came around the desk to inspect the shelves as if for the first time. 'Ah, now, there you go.'

The Complete Works of Oscar Wilde. This was more, so much more than I could possibly have hoped for. Once again I flung myself on my bed and started to read. Some of the dialogues written in the Socratic style in essays like 'The Decay of Lying' and 'The Critic as Artist' confused me a little, and parts of 'The Soul of Man Under Socialism' were quite beyond me. The poems I frankly disliked, save for 'The Ballad of Reading Gaol', which seemed an odd subject for such a glamorous and flowing lord of language to have chosen. The stories for children made me weep, as they do to this day, and *The Picture of Dorian Gray* touched a part of me that I couldn't quite define but disturbed and excited me very deeply indeed. 'De Profundis', too, I found beautiful, but puzzling. I wasn't sure what the allusions to 'prison' and 'shame' and 'scandal' and so on were supposed to mean. Indeed, I assumed the letter to be a work of fiction that held some allegorical meaning beyond my reach.

I kept this collection for four weeks, and the cosily obliging librarian waived the late return penalty of sixpence when I at last brought it back to the mobile library. I asked if she had anything else by this Oscar Wilde.

She pointed at the book. 'If that says "The Complete Works", then I should think that's the complete works, wouldn't you, young man?'

'Hm.' It was hard not to see the justice of this. 'Well, do you have anything *about* him, perhaps?'

Her soft, powdered cheeks pinkened a little, and in a rather quavery voice she asked me how old I was.

'Oh, I'm a very advanced reader,' I assured her. Being tall and with a voice that never broke but slowly deepened, I could usually pass as older than my real age; at this time, unless memory plays me false, I had just turned thirteen.

'We-ell . . .' she fossicked about the lower shelves and came up with a book called *The Trials of Oscar Wilde* by an author called H. Montgomery Hyde.

The book was like a kick in the teeth. A kick in the gut. A kick in the groin. A kick most especially in the heart. After reading about the character of this brilliant, engaging, gentle, exceptionally kind and quite remarkably gifted Irishman, to discover the truth of the sudden and calamitous third act of his life, the three trials (it is often forgotten that following the legal action he foolishly took against the Marquess of Queensberry, there were not one, but two criminal trials against him, after the first ended in a deadlocked jury), the exile and the squalid and unhappy travels and subsequent penurious death in Paris, all this was almost more than I could bear.

Yet.

Yet it also confirmed in my deepest heart something

that I had always known. That he and I shared a similar 'nature', as he would say, or 'sexuality' as we would call it today.

My heart was wrenched by the story of Oscar. The mobile library was no longer enough. The only place for me now was Norwich City Library, twelve miles away. Sometimes I had the energy to bicycle, sometimes I took the daily coach that stopped at that same meeting of lanes at twenty to seven every weekday morning.

Before the internet and Berners-Lee's miraculous World Wide Web, the closest you came to metadata or hyperlinks were the bibliography and the index cards in the wooden drawers of a library catalogue.

I started by seeing what else this Montgomery Hyde had written. *The Love That Dared Not Speak Its Name* was one book. *The Other Love* was even more astonishing. I found myself endlessly in Norwich City Library, scribbling down names from the bibliographies at the end of each non-fiction book (bibliographies are the lists of titles and writers that the author has used as sources) and then haring to the catalogues to see if the library might hold a copy of anything related to a newly acquired lead to the world of forbidden love. Through such means I learned about the infamous Baron Corvo, aka William Rolfe, and his eye-popping, trouser-shifting 'Venice Letters', Norman Douglas, T. C. Worsley, 'Y' (an anonymous gay autobiographer), Robin Maugham, Angus Stewart, the scandalous Michael Davidson, Roger Peyrefitte,

Henry de Montherlant, Jean Genet, William Burroughs, Gore Vidal, John Rechy and dozens and dozens of others. It was the equivalent of clicking on web links, more cumbersome and time-consuming, of course, but breathlessly exciting. Along the way, as a happy accident, I acquired a kind of alternative literary education that ran in parallel to the one I was receiving at school. You cannot read Genet or about him without encountering (the entirely heterosexual so far as we know) Jean-Paul Sartre, and you cannot brush up against Robin Maugham without making the acquaintance of Paul Bowles and the Tangier set. Burroughs leads to Denton Welch, Corvo to the Bensons, Ronald Firbank, Stephen Tennant, Harold Acton and so on until by fortuitous and serendipitous circumstances, fuelled by inner erotic curiosity and stimulation, I found a world of artists and writers, straight and gay, who were their own reward.

Suppose I had been born in the 1980s? All the vindication and support I might ever have needed to make me comfortable about my sexuality could have been found in television programmes like *Queer as Folk*, by the pioneering gay kisses on *EastEnders* and *Brookside*, in Pride marches along the streets of London and in the billions of pathways, savoury and unsavoury, offered by the internet. The fact that my childhood, youth and early manhood preceded all of this diversity, freedom, tolerance and openness I, of course, regret to some degree – the brave new gay world would have saved me the doomed feeling I had that my life was inevitably to be one of secrecy, exile, seedy sex shops and the police courts – but I am very, very glad that the only available route to a proud acceptance and endorsement of my gay nature should have come through literature. I think I would always have loved Shakespeare, Keats, Austen, Dickens, Tennyson, Browning, Forster, Joyce, Fitzgerald, what the bluff English master of one of the private schools I attended called 'the big hitters', but I cannot thank my sexuality enough for giving me, in my particular case, a love of all reading and an introduction to the gay identity which offered so much more than gaytube and xhamster.com.

So, here I am now at Uppingham School, knowing that I was technically one of a despised and secretly special tribe, but little suspecting that the big issue in life was never going to be the gender one masturbated over; that was small potatoes. What smacked me amidships, holed me below the waterline and sent me bubbling to the bottom of the ocean was love. Love made a wreck of me. Love, the silly word that lyric writers and pop songs endlessly overused; love, the subject of so many plays and poems and films; love, that soppy plotline that got in the way of a good story. Love came up and punched me so hard in the face that I have been giddy and brain-softened ever since. I'm flattened on the canvas, towel thrown in and having barnacles affix themselves to my rotting decks on the sea bed, if we are to allow me to mix metaphors.

The fact is, real life is sometimes so complicated that a pure unmixed metaphor would be unconvincing. And the truth about love . . . well, as Auden wondered:

> Will it come like a change in the weather?
> Will its greeting be courteous or rough?
> Will it alter my life altogether?
> O tell me the truth about love.

The third line was answered by an emphatic 'yes'. Add together a manic and disruptive nature in the classroom, an addiction to sweets (as covered in loving, meticulous detail in *The Fry Chronicles*), a fear and hatred of compulsory games (absurdly replaced today by a love of almost *all* sport) and this new heart-pounding, soul-lacerating feeling that consumed my every waking hour, and a Stephen emerges who is simply too hot to be handled by any school, teacher or parent, let alone by himself.

I was finally expelled from Uppingham School in my first term in the lower sixth form, just as I was embarking on a two-year course of A levels. I had taken all my O levels when I was fourteen, a normal procedure then: if they thought you could get them, they put you in for them. I may have been academically mature but I was as physically and emotionally mature as a newborn puppy. And so much less adorable.

Why was I expelled? Some fraction of you reading this will want to know, another (perhaps larger) will be really seething now. 'This isn't a book, it's a retread!' they'll be shouting. On the other hand, it seems so rude to gloss over the whole episode as if expecting those in the dark to guess or spend money on a previous autobiography. So once again, I will remind those who don't want to watch a repeat that they can change channels, mix themselves a liver-and-whey protein shake, knit a smartphone-cosy or simply take a nap.

I was sacked from school because I had received permission from my housemaster to go to London for a meeting of the Sherlock Holmes Society of London, of which I was, at the time, the youngest member. I was to deliver a paper on T. S. Eliot's metrification of Sherlock Holmes's description to Doctor Watson of the life, appearance and habits of Professor Moriarty, who, in Eliot's *Old Possum's Book of Practical Cats*, becomes Macavity the Mystery Cat. The idea was to do the evening, which was on a Saturday, be free in London for Sunday *and* the following Monday, which was a public holiday to celebrate the Queen and Prince Philip's silver wedding, and return by the last train that day. As it is, I (and my friend Jo Wood, who was not so natural a lawbreaker, but loyally attended me) were suddenly gripped by cinemania. We saw *Fritz the Cat*, *A Clockwork Orange*, *Cabaret*, *The Godfather*, all of them, time after time after time, as they ran and ran repeatedly on all-day programmes in the major West End cinemas. By the time we woke up from our binge it was Wednesday.

Sheepishly we returned and wolfishly we were devoured. Jo, having no form, was rusticated until the end of the term. I was shown the full red card.

My parents tried another seat of learning, the Paston School, a local direct-grant grammar with the distinction of having educated the young Horatio Nelson. Its allure was lost on me, and I developed the habit of hopping off the bus that took me there in the small town of Aylsham, halfway between my house and the school in North Walsham, and spending all day and all the spare money I had managed to find in my mother's handbag on pinball, cigarettes and Fanta. Before long the Paston had had enough of me too. For one thing they had wanted to put me on a course of O levels. I indignantly (and I daresay defiantly and arrogantly) declared that I had a very good set of O levels already and had been expelled from Uppingham while in the sixth form half a term into an A level course. Why should I have to sink down to the fourth form again? 'Because we do things by age here,' was the unsatisfactory reply. Or possibly they sensed that I was all show and no substance. At any rate I was slowly turning into one of those sneering, 'I've had it up to here with edu-bloody-cation' teenagers. Pinball and smoking were my highest ambitions.

To pursue even these minor pastimes I needed money, however, and when the Paston had hurled me out on my ear, my parents sent me as a last resort to NORCAT, the Norfolk College of Arts and Technology in King's Lynn. Here I developed the even more expensive habit

Chelsea. Oh dear.

Chelsea – seems a waste of time to take trouble over tying a bow tie but neglecting
to shave properly . . .

Kim Harris, Chelsea.

Kim in Draycott Place, taken by self (I solved that Rubik's Cube too, but months after my father cracked it).

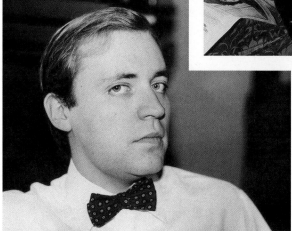

Kim Harris in our Chelsea flat.

My beloved parents . . .

My Personal AsSister doing what she does better than anyone.

In 1986, I spotted a house for sale in classic west Norfolk brick. Reader, I bought it.

Remsenburg N.Y.
April 30.1974

Dear Mr Fry.

Many thanks for your letter.   Much appreciated.

I found what you told me about yourself very interesting. Here is a little about myself. I have been living in this hamlet, eighty miles from New York. for twenty years with a wife, a sister in law, two dogs and six cats. I am a terrific enthusiast on baseball, never missing a New York Mets game on TV. My legs having gone back on me, I do nothing these days but read and write. I have just finished a new Jeeves novel which my London agent and published think is the best I have done, and am now trying (vainly at present) to get a plot for another.

All the best

Yours

P. G. Wodehouse

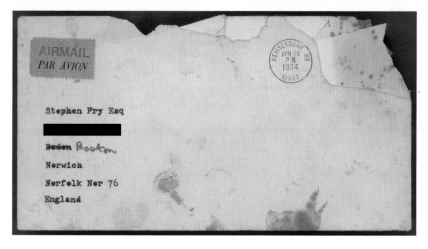

Stephen Fry Esq

Boden Booton
Norwich
Norfolk Nor 76
England

From P. G. Wodehouse.

Chelsea: Pipes are hard work. P. G. Wodehouse signed photograph evident.
As is Rubik's Calendar, which is just showing off.

Chelsea flat, at work on something. You can just see the signed photograph
of P. G. Wodehouse on the left.

owan's inexplicable ability to find something more interesting than me.

tempting a carol. Christmas Day, Norfolk, 1987.

Chelsea – damn, I wish I still had that pullover . . .

of gambling. A set of us would smoke and drink beer in a pub called the Woolpack, playing three-card brag for hours on end. I happily fell in with a group of highly literate and fascinating young eccentrics from the town. We met together to talk Baron Corvo, contribute to a strange magazine called the *Failure Press* ('failure' was deliberately misspelled in some way), devise a unique alphabet and arrange Paradox Parties, parties to which you could not be admitted unless you submitted an original paradox. Pretentious, you might think, but to find such a group in King's Lynn was thrilling for me. It was like finding not water in the desert, but a flask of quince, starfruit and lychee juice. Original. Strange. Testing. Provocative. And, as we would say of almost everything we liked, highly conducive.

At least NORCAT let me take A levels. But what with falling for a very lovely and smart girl from that group (yes, I have that 10 or so per cent of me that is entirely capable of being attracted to girls), feeling wholly uninspired by the academic side of life and still burning inside with that desperate first love that had made such a mess of me at Uppingham, I was becoming a less stable, predictable or hopeful entity.

It is a terrible thing to look back and realize that one grew up in a kind of golden age. Tarnished, but golden nonetheless. The 1970s are typically portrayed as grey, hopeless, hyper-inflationary, riddled with failure, strikes and sullen class warfare. Certainly, if you watch an episode of *The Sweeney*, it's hard to square John Thaw's menacing, jaw-crunching, whisky-slugging, cigarette-puffing, convention-defying Flying Squad detective Jack Regan with the unconvincing-Oxford-English-accented, crossword-solving, classical-music-loving, vintage-Jaguar-driving, tweed-jacketed Inspector Morse, who appeared a generation later. The brutal realism of the one contrasted with the cosy nonsense of the other is revealing. Similarly, the excellent balance of *Upstairs Downstairs* stands up very well against the ghastly snobbery and tacked-on *noblesse oblige* of that horrible Abbey programme. I say this guiltily, having actor friends I like very much who play in it, and play excellently, but truth must out.

Musically the 1970s were astonishing, even for someone like me, who is not especially attracted to pop or rock. You can distinguish early 1973, for example, from late 1973 in terms of both musical and fashion styles. Loons came in and bellbottoms bowed out. Every week you could see the young Elton John, David Bowie or Marc Bolan on *Top of the Pops* (admittedly Gary Glitter and Jimmy Savile too), not to mention Mud, Slade, Wizzard, Roxy Music and a myriad of freakish novelty songs and eclectic mixes. Meanwhile Led Zeppelin, The Rolling Stones, The Who, Pink Floyd, Genesis, Yes ... giant album artists were dominating the world. A few years later punk exploded – all this a heartbeat away from the dissolution of The Beatles. Music, unless my ear is staggeringly dysfunctional, hasn't undergone anything like such re-markably swift, imaginative, colourful and fundamental changes of style in the twenty-five years between the arrival of rap and now. Bits of acid house, trance, garage and other electronic dance music seem to have coincided with hip-hop in a more or less unbroken line. A photograph of an eighteen-year-old in 1990s clothes looks exactly like a photograph of an eighteen-year-old in twenty-first-century clothes.

But that is not the point, not the point at all. We moan about the sense of entitlement the young are said to have today. I think it is nonsense. It is simply that they are aware of the *actual* entitlement my generation enjoyed. Despite coming from a comfortably off household, since expulsion from private school all my education was at the expense of the state. Grants to cover living costs, tuition fees, everything. I even, while I was in debt to a bookshop at Cambridge, had the cheek to send a photocopy of their bill for the due sum of four hundred or so pounds (the equivalent of well over a thousand now) to the Norfolk and Norwich Local Education Authority. A tutor had added a paragraph to say that, as a scholar and potential academic of the future, these books were necessary to me. A cheque to cover the bill was immediately sent. I tell stories like that to my godchildren and nephews, who are just emerging from their university careers, burdened with debt, and I can see them wanting to punch me in the face. Hard.

I left university and shared a flat with my friend and Cambridge lover Kim in Chelsea, and life seemed infinitely interesting and straightforward. For the emerging graduate today there seems to be little on offer but a McJob, endless unpaid internships (only then if you know the right people) and a first rung on the property ladder that is higher and less attainable than the middle rung was in my early days.

But wait a minute – you've made me leap ahead of myself again. So, NORCAT. Three-card brag, beer, a girl, absolutely no interest in the curriculum and . . . a disappearance.

My memory cannot quite summon up the absolute circumstances of the First Great Escape. I was seventeen, it was 1974, I think I had agreed to go to some kind of musical festival and meet up with my friend Jo Wood. To cut a long (well it's fairly long in *Moab is My Washpot*) story short, some credit cards fell into my possession. Which is to say that I stole them. The short arm of the law had been reaching out feebly for three months or so before I was finally apprehended at the Hotel Wiltshire in Swindon, which stood, conveniently, absolutely opposite the police station.

I refused to give my name. My poor old mother and father had been through enough, surely? A sly officer, who unbeknownst to me had been going through my luggage in another room, returned and slowly whispered names that had been written on the flyleaves of the books

I had been lugging around with me during my adventures. A lot of them had been stolen from libraries, bookshops or friends' shelves, of course, and had all kinds of names scrawled on their title pages. Eventually, as I was being questioned by the detective sergeant in the interview room, I heard 'Stephen Fry?' being said in a low voice behind me. I had swung round and answered 'Yes?' before I was aware of the trap I had fallen into. I was, of course, on a missing persons list, and it was not long before my parents had sorted out a solicitor – my godmother's husband, who lived not far away. The game was up, and the goose cooked.

Some months of custody followed in the delightfully named Pucklechurch Prison. I had declined bail (not that I think my parents would have offered it anyway) and stayed at Pucklechurch for two weeks before another magistrate's appearance in Swindon, at which I was expected to plead. I announced my unquestionable guilt and was sent back on remand while the police took an embarrassingly long time to collect and assimilate the paperwork from the seven counties in which I had fraudulently used the credit cards. Back inside now as a con, as opposed to a non-con, the colour of my uniform changed and I was set to work.

The time passed easily and pleasantly enough. I had spent fourteen years in the private school system for heaven's sake: this was nothing. Other inmates at this young offenders institution, all tougher and mostly older than me, sobbed themselves to sleep. They had never spent a night away from home before.

At my trial, a dear friend of my parents, the imposing Sir Oliver Popplewell, then a noted QC, now a retired judge, represented me. I had worried that his distinguished name and reputation might rile the magistrates, a metropolitan sledgehammer sent to crack a provincial nut could seem offensive to their *amour propre*. I was also concerned that they might have little patience with one who, unlike most young offenders, had been given every opportunity and simply pissed his good fortune against the wall each time. I was guiltily stricken myself by the obvious difference in the 'life chances', as we would say now, of most of my luckless fellows back at Pucklechurch, who had been born into backgrounds of poverty, ignorance, squalor and abuse.

The magisterial bench, however, concluded that, since I had a solid family background (and perhaps came from the same class as them, I crimson at the thought), there was no need for a prison sentence, which would in those days and at my age have taken the form of Home Secretary Roy Jenkins's 'short sharp shock', the notorious detention centre, which was all the rage at the time. I had been dreading this: fellow cons at Pucklechurch told me it was all about running around and gym and weights and eating standing up and running about again like someone in Olympic training. DC provided the world with marvellously fit villains, ideal candidates for posts like nightclub bouncers and drug dealers' debt enforcers. Fortunately for me, taking into account the months I had already served (plus the other possible reasons I have indicated) I found myself sentenced to two years' probation in the care of my parents.

We move then from the image of the wretch lying on the stone flags of the prison cell, shadows of the prison bars cast across his sobbing frame, rats squeaking, gibbering and weeing in the corner, we move from this unhappy (and wholly inaccurate) picture to the solemn silence of the journey home from Swindon Magistrate's Court, father's stern face at the wheel, jaw tightly clamped and eyes sternly on the road ahead.

I seem to be sketching the biography of a Cambridge spy, a whole genre of literature in itself, factual and fictional. But whenever Kim Philby or Guy Burgess and their circle are written about, or (spoiler averted) the mole in Le Carré's *Tinker, Tailor, Soldier, Spy*, for example, there is repeated (to the point of cliché) emphasis on how withdrawal of the parental presence at an early age, the very nature of an old-fashioned classical English education given to a certain kind of person equipped with charm, intelligence, duplicity, guile (I was always called Sly-Fry, from my earliest memories of my very first schools) who had an almost pathological need to prove himself, to *belong*, could provide all the ingredients of a five-star, twenty-four-carat traitor and spy. I was and am neither of course, but had I been at Cambridge in the 'low dishonest decade' of the 1930s, instead of at the beginning of Thatcherism – between the 'Winter of Discontent' and the Falklands War essentially – then perhaps I would have been drawn into the Ring of Five and made it a Ring of Six. I doubt it: I'm not sure that the SIS, or MI6 as it's usually called these days, the most exclusive club there ever was in Great Britain, would have taken a Jew. Victor Rothschild came the closest, being a Cambridge Apostle like Burgess and Blunt, but even he, glamorous first-class cricketer, decorated war hero and Bugatti-riding adventurer that he was, was MI5, not 6. Some people still believe that Rothschild was the fifth man who closed the circle. We will probably never know. But there was a world of difference between the two services: 6 was pukka, 5 much less so. I am sure that is not so today, but what *is* true today is that I possess so many of the similar qualities, right down to a love of cricket, claret and clubland.

An upbringing that might under different circumstances have been used for a complex secret betrayal of my tribe became instead a simple public mockery of it in *Latin!*, my first piece of proper writing, followed by Cambridge Footlights sketches and, in the outside world, *Blackadder*, *Fry and Laurie* and so on. Like the satire of the 1930s Berlin cabarets that, as Peter Cook observed, 'did so very much to prevent the rise of Adolph Hitler', the satire in *A Bit of Fry and Laurie* such as it was – privatization, obsession with the free market and so forth – had the force and effectiveness of a kitten armed with a rubber bayonet, but we never expected anything else. We probably didn't imagine, however, that Old Etonians would still be ruling the country a quarter of a century later. Or indeed that they would be ruling the American TV and movie box office in the form of Damian Lewis, Dominic West, Tom Hiddleston, Eddie Redmayne and – ahem – m'colleague Hugh himself.

Male writers in Britain between the wars, as Martin Green brilliantly observed in *Children of the Sun*, could be divided into two classes: those that went to Eton and wished they hadn't, like George Orwell, and those that hadn't and wished they had, like Evelyn Waugh. I certainly cannot convincingly deny that I fall into the second category. The great advantage of an Oxbridge education is not that some mafia pushes you up the ladder as soon as you leave, nor is it in the education and living standards that you enjoy at either university: the real advantage is that you never have to deal with the fact that you didn't go there. Many genuinely never wanted to, many brush it all off with a 'Yeah, I could have gone, but the course at Warwick was so much better', others simmer in rage at the number of us in comedy, television, the law and all the other establishment trades. As would I, had I not got in. So it is with Eton. It would have been nice to have gone there, but on the other hand I would probably have been expelled even earlier, and who knows what criminal abominations I would have committed with an OE tie and that spy-like deceitful manner?

Where were we? Travelling with my parents in a silent journey from Pucklechurch Prison back home to Norfolk.

The twelve months between 1976 and 1977 followed. My first ever year of self-control. Possibly my first and *only* year of self-control. Every day I worked on the one-year course of A levels that I had managed to persuade Norwich City College to allow me to sit for. Aside from the syllabus, I read every Shakespeare play, writing synopses and notes on each character and scene. I devoured Chaucer, Milton, Spenser, Dryden, Pope and all the literary giants that I supposed I would have to be expert in before Cambridge would even look at me. I read *Ulysses* for the first time, with the help of a reading companion written by Anthony Burgess. I worked part-time in a department store in Norwich. I didn't steal or transgress. I was, it must be said, quite extraordinarily focused, sober, clean and concentrated.

Fortune favoured me, and I won a scholarship to Queens' College to read English Literature. If you have read *The Fry Chronicles*, you shouldn't be here, you should still be descaling the rabbit or tread-milling in the gym to the varied stylings of Jack and Meg White. You already know all of this, so I shall steam through for the others, and you'll find out where to pick up from where I last left off.

I performed in lots of plays when I got to Cambridge.

I fell in love with and shared rooms with a brilliant clas-
sicist and chess player (and more importantly wonderful
person) called Kim, as in Philby. I produced articles for
university magazines. I wrote the aforementioned play
Latin! or Tobacco and Boys, which was performed at Cambridge and then taken to the Edinburgh Festival. This led
to my meeting a tall fellow with a red flush to each cheek
and a rather endearing way of saying 'Hullo!' He was
James Hugh Calum Laurie, a name which can be convincingly expressed sixteen ways.

'Hi, I'm Calum Laurie Hugh James.'

'Laurie James Hugh Calum, at your service.'

'James Laurie Calum Hugh, how may I help?'

Et cetera. So many permutations, but he chose to call
himself Hugh Laurie, which is how the little world of
Cambridge then knew him and how the wider world of
the . . . er . . . wider world now knows him.

Together with friends Emma Thompson, Tony Slattery, Paul Shearer and Penny Dwyer, we put on a show in
our last year. It won a new award called the Perrier Prize,
which resulted in us going to perform our show in London, then Australia, before coming back to record it for
the BBC.

This is the linear bit and dull even if you haven't read it
before. Kim and I shared a flat in Chelsea, while Hugh,
Emma, Paul and I started to do a show for Granada Television in Manchester. We were, as it were, boy-banded
together with Ben Elton, Siobhan Redmond and Robbie

Coltrane to create a new sketch comedy troupe. The resultant show, *Alfresco*, was not much of a success, but we liked each other's company, and new opportunities arose.

Kim and I drifted apart, but are still the warmest and best of friends. My fifteen years of so-called 'celibacy' began. Work started to come in the form of newspaper and magazine articles, a West End play, a stage run of Alan Bennett's *Forty Years On*, and then *Blackadder II*.

Noel Gay's musical comedy *Me and My Girl* came next. I worked on the 'book', in other words the story, dialogue and some of the lyrics. 'The Sun Has Got His Hat On' was a charming number from Noel Gay's back catalogue, and the director Mike Ockrent and I managed to make it a suitable opener for the second half of the show. The verse

> He's been roasting niggers
> Out in Timbuktu
> Now he's coming back
> To do the same to you

needed a little tweak, one could not but feel.* With pulsating lyrical talent, Gilbertian wit and astounding geographical, agrarian and botanical understanding the verse now became, under my magical weaving fingers,

---

*Since I wrote this passage some poor sod of a local radio DJ was forced into resignation for playing an old recording of the song. Oh lawks.

He's been roasting peanuts
Out in Timbuktu
Now he's coming back
To do the same to you

Nobody seemed to notice. No letters from outraged Malians denying that they had ever roasted a single peanut, not even in fun. No death threats from the guild of professional peanut roasters of Atlanta, Georgia. But the show was a success in the West End and then on Broadway. It made me money. I went mad buying classic cars, a country house, all kinds of things.

I filled every day with writing: book reviews for the now deceased *Listener* magazine, general articles for magazines like *Arena* and radio pieces for any number of programmes hosted by Ned Sherrin.

I became friends with Douglas Adams and began a lifelong love affair with all things to do with computing and the digital world.

In 1986, sharing a house with Hugh and others, just having finished recording the *Blackadder II* series, I was offered by an actor, who for obvious reasons shall remain nameless, a line of the illegal stimulant cocaine.

Right, all those who feel they absorbed *Moab is My Washpot* and *The Fry Chronicles* can come back in now. You will know from the latter that I seemed to have been born with a propensity to become addicted to things beginning with c. Sugar ($C_{12} H_{22} O_{11}$) – in the form of Candy, Confectionery and Chocolates – Cigarettes, Credit Cards (other people's to begin with), Comedy, Cambridge, Classic Cars, Clubs and so on.

But Cocaine. Oh dear. This has to be played delicately. If I go on about it too much it will sound like repellent braggadocio: 'Wow, what a wild crazy-head this guy Steve-o is. Taking blow like a crazy rock star. Cool.'

If I drown myself in pity it's no better: 'I was in the grip of a disease, and the name of that disease was addiction.' There's something po-faced, self-pitying and sanctimonious about that, true interpretation as many would insist that it is.

We have heard it all before. In short-form magazine articles, in long tearful confessionals. It is yesterday's news. Kind of. But it was fifteen years of my life, so it would be wrong of me at least not to – as it were – give you a sniff of the coke years.

Moral or Medical?

The Line-up

- Buckingham Palace
- Windsor Castle
- Sandringham House
- Clarence House
- The House of Lords
- The House of Commons
- The Ritz
- The Savoy
- Claridge's
- The Dorchester
- The Berkeley
- The Connaught
- Grosvenor House
- White's Club
- Brooks's Club
- Boodle's Club
- The Carlton Club
- The United Oxford and Cambridge Club
- The East India, Devonshire, Sports and Public Schools Club
- The Naval and Military Club

- The Reform Club
- The Travellers Club
- The Army and Navy Club
- The Naval and Military Club
- The RAC Club
- The RAF Club
- The Beefsteak Club
- The Garrick Club
- The Savile Club
- The Arts Club
- The Chelsea Arts Club
- The Savage Club
- Soho House
- The Groucho Club
- BBC Television Centre
- Fortnum & Mason
- ITV HQ
- The London Studios/LWT
- Shepperton Studios
- Pinewood Studios
- Elstree Studios
- 20th Century Fox
- *Daily Telegraph* offices
- *The Times* offices
- *Spectator* offices
- *Listener* offices
- *Tatler* – Vogue House
- *Vanity Fair* – Vogue House

I take this opportunity to apologize unreservedly to the owners, managers or representatives of the noble and ignoble premises above and to the hundreds of private homes, offices, car dashboards, tables, mantelpieces and available polished surfaces that could so easily have been added to this list of shame. You may wish to have me struck off, banned, blackballed or in any other way punished for past crimes; surely now is the time to reach for the phone, the police or the club secretary. There is no getting away from it. I am confessing to having broken the law and consumed, in public places, Class A sanctioned drugs. I have brought, you might say, gorgeous palaces, noble properties and elegant honest establishments into squalid disrepute.

That was then, this is now, yet some of you will be reading this in horror, not because you are easily shocked, but because *you thought better of me than this*. You might have children who will read of my pathetic exploits and you fear that they will take them as permission or encouragement to imitate the chopping-out of that long line of cocaine that stretched from 1986 to 2001. Oh Stephen, *how could you?* Such weakness, such feeble-mindedness, such self-indulgence. Such an insult to the efficient and admirable brain with which nature graced you and the warm and loving home in which your parents brought you up with such care.

This is where it all gets damnably difficult. We come to choosing between what we might call the addiction approach and the personal responsibility approach. There are those, there will always be those, who simply do not buy this addiction concept. Most especially they repudiate the premise that addiction is a disease, one that grips you as permanently and assuredly as any chronic affliction such as diabetes or asthma. They only see weakness, lack of grit, absence of will-power and feeble, self-justifying excuses. They hear, most especially, figures in the public eye talking of 'pressure' and 'stress' and they want to puke up. Here are rich, overpaid, over-praised, over-pampered, overindulged 'celebrities' who scrabble and snuffle and snort like rootling truffle pigs at the first bump of naughty powder they are offered and then, after years of careless abuse, when their septum finally surrenders, or their mind turns so paranoid on them that they lose their only true friends, they bleat, 'But I've got a disease! I'm an addictive personality! Help!'

I'm painting it as blackly as I can, yet I know some of you will see the foregoing as the correct, or at least as a convincing, analysis. Addicts are looked at with the same wrinkled-nosed disgust that is directed at the morbidly obese waddling through Target and Walmart stores in the Midwest states of America. Those poor clams can at least claim indigence and ignorance as the root cause of their addiction to the high-fructose corn syrup, ice cream and corn dogs that are slowly killing them. Does a rock star, City whizz-kid, actor, journalistic feature writer, best-selling novelist or comedian have the same excuse?

In the opposite corner there is the straightforward reverse of this pitiless verdict. It argues that addiction is indeed a condition, often inherited or congenital, and that the only way to defeat it even if it is not a 'real' disease is *to treat it as if it is.*

I can quite see how one view speaks to the contempt, envy, resentment, scorn and impatience many in the modern world have for what is so revoltingly called and yet so revoltingly *is* 'celeb culture'. A spoiled minority, to which I find myself belonging willy-nilly,* seem to be encouraged to believe their views on everything from politics, art, religion and society are more valid than that of everyman or -woman. Oh how we oh so modestly and smilingly lord it over the rest of society: unto us is given more than we need by way of freebies, attention and opportunity, while ordinary, *real* people struggle with the daily round, unattended to, unheard, bulldozed or at least elbowed aside by a brutish, shallow culture which values fame even above money.

I have been fairly well known in my own country for a quarter of a century, and beyond, in Russia, Canada, New Zealand and Australia, for perhaps fifteen. My books have been translated into dozens of languages, but mostly I find when wandering in Eastern Europe or South America that I am taken for a strangely morphed compound of Jeremy Clarkson and James May from BBC

---

*In the *real* sense of willy-nilly. Not in the sense of harum-scarum or all over the place.

Television's *Top Gear*. Something to do with being a tall, fleshy Englishman with odd hair who rings a faint bell in the eye of the average Bulgarian or Bolivian, if bells can be rung in eyes, that is.

I remember a marvellous line of Anthony Burgess's when he reviewed, in, I think, the *Observer*, William Goldman's peerless *Adventures in the Screen Trade*. Burgess used the phrase of film stars: 'those irrelevantly endowed with adventitious photogeneity'. Or it may perhaps have been 'those adventitiously endowed with irrelevant photogeneity'. It so happened that I got to know William Goldman well in the early to mid-1990s when John Cleese, in a breathtaking act of generosity, chartered a boat for about thirty to go up the Nile. All we guests had to do was turn up at the Cleesery in London, and the rest was taken care of: carriage to the airport, flights, laundry, food, sight-seeing, informative evening lectures – everything was looked after for us on the floating Claridge's that glided up from Cairo to the Aswan Dam.

One afternoon comes back very clearly to me. We were shading ourselves in the shadow of an ancient pylon in Luxor while our tour guide spoke of hiero-glyphs and higher things. I asked Bill a few questions that I had been too shy to previously. He was hero enough for having written *Adventures in the Screen Trade* and earlier *The Season*, a still perfectly relevant and never less than insanely readable summation of one year in the life of Broadway. But Goldman was the screenwriter who wrote *Butch Cassidy and the Sundance Kid*, *All the President's Men*, *Marathon Man* and *The Princess Bride* and was, even then, chewing over whether he would accept the offer from Rob Reiner and Castle Rock to adapt Stephen King's *Misery*.

Unforgivably gauche as it seems, I found my mouth forming the shy sentence: 'So, er, what's Robert Redford really like?'

'Well,' said Bill, 'tell me what you would be like if for twenty-five years you had never heard the word "no".'

Which is as good an answer as could be given. It is far from necessary and sufficient not to have heard the word 'no' for decades to become a brat, or spoiled or impossible to deal with, but it goes a long way to explaining some of the more painful characteristics of those who are called stars.

It's rather like the argument used to defend those brought up in poverty and abuse, however. It fails to explain those many who, under the same intolerable, horrific circumstances, do *not* become members of gangs or crack-smoking thugs who could remorselessly beat an old man to death for asking them to keep the noise down. There are those who have endured childhoods we can't even imagine who go on to university and lives of fulfilment, kindness and familial bliss. Similarly there are long-established stars, Tom Hanks to pull a random name out of the Starry Sorting Hat, who are as kind,

75

self-deprecating, professional, unspoiled and modest as it is possible to be.

So we return to drugs. How can I explain the extraordinary waste of time and money that went into my fifteen-year habit? Tens if not hundreds of thousands of pounds, and as many hours, sniffing, snorting and tooting away time that could have been employed in writing, performing, thinking, exercising, *living*. I can't begin to explain it, but I can at least attempt to describe it.

The Early Days

The first effect of cocaine is of . . . nothing. You don't get the huge, whoomping, rushing high that is said to be the reward of heroin or of crystal meth and crack. I haven't tried any of those because I am a squeamish wimp. Perhaps this denies me any credit as a true addict. Friends like Sebastian Horsley and Russell Brand, the late Philip Seymour Hoffman and all those rock stars of the 1970s who were unafraid to put a flame under a spoon, suck the juice into a syringe, tighten a tie round their biceps with their teeth, pump their fists and tap with two fingers until they found an available vein, whether it be, once the more available ones had hardened into uselessness, a vein in their eyeball or their penis, then plunge the plunger, they were surely the true addicts. I got the word 'squeamish' from an article I read by Aaron Sorkin, the screenwriting phenomenon who gave the world *A Few Good Men*, *The West Wing*, *The Social Network* and *The Newsroom*. He was taking a break in rehearsals with Philip Seymour Hoffman and, as an ex-coke fiend, was saying to him that he'd always been too squeamish to inject himself, otherwise he supposed he'd have been a junkie. 'Stay squeamish,' was Hoffman's (typically) curt reply. It wasn't too long after that that he himself was dead. Twenty-three years 'clean' and then one back-slide and it was all over. It's rather like nuclear weaponry: you can never say it is safe because it has only been safe *up until now*; it needs to be safe for all time: one moment of not being safe, and the whole game is up.

So, back now in London in 1986 for my first experience of taking coke. I nervously watch my friend take out a folded wrap of paper, open it and shake out a heap of granular white powder on to a metal tray on the table beside him. He takes out a credit card and with its edge chops gently until the powder is as fine grained as he can make it. He uses the edge to sweep this pile into five equal lines, rolls up a ten-pound note, bends down, applies the end of the tube to one nostril and the other end to the first line and with a sharp snort sucks in half of it. He takes the remaining half of his line up the other nostril and then passes me the rolled-up tube.

With as much nonchalance as I can muster I reproduce his actions. My hand is trembling a little, and I am more than a little anxious not to imitate Woody Allen's notorious sneeze in *Annie Hall*. My bent nose has gifted me a deviated septum, which means that it is uncommon for both nostrils to be in full working order at the same time. I force as much suction as I can on my line with the weak left nostril and nothing moves. Embarrassed, I take the whole line up my clear right nostril with one huge snort. The powder hits the back of my throat and my eyes sting a little. The other three, also neophytes at this ceremony, take their turns.

I sit back, expecting hallucinations, a trance, bliss, euphoria, ecstasy . . . *something*.

Our host, as is his right, licks his forefinger and sweeps up the residue of powder, pushing it round his gums.

'Er . . .' says one of our number braver than me, 'what are we supposed to feel?'

'You get a bit of a buzz' – the expert claps his hands together and exhales loudly – 'and you feel just . . . good. That's what's so great about coke. It's kind of subtle?'

Up until this time the only illegal drug I had ever tried had been dope, which I had been rather ashamed of strongly disliking. Cannabis, even the milder versions of grass and resin available back then before the age of skunk and buds, was certainly not subtle, neither in effect nor in after-effect. In 1982 I had once vomited all over, around, above and below the lavatory of a friend's house only a few months after coming back from our Footlights tour of Australia. I can't remember any discernible pleasure at any stage and had more or less foresworn the weed. Most people have a drug that suits them, whether it is nicotine (not much of a behavioural modifier), coffee, cannabis, alcohol, ketamine, crystal meth, crack, opium, heroin, speed, MDMA/Ecstasy. I had decided early on that cannabis was not for me, but I hadn't for one second considered replacing it with another one.

Sitting back now and inspecting the effect of the

cocaine, I have to confess to noticing finally a benevolent stimulation. I observe too that we are all inclined to talk a little more. Mostly over each other, without listening, a feature I will soon come to recognize very clearly.

A Brief History of Blow

Cocaine (if you call it 'blow' you sound hipper and cooler), as most people know, derives from the coca plant, indigenous to South America, principally Colombia, Peru and Bolivia. The leaves of the plant are freely and legally available in those countries to chew or to make into a tea known as a *mate* and are said to help humans cope with the fatigue and altitude sickness associated with the high Andes. Ingestion of these leaves or infusions doesn't impart a fraction of any of the euphoria or stimulation associated with cocaine, but they are said to be rich in all kinds of vitamins, minerals and fibre.

When I was in South America in my puffing, wheezing cigarette-smoking days, locals there encouraged me to chew the leaves with lime, or to add lime juice to the *mate*, in order to speed up the (very mild) effect of coca and help me with the exhausting altitude. I suppose the process of adding lime is a gesture towards the acid/base extraction which turns coca into cocaine, the Class A scheduled drug, the billion-dollar industry, the working-class, media-class, rural and urban community must-have weekend companion that has been growing and growing in popularity since the 1970s and still shows no sign of declining. A chief constable told me not long ago that it is easier to score cocaine in a market town in East Anglia than it is in Soho Square. It's Lombard-street to a China orange* that there is more coke consumed on Friday and Saturday nights in Doncaster than in Chelsea. No one can call the substance cheap, but it has held its price pretty steadily over the past decade or so and it is now far from the preserve of the members of 'trendy' – as the word then was – Soho or Mayfair private clubs.

It was in the nineteenth century that the breakthroughs were made that turned this harmless, utterly non-addictive Andean bush-leaf into coca-ine ('-ine' is a suffix chemists give to alkaloids: coffee's alkaloid is caffeine; the alkaloid of *Atropa belladonna*, or deadly nightshade, is atropine; and so on). Heroin, on the other hand, was so called by the Bayer Company of Germany, who gave us aspirin, because it was thought to confer heroic properties on the user.

No less a figure than Sigmund Freud was one of the first major medical figures to write on the properties of cocaine, which was a *rara avis* in the nineteenth century, inasmuch as most major drugs were narcotics, usually derived from the poppy family: morphine, opium, codeine and Queen Victoria's favourite tipple, laudanum, which is

*A once common phrase that no one seems to know any more, but is worth looking up.

morphine and alcohol combined: blissikins, as Nancy Mitford used to say. Freud's book *Über Coca* contains some fascinating insights into the effect of this new drug on himself and his patients/volunteers/kidnapped tramps.

> It seems probable, in the light of reports which I shall refer to later, that coca, if used protractedly but in moderation, is not detrimental to the body. Von Anrep treated animals for thirty days with moderate doses of cocaine and detected no detrimental effects on their bodily functions. It seems to me noteworthy – and I discovered this in myself and in other observers who were capable of judging such things – that a first dose or even repeated doses of coca produce no compulsive desire to use the stimulant further; on the contrary, one feels a certain unmotivated aversion to the substance.

As *if* and I wish . . .

> The psychic effect of cocaïnum muriaticum in doses of 0.05–0.10g consists of exhilaration and lasting euphoria, which does not differ in any way from the normal euphoria of a healthy person. The feeling of excitement which accompanies stimulus by alcohol is completely lacking; the characteristic urge for immediate activity which alcohol produces is also absent. One senses an increase of self-control and feels more vigorous and more capable of work; on the other

82

hand, if one works, one misses that heightening of the mental powers which alcohol, tea, or coffee induce. One is simply normal, and soon finds it difficult to believe that one is under the influence of any drug at all.

Freud *drank* while he worked? Oh, well, that explains everything . . . Just to repeat:

It seems probable, in the light of reports which I shall refer to later, that coca, if used protractedly but in moderation, is not detrimental to the body.

We'll ignore the happy-sounding 'sudden cardiac death' that today's doctors and rehab clinicians like to harp on about with what I can only call tactless relish.

Coca is a far more potent and far less harmful stimulant than alcohol, and its widespread utilization is hindered at present only by its high cost.

The cost issue is still true, I suspect, and there are certainly many, many more deaths from alcohol in the world than from cocaine. Even taking into account the wider use, death from sustained cocaine ingestion is, I think, moderately rare, but certainly not unheard of.

Long-term use of coca is further strongly recommended and allegedly has been tried with success in all diseases which involve degeneration of the tissues, such as anæmia, phthisis, long-lasting febrile diseases, etc.; and also during recovery from such diseases . . . The natives of South America, who represented their goddess of love with coca leaves in her hand, did not doubt the stimulative effect of coca on the genitalia.

Ask any seasoned cokehead, certainly a male one, and they will probably agree with those lines of the Porter in *Macbeth*, who is discoursing here about alcohol but may as well be referring to Charlie.

> Lechery, sir, it provokes, and unprovokes;
> it provokes the desire, but it takes
> away the performance: therefore, much drink
> may be said to be an equivocator with lechery:
> it makes him, and it mars him; it sets
> him on, and it takes him off; it persuades him,
> and disheartens him; makes him stand to, and
> not stand to; in conclusion, equivocates him
> in a sleep, and, giving him the lie, leaves him.

Save that cocaine doesn't 'equivocate one in a sleep' so much as leave one wide-eyed and drippy-nosed for hours upon end, staring at the ceiling and making promises for the morrow that one knows one will not keep.

> Mantegazza confirms that the coqueros sustain a high degree of potency right into old age; he even reports cases of the restoration of potency and the disappearance of functional weaknesses following the use of coca,

although he does not believe that coca would produce such an effect in all individuals.

Marvaud emphatically supports the view that coca has a stimulative effect; other writers strongly recommend coca as a remedy for occasional functional weaknesses and temporary exhaustion; and Bentley reports on a case of this type in which coca was responsible for the cure.

Among the persons to whom I have given coca, three reported violent sexual excitement which they unhesitatingly attributed to the coca. A young writer, who was enabled by treatment with coca to resume his work after a longish illness, gave up using the drug because of the undesirable secondary effects which it had on him.

So one patient became so embarrassed by the increased libido of the drug that he discontinued it. 'Undesirable secondary effects', indeed. A Viagra, a workhorse, a cure for numerous debilitating ailments, less dangerous or mind-altering than alcohol, cocaine was welcomed by the late nineteenth century and, as is well known, gave the drink Coca-Cola the first half of its name, although the company dropped it from the list of ingredients in 1929. It was available everywhere legally in pastille, pill or potion form as a tonic and often self-contradictory treatment, being most efficacious in the cure of constipation and magically helpful too for the firming of loose or watery stools. It aided concentration and work rate, it cheered melancholy and in smaller doses was remarkably effective in the calming of recalcitrant children.

This was all during a period known as the Great Binge, roughly designated by social historians as 1870–1914, after which the First World War came and spoiled everything: almost at the sound of the first martial trumpet, beer was weakened, licensing hours were decreased, and, in 1915, the French banned absinthe, the poster child of the Great Binge. In between, during the Binge itself, however, every-thing was on sale at your local chemist or drug store over the counter, no questions asked. Fortnum & Mason, the elegant and grand Grocers' Royal of St James's, sold tasteful hampers which included silver boxes containing syringes and *étuis* for doting parents to send heroin and cocaine to their sons in the South African War and early years of the Great War. Indeed, Benzedrine, the trade name of a kind of amphetamine or 'speed', was supplied to commandos throughout the Second World War as part of their usual rations. In the Ian Fleming novels, James Bond is hardly ever off the stuff. It was just my luck to be born into an era when virtually anything exciting, beguil-ing, enchanting, naughty and nice was furiously illegal. Those comedians and actors a generation above me who were worried about their weight would regularly go to their doctors and be prescribed as many 'bennies' as they wanted. Generally speaking, anything that speeds up and stimulates your metabolism will suppress your appetite. Downers like cannabis produce, as is well known, that undignified state known as the munchies. Groups of young men and women invading a twenty-four-hour petrol station loading up on Mars Bars, Doritos and great basketfuls of junk food are as clear a statement of an evening of passing joints around as you could get.

Maybe it is the very illegality of cocaine that drew me to consider becoming a user. Perhaps an echo of Sherlock Holmes and his Seven-Per-Cent Solution resonated in the back of the mind. Perhaps my sexuality, or even my Jewishness, had always made me believe deep down that I would never be *normal.* That I was forever to be an outsider, a transgressor.

Nowadays there is a war of catch-up going on: a running war between the drug enforcement agencies and the enterprising chemists out in the world. Change a molecule here and a molecule there and you've got yourself a 'legal high' – some kind of pill (advertised as not for human consumption but 'for promoting healthy plant leaf shine') which will send you completely wild for about a day and a half. Which is probably overdoing it if you have a schedule like mine.

Here is a truth so obvious that people fail to notice it: *precisely* the same substances may, in fact usually do, have entirely different effects on different people. We see this clearly with allergies: Person A can down a bag of peanuts in one and then, with a satisfied eructation, ask for more, while Person B is on the floor choking to death with anaphylaxis because he took a bite out of an apple

87

that grew on a tree near a factory which ten years previously used nuts in its food processing plant.

We are used to it with alcohol too: we can sit at a table and match a friend glass for glass until that moment, that ghastly moment, mortifying for all, when the friend's eyes will snap down like shutters, he or she will start arguing with the waiters, they will start to repeat themselves, get spoiling for a fight and generally become a foul and unspeakable embarrassment everyone is anxious to be as far away from as possible. They will have had exactly, to the sixteenth of an ounce, the same amount of alcohol in their body as you have, yet you are capable of walking in a straight line, reciting 'Ozymandias', doing the crossword and drinking another four glasses without feeling anything more than a little merry. The number of times I have had to tell friends of mine who have had trouble with the bottle that they just must face up to the fact that they are, unfair as it seems, to all intents and purposes, allergic to it . . . you can't even make a rule out of body size. I have had huge friends who just can't take a drink, and have known dainty girls who can drink continuously without showing any sign of instability, aggression or wobble.

I am very lucky, or perhaps unlucky, in that I have a high tolerance for alcohol myself. Sometimes I've been known to mix it with an injudicious pill and found myself in bed the next morning without the faintest recollection of how I got there or how the whole evening panned out.

Another characteristic that I must be really clear and

88

straightforward about is that I *hate parties*. I absolutely detest them. I don't think I have ever liked a person as much as I have hated a party. The moment I am there I want to leave. I discount meals around a dinner table in a private house or restaurant. But parties with music, with people standing up, parties with music, parties with buffets or canapé waiters, parties with music, bring-a-bottle parties, parties with music, poolside parties . . . did I mention music? There's a famous speech in Evelyn Waugh's novel *Vile Bodies*, which I lifted almost whole for a screen adaptation I made in about 2002. 'Oh, Nina, such a lot of parties . . . all that succession and repetition of humanity. All those vile bodies.' Waugh was a rude snob, a bully and a rascal, but he wrote like an angel, and he and I (or at least I and Adam Fenwick-Symes, his hero) are as one when it comes to parties.

In the gay community, to which I did not belong, despite the sexual visa issued to me at birth which told the world that I was a citizen, musical comings-together were the least squalid form of finding a partner for the night and – who knows? – for the long term. These comings-together were in gay bars that pumped out Donna Summer, Blondie and the Eurythmics or in places like Heaven, down behind Charing Cross, which was supposedly the largest disco in Europe. I went to Heaven precisely once and found it hell. The noise, those awful up-and-down raking inspections that greeted you wherever you went. I knew that I fell short of the ideal, which in those days seemed to involve string vests or plaid shirts, moustaches, jeans and plenty of muscle. The clone look, as it was known on account of its duplicated prevalence.

That one time I went to Heaven (I know, a clever name for a nightclub one must admit) I saw Kenny Everett dancing frenziedly and happily. He coo-cooed and blew me his special brand of extravagant kiss and threw back his head as if to say 'Dahling!' before being swallowed up in the bopping mass.

I saw too my friend from Cambridge, Oscar Moore. He was to go on to write *A Matter of Life and Sex* under the pseudonym Alec F. Moran (an anagram of *roman à clef*) and to edit the film magazine *Screen International*. Everett continued to be sacked and rehired, sacked and rehired, sacked and rehired every six months or so by the BBC.* Before too long both Moore and Everett would have died painfully and unhappily.

Sex

I do apologize for leaping about like this, but I did warn you. In my mid-twenties a sexual relationship, aside from

---

* After three series a BBC executive eventually cottoned on to the terrible truth that the name of Everett's female vulgarian, Cupid Stunt ('all in the best *possible* taste'), could be crudely spoonerized. She was forbidden from reappearing. A new, seemingly identical, character called Mary Hinge popped up in the next series. 'Now you see that's better,' said the executive. 'You don't need to be smutty to be funny.'

the usual schoolboy larks and nervous cottaging, had come to me but once. It took the shape of my partnership with the aforementioned remarkable, brilliant and loyal friend Kim. We were lovers at Cambridge, and only the necessity of driving weekly up to Manchester to work on my first television series, *Alfresco*, kept us apart. Perhaps too much, for this marvellous lover in one arena loved what I exactly most didn't: the 'scene', those gay clubs and pubs and their music. Conversation was what I adored. Sometimes even other people's. How can you converse with 'Pump Up The Volume' vibrating your tummy and hoarsening your voice to a whisper that wouldn't be heard in a nun's cell?

Well, I returned one weekend to find a Graeco-American young man there, called Steve. In a perfectly happy, loving way I moved to the spare room in the Chelsea flat, while they took the master bedroom. Yes, in those rosy years one could live in a two-bedroomed flat in Chelsea just between the King's Road and Brompton a year after coming down from university. Well, I say 'one' – Kim's parents had money, and not all my contemporaries were as lucky: some had to live as far out as Clapham and Islington. To have been born clutching the coat-tails of the baby-boom was to have drawn first prize in the lottery of life. I am quite sure the young don't want my pity, but they do have my wanted or unwanted sympathy.

Everything continued swimmingly, Steve was very

charming, I didn't feel the least betrayed, and Kim and I have stayed the best of friends ever since.

A perfectly accidental advantage of this celibacy and my loathing of gay clubs and pubs was that at precisely the same time I emerged from university HIV emerged into the world too, although the first name I ever heard it given was GRID – Gay Related Immune Deficiency. By the decade's end I would have sat at the bedsides of many friends and attended the funerals of more. There is no virtue in my having survived the swathe of death that AIDS cut through a whole generation of gay men and intravenous drug users any more than I am prepared to say that there was any vice in the infection and deaths of those who did succumb. Once the facts were out, it was pretty dumb to be caught by the virus, it must be admitted, but my fiercest feelings at the time were for the hysterical untruths and myths perpetuated by the tabloid newspapers. I began to involve myself in Britain's first AIDS charity, the Terrence Higgins Trust, and have worked with them ever since.

We mounted in the late 1980s and early 1990s three or four benefit shows for THT called *Hysteria*, two of which were televised. In one of those Eddie Izzard made his television debut, in another Vic Reeves and Bob Mortimer. At these packed-with-stars benefit evenings the audience will be very stoked up, and when one comes on, as master of ceremonies, to announce, 'And now ladies and gentlemen, loosen your girdles and clamp your thighs, it's . . . Mr . . .

Rowan Atkinson!' or '. . . Miss Jennifer French and Dawn Saunders!' there will be an explosion of cheers and foot-stomping and whistles of joy and welcome that hit you like a force field. Unless the material they perform is entirely astonishing, the sound that accompanies their exit is necessarily a little less wild. That is no sign of failure, naturally. It was then a thrilling pleasure to announce, 'I know you're going to love him, please welcome the extraordinary Eddie Izzard!' There wasn't exactly the lone cough, tolling of a bell and bouncing of tumbleweed so beloved of *Simpsons* scriptwriters and others, but the reception was little more than cheerfully polite. His exit though – oh my word. The audience actually stood as they cheered him off, and I, in the wings, had to push him back on to take another roar of approval. I turned to one of the producers, and we both mouthed simultaneously, 'A star is born.' I know: what a cheesy showbizzy cliché, but you have to accept some.

Weird truth: since I began this paragraph an email just hit my inbox, reminding me of this June's Terrence Higgins Trust Gala Dinner. For the last twenty-odd years I have made a fundraising speech on these occasions and before each I have the same panic attack about what I'm going to say. It becomes harder and harder not to repeat myself. Maybe I'll cheat this year by reading out passages from this book.

A surprising number of you (surprising to me because I think, despite the evidence of my passport, that I still hover somewhere between my mid-twenties and early thirties) won't really know quite how disastrous, ugly, desperate, upsetting and frightening the AIDS epidemic was. The transition from being 'HIV positive' to having 'full-blown AIDS' – always 'full blown', no one ever managed to find another phrase – meant that death was a certainty. Well, not entirely a certainty. I have two friends who were diagnosed early and seem to possess some inbuilt antibody. Naturally, virologists have swarmed all over them, attempting to determine why they are to all intents and purposes immune.

Those dying of AIDS resembled the survivors of Nazi death camps: the gaunt, hollowed cheeks, the total emaciation, the dry, crusted lips, the dull glimmer of fear and pain and hopelessness around the eyes. And always the shallow panting from infected lungs that denied any conversation but the most banal and forcedly cheerful from visitor and visited.

Perhaps the most upsetting sights I ever saw were anxious parents sitting on one side of the bed, looking down at their wasted and withered child, while on the other side sat the (for whatever reason) healthy and uninfected partner. The parents would flash sidelong glances that seemed to say, '*You* did this to our boy. *You* killed him. Why aren't *you* dying too?'

If I had enjoyed the 'gay lifestyle' and cruising and bars and clubs, it is very probable that I would be long dead. Anyone who ever saw someone suffer from AIDS knows it was not the release of death but the agonizingly drawn-out manner of dying that was so cruel and unendurable.

Very often friends of mine had to give their parents two pieces of shattering news in one.

'Mum, Dad, I have something to tell you. I'm gay.'

'What?'

'Yes. And, um, I have AIDS.'

Imagine a family having to deal with that. I met some heroic parents along that troubled fifteen to twenty years, when to test seropositive, as doctors called it, was to receive a certain sentence of death.

Religionists from pulpits and evangelical TV stations announced that this was all God's punishment for the perverted vice of homosexuality, quite failing to explain why this vengeful deity had no interest in visiting plagues and agonized death upon child rapists, torturers, murderers, those who beat up old women for their pension money (or indeed those cheating, thieving, adulterous and hypocritical clerics and preachers who pop up on the news from time to time weeping their repentance), reserving this uniquely foul pestilence only for men who choose to go to bed with each other and addicts careless in the use of their syringes. What a strange divinity. Later he was to take his pleasure, as he still does, on horrifying numbers of women and very young girls raped in sub-Saharan Africa while transmitting his avenging wrath on the unborn children in their wombs. I should be interested to hear from the religious zealots why he is doing this and what kind of a kick he gets out of it. But we are wasting time on those beneath contempt.

I suppose we will return to sex at some later point, but for the moment, where are we? Before you distracted me with your fevered and filthy red herrings and irrelevant erotic diversions, we were examining that first intranasal introduction of cocaine into my system. I wrote that the effect upon me had been between zero and minimal. A slightly increased propensity to talk and a little jigging up and down of the knees. Nonetheless that momentous evening will never leave me. We all had a second line, finishing up our friend's supply – he was only an underpaid actor after all. It was that second line that got hold. Don't misunderstand me, it didn't hook me and turn me instantly into an addict. Just a few smokes or shots of heroin won't make a junkie out of you, even if twenty or more just might. The second line gave me enough of what Freud had called 'euphoria' and enough of a sense of energy and optimism to make me think that this was a drug tailor-made for me.

The strange thing about cocaine is that it is said to cause a *dependency* rather than an addiction. Tallulah Bankhead put it this way: 'Honey, cocaine is not addictive. I should know, I've been taking it for twenty years.' Alcoholics, smokers and junkies are addicts. That is how I looked at it as the habit grew after that first simple encounter. Not one of the others in that room, all close friends, responded in the same way. There was ever something darker, more dangerous and – let's be frank – more stupid about me than about my friends. Socially, psychologically and inwardly stupid. Imbecilic. Self-destructive. More of a fool.

By the end of the 1980s I would no more consider going out in the evening without three or four grams of cocaine safely tucked in my pocket than I would consider going out without my legs.

Yet I was after all able to find it perfectly simple to go to the country and write my first novel, *The Liar*, sitting at the computer in Norfolk for four months without even the *thought* of cocaine crossing my mind; and this was when I must have been already regularly using it for five years. Just about daily.

I dare say cocaine was ready and waiting for me, but the real reason I embraced it is that I found it could give me a second existence. Instead of performing and being in bed with a mug of Horlicks and a P. G. Wodehouse at 11 p.m., coke gave me a whole new lease on nightlife. It made me for the first time in my life actually enjoy parties, though still never parties with music, no matter how wired I was. So long as I had two or three wraps in my pocket and access to a lavatory that wasn't too squalid or have too long and obvious a queue for the stalls, then I was a new, sociable, fun-loving Stephen. No longer the Stakhanovite drudge, producing column after column for magazine after magazine, voice-over after voice-over for face creams and dog biscuits and TV appearance after TV appearance for anyone who asked, I was Stephen the party animal, always to be seen at the now defunct Zanzibar in Great Queen Street, Covent Garden or its famed and 'storied', as Americans would say, successor, the Groucho Club in Dean Street, Soho. Bed by four or five in the morning and then up at ten feeling fine, ready to get through the backlog of magazine articles, reviews, radio scripts and whatever else the day demanded.

There again, I was lucky and unlucky. I know many, many people who profess to liking coke but who just can't recover the next morning and will feel like hell for two days afterwards. For some reason it never had that effect on me. I would awaken with a spring and a bounce and Tigger my way down to the kitchen in search of breakfast, much to the grumpy annoyance of Hugh, with whom I still shared a house at that time, along with his girlfriend and other Cambridge friends. Never the larkiest bird in the morning sky, Hugh, after a day in the gym, bed at 11.30 and not so much as a gin and tonic in between, still managed to feel like hell until mid-afternoon and seven coffees the next day.

I felt blessed. I was meeting new people at all kinds of parties, not just coke parties with fellow cokeheads, but ambassadorial, political, social and geeky-digital parties. I would never have accepted invitations to any kinds of parties like that without the little friend in my wallet.

Paraphernalia

Not the most important issue: if you've got a gram or two about you and any available surface on which the powder won't get trapped or soaked in then frankly a currency note and a credit card will get the job done perfectly adequately. Or you can even transfer by the corner of the card or a pinch of the fingers a 'bump' on to your fingernail or the side of your clenched fist and sniff it in like a Regency snuff-taker. Nothing can keep an addict from his supply. But for a cleaner, neater, altogether *purer* experience I had put together quite the little kit. During my visits to the sound studios of Soho for the purposes of lending my larynx to the allure of L'Oréal or the double-action brilliance of Bold Automatic, I had taken every opportunity to snaffle, when no one was looking, a useful collection of those editor's razor blades with a protective bar on the top that they used for cutting tape back in the days of old analogue reel-to-reels. Whenever I passed a McDonald's I popped in to make another haul. Ronald McDonald's red, white and yellow drinking straws, stored in glass carousel jars by the napkin and ketchup sachets, were the coke sniffer's ideal. Hygienically protected in paper with a wider bore than the average straw, fistfuls could easily be taken home, and each straw neatly snipped in half with scissors to make the best possible sniffing tube. Washable too. I mean, for heaven's sake, when one is generous with one's supply, as I always prided myself

99

on being, who knew what germs lurked within the snotty nostrils of the user to one's left as one passed on the straw?

Storage? I won't believe a single coke user who tells me they haven't at least once opened their wallet only to watch, with a shudder of horror, their precious packet or baggy fall out and splash into the lavatory bowl below.* So, aside from the obvious advice to make sure you always close the seat before opening your pockets and getting down to business, consider the container. For a short time I favoured the highly fashionable, for sadly obvious reasons, condom holder. You could slip three well-packed wraps and a blade in this two-piece plastic container and then slide the two halves together. It was compact and safe. I would keep two straws in the other pocket. In later years I discovered Californian head shops, where simple grinders were on display in the window. Even smarter ones allowed you to grind out a dose and then quickly sniff it up, concealing the action behind a handkerchief. No visit to the loo, no waiting for said loo to empty so that the sounds of one's chopping and snorting went unnoticed, just a simple indiscernible action. Of course, buying such a thing and several spares too is an unspoken – even to oneself – concession of one's addiction.

Incidentally, using the phrase 'getting down to business' when describing a men's lavatory may seem a little

* As with smartphones, coke lore had it that storing the damp wrap in rice would eventually dry it out, but it never worked for me.

'ho ho', but during the 1980s the epidemic of cocaine fever sweeping through the mewses, squares and side-streets of Mayfair had reached such a pitch that I remember sitting one evening in the bar of the wildly successful nightclub Annabel's when a friend, a great wit, known by just about everyone in the world of London fashion and parties, a man one could genuinely call a play-boy, came up from the men's room with a look of outrage on his face.

'Do you know what just happened?' he asked, a frown of indignant disgust clouding his otherwise fair features.

'No.'

'Some arsehole just came into the coke-room while I was chopping out a line and, without so much as a by-your-leave, he took his cock out and had a piss in one of those porcelain bowl things . . . I mean, should we get Mark to fling the man out and have him thrashed on the steps of the club?'

That really is how prevalent the white stuff was then and how utterly unremarkable the taking of it in public was. Inasmuch as the gentlemen's lavatories of Annabel's can ever be called public.

Incidentally, some of the paragraphs above look like I am writing out a template of instructions and encour-aging advice for the coke novice. It should go without saying and must be apparent if you read on and find out what damage I believe this noxious yet maddeningly be-guiling substance did to me that *I wouldn't recommend cocaine to my worst enemy.* Which won't, of course, stop someone taking it out of context and damning me. Goes with the turf. Chap gets used to it. Barely a day goes by without someone on Twitter favouring me with the information that 'I thought better of you than that' – the 'that' being anything from passing on the blandest of off-colour jokes, to employing a swear word that 'offends' them (don't get me started), to using a epithet that apparently slights a minority of some kind. Which I don't really get. 'God, there have been a lot of clever yids' doesn't seem in the least problematic. Nor does 'Amazing how many of the greatest ever American comedians have been kikes – must be something to do with their 2,000-year need to stay together and keep themselves amused', or whatever. Perfectly charming observations that don't need someone to say, 'Excuse me, those words are offensive. Kindly use the word "Jews" or better still the phrase "Jewish people",' (as if the latter takes the sting out of being a Jew, as if even that word is too strong). 'All Jewish people should be beaten up' and 'Fucking Jews run everything – you know they conspire to keep others out?' How is it better that whoever writes something so ghastly is using 'acceptable' words? It is the sentiment expressed that is repulsive or not repulsive, not the words. Hell, I'm turning into a foaming 'political correctness gone mad' animal. I shall shush on that topic. Paraphernalia then is described not for the purposes of an instruction manual, but as a warning: permanent sniffles, blood from the nose and other unwelcome parts, sleeplessness, diarrhoea, head-aches, itchy skin . . . and on top of these indignities, that of dealing with your dealer. We'll come to that interesting, intriguing and inscrutable being in a little while. Hold that thought.

Unexpected Diversion Ahead

Now this section isn't a diary (diary entries lie up ahead, waiting for you) but I do feel I have to insert here, by way of flavour, the unexpected nature of today, this day of my writing this sentence. A not untypical day in my life except for one rare but wild circumstance. In this interruption itself, as throughout the book, there will be plenty of unexpected excursions, which I hope will not annoy.

I awoke early this morning, still tingling. Last night I experienced one of the strongest manic episodes of my life. It had been stealing up on me for some days, but last night I felt almost possessed. I texted everyone I knew furiously, knowing that safety with cyclothymia (my particular variation of Bipolar Disorder) lies in the support of friends and family. They can tell from one's voice how over-sharp the edge of hysteria might be and talk one down or insist upon one accepting help. Hypomania (I know, one would have thought it should be called hyper-mania) often presents with a euphoric need to be in touch with people and a garrulity and excitable chattering manner that can make one barely comprehensible. It is, I am told, much harder to live with someone manic than someone depressed. The worst state for a family member, spouse or companion to deal with is the transitional mood that develops as one cycles between the two. I realized last night that this was what I had been going through the previous week, when I had felt angry and prickly about everything. I was energetic but in what you might call a negative manner.

But last night I was so charged, flying so high, feeling so positive and convinced of my worth that I suddenly understood historical figures like Joan of Arc and the wild prophetic ravings of Howard Beale, the radiant seer of broadcasting played so memorably by Peter Finch in his posthumous Oscar-winning last hurrah in *Network*. I'm sure you remember the scene where, raincoat over pyjamas, he comes dripping and possessed into the network building to take up his position in the newsroom as anchorman and, live on air, stands with arms outstretched exhorting all his viewers to go to their windows and shout, 'I'm mad as hell and I'm not going to take this any more!' God knows what drivel I might have come out with had I been in front of a camera last night.

If I didn't have a tiny core of sanity inside me I quite seriously would have believed myself imbued with some great spirit. Only those who have endured, or perhaps enjoyed, hypomania will understand quite what I mean. I am still today rattling away at top speed, though I dare say I will come back to revise this passage when I've either floated down (as I earnestly hope) or crashed to earth (as I worriedly fear).*

The nature of depression, mania's sinister twin, is that it is opposite in *every* regard. The one gives you hope and a vainglorious, grandiose belief in the future; the other convinces you of life's entire and eternal futility. The one gives an urge to communicate by text, letter, phone call, Twitter and personal visit. The other casts one alone into a darkened room, refusing visitors and rolling away to turn one's back on those poor concerned ones who love you and want to speak to you. Two poles.

So, I repeat. Yesterday was as high a day as can be. As a matter of fact I went to see my team, Norwich City, suffer a catastrophic and wholly undeserved defeat at Craven Cottage, the home ground of Fulham Football Club. How we will avoid the drop from Premiership to Championship I don't know.† But that is entirely another matter, and one that holds no interest for you. I mention it only because being in the directors' box in the company of Delia Smith and fellow board members and club staff allowed me to squawk and scream and jabber and joke and yell and yodel without it seeming the least odd. By the time I got home, undefeated even by the terrible loss of the match, I found myself in a state of unparalleled OCD busy-ness.

*I haven't . . . except to correct hasty typos.
†We didn't.

You will have the pleasure of learning more about my strange mind later as we go, but for the remainder of yesterday evening I polished shoes, tidied cupboards, reorganized stationery, cleared clutter and cooked a supper which took about half an hour to plate up, so fantastically symmetrical and exquisitely layered were its ingredients.

When I had finished this Adrian Monkish meal I began to feel my hands shaking, the blood singing in my head and a pressure pushing down on my chest. I was alone that evening so I set about sending long, long texts to those I knew best. I told them that I was manic, but that I was safe and had no feeling that I was going to do something mad, embarrassing or unsafe. Finally, I took the decision to text my psychiatrist, who was just returning from Marseilles, and he texted back with a suggested tweak to my medication and instructions to call him tomorrow, Sunday, by which time he would be home.

I slept well last night despite such an extraordinary and quite unexpected swing of the internal weather-vane. This morning I worked on a passage of this book, words tumbling furiously from me. I do hope, by the way, that this doesn't show. Marry in haste, repent at leisure, as Congreve wrote. Tweet in haste, repent at leisure, as I have learned. Sorely. Write in haste, revise at leisure, as experience has also taught me. 'I can write drunk, but must revise sober,' F. Scott Fitzgerald is said to have told his editor, Maxwell Perkins.

At two-thirty in the afternoon I slipped into a good shirt, knotted the silk salmon-pink and cucumber-green Garrick Club tie around my neck, selected some unassuming trousers and a pleasing jacket and trotted over to the Criterion Theatre, that little Thomas Verity jewel-box right by Eros* on Piccadilly Circus. The bar next to the theatre (the Cri, as it used to be known in its late-Victorian, early-Edwardian heyday, the age and locus of Wodehouse's Hon. Galahad Threepwood and his nemesis, Sir Gregory Parsloe-Parsloe) is where Doctor Watson met up with his old dresser from Barts Hospital, 'young Stamford', who was to go on that very afternoon to introduce him to Sherlock Holmes. So for me, despite the hordes of Chupa Chups-coloured tourists who clamber up to be photographed as they mime sucking the aluminium figure's elegantly veiled little dick while fingering his pert botty,† carelessly breaking the bowstring as they do so, despite their moronic, thoughtless littering of the surrounding area and despite at night drunks pissing into the trough at the base of the bronze fountain, despite all this, Piccadilly Circus – 'the hub of the Empire', as they used to call it – is sacred turf to me. Sacred paving, I should say.

*Technically Anteros, of course, but what the hey?
†The second best in central London. The best is, of course, that of the young man memorializing the Machine Gun Corps in Wellington Place. His matchlessly perfect buttocks present themselves to anyone travelling south along Park Lane towards Hyde Park Corner. One never minds a red light there.

I have the honour of being the chairman of the Criterion Theatre. It involves little more than a board meeting every now and then, but it is such a beautiful playhouse, and it does give me a little kick to see my name in the back of the programme, lost in the tiny print somewhere amongst the producers, investors and other board members. Our proprietor is the munificent Sally Greene, whose bountiful patronage (should that have been proprietress and matronage?) has also breathed life into the Old Vic and the great Soho jazz club, Ronnie Scott's.

So, I arrive at the theatre and descend to the stalls (the Criterion is one of the rare theatres where everything is underground: bars, dressing rooms, stage and auditorium) for an afternoon celebrating the life of the actor Richard Briers, who died some months ago. He was a fellow Garrickian, hence the choice of tie. Everyone who worked with him and is still breathing seems to be here. Pennies Wilton and Keith, Peters Egan and Bowles, Dickie's wife Annie, of course, his daughters and grandchildren and the great Sir Kenneth Branagh, a man as busy, if not busier, than I am, and whom I rarely get to see these days. Before the event begins I stand gabbling away with him, for once matching him in verbal pace and energy. I tell him of my current mental state. Like so many he responds with understanding and experience, recommending, of all things, meditation. The Kenneth Branagh I knew in the days of the film *Peter's Friends* would have sprayed out his tea derisively at the idea of meditation and embarked upon a hilarious, vituperative and brilliant extemporized monologue exposing the idiocy of staring at nothing and chanting, 'Om mani padme hum.' This is one of the many things I enjoy about ageing: I discover that I am so much less likely to find things twatty, pretentious and scorn-inducing, and I must assume KB feels the same.

Just as the houselights dim I approach the stalls seats from the wrong end and have to scuttle all the way round. I am rewarded with a hard glare from Penelope Keith, who is well known for . . . well. It is not my place to say.

She reads, however, the verse that Sir Henry Irving wrote as a farewell on his final stage appearance – a plea for the public to be charitable to lesser-known actors – very well. Everyone in fact is on top form as they summon up memories of a man who charmed all who knew him and swore more regularly and fantastically than anyone I ever met. Never having met myself, who would count as the one exception, I might boldly claim. Although the best swear I ever heard came from a close friend of both mine and Ken's, an actor who, forgetting his lines on a film set, reprimanded himself with the savage cry of 'Cunting Auschwitz!' Being Jewish, he could get away with it, I suppose. Just. But it's a curse one needs to keep for a serious moment of distress or fury, one can't but feel. For this person, forgetting his lines while filming was as serious and infuriating as anything could ever be. I am afraid I am more dilettante about such occasional lapses.

A remembrance of a much-loved man without a dud moment, although it is KB who, family aside, wins the afternoon by several lengths. Celebrations, memorials, funerals and charitable evenings are not competitive, you are thinking. To an actor, let me assure you, every single opportunity to open your mouth and perform to an audience alongside other actors is always a fierce and biting adversarial combat, and do not believe anyone who tells you otherwise.

Every story Ken tells about Briers (whose career direction he helped transform astoundingly to the extent of casting him, very successfully, as King Lear) I have heard many times before, yet I am reduced to an asthma attack strong enough to need a gulp or two on the inhaler I laugh so much and so uncontrollably. Branagh is always referred to as an exemplum of the self-regarding thespian lovie, or luvvie, or however you choose to spell it. This is rather unfortunate for me, since the Oxford English Dictionary cites *my* employment of the word (as it is commonly understood in reference to the acting trade) as the first known publicly printed usage. As a matter of fact, if he belongs to any class or subspecies of actor at all, I would say that Kenneth is blokey rather than luvvie. He is also – and for some reason people find this hard to believe – amongst the five funniest people I have ever met. We'll meet him again later in this unpredictably juggled narrative too.

I am sitting next to the legendary Frank Finlay, who

barks out the occasional laugh. I cannot say that he was entirely friendly to me when I breathlessly took my seat at the last minute, but then he is a devout Roman Catholic and perhaps he has heard of the debate in which I argued alongside Christopher Hitchens against the proposition that the Catholic Church is a force for good in the world. The number of people since who have accused me of being 'anti-Catholic' depresses and upsets me. Perhaps someone reported to him that I had rudely insulted the Mother of Churches and had harsh words for the pontiff (at that time Joseph Ratzinger, Benedict XVI, RC Ret'd).

I leave the event speedily to avoid being stuck with too many people. I am sure there is no one there whose company I am specifically avoiding, but I want to come back to this: the computer screen. My mind is still spinning, but I seem to need to share my afternoon with you, the uncomplaining reader.

The Richard Briers afternoon was typical in some ways of the kind of event that actors attend. Gossip and tales of thespian tradecraft and unspeakable theatrical disasters are told, retold and mistold. Academics, spies, doctors and lawyers are no different, give or take the dictates of their professional ethics. My life is so fragmented that I live the life of an actor and then the next day another life entirely. It may be the life of a writer or that of a sort of television presenter and host; I dine with classical musicians, with restaurateurs, playmates from the old drug days, plain downright socialites, chefs, fellow cricket lovers and new-found friends from the world of online networking. Unlike an envied and admirable few, I separate my friends and almost never dare mingle one group with another. When I do, it is usually a social disaster, like mixing drinks. I love good beer and I love good wine, but you cannot drink both on the same evening without suffering. I love the friends with whom I play or once daily played snooker and tooted quantities of high-grade pulverized Andean flake; I love the friends with whom I dine at preposterously expensive restaurants; I love the friends with whom I'm film-making or mincing on the stage. I love and value them all equally and don't think of them as stratified or in tiers, one group in some way higher or more important than the rest, but the thought of introducing them to each other makes me shiver and shudder with cringing embarrassment.

So today I walked away from the theatre, stopped off at a passing supermarket to buy some ice, turkey breast and tomatoes – an entirely random raid – and found myself, after I had escaped the usual struggle with the automated checkout (unexpected item in the bagging area *again*), trotting along the street in the company of the sartorially point-device Peter Bowles and the ever gentlemanly Moray* Watson†. For a hundred yards I was an actor, as I

---

* Pronounced like the mint you were a long time ago urged not to hurry and Andy the tennis champion.
† Moray played the definitive Colonel Bantry all those years ago with Joan Hickson's equally definitive Miss Marple.

tattled and swapped anecdotes with them before peeling off and making my way home and finding myself here. Still high on my own erratic and mercurial endorphins, I sit myself before you and think about what to write next.

We shall pick up the thread and theme of this chapter.

I mentioned in my list of shame that amongst the places I had taken cocaine was the House of Commons, and this is true. I was sitting in a low, satisfyingly old and comfortable leather armchair after a pleasant, but not too pleasant – it is a club after all – lunch with a Member – we needn't drag his name into it – and expressed a wish, as we swirled our brandies happily around, to betake myself for a young piddle. The MP pointed me to a door at the corner of the room and told me to take the second right in the corridor which would present itself. I swaggeringly entered until I saw to my alarm that this was a urinal only lavatory. And only one urinal at that. No single stall with a door. The shit, as William Morris predicted so accurately all those years ago in his utopian novel *News from Nowhere*, must be confined to the Chamber, I thought. So, heart beating like an engine, with the slightly trembling devil-may-care desperation of the true druggy, I wiped dry of condensation the rear section of the top of the urinal with the back of my tie, chopped a line there, drew out my straw and was just bringing it up to my nose when a merry, florid, well-lunched parliamentarian who would never see seventy again came in, humming happily.

'Sorry!' I said, in a rather muffled way, my shoulders shielding my shameful line. 'Thing is, silly I know. But I'm a little pee-shy. If there's someone waiting it just won't come.'

'Quite understand,' the man said cheerfully, backing out. 'You wait till you get to my age. Damned prostate won't let you get a drop out unless you curse and cajole it. Carry on.'

I took my courage in one hand and my straw in the other and with a sort of coughing House of Commons 'hear, hear!' roar, sucked in the line and straightened up. The old buster lurking outside was still tunefully and now tactfully humming. I swept away what little residue there was with my index finger, gummed it, contrived to achieve a genuine desultory wee and noticed in shame that I had left rather a puddle for this man's feet. I dived for the taps and the towels and made my escape back to the Smoking Room, as I seem to remember it was called in those days. It is probably known as the Herbal Tea Salon now.

Truss, Tweed and Intoxication

I may have mentioned before in book, blog or broadsheet that, as I grew to fame, I became more and more astonished at how even apparently observant and intelligent journalists would either tell blind lies, fail to notice the obvious or deviously ignore what was before them because it didn't fit with an image that they or their editor wished to project.

One sunny morning I was assigned to be 'profiled' by Lynne Truss, formerly my literary editor on the *Listener* magazine and soon to achieve fame in all English-speaking territories and beyond on account of her *Eats, Shoots and Leaves*, a declaration of war on what for linguists and those who love language are the ever-dancing, ever-dazzling, ever-changing particles, diacriticals, apostrophes and mutations that allow language to live, breathe, thrive and evolve. But that's another story. Lynne and I were to meet at the then very fashionable L'Escargot restaurant in Greek Street, run by Nick Lander. Lander's wife, Jancis Robinson, Master of Wine, caused L'Escargot to be, unless I am wildly mistaken, the first British restaurant whose wine menus were listed varietally.* You're very bored now, and I can see why. I am getting there.

So I arrive, and the delightfully frisky and beaming four-foot-nine-inch figure of Elina Salvoni, the maîtresse d', is there to welcome me. Lynne is already at the table. Now, a month or so earlier I had decided that it was about time to transform myself. I do this from time to time, rather like Doctor Who, only not like him at all. I had reinvented myself from nerdy bookworm to thief and

---

* In other words by grape variety – Sauvignon Blanc, Shiraz, Merlot, etc. – as opposed to the confusing traditional British manner of listing by estate without any mention of the grape. This once pioneering approach is now standard practice, of course.

convict, from thief and convict back to nerdy bookworm, from nerdy bookworm to tra-la-la acting and writing performer, from tra-la-la acting and writing performer to nerdy first-adopting computer user, and so on. And within those transmogrifications were so many more. My most recent mutation was from ponderous, tweedy, pipe-smoking paragon of pomposity resembling nothing so much as a Latin teacher at a school which was just going to be closed down in a blaze of scandal to leather-jacketed, jeans-wearing, trail-bike-riding, aftershave-slapping dude who knew which bands were going to be the Next Big Thing and could wear shades indoors without looking a prick. I know what you're thinking: every fibre of your being must be screaming that this must not be so, but for a year or so that is in truth how I was.

The fact is (I'm sure I shouldn't be so forward as to call it Fry's Law), such drastic and dramatic outward differences cut no ice at all. Any more than cosmetic surgery would have turned Heinrich Himmler into a pleasant companion for a spring walking tour of butterfly-filled alpine meadows.

Anyway, at the L'Escargot restaurant, I checked in my 'skid-lid', as we crazy two-wheeler sons of bitches called them, and joined Ms Truss at her table. We chatted amiably, old colleagues. I had a book to sell; perhaps it was my first novel, *The Liar*, I can't remember. She seemed very enthusiastic, the lunch and the Sémillon were well above par. Princess Diana shyly swept up to the first-floor dining room; security men dotted discreetly about down-stairs and upstairs tables, rendered conspicuous by their inconspicuousness. That was fashionable London in the 1980s for you. I had another appointment, and my Yamaha beast was growling for release in Soho Square, so I escaped the confining truss of Lynne and roared away, thinking little of the encounter.

Two weeks later the issue of the magazine Lynne had been writing for came out. The first words of her copy?

'Tweedy Stephen Fry . . .'

I had sat in front of her, radiating Guerlain *Eau de Verveine*, a goatskin US Airforce Golden Bear bomber jacket creaking and gleaming about my person before I took it off and hung it on the chair to reveal the pure white, captionless T-shirt beneath, a pack of Marlboro Red tucked, Brando-styley, into the sleeve. My legs were sheathed in Levi 501s and my feet shod in acid-resistant, heavy-duty Doc Marten working boots, the footjoy of choice for any Soho media fashionista (not a word yet in currency then) or fashionisto (not a word yet in currency now). The front upper of the left boot was already worn from gear-changing my hog, and the first word she can come up with is *tweedy*? Well, who am I to tell her that she is wrong? Webster was much possessed by death. He saw the skull beneath the skin. Or so claimed T. S. Eliot. Maybe Truss saw the tweed beneath the leather jacket and boots. Where others have cartilage and sinew, I have corduroy and cavalry twill, it seems, and always will. We see in people what we want to see, and nothing can change that.

The first rule of being a rebel is that you can't *make* yourself a rebel. It is an action not an identity, a process not a title. You *rebel*. When I was a distressed, confused, manic, disruptive and disrupted schoolboy, rebellion did not come as a choice.

It is extraordinary how some single concentrated occasions seem to combine so many features of your life in one dreadful moment so as to stand as symbolic of your entire character and destiny at that point in time.

There came one such critical culmination of all that I was in the summer of 1989. I found myself in a restaurant in Soho's Dean Street, an establishment long since passed into memory. It was called Burt's, I think in honour of Burt Shevelove, the little-remembered (by most) lyricist and librettist – *No, No, Nanette* and *A Funny Thing Happened on the Way to the Forum*, those kinds of works. We had booked the whole of Burt's to give Kenneth Branagh some kind of stag party, for this was a Saturday night, and he was to wed Emma Thompson on Sunday at Cliveden, the country house hotel that once belonged to the Astor family and gave its name to a 'set' of supposedly appeasement and Germanophile aristocrats and politicians that flourished in the 1930s.*

---

* As in Ishiguro's *The Remains of the Day*, only more lively and convivial.

All the details are on the clapperboard.

Quiet, dignified downtime: Eilean Aigas, Inverness-shire, 1993.

Hugh, perfectionist as he is, always stays within his character: a drivelling poltroon from dawn to dusk while *Jeeves and Wooster* was being filmed . . .

Everyone always anxious to sit next to me on the *Jeeves and Wooster* set.

Official publicity still for *Jeeves and Wooster*. I remember it as if it were twenty-five years ago.

Filming *Jeeves and Wooster* at Farnham, 1989. Sister Jo visiting the set.

Giving Charlie Laurie
his daily vodka and
yogurt smoothie.
Christmas, 1988.

It's that butch look.
Christmas, 1988.

Newborn Charlie Laurie,
adoring godparent, 1988.

My butch look,
1987.

Hysteria publicity
shot, 1991.

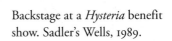

Backstage at a *Hysteria* benefit
show. Sadler's Wells, 1989.

...eading at, I think, a *Hysteria* show.

(*See over*) I know what you're thinking, and you're to stop it, January 1991.

All week Hugh, Rowan and my fellow Blackadderists had been rehearsing the final episode of *Blackadder Goes Forth*, so by the time we got down to Soho from Television Centre and the tech rehearsal we were rather tired. I had ridden in on my rearing, snarling trail-bike, which I parked dead opposite the restaurant in Bourchier Street, commonly known as piss alley. I worry to this day whether the lane's official name should be pronounced as spelled, 'Boor-she-A', or weirdly to rhyme with 'voucher'. The trouble is, I don't suppose there is anyone alive who can tell me the answer. I only fret over this question because a) I am a verbal nerd who does get in a tizzy about such things and b) I once judged a reading competition at Harrow School which was called the Lady Bourchier Reading Prize and was most definitely pronounced to rhyme with Sloucher and Croucher, solicitors at law and notaries public. I awarded one of the schoolboys, who went by the exotic name of Benedict Cumberbatch, second prize. *Second.* I cannot remember the name of the boy who won first, but I hope he will suddenly burst on to the acting scene, blow Benedict out of the water and finally vindicate my judgement. Something tells me that the contingency is a remote one, and I shall continue to look upon myself as the fisherman who let the big one go.

Whichever and however I parked my Yamaha, conveniently facing the entrance to Burt's restaurant, where Kenneth Branagh and friends were celebrating his last night as a bachelor.

I fully intended to be a good boy that night, for the following day we would be recording that last episode of the series *Blackadder Goes Forth*. I drank no more than a few vodka and tonics, my favoured drink back then, before turning to give Ken his obligatory farewell hug.

'Here,' said Ken, 'have this.' He passed me a large glass half full of whisky.

'I really . . .'

'Go on! Down in one.'

'Oh well, here goes.'

I swallowed it all down and weaved my way through to collect the skid-lid and gauntlets that, together with the previously described goatskin leather jacket, were all that might come between me and a skin-peeling 'moment', as two-wheel riders call anything from a slight loss of the back wheel to a somersault over the front on to the road.

This was a time when motorbikes swarmed over London streets. The *soi-disant* service industries were thriving in post-Big-Bang Thatcherite Britain, especially, of course, in London. The internet was in its hobbyist infancy, and fax machines were limited. I described the ubiquity of the motorcycle courier in the still in-print and still entirely fascinating *Fry Chronicles*. The noise and smell of them was all-pervasive (the motorbikes, not the chronicles, which are but lightly and pleasantly perfumed) and library footage of the era reminds one with a start how empty of them the metropolis now is. The delivery of scripts and documents could be achieved no other way, and many a student topped up his savings by haring about the city on delivery runs with scant regard to his or her or pedestrian safety.

I suppose we riders were easy meat for the busies.

I crossed Dean Street, pulling on the gauntlets and pushing the tightly fitting crash helmet down over my head with a smack on its crown, unjacked the beast and swung my leg over. I started the engine and was just easing forwards when a heavy hand descended on each shoulder. Fuck, I was going to be mugged. My adored motorcycle was going to be stolen. If I revved the engine and tried to escape, the bike would jerk forwards, and I would be left behind in Wile E. Coyote midair before thumping to earth with a coccyx-jarring thud.

I turned to face the aggressor.

Double fuck and twenty rotten arseholes. Uniformed police. What the hell?

Another constable stepped forwards from the shadows, signalling with a throat slit gesture for me to cut the engine. I complied, jacked the bike up, prepared a charming and conciliatory smile and pulled off the helmet.

The helmet, most unfortunately, almost airtight with the visor drawn down – which it had been – released right into the face of Second Constable a warm aromatic ball of something malty, peaty and Scottish.

'Oh dear. Oh dear, oh dear, oh dear,' said Second Constable to First. 'Whisky.'

First Constable had released his grip from my shoulders and allowed me to swing from the bike.

A van was parked opposite the Groucho Club.

'You seemed to be tottering a little unsteadily as you crossed the street to your motorcycle, sir,' First Constable explained.

I knew he was giving me his 'due cause' explanation. Since the repeal of the ancient sus laws, which had given the police the right to stop anyone 'on suspicion', a plausible reason had to be given. The police are very good at plausible reasons. *Not the Nine O'Clock News* had made merry fun with them on that very head some years earlier: 'walking in a built-up area in a loud shirt', and so forth. It was no good my protesting that I hadn't 'tottered' in the least. Crossing a street while donning a crash helmet is not a task easily undertaken, and while I may have wound and woven this way and that a little, it was certainly not in a manner that would cause a reasonable onlooker to suspect me of being inder the unfluence, ossifer. But none of this was of any use: they had me and doubtless they were going to invite me to blow down a tube of some kind.

Two vodka and tonics (doubles) and one very large whisky. Would that propel me over the limit? It was shock enough to think that a bike rider would be stopped at all. One of the reasons I had bought the damned thing, I reflected, was that I had had the idea that it would offer me a modicum of freedom from police interference.

A white tube was attached to a device, and I was invited to exhale.

'This reading indicates that your blood alcohol level is over the legal limit for the operation of a licensed motorized road vehicle, sir. We will now take you to the main station, where you will be asked to offer another breath sample to a Lionizer machine. This will be compared to the reading you have given us. The lower of the two readings will be used. If you do not wish to blow into the Lionizer, a blood or urine sample is acceptable. Failure, however, to provide any of these is a criminal offence. Do you understand this, sir?'

I nodded. Second Constable took my helmet and gloves, opened the rear doors of the van and hauled himself in. I was invited to sit on the bench opposite him. First Constable went round to the driver's seat, and we moved off. It was only as we turned right into Old Compton Street, which you could do in those days, that I realized my predicament. In my left-hand jacket pocket was a condom holder containing three grams of the best-quality cocaine, bought yesterday with a view to larks and fun at Cliveden. Surely I was certain to be searched or asked to empty my pockets when we got to the station?

I slowly moved my right hand to the jacket's right pocket, where I had some mints. This, I hoped, was where a decade of being obsessive about magic might pay off. I pulled out the mints and offered the bag to Second Constable, while at the same time putting my other hand into

123

the left pocket and curling my fingers around the condom holder. A very simple act of misdirection which seemed to work.

'Thank you, sir. And if you don't mind, I'll keep these. Nothing is allowed in your mouth until you have completed the Lionizer test. I'm sure you understand.'

'Of course.' I spread both hands wide in a gesture of complete comprehension. The condom holder was now on my lap and I was leaning forwards, allowing the groin-crease of my trousers to conceal it in the half light of the police van. 'So which station are we going to, if I may ask, officer?'

'West End Central,' was the reply.

West End Central. How grand. I had heard of it. The name cropped up in news reports and police dramas. George Dixon (of Dock Green) would often say to his son-in-law, Detective Sergeant Crawford (played by the eyebrowy Peter Byrne), 'Now, now, Andy, we don't want to go treading on West End Central's corns,' and things like that. Famous as it might be, I had no idea where it was. Somewhere central in the West End would be a good guess. It was a pleasant surprise when we drew up in Savile Row.

As I had hoped, Second Constable rose to his feet before me. I stood up fractionally later, just as the brakes were applied. I slapped my hand to the metal roof of the van, and my right foot stamped forwards to give me balance.

'Oops,' I said cheerfully. My foot had kicked the condom holder deep into the shadows below the bench I had sat upon. Surely it would not be discovered for a few days, by which time dozens of malefactors would have had rides in the van?

I sprang down and allowed myself to be led into the station. Relief flooded me. Whatever punishment might be meted out for the infraction of driving a motorbike with a glass or so more alcohol in the blood than was permitted could not compare to the scandal, shame, possible imprisonment and career ruination that would follow the discovery of three whole grams of a Class A drug on my person.

It was generally understood in the druggy world that one or two grams would be taken to be 'personal use' but that much more might be construed by a bolshy or ill-disposed policeman to be 'intent to supply'. The first might result in confiscation and a warning; the second would certainly, if the judge was in accord, lead to a prison sentence. Three grams lay on the borderline, and although my poor, stupid, addicted mind was running through a plan to get hold of my dealer between now and tomorrow, I felt well rid of my stash.

The Lionizer gave a reading that was jeeeyust over the limit, and I hoped for clemency. They led me into a room where a female sergeant was sitting across a desk. She asked me to empty my pockets. I complied with scrupulous obedience, turning the pockets inside out. From my inside jacket pocket I drew a wallet and four tickets for the following day's audience recording of *Blackadder Goes Forth*.

'Oh,' said the sergeant, 'you're doing another series, are you?'

The problem with new series of *Blackadder* as they came along was that people were used to the one before. They were never broadcast until all had been recorded, so when the audience came into the studio expecting to see Queenie's throne-room and Blackadder's low-beamed chamber, they were puzzled by the Regency wallpaper of Prince George's suite. Our audiences over the last few weeks had come expecting Mrs Miggins's pie shop, and we had to hope they would get used to Captain Blackadder's trench and Melchett and Darling's Staff HQ.

I saw my opportunity. We were given four studio tickets every week as a matter of course, and I hadn't yet thought about whom I might invite.

'Would you like to come along to a recording? It's at BBC Television Centre tomorrow evening. As it says on the tickets . . .' I pushed them forwards.

The sergeant looked up, and First and Second Constables nodded enthusiastically. They came forwards to collect one each, and she kept the remaining two for herself.

'Right,' she said. 'Well. You were over the limit, Mr Fry, so we will be charging you with the offence of driving or attempting to drive while above the legal limit or unfit through drink. It says on your driving licence that you live in Islington?'

Well, so much for the corruptibility of the Metropolitan Police. I was scandalized. Was no one to be mistrusted?

And so much too for the slow turning of the mills of justice. I would be expected to make an appearance on Monday morning, complete with insurance documents and licence, at Clerkenwell magistrates court, which, as it happened, was situated at the end of Duncan Terrace, where I was house-sitting for Douglas Adams. I was not to drive home on the motorbike, but could collect it the following day – Sunday – morning.

I descended the station steps, crash helmet and gauntlets under my arm, thinking furiously. I wanted the next day to drive my Aston Martin V8 Vantage to the BBC, and then after the *Blackadder* recording to 'motor down to Cliveden', as one imagined Asquiths and Grenfells doing, back in the palmy days. At some point I would need to meet up with one of my three tame coke dealers, who might be induced to rendezvous either at the BBC (in that event I must remember to get another studio ticket, I told myself: funny if they end up next to the policemen and -woman) or somewhere in Soho early the next day as I collected my bike. Perhaps they could come to Islington that night? Damn! I realized that I should have brought my mobile phone with me. I rarely took it on the bike, as its bulk prevented me taking anything else in the limited storage area. Anyway, I would somehow get hold of a wrap or two of good gear, get happily wrecked at Cliveden and then up early next morning, that is if I went to bed at all, and gun the Aston – perhaps for the last time in a year – back to London in time for my court appearance, which was fixed for 11 a.m.

Then another, truly dreadful thought crashed into my mind. Suppose they found the condom holder under the bench in the police van, saw that it contained drugs and then brushed it for fingerprints? As I had a criminal record,* mine would be on file. But no, if they picked it up, they wouldn't do so with gloves. It was a van, not a crime scene. They would be lucky to find any 'latents' surely?

'Mr Fry? Mr Fry?'

It was the police sergeant. I turned to see her standing at the bottom of the steps waving her arm above her head.

'Yes?' I approached her nervously.

'I believe you left this in the van, sir.' She pushed the condom holder into my hand.

'Er . . . I . . . thank you . . . the . . .'

'Be careful, sir. And thank you for the tickets.'

I simply did not know what to say. It was already too late to disown it. She turned with an inscrutable look on her face, leaving me standing there, my mouth opening and closing like a landed fish.

*See *Moab is My Washpot.*

A taxi was rattling towards me from the Piccadilly end, so I hailed it and climbed in. En route to Islington I privily and gingerly slid apart the two halves of the condom holder. There, perky as a stripper's tits, lay the three wraps. I could have sworn they winked at me.

To this day I am at a loss as to the how and the why and the what-the-hell of it all. Did the sergeant think it rude to open a private condom holder in this, the age of AIDS? Did she open it and think, hell, I'm about to go off duty, I just can't be arsed to bust this man. We already had the paperwork on the drink driving, so we had to follow through, but this . . . not inclined to blight his chances. I shall never know. Unless she happens to read this, in which case she is very welcome to be in touch.

I do not watch myself in old films or television programmes, or even new ones, unless I am in the cutting room and a part of the process of putting them together, but if I do catch (it is repeated so often) the final episode of *Blackadder Goes Forth*, the one which ends with the Blackadder trenchful finally truly going over the top and the image of a field of poppies bleeding through to the sound of raking machine-gun fire and a final mournful version of the Howard Goodall theme tune, if I do catch it or a scene from it, I cannot but say to myself, 'That was the day after I was busted for drink driving. The day after the woman police sergeant handed my coke back to me in a condom holder, cool as you please. And that evening I took the Aston down to Cliveden, parked it and partied through the night in honour of Emma and Ken's union. And the following day was the day I lost my licence for a year.'

Waiting for My Man

I have always, since I can remember, been a – what word does one choose? A handful? No, that's a bit nannyish. A rebel? Too cool. A transgressor? The John Buchan generation would've called me a wrong'un. An outsider is the closest I can come to it. Perhaps it is just that, as those who had the pleasure of reading the opening chapter of *The Fry Chronicles* will know, I was a pre-teen crazed with a love of sweets and never felt I had enough money for them; this triggered an addictive path upwards, a desire for the illicit and the unattainable. Next came cigarettes. Being caged in prison took my mind off this, and I concentrated on getting out and getting into university. Once at Cambridge, I barely drank anything more than coffee and certainly didn't take drugs: I just threw myself into comedy, drama, smoking and writing.

So, two or three years later – already lucky enough to have a TV show in Manchester with Ben Elton, Robbie Coltrane, Hugh Laurie and Emma Thompson – Hugh and I were also starting on *Blackadder II*. Physically, I was, if it can be believed now, lean; socially, given to few nocturnal exploits: parties, as I have said, being abhorrent to me.

But those two toots of cocaine had awoken a long-sleeping giant. The same dragon that got me expelled from so many schools and that landed me on the flag-stones of a prison cell was beginning to uncoil and rear up at me, snorting flame.

I cannot understand why, from the earliest days of my childhood, I had always been a problem. No uncle, god-father or family friend or (thank heavens) family member dandled me on his knee in a way which would prissily be called by my generation 'inappropriate' and more grace-fully by the younger generation 'awkward'. It is true that I had, from the first, grandiose plans to be a scholar, a writer, an actor, a somebody. But I was never discouraged in these fields of endeavour. Only my own frantic wild behaviour got in the way until it seemed, lying on that previously evoked straw-strewn prison floor, something in my brain snapped, and I knew that I had one last chance, if I may mangle Tennyson, to rise on the step-ping stones of my dead self to higher things.

And so we come round again to the unbelievably good fortune to have got that scholarship to Cambridge, to have been all-consumed by the acting and then writing bug and foolishly to have allowed myself to believe that every problem, propensity to bad behaviour and tempta-tion to library book theft and wild destructive pranks was way behind me. I didn't really like alcohol so very much; I didn't like late nights, I liked work. My last book, *The Fry Chronicles* (I'm simply astonished and only slightly wounded that you haven't read it), had written on its title page a line of Noël Coward's: 'Work is more fun than fun,' something I am lucky enough still to find true. 'Young men sow wild oats, old men grow sage,' Churchill is reputed to have said. It almost never is Churchill. In fact collectors of quotations call such laziness in attribution 'Churchillian creep'. I made the mistake of thinking all my oats were sown and falling asleep on my watch over myself.

Unless you have been a user of illegal, street, or recreational drugs yourself at any time in your life, you probably have a clear view in your head of what a drug dealer is like. As younglings we were sat in front of terrifying films and taught to call them 'pushers'; they were rated on a moral scale somewhere between Fleet Street royal correspondents and dung beetles.

'I Blame the Evil Pushers,' parents and editorial articles would squeal, wringing their clean hands in despair, incapable of even imagining such unalloyed evil. 'Pushers' hung around the school gates, waiting for a chance to get a child addicted. At first they weaned them on legal solvents like glue, fast-drying wet cement, toluene, butane and propane. Once the dopamine and norepinephrine and noradrenaline – I am not an endocrinologist, but drug use is all about the body's pleasure/reward system, as I'm sure we all know – have introduced themselves, offered a handshake and a moment of bliss, usually followed by a wild arc of vomiting, the substances bind themselves to the young users' brains, who find their pleasure centres tickled and massaged and unconditionally adored as they roll on the grass of the local park and look up at the sky with new loving eyes that ice cream and family life won't give them. Next, according to this mythical and inevitable wicked process (cheap cider aside, the most dangerous and most overlooked of them), illegal weed is offered and before the defenceless infant has a chance their 'friendly', 'low-price' suppliers are introducing them to cocaine and heroin. And once those dependencies are formed, the price ratchets up, the threats for non-payment become very real and Little Jack is raiding his mother's purse, burgling gran's flat, snatching mobile phones from younger kids, and the monstrous social malaise that we call drug culture is upon us. Sink estates, gangs and random violence, Ladybird Book Britain transformed into a moral, civil and derelict wasteland in fewer years than my lifetime, which, dear reader, despite this being my third autobiography, is not really so very long after all. That is what drugs have done to blight Britain.

All the foregoing is, of course, horse-shit. No, it's worse than horse-shit; horse-shit is strawy and pleasant smelling. It is human shit, which is malodorous in the extreme. Successive government-employed 'Drug Czars' who knew what they were talking about physiologically, sociologically and neurologically have been fired for telling their masters of either political stripe the real truth. If drugs are not soon legalized and controlled, taxed and categorized, the situation will get worse and worse and worse. Coca bushes are now immune to the vile airborne pesticides sent over from America to Colombia in the 1990s; the drug wars in war-torn Mexican drug-gang cities like Juárez in the noughties and teens of the twenty-first century make 1980s Medellín in Colombia look more like Moreton-in-Marsh in the Cotswolds; the profit margins have become so colossal that at every stage of 'cutting' or diminishing through additives the purity of the original cocaine block, each player in the journey from peasant leaf-grower up to the nightclub dealer is going to make a pleasant living.

From what I believe are unimpeachable sources, the end purity level for the user who doles out £50 or £60 for a gram (twenty-eight and a third grams constitute one old-fashioned imperial ounce) usually comes out at between 20 and 30 per cent. The dealer is a tiny fish in all this. He or she (and yes there are plenty of shes) may have taken a career path that goes something like this: not having done so well at school, they drifted perhaps into the music business as a DJ or bouncer and found that they liked a gram or two of coke in the evenings. So they went into business with an existing dealer they knew, having a different circle of friends. They told some of their friends they could be relied on for whatever they wanted, and those friends were overjoyed. It's a sellers' market, they don't need to push drugs on people. They are more likely to need to push people *away*. They frequently don't have enough on them to supply a clubful of desperate potential clients (dealers often like to use the word client) keen to party away.

I cannot tell you much about what goes on further up the chain. Of course, there is violence, just as there was in America during the blockheaded days of Prohibition. A gap is left when a desired substance is banned; that gap will offer such profits that no amount of violence will be considered too great to get hold of a great share of the market. But I can tell you I have yet to meet a doctor, policeman or probation officer who does not believe that street drugs should be licensed, legalized and controlled. Only politicians who stick their fingers in their ears and go 'La, la, la, la!' until they think the people who actually understand the problem will shut up are obsessed with the unwinnable 'war on drugs'. That, of course, is because voters are misguided.

Aside from anything else, just think what coke is cut with in order to maximize profits at every stage. In my early days it used to be baby laxative, with an all-too predictable outcome. More recently sugars, creatine, benzocaine (to mimic the numbing effect on the lips that makes you think you are getting plenty of the real deal) were favoured and especially these days levasimole, a cow dewormer, is now found in anything from 50 to 90 per cent of street cocaine. Not only does it dilute, but it also uses its own properties to stimulate and set off our inbuilt happy drug, dopamine. Other additives include hydrochloric acid and potassium permanganate. Not nice.

If alcohol were banned today, you can be sure criminal gangs would do the same with their bathtub gins and moonshine whiskies. Ethyl and isopropyl alcohol, methylated spirits and all kinds of cheapening and dangerous additives would go into the illicit brews. We know this because history has shown us that it was so. Cocktails were invented to sweeten and diversify the rancid effects of chokingly foul speakeasy booze.

But let us return to the dealer – Mitch, Nando or Jacquie we'll call them. I have known dozens of Mitches, Nandos and Jacquies in my time. Not one of them violent, not one of them morally inferior to me or anyone else I know. In fact they have often stood out as incredibly decent friends, wonderful parents, kind, attentive, funny people, no more branded with the Mark of (Co) Cain than your mother is.

Business is straightforward. You, the user, have your wad of cash; you meet in a café, bar, the dealer's flat or (less likely) at your home. If it is a public place or space, you have already secreted the money in a newspaper, which you oh so casually slide across the table towards Nando, and he returns by pushing over a packet of cigarettes which contains the gear. This is followed by talk of football, music, fashion, gossip, friends, children and a hasty draining of the cappuccino mug before we go our separate ways. Most dealers follow the rule 'don't get high on your own supply', but a user will be slightly uneasy in the presence of a Mitch or Jacquie who *never* took a line. At their flat, say, when you pop by. On the other hand, one tends not to like a dealer to come to one's own house, especially dealers who really like the stuff. How do you converse with them in a personal way? When is it decent to ask them to leave? How much of the expensive powder that you have bought from them and are now sharing with them is she going to hoover up? All in all, it is a most strange unwritten contract. You are anxious not to treat them like servants and probably overdo the deliberately non-patronizing talk, just as one does in conversation with bin-men and builders, yet all the while one is slave to them and the service they provide.

There has only ever been one significant and maddening problem with dealers: it is almost unique to them as a class and it drives one *insane*. Punctuality. Hence the quotation from Lou Reed that heads this section. The poor, late-lamented rock god must have put together, as have I, hours on street corners, in cafés and bars wondering if ever the *hell* they'll come. Have they been arrested? With your phone number in their directory? Please God they use a code name for me . . .

I know you want to think of the dealer as the evil link in this chain, but the truth is dealers spend most of their time pushing clients away. Their phones are ever buzzing (pagers back in the day): 'I need four grams now, where can I meet you?' 'Be at the usual café at ten.' 'I'm having a party tonight, six of us want two grams each.' The dealer dashes from client to client, getting cash up front before they can then visit *their* suppliers (who are the big, scary, silent ones who don't take credit and you really don't want to mess with), pick up the gear, go back home to cut it to whatever degree they can get away with, fold it into wraps before haring round town, dropping off to each client as discreetly as possible. That is your average dealer, caught between gangsters and clients. It's a sellers' market, yes, but that doesn't make life easy. They never have enough to meet demand. Some bullying rock star, pockets stuffed with currency notes, will catch sight of them and buy all they've got: 'No, but I've promised Jack and Rosie and Bill and Tom . . .' the dealer will protest, but to no avail. Now he or she has to start the whole process again. *That* is why they are always late. No wonder Lou Reed wrote that song.

A dealer's five minutes is therefore, if you're lucky, an hour and a half. Well, you have to wait for the good things in life, I suppose. A pleasure deferred is a pleasure increased.

The good things in life? A pleasure? Stephen, have you run mad? Are you telling your readers that cocaine is one of the good things in life?

No, no I'm not. Do believe me. I'm treading that difficult balance here. When I started taking coke my life was more or less perfect. I had enjoyed preposterous success.

So let us just return one more time to that first evening, where our actor friend introduced our little group to two lines of coke. I think – if I remember it rightly, and you really must forgive me either if my memory is faulty *or* if it is correct – I think that I wanted from that moment to define myself as a coke user. What a ludicrous and incomprehensible ambition. Many of my 'life choices', looking back, have been incomprehensible from today's viewpoint, so this is just one more. Perhaps a little more sensational, but no less incapable of understanding.

A few days after my first encounter with the Devil's Dandruff, as Robin Williams so memorably dubbed South America's glittering granular gift to the global billions, I embarked upon the first of what were to become regular appearances on Ned Sherrin's Saturday-morning BBC Radio 4 programme *Loose Ends*, along with Emma Freud, Victoria Mather, Victor Lewis-Smith, Brian Sewell, Robert Elms and many others. I had invented for the show a character called Donald Trefusis, who claimed to be a fellow of St Matthew's College Cambridge and the Regius Professor of Philology there. I used him as a vehicle for what may as well be described as derision or querulous indignation about this Thatcherite thing or that dismal dumbing-down disaster that was beginning to infect the BBC. Being in my early twenties but satirizing in the voice of a piping old man somehow took a lot of the offence out of what I was writing. My natural speaking voice at the time, when I hear it now as it might occasionally survive on some scrap of old MP3 or You-Tube material, shocks me with its fey public-school youthfulness. You will be happy to know that a collection of the Professor's thoughts is still available in the in-print masterpiece *Paperweight*. The ideal lavatory book, and one where you can decide for yourself how the voices of Trefusis and other characters I made up should sound. While in mercantile mood, I believe there is an audio book on the market too, read by myself. All proceeds to the cattery of your choice. That is negotiable. Actual offer may vary. Terms and conditions apply.

I am not comfortable writing about the dead, or upsetting the public's preconceived view of them, but I noticed in the Broadcasting House studio the Saturday following my coke experiment that there was a little flake of white in Someone Who Shall Remain Nameless's nostril and the occasional telltale snuffle. At the George, the pub round the corner from Broadcasting House we all flocked to after a recording, I managed to get SWSRN aside and shyly asked if he could recommend a dealer.

'Oh my dear,' SWSRN said, putting his hand on my leg and shooting an almost pitying smile at my naïveté, 'you couldn't do better than ask Mitch.' This particular Mitch was well known to me, and it was a surprise that such a brilliantly educated and literate person dealt in a highly illegal Class A substance. Never having bought it before, I was in paroxysms of fear when I called her up and asked if she might have some 'COFFEE' for me and that if I popped round maybe a couple of jars of 'COFFEE' would be possible? Mitch giggled that this would be fine and that it was 'SIXTY PENCE A JAR' and very high quality. These codes used by dealers and users alike can be absurd. Jezzer is a common one, as a reference to Jeremy Clarkson, who I'm sure has never snorted except derisively, but the title of whose programme, *Top Gear*, suggests precisely what the client was seeking of the seller, material of the least-cut highest quality: absolute top gear . . .

So for my first drug deal, I called up Mitch from a phone-box to confirm the time, found a cash machine, took out £240, which was a matter of two credit cards in those days, and, after rapping lightly on Mitch's door (convinced there were police snipers on every rooftop), found myself shortly in possession of four grams of my very own supply of coke, in four tightly, neatly folded wraps. A part of me wants to show you what a wrap looks like, using an origami-style diagram with dotted lines, but I really do not think that necessary or desirable. The point of a wrap was that any square of reasonable-quality paper could contain the powder without there being any chance of it spilling from the corners. Some dealers, in an almost foolhardy manner you might think, had their signature wrap paper. Lottery tickets, for example, or squares cut from specialist magazines.

Mitch had, and has, a very successful broadcasting career, and I think in those days she and her boyfriend were having trouble making ends meet, and this little business on the side helped keep the wolf from the door. I always had too much respect for them to use them as regular dealers; it seemed like an insult. Soon enough they had introduced me to Nando, who worked in the Petticoat Lane market, a corner pub nearby being our regular meeting and dealing place. Nando introduced me to Midge, who passed me on to Nonny, until I had quite the network, and I don't think a day could go by without my being sure of a supply of a wrap or two in my pocket. Nonny was a great girl, and she had the best supply. The B-quality Charlie for her 'ordinary' customers and A-Charlie for actors, comics, musicians, loyal regulars, Euro-trash, wild childs (children seems wrong in that context), supermodels and aristos.

I didn't take coke because I was depressed or under pressure. I didn't take it because I was unhappy (at least I don't think so). I took it because I really, really *liked* it. Most of my friends screwed their face up at the thought of it, or at most had one or two lines at weekends. Over the years they began, I think, I *know*, to worry about me. But I had drug friends, very well-known artists and musicians and actors with whom I would regularly hang out and play snooker, smoking, drinking and snorting day after day after day. Amongst this crowd there was always a friend wilder by far than me, one who could pull two or three all-nighters in a row and then go filming on the third day bright as a button. I cannot tell you how much better that made me feel about my own growing dependency.

Underneath it all, I still valued my work above everything. Hugh and I had started *A Bit of Fry and Laurie* for the BBC, and it would no more occur to me to write, rehearse or perform in front of the cameras with coke up my nose and in my bloodstream than it would for me to drink all day and bumble into the studio tanked up. Coke was 'pudding', it was the reward that meant I could grant myself an extra three or four hours at a members' club somewhere, discreetly (but frankly back in those days, not so very discreetly) powdering my nose.

Snooker and poker played a large part: there was no appetite for food, but a gigantic one for alcohol. Cocaine, in sharp contradistinction to MDMA and cannabis, seems to increase one's threshold for pure liquor more than anything I've known.

I have tried to make this book as balanced as possible, by which I mean *true*. I am not going to squirt out a great list of famous names with whom I have shared lines – that simply is not my business. I don't want this book to be a snivelling apology, nor a boastful 'Coke, fuck-yeah!' So I have to be honest and say that the first ten years of my coke dependency seemed to cause me no trouble whatsoever. Sometimes, very rarely, I had to postpone or cancel an early-morning appointment, but generally speaking I lived a high-functioning life. As my prosperity rose my ability to acquire higher-quality cocaine increased commensurately (hence Nonny), and that cannot have hurt either. Better purity meant less diarrhoea, nasal bleeding and nausea.

Was the presence of coke in the system noticeable to others? There is an old Greek saying: 'It is easier to hide two elephants under your arm than one pathic.' You may need to stop and do a little poking around and looking up to parse that, but what it is essentially saying is that if you walked through the Athenian marketplace with the boy you were sleeping with – your pathic or catamite – it was more conspicuous and obvious to all than walking with a pair of elephants. Much the same with coke, certainly with a chronic habit. Tooth grinding, the telltale running nose, the chattering, the lack of appetite. Much as I hate to disagree with Professor Freud, one line leads to another and another, certainly not to 'aversion'. Most coke users will acknowledge one particular rule of the stuff. There is either not enough or there is too much. Not enough, and you start to ring dealers at three in the morning. They will be far from best pleased. Too much, and you fill yourself up with it and won't be able to sleep till noon or later.

Another stroke of good fortune, which is something to do with my ambition or my constitution or some mixture of them both, is that I have always known when to stop, especially if I am working the next day. I am nearly always the first to leave the party, murmuring excuses about a film call the next morning or whatever it may be.

I was once standing at the bar of the Groucho Club with the painter Francis Bacon, the art dealer James Birch and those two inseparable art works in themselves, Gilbert and George. Everyone was in a very jolly mood when Bacon ordered a bottle.

'Oh, not for me,' I said, 'I'm up pretty early tomorrow morning.'

'Oh, don't be a cunt,' said a Gilbert or a George. 'Drink with us, ducky.'

'I'm really sorry . . .' I insisted.

Francis tapped me on the shoulder. 'Ah, you're like me, you've got a little man.'

'Well actually, I'm single,' I said.

'No, no, no,' he prodded the side of his temple. 'A little man in here. A little man who tells you when to stop and go home. Oh, the people I knew. So talented, but no little man to stop them. Minton, John Deakin, Dan Farson . . . no little men, you see? I understand. Off you go.'

I was profoundly touched (and flattered of course) by this fellow-feeling and thought myself lucky to have this little man and that such a legend as Bacon recognized it in me. For all I know, he thought I was a total arsehole and made the whole story up just to get rid of me. But it is certainly true that Francis himself would go on outrageous binges, drinking and drinking like a man who wanted to die and then *his* little man would intervene and say, 'No, Francis. Time for the studio.' And back he would go to work for another four or five weeks, producing some of the greatest paintings of his time. So far as I know, he was never much interested in drugs.

There is, however, a wonderful story that has done the rounds enough for me to believe it to be true. Skip if you know it. Lionel Bart, the endearing but woefully hapless songwriter and creator of the musical *Oliver!*, came round to dinner with Bacon and his boyfriend, John Edwards, some time during the late 1970s. They couldn't help noticing that every now and then Bart would disappear under the dining-room table, and a snorting, snuffling noise would ensue, accompanied by the unmistakeable rustle of a plastic bag. Bart would get up, apologize and then carry on with the merry conversation.

An hour or so later he left, with many hugs and thank yous. Francis and John (no staff, fantastically rich as Francis already was by then) started to clear the table.

'Oh, what's this?' said Bacon, who had found under Bart's seat a bag of white powder.

'Heavens, Francis, you're such an innocent. That's cocaine.'

'Ooh, ooh! What shall we do with it?'

'I know,' said John with a flash of inspiration. 'We'll go to Tramp.'

Tramp was a well-known nightclub in Jermyn Street run by the excellent Johnny Gold. It is almost always mistakenly called Tramps, with which Johnny would put up with sighing resignation. In the 1970s it hosted the wedding receptions of Liza Minnelli and Peter Sellers,* it was

---

*Not to each other. Two separate ceremonies.

the chosen watering-hole of sporting naughty boys like George Best, James Hunt and Vitas Gerulaitis, all kinds of models (before they were ever prefixed as super), various cashmere-cardiganned European playboys and film actors from both sides of the Atlantic. Nothing like as smart as Annabel's, but enduring and not without its own character and likeability. It is still going, but without the enlivening presence of Johnny Gold.

The pair arrived at the door to be met by a large doorman who had no more idea of who Francis Bacon was than Francis Bacon knew who Kenny Dalglish might have been.

'Sorry, mate, we're full. Queue over there,' he told Edwards.

Daringly, Edwards – who had an idea about club doormen that was more or less infallible in those days – let the man see a glimpse of the bag of white powder.

'Would you like a . . .?' he said.

'Just a sec, gents . . . follow me.'

The doorman beckoned to a second-in-command and pulled Edwards and Bacon into a little alcove next to the door. John tentatively proffered the bag, and the doorman took a healthy scoopful, which he transferred into a little bag he had ready in his waistcoat pocket. He next led them to an occupied table, which he swiftly de-occupied with a growl of 'reserved' and a sweep of his well-muscled arm.

'Juanito, the best champagne for my friends . . .'

Well, thought Bacon and Edwards. This is the life and no mistake.

A bucket of Dom Pérignon arrived and was poured out into glasses by the fawning and chattily verbose Juanito. All the while, John and Francis were impatiently planning their discreet visit to the gentlemen's lavatories, which they had noticed were being visited with great frequency by a steady line, as it were, of glamorous, well-known faces.

They had hardly taken one sip of the Dom Pérignon before the bouncer was clattering back down the stairs.

'You two, out! Out this fucking minute. If I ever see your fucking faces again, I'll fucking beat the living crap out of you. Got it, you fucking fuckers?'

Disconsolately they taxied their way back home, wondering what could have gone wrong.

'Did you notice,' said Francis, 'that his nostril was *frothing* slightly? And rather pinkly, as if blood had been drawn? Is that usual?'

They put the matter out of their minds, had some drinks – alcohol being a drug they well understood – and went to bed.

The next morning Lionel Bart called to thank them for the dinner party.

'Oh, by the way,' he said, 'did I leave my bag of denture fixative powder behind? Can't find it anywhere.'

The Groucho

Play by the Rules: The Groucho Club Rules

Upon arrival at The Club, Members shall approach the Reception desk to sign and print their names in the signing-in book – this Ancient Ceremony being a necessary preliminary to entry into all the Club Rooms.

The use within The Club of Mobile, Cellular, Portable or Microwave-controlled Telecommunication Instruments is an anathema, a curse, a horror, a dread and deep unpleasantness and shall be prohibited in all locations, save the Reception area and the Soho Bar, until 5 p.m. Please be alert to the acknowledged misery of Ring Tones and silence all such mechanisms before entry into the Club Rooms.

The ingestion into the bloodstream of powders, pastilles, potions, herbs, compounds, pills, tablets, capsules, tonics, cordials, tinctures, inhalations, or mixtures that have been scheduled by Her Majesty's Government to be illegal Substances of whatever class is firmly prohibited by Club Rules, whether they be internalized orally, rectally, intravenously, intranasally or by any means whatsoever. So let it be known.

149

A Member may invite into The Club up to four (4) Guests at any one time, for whose behaviour and respect of the rules the Member is responsible. Be it understood that a Guest will not be allowed into the Bar save that they be accompanied by a Member.

The wearing of String Vests is fully unacceptable and wholly proscribed by Club Rules. There is enough distress in the world already.

To step out into Dean Street owing money to The Club leaves a stain on a Member's character that cannot be pleasing to them. For this reason all bills and monies owing to The Club should be settled in full before a Member may leave The Club.

Upon settlement of aforesaid bills and levies, all Members are reminded that Soho is a neighbourhood containing many residents. Show dignity, consideration and kindness by leaving The Club quietly and with as little brouhaha as may be contrived.

The Club is a club. A place of sociability in which to relax and be affable and friendly. Respect the views of your fellow Members and ensure that your Guests do the same. Let amiability and charm be your watchwords.

It seemed to me from the late 1980s through the naughty 1990s and into the opening years of the twenty-first century inconceivable that there was anyone in London *not* doing coke. Every time I saw somebody in a restaurant rising from their table and moving towards the gents or the ladies I assumed they were off for an energizing sniff. It didn't stop me writing or performing or pursuing any other occupation that required hard work and concentration. It was only, as I have said, the reward for that hard work, the pudding or savoury that I had earned and that would give me five or six hours of convivial social immersion.

My usual port of call was the Groucho Club, from 1985 onwards the watering-hole of choice for almost all in publishing, music, comedy, drama and the arts in general. That section of society that the hero of my 1994 novel *The Hippopotamus*, Ted Wallace, cholerically called the mediahadeen* and was later scornfully to be assigned the sneering ascription 'the chattering classes' from another class of chatterers that chattered in other watering-holes.

As well as writing the official club rules (above) I also coined one evening in the late eighties the 'Groucho Rule', which states that any remark, apophthegm, epigram, aphorism or observation, be it never so wise, well intentioned, profound or true, is instantly rendered ridiculous and nonsensical by the addition of the phrase 'he said last night in the Groucho Club'.

*Feeble ref. to the Mujahadeen, who were one of the Afghan insurgency forces in the old Soviet–Afghan war.

Thus: 'Workers of the world unite! You have nothing to lose but your chains,' remarked Karl Marx in the Groucho Club last night.

Or: 'For evil to flourish, all it takes is for the good man to do nothing,' pointed out Edmund Burke in the Groucho Club brasserie late last night.

And so on. The Athenæum it is not and nor does it pretend to be.

Tony Mackintosh (of the Norfolk chocolate family which gave the world the Caramac and Quality Street amongst other memorable masterpieces) was a noted figure in the world of London hospitality, running for many years 192, a popular Notting Hill restaurant whose first chef, Alistair Little, was *the* premier metropolitan skillet-wielder of the mid-1980s. Mackintosh was also in charge of the Zanzibar, a very pleasant drinkery in Great Queen Street, Covent Garden. It was here that I learned to queue up for the single gentlemen's lavatory. Its seat had long disappeared, and there was no cistern lid. I assume this was an attempt by Tony to deter drug-taking. Although he was one of London's foremost and most fashionable restaurateurs (there is no *n* in 'restaurateur' despite the number of times you hear 'restauranteur') he resembled a kindly old-fashioned schoolaster (there is of course no *m* in 'schoolmaster', a little known fact), and to this day I am not sure that he knew what went on in his establishments. He was certainly present the night Keith Allen went crazy. Well, that is a preposterous thing to say. The night when

Keith Allen went *crazier*, I should have written. The wild Welsh whirlwind stood on the bar and hurled glassware at the mirror behind the bottles and optics. He was effectively Zanzibarred for the rest of that club's life, for it was only a few months later that the Groucho was born from its shards and ashes.

Originally the idea of publishers Carmen Callil, Caroline Michel and überagent Ed Victor, the club was conceived as a place where authors and their editors could meet for a mid-morning breakfast and talk in comfy chairs without the formal dignity of an old-fashioned West End club or the passing human traffic and distraction of a hotel lobby or dining room. This was the era of croissants, orange juice and newly enthralling Italian coffees. I cannot think of those days without the memory of buttery pastry flakes and marmalade. The evenings, however ... the evenings were very, very different. More of them in a moment.

Tony, always a benign but hazily distant figure, had, as much more hands-on fellow managers, a radiant being called Mary Lou Sturridge, sister of Charles, the precocious director of Granada's barnstorming *Brideshead Revisited*, and Liam Carson, who was to become a very close friend. Mary Lou, Liam and their various colleagues, notably Gordana, a Serbian of magnificent charm and a voice like a factory foghorn, kept order and created the ambience of the club, which was an instant and stunning success. Indeed, such was the nature of the success that those who were not members made no secret of how much they despised the place and how posturing, pretentious and 'up themselves' the members were. As a matter of fact the only people I have ever seen behave revoltingly and unacceptably at the Groucho Club have been members' guests, who can become (or certainly could in those early, heady days) overheated by alcohol and the presence of well-known faces. Members and the staff know how to comport themselves in the club.

I cannot deny that for me such a place was something like an oasis. The better known I became, the more difficult I found it to go into a pub. This has become more and more the case over the years. Whenever I do, the chances are that someone will come up and offer to buy me a drink. This is charming and kind but places me in an unwinnable bind. If I refuse the drink I am considered top-lofty, lah-di-dah and hoity-toity; if I accept it I have been functionally purchased for half an hour. You can't take someone's drink and then make your way to the other side of the saloon and ignore them. It is often pleasant to speak to strangers, but there are times when one wants to spend time with one's friends, uninterfered with. So pubs, unless I am in my home county of Norfolk, where there seems to be an inbuilt understanding that people should be able to come and go unmolested, famous or not,* are off limits to me.

*After all, the royal family have a house not far from me, and Princes William and Harry have been known to pop into one of my favourite

It is unfortunate, then, that the well-known are excoriated for not being 'real' enough to go to ordinary places like pubs, whatever 'real' might be taken to mean. I do shop in supermarkets and high streets and often, absurdly, people say to me – sometimes almost in the most put-out fashion – 'What are *you* doing *here*?', to which I am tempted to reply, as I push my trolley along the aisle, 'Playing badminton / sitting my History A level exam / performing a tracheotomy on Jeremy Vine . . . What are *you* doing?'

I have mentioned before in blog or perhaps in interview that fame is wonderful, a picnic. Instant tables in fashionable restaurants that others have to wait weeks to book for, tickets to premieres, sporting occasions and gatherings of genuine interest and excitement and the opportunity to meet heroes in all walks of life. But, as at any picnic, there are wasps. Sometimes the wasps are no more than a nuisance and sometimes they cause you to pack up and run indoors yelping. It was Fellini in *La Dolce Vita* who called his 'society' photographer Paparazzo, a word that suggested to him an annoying buzzing insect. The Italian for wasp, *vespa*, was already taken of course . . .

Certainly paparazzi can be a nuisance, especially if you are with someone who is not in the public eye and would rather not have their features printed in a newspaper accompanied by speculation as to their identity. Then, of course, everyone is a paparazzo today, for everyone has a

---

pubs in the county: that being the case, some git off the TV is hardly going to cause excitement.

camera, one of higher and higher quality as year succeeds year.

To this day there are often amateur paparazzi every night waiting outside the Groucho Club, the Ivy Club, the Chiltern Firehouse, Annabel's, Hertford Street and sundry other 'haunts of the rich and famous'. They only need one photograph of a celebrity vomiting, or trying to punch a colleague, or snogging the wrong man or woman, and they have paid their rent for the week.

One Day in the Life of the Groucho Club

So, back to the Groucho. I will take you through a day. It is in fact an amalgam of many days, but it may suffice to give you a flavour of the club's high-water mark, or scumline if that is your point of view.

Let us say it is a sunny autumn afternoon in the early 1990s. I have had a late-morning meeting about a new book with my publisher, Sue Freestone, in the bar area of the Groucho and am due to lunch with my agent, Lorraine Hamilton, who tells me, over the navarin of lamb, that a producer called Marc Samuelson would like a meeting to sound me out about the possibility of playing Oscar Wilde in a new film.

Buoyed and excited by the very thought of such an idea, I take my post-luncheon brandy to the bar. A pair of adorably cute boys are sitting there, rhythmically drumming the bar-rail with their feet and looking nervously about them. I estimate that they are in their mid-twenties.

I have always felt that the Groucho should be a club within the most sociable meaning of the act and that open friendliness ought to be a very part of its nature. People should be made to feel welcome and at home, not snubbed or avoided. Which is not to say that they should be interrupted or have their conversations crashed. It seems to me that these two young men are certainly in need of a solacing word or two.

'Hello,' I say, slipping on to a stool next to them.

They nod and smile.

'You look as if you are a little bewildered?'

'Well,' says one of them, who had charming mousy hair, 'it's the Groucho Club. You hear things . . .'

'Goodness,' say I. 'What sort of things?'

'That it's a bit, you know . . .' says the other, who has perfectly black hair and the deepest brown eyes, 'not for the likes of us.'

'Oh now, pish,' I reply. 'You look like just the kind of young bright people that the Groucho would most welcome. Tell me, what do you do?'

'We're musicians,' says the mousy-haired one with just a hint of endearing mockney.

'Ah, well then. You're *exactly* the kind of members the club needs. I'll make sure your candidacies are fast-tracked. Don't you move a muscle. I'll be right back.'

I nip to the front desk and ask – Lily would it have been? – to give me a couple of membership forms. I return, brandishing them.

'Let's fill these in then,' I say. 'Hm. "Profession?" . . . Musicians. "Address?" . . . I'll leave you to fill those in, along with telephone numbers. "Proposer?" . . . I'll sign that. "Seconder?" . . .' I scan the bar area. 'Tim!' I call to an old friend and Groucho regular. 'Come and second these two splendid fellows. They're called . . . sorry, I'm afraid I don't know your names . . .'

'Alex,' says the one with the black hair and brown, brown eyes.

'Damon,' says the one with the mousy hair and, now that I look more closely, wonderfully blue, blue eyes.

'And they're musicians!' I tell Tim.

Tim takes the form and signs.

'Are you currently in work, or do you have a band or something?' I inquire of the pair.

'Stephen,' says Tim, 'this is Damon Albarn and Alex James. They are Blur.'

This is not very helpful to me.

'*Park Life*?'

'It's OK,' says the dark-haired one called Alex, extending his hand to be shaken. 'Big fan.'

Hands are shaken, and drinks ordered all round. I leave the filled-in proposal forms with the front desk and bump into Khaki Joe, another dealer. Currency notes are discreetly swapped for small, tight wraps. I am now, as

Americans say, loaded for bear. Ready for a full-on Groucho evening.

The afternoon takes shape. Damon has to leave, but meanwhile Keith Allen has arrived. Keith has entered in bonhomous mood. He already knows Alex James. In fact they are to go on and have a long and productive friendship. Aside from anything else, they give the world Fat Les and the hit single 'Vindaloo', for which the world will always be dizzy with gratitude.

Pages could be written about the strange and extraordinary Keith Allen: throughout the late 1980s (following his Zanzibarring) through the 1990s and up until the mid-2000s he was to be found in the Groucho Club most days and nights. He could be bruisingly rude. 'Some people are crap, some people are brilliant,' he once told a well-known TV comic loudly. 'You are mediocre, which is worse. So much fucking worse.' It's very hard to recover from this kind of assault. I sat with the poor recipient of this onslaught for two hours, trying to convince him that vitriol from Keith Allen was as healing balm from a seraph, a compliment of the highest order. Keith was an early figure in the alternative comedy world, and anyone who came after him or perhaps Malcolm Hardee* was a

---

*Famous in the wider world for his naked balloon dance. He drowned, aged fifty-five, much mourned by what was then the oxymoronic alternative establishment. His stand-up act was, I need hardly add, staggeringly unfunny in a way that must have taken enormous effort. He himself was astonishingly funny, however. Go figure.

sell-out in his eyes. For months in the Zanzibar and then the Groucho I tried to avoid him. One day he had come up with a drink, sat down and told me that I was great. This was most discomfiting. He had told almost everyone I liked and admired that they were complete wankers and that their work was shit and derivative. How should I take a compliment from this terror? Naturally, wuss that I am, I absorbed it gratefully, and we became friends, albeit warily on my side. Griff Rhys Jones, a man of exemplary forcefulness and courage, once confided in me that Keith scared him half to death. Long Groucho poker evenings drew them closer together. Griff is a non-drinker and good boy (unless you count poker as a vice), so Keith's acceptance of him could be counted as highly complimentary.

Why would one want to be liked or accepted by someone so loutish, rude, uncontrollable and horrific, you might wonder? Charisma, I suppose. Famed for his amatory adventures and now for the success of his children (Alfie the Greyjoy in *Game of Thrones*, and Lily the singer-songwriter), he has a quality of playfulness and boldness that naturally more cautious and bourgeois figures like myself cannot but be drawn to. And whatever your instincts may tell you, I can assure you that he is a very loyal and generous friend to those in need.

*

We decide to go upstairs to the snooker room. Oh, the hours and hours and hours and hours I spent there. I bought many of the accoutrements. A device for respotting a ball. Rests, spiders and extensions. Chalk. My own cue made from finest English ash. They rarely lasted more than a week before being broken or stolen. The room is only just big enough to fit a full-sized table. You almost have to open a window to play some shots. You certainly have to ask anyone sitting and kibitzing to lean to the left or right if you need to cue either side of the blue pocket. 'Lining up on the white' became a favourite, if obvious, joke. Coke, snooker, vodka, tobacco, chat.

There is a strange stumbling noise on the stairs. Up comes a round-faced, shaggy-eyebrowed young man.

'You're all fucking wankers,' he says. 'And you . . .' he points at Alex. 'Where's that shithead All Bran?'

Alex smiles dozily.

'Fuck you all. You can't play for fucking toffee.' This strange interloper grabs my cue. 'And you,' he says to me, 'you are a poncey tosser.'

'Right,' I say. 'OK. Poncey tosser. I shall make a note of that.'

'Fuck off!' he shouts, stabbing the cue up in the air. The round end of the butt bangs violently into the low ceiling. Dust descends.

He drops the cue and throws himself back down the stairs.

'Well,' I say. 'Who on earth . . . ?'

Keith is stepping on to a chair, magic marker in hand. 'Fuck's sake, Stephen. Don't you know *anything*? Liam Gallagher.'

He draws a ring round the circular dent left in the plasterwork and writes: 'The mark of a cunt.'

'Oasis,' Alex explains. 'There's this really dumb thing about which one of us bands is better.'

'Oh,' I say. 'Ah. Yes. Quite. I see.' Not seeing at all.

The afternoon folds itself into an evening. Other people, including many rather desperate known figures who never can or never will buy their own supply, drift in and look longingly at us as we now more unobtrusively flit from loo to table and back, sniffing up the residue from our nostrils as discreetly as we can. A coke addict's discreet sniff is like the trumpeting of an elephant and deceives no one but him- or herself. It is of a piece with the whisky drinker's mouth-freshening mint or the odorous farter's suspicious darting glances at other people. Futile fabrication, fooling none.

The pretty-please puppy-dog eyes of the liggers is distressing me. As usual, Keith ignores them. Liam Carson arrives up the stairs to join me as a partner in doubles.

Only the day before I had had an opportunity to watch Liam in action. The daily management of a club like the Groucho presents all kinds of unique problems. How to deal with the notorious Soho bohemian Dan Farson drunkenly pulling rough trade up the stairs to the bedrooms? Vomit in unexpected places. Indiscreet snorters ruining it for the rest of us by tapping out lines on the dining table. Out-of-control revellers who think the place is open to all trying to pile in after pub hours (the club is licensed to serve drinks until two in the morning). Liam calmly deals with all these issues. There is a steely Irish resolve inside what appears to be a placid, rather doughy exterior. He was taught by the legendary Peter Langan, father of all London's better restaurants. Peter begat Liam, Peter also begat Jeremy King and Chris Corbin of Le Caprice, the Ivy, J. Sheekey, the Wolseley, the Delaunay, Colbert's, Brasserie Zédel, Scott's, the Mark Hix group of restaurants, etc., etc. The better elements of London's hospitality industry can all be traced in a direct line back to Langan.

As we were: the previous night I was sitting in the back corner of the Groucho brasserie, chatting to Liam and sipping a vodka and slimline* tonic. He would have been on a glass of Chardonnay, this being the era before that grape and its wine were mocked into an unfashionable corner and a preposterous Essex girl Christian name to make way for Sauvignon Blanc. Liam was enough of an alcoholic to think that drinking wine by the bucketful didn't really mean anything. Only the hard stuff counted. We are interrupted by a flushed girl from the front desk.

'Liam, there's an awful tramp in reception. He's just standing there in a manky old coat with his hands into his pockets staring. What do we do?'

---

*Slimline it may have been called, but it imparted no such thing to my increasing bulk.

Liam slowly gets to his feet. 'Don't worry, darling. I'll deal with it.'

'Oh, do you mind if I come too?' I had never seen Liam handling street interlopers. I knew he would never be mean or threatening. He is a kindly man. Besides, part of his job is to avoid scenes.

In Soho, where the fashionable, successful and prosperous dine, drink and thrive in such close proximity to a parallel world of destitution, prostitution and misery, a bitter hiccup of liberal shame, embarrassment and guilt (which are of no use to anyone) rises in the breast of people like me, a kind of social acid reflux, which is the price we pay for too much good living. And useless, as I say, to the poor, who would rather have our money than our pink-faced, hand-wringing apologies.

I follow Liam as he opens the doors that lead from the bar area to the reception. The frightened girl from the front desk is next to me, just as anxious as I am to see how Liam will deal with this 'tramp', a word from childhood but what other does one use? Bum? Hobo? Panhandler? All rather American.

The tramp in question has his back to us, but I can see a thick overcoat a size too big for him into which his hands are thrust. As he turns, Liam quickly extends a cordial hand. 'Mr Pacino, welcome. How can we help you?'

The girl by my side quietly melts into a puddle on the floor. I can understand her mistake. The great actor has eyes, in the old phrase, like piss-holes in the snow. He is

unshaven, and his 'affect' is ungiving. It is possible, probable even, that he is researching for some role. I think this
was before his Richard III project, but maybe this was
where his mind was at the time.

Back to this evening of evenings. Liam and I play Keith
and Alex, our new best friend, at snooker. We are joined
by Charles Fontaine, chef patron of the excellent Quality
Chop House in the Farringdon Road, a 'working men's'
restaurant more or less unchanged since 1869. As ever, he
is anxious for poker, so we decide to go upstairs to the
Club Room to play. Alex excuses himself from this and
slides in a happy, lazy shuffling way downstairs. Something rather Bazooka Joe about him.

Charles, a French 'man of the mountains', as he likes
to call himself, is passionate about poker. His skill is not
in proportion to his enthusiasm, but he seems not to
mind. We play Seven Card Stud, Texas Hold 'Em, Five
Card Stud, Five Card Draw, Omaha, High Low, dealer's
choice. A card-table to make modern purists shudder. We
even allow the dealer to nominate wild cards. I have provided the packs and a neat wooden carousel of chips,
plastic but serviceable enough.

'Oh, Stephen,' Charles says to me excitedly during a
shuffle, 'you know the Peter Blake? I buy it.'

'I'm sorry?'

Charles has been in London for the best part of fifteen
years, working in the kitchens of Le Caprice under Mark
Hix, yet still his command of the English tongue is far

from secure. I manage to grasp what he is trying to tell me. He has bought a découpage artwork representing me that the pop artist Peter Blake had been commissioned to make to accompany a profile for *Harpers & Queen* or *Vogue* or some such magazine the previous year. Somehow Charles had tracked the original down and hung it in the Chop House. As I look up from the computer this very minute I see it hanging on *my* wall now. Charles called me up a month or so back from Spain, where he has a restaurant these days. Spanish sovereign debt crisis, money tight, he wondered if I might be interested in buying the piece? A price was agreed, and now it is mine.

But back to that day in the early nineties.

Usually a poker game lasts from around midnight to four or five in the morning. Liam will be in charge of locking us in and letting us out. The greatest fear is his wife Gabby coming round and tearing a strip out of him. They have a daughter, Flossy, and how she would love him to settle down to something sensible and secure and unconnected to alcohol and druggy people like Fry and his fiendish friends.

Tonight, however, is a very special night. At round about midnight word reaches us that we should go downstairs. There is a palpable buzz at ground-floor level. The doors that lead from reception to the bar area are thrown open, and in charges Damien Hirst, accompanied by Jay Jopling, the gallery owner, followed by Sarah Lucas, Tracey Emin, Sam Taylor-Wood and Angus Fairhurst.

These are the leading YBAs, Young British Artists, graduates of Goldsmiths College, London. Collected by Charles Saatchi, reviled by bourgeois tabloids, they are all making a serious noise in the art world.

Damien, leader of them all for shock value and fame, is waving a piece of paper over his head like Neville Chamberlain on his return from Munich. It is not peace in our time, however, but a cheque.

'Here!' shouts Damien, pushing his way to the bar and handing it across. 'I've just gone and won the fucking Turner Prize. There's twenty grand there. Lock us all in and let me know when it's spent.'

A huge cheer. At round about six in the morning the barman wearily but cheerfully rings the cheque through the till. 'That's your twenty grand spent,' he says.

'Another twenty grand on me,' says Damien to another great cheer.

Six hours later I'm sipping a Bloody Mary. Somehow the club has been tidied, shifts have been relieved. Only we hardcore imbeciles are left.

Tracey and Damien vie with each other, trying to shock the shoulder-padded power-dressed publishers who are starting to come in for lunch.

'Oi,' shouts Tracey, sitting on the bar, 'are you calling my cunt a pussy?'

A knot of publishers scuttle away, baffled and alarmed.

'You,' says Damien to a couple as they enter, 'how do you make a queer fuck a woman?'

'Errrr . . . ?' They know who this terrifying man is and don't for one minute want to look unsporting. 'I don't know . . .'

'Shit in her cunt.'

Ah, les beaux jours . . .

Ach, die schöne Zeiten . . .

Those were the days . . .

I have almost certainly conflated several days into one. I expect Keith Allen will call me up to say that he can't have been playing poker with me the night Damien won his Turner Prize because he was there at the Tate for the ceremony. Alex will let me know that I proposed Damon Albarn and him for Groucho membership in '93 and Damon will say it was '94. Everyone's memory will be different, but none of them, I think, will dispute my representation of the spirit of the age as we lived it, foul as it may stink in your nostrils, self-indulgent as it certainly was: precious hours wantonly pissed away, good money spunked, valuable brain cells massacred, execrable shit talked. At the time I loved it. Lived for it and little else. But I was fortunate, very fortunate, for I had a little man. I know because that genius Francis Bacon told me so, as related above.

The truly monumental Soho drinkers, carousers, wastrels and rakehells preferred the Colony Room to the Groucho. In the era of its founder, the fabulous Muriel Belcher, Francis Bacon was one of the first habitués. Dan Farson, author of *Soho in the Fifties* and *Sacred Monsters*, drew a splendid portrait of the early years of this tiny after-hours first-floor bar. When Muriel Belcher died, she was succeeded by Ian Board, the barman. Generally known as Ida, he had the most enormous spongy drinker's nose I've ever seen and was one of the few people I ever met who still used, well into the 1980s, in a cracked, camp sixties voice, the appellation 'ducky'. If he liked you more it was 'cunty'. Someone told me, I can't remember who – perhaps Michael, his assistant behind the bar – that when Ida died in the club, in harness naturally, everyone in the room, as he slumped to the ground, saw his great nose shrink down like a deflated balloon. The stopped heart no longer pumped blood to his scattered network of broken capillaries.

Jeffrey Bernard (whose drinking gave rise to the magnificent comedy *Jeffrey Bernard is Unwell*, for many the last chance to see the greatness of Peter O'Toole on stage) started to frequent the Groucho rather than the Colony Room or the French House the other side of Old Compton Street, another haunt of the old guard. He grudgingly grunted good mornings to me when I came in. Perhaps because his niece Kate Bernard was a schoolfriend of my sister's. I always felt that the pioneering generation regarded us as soft. Alcoholic dilettantes. And the coke they regarded as pretentious and pathetic. Which it is, of course. We were amateurs. Bernard was a warning to all, however. Stick-like, he was as withered and fragile as Tithonus, on whom Zeus finally took pity, turning him into a cicada. You felt you could snap him in half over your knee. In his later years he sat in a wheelchair in front of the bar, cigarette in mouth, vodka and soda in hand. First one leg was amputated, then the other. I saw him and Dan Farson at the bar together once. They each subsisted on almost identical diets of pure alcohol, yet one was as round, red and shiny as a balloon and the other dry and paper-thin.

Francis Bacon started to come into the Groucho too, overcoming whatever initial distrust of the place he may have had. Rather as email and then Twitter were to be met with howls of displeasure and sceptical derision when they arrived in the world, only to be embarrassedly embraced later, so it was amongst the founding fathers of SohoBoho degeneracy that the Groucho Club – sneered at and despised by right-thinking roués at first – came finally to be accepted and enjoyed in the evening of their years.

Heigh ho, twenty years have passed since those days. Jeffrey Bernard and Francis Bacon are dead. Charles Fontaine lives and works in the south of Spain. Alex James has moved from the Groucho Group to David Cameron's Chipping Norton set and makes award-winning cheeses in Gloucestershire. Damien Hirst lives and works in the West Country too, as does Keith Allen. Tracey Emin is one of the few YBAs, it seems, to have kept the bohemian candle alight. Not that she ever sucked things up through her nose to my knowledge. But she can drink. Yes, she can do that.

People, groups, movements, energies gather themselves into a ball sometimes and hurl themselves into history. Then the time comes when the fire dies. The great mass deflates like Ida's purple, spongy nose. Many will regard the Britpop and YBA movements as shallow and unimportant. But damn, it was fun to be caught up inside as an amused, amazed observer.

Today and for many years the Groucho Club has been as clean as clean can be. The surfaces in the bathrooms are free of white powder, and no one sits on the bar telling shocked arrivals frightful, yet appallingly funny, jokes. There has been no lock-in for a Turner Prize-winning artist there since 1995. But it remains a good place to eat and drink. It is ruled by Bernie Katz, the Prince of Soho. He stands four foot ten in elevated shoes, but he can throw out four unruly drunks without thinking. There is a yearly quiz (for which I have from time to time set questions), a staff party, at which favoured members serve the waiters, kitchen, management and bar staff, and a Gang Show, at which money is raised for the Soho homeless. The art on the walls betrays the long connection with Hirst and Emin and others. Securely screwed into the walls, they are worth a king's ransom now. Some may regret the passing of the old days and the inevitable deflation of that pumped-up, alcoholic, coke-fuelled nose, but all things change. Another time of energy and innovation will come and then go too. A compensation of age is a realization of the cyclical nature of fashion, politics and art.

Notes from a Showbusiness Career

From the mid-1980s onwards I was kept busy with a more or less huge writing workload and, after attending to new *Me and My Girl* openings on Broadway and in Australia, I found myself in the grip of a persistent, ankle-nipping producer called Dan Patterson. This, you should know, was before the coke days. We're looking at 1985 or '6, I think.

Dan and I met when he shadowed Paul Mayhew-Archer, a BBC radio comedy producer later to find more acclaim as the man in charge of most of the numerous series of *My Family* featuring *Me and My Girl*'s star Robert Lindsay. Paul was directing me in a series called *Delve Special*, in which I played a hapless investigative journalist. The series was written by Tony Sarchet and recorded, unusually for radio, 'on location'. Which is to say that, rather than using the standard sound effects gravel tray for walking and the three-textured staircase (wood, stone and carpet) and stand-alone car doors and front doors and bedroom doors with which studios were comically furnished, Paul decided for reasons of verisimilitude that we should take a Uher recording device up to the Broadcasting House roof, or on the street in Portland Place, or in some cupboard or busy *Woman's Hour* or *The World At One* production office.

Dan Patterson arrived as a work-experience observer and within seconds was bombarding me with questions. In Oxford, where his father David was a pioneering professor of Hebrew studies, Dan had seen our 1981 Cambridge Footlights revue and could quote huge chunks of it by heart. He was recently back from a trip to America, where the new world of improvisation had opened up before him like some beautiful flower. Now he was back and keen to get going as a producer himself. I have never met anything that wasn't a puppy so boisterously excitable, keen, persuasive and determined.

Before I knew what I was doing I had agreed to write six radio comedy programmes and to be in a new series featuring the kind of improvisation that Dan had seen and been so struck by in America. This latter was *Whose Line Is It Anyway?*, a jokey approximation of the title of the hit play and film *Whose Life Is It Anyway?* The show was hosted by Clive Anderson, who had been a coeval of Griff Rhys Jones and others at Cambridge, but taken a different course into law, where he had eaten his dinners, as their jargon has it, and been called to the Bar, or is it inducted? In other words, as any less magnificently potty country would put it, he had qualified as a legal advocate. He was a barrister.

The only other regular in the series was John Sessions, a phenomenally talented mimic (he had worked regularly on *Spitting Image*) whose one-man shows combined imper-sonation, deep learning and almost unbelievably vivid and poetical writing.

The show suited his talents perfectly. He could instantly tell the Red Riding Hood story in the style of Ernest Hemingway or D. H. Lawrence or whichever author, actor or indeed rock star was thrown at him by Clive or a frenetic studio audience. Anyone from Anthony Burgess to Keith Richards, by way of *EastEnders* stars and BBC weather reporters, was grist to his remarkable mimetic mill. From our Footlights days the ever-huggable Tony Slattery forged ahead on the show too, as did Josie Law-rence, who specialized in improvising song lyrics and tunes with astonishing rapidity and brilliance with the help of pianist Richard Vranch, who had been with us at Cambridge and whose remarkable ear and talent for impromptu accompaniment to this day regularly sup-ports performers in London's Comedy Store. As far as I can recall, and nothing would induce me to listen to a minute's worth of tape to confirm this, I just stood there saying 'botty' or occasionally managing some kind of actual joke or apt remark.

It was a remarkable success, and, as did a lot of radio comedies (including *Delve Special*, which changed its name to *This Is David Lander* for reasons that I cannot recall), it soon transferred to television. I baulked, agreeing reluc-tantly to appear twice. It made household names of John, Tony, Clive and Josie – well, in the kinds of scrubbed-pine households that marked out the middle-class viewer in those days. I only consented to do a second appearance because Peter Cook was going to be on. We were both a little the worse for drink, and both deeply uncomfortable. The funniest man alive, the most brilliant extempore wit that ever breathed in my lifetime, was not suited in any way to the ordeal of the programme. Nor was he. *Kidding*.

I think it was the upstage stools that I could not abide. Having to dismount from them, as if summoned down to the play-mat by Miss Spanky at some frightful kindergarten. Dan has continued his stool obsession (that sounds so wrong) with his highly successful *Mock the Week*.

But the other programme Dan pushed me into – well, it was hardly pushing – was one which would be of my own devising. It was called *Saturday Night Fry*, it is still available online, and, though I shouldn't say so, I really am very proud of it. I wrote all the episodes in one huge burst of energy over little more than a week and I think I was genuinely inspired. All my love of radio, a love that went back to my earliest memories, was poured into the construction of the scripts. I was helped knowing that Hugh and Emma and the matchless Jim Broadbent had already agreed to be a part of it.

At this time I was sharing a house in Dalston with Hugh, his girlfriend, Katie Kelly, and Nick Symonds, a mutual friend from Cambridge. I related in *The Fry Chronicles* how Paul Whitehouse and Charlie Higson, our painter decorators recommended by new friend Harry Enfield, seemed unusually gifted and amusing.

This was, looking back, a very productive time for me. Aside from *Saturday Night Fry*, I produced occasional pieces for *Arena* magazine and every week an article for the *Listener*. One of these, called 'Licking Thatcher' (a feeble title playing on the title of the David Hare theatre work* *Licking Hitler*), was a more than faintly impertinent call for Neil Kinnock to be more assured, confident and self-possessed when facing Margaret Thatcher across the dispatch boxes in the then twice-weekly verbal fencing matches of parliamentary Prime Minister's Question Time, popularly known as PMQs. 'He should give the impression that being Leader of the Opposition is the best job in the world under this régime,' I wrote, or some such twaddle. 'He should smile not snarl, shake his head with laughter at her crudeness, philistinism and asininity rather than shouting his head off in a lather of righteous indignation.'

I was very delighted to receive a letter a few days later with an embossed portcullis on the back of the envelope declaring in green heraldic splendour its House of Commons origin. Neil Kinnock was inviting me to join his team of speech-writers. I thought it rather classy of him to read a pissy critique of his manner from some Oxbridge upstart and, rather than dismiss it, invite him on board. I

---

* I once heard someone say they'd really enjoyed the new Hare piece at the National . . .

cannot claim for a second that I actually wrote an entire speech for him or for the two subsequent Labour leaders, John Smith, loved by all who knew him and sadly wrenched away from the world by a heart attack well before his time, and his successor Tony Blair, loved by . . . well . . . Once Tony had won in 1997 let's just say it stopped being fun. Writing for the underdog is infinitely more challenging and amusing.

Bit of gossip, though, which isn't too mean. I'm holding back on cruel revelations until I'm dead. A few weeks after he had been elected Prime Minister in 1997, Tony and Cherie Blair sent me an invitation to dinner at Chequers, the Prime Minister's *ex officio* country house. The invitation said 'informal', which in the strange British world of etiquette means, when referring to a dinner, 'not black tie'. Similarly, the phrase 'we don't dress for dinner' indicates that dark suits shall be worn, rather than dinner jackets. Well, so I understood, having grown up in this preposterous nobby British tradition. Yes, you are right: I secretly love it. Not so secretly.

As it fell out, I was the first to arrive at the grand Tudor mansion, ushered into the great hall by a pretty and slightly nervous blonde WAAF. Servicemen and -women customarily take turns to serve at such occasions. I sipped sherry and admired the furnishings and fitments for five minutes before Tony Blair, twenty days into his premiership, doe-eyed enough to have been nicknamed Bambi, pattered down the stairs before skidding to an abrupt halt at the sight of me. He was wearing a denim shirt and pale chinos.

'Oh,' he said, 'didn't the invitation say "informal"?'

'I took that to mean no dinner jacket,' I said.

He looked aghast. 'Do you think everyone else will think that?'

'There's a strong chance,' I told him.

By this time Cherie had arrived, and there was much confabulation before the PM hared upstairs to change.

Everyone else did indeed arrive in dark lounge suits, as they are revoltingly called. I thought Tony's (as one was always encouraged to call him) ignorance of these matters was rather touching. It is all absurd snobbery and unguessable usage after all.

I was impressed that the Blairs had invited Betty Boothroyd, the retired Speaker of the House, and Giles Wilson, mathematician son of Harold and Mary Wilson. Wilson Junior had never been back to the house he might have been said almost to have grown up in, and not once had Betty been asked to Chequers throughout her Speakership during the days of Thatcher and Major.

I recall getting rather drunk on a very fine cognac that was one of the gifts Jacques Chirac had brought the week before when he had been the first Chequers guest of the Blair premiership. Upstairs after dinner I found the red box that all government members are given by their civil servants at the end of the day. I knew they contained papers that our leaders had to work through. A scarlet leather case, stamped with the royal arms, the red box is one of the great mystical fetish objects in British politics. When no one was looking I committed the treasonable act of flicking the latches and lifting the lid. I was rather astonished, which I should not have been, to see that instead of papers, the box revealed the keyboard of a laptop computer. The astonishment came as much from my knowledge that Blair had no understanding of computers at all, despite his call of 'a laptop for every child' in the recent election. Still, it was a sign of the times.

My task for the Labour Party, from Neil Kinnock onwards, had been to write what I called 'bolt-on modules', paragraphs that addressed whatever it was that Jonathan Powell and others in Neil's/Tony's office thought needed addressing. I am pleased to say I had nothing to do with the disastrous Sheffield triumphalism that many believe dashed Kinnock's chances of defeating John Major in 1992, but I cannot claim that a single paragraph, sentence, phrase or word of mine made the slightest impact on British politics. It probably only served to annoy more people who found 'Labour luvvies' instinctively repellent than it attracted to the party. The idea that I would vote Conservative because Kenny Everett or, heaven help us, Jimmy Savile encouraged us to do so is clearly nonsensical and insulting. I always wanted to keep my name out of the list of prominent Labour supporters for just that reason.

*

While we're in gossipy mood, I suppose I might as well get His Royal Highness the Prince of Wales out of the way. It is fairly well known, amongst those who know these kinds of things fairly well, that I am an admirer of the PoW, and, I believe, vice versa. This puzzles, confuses, angers and distresses some who think that either I am blind to what they consider egregious faults in the Prince, or that I am sycophantic to, and glamourized by, an institution for which they have nothing but contempt. I don't mean in this book to defend the monarchy, which institution must of course appear like an oddity to many. My own view is that, since we have it and since it gives such pleasure to so many, especially around the world, it would be folly to get rid of it. The backside of whom are we going to lick when we send a letter in the Republic of Britain? William Hague? Harriet Harman? An elected British President will not glamourize the heads of state of other countries when they come on a state visit. Compared to carriages, crowns, orbs and ermine, an entry-level Jaguar and Marks & Spencer suit offer no edge over other nations when vying for trade advantages. By definition half the country will despise a Labour President or a Conservative one, and you can bet your bottom dollar that politicians will ensure that, if we do become a republic, there will be little other choice than the major parties. Which, at the time of writing, might include UKIP. Lovely.

I also admire the tradition of the Prime Minister having

to visit the monarch weekly and use him or her as an echo-chamber. I tell Americans that it is the equivalent of their President once a week being obliged to pay a call on Uncle Sam, assuming that that universally recognizable symbol of the nation were a real, bearded fellow in striped trousers and spangled coat. If a man as powerful as a President or a Prime Minister has to explain what he is doing, what he has enacted, how he has responded to this crisis or that, to someone who represents the nation in a way he or she cannot, I think it keeps them from going too power-crazy.

Many people, to return to the man in question, know more about military history than the Prince of Wales; many know more about architecture; many know more about agriculture; many know more about painting; many know more about flying; many know more about sailing; many know more about riding; many know more about horticulture, cheeses, geography, botany, environmental science and so on and so on and so on. You see where I am going. I can honestly say that I have never met anyone who knows more about all those things. This makes him, at least as far as I am concerned, good and interesting company. He was way ahead of the curve when it came to many environmental and agricultural issues, but there remain many things I fundamentally disagree with him about. Homoeopathy for one, and what seems to me his dangerous instinctive distrust of science and fondness for 'faith' for another. I am much more disposed to like

elf, Ben Elton, Robbie Coltrane, Griff Rhys Jones, Mel Smith, Rowan Atkinson.

An idiot and an imbecile.

Ready to lay down their lives for my country.

A blithering idiot and a gibbering imbecile.

Radio Times 1988 Christmas
Edition: *Saturday-Night Fry* feature.

11.00 Saturday-Night Fry

A programme in the direct line
of comedy that runs like a
silken vase from Aristophanes
to the *Today* programme.
A show identical in spirit to
the great Mary Queen of Scots
tapestry that hangs in
Osterley House.
Starring **Stephen Fry**
Hugh Laurie and
Emma Thompson
A special guest appearance
by a special guest
Written by STEPHEN FRY
Additional material by IAN BROWN
and JAMES HENDRIE
Producer DAN PATTERSON. *Stereo*
(Re-broadcast Wednesday at 7.45pm)

Frying tonight

Saturday-Night Fry is, according to Stephen Fry (right), 'a radio comedy
that roams between E. M. Forster, Jimmy Savile and a small town in
Venezuela with the graceful ease of a mastodon migrating from grassy
uplands to a marshy swamp'. It's written by Stephen himself and co-stars
old chums Hugh Laurie (who also joins Stephen in a BBC2 special) and
Emma Thompson (of *Fortunes of War*).

'The show is Stephen's own peculiar brand of humour,' explains Emma
(currently writing her own comedy for BBCtv). 'It's got a sort of story
running through it, but basically it's a continuous stream of madness.'
Q. Who did Stephen play in *Blackadder II*?

Hugh, Jo and I.

With sister, Jo

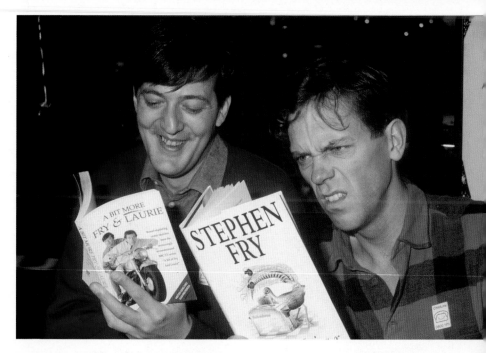

A signing at a Dillons bookshop. London, 1991.

Hugh's warmest, most approving look, 1991.

Despite his resemblance to a 15-year-old shuffling schoolboy, Stephen Fry has numerous television series, charity benefits and now a novel behind him. His sister Jo, *opposite page*, runs operations from his house in Islington

A profile of a liar for the publication of *The Liar*, 1991, with sister Jo.

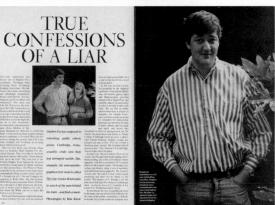

TRUE CONFESSIONS OF A LIAR

Stephen Fry has confessed to everything: public school, prison, Cambridge, homosexuality, credit card theft and attempted suicide. But, strangely, his semi-autobiographical first novel is called *The Liar*. Jessica Berens goes in search of the man behind the truth - and finds a weak.

Photographs by Kim Knott

Tourrettes-sur-Loup
– my best audience

Tourrettes-sur-Loup – picking
on someone my own size.

some modern architecture than he seems to be. But if disagreements over such matters were causes for scourging and falling out, then who would 'scape whipping, as the man said?

I first got to know him quite well when I found myself at one of those line-ups after a comedy show of some kind in 1990 or thereabouts. He had heard, I think through Rowan Atkinson, that I had a house in the country not far from the royal residence at Sandringham in Norfolk.

'I believe we're neighbours,' he said.

'Indeed, sir,' I said. (Oh! Remind me to tell you a story about Penn Jillette. You'll love it.)

'We absolutely adore Norfolk,' the Prince said. Quite the right thing to say.

'You must come and visit me over Christmas,' I said, knowing that this was the season when the royal family spent most of their Sandringham time.

'Indeed, indeed,' he murmured as he moved on to the next bowing comic in the line.

I thought very little more about it. That Christmas in Norfolk I had a houseful. Something like fourteen people, I believe. I had somehow managed to provide stockings for them all on Christmas Eve (a fantastical effort of wrapping and Sellotaping on the snooker table, an ideal surface for Christmas) and made a chestnut soup, roasted a turkey and provided the approved pudding, bedight with Christmas holly on top, as Dickens phrases it. A week of game playing, film-watching, snoozing and light walking had followed. It was a period when I was off the powder and all the better for it.

One morning I was making hollandaise for Eggs Benedict, a breakfast dish I pride myself in having mastered to the point of professional excellence. Hollandaise, like mayonnaise or any emulsified sauce, takes concentration. The melted butter mustn't be poured too quickly into the egg yolk or the mixture will split. A thin, steady stream is called for. This I was achieving when the phone went.

'Someone answer it!'

Fourteen people slumbering, showering or shagging . . . not one of them, it seems, capable of answering the bloody telephone.

'Will someone just . . . oh never mind!' Abandoning that consignment of hollandaise to failure, I strode to the phone and yanked it from its bracket.

'Yes,' I barked testily.

'Um, can I speak to Stephen Fry, please?'

'This is he.'

'Ah, it's the Prince of Wales here.'

A moment. A heartbeat, no more. And in that short series of milliseconds my brain had instructed my mouth to say: 'Oh fuck off, Rory.'

But somehow one always knows when one is listening to the real thing, not to Rory Bremner or any another impressionist, no matter how skillful. That same brain sent an even faster order to overtake and countermand the first.

'Hello, sir!' I managed to choke. 'I'm afraid you caught me trying to make a hollandaise sauce . . .'

'Ah. I'm so sorry. I was wondering, um, wondering about taking you up on that offer and, um, coming for tea?'

'Of course. That would be marvellous. Absolutely splendid. When did you have in mind?'

'How about New Year's Day?'

'Fabulous. I look forward to it.'

I replaced the phone carefully in its cradle. Hmmm.

I stood in the hallway of the house and, like Rik or Mike in *The Young Ones*, called 'House meeting!' at the top of my voice. Slowly people appeared at the heads of stairways and grumblingly made their way down, like the guests in the fire-alarm scene in *Fawlty Towers*. It was probably about eight in the morning, and I am long used to the dislike and annoyance my being a cheerful morning lark engenders. Most people are owls and take a lot of getting up.

'Look, sorry everyone, but the day after tomorrow the Prince of Wales is coming for tea.'

'Yeah, right.'

'Ha fucking ha.'

'You woke me up for *this*?'

I held up a hand. 'Seriously. He really is.'

But I had lost my audience, who were already tightening their dressing-gown cords and trudging back up the stairs.

It was only when, on the following day, a dark green Range Rover appeared that I was finally truly believed. Two detectives and a dog got out, cordially welcomed a proffered tea and poked around ... for what we were unable to ascertain. After this cursory security screening of the house and a multitude of chocolate Hobnobs they had gone. My house guests swarmed around me.

'Well!'

'Oh my lord!'

'What on earth am I going to wear?'

All of us adults were traditionally and pleasingly left-leaning without being rude, yet now we found ourselves to be as flushed and excited as a kennelful of beagle puppies hearing the clink of the leash.

We all arose early the next morning. Why I didn't photograph Hugh Laurie hoovering the drawing-room carpet I have no idea. It would be worth millions in blackmail money today. Ah well.*

Everything is polished, swept, cleaned, washed, waxed and prepared. Teapots are at the ready, kettles half on and half off the hottest ring of the Aga. Bread, crumpets and

---

* I was wise enough to run the manuscript of this book by Hugh to check for accuracy. I am sometimes accused of a good memory, but it is only good for useless things. Hugh's is both compendious and useful. I quote his response to the paragraph above: '... not that it matters, but it was definitely Rowan who did the hoovering. I also distinctly remember him driving to the petrol station – the only place open on New Year's Day – and coming back with fig rolls, for God's sake. They might have been there since the previous New Year.'

muffins piled up for toasting. Butter softened. Jars of homemade blackcurrant jam and lemon curd (two Christmases' worth of presents from my brother's sister-in-law). Sandwiches are cut. Honey! I know he likes honey in his tea! A pot of runny honey is found somewhere. Has it gone off? Honey can't go off, I am assured, a fact that is many years later confirmed for me by a *QI* elf. A wooden honey spoon is discovered in a drawer. The drawer also reveals a better tea-strainer, a proper silver one, not the rather naff Present From Hunstanton which was all I thought I had. Another teapot and a big Dundee cake for his police security men, who will be able to eat in the kitchen. Oh God, have we overdone it? Battenberg cake . . . hell, he might think we're taking the piss. Battenberg was his family name once.

We leave the kitchen and crowd into the drawing room, which has a view through the drawn curtains of the driveway. It is dark, of course, and has been since early afternoon. It is only a week and a few days since the shortest day of the year. Hugh, who is diligent at this kind of duty, takes the log basket out to reload it. The fire is roaring splendidly, but you cannot have too many logs. Jon Canter, writer and friend, checks the candles that are artfully disposed around the room. I am still twitching one curtain and looking out into the night. Kim and Alastair are twitching another curtain and giggling like Japanese schoolgirls.

Headlamps, as in Dornford Yates novels, stab the air

and sweep the hedgerows. But they are bypassing the driveway. We all look at our watches. Was it after all some gigantic hoax?

Then, before we even seem to know what is upon us, the gravel is crunched alive with the sound of two cars skidding to a halt before the front door.

'Right,' I say, 'let's . . .'

They have all scrammed. Skedaddled. Vamoosed.

'Cowards!' I just have time to shout before gulping, breathing deeply and placing myself on the mat. The front doorbell is rung. If I open the door immediately it will look as if I have been waiting like an uncool cat, which I have been and am, but I count to fifteen to dispel the idea and, just as the second peal begins, swing open the door with a smile.

'Your Royal Highness . . .'

'Hullo. I hope you don't mind, but I've brought my wife.'

Out of the shadows steps Princess Diana. She lowers her head and looks up in that characteristic fashion, captured so many times by Mario Testino and a thousand other photographers, smiling from under her lashes. 'Hello, Stephen,' she sweetly murmurs.

I conduct them into the drawing room. They look around and say approving things about my house. It has six bedrooms and is by no means a cottage, but it would fit comfortably into a half of one Sandringham wing. Well, it is all mine, inasmuch as I earned it and didn't inherit it, so I can't be that ashamed. I am not sure 'earned' is the right word, but this isn't the time to go into that.

Slowly the house guests emerge like shy, hungry zoo animals at feeding time. Introductions are effected, the policemen shown into the kitchen by the back door. Is that rude and disrespectful? They don't show offence, but then they wouldn't. Of the Dundee cake not a crumb was left behind, so I must assume they felt at home.

Back in the drawing room. Hugh and Jo's first child, Charlie, is just at the toddling stage. He lurches zombie-like towards the television (yes, there is a television in my drawing room, which the Prince and you persons of tone and breeding must think grotesquely common, but there we are) and switches it on, a child entirely of his generation. Jo screams out 'Charlie!' and the Prince of Wales, one assumes unused to being addressed in this forceful, matronly manner, jumps sitting down, a clever trick. Meanwhile, to my mortification and that of his mother, *EastEnders* comes on to full blaring cockney life. She leaps to her feet to find the remote control. (That reminds me. Very funny Queen Mother story. Remind me to tell you.)

'No, leave it on,' says the Princess. 'It's the special New Year's edition. I want to find out what happens to Ange.'

The Prince is relaxed and cheerful, the Princess charming and beguiling. She wears cowboy boots that suit her very well. The Prince does not wear cowboy boots, which suits *him* very well.

The honeyed tea and the buttered crumpets and the toast and the cakes last out until it is time for the royal pair to depart.

At the front door the Prince thanks me and bids everyone else farewell. Princess Diana holds in the threshold for a second longer, checks over her shoulder that her Prince is out of earshot and whispers softly in my ear, 'Sorry to leave early, though secretly I'm quite glad. It's *Spitting Image* tonight, and I want to watch it in my room. *They* hate it of course. I absolutely adore it.'

And there you have her in a nutshell. By telling me this she was putting me in her power. It was a statement then worth tens of thousands of pounds. 'Princess Di Loves Anti-Royal Smut Puppets!' All I had to do was pick up the phone to any tabloid. But by confiding in me she had made me in some measure her slave: to be trusted with such intelligence was to be appointed one of her special courtiers. Even as intellectual, sharp, brilliant, knowledgeable and impossibly well-read and sensible a man as Clive James was utterly devoted to her.

I closed the door and leaned back against it in that afraid-it-will-soon-be-opened-again-but-I'll-defend-it-with-my-last-breath manner much noted in fast-paced Leonard Rossiter sitcoms.

'Well!' I said.

'Well!' said everyone else.

'Awfully nice couple,' said Jon Canter, 'awfully nice. I didn't get *her* name.'

For the post-mortem we opened a whisky bottle in the drawing room, caring nothing for clearing up the tea things.

'Unbelievable,' said one of the heterosexual male house guests, of which there were a more than ordinary percentage that Christmas. 'Did you see how she looked at me? I was in there . . . she was practically looking up at the ceiling as if to suggest we go upstairs. Jesus!'

'What are you talking about?' another man interrupted. 'That was me she was giving the eye to.'

'No *me*!'

In the PR war the Prince of Wales never had a chance. His tireless work, his initiatives, the Prince's Trust alone, none of these could compete with so perfect a piece of seductive nature.

For his fiftieth birthday (this is one of the stories I was going to tell you) I emceed an entertainment at the London Palladium. Afterwards I stood once more in the line-up. Next to me was Penn Jillette, one half of the brilliant Penn and Teller, American magicians, pro-science, sceptics of the highest rank.

Penn turned to me as he watched the Prince slowly coming down the line.

'Do I have to call him "Your Majesty" or any of that shit?'

'No, no. Not at all. If you were to use a title it would be "Your Royal Highness", and from then on "sir", but there's no need. After all, I haven't called you Penn once in this conversation until now, have I, Penn?'

'Oh, OK, just so long as he understands that we don't talk like that. And what about bowing? I have to bow? We don't bow in America.'

'No, no,' I reassure him, 'no bowing necessary.'

'Cuz I'm an American, and we don't bow.'

'Yes, he knows you're an American.'

'I won't get put in the Tower of London or anything?'

People always think that sojourns in the Tower of London, like knighthoods, are somehow in the gift of members of the royal family.

I reassured him on these points. No Highnessing, no kowtowing.

At last the Prince reaches Penn, who immediately falls almost prostrate to the floor. 'Your Majesty Highness. Your Royal Sir . . .' and so on and so forth, babbling like a gibbon on speed. The Prince passes on to me and whoever was the other side of me without turning a hair. Seen it all before.

After he had gone, I watched Penn, an enormous man, crouching on the floor, rolling about, beating the planks of the stage, sobbing, stuffing his fist into his mouth and moaning up to the fly-tower: 'Why did I *do* that? What came *over* me? What power do they have? I betrayed my country!'

During the course of the early 1990s, I got to know Sir Martin Gilliat quite well. An extraordinary man. If you didn't know him yourself I assure you you would have loved him. He was of a type that no longer exists and whose very background and manner would now, I suppose, be looked down upon very snootily. Ludgrove House, Eton and forty years Equerry and Private Secretary to Queen Elizabeth the Queen Mother. 'All Sir Martin's geese are swans,' was a popular saying in royal circles. Which, being interpreted, means that everyone was alike in splendour to him, low, high, of whatever background, breeding, race or gender. I never met a man of such natural charm, kindness and vivacity. He had had a 'good war', of which, naturally, he never spoke. He escaped the Nazis several times but was always recaptured. At last, like all serial escapers, he was sent to Colditz, the Eton of prison camps. I was told that he had never slept since. Not properly. Apparently doctors examined him until he got tired of it* and sent them packing. This made him ideal for the Queen Mother. She would dine festively, play amusing games and then go to bed round about one or two in the morning. He would sit up writing letters until she came down. They would walk the dogs together in the park. Ideal companions.

There is a story told in Hugo Vickers's biography of Queen Elizabeth, as she was known in the Household. She liked pranks at parties. One evening after dinner at the Castle of Mey, her favourite residence, right up in the very north of Scotland in Caithness, she and the ladies, having retired to leave the men to their port, decided it

---

*Not tired enough to sleep, obviously . . .

would be a lark if they all hid behind the curtains to surprise the men when they came out after their port and cigars.

Sir Martin led the men out and said in his very loud voice, 'Thank God for that, they've all fucked off to bed.'

I got to know him because he was an inveterate punter in the West End stage, what is known as an angel. He hit the motherlode with *Me and My Girl* and was forever grateful. He invited Rowan Atkinson (who also knew him) and me to Buck's, his club, for lunch. Over the gulls' eggs and asparagus he confessed that there was an ulterior motive for his invitation.

'Marvellous to have you chaps to luncheon of course, but I have to ask you. Do you know the Dowager Duchess of Abercorn?'

We both regretfully disavowed ever having had that pleasure.

'No? Well. She was a lady-in-waiting of Queen Elizabeth's for many years. It is her eightieth birthday in July, and we, which is to say Queen Elizabeth, are going to throw her a birthday party at Claridge's, and I thought perhaps you might provide a little light relief? We have a band, but comedy is always popular.'

Rowan and I digested this and exchanged speaking glances. The year before he and I had descended on the Middle East, a swoop known in Rowanese as a bank raid. Rowan and I performed in his amusingly entitled *One Man Show* in Bahrain, Abu Dhabi, Dubai and Oman, brightening the lives of expat oil executives with high-quality, high-priced comedic entertainment. So we did have a show.

Rowan expressed our reservations perfectly.

'Well now,' he said. 'We do indeed have material, b-but if most of the audience is the same age as the Duchess and the Queen Mo . . . Queen Elizabeth, then some of it might seem a bit . . .'

'A bit fast? A bit racy?' boomed Sir Martin, his resonant voice echoing off every surface of the dining room and rattling the glassware. 'Oh I wouldn't worry about that. The royal family loves the lavatory. I mean obviously not yer fucks or yer cunts.'

'Well quite,' said Rowan, swallowing and looking down at his plate. 'No indeed.'

Sir Martin, as a loyal servant, was not one prone to gossip but he could not help telling me this story of his employer. One morning in the upstairs drawing room of Clarence House she said to him, 'Martin, I think our television is on the blink. Do you think we might need a new one?'

'I shall have a look, ma'am.'

Sure enough the television – this was many years ago – was suffering from that annoying rolling horizontal bar affliction that was the bane of many an ageing cathode ray tube.

'Ma'am, I shall be straight on the telephone to those nice people at Harrods, and while you're at luncheon they will install a new one.'

'Lovely, Martin. You're an angel.'

This was, of course, before the days of the not-so-cold war between the royal households and Mohamed Al Fayed's Harrods.

After her luncheon the Queen Mother – Queen Elizabeth, I beg her pardon – tottered upstairs to watch the three o'clock from Chepstow or whatever it may have been, and there was Sir Martin, standing proudly by a brand-new, very large television set.

'Oh, how grand!' said Queen Elizabeth.

'Yes indeed, ma'am, and I'll tell you something rather special.'

'Oh do, do!'

'You might notice that it has no buttons for changing the channels.'

'Oh no,' she squealed, 'they've forgotten the buttons. How dreadful!'

'Ah, but no, ma'am. Do you see that grey box next to your gin and Dubonnet on the side table there?'

'Oh, now whatever can that be?'

'Well that is what they call a "remote control", ma'am. If you'll allow me . . . I press the button marked 1, so, and up comes BBC 1. I press button 2 and up comes BBC 2. And then button 3 for ITV. You see?'

'Oh, how clever!' Queen Elizabeth beamed approvingly and then added, 'I still think it's easier to ring.'

Living the Life

Over the decades I have been asked to deliver lectures, disquisitions and addresses on numerous subjects and for the most part I manage to excuse myself. Just occasionally, however, a subject is so appealing or a cause so close to my heart and my diary so surprisingly and unwontedly amenable that I find myself under an obligation to disgorge as requested. I offer you the opening of a lecture I gave in the Royal Geographical Society's lecture theatre some years ago: the first Spectator Lecture, or Speccie Leccie, as I called it. I have scavenged from it and present the exordium so as to make coherent some of my thoughts about America, a country I was becoming more and more fond of and anxious to visit more and more often.

Thank you. Thank you very much. Good lord. Well, well. Here we are. Gathered together in the very lecture theatre where Henry Morton Stanley once told an enraptured world of his momentous meeting with Dr Livingstone. Charles Darwin was a member and gave talks in this same hall. Sir Richard Burton lectured here, and John Hanning Speke ... spoke. Shackleton and Hillary displayed their intimate frostbite scars to a spellbound RGS audience. Explorers, adventurers and navigators have been coming here for the best part of 180 years to tell of their discoveries. If only at school, geography teachers, surely the most scoffed and pilloried class of pedagogue there is, if only they had concentrated less on rift valleys, trig points and the major exports of Indonesia and more on the fact that geography could promise a classy royal society with the sexiest lecture theatre in the land. Actually, now that I think of it, one reason for me to be fond of the subject was the circumstance that in my prep-school geography room there were piles and piles of shiny yellow *National Geographic* magazines available for skimming through. These, with their glossy advertisements for Chesterfield cigarettes, Cadillac sedans and Dimple whisky, gave me my first view outside television of what America might be like. But there was another reason religiously to scan the magazines . . .

National Geographic, before it became best known for an imbecilic and embarrassing suite of digital TV channels, was – thanks to its anthropological coverage in a pre-internet, pre-Channel 4, pre-top shelf age – the only place where a curious boy could look at full colour pictures of naked people. For that alone it deserves the thanks of generations. One did get the false impression that many peoples of the world had protuberances shaped exactly like a gourd, but never mind.

National Geographic made films too, and at my school these would be run through an old Bell & Howell projector by the geography masters to keep us quiet and to give them time to beetle off and pursue their amorous liaisons with matron or the whisky bottle, depending on which teacher it was. 'Fry, you're in charge,' they would never say on their way out. But what strange films they left us to watch. I seem to recall that the subjects were usually logging in Oregon, the life cycle of the beaver or the excitements to be found in the National Parks of Montana and Wyoming. Very blue skies, lots of spruce, larch and pine, and plenty of plaid shirtings. The unreliable speed of that hot and dusty old Bell & Howell rendered the soundtrack and its music flat then sharp then flat again in rolling waves of discord, but it was the commentators that gave me raptures with their magisterially rich and rolling American rhetoric. What a peculiar way with language they had, employing poetical tricks that had been out of date a hundred years earlier. My favourite was the 'be-' game. If a word usually began with the prefix 'be-' it was taken off. Thus 'beneath' became 'neath' and so on. But the 'be' of 'beneath' wasn't simply thrown away. No, no. It was *recycled* by adding it to words it had no business being anywhere near. Which would result in preposterous declamatory orotundities of this nature: ''Neath the bedappled verdure of the mighty sequoia sinks the bewestering sun,' and so forth. And what is the proper name for *this* rhetorical trope, also much deployed? It would start with the usual 'be-' nonsense: ''Neath becoppered skies bewends ...'

but then this: 'the silver ribbon of time that *is* the Colorado River'. The weird and senseless maze of metonym and metaphor that *was* National Geographic Speak in all its besplendour was a great influence on me, for where others had rock and roll music, I had language . . .

And so I bewended and bewittered like the large slab of humanity that *was* Stephen Fry. Despite my passion for all things American and my obsession with its language, literature, history and culture, I didn't visit the country until I was well into my twenties. I had adapted and rewritten the book of the British musical *Me and My Girl* as alluded to *passim*, and it was decided that a Broadway production might be worth attempting. With Mike Ockrent, the director, and Robert Lindsay, the star, I took a PanAm flight from London to JFK. I had never been so excited in my life. My first view of the Manhattan skyline was like Dante's first view of Beatrice, Cortez's of the Pacific and, I dare say, Simon Cowell's of Susan Boyle. I fell for New York quite as much as Wodehouse, W. H. Auden, Oscar Wilde and my other literary heroes had before me. But we were only there for rehearsals. The musical was to try out and open in Los Angeles, California. My first visit, and I was to live for a while in both Manhattan and Beverly Hills. My cup ran over like a blocked gutter.

In Broadway's theatre district there is a famous eatery called the Carnegie Deli. It features in Woody Allen's

Broadway Danny Rose, you may remember. It was on my first full day in America that I went in there and ordered a pastrami sandwich. Big deal, you may say. Oh yes. Big deal. Huge deal. For those who have not had the pleasure, a proper New York deli pastrami sandwich is about the size and thickness of a rugby ball. Two thin layers of rye bread and in between slice after slice after slice of warm, fatty, delicious pastrami. On the side is served a pickle or so. Hold that image. Me facing off with a vast pastrami sandwich. Right. We now scuttle to LA. I blew all my per diems on a single weekend in the Bel Air Hotel, luxury on a scale I had never even imagined, let alone contemplated. Robert Redford winked at me from across the breakfast room. I nearly trod on a dog belonging to Shirley MacLaine. My over-running cup ran over even more till it was more like the Trevi Fountain than any sort of cup I know.

Then back to New York. I am happy to say the opening night of *Me and My Girl* was everything one could have hoped for. The *New York Times* raved; we were a hit. I won a Drama Desk award and a Tony nomination; Robert Lindsay went on to win a Tony and a hatful of other trophies for his brilliant performance. There and then I promised myself that one day I would live in New York, this city from whose sidewalks you drew electricity like a tube train from its tracks. At the time I had been staying in an apartment belonging to my friend Douglas Adams. On the flight back I garrulously chattered away to an

American lady sitting next to me about how I loved America and was planning to live in New York.

'But honey,' she said – she was rather in the Rosalind Russell Auntie Mame mould – 'honey, you told me you'd only ever been to New York City and Los Angeles.'

I confessed that this was true.

'Then you have never even *seen* America,' she said.

I suppose regarding a *part* of something as being congruent to its *whole* might be viewed as a kind of *pars pro toto* fallacy or lazy synecdoche, but I didn't truly understand what this woman meant until, as the *National Geographic* might say, I bethought me of the colossal continent of succulence that *was* a Carnegie Deli sandwich. How could anyone say they had eaten a Carnegie Deli pastrami sandwich if in fact they had only gnawed at the thin slices of rye at either end while the whole continent of meat lay untouched? How could anyone say they had experienced America who had only nibbled at New York and Los Angeles?

One of the tasks I was – er – tasked to do when in Los Angeles some time in 1990 or 1991 was to pick up a script in Las Vegas and transport it to London. To fax an entire 120-page script from Las Vegas to London might have been within the budget of a major studio, but not within the budget of Renaissance Films, Ken Branagh's production company, founded with a City gentleman turned producer called Stephen Evans. Email attachments were but a glint in the eye of the future. If you had a document to send you used a courier. Couriers came in the shape of DHL and FedEx or possibly in the shape of Stephen Fry.

I cannot remember what had taken me to Los Angeles in 1991, or even if I have the year right, but I do know that the previous winter I had invited Emma Thompson and her new husband, Ken Branagh, for a week at my Norfolk house. They had seen me chopping wood. We had talked of this and that and somehow, as is the way with Ken, a story idea had been born or confirmed in his head.

I think perhaps on reflection that I may have got this wrong. Maybe it was Martin Bergman* and his wife, the American comedian Rita Rudner,† who had been up to Norfolk, for it was certainly they who wrote the screenplay in question. Oh memory, what a ditzy queen you are.

Well, well. The facts of the matter are that Ken knew I was in Los Angeles and asked me to stop off in Las Vegas and pick up the latest version of the script. I had not read *any* version of it, but had agreed to be in it, such was my instinctive trust of Ken and such were his extraordinary powers of persuasion.

The film was to be called *Peter's Friends*, and I read it on

---

* Ex-President of the Cambridge Footlights. Before my time, but he co-produced our 1981 tour of Australia, magnificently described in *The Fry Chronicles*.

† Terrifically funny American stand-up comedian. 'I can't understand why cosmetics manufacturers make perfumes that smell of flowers. Men don't like flowers. If they want to attract men they should bring out a scent called New Car Interior . . .'

the plane back from Los Angeles with a mounting sense of horror. It was funny, I thought, but it was about *us*. About Hugh and me and Emma and Tony Slattery and our Footlights generation seven or eight years on. Ken had enjoyed great success with the film version of his triumphant Stratford *Henry V* and now he wanted to make a kind of British *Big Chill*.

Hugh and I, perhaps because of the permanent guilt derived from our perceived privileged upbringings, instinctively recited in our minds the likely response of critics whenever a new project arose. We had in mind some kind of antagonistic *Time Out* reviewer. The wrinkle in his nose, the snort of his derision, the slow downward curl of his lips – we were there before him, writing his copy as if inside his head and the heads of everyone else. This we will return to in a moment.

In the spring of '88 I played the part of the philosopher Humphry in Simon Gray's *The Common Pursuit* in Watford and at the Phoenix Theatre in the West End. During that time I had been making the television version of *Delve Special*, which had been retitled *This Is David Lander*. Filming all day and then just making it in time to the theatre and after *that* being naughty in the Limelight nightclub with rock stars, snooker players and other disparate low-life legends seemed to be something I could manage, although my doctor popped into the dressing room at the Phoenix twice a week to inject me with B12 to keep my energy levels up. I don't remember asking for this, so I assume it was the show's producer who probably worried, as producers do, that I might be running out of fuel. The run of the play was followed by a period Hugh and I had set aside to write all the material for a comedy sketch show that we decided after much agonized debate to call *A Bit of Fry and Laurie*.

In the early spring of 1989 we began taping the first full series of this ('a lacklustre throwback trapped in an irrelevant Oxbridge past', we imagined *Time Out* snarling furiously). In the summer of that year we recorded *Blackadder Goes Forth* ('a sad dip in form after the delights of *Blackadder the Third*', *Time Out* would be sure to mutter) and immediately after that Hugh and I filmed the first series of *Jeeves and Wooster*, again sharing throughout the shoot what we imagined would be *Time Out*'s verdict: 'while the rest of the world leaps ahead in innovation and edge, Fry and Laurie welter feebly in a snobbish and puerile past'.* This had come about when a fellow called Brian Eastman had asked for a meeting. Eastman had previously worked in music for the Royal Philharmonic Orchestra and the British Council and now had a company that produced most notably the series *Poirot* on ITV.

---

*For all I know this is deeply unfair, and *Time Out* welcomed us with lavish praise. We were too scared to look. I remember years earlier Rik Mayall opening a *Time Out* to see a review of the second series of *The Young Ones*. '"Nothing like as good as the pioneering first series,"' he read, then spluttered, Riklike, 'but they *hated* the first series. Bastards!'

It was his plan to bring Wodehouse's Bertie and Jeeves to the screen, and he felt that Hugh and I were good casting. Strangely, to us at least, he was quite open as to which roles we felt each should play. It seemed obvious to us that Hugh was a natural Bertie and I more suited to Jeeves. Hugh put it this way: Bertie's voice is a trumpet, Jeeves's a cello.

Actually, such was our insecurity and fear of failure we didn't really believe it could be done and might easily have turned Brian down, had it not been for a fear of any other two actors playing the parts. The pessimism in this case wasn't entirely our usual flabby lack of confidence, so much as an immense respect of, and devotion to, Wodehouse's work. His novels and stories, like any writer's, are composed of plot, character and language. What makes Wodehouse stand head and shoulders above any comic writer of the twentieth century (indeed almost any writer, regardless of genre) is his *language*. In the end we decided if we could get across character and plot and only a small amount of that peerless prose then we might turn enough people to reading the books, consigning them to a lifetime of endless pleasure. Clive Exton, who wrote the adaptation, was best known for his chilling screenplay *10 Rillington Place*, the grim, murky retelling of the Christie murders. But he had since moved to another world of Christie murders altogether as one of the lead writers on the *Poirot* series.

Fry and Laurie seemed sometimes to be a desperate affair,

writing and staring at the wall and not believing we were at all funny, performing dozens of sketches before a live audience on each recording evening and then worrying straight away about the next week. But I was working with Hugh, my best friend in the whole world, and while sketch delivery, like any kind of birth, involves pain and squealing, it was a period of fecundity, laughter, freedom and friendship that I would have been lucky to have experienced had I lived a hundred lives. Sometimes I will be sent a YouTube link on Twitter and out of curiosity follow it up only to discover that it is an old *Fry and Laurie* sketch that I have almost entirely forgotten. Forgive me if occasionally I find myself laughing and actually feeling proud. Naturally, as we all do, I wince and writhe in embarrassment at this mannerism or that, but I do really believe that some of our writing and performing was . . . well . . . top hole . . .

Straight after *Fry and Laurie* we made *Blackadder Goes Forth*. The audience that came into the BBC studios, as I have mentioned, had almost certainly seen *Blackadder II* and *Blackadder the Third* on their televisions at home and were somewhat alienated by new characters and settings. In rehearsal there was a lot of pacing, smoking, coffee-drinking and throwing out ideas, not to mention having ideas thrown out. We were young, we were buzzy and we were also, although we had no idea of it at all, making a comedy series that for whatever reason appears to have stood the test of time. The character drawing and imagination of writers Richard Curtis and Ben Elton, our own additions, I would modestly suggest, the extraordinary talent of Rowan, Hugh, (Sir) Tony Robinson, Tim McInnerny and the late and hugely lamented Rik Mayall all seemed to combine in a way that simply clicked. John Lloyd, the producer, kept us all on point, as Americans like to say, but on a couple of occasions we made such drastic changes to the storyline that whole new sets had to be ordered from the production designer just two days before recording, and it was John who manfully took the blame each time. My own proudest achievement is perhaps not the playing of the insane General Melchett, but the suggestion after the first read-through that Tim McInnerny's character's name be changed from the proffered 'Perkins' or 'Cartwright' to something that might explain his animosity, suspicion and hostility to all around him. I wondered if 'Darling' might not work, and Rowan and Tim ran with the ball as only actors of their quality could.

Jeeves and Wooster, which started more or less straight after *Blackadder* finished, was unalloyed pleasure. Hugh and I both took to single-camera filming (as opposed to the multi-camera TV studio set-up then customary in which sitcoms were recorded on tape) like ducks to bread crusts. We had wonderful fellow actors to work with and lively, funny crews full of banter and inventiveness. Between them they had been involved in many of the best films ever to have come out of Britain, from *Dr No* to *Dr Strangelove*.

Somehow during this period as well as my involvement in those three television series I had also written four or five twenty-minute films for John Cleese's company Video Arts. Video Arts specialized in training films for business and industry. These films had been constructed around psychological ideas all vetted by John Cleese's pet psychologist, Robin Skynner, with whom he'd written the book *Families and How to Survive Them*. They had thrilling titles like *How to Schedule a Meeting, How to Run an Interview, How to Succeed in a Job Application*. I secretly called the whole project 'How to Make Money by Stating the So Fucking Obvious It Makes Your Nose Bleed'. If businesses needed to be told in firm language:

- make a list
- stick to it

then no wonder the British economy was swirling round the lavatory pan. They were fun films to make, however, and to be around John Cleese, a towering hero from my early teens, still made me rub my eyes with disbelief. I had written roles for myself, John, Hugh and Dawn French. Other parts were played by Ronnie Corbett and Julian Holloway.

It was during this period, post *Fry and Laurie*, *Blackadder* and *Jeeves and Wooster*, that I made simply the best decision in my entire life. It saved my health, my career and (for a time at least) my sanity.

While I had been deep in this absolutely brutal schedule (although it seemed natural to me), my sister Jo had completed a TV and film make-up course in London, and one evening we had dinner in Orso, the popular Covent Garden restaurant.

I had been turning something over in my mind and finally, over the *panna cotta alla fragole*, I ventilated it.

'Jo, I know there's always the possibility of your going off to do make-up work on a film or something. And I know Richard might get stationed abroad,* but do you think you might like . . . ?'

'Yes?'

'Well, if this is out of order just spray wine at me, but how would you feel about . . . ?'

'Go on.'

'Well, over the last few years I've started to get more and more fan mail, more and more requests for appearances and after-dinner speaking and the lord knows what else. It's kind of out of control . . .'

'Right . . .'

'My diary is so packed that I can hardly keep up with what I'm doing, and I need, well I need a . . .'

'A secretary?'

'Well, the term for it is Personal Assistant. PA. But in your case, being a personal sister, you'd be a Personal Assister.'

'Oh God, that is so exactly what I hoped you'd ask me. I was going to suggest the same thing. I'd love it. I'd love it more than anything.'

* Her husband, Richard, was an RAF pilot.

For the past twenty-six years, then, Jo has been my PA. She is the best PA anyone ever had. Naturally I would say that out of family loyalty, but a story illustrates the point.

During filming with John Cleese somewhere in West London for a Video Arts project, Jo visited the set with her Filofax to go over the next week's diary business. This was before you could electronically sync diaries over the air, well before PDAs and smartphones. She stayed for lunch, joined John in watching me film a scene with Ronnie Corbett and then biffed off.

About ten minutes later John stalked over.

'Well, don't I feel a total dick.'

'What's happened?'

'All my working life I've looked for the perfect assistant, and you, you bastard, have found her. So naturally I said to her while you were on camera, "Whatever he's paying you, I'll double it."'

'Ah. What did she say?'

'She smiled very sweetly and said, "That's very kind, Mr Cleese, but he is actually my brother." I don't know when I last felt such a complete tit.'

'Well, you weren't to know . . .'

I was, of course, very pleased to hear such praise. It was entirely typical that Jo herself never mentioned this story to me. I finally raised it a week or so later.

'You do know John told me about trying to poach you?'

'Oh that! That was funny . . .'

'You could have told me, and I'd've had to double your pay . . .'

Which I think, I *hope*, I did.

It is no exaggeration to say that I would not be alive now were it not for Jo's gentle but firm control of my life. I tease her by calling her Martina Bormann, my diary Nazi, but it would have been impossible to have done a tenth of the things I have done without her understanding of how diaries, film schedules, call sheets, production companies, television executives, airports, drivers and above all her capricious, weird and impossible boss/ brother operate. Or fail to.

I was called one week the following year, which was probably 1990 but don't quote me, to visit a certain Roger Peters, who was installed in splendour in Suite 512 of the Savoy Hotel. The man turned out to be an American of middle years. He gave me to understand that he was the heir and last lover of the American composer Samuel Barber. I had always believed that Barber had died of a broken heart after his long-time partner and fellow musician Gian Carlo Menotti traded him in for a younger model, but it seems he found Roger Peters at the end.

Roger, it seemed, had the film rights to Noël Coward's *Hayfever* and wondered if I was interested in writing the adaptation. I politely demurred, knowing that: a) *Hayfever* was Coward's favourite play and he had specifically given orders that 'no cunt ever be allowed to fuck about with it';

and b) it was all set in one place and just about one time, adhering as closely as possible to the Aristotelian unities, making it a bugger to adapt for the screen. Not that Reginald Rose and Sidney Lumet didn't do a bang-up job with *12 Angry Men* . . .

He didn't seem too offended, and we drank and chatted and gossiped. I guessed that he had asked just about everyone who had ever held a pen or tapped at a keyboard to take on this job, starting, as one did, with Stoppard, Bennett and Pinter and then reaching after exhausting weeks of refusals the bottom of the barrel. Not false modesty, just realism.

The suite was magnificent, with spectacular views that gave out on to the Thames. The idea of living permanently in such splendour filled me with a perfectly unforgivable mixture of envy and ambition. One day, I thought to myself, one day . . .

The calendar pages peeled and blew away, as Vivian Stanshall phrased it, and it is now early 1992, and I find myself window-shopping along Piccadilly.

'Hello, Stephen!'

I have a mild case of prosopagnosia, absolutely maddening. Nothing like the severe face-blindness that afflicts some. I have a friend who cannot distinguish his own family members until they say their name. My level of this disorder may not be severe, but it does mean I frequently appear rude. So if you know me and I cut you in the street, it doesn't mean that I don't like you and wish to

blank you out of my life, it just means I haven't the faintest idea who you are. Tell me your name, and I'll be
absolutely fine. Most people are the other way about and
remember faces but not names.

This fellow, fortunately, was happy to supply the name
without prompting.

'Roger Peters!'

'Of course,' I said. 'How's tricks?'

'Well, you know,' he said, falling into step. 'You're just
the fellow. Do you know of anyone, *anyone* . . .'

Oh God, he's going to harp on about the bloody *Hayfever* script again, I moaned inwardly.

'. . . *anyone* who'd be willing to live in my Savoy suite for
four or five weeks. I have to go to America for family
business and I don't want to move all my stuff out. I have
a deal with the hotel whereby I pay by the year anyway, so
it's just a question of someone suite-sitting. Anybody
come to mind?'

'We-e-ll . . .' I said doubtfully, 'there is one person it
might suit. He's about this high . . .' I raised my hand to
the level of my head. 'About this wide . . .' I parted my
hands to the width of my body. 'He has a bent nose and
he's talking to you right this minute.'

'Oh, that's fantastic! I'm leaving Wednesday. Why don't
you come round tomorrow afternoon, and I'll introduce
you to the floor butler and show you where everything is.'

And so it came to pass that the Savoy Hotel became
my home for just over a month. For eleven days of that

time we filmed *Peter's Friends*. The script that I couriered over to London the year before had been polished and burnished and buffed to a light sheen, but Hugh and I were still, to our eternal discredit, deeply embarrassed about the whole thing. Occasionally in the hallways, corridors and drawing rooms of Wrotham Park (the grand house outside Barnet where we had already shot some scenes in *Jeeves and Wooster* and where I was many years later to shoot scenes in Robert Altman's *Gosford Park*), occasionally, Ken would see Hugh and me looking hangdog and licked to a splinter between set-ups.

'Everything all right, darlings?'

'They're going to hate us,' I moaned.

'Who? What do you mean?'

'"This incestuous, up-itself tale of Oxbridge wankers who reveal their feeble, wimpy and effete so-called 'problems' over a weekend of excess in a country house . . ." Can you imagine how *Time Out* are going to react?' (I've no idea why *Time Out* was still the symbol and focus of all our insecurities.)

'*Time Out*? Who gives a fuck? It's read by about twelve people. Seriously, loves, why would you worry about what they think?'

We admired Ken Branagh, and still do, for many reasons, but his magnificent ability not to be downcast or diverted by concerning himself with how some reviewer was going to react to his work was near the top of the list of his accomplishments. Daring and courage are half the battle with acting, directing and film-making. If you have a newspaper reviewer or even the ghost of a generalized and antagonistic public over your shoulder tutting and hissing in through their teeth as you try to concentrate then you are doomed to failure.

Ken, of course, does not associate his place in the world with guilt. He grew up in Northern Ireland in no position of prosperity. His love of theatre was in-born and absolute; any money he managed to earn he would spend on the ferry to the mainland and the bus to Stratford-upon-Avon, where he would watch every season from his early teenage years onwards. It is no accident that he arrived for the first full day of shooting for *Peter's Friends* already filled with knowledge, courage and self-belief. It is also, I would argue, no accident that Hugh and I arrived almost sick with apprehension, shame and foreboding. The very good fortune that took us from our public schools (by way of other schools and prison in my case) via Cambridge, the Footlights and into *Blackadder, Jeeves and Wooster* and our own sketch show, far from filling us with confidence, made us feel utterly unworthy. Please do not think we are asking for sympathy and certainly not for admiration. I speak as it was in our befuddled minds, and you may take it as you will. Perhaps if you have imagination you can see yourself feeling the same way under the same circumstances. Perhaps we were just peculiarly weird.

That a whole feature film could be shot in eleven days

was testament to the work ethic of Ken and his crew, the tight unity of time and place within Martin and Rita's script and, of course, the sparsity of the budget.

Meanwhile, the pleasure of having a car coming to pick me up from the Savoy and dropping me there in the evening was almost more thrilling than anything I had ever experienced. The top-hatted 'linkmen', often incorrectly referred to as doormen, were unfailingly polite to me, and I soon got to know the rest of the staff. If you want to know anything about the depths of degradation of the human being, make the acquaintance of the executive housekeeper of any large hotel. You will never be the same again. Discretion prohibits me from going any further, this is a journey you must undertake yourself. It is a bit like telling someone to look up the word 'munting' in urbandictionary.com. I take no further responsibility.

Otherwise the joys of suite-sitting were altogether delicious. No bathrobes were ever softer and fluffier, no shower-rose wider and more generous in its precipitation. One small and entirely preposterous annoyance however, a something that got under my skin, was the daily *sameness* of it all. That ashtray on that table in the drawing room was always placed *exactly* there. That chair always angled *exactly* that way. One day I mentioned this to the floor butler.

'Whenever I come back from filming or from a walk,' I said, 'the suite has been wonderfully cleaned and tidied, but – and I really don't mean this as a criticism – everything is always in exactly the same place. The ornaments on the mantelpiece, the . . .'

'Sir, say no more. From tomorrow we will surprise you in small ways each day.'

Which they did. It made me, and I like to think the chambermaid and other staff members, giggle, each time they made a small alteration. Playing Hunt the Ashtray kept me on my toes and freshened the experience of hotel living.

One spare evening I had gone to see a production of *Tartuffe* in which my good friend Johnny Sessions played a role. Also in the production was Dulcie Gray, whose husband, Michael Denison, had played Algernon in Anthony Asquith's *The Importance of Being Earnest*, delivering the line: 'I hope, Cecily, I shall not offend you if I state quite frankly and openly that you seem to me to be in every way the visible personification of absolute perfection?', that very joyous progression of words that had so made me wriggle and writhe and squirm with delight when a young boy.

Michael and Dulcie, a grand and much-loved theatrical couple, made a tradition of having a summer party at Shardeloes, a marvellous eighteenth-century house in Old Amersham with noble Robert Adam interiors and a 1796 landscaped garden by Humphry Repton. The house had been saved, restored and divided up in the 1970s after falling into the customary nursing-home use and further slow decline. Dulcie and Michael had the best ground-floor rooms, giving out over the great lawn; their party, when I arrived, was already crammed with figures from the British film and theatre world. I found myself falling into conversation with Doreen, widow of the great Jack Hawkins, one of my favourite British film stars. Then who should I see across the room? Did my eyes believe it? My favourite of them all, John Mills. A certain amount of excited hopping on one leg, a little light coughing and I found myself sitting on a sofa next to him. He twinkled, just as I expected him to, this nimble, unutterably charming and deeply gifted man. His wife, Mary Hayley Bell, author of *Whistle Down the Wind*, barked and laughed just as I expected her to.

John Mills was the man Noël Coward wrote 'Mad Dogs and Englishmen' for. In the mid-1930s he had been a singer, hoofer and all-round entertainer for a company with the unfortunate name of 'The Quaints'. Coward, on a journey back from Australia, stopped off in Singapore and saw a poster offering the unlikely double bill (surely not in one night?) of *Hamlet* and *Mr Cinders*. It was in the latter that the lithe, lissom and perky Mills impressed. Coward went round afterwards and told him to visit him in London, where he would find a part for him.

Johnny Mills had a genius for friendship. Coward (whom Mills was the first to dub 'the Master'), Laurence Olivier, Rex Harrison, Richard Attenborough, Bryan Forbes and many others benefited from his selfless and sweetly unegotistical charm.

As we sat on the sofa at Shardeloes I must have bombarded him with dozens of questions about his films and career. *The October Man*, *In Which We Serve*, *Ryan's Daughter*, *Hobson's Choice*, *Tiger Bay*, *Swiss Family Robinson* and above all *Ice Cold in Alex*, *Great Expectations* and *Tunes of Glory* had affected me profoundly.

When I paused to draw breath, Johnny asked me what I was up to. I explained that I was in the middle of making a picture with Kenneth Branagh.

'Oh, no, really?' said Johnny. 'I wonder, would you do me a favour?'

'Anything.'

'Could you tell Kenneth that, as a friend of Larry Olivier's, I just know how much Larry would have loved Kenneth's *Henry V* and how much he would have loathed the vile comparisons the critics have made. Can you tell him that?' Johnny was referring to the fact that, while Ken's *Henry V* had been an undoubted success, many snarky responses along the lines of 'Who does he think he is? He's no Laurence Olivier' had greeted its release.

'I'm afraid I can't pass that message on,' I told Johnny.

'Oh.' He looked rather nonplussed.

'I'd much prefer you to pass it on yourself. If I gave a dinner party, would you and Lady Mills come along?'

He beamed assent, telephone numbers were swapped, and the thing was fixed.

There is nothing quite like hosting a dinner party in a five-star hotel suite. Yes, of course, I'm aware of how utterly appalling that sounds, but I might as well get the story out.

Here's how it goes. You tell Alfonso and Ernesto on your floor that you plan to have six guests for dinner next Friday, and they bow with pleasure.

When the day dawns, Ernesto comes in with a menu card and the suggestions from the executive chef and his team toiling in the hypocausts six floors below. You select what you hope is an agreeable dinner* and then, at round about six o'clock, Alfonso, who doesn't want you under his feet while he sees to the flowers and place settings, comes in and commands that you go on a walk. When you arrive back at the suite everything is simply perfect. The armchairs have been moved back to the window, in a semi-circle looking out over the Thames at dusk. In the centre of the room the main table has had an extra leaf inserted to accommodate seven people: I have invited Hugh and Jo Laurie, Emma Thompson and Ken and of course Sir John and Lady Mills.

Starched white napery, crystal glassware and silver

---

*I bore in mind the fact (told to me years ago by my mother, who knows these things, when watching a Mills film) that Sir John had been for fifty years on the Hay Diet. When he was a young man he had developed a stomach ulcer, then the most common cause of death of men under forty in Britain. Today, of course, suicide is the most common. Someone recommended to him the Hay Diet, in which protein and carbohydrates are never combined. Vegetables are 'neutral'. You can have steak and salad or pasta and salad. You can have cucumber sandwiches, but not cheese rolls. Ham and eggs for breakfast or just pancakes. You get the idea. His ulcer was allayed, and for the rest of his life he remained trim.

cutlery gleam in the candlelight. Two low bowls of perfect peonies on the table, vases of roses and exquisite
flowers I cannot identify distributed about the room. On
occasional tables occasional nuts, olives and cornichons.
Fortunately this is the age before the uneatable Bombay
Mix or palate-destroying pretzel assortment. A bottle of
champagne in a silver bucket shifts slightly in the ice. I
pour a solacing vodka and tonic, light a cigarette and pretend to myself that I am not a little nervous. When out on
my walk I withdrew enough cash to tip Ernesto, Alfonso,
Gilberto, Alonso and Pierre as lavishly as might be appropriate.

I have arranged with Alonso that as soon as the first
guest has arrived he will come in to serve cocktails and
the fizz. If he has not been alerted by reception I will
press the bell by the fireplace.

A thought strikes me: perhaps the front desk won't
know who John Mills is! It would be dreadful if so august
a figure should slip anonymously in without being treated
with the respect he deserves. I call down.

'Good evening, Mr Fry.'

This was a time when I still got a little disconcerted by
the hotel staff being able instantly to identify me as soon
as I called.

'Hello, yes it's me. Stephen here in 512. I just wanted to
say that I'm having a dinner party, and the thing is, the
guests of honour are Sir John and Lady Mills, and I hope
you will –'

'. . . Oh, sir, we know Sir John very well indeed. Rest assured we shall welcome him most enthusiastically. Most enthusiastically!'

Hugh, Jo, Ken and Emma arrived together. We were still young enough to be excited by such a preposterously grown-up business as holding a dinner party in a place like the Savoy.

Alonso made cocktails and stood discreetly by the drinks trolley as we giggled and shrieked.

The buzzer sounded, and we all straightened up and put on serious but welcoming faces.

I opened the door, and there stood Sir John and Mary. He stepped in and looked blinking about him.

'Oh . . . oh! It's . . .'

I noticed with alarm that he had started to weep.

'Sir John, is everything all right?'

He took my arm and squeezed it tight. 'This is *Noël's* suite!'

He let go and walked about. 'Every first night, this was the suite Noël took. Oh gracious!'

It was a perfect evening. Johnny and Ken quickly made friends. Anecdotes rained down, and many beans were spilled. The front desk had already made a great fuss of Johnny and Mary, lining up to greet him at the famous porte-cochère as soon as his splendid old Rolls-Royce had arrived with his faithful driver, factotum and friend John Novelli at the wheel.

It was the beginning of a long friendship between

John, the Mills family and me. Not long enough as far as Johnny was concerned of course; he died in 2005 at the age of ninety-three, and Lady Mary, who had lost herself to dementia many years earlier, joined him in death later that year.

Their sixty-four-year marriage was an extraordinary achievement. I bumped into Johnny in 1996 in an artist's green room at the Sitges Film Festival. He peered up at me.*

'Oh, Stephen. Do you know something? This is the first time Mary and I have spent a night apart since we were married.'

Astonishing. I once asked him what the secret of so strong a marriage might be.

'Oh, it's very simple,' he said. 'We behave like naughty teenagers who've only just met. I'll give you an example. We were at a very grand dinner a couple of years ago, and I scribbled a note saying, "Cor, I don't half fancy you. Are you doing anything afterwards? We could go to my place for some naughty fun . . .", something like that. I summoned a waiter. "You see that ravishing blonde at the table over there?" I said, pointing towards Mary. "I wonder if you'd be good enough to hand her this note?" I was then rather horrified to realize – my sight was just going at this stage, you have to understand – that he was hand-

---

*He had been unable to see properly for at least five years by this time and spent much charitable energy helping the Royal London Society for the Blind.

ing the note to Princess Diana. She opened it, read it and with her eyes followed the waiter's pointing hand back to me, squirming in my seat. She smiled, waved and blew a kiss. Oh dear, I did feel a fool.'

Two events gave me especial delight during my years of friendship with Johnny. One was the good fortune I had in spotting that Christie's were selling an old dressing gown of Noël Coward's. I won the auction and gave it to Johnny on his eightieth birthday. He remembered Coward wearing it, and owning it gave him a remarkable amount of pleasure, which in turn, of course, gave me a remarkable amount of pleasure.

The second event took place on a freezing winter's day in the grand old house Luton Hoo, former seat of the Marquesses of Bute and latterly the diamond magnate Julius Wernher, much of whose famous Fabergé collection was stolen from the house in a daring motorcycle raid. I was using it (some time after this burglary) as a location for scenes for the film *Bright Young Things*, an adaptation of Evelyn Waugh's second novel, *Vile Bodies*. I tentatively asked Johnny one day whether he would consider playing the part of Old Gentleman at a Ball. He immediately consented. I explained that what I wanted him to do in his scene was to spot Miles, a fey young man played by Michael Sheen, apparently taking a pinch of snuff from a small silver box. Miles would offer the old gentleman a pinch of this 'snuff', which was peculiarly white for milled tobacco, and then resignedly allow him to take more and more in odd moments when we returned to them as the ball progressed. Johnny was very excited to be playing his first drug scene so late in his life and took it, as he did all his work, very seriously. Though just about stone blind and in a large chilly house, he asked for nothing extra. We had made up a small interior tent for him, however, which we furnished with a day bed and five-barred electric heater.

A few years later Johnny lay dying in a new house in Denham Village (The Gables I think it was called), up the road from Hills House, where they had spent so many years. I went to visit him. He had a chest infection and couldn't really speak, but I sat and held his hand. I had brought with me an iPod, on which I had uploaded as many Noël Coward numbers as I could find. He was dressed, as he liked to be, in a velvet jacket, his KBE and CBE medals proudly attached to his chest. I put the iPod down by his side and gently pushed the earbuds in. As I heard Coward's voice crooning 'I'll See You Again', I saw his mouth form a smile and tears leak from the corners of his eyes.

Back at the Savoy Hotel a few days after the Mills–Branagh dinner party I am waiting at six in the morning for my car to take me to Wrotham Park for the day's filming on *Peter's Friends*. I find myself chatting to Arturo, one of the linkmen.

'You a fan of Frank Sinatra, Mr Fry?'

'Am I? You bet I am.'

'Ah, well. He's coming to stay with us today.'

'You're kidding!'

On the ride up to Hertfordshire I rehearsed what I'd say if I bumped into the great man. Ol' Blue Eyes. The Chairman of the Board. The Voice.

The filming, as it does, went on and on and on and on and on. It must have been past midnight before I drew up again at the Savoy. Arturo opened the door for me.

'That was a long day, Mr Fry.'

'Looks like it was for you too.'

'Just started my shift, sir. Now, why don't you follow me? Something I'd like you to see.'

Baffled and faintly irked – all I could think of was bed – I trailed after Arturo along the passageway that led, and still does, to the American Bar. We went down the steps, and Arturo pointed towards a man sitting in a pool of light, head bowed over a crystal lowball glass, backlit cigarette smoke ribboning up. A living album cover.

'Mr Sinatra, I'd like you to meet Mr Fry, a long-term guest.'

The man looked up and there he was. He pointed to the chair opposite him.

'Siddown, kid.'

'Kid'. Francis Albert Sinatra had called me 'kid'. It reminded me of the moment in Richard Lester's *The Three Musketeers* when Spike Milligan says in a stunned, reverent voice, after Charlton Heston has grasped his wrist and whispered him into conspiracy against his wife (Raquel

Welch), 'The Cardinal has taken me by the hand and called me friend!'

I think I had about three minutes alone with Frank before the room was filled with old friends and I found myself pushed to the edge of the party. But it was enough, and I wound my way back to 512 as one in a holy dream.

A few days later I saw Arturo on duty again. I pumped him by the hand and pushed a fiver on him.

'As long as I live I will never forget that moment, Arturo. What a favour you did me. I can never thank you enough.'

'It was my pleasure, Mr Fry.'

'Is he still here?'

'Left this morning. Quite funny actually.'

'Oh yes?'

'Well, just before he got into his car for the airport he gave me a roll of cash. Great thick roll it was. "Thanks for a terrific stay, Arturo," he says. "Well, thank you very much, Mr Sinatra. Always a pleasure for us to have you at the Savoy." "Tell me," he says, "is that the biggest tip you've ever had?" I look down at the money. Huge roll of twenties and fifties it was. "Well, as a matter of fact, sir, no it isn't," I says. He looks most put out. Most put out. "Well tell me," he says, "who gave you a bigger one?" "You did, sir, last time you stayed," I says. He got into the car, laughing his head off.'

'And next time he stays you'll get an even better tip,' I said.

'Ooh, the thought never crossed my mind,' said Arturo.

Dear Diary

By 1993 *Peter's Friends* had come out, *Fry and Laurie* had had a second series, and I had written my first novel, *The Liar*, and a collection of journalism, essays and other scraps called *Paperweight*.

I am an irregular diarist, but the months leading up to the completion of my second (and favourite) novel, *The Hippopotamus*, and the delivery to my flat of its galley proofs were well covered by me. I offer them to you because I think they recapture better than my memory ever can the hectic, intensely busy and fractured nature of my life back then. That it was leading to a catastrophic explosion I did not realize. Perhaps it will be apparent to you as you read. I have remained loyal to the intentions laid out in the first entry and have not altered or added, except for the sake of respect for those who would rather be kept out or have their identities masked. From time to time footnotes have been added for the sake of clarity.

Monday, 23 August 1993 – London

I'm going to be 36 tomorrow: three dozen, a quarter of a gross. A very factorable number, but otherwise nothing special. Nonetheless it seems a good time to restart my diary. (*First resolution*: no going back and altering this chronicle. No reading back, no emendations, no retrospective editorials. It must come out of me absolutely in one. Otherwise, what's the point?) Ha! 'Oh, what's the point?' . . . the last words in Kenneth Williams's diary, just published and just skimmed through by me. I'm mentioned once in the index, a reference to an appearance on a *Wogan* that KW guest-presented. 'Stephen Fry OK', that's my reference. An epitaph. Listening to Strauss's Alpine Symph. while writing this. It's on Radio 3 as a prom. Rather wonderful version by some Russian conductor I've not heard of.* Introduced in traditionally hushed tones by James Naughtie. Naughty James sat next to me at the John Birt Cup Final lunch earlier in the year. Nice chap.

Lazy day today. Very lazy: like all the days I've spent recently. Having such a reputation for hard work is satisfactory and bolsters my *amour propre* but it is *such* a lie. Spent most of the day polishing off the seating-plan for tomorrow's birthday dinner. How can it take that long? Well, I've decided to do anagrams for the guests' names. Here's a list, with explanations:

- Henry F. Pest – Me
- Lacey Easy-Fleece – Alyce Faye Cleese (wife of John Cleese, Okie psychotherapist)

---

*Almost certainly Valery Gerghiev, who has since become a kind of friend.

- Irma Shirk – Kim Harris (darling friend from Cambridge)
- Lady Orlash – Sarah Lloyd (wife of John)
- Mercie H. Twat – Matthew Rice (sweetie designer and splendour)
- Sonia Wanktorn – Rowan Atkinson
- Katie Labial-Scar – Alastair Blackie (friend of Kim, agent, and my gardener)
- Martie Badgermew – Emma Bridgewater (wife of Matthew Rice, designs crockery)
- Jones Leech – John Cleese
- Maria Sillwash – Sarah Williams (producer, currently back with Nick Symons)
- Harold Clit-Shine – Christian Hodell (assistant of Lorraine)
- Julie Oar – Jo Laurie (wife of J. H. C. Laurie)
- Coke Toper – Peter Cook
- Reg Gowns – Greg Snow (friend from Cambridge)
- Slim Noble – Simon Bell (Oxonian layabout and charmer)
- Nik Cool – Lin Cook (wife of Peter)
- Dolly John – John Lloyd (producer of *Blackadder* etc.)
- Mario Nolan–Hitler – Lorraine Hamilton (my agent)
- Miss Nancy L. Soho – Nicholas Symons (old Cambridge chum producer of *Bit of F&L*)

- Antonius Stanker – Sunetra Atkinson (wife of Rowan)
- Eli Cider – Eric Idle
- Uriah H. Glue – Hugh Laurie

Anyway – spent all fucking day working out those anagrams (Alyce Faye Cleese way the hardest – all those bloody E's and Y's)* while I should have been working on the nov. Satisfactory in its way. In the background Radio 3 (not music this time but the Test Match – England *won* can you believe it? Never doubted them. Atherton clearly good captain; he'll have his hellish moments in the years to come, but a sound fellow) while I strained my verbal skills on this useless anagrammery which will probably annoy the guests tomorrow anyway. No bloody *fun* in the world any more: no one doing mad silly things, no one playing practical jokes or organizing stupid parties with games and tricks like they did in the 20s. Even melancholy Virginia Woolf (heard Dame Edna on *Kaleidoscope*† a year or so back: 'Darling Virginia, a woman with whom I have so much in common, except of course that I can swim.') even she and her set used to love practical jokes. Everyone's so sodding *serious* and ordinary now.

God knows whether the seating plan will work. If

---

*Some might think the anagram rather appropriate given the astounding settlement awarded her when JC and she divorced. I couldn't possibly comment.

†A BBC Radio 4 arts programme, forerunner of *Front Row*.

Simon Bell is sober it'll help. Well I'll report the day after tomorrow.

Talking of the morrow, although my birthday, I seem to have filled it up with interviews to publicize *Stalag Luft*,* endless TV magazines and similar.

Bottle of wine at my elbow, Kanonkop, a S. African claret mimic, not enough tannin. Strauss's storm is brewing up, all those flutey interjections seem borrowed from Rossini's Wm. Tell overture or I'm a Flying Dutchman.

Tuesday, 24 August 1993 – London

Well – thirty-six then. Usual cliché of searching for grey hairs in the mirror. Some individual white flecks around the temples, but it's hard to tell whether they're real or a trick of the light.

The whole morning given over to publicity interviews for *Stalag Luft* at the Groucho. Endless stream of women from *TV Quick*, *TV First*, *TV Super* and *TV Cunty* all wanting to talk about my celibacy. 'Surely you must fantasize? Surely you must meet people and . . . *fancy* them?'

Basically, they want to know what pictures go on in my mind when I masturbate. Had the same thing a few weeks ago when I went to dinner at Ken and Em's. Ken got a bit in his cups (it doesn't take more than a glass with him)

---

* Comedy POW drama written by David 'Reggie Perrin' Nobbs. I had filmed it with Hugh Bonneville, Nicholas Lyndhurst and others earlier in the year.

and he was all, 'Come on, *darling*, what do you think about when you wank?' Em tried to slap him, but I bet she was too intrigued really to mean it.

Very pleased that my dreams and fantasies aren't too out there. I mean, only today the papers are full of this Michael Jackson thing. Some woman apparently reporting him for abusing her son. Let's face it, whoever doubted that Jacko was a boylover? My God, there's going to be a fall there if they find anything at his ranch. Porn, film, whatever . . . poor deranged sod, I don't think his own childhood fell far short of abuse in its way.

Then – the party. Everyone turned up. Everyone got me presents though I told them not to. The anagrams seemed to tickle them all too. Most people in a good mood and seeming to enjoy it, even Rowan managed to last to the end.* I sat next to Jo Laurie and Alyce Faye Cleese, I put Hugh down the other end near Eric and John C. Peter Cook in great form, talking about *Derek and Clive* which is about to be re-released, most people lightly drunk by the end. The bill came to almost exactly £1,000, which is reasonable, I would say. Damn good tuck. Did I mention earlier that it was at 190 Queensgate, run by Antony Worrall Thompson, who was there and joined for a drink earlier on? Turns out he was at school with John Lloyd. Home with Simon Bell, whom I gave a whisky before he eventually left.

* Usually notorious for bowing out of parties with a gentle yawn at about 9 p.m.

Wednesday, 25 August 1993 – London

Voice-over with Hugh this morning, for Energizer batteries. Hugh in good form, which is always a treat. A fun one and a half hours. Bumped into Norman Beaton before going into the sound studio. Mad old duck, rather a fan. Wants us to write a sketch for him to be in. Hum.

Afterwards a lot of leisurely shopping down Cecil Court. Bought an original *Vanity Fair* print of Gillette as Holmes and a signed photograph of Basil Rathbone. Don't ask me why. Might make a good present. Also got hold of a copy of Ricky Jay's book *Learned Pigs and Fireproof Women* which I have been after for ages.*

Eventually got home in time to read a little before popping out to the Institute of Directors in Pall Mall just around the corner. This was to meet a man by the name of Robin Hardy who is producing a film called *Bachelors Anonymous* (nothing to do with the Wodehouse story of the same name). He wants me to play the second lead and to DIRECT it. Flattering and pleasing that he can be confident enough to give such a relatively big movie to a first-time director, but there is a problem. Firstly, is the script good enough? He has written it himself from a novel called *Foxprints* by Patrick McGinley. Really rather fascinating, but needs improvement so as not to look misogynistic or just plain silly. The major problem

---

* Wasn't so easy to 'source' a book in the days before the World Wide Web and Amazon and so on . . .

though, is WHEN. I have *got* to try and finish the novel soon. Then I spend from October to January writing with Hugh for *A Bit of F&L* series 4. Then we make the thing, six weeks of studio, rehearse/record. That takes us to the end of March. John Reid will, I assume, want to go with the Elton musical next and the BBC will make noises about filming the adaptation of *The Liar*. There is no chance I could start pre-production prep on *Bachelors* until end of June, which would mean shooting it in September, over a year from now. Mad to think my life is that booked up. And where does that leave a second script for Paramount and Hugh's film *Galahad*? WHY is my life always like this, and why am I complaining about it?

He seems a reasonable fellow, this Hardy. Strange place to meet, the IoD. He fits it well, having a rather box-wallah version of an upper class accent. He did, on the other hand, write and direct *The Wicker Man*, a great classic. I feel it odd that I've never heard of him. Lorraine (Hamilton) is running a background check to see what she can see. Perhaps it will be a good thing to do, direct a film. I feel I can. I lack a lot of common sense, always have done, but I think I'll keep my head above water with a good operator, a good First and someone like Dougie Slocombe to light the film. Lor . . . what to do, what to do. Just aren't enough hours in the frigging day, are there, Stephen old love?

Thursday, 26 August 1993 – London

Parents are going to arrive at any minute. Father's birthday. I'm taking them to the premiere of Ken's *Much Ado* tonight at the Empire, Leicester Square and then to a party at Planet Hollywood of all places. So I'll do this entry now, rather than tonight when they'll be hanging around the flat.

Actually spent most of the day doing no more than preparing for their arrival. Hiding all the Euroboy videos, tidying up, trotting over the road to Fortnum's to buy fruit, flowers, tea things and so forth. Spent a merry hour in Hatchard's buying books. Got Alan Clark's diaries (signed) for Father, as well as the new Bill Bryson, as he likes him and a biography of Einstein (*not* the salacious one). For myself I rounded up a lot of books on theology ... mostly beginner's stuff. All this reading of Susan Howatch recently has got me interested in knowing more about the subject. I don't believe in God of course, but I sometimes think I *want* to believe. And then there's that foolish vision of myself as a bishop, sermonizing and saving the poor old C of E from itself. So fond of the C of E. The 'broad backed hippopotamus' as T. S. Eliot called her. So much better a liturgy ... and the music! Russell Harty* once confidingly said to me, while playing hymns at the piano (he had a perfect ear and could play anything you named that he knew), 'I don't think I could

---

*TV chat-show host: a simply adorable man who died from Hepatitis B in 1988.

ever love anyone who didn't love English hymns.' Mind you being a roamin' cat-lick his last lover the sweet Jamie O'Neill can't have known much Anglican church music.*

Appalling arrogance of me to think that I would be a good church leader without a concomitant shred of faith. Very Henry Crawford.† Mind you, probably a better life than my other footling fantasy, Fry the politician, Fry the scourge of the Right and the hero of the Chamber.

Also, bought a first novel called *In the Place of Fallen Leaves*, simply ghastly title but Roger, the sweet old queen at Hatchard's, recommended it.‡

Still haven't been able to face my own novel. I'm banking on being able to work when I get to Grayshott on Saturday, but how is one to tell? I'm always assuming that words will come and that I'll be able to get down that tunnel of concentration when I put my mind to it, but there's so much to do and I do desperately want it to work. If I don't finish it this year it'll spill over into next and then what happens to the idea of directing, or the TV version

---

*Jamie struggled after Russell's untimely death in 1988 but then wrote the wonderful *At Swim, Two Boys*, one of the best Irish novels of the past however many years.

†The wicked cad in Jane Austen's *Mansfield Park*, whose casual allusion to how good a parson he would have made had he minded to become one so shocks Fanny, the heroine, who is shocked by everything, to be honest.

‡And rightly. It went on to win the Hawthornden Prize (which had been recently resurrected by the munificent Dru Heinz, widow of the 57 Varieties chap), and the author, Tim Pears, went on to write the hugely successful *In a Land of Plenty*.

of *The Liar*, or the Elton John thing, or *Galahad* or God knows what else besides.

I'll report on *Much Ado* tomorrow. I've seen it already, at a preview cinema months ago. Really enjoyed it then, but perhaps it'll be less fun in front of a bigger audience and now that I have expectations. Hugh made a good point about how Ken on film sometimes does this thing of laughing and throwing his head back and slapping people on the back when wit is being offered. He did it in *Peter's Friends* and he does it in *Much Ado*, clearly encouraging his cast to do the same. Especially of course, the blissful Brian Blessed who roars like a speared ox through most of his scenes. Hugh's theory is that actors laughing prevents audiences from laughing and that this is perhaps true of screen or stage tears as well. Rather a convincing idea. And no doubt the Branagh haters and Ben Elton* haters will be out in force anyway. I'm so lucky that I don't seem to be quite so despised as they do. Mind you, not as admired either, which is only right. I suppose people think of me as some kind of reliable old thing, rather than as a threat. Ken and Ben are certainly threatening, those who dislike them regard them as the kind of yappy Jack Russells who leap up and spunk all over your trouser crease. The snobbery in Britons makes them believe that I, on the other hand, however rude or leftie I may seem, am fundamentally sound and reasonable, like a trusty labrador.

*Ben played Verges.

Frankly, I'm too lucky. Filled in a *Guardian* questionnaire the other day. In answer to the question 'When and where were you happiest?' I answered, 'At the risk of tempting providence, I'm pretty chipper at the moment, as it happens.' Tempting prov. is right. Even now, in Plum's immortal phrase, Fate must be lurking around the corner quietly slipping the horseshoe into the boxingglove. Shit, there goes the doorbell, here are the parents.

Friday, 27 August 1993 – London

Well, they arrived yesterday, admired the flat and seemed in good order and spirits despite a visit to their accountant. Impossible to imagine how things are with them. They just carry on as always, the business continuing in its gentle way, Mother doing the VAT, Father exercising his extraordinary mind. I am more certain that that man could have been absolutely anything he wanted to be in the world than I am of almost anything else. The gloss of complete admiration may well have worn off in some regards. There's no question that he seems curiously unsophisticated to me now, but his mind is still a remarkable thing.

Anyway, after tea-ing them and cocktailing them we sallied forth on foot for the Empire Leicester Square. *Unbelievable* crowds ... a greater number, according to today's papers, than turned out for the opening of *Jurassic Park*, which says something for Ken and Em. We approached, naturally, from the West, only to discover that the crash barriers were arranged such that we had to walk all the way round and enter from the Charing X Road end. Highly embarrassing. Many cries of 'Steve!' and applause as I trotted the gauntlet, parents in tow. I suppose it must have been strange for them, really, to walk with me and know that everyone there was cheering their son and knew who he was. Lot of posing for the paparazzi outside the doors and then I managed to get inside. Naturally, the really smart ones were indoors, including Richard Young, who really is extraordinary. He instantly sidled up and said, out of the side of his mouth, 'Those your parents, then?' I said, amused, 'Yup' and he asked for a shot with them. I reckon that man could tell, instantly, if two people enter a party, whether or not they are sleeping together. Remember that Greek saying? 'It is easier to hide two elephants under your arm than one pathic.'

After Richard there were endless TV crews. God knows how many showbiz and local news programmes there are these days.* All wanting pre and post screening comment. (Oh, dear me, on TV as I type this there's a documentary about a man with cystic fibrosis going on in the background. Sounds of a great quantity of mucus expression going on.) Up at the party there was a sprinkling of theatrical knightage, Sir John Mills and Mary, who both kissed me sweetly. Johnny kissed my mother, which

* A lot fewer than there are now, Stephen young sausage.

was divine of him. Dickie, now Lord, Attenborough was there and Sir Peter Hall. A couple of *Peter's Friends* stalwarts, Alphonsia and Tony S.,* and of course Ken and Em, the latter looking divine, the former surprisingly like Noel Edmunds. Kim Harris turned up with Hugh. Kim looks absolutely zonked. A few months ago, Ken rang up and asked me to rewrite *Frankenstein*. It was exactly when I was shooting off to Texas to make an episode of *Ned Blessing*, a new Western series for CBS. (I played Oscar Wilde, directed by David Hemmings of all people). I told Ken I couldn't do it, but suggested that he try Kim. Well, it seems Kim has turned out well, but is being driven like a dray-horse by Sir Kenward. Just as well I said no, I suppose, though it would have been fun to meet Robert de Niro. I hope Kim is alright. One worries when he gets so tired.

Eventually the reception broke up to go into the cinema and we watched the movie. Speeches by Stephen Evans the Renaissance Films supremo and Ken. The film was even more moving the second time around. Still thought that Michael Keaton and Ben were a little out of their depth, but Em was staggeringly good (of course) and Ken fabulously likeable and witty. I hate the way I've been influenced by the critics: as I watched I started to

---

*Alphonsia Emmanuel and Tony Slattery, who were also in *Peter's Friends*. Richard Curtis of *Four Weddings* fame unkindly remarked that surely Alphonsia Emmanuel is a drag name . . . you might think that, but I c. p. c.

notice flaws in the lighting and background action. Brian Blessed's heartiness and the general laughing and merriment now grated a little. Nonetheless a wonderful movie and what a reaction! The whole place stood and cheered for ages. A genuine spontaneous standing ovation. It made me cry, I'm afraid to say. Ken really is a mensch and a half.

The party afterwards was at Planet Hollywood, which I hadn't visited since that bizarre opening party with Bruce Willis, Schwarzenegger et al. Parents still excited and merry. Richard Briers, who is about the kindest man in the universe, stopped and chatted to them for ages. They were the only people in the room for him. I do hope I'm not a starer-over-the-shoulder type person, but give whomever I'm talking to my full attention as Dickie B does. Mother and Father are the same. The only difference was that Dickie toned his language down a bit: normally he starts every sentence with 'Fucking hell love,' no matter whether he's bumming a cigarette or admiring a building. After next standing about with Richard Curtis and Emma Freud for a bit we were invited over to the area where Ken and Em had booked a table. Chatted a lot to Paul Boateng the MP, who was in merry form and wearing rather startling clothes. Cozed a bit with Slatbum* and his boyfriend Mark, who's just won a Drama Desk award in New York. They met on *Me and My Girl*

* Tony S.

years ago.† Rather touching. Dan Patterson turned up, despite a recent operation. Anthony Andrews has absurdly petite hands and feet (sounds like a clerihew) and ludicrous Prince Charles mannerisms, but otherwise seems a very charming cove. There was an unbelievably choice young man with blond hair with whom I exchanged smiles.

At half past one or so I managed to tear the parentals away and we sloped off back home. *Still* an enormous crowd outside the place when we left. Lots of photography and signing before we could get away.

Now we're back to today. Arose at nine-ish, said goodbye to M and P and joined Hugh for a VO. Alliance and Leicester radio commersh. In Tottenham Court Road bought a load of jockstraps, trainers and so forth ready for Grayshott. Watched a video when I got home: a film called *The Living End*, billed as 'an irresponsible movie'. It's about a couple of guys, both HIV+, who decide to let the world go hang and jag about the States, fucking and shooting. Sort of *Henry: Portrait of a Serial Killer* for the smart gay set. Witty, neatly done, despite abominable sound-recording. At three I wandered about Soho, fetched up at the Groucho where Simon Bell (surprise, surprise) was propping up the bar, had a couple of glasses of wine and biffed off to Magmasters for another VO.

I rang Johnny Sessions to see if he felt like hitting the

† Still together *sentimental gulp*.

West End this evening, but he was having another of his old chums to dinner, plus wife, so I've decided to stay in with a bottle of Fleurie and some videos. Just watched the original episode of *The Sweeney* and must now decide on another. But tomorrow, ha! *tomorrow* sees a new Stephen. A hardworking, concentrating, noveliz-ing, non-drinking Stephen.

Jo Laurie rang to say goodbye. Her new baby will be hitting the straw while I'm away. She told me Kim was okay, just healthily tired. But one day, one day, I am going to hear that he is ill and I am going to know what that 'ill' means. It's impossible to believe. Fuck it, he's 35 and there's a time-bomb inside him. It's all just happening too, the *Frankenstein*, the relationship with Alastair which seems so good. Makes you vomit, doesn't it. God blast AIDS.

Spent a merry hour writing notes for my brother Roger, who's going to be borrowing the flat with his wife and my two nephews Ben and William. Arranged with the manager of Planet Hollywood that they could barge the queue with my special celebrity card (eugh!) which I left for their use.

Showed on the map where it was and where the near-est shops were. Hope they have a good time.

Saturday, 28 August 1993 – Grayshott Hall, Surrey

Well, for heaven's sake.

Grayshott Hall, once, apparently, the home of Alfred Lord Tennyson, is now a 'Health Retreat', featuring spas, hydros, gyms, golf, tennis, badminton (it's beginning to sound like that speech of Lucky's from *Waiting for Godot*), swimming, snooker, scrabble, bridge and the lord knows what else besides.

I arrived for lunch and found myself in what I subsequently discovered to be the 'Light Diet Room', where salads and a gently cooked poussin seemed not unconscionable. At 1.30 I had an appointment with 'Liz' who checked my blood pressure, weighed me (16 stone and a lot, yuk) and asked me what sort of 'treatments' I required. Everything here is a treatment. If you had sex with one of the waiters it would be called an erotic treatment. Drink (alcohol treatment) is not offered here, no bad thing, there is a smoking room, complete with card tables and so forth, which hasn't been made impertinently uninhabitable, which is something. I haven't volunteered for any particular treatments, though reflexology is something I've had before and is rather relaxing and splendid. I might, for the hell of it, try smoking hypnotherapy too. And there's some kind of men's 'facial' which teaches you how to shave. Come to think no one has *ever* taught me to scrape the face and for all I know I've been doing it wrong all my life. Included in the price, £150 p.d.* there is a 'heat treatment' (steam room, hot box or sauna) and a Swedish massage. Reminds me of Shrublands, the health resort you see in *Never Say Never Again*† but

*Now between £300 and £700 p.d.
†Sean Connery's 1983 remake of *Thunderball*. Rowan Atkinson made a brief appearance in it.

not quite so grand. I book myself a 'deep tissue massage' which sounds potentially painful for 10.00 am tomorrow.

Actually the place is quite pleasant. Mostly women here. Everyone is encouraged to go round the place in dressing gowns and tracksuits all day, so no formality, which is a blessing. I suppose the fellow guests are what you would expect, rich Totteridge Jewry, executive wives and thin girls who certainly have no need of this kind of regime. My room is pretty spartan actually. I applied this afternoon for a suite should it become available. Started work on the novel anyway, which, let's face it, is the point of being here. I don't know . . . I really don't know. I am going to have to plan it out, and that's a fact. I know how bad I am at planning. Never did any with articles, with essays at Cambridge or school, but in this instance it's got to be done. There are so many threads. The novel has to be about the redemption, if that isn't too ghastly a word, not of the hero, Ted Wallace (that's his current name, anyhow, though I'm getting annoyed with having to avoid the inelegant 'said Ted') which everyone will think it's about, but rather of those around him. He's a poet and knows that poetry is chthonic not ethereal. Of earth and water not fire and air. It's also seemingly about Purity and the Operation of Grace and horrifically dull and off-putting Bridesheady things. But that isn't my problem, my problem is structural. I have to find a way of pulling together the past and present and getting the characters introduced properly.

At the current pace, the novel won't get to the half way stage till I've written 100,000 words. I'm quarter of the way to 80,000 which is an acceptable novel length, but it looks as if this is going to be longer, which is the last thing I want. And there's nothing worse than reading a novel where you sense the writer has speeded up towards the end. I've got to remain true to the idea of it. One of the problems with *The Liar* was my lack of confidence that people would be interested enough in Healey and Cartwright and so I shoved in all the spying crap, which, in fact, most people found less interesting than Adrian in love. I mustn't make the same mistake again.

Anyway, I wrote for a few hours, then dined on plaice and vegetables, washed down with plain water and followed by fruit. Came back to the room, couldn't work any more, watched some dreadful Brian Dennehy film called *The Revenge of the Father*. Tomorrow, massage and a quick nine holes before breakfast excepted, must see me At Work.

Sunday, 29 August 1993 – Grayshott

Not much to report. Up at 7.30, breakfast was a mess of cottage cheese, All Bran and coffee. Whether or not the coffee here is decaffeinated I can't really tell, which I suppose means that it doesn't matter. Played 9 holes on the golf course. No hole is longer, which suits me, than 150 yds. Tried out for the first time the 'Killer Whale' which

John Lloyd* gave me as a thank you for doing his *South Bank Show* comedy spesh. Sliced it, which is a first for me as I usually slice.†

Had my massage after that. I didn't realize you were supposed to arrive half an hour earlier for the 'heat treatment' so I missed that. Kept my swimming trunks on all the time under my towel. All the fat men with hairy backs (who all resemble Ari Onassis and Picasso) waddled around slapping their bellies and showing their acorns, but I was damned if I was going to. I'm not having some *For Women* magazine telling the world about my cock length.

Had the Swedish massage, which was nothing special and went back to the room to work. Making *some* progress, but I need a breakthrough, there's no question about that. The chances of my finishing this novel for publication in the spring are remote in the extreme.

Spoke to the front desk about changing the room, I'll be moving into more luxurious quarters tomorrow.

Monday, 30 August 1993 – Grayshott

Yup. I'm in Room 5, now. It has coffee-making equipment, a mini-bar containing mineral water and skimmed milk, complimentary flowers and fruit basket and all the

---

* Producer of *Not the Nine O'Clock News*, *Spitting Image*, *Blackadder* and – in 2003 – *QI*.
† I meant that I usually hook.

things one has come to expect in one's life these days, tee-hee.

They sent me a letter telling me about the new room rate, this suite is £298 per night as opposed to the old rate of £195, but what the fuck. In this letter they said, and I quote 'We are now requesting all guests to refrain from smoking in the bedrooms however, the functions of the Billiard and Smoking Rooms have not changed.' What a fucking nerve. Some slatternly skivvy has gone and squealed, by which I mean some plump, curranty sweet-ness of a chambermaid has informed the management of my 'in-room self-administered tobacco treatment' . . . thing is I'm turning into that character Ted Wallace in my frig-ging novel, it's not like me to call chambermaids slatternly.

Another nine holes this morning and then waddled off in my dressing-gown to experience the steam-room effect. Horrific place. Some old boy sweating it out next to me said it was newly installed. He's a regular, must be rich as Croesus. It's like a sauna, but to be frank, not quite as unpleasant, as the humidity is exceptionally high. A minute takes a quarter of an hour to pass. Horrifying. Still contrived to keep my bathers on, though. Everyone must be beginning to talk about my strange modesty . . . much better massage, however. Chap called Pete, I'll try and stick with him.

Midway through the afternoon I genuinely despaired with the novel. I've changed its working title to *The Thauma-turge* as much to annoy the critics as anything. I came within an ace of packing up and moving either back to London or to some country house hotel where I could drown my sorrows in lonely jugs of claret. Then, two things happened. Firstly a man came in with an ashtray and said I was welcome to smoke in the room, they must have seen me nipping down to the smoking room and billiard room every half an hour and taken pity. And then I had an idea. A whole chapter that I've written should be in the form of a letter from Ted to his goddaughter Jane. It may not work out fully, but it's driving me along a little. Wrote a couple of thousand words after that. Still not enough, but let's hope it's a good sign. Have to go to London tomorrow, chiz. A VO for Compaq computers. I'll drive to Haslemere, get on a train and hope to be back by two-ish. Wonder if I'll be a naughty boy and guzzle sandwiches on the train. Nothing but chicken and fish and fruit and veg. so far. Night, night.

Tuesday, 31 August 1993 – Grayshott

Well, frankly. Rose with the lark, lark rise under candlewick you might say. Drove like stink to Haslemere, parked the car and discovered that I'd left my wallet back in the room at Grayshott. Fortunately, God knows how or why, I'd got my cheque-book with me. Avoided the queue for the tickets and jumped straight on the 08:06 to London. Sat all of a quiver in a second class smoker wondering what the issue would be. A ticket conductor arrived some time after Woking (Lord, Home Counties place names have such negative evocations, don't they) and I explained the posish. Thank God for fame, he recognized me and seemed tickled pink (as did my fellow passengers, regular commuters to a man, and I mean man), said something about it being a good way of making his quota (there's a surcharge, natch) and waddled off.

Fetched up at Waterloo at 0900 precisely and, having not a bean to my name (well 40 odd pence) I walked all the way over the bridge, along the Strand and to St James's. Half-way up the Strand I remembered that Roger, Ruthie, Ben and William were all staying in the flat. Thought they may have left for Norfolk but arrived to find plenty of traces. Assuming they were out for brekker at Fortnum's or some-where I left them a note and hared off to Lexington Street where the Voice Over was. The sweet girl at the Tape Gal-lery, the studio, cashed a cheque for fifty quid, thank God. The VO for Compaq Computers (yah, boo) was booked as a two hour session, but I finished it to their satisfaction in twenty-five minutes. My internal clock going great guns. They wanted each of the VO's to last 18 seconds and I duly obliged first crack out of the box with each of the seven scripts. Scuttled back to the flat, Breda the cleaner was there, but no sign of R & R. Hung around for an hour in case they showed and then got a cab back to Waterloo.

Car at Haslemere amazingly not towed away, so I was back at Grayshott in time for a nutritious lunch. A chap-pie told me that Imelda Staunton was staying, so I arranged to meet her at the cocktail hour, 6.00.

Heat treatment and massage at 3.00. Actually took my clothes off this time! Mustn't do exclamation marks, it's so Adrian Mole. That's all Mummy's fault, she does them in letters to the milkman, everything 'Thank you!' and so on.

The less efficient masseur, Steve, did the business, must remember to ask for Peter next time. Got back to the room, worked on *The Thaumaturge*, which seems to be coming along okay and dipped down for revivifying cocktails with Imelda and her mother, Bridie, an Irish poppet the spit of Imelda. Cocktails, you should understand, comprise either cucumber or tomato juice, but actually that's fine. Imelda, who's eight months pregnant, was telling me all about Jim Carter, her man,* and his nightmare shooting on a film of *Black Beauty* for Warners. All the horses misbehaving and that kind of thing. Peter Cook's in it too.

Anyway, then dinner and now, before I hit the mattress (not like a Mafioso fortunately), a video. I collected an armful from the flat. Time I think to enjoy Jeremy Brett once more, this time in 'The Dancing Men', one of the best Holmes stories. Sleep tight.

Wednesday, 1 September 1993 – Grayshott

And a pinch and a punch to you.

Doing this diary must be good for me, I had an inspiration last night after writing yesterday's entry. I suddenly saw that of course the thaumaturge is not David, but

---

*Now known the world over for his portrayal of the Downton butler.

Simon. I had thought all along that David, the pure poetical son of the Logan family would be the miracle worker, but of course it must be the apparently dull, ordinary, less intelligent or sensitive boy. That's the poetic truth as opposed to the poetical one. There's a sense in which I'm saying my brother Roger is the miracle worker of *our* family, not me and I think that's true. He's decent, no, more than decent, he's *good*, decent in the way Tom Wolfe means it in *Bonfire of the Vanities*, he's hard-working, he's loyal, he's true, he's . . . well he's what makes man great. Sounds sententious put like that, I suppose. The key to it in the novel though means that at least some kind of twist or surprise can be guaranteed. Everyone was fooled by Davey (who deliberately allows Jane and Ted to believe that *he's* the one).

Talking of the diary, this being the first of the month, I've decided I will print out an entry at the end of each month. This will guarantee that I can't go back and change things. That's the devil of a computer-kept diary, it looks impersonal and there's no assurance that it hasn't been tarted up. When I get back to London, I will print out all of August, it only started late in the month, of course.

Usual nine holes. Got a birdie! Yippee! My first. I was playing the six iron as Brendel plays a Bösendorfer today. Usual steam business followed by a massage from Peter, who is infinitely better than Steve. I have asked the desk if I can always have him, there should be no problem. Then I had a consultation with the Sister. I have lost 8

pounds in the time I've been here. Eight pounds. Unbelievable. I only arrived halfway through Saturday
(hogged a load of sandwiches on the road on Saturday
morning anyway), three and a half days, over two pounds
a day. I won't be able to keep it up at this rate, but still.
Not bad, eh?

In the afternoon (Sister's advice) I had a holistic massage. All kinds of bollocks from Janice the masseuse about
energy and channelling and healing and so forth, but I
have to say it was a wonderful feeling. An hour and a half
of intensely gentle, yet intensely deep massage. Felt very
woozy afterwards, but then keyed up and raring to go.

Imelda and Bridie joined me in the Light Diet Room
for dinner and we chatted about this and that. Since then
I've been working at the nov. Spent most of this evening
trying to write a poem that David Logan (who's aged 15)
could have written. Tricky. Can't be too sophisticated, but
no point if it's too childish. Takes bloody ages, poetry.
Can't wait to get back to dialogue and description. I need
words by the thousands!! Oh no! More Adrian Moling!!!

Nighty night.

Thursday, 2 September 1993 – Grayshott

Well, usual thing really. Nothing too outrageous to report.
Nine holes in the morning. Started badly, but really began
to hit the ball well (yawn, yawn, yawn) and felt good about
the game. Came back, steam room and massage as per

usual. Lots of work, then lunch. Some work after lunch then decided to take half an hour off to play another 9 holes. Really genuinely actually frankly properly hitting the ball. Very exciting. On the ninth, the pro was walking past as I hit the ball from the tee, spang on line with pin, right onto the green. 'Good shot,' he said. From a pro!

Back to the novel, it continueth. I've done an exhaustive word count. 30,034 words so far. That means I've written 9,174 since I've been here. That's an average of 1,529 per day, which isn't frankly enough to get the thing finished when I want it finished. But, and it's a but the size of Hyde Park, I am sure I am writing more each day. It started slowly, after all, so perhaps things aren't going too badly. Do wish I was in Norfolk, though. I'd've had the thing finished a fortnight ago if I could have been in Norfolk. And I'd've saved myself the three or four thousand pound bill I'm going to get for this little lot (let alone the gigantic cost of the building work that's being done): by fuckery it'd better be worth it.

Heigh ho. *Fry and Laurie* on in half an hour. Might as well catch it. Sleepums wellums.

Friday, 3 September 1993 – Grayshott

Well, watched *F&L* all right. Not bad, actually. Laughed in places, but Christ I wish I didn't always wear such a smug expression. My face in repose always looks as if it's smirking which is peculiarly repellent.

Usual thing this morning: nine holes (a step back in competence this am, but made up for by a screamer at the ninth again), steam, massage, lots of writing and then, as a treat, a Flotation and Facial in the afternoon. The Float is a strange bath, barely long enough for me to lie in, filled with salts so that the water takes on the buoyancy (and viscous consistency) of the Dead Sea. You go into an ante-room, shower, smear Vaseline over any abraded skin, bung wax in your ears like Odysseus and then lie down and float. There is an open intercom with a floozy at the desk in case you panic or something. Music (well, I say music, whale song in fact, as you might have guessed) is then played which, on account of the earplugs and something else besides, Boyle's Law* possibly, you can hear best with your ears below the level of the water. You have control over the light switches too. The idea is that you bob there, completely buoyant, utterly blind, listening to bull whales telling cow whales to get their knickers down. I sort of enjoyed it while it happened and did feel good afterwards. Next treat(ment) was a facial, actually just a big plug for Aramis products (scalp revitalizer, cucumber face mask, that sort of tosh). Lovely feeling to have your face woman-handled, though. Like being made-up for film or TV without the silly gossip and drivelling on about horoscopes. The popsy also shaved me, which is always pleasurable.

---

*Not even *vaguely* like Boyle's Law, Stephen, which is to do with gases.

Then, basically, back to the nov. I've now decided to call it *Other People's Poetry*, which the publishers will hate, if anything, more than *The Thaumaturge*. I stupidly gave Sue Freestone, my editor, the working title *What Next?* a few months ago and she loved it. I think it's too junky or possibly Joseph Heller-y (not that JH is junky). Sounds like the kind of title people give books that they are desperate to become best-sellers. Not that I am desperate for anything else, naturally, but it's also a hostage to fortune as far as critics are concerned. 'What next indeed, Mr Fry? A proper novel we hope, snicker, snicker . . .'

I wrote over 3,000 words, anyway, which is an improvement. Mind you, I've written 7,061 words in this diary so far, which is an average of (as you can surely work out for yourself) 588.416666 per diem; time which you might believe would be better spent novelizing. Actually though, I feel this diary, if nothing else helps prime the pump (that *must* be drivel because I always write it *after* I've been working, well, you know what I mean).

Well, bed time. Cricket tomorrow and my first real food for ages. Lost nine pounds so far, don't want to put any on. Must be careful not to drink too much.

Bedly beddington now.

Sunday, 5 September 1993 – Grayshott

Went up to London for to see the cricket. *Bloody* good match. Sussex v. Warks. Nat West final, Lord's. Settled by

the last ball. Warks needed 2 runs from the final delivery
to score a winning 322. Actually, one run would have
done, as they'd lost fewer wickets, but in any case a hum-
dinger. Was so dark by the end I'm amazed the batsmen
could see the ball. Just shows what gamesmanship there
is when they appeal for bad light when things are going
against them. Went because Will Wyatt invited me to a
BBC box. Mostly full of corporation figures, Roger
Laughton, Michael Checkland* etc. But spent most of
the match as the ham in a playwright sandwich. David
Hare to the left, Simon Gray to the right (in every sense).
David turns out to be a manic Sussex fan. Poor man: for
the first time I really warmed to him as he sat gnawing his
knuckles and turning into a closer and closer simulacrum
of Munch's *The Scream*. His tonsure was purpling with
passion. All this seemed to matter far more to him than
the opening next week of his new play, *Murmuring Judges*.
Turns out he is also working for Scott Rudin. We compared notes on the impossibility of getting in touch with
him. Scott's office has been ringing my London number
daily as usual, as if they know I'm away in Grayshott.
Scott himself is in Venice for the film festival, so it's
rather pointless my ringing back anyway.

Simon, whom I haven't seen in a pig's age looks frankly
bloody awful. Rheumy, weeping eyes and squashed pug's

---

*Last three named all BBC high-ups of the time. Checkland (known as
 'Chequebook' as he came up through the ranks of admin and business
 rather than programme-making) was Director-General.

face in no way enhanced by a deep tan. The thick hair with its characteristic flick looks no longer boyish, simply the-portrait-in-the-schoolroom-ish.* He's been in Greece, the island of Spetses, writing a novel of all things for Mark McCrum's brother Robert at Faber's. Still drinking clearly: Simon not Robert McCrum. Confessed to some guilt about leaving Beryl and gave me the lowdown on how Eddie Fox trampled on the possibility of taking the revival of *Quartermaine's Terms*† into the West End. The best ever prod of *QT* Simon thinks, but Fox scared of being compared to his original performance, despite his mother's firm statement that the revival outshines it. Amazing thing is that Simon is still very very prolific: as well as the novel there's a new play waiting, a couple of radio plays just written and two films for Verity Lambert's 'Cinema Verity' (ho, ho) outfit.

David Frost turned up a little late: he'd just got in from Moscow where he'd been interviewing Mikhail and Raisa Gorbachev. I swear that man still talks and acts as if he's just left Cambridge and is desperate to make a name for himself in television. Wonderful really. Can't help adoring him. It's been a week of Frost on TV lately, as it happens, coinciding with the issue of a fat First Volume of auto-biography and at least five TV programmes about him. He

---

* In *The Picture of Dorian Gray* it's a schoolroom in which the eponym hides his portrait, not – as everyone says – an attic. But only I would be so pedantic in a diary.

† Subsequently re-revived by Rowan Atkinson.

tells me that the one being shown this very night, 'Frost-bites' (ho, ho), which is a compilation of interviews over the 30 years, includes a section of one he did with me earlier this year. He leaves early to edit the Gorbachev material.

John Sullivan, author of *Citizen Smith*, *Only Fools & Horses* etc. is also amongst those present. We swap stories about Nick Lyndhurst and David Jason. I've just been filming with Nick all June doing the *Stalag Luft* film for Yorkshire TV. Bill Cotton is here too. He tells a story of how he is in a train compartment with Peter Sellers, Tommy Cooper, Barry Cryer and Dennis Main Wilson.* Dennis is telling one of his stories when Tommy gets up to go to the loo. After about ten minutes they start wondering where Cooper has got to. Sellers and Cryer get up and go down the corridor to the lav., which is locked. They bang on the door. No reply. Worried, knowing that TC is well-sauced, they search for the ticket conductor. 'Mr Cooper's in there,' they say. 'Can you open the door somehow?' The conductor does so. Tommy is sitting on the bog, lid down, trousers up. He gives them his signature creased eyebrow look of worry and asks 'Has Dennis stopped talking yet?' No good unless you know D.M.W. of course, but we did.

The match takes up most of our attention from then on. I've been a good boy, combining food like Hay him-

---

* The splendidly mad old producer of *The Goon Show*, *Till Death Us Do Part* and, in 1982, Cambridge Footlights for the BBC with me, Hugh, Emma and Tony S.

self and sticking only to one sipped glass of red and a small vodka and tonic. As the ante-penultimate over is about to be bowled I ring up the cab company and order a taxi to be waiting outside the Grace Gate so that I can go on to Hugh and Jo's for dinner, where Ben Elton will be, having just returned from Oz. Simon asks if he can borrow my phone to do likewise.

Leave as soon as the result is clear, having thanked Will and commiserated with David H. Taxi not there, hang around feeling a fool. People approach, but are not too pesky or autograph hungry. Then, amazingly, *Nigel Short* bounds up! He's spent the whole day watching the match. He's about to sit down and face Garry Kasparov for the World title on Tuesday and there he is . . . I'd be covered in a wet blanket forcing coffee down myself while I sweated over variations of the Maroczy Bind and the Winawer. I suppose he knows what he's doing. He begged me to come along to the match and say hi. May do. We'll see. So far I have resisted the blandishments of Channel 4 and BBC2, who are both covering the match. What can I actually say on air? I can't keep up with Ray Keene as an analyser and I'll be reduced to a sort of media hack who says clever things about the psychology and witty nonsense about the body language. Pyeuch. There's a programme on as I write this: Dominic Lawson, Bill Hartston, David Norwood GM and Florencio Campomanes, the President of FIDE. It does begin to look as if Nigel has blown it before it's started.

Hugh and I revealing our weekend recreational identities.

Mandela Birthday Concert, Wembley Stadium, 1988. About to perform in front of 80,000 people. Not in the least nervous. Oh no.

felt comfortable and ALIVE.

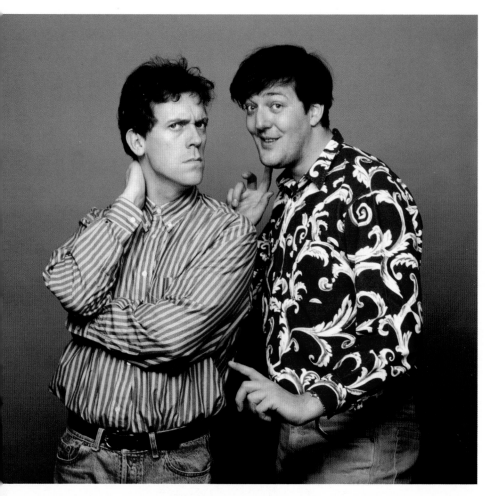

Incredibly, I still have that shirt. Haven't burnt it or anything . . .

Self and Hugh wining,
dining and pointing at
Sunetra Atkinson.

A bit more Fry and Laurie.

Cap Ferrat with Mrs Laurie.

Cap Ferrat, 1991 – Charlie Laurie, by this time, rightly, bored of my attempts to amuse.

Stripey me.

Self and self at the National Portrait Gallery. Maggi Hambling's completed work.

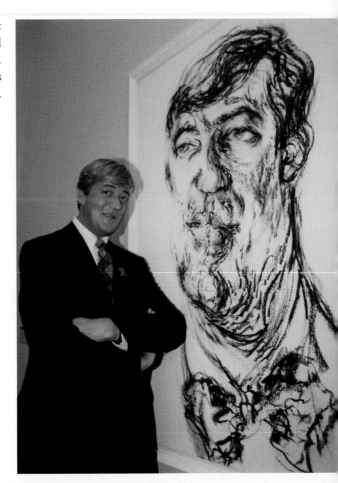

Next to Maggi Hambling charcoal portrait of me commissioned by the National Portrait Gallery. Do NOT mention the hair.

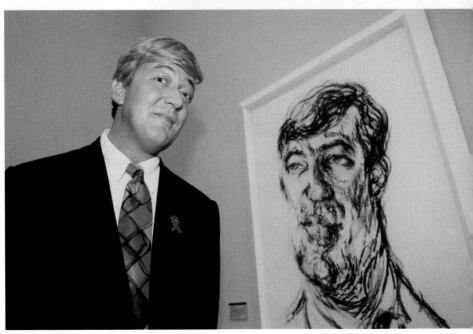

Maggi Hambling's National Portrait Gallery picture of me.

Taking pleasure in red wellies: life gets no better, 1990.

Simon totters out and his cab is waiting. Bugger those
Computer Cab sods. But Simon, sweetly, suggests I hop
into his, so we go first to Tufnell Park before it takes him
on to Notting Hill . . . a long distance out of his way. Blimey
. . . they'd just finished the chess programme and started
Blow-Up . . . I think David* looks better now than he did
then. No that's not true. It's just that in *Blow-Up*, as an actor
he doesn't communicate a tenth of his amazing *energy*.

At the Lauries' everything hunky-dory. Jo desperate to
drop now. She had told me a couple of days ago that Ben
and Sophie were going to get married *and I completely forgot*. Christ I'm hopeless with gossip. Not that that was
gossip, but you know what I mean. Other people's news.
Other people's poetry. (I'm surer than ever that this is the
right title and that Sue will hate it.) Sophie is going to
come and live in England. Ben thinks April or May for
the wedding.

I told him May was traditionally looked upon as unlucky
for weddings. Like the colour green. Don't know what I
was thinking. I'm not in the least superstitious and I could
see it rather rattled the happy pair. Was I subconsciously
being malicious? I'm sure not.

We talked a little about our respective novels. Hugh's
writing a thriller: I've read about a third of it and it's *very*
funny.

Next day: ie today, got up early, trained to Haslemere

---

* Hemmings.

263

and had played my 9 holes at Grayshott by half past ten. Toyed with the nov. a bit, but just that one day away has lost me a lot and I couldn't concentrate properly enough to write anything new, so spent time rewriting and rejigging here and there. Had a massage at 3.00. Steve's away so it was Willy Blake, well named. He's a Norfolk friend of my sister Jo and a rather endearingly nonsensical New Age freak. Gibbered on, while rubbing away, about channelling and auras. I asked him if he'd ever seen anyone's aura himself. 'No,' he said. 'Not a proper aura, but I once saw a very clear etheric sheath.' Well I mean frankly.

Mostly watched TV after that, the Muse having taken a powder. Then dinner, bit more telly and this diary, really.

Monday, 6 September 1993 – Grayshott

Very little to report today. An absolutely bog standard Grayshott kind of a day. Nine holes, slightly disappointing, heat treatment, massage, work, bed. Another nine holes in the afternoon, adequate play. Not much more to it than that I'm afraid.

Tuesday, 7 September 1993 – Grayshott

Much the bleeding same. Sister Jo is back today and I spoke to her on the phone. She and Richard and the baby* seemed to have a good time in France. No vital

---

*My beloved nephew George. All three of my nephews are equally beloved of course. No nieces sadly; sister and sister-in-law just weren't

messages: Greg Snow's present of a Lesbian Cunt Coloring Book from Florida is being despatched, to which I look forward eagerly. I've been invited to the first night of *La Bohème* at the Coliseum next week, which might be a lark.

Sue Freestone, my publisher, sent a fax saying she is insanely excited that I am getting on with the novel. She seems to think it will be finished as a matter of course. Gulp. Wants to know what ideas I've got for the cover. I'm not half way through and she wants a cover. Oh shit.

Spoke to Maggi Hambling† on the phone. She wants two more sittings for her portraits. I have arranged to go over on Tuesday and Wednesday next week.

In the afternoon I watched some of the opening game in the Kasparov v Short match. Both Channel 4 and BBC2 are giving it plenty of air. Channel 4's coverage is taking populism to new depths. The presenter can't even let Daniel King or Jonathan Speelman use the phrase 'queenside' without jumping down their throats. 'So that's the left-hand side of the board is it?' 'Yes, that's right.' Well it isn't the left-hand side to Nigel, playing black, is it? She is trying desperately to find dramatic phrases culled from

---

concentrating. Actually, it's the sperm that determines gender come to think, no pun intended. Help, I've become infected. Writing footnotes in diary style now. It'll be exclamation marks next!! Oh merciful heavens!! No!!!

†The painter and sculptor. She had been commissioned by the National Portrait Gallery to paint a picture of me, which she had long wanted to do anyway.

any other arena than chess, to describe what is an intellectual battle utterly beyond her grasp. Or mine for that matter. Granted, it's a good idea to widen the audience, but treating it like a benzedrine-driven joust between two wild-eyed exponents of gamesmanship is hardly helping.

Sadly Nigel lost *on time*. He had weathered a storm, a battering in fact, from Garry K, but as he was preparing to make his *very last* move in time control, his flag fell. Disaster. He must be sick to his soul. It was good that he ended in a position that was at least drawn, but calamitous that he should have lost the game so stupidly. Went to bed in a thunderstorm. Lovely feeling. It wasn't attacking my king.

Wednesday, 8 September 1993 – Grayshott

No golf this morning: wind blowing hard, grass sodden. Lots of work, now definitely half way through. I've written over twenty thousand words in 9 days, which isn't bad. Unfortunately I won't get another stretch of time like this. I spoke to Sue Freestone on the phone. She's coming round next Thursday to look at what I've got. My novel, which she still insists on calling *What Next?* is going to be 'the biggest publishing event of Spring '94.' Great.

Ian McKellen rang too. He wants me to present some bloody Age of Consent* benefit at the London Palladium

---

*The sainted Edwina Curry was bringing a Private Members Bill before the House of Commons to make the age of homosexual consent equal to the heterosexual age. At the time the gay age of consent was twenty-for Stonewall. Well, not present, just introduce. I've also agreed to do a debate at the Cambridge Union on the same issue. All these things are going to take up time I cannot spare. After all, there's the Sam Wanamaker Globe bash at the Albert Hall too.

Talking of the Albert Hall, I'm going to the Last Night of the Proms on Saturday, after Charles and Carla Powell's wedding. Well not *their* wedding, their son's.

Played golf in the afternoon, during a lull in the weather and a lull in my inspiration. *Played like a fucking genius.* As I was addressing the ball I just *knew* that it was going to go long and straight. For the first time in my life I consistently hit overlong and had to go down a club at almost every hole. Birdies and pars and virtually nothing else. Ridiculous because I am the most uncoordinated, least able striker of a ball who ever pulled a club from a bag. But every dog has his day, I suppose. I will probably never play another round like it, so it is as well to be pleased.

The novel steaming along too. Not that it's anything other than balderdash, but at least I feel as if I'm achieving things. Elements are coming together. So far, however, it is lacking in any passion. I want people to cry at parts of it, and those stages haven't yet been reached. Gonna be tricky. Ner-night.

---

one, the original Wolfenden Report recommendation, passed into law thirty-odd years earlier. Final equality had to wait until 2000, three years into the Blair administration.

Thursday, 9 September 1993 – Grayshott

Reasonable day. Fair old quantity of work done, over 4,000 words. The post contained Greg Snow's present from Florida: *The Cunt Coloring Book* by Tee Corinne. I quote from the introduction. '*The Cunt Coloring Book* published in 1975, was immediately and wildly popular, although many people complained about the "awful" title. Three printings later, in 1981, the title was changed to *Labiaflowers* and the book virtually died. So much for euphemisms. Welcome once again to the *Original Cunt Coloring Book* (with a few additions). May you color it with pleasure. The drawings in this book are of real women's cunts. My love and thanks to the many women who participated with me in this project and to those who encouraged and counseled me. These pages are a celebration of your energy.'

That was from the foreword by Tee herself. There is also a little prefacing essay entitled 'In The Beginning' by one Martha Shelley.

In the beginning we come from the cunt, not from some man's side; and we are washed in the water and blood of birth, not the spear-pierced side of some dying god. In the beginning women made pots and jars shaped like wombs and breasts, and decorated them with triangles, which were symbols of the cunt.

So the first art was Cunt Art. The bones of the dead

were laid in jars – perhaps to speed the soul to its next womb? Did the ancient women sing, how delicate, sensitive, delicious, how strong the ring of muscle between one life and the next? There are tribal women today who sing praises of their cunts, how pretty and long and full their lips are, how the hair curls and glistens with moisture.

Well, I mean dah-ling . . .

Naturally the pages themselves contain hideous warped oysterish things that look like the result of an explosion in an organ-donor depot. I hope that doesn't sound misogynistic – a Cock Coloring Book would be just as beastly.

The book even has an ISBN no.* can you credit it? For the rest, there is sadly, no text, just these line-drawn quims.

Otherwise, the only other post was a card from Rory Bremner, asking me to be a 'guest-writer' on one of his new Channel 4 shows. Kindly offer but I think I'll pass.

Rang Kim during the second Short/Kasparov game. He seems to think, with me, that Nigel's blown it again.†
Invited K to accompany me to the opening of *La Bohème* and *Oleanna*, the new David Mamet. Still no news from Hugh and Jo L. They *must* be dropping even now, surely?

---

*0-86719-371-9.
†Kim was seven thousand times more likely to know. He was a chess master and had been at school with Nigel Short. Taught him the French Defence and its many variations, Kim's favourite for black.

Had a reflexology and aromatherapy massage. Not bad. Still feel pretty energized. All my masseuses now seem to be in agreement that I am 'balanced and relaxed', which is pleasant.

Spoke to Scott Rudin. He's pleased I had the session with Terry Gilliam about T's new film *The Defective Detective*, but wishes I was harder on Terry about the script. Hyuh! What's it to do with me? I'll try and liaise with Scott about my next script for him when I've done with the novel.

Sue F. faxed me with a suggestion for the jacket. 'How about Michelangelo's David wearing Y-fronts?' Well, I mean really! A tad homo-erotic, for a novel that is primarily non whoopsy. Thought of a scene today in which Davey will fuck a horse to heal it from some mysterious illness like ragwort poisoning. Could be good.

News just in. Nigel drew the game. Phew. Ho-hum.

Friday, 10 September 1993 – Grayshott

Last full day here. Arose in time to do some work, biffed off for the massage and heat treatment and returned to the room to find a message under the door: 'Please ring Rebecca Laurie, 071 580 4400, Room 101.' Just for a moment I thought I'd gone mad and then . . . of course! Jo decided to have a Caesarian today. The child had been up there for too damned long, putting on too much bloody weight. 8lb 13oz. Jo was barely able to walk or breathe. The doctors thought it would probably stay up there for another two weeks, just liked it too much. University College Hospital said they wouldn't do a section for another fortnight, so Jo and Hugh took the reluctant decision to go private at the Portland. A big bonny baby girl. I shall see her on Sunday.

Plenty of work, then a holistic massage, pleasure as always, followed by a swift nine holes. Some great shooting, some average (as if you care).

Then more work: reached three hundred words shy of the fifty thousand. That means I've written just about 30,000 words in the last eleven days. Not bad. I've just finished writing the scene in which Davey fucks the horse. My lord I'm going to get some stick for that. 'So, did you try it out, Stephen? . . . in the interests of research naturally . . . hyerk, hyerk . . .'

It might be dreadful I suppose, we shall see. Wonder what Sue Freestone will think. Final treatment tomorrow will be a facial with which to present a smooth and glossy countenance to the wedding and the Proms. All in all, this has been a truly splendid stay, I've lost over a stone in weight. I've enjoyed the work once it's started flowing and I've been more relaxed and happier than for years. And I've kept off the booze, plenty tomorrow though . . .

It's past 11.00 now and I shall hope to be asleep by twelve. Nightly-nightington.

Sunday, 12 September 1993 – London

Back in town, one stone two pounds lighter and thirty thousand words to the good. Finished off with a facial yesterday and hit the A3 looking shiny, fit and relaxed. Those fine dryness lines the commercials love so much didn't have a chance. I challenged the visible signs of ageing.

Arrived in time to zip over to Lipman's in the lower Charing X Road where I hired a morning suit, my own being stuck up in Norfolk. Then I bought a print at the Chris Beetles Gallery for the happy pair, quick change in the flat before high-tailing it by taxi to the Old Church, Chelsea. Charles and Carla Powell looked in great nick. Well Sir Charles has aged a spot, but that's hardly surprising as he regularly jets to Hong Kong for half hour meetings with Chris Patten* before jetting back again the same day. Takes a toll. Carla, on the other hand in supreme shape. Spending most of her days in Italy looking after her father. Their son Hugh was marrying one Catherine Young, daughter of Sir William and Lady Young, whoever they might be. He is a director of Coutt's the bankers but chaps of his background are directors of banks much in the way they might be members of a squash club. Dennis Thatcher was there on the groom's side, as were poor

---

*The last Governor of Hong Kong, who oversaw the rain-sodden handing over of the Crown Colony to China in 1997. At time of writing Chairman of BBC trustees and may well be the last of those too, given the corporation's plight.

old Rosemary and Norman Lamont.* Ha! That'll teach him to be a loyal Tory.

Good service: Schubert's *Ave Maria* and Mozart's *Ave Verum*, beautifully sung. Good trumpeter in evidence for inevitable Jeremiah Clarke† and Grand March from *Aida*.

Soon as the service was over I cabbed back to the flat to change for the Albert Hall. Arrived good and early so I could track down Patrick Deuchars who runs the place. He had invited me for the Prom's Last Night and I had initially turned him down, thinking I'd stay for the wedding reception. It occurred to me last week that this was silly as I really wouldn't know that many people at the wedding and the L. N. of the P's would be larkier. So I rang John Birt's‡ office and said I could come after all. That's right. John Birt's office. Like an arse I had thought it was *he* who had invited me, not Deuchars. John is always inviting me to *something* after all . . . Wimbledon, Cup Final etc. His office had said 'fine, help yourself . . . no problem. You'll be squiring Lady Parkinson (wife of Cecil).' Only then did I realize my bloomer. At the RAH therefore I found Patrick who was highly amused and said not to worry. John Birt when he arrived was similarly tickled,

---

* Norman Lamont had been sacked a few months earlier as Chancellor of the Exchequer by Prime Minister John Major. He made a snidely neat resignation speech in the House: 'This government gives the impression of being in office but not in power.'
† Supposedly the composer of Purcell's 'Trumpet Voluntary', although I have heard a theory that it was by someone called Mud.
‡ Then Deputy Director of the BBC.

so was able to play the self-lacerating idiot and make them feel good.

Who was there? Well, a load of old Tories really. Michael Heseltine and his wife. They turned out to be enormous fans of *J&W*. 'We've got a butler who absolutely bases himself on your Jeeves,' trilled Mrs H. 'Lah-di-fucking-da, darling,' as I stridently didn't say. Peregrine Worsthorne and his wife Lucinda Lambton, who came in the most extraordinary Union Jack frock, Alan Coren and his wife Anne, Terry Burns of HM Treasury, Debbie and David Owen, the latter hot-foot from his notable failures in Switzerland.* Jane Birt and self made up the numbers. I like Jane I must say – American, as is Debbie Owen.

Pretty good time had by all, though the event is significantly less moving in the flesh than on TV. Secretly I felt it all rather anticlimactic, as if I had been expecting some other element that actually wasn't present. We dined afterwards at Launceston Place, the Owens giving me a lift in their brand new Volvo. Rather comical actually. They argued about absolutely everything. The way to the car, how to get to the restaurant, how to park once there. I said, 'Well, if you can't decide how to walk to a parked car, no wonder there's such hell in Bosnia,' a bit obvious, but really ... U.N. negotiator and he can't negotiate a one-way system.

Sat at one end of the table flanked by Lucinda and

---

* Trying by diplomatic means to stop the slaughter in the wreckage of the former Yugoslavia.

Lady P. She's all right is our Lucinda I think, in a batty aristo way. A professional enthusiast, and therefore slightly overdone, but I think not a fraud. Home to bed at two-ish, my latest night for a fortnight.

Today I went to the Portland to inspect young Rebecca Laurie, who is stout and sweet. Jo, poor thing is absolutely knocked out, pneumonia, the works. She's got either a nebulizer or an oxygen mask on at all times. Hugh showed up and seems, for him, rather confident about the novel he's writing. I bet it's blissfully funny.

Strange things, private hospitals. You ring a number on the phone and get the answer 'Room Service . . .' I had noticed a TVR parked out the front which had the number plate A1 OB ST, which turned out to belong to Mr Armstrong, the consultant who did Jo's Caesarian. He turned up too, all jeans, Kickers, navy blue Guernsey sweater, your casual Home Counties weekend uniform.

Then back home and a bit more work on the nov. I *think* I may be able to do things here. I damned well hope so. Only a thousand words today. A lot of fucking about with the formatting of a couple of faxes that are contained in the novel.

Well, it's past midnight and I'm for sleepies.

Monday, 13 September 1993

A quiet day. Barely stepped out of the flat. A lot of letters to get out of the way, which I managed. The world has gone wild today on account of the PLO Israeli agreement being signed in Washington. Henry Kissinger and other so-called wise old birds are being very cautious. Not surprising, really. A lot of work to do yet, if right wing Israelis and nationalist Palestinians are to be quietened.

Worked on a different kind of chapter of the novel. The third person narrative of Michael Logan's upbringing, vaguely based on my grandfather's life. Where else would I get the idea of a Hungarian grower of sugar beet?

Not much else to report. Still trying to eat well, but it's so hard not to raid the fridge. Must buy a set of scales, that would help.

Tuesday, 14 September 1993

Up early to sit for Maggi Hambling again. It started badly, both of us a little nervous. She grew in confidence however, drawing with a stick of charcoal that was roughly the size of a milk-bottle. Amazing implement. Christ it's a chore standing stock still for so long. Towards the end she played some Ink Spots on the cassette player and wanted to draw me as I danced, a procedure she finds endlessly amusing, as does anyone fortunate enough to witness so rare and unwilling an occurrence. A car came to pick me up at 12.45 to take me to a studio in Islington for photographs for the *Radio Times*. All to do with *Stalag Luft* whose screening date they really can't decide upon. I think it's back to late October again now, having been the 8th at one point. The photoshoot, by Brian Moody, absolutely sweet guy as a lot of good photographers are I've noticed, was followed by an interview. Reasonable outcome I hope. Must say I felt good all through, despite longing to be at the keyboard novelizing. The Grayshott effect still keeping me relaxed and cheerful.

More work in the evening, hours of it. Continuing the chapter in which we go back to Europe to see Michael Logan's father as a Hungarian Jew.

Wednesday, 15 September 1993

Another sitting with Maggi. She wanted me to bring a DJ this time, more consonant with whatever image she has of me. As we progressed I realized these sessions weren't enough for her. She has a large black canvas she wants to paint in oils, and we clearly didn't have time to get near it. I suggested another couple of sessions and she was clearly relieved. Next week then.

Back home for more work before Kim could arrive to accompany me to the Coliseum for the opening of *La Bohème*. Helen Atkinson-Wood* rang to ask if I would talk into a cassette for a boy who is a friend of her family. He had a cycling accident and is now in a coma. Turns out to be a huge *Blackadder* fan. Said I'd do what I can.

* *Blackadder the Third*'s Mrs Miggins.

Naturally I have now discovered that I have no recording facilities here.

Kim arrived looking well and smart and we shogged off to St Martin's Lane. What a disappointment! Dreadful production, simply dreadful. The work of Steven Pimlott. Chorus abominably handled, no interval, which enraged Kim who thought it made the thing stink structurally. He knows it better than me, so I took his word for it: very short evening even without interval. I would otherwise have assumed that the opera itself was a structural mess. The Rodolfo was ghastly, barely audible above the band, and the whole thing sounds so foul in English. Mind you, I wept like a baby at the end, who couldn't? Saw Melvyn Bragg there: he's lost a ton of weight and looks twenty years older for it. His chubbiness was what gave him the boyish, almost cherubic look for which he is famed. Jeremy Isaacs* present also, and Anna Ford and Frank Johnson and assorted Mediahadeen. Kim and I went to The Ivy afterwards. Saw Harold and Antonia, Mike Ockrent (also looking older for weight-loss)† and Tim Rice, mercifully at full weight.

Back in time for bed.

---

*Then running the Royal Opera House, Covent Garden, formally head of Channel 4.

†He was sadly to be wrenched away from the world by leukaemia six years later, while working on the musical version of *The Producers* with Mel Brooks.

Thursday, 16 September 1993

Sue Freestone today! Great nerves. Final checks, then a print out. She read half before we went to Green's for a quick oyster or two. Then back to finish. She seemed immensely pleased. Great relief. No real criticism. I worked on her as regards the title *Other People's Poetry* and she seems to be warming to it.

At 5.00 I trotted off to the Lauries' to inspect Rebecca again and deliver my nebulizer, which Jo and Hugh feel they ought to have on hand, given Jo's recent pneumonic state. Stayed for supper and *Die Hard 2*.

Friday, 17 September 1993

Frustrating morning wandering up and down Regent Street and Mayfair looking for a tape-recorder. Maddened by being ignored by the five or six staff at Wallace Heaton in Bond Street. Can't kick up a fuss or they'd think I was annoyed because of 'who I am'. Eventually had to go all the way to 76 Oxford Street, where I got a Sony Professional Walkman. Wrote and delivered a monologue as Melchett for the boy in the coma, printed out the novel thus far for Anthony Goff my lit. agent and got a taxi to deliver the tape and the manuscript. Anthony said on the phone that Sue sounded frankly ecstatic about the work so far. I MUST NOT LET THIS DIVERT ME FROM CONCENTRATING.

Then, down to work. It all seems to be coalescing in

my head, and as always when things are apparently going well, elements I had put in the novel frankly on spec early on in the writing, when I had no idea what the plot was doing or what the outcome would be, suddenly make absolute sense and look natural and right, as if I had always known they should be there. What does that mean though?

Heigh ho.

Saturday, 18 September 1993

Mostly work, as usual. Had an idea that each chapter should be headed with a verse from Eliot's poem 'The Hippopotamus'. It seems so appropriate. I know the poem is really supposed to be about the C. of E., but it fits the character of Ted to see him as an apparently mud-baked hippo who is in fact more likely to rise and be washed by the angels and martyrs than anyone else. Should the novel itself be called *The Hippopotamus*? Is that over-egging the pudding?

Skipped around St James's and the Burlington Arcade, trying to find a present for Alastair's b'day. Ended up getting a rather splendid dressing-gown at Turnbull & Asser. £390 odd but worth it. Kim and he held a party at their place in Dalston. Nick and Sarah were there, but Hugh never showed. Trevor Newton back from his year's sabbatical in Australia, teaching at Rochester again. He seemed good, if a tad subdued and self-conscious.

Strange: at Cambridge he was infinitely more urbane and polished than any of us, but since he's become a dominie he's grown away from London; it must be hard for him now that Kim is doing well writing for Ken B. and Greg Snow (also present) is getting on with things as a writer. Why a schoolmaster should feel inferior . . . yet we know they do. We are the ones who should feel inferior.

Kim and I talked a bit about Oscar. K is getting on with the screenplay for Ken. They showed the Peter Finch film this afternoon, I was writing, so I've recorded it to watch tomorrow. Bet he's unsurpassably good: it'll only depress me to see him.

I had some lines of coke for the first time in months and months. Weird having that old feeling coursing in the blood again. A large hammer of guilt was banging away in time to the accelerated beating of my heart. All that health and weight loss at Grayshott and now I was guzzling pink champagne* like a beast. That's the trouble with the old nose-candy: it may suppress your appetite but it sure as hell increases your intake of alcohol. Still, one night in five hundred can't be fatal. Fuck me, it's appealing stuff though. Simply too gorgeous and delicious to be trusted. I could fall back into my old ways oh so easily.

Stayed and chatted for much longer than I otherwise

---

* Allergic to standard champagne, but not pink. Go figure. A pink champagne socialist.

would as a result of the Charlie. Ian, Ceri and other of Alastair's Oxford friends made up the majority of the guestage. Quite fun. Got back at two-ish. Not an excessive amount of leg-thrashing, skin-twitching insomnia. Probably clocked out at three.

Sunday, 19 September 1993

Awoke at 11.00-ish feeling worse than I have for ages. But not a massive hangover. Knew I'd be able to work when it came to it. Took things easily and wrote two and half thousand words . . . not as good as I have been, but that's understandable under the circs.

Watched the Peter Finch Oscar. Christ he was excellent. Terribly moving. The witty lines excellently thrown away. How will I ever beat that? Lionel Jeffries splendid too.* Very painful.

So far we have 69,009 words for the novel. Have written a diary entry for the queeny character Oliver Mills who gets 'cured' by Davey rather as the horse did. Decided against actually writing the scene itself.

The thing seems to be taking shape. Oh God, it's so hard to tell any more. When you're inside something for so long, what do you really know about it?

Humpy-hip. Beddly-poos.

---

* As Wilde's nemesis, the Marquess of Queensberry.

Monday, 20 September 1993

More work. What else can a chap do? Again, seems to be proceeding all right. But Christ knows if it means anything.

My taxi returned from the garage, new radio and cassette fitted, the kind with a removable front. They've done a lovely job on the cab itself, but the fucking radio is dead. Boo.

At six-ish Kim came round, with a line of coke for us each to enjoy before the theatre. While he was chopping up I printed out the horse-fucking scene for him to read. He seemed to take to it well: really liked it I think.

Fortified artistically and nasally, we trolled to the Duke of York's for the first night of *Oleanna*. Rather ordinary first act, which disappointed me and then – kerboom! – the thing exploded and you had the ordinary nature of the pre-interval set-up reinterpreted in front of your eyes. Wonderful stuff.

Never seen so many people streaming out of a theatre *talking*. Everyone had something to say. I discovered that I was sitting next to Edwina Curry of all people. She, naturally, had *very* firm ideas about it all. Piffle, as you would expect. 'He failed her.' What, so he deserved to lose his wife, house and job, did he? What would Edwina's life be like if she was punished for a sexual indiscretion of that kind?*

---

* Ha! We didn't know at the time that she had had an affair with the future
  Prime Minister, John Major, in the mid-1980s.

We avoided the party afterwards and wound our way to the Brixtonian in Neal's Yard, where Alastair's friend Ian Poitier was having a birthday party. A sweet poppet from the W. Indies, Ian was at Oxf. with Al. and says he's a cousin or nephew of the great Sidney. We left there, however, and went to the Ivy actually to eat. Bumped into Simon Gray who, natch, hated *Oleanna*. Then home for kip.

Tuesday, 21 September 1993

Sat for Maggi *again* all morning. She has started the big oil now and I hope will be done by Friday. It's fun but intense. Nipped back home for a spot of work and then off to Mount Street to see Dougie Hayward the tailor to be measured for a suit. He's going to make a dark blue job. Never had one that colour before, but it could work. He makes for Michael Caine and John Cleese (who recommended him) very much *the* man of the 60s along with Tommy Nutter, tailoring for Terence Stamp and those kind of people. Not sure my bulk will bring out the best in his snipping, but we'll see.

At seven-thirty, after a lot of heavy writing, which went pretty well I think (did the scene in which Davey persuades the fourteen year old with a brace on her teeth to give him a blow-job) I taxi-ed to Ben's flat. He's in a bit of a state, poor love. His psoriasis is spreading vilely. He's trying this Chinese figure, Tong, who did so well for Jo Laurie, but so far no success. He's told Ben to steer clear of yeast, which means no beer, which Ben hates. But if tension is a cause, then it's amazing Ben hasn't got it worse, frankly. Neil and Glenys Kinnock came round and we walked to the Bombay Brasserie. Both N & G in excellent form. I was delighted and amazed to hear that they had come to the same conclusion as me, which I would never have dared raise otherwise, thinking it sacrilege . . . viz. it's time the Lib Dems and Labour got to-bloody-gether and prepared to kick the Tories out. Very good fun.

Trailed back home at one-ish.

Wednesday, 22 September 1993

A frustrating day, if the truth be told. Not enough chance to work. David Tomlinson* had invited me to lunch at Carluccio's restaurant in Neal Street. Wonderful place, fabulous funghi, good wine and the company of David, Richard Ingrams, his assistant at the *Oldie* Isabelle, and Beryl Bainbridge, who's always a lark. But too much incredibly fine whisky. Woozily wandered home and got into the cab to go for a costume fitting for the Juvenal thing I'm doing next week. Cabbed back, fell asleep for half an hour and then had to get ready for the theatre. Went to see Simon Donald's new play at the Donmar *The Life of Stuff*: started badly but perked up. Very much a young inexperienced playwright's work, but full of heart and shocks and

* *Mary Poppins, Bedknobs and Broomsticks* and so forth.

some wit (mostly derivative and inconsistent if the truth be told). Was with Lo and Christian (Simon's a client of Lo's) as well as someone called Sarah and her boyfriend Dominic Minghella, brother of Anthony, also a writer apparently. They've built some whole new complex by the theatre called Thomas Neal's, sort of mall really. We dined at a new Mezzaluna there, part of the same chain you find in LA and New York. Then off home again.

Thursday, 23 September 1993

More productive day. 77,000 words done! Gosh I hope it's all right. Did a VO for Matchmakers at 11.00, with John Junkin of all people. Stout fellow, friendly, not sour, curmudgeonly and feeling passed over like so many his age . . . Barry Took etc.

I'm writing this at 4.45. Have to shower and change for the premiere of *The Fugitive*. I'm taking Alyce Faye: sending a stretch limo round to pick her up, the works. It's at the refurbished Warner West End, thence we go to a party at the Savoy, though we've also been invited to a party Michael and Shakira Caine are giving, so we might pop there first for an hour or so. I'll tell you all about it tomorrow, Daisy Dear. (Daisy is short for Daisy Diary, it's what the character Oliver Mills calls his diary in *The Hippopotamus* – that's definitely the title, I'm sure of it now). Must go and dress for tonight. Tell you about it tomorrow.

Friday, 24 September 1993

Well, last night was amusing enough. The limo that arrived was longer than a cricket pitch and whiter than a cricket boot. Alyce Faye highly amused. We had a voddie together and then hit Leicester Square. Absolutely *thousands* of people. What are they all *doing*? Most peculiar. In the foyer, hundreds milling about and, on TV screens, an in-house *Ent. Tonight* style show with comedian Andrew O'Connor, some bint called Amanda and good old Iain Johnstone all conducting interviews, with street people, celebs and film people respectively. Highly embarrassing. We went in and took our seats early. Only to discover that actually we were in cinema number 5, out of 11. *The Fugitive* was being shown in 9 of them. We were *not* in the same one as Princess Di and the A list. Feel acutely embarrassed and hope Alyce Faye isn't affronted. Doubtless John Cleese, had he come, would have been in amongst the big nobs. They are showing the TV celeb show on the screen. Insane. Baz Bamigboye appears and says that only the nobodies would have turned up this early . . . glunk.

Anyway, film happens: damned good thriller. Tommy Lee Jones absolutely top hole. We streak for the exit. See a big white limo passing, but being moved on to do another circuit. I go out to stop it. Huge cheer from crowd.

It's not our limo. I walk back to the foyer: huge laugh

from crowd. Get trapped by a genuine TV crew and chat to the interviewer for a bit. Limo comes and we go. Weird feeling being pressed upon at all sides. People think it might be Madonna inside.*

We go first to the Hyde Park hotel to Michael Caine's and Marco Pierre White's new restaurant. We're in time for wine and *friandises* . . . very fond of Shakira Caine. Michael is fine, but seems a bit pissed. Very sharp man in his own way but often cross and bitter. What he has to be resentful of I can't quite guess. I think he still feels the British class system held him back. Seeing that he and Sean Connery are far and away the biggest film stars we have produced since the war, with maybe the exception of Richard Burton who's hardly aristocratic either, I don't quite get it. But Caine can do no wrong in my eyes. He was Harry Palmer in *The Ipcress File* for heaven's sake.

We get back in the limo and head for the Savoy. More interviews on camera and then I'm left in peace. Gobble some lobster, command a table and some wine. Chat to Mo and Iain Johnstone. Michael White† and Jerry Hall pop by. We decide to leave. Home by 2.00.

Why does one attend such things? Well, it's honestly the only time I ever go to a cinema. You can just about

---

*I simply don't know *what* I was thinking of. A white stretch limo? Maybe they weren't so hen-party back then. But still . . .

†Producer of the first Monty Python film and impresario responsible for popularity of *Oh, Calcutta!*, *The Rocky Horror Show* and too many others to mention. Mad on tennis.

guarantee that people will behave at premieres and they certainly won't ask for your autograph or giggle. I don't think I've got many more in me though.

This morning up early, not hung over, another sitting with Maggi. Goes all right. Leave her place after four solid hours of standing and drive off to do some shopping for dinner on Sunday. Did I mention that Nigel Short and his wife Rhea and Dominic and Rosa Lawson and Kim Harris are popping in for dinner then?* Can't shop tomorrow because I'm off to Cambridge.

Anyway shopped and got back to the flat. No real concentration enough to work on the penultimate chapter, which is where I'm at. The Ryder Cup has started, for one thing. Oh – Manchester has lost its Olympic Bid.† No real surprise. Absolutely typical John Major failure, however. Australia, the Lucky Country . . .

Anyway spent most of the afternoon half-watching the golf and going back to clean up and rewrite the last few sections. 78,685 words. Lumme. When I think back to how depressed I was on the first Monday at Grayshott. How within an ace of calling it all off I was . . . not that it's necessarily *any good* what I've got. I have to keep reminding myself of that.

Well, it's 11:03 now, best be making an early night of it. We'll chat tomorrow, 'if I'm spared' . . .

* No, Stephen, it would appear that you didn't.
† For the 2000 Summer Games.

Saturday, 25 September 1993

Strange kind of a day. Had agreed, somewhere back in the mists of time, that I would drive to Cambridge and appear in a kind of 'celebrity' *University Challenge* game, hosted by Bamber Gascoigne. It was for the Alumni Weekend, which rather American sounding thing is an innovation. I arrived in time to do some shopping before the lunch. Bugger me Cambridge gets crowded these days: it's almost an unworkable city now. You have never seen such crowds, and if London had to put up with that kind of traffic there would be riots. Riots. Bought some books on equine anatomy and health to see if I can get Lilac's disease right in the novel. Also finally bought Donna Tartt's *Secret History* which everyone has been going on about and I suppose I ought to read. No sign of a book called *Trainspotting* which Simon Donald had told me to catch up on. By a Scot called Irvin(e) Wels(c)h I think the name is.

Got to the Grad Pad* in time for the lunch. I was on the Vice Chancellor's table, opposite Bamber and Germaine Greer and wedged between a couple of dons. Nice guy called Harcourt, Australian economist, on my right, zoologist called, I think, William Foster on my left. Sebastian Faulks was there too, which is good because I've just started on his novel *Birdsong*. Our team was completed by Valerie Grove.

The actual game was played in the Lady Mitchell Hall

---

*Deeply unpleasant soubriquet for Cambridge's Graduate Centre.

on the Sidgwick Site. Needless to say we *trashed* them. Germaine Greer said to me afterwards 'Jeez, you're so *competitive*' which I thought was *highly* revealing. She's a good stick though, for all that. It's clear in her conversation however that she still feels the need to prove herself all the time, which given her intelligence and confident eloquence is odd. No it isn't. We're all like that, eloquent or not. We just show it in different ways. Kept back for a few interviews and the like, one for *CAM* magazine, some graduate thing, and another for Varsity.

Drove back home listening to Day 2 of the Ryder Cup. It's going to be *fucking* close. Bit of telly, some small amount of work on the novel. London is not as good as Grayshott . . .

Ner-night.

Sunday, 26 September 1993

Up fairly late, tiny bit of novelizing, but most of the day spent chewing my nails at the Ryder Cup. We lost, boo-hoo. All a bit embarrassing, because it was down to Barry Lane chucking a three hole lead and turning it into a one hole loss all in the course of the last five holes. Also Costantino Rocca fucked up. All a bit of a shame. More English Majorite loss and gloom.

In the afternoon prepared dinner, just about got everything ready in time for Kim, Dominic Lawson, Nigel and Rhea Short and Dr Robert Hübner. Nigel in tremendous spirits considering he is on the brink of another famous English defeat. Well, not yet on the brink, but he was seriously outplayed by Kasparov on Saturday. A good evening though. Kim on good form, we talked a little about the chess. Then we got into a stupid argument with the rather vain figure of Hübner on the subject of whether or not things are altered by one's perception of them. He was poo-pooing any kind of thinking which veered from his *Ding an sich* Germanism. Bit of a prat, if the truth be told. After all, Schrödinger was just as German.* And Heisenberg. And they proposed that things are certainly altered by our perception. Certainly at the quantum level.

Kim and I promised we'd go next week to one of Nigel's games. I suspect we'll make it Saturday, when he'll be white and have a chance. They left and Kim and I stayed up for another hour. Kim had to shog, because tomorrow is the first day of *Frankenstein* rehearsals at Shepperton.

Monday, 27 September 1993

Day of some novel writing, but I'm finding it so hard to finish. Over 80,000 words done: never thought *that* day would dawn . . . but two chapters from the finishing post. Very hard to get them right. Didn't step out of the flat once. Rang a vet in Newmarket whose name was given to me by the Royal College of Veterinary Surgeons. Didn't seem to have much of a clue about an illness that could

* Well, all right, he was Austrian, but you know what I mean.

be misdiagnosed. Pathetic. I'm going to have to find a vet I can take out to dinner so I can explain it properly.

Watched Robbie's new series, *Cracker*, damned good stuff. He's on excellent form, really good. Not overacting, just perfect. Then wrote this. Highly dull, I'm afraid.

Time for boo-boos.

Tuesday, 28 September 1993

Oh Nigel. Oh Nigel, Nigel, Nigel. He missed a win. He missed his first great win. Oh damn, damn, double damn. Just been watching it on TV. He could have had Kasparov right there on the ropey-rope ropes. He fluffed it. Poor sod, he must be sicker than sick. He made a gigantically wonderful queen sacrifice and should have won. It's so clear that he should have won. Even I could fucking see it. Blastly damington. What a year for British sport. Is there a chance we can beat Holland to get into the World Cup finals? If there is it's far from a fat one. Poo and miz and boo and horridy-horridy-horrid.

Another day spent entirely in the flat. Not a breath of outside air. Getting unshaven and foetid so I lit some joss-sticks or 'incense sticks' as everyone now insists on calling them, but the novel proceeded better today. Now up to round about the 86,000 words mark. Man from the Newmarket vet rang today and suggested timpanic colic, which can be diagnosed as spasmodic colic which is worse. Might suffice, we shall see.

I shall watch *Tales of the City* which starts in half an hour on C4 and then go to bed. Boo-hoo.

Wednesday, 29 September 1993

90,113 words! Had a sudden and depressing realization last night at one in the morning that everything I'd written yesterday was wrong. Well, not everything, but nearly. I realized the final chapter had to run on immediately from the previous. Yesterday I'd set it the following morning and had the show-down in which Ted reveals the fruits of his researches taking place after lunch. As it is, it now takes place at dinner, which I think is better.

Got up early-ish, worked a bit and then did a voice over at ten. Got back, buying a pair of Doc Marten's on the way, and wrote till 6.00. Had a meeting with Dave Jeffcock at the Groucho Club at 6.30. He's producing the Juvenal thing I'm doing tomorrow and Friday and which, dear Daisy Diary, you will hear all about. Wish I wasn't doing it, though. I could bloody finish the novel this week otherwise. Drank one and a half glasses of red wine. No more. Came back, titivated a bit and counted the words. The novel is now longer than *The Liar* already. As if that makes a fucking bit of difference, Stephen, you total arsehole.

Really enjoyed *Tales of the City* last night. Damned fine. Followed by a highly depressing documentary on ITV about child abuse. The horror of it all.

John Smith has won his vote on OMOV today, thank Christ. Very, very close. The TUC loses its block vote.

Heigh ho. Better go and learn my lines.

HORRIFIED POSTSCRIPT: after doing this diary entry I decided to do some backing up of work on *The Hippo*. After my return from the Grouch I had worked for 2.5 hours rewriting the work of the day. Saved the wrong file and overwrote the rewrites, if that makes sense. So I might as well have stayed all night at the Grouch. Lost all my rewriting. Piss and fuck.

Thursday, 30 September 1993

Well, bugger me with a cocktail onion, what a day. What a day. Up earlyish and then a walk to the Groucho Club where the BBC had set up base camp.

The programme is called *Laughter and Loathing,* it's presented by Ian Hislop and purposes to analyse and document satire. Programme One, pilot and first ep., is all about Juvenal, played by me. Well, as you can imadge, the only way to play Juve is to get yourself dolled up in a toga and pace the streets of London, declaiming satires. No point doing it in a Tuscan Doric decorated studio looking like a historical figure. Juve was very much now and in the streets. There can be nothing in the world more embarrassing than standing outside the Bank of England in a toga, with a camera crew on a long lens miles away, shouting irate verse into a hidden radio mike. Tourists think you're a guide of some sort, punters who recognize you come up and nudge you or hound you for autographs. Unspeakable shame. Add to this a pair of thin boot/sandals and the rainiest late September day in living memory and you have a recipe for disgrace and horror. Filmed all morning in the City, Bank underground station and, mercifully, in the Conway Hall.

The evening was taken up with this party: brainchild of our prod./dir. Dave Jeffcock, the idea was that in the Gennaro Room of the Groucho a load of celebs and liggers would turn up for a free party in which self would be filmed (still in toga) being rejected and cold-shouldered by these media types. This would be edited with a VO of self reciting a Juve satire in which the poet complains about being a reject who has to go to smart parties and be ignored, just in order to eat. As we started filming the mood came upon me and – *eheu fugaces* – I asked Liam Carson whether or not he might be able to find me a couple of grams of Devil's Dandruff. This he duly did and I spent most of the party slightly wired. The guests included Clive James, Jeremy Paxman, Charles Kennedy the leader of the Liberal Democrats, a man who likes a drink, Angus Deayton, Danny Baker and Melvyn Bragg, the latter turning up with Cate his wife. The filming finished and I stayed on for a while.

Danny introduced me to a man with long hair that I realized was Rob Newman of Newman and Baddiel infamy. They had been a year or two below us at Cambridge but we never knew them. This frightening pair have been so rude about everyone I love and like that I assumed that he would snub me. In fact he was rather sweet and naturally I told him that I thought his show, currently on BBC2, was splendid. Haven't actually seen any of it and am sure it isn't quite my tasse d'oolong.

After this played Perudo* with Liam and a couple of other degenerates and flew off home when I realized that Tina Time had stolen some hours from me and it was twenty past one in the fuck-mothering morning.

Not ending September as I began it. Wine, coke, late nights. Shucks.

Friday, 1 October 1993

Pinch, punch – yeah, yeah, yeah. Another supremely embarrassing day, filming in Soho and Covent Garden in a toga and rain. Used up the lunchtime buying birthday presents for Nick Symons and Griff Rhys Jones, both of whom had parties tonight.

Finished filming at 8.oo-ish and biffed off to Primrose Hill for Nick's party. Hugh was there and Paul Shearer and Kim and Alastair. Helen Napper and Jon Canter too. Had a gram and a half left over from the previous night.

Nick's party finished at eleven thirty and I cabbed it to Clerkenwell for Griff's. Usual suspects present and incorrect. Angus, Phil Pope, Helen A-W, Clive Anderson, Nick Mason (drummer from Pink Floyd) those sort. Mel Smith

---

* Perudo is a dice game that uses bluff, often called the Liar's Dice of the Andes. I described it as the second most addictive thing to come out of South America.

in US filming, but his wife Pamela in attendance. Got coked and drunk and at three-ish managed to retain the sense to call for a cab which I shared with Simon Bell to the centre of town: dropped him in Soho and fell into bed. Oh dear, Stephen, what a case you are.

Saturday, 2 October 1993

Up at 10.30, in no mood to work. Filled in time watching videos and then Kim arrived to accompany me to the Savoy Theatre to watch Nigel playing Gazza Kasp. We cabbed it after a cup of tea and arrived half an hour early. Sat in the front row and chatted. Rhea, Nigel's wife fetched up and we watched the first three quarters of an hour unfold. Nigel was white and it developed, as always, into a Najdorf Sicilian, with Nigel playing the Fischer favourite, Bishop c4. Kasp unwound a piece of preparation beginning with Nc6, and had taken 11 minutes to Nigel's 52 by the time we left the hall and went to Simpson's in the Strand where the grand-master's analysis room was. Most of the GMs in agreement that Nigel was in trouble. Kim had accurately predicted the course of the game and reckoned that Nigel stood all right, considering how taken by surprise he was. Tony Miles, ex-England #1 was presiding at the roundtable of GM's and making bitter foolish remarks about N's play. Dominic Lawson explained how completely asinine and childish Miles is. He cannot bear the fact that Short is so much better than him and has always beaten him. At one point he laughed out loud at a move of Nigel's which was absolutely necessary, precise and accurate. Really sad. He's spent some time in a funny farm, so one mustn't hate. Speelman turned up and was friendly. Chatted to Ray Keene and others. Nigel managed a draw and acquitted himself well over the board. Beaten in preparation perhaps, but excellently played.

Alastair then arrived and we had a drink and stepped over to Joe Allen's for dinz. Saw Maggi Hambling and, of all people, Amanda Barry* sitting at a table with Percy, Maggi's terrier. Then came home, drank a bottle of red wine and wrote this.

Now must bed myself. Off to Wyton† tomorrow for Jo (sister) and Richard's christening party for my nephew George.

Sunday, 3 October 1993

Drove to RAF Wyton. You have to report to the guardhouse and get a chit which you stick on your dashboard. Found Jo and Richard's quarters. Arrived same time as Roger, Ruthie, Ben and William. Ben and William v. affectionate and sweet. Jo looking fearfully well and George bouncing fit to bust. Splendid fellow. None of the usual stickiness you expect from these family affairs.

---

* *Carry on Cabby*, *Coronation Street*. Once I'd got to know her better it wasn't that surprising she was in Maggi's company.

†RAF station where Richard, husband to Jo and father to George, was based.

Almost frighteningly English. The X'ening itself took place in the church on the station, a rather cute little affair with shiny rafters. Simply *ghastly* ASB (Alternative Service Book) form of Christening. Even the Lord's Prayer was tampered with. Nice padre, but v. low. Came back for buns and cake.

Got away sharpish and returned to London, spot of TV and bed.

Monday, 4 October 1993

Well, a day spent entirely in the flat once more, and a day that has seen me finish the novel. Well, I say that, but when is a novel ever finished? I dotted the *point final* as the French say at round about six-thirty and ever since have been combing through the main body, rewriting. I suspect the length will be round about 96,000 words when we're done (Stephen, you are *such* a size queen).

Stopped off to watch the second ep. of Robbie Coltrane's *Cracker*, even better than the first, simply spot on. This was followed by *News at Ten* with all the pictures of Moscow's new October Revolution. It'll all drift into dim memory in a fortnight or so, but what a day . . . tanks blasting holes in the side of the Parliament building, hundreds killed. Could it happen here, we wonder?

Only worrying thing is that I somehow succumbed and opened a bottle of wine at nine-ish, most of which

I've consumed. Really must get into the habit of passing through a day without any alcohol.

Heigh ho. Up earlyish tomorrow please, Stephen, and perhaps it will all be really, really, really done.

Ner-night.

Tuesday, 5 October 1993

FINISHED ... well perhaps there's more work to do, but I've printed it out, sent a copy to Hugh Laurie and feel that it's out.

Immediately rang Sue, but she's at the Frankfurt Book Fair and so I won't send it to her until tomorrow or Monday even as she won't be back for the rest of the week. Rang the Lauries though and have cabbed it off to Hugh.

God knows what it's like. Feel hot and cold about it.

The evening saw a dinner at W. H. Smith's headquarters in Holbein Place off Sloane Square. Sir Simon Hornby, the chairman had invited me to dinner. Turned up in time, after a couple of lines, still left over from Liam's kind sale on Thursday. Drove the taxi. Interesting people there: the Roux bros., Hugh Johnson the wine writer, Edward Cazalet, Plum Wodehouse's grandson and others. Strangely serendipitous going to a Smith's dinner on the very day I finished the nov. They served Chateau La Tour and Meursault. Highly enjoyable, I got very drunk indeed.

Wednesday, 6 October 1993

Spent the day sorting out all the correspondence that had built up over the weeks since I'd been concentrating on *The Hippo*. Then I posted it and went shopping. Had lunch with Lo and Christian at the agency. Then ... walked to Mortimer Street and bought an Apple Newton. Wow! What a piece of kit. It's going to take a little time before it can read my handwriting, but this is the way technology is going, no question.*

In the evening went to Victoria Wood's concert at the Royal Albert Hall. Met up with Hugh and Ben Elton: Ben's manager Phil McIntyre is the promoter of VW and arranged a good box for us. Afterwards we trotted off to the Bombay Brasserie (where Ben and I and the Kinnocks dined the other night) and spent a wondrous evening chatting. Hugh is reading Ben's novel as well as mine at the moment, so I've got a fluttery tummy. Especially as I've suddenly lost confidence in *The Hippo* and wonder what on earth I was at writing such a hard-to-define novel.

Thursday, 7 October 1993

Hugh came round this morning to start writing on the next series of *A Bit of Fry and Laurie*: no two week holiday after the intensity of *The Hippo* and all else. Come to think

---

*Sadly the Newton was somewhat before its time, but it was indeed the way technology was going. Hand held, touch screen (although with a stylus) ... many things to like and admire in it.

of it when did I *ever* have a holiday? We didn't get much done, but it was *so* good to have him here. In the afternoon, Griff Rhys Jones rang up to invite me to a poker game at the Groucho.

After Hugh left I wandered to the G and the game happened. You have never seen so much coke in your life, how Griff resists it I do not know. XY was there too and the white powder simply flowed. I played poker pretty well, despite some very bad hands and managed to exploit what little luck I had. The effect of the C and a lot of red wine began to take its toll on me (but on no one else) and towards the end of the evening I (embarrassingly) threw up out of the window onto Dean Street below. Liam had a look and said there was no one there, no policemen, no unfortunate victim of the chunder. Shame, indignation and horror. It reminds me of the time when I was with *insert names of huge rock star, huge acting name, huge producer name here* in the back office of the 24 hours café in Kingly Street and we decided to have a Longest Line Competition. Each of us chopped out a line, mine being the longest. But the point was we had to take it up in one. A vile version of the shot-glasses down-in-one horror. On that occasion I took the line up my nose, it must have been seven foot long, but thin, hoovered it up, and as I got to the end of the table opened my mouth and let out gallons of pure, bright red vomit.

Not quite as bad as that this evening. Everybody very

nice about it, but what a humiliation. Struggled home somehow.

Friday, 8 October 1993

Quieter day. Hugh arrived late and we worked a bit. I wrote a sketch of appalling double entendre quality* and then he left. Played with the new Newton, watched a few videos and then went to bed.

Saturday, 9 October 1993

Bought some French videos to watch actors for the movie *Bachelors Anonymous* that I've been asked to direct next year. The Lauries invited me to dinner and I popped over. Nigel Short lost his match today, for the first time for weeks. Big shame. Came home, got a bit drunk and wrote up these last few days. Forgive my brevity of late.

Ner-night.

Sunday, 10 October 1993

Woke up good and dominically† late. Had a lunch at the Ivy with John Reid, Elton John's manager, and Arlene Phillips the choreographer. They had asked me some

---

*Known as 'The Understanding Barman'. Quite proud of it now. I think we thought it was a satire on Ronnie Barker-style innuendo, but of course such innuendo is funny: https://www.youtube.com/watch?v=U8ko2nCk_hE.

†My electronic calendar confirms that 10 October 1993 was indeed a Sunday.

time ago to see if I couldn't come up with a narrative framework for Elton's songs, with a view to putting on a West End Show. I wrote the book in February/March this year. Reid and Arlene like it, John R. has just come back from LA where he showed it to Bernie Taupin, Elton's lyricist who, as I suspected, did not like AT ALL. Accused it of being cliché-ridden, which is true, but inevitable for a West End/Broadway musical, and Elton's early life of transgressive sex, excess, drugs, rock and roll *was* frankly cliché-ridden. Still John and Arlene want to go ahead, so I'm to ring Sam Mendes tomorrow, as John likes the idea of his being the director. John, who'll produce, will see Sam when John gets back from Hong Kong next week. As well as being Elton's manager, he's also Billy Connolly's (and until a month or so ago, Barry Humphries').

Well, it may or may not take. The story is full of gay stuff, which will at least make it different. It's unhip and uncool, which is what Taupin dislikes, naturally. Taupin thinks of himself as some kind of hep Village guy from the 60's. Sort of Neurotica-Beat generation cool dude poet. Still trying to escape the fact that he's a Lincolnshire farm lad gone middle-aged and millionairoid.*

Came back, watched TV and wrote this. Still haven't watched any French stuff to see what I think of French

---

*This is awful. I met Bernie Taupin a year or so later and found him to be just about the most endearing fellow you could ever encounter, not in the least self-deluded or spoiled by his enormous success with Elton.

actors for *Bachelors Anonymous*. Hugh round again tomorrow for more *F&L* writing. Glunk.

Monday, 11 October 1993

I'm a bit behind diary-wise and I'm writing this later. Damned if I can remember what happened today. Wrote with Hugh in the morning and afternoon and then what . . . ?

Tuesday, 12 October 1993

More writing with Hugh during the day and then popped over to the Groucho to see if I could find some coke to ingest before dinner at L'Escargot with Pnina my second cousin's wife and Liora, her daughter. They were alright actually, could have been a lot worse. Desperate to know what the rest of the world thought of Israel's peace moment with the PLO. L'Escargot just recently reopened and Jimmy Lahoud, the new owner, was absolutely thrilled to see me there and stood me cognacs and all the rest of it. Okay evening. Walked home nearly sober.

Wednesday, 13 October 1993

Strange day. Wrote with Hugh up until about 5.00 when Mother came round to pick up a copy of *The Hippo* which she wants to read. We gossiped for a while and then I had to change for the evening. Tristan Garel-Jones had invited me to dinner. Arrived first at his Catherine Place address. Highly bonhomous cove, far too civilized to be a convincing Tory. Other guests included the Chancellor of the Exchequer, Kenneth Clarke, the Chief Whip Richard Ryder and assorted sprigs of the nobility, chiefly female (Leonora Lichfield, Jane Grosvenor that kind of thing). Had damn good chat with them all and raised the subject of tomorrow's debate at the Cambridge Union, viz. the age of consent. Tris was all for a free vote if ever it gets to the House of Commons, Richard Ryder (Ma and Pa's local MP in Norfolk as it happens) was being very tricksy about it. This horrific shite that the government have been spewing about 'family values' recently, since Blackpool in fact, may mean that they are not interested in things like justice and equality at the expense of the blue hair vote.

Left the dinner early because Griff had invited me to a card game at the Groucho. Eventually it took place: rather knackering business, lots of C. Managed to struggle home at two-ish.

Thursday, 14 October 1993

Had to be up very early in time for the *Today* programme on the consent and Cambridge debate issue. Felt like shit, as you can imagine after the excesses of the evening before. Eventually, after a great deal of hanging about, I got to the studio where Anna Ford and Brian Redhead were at their microphones. I was to deliberate with a

Conservative MP, David Wilshire, a sponsor of the Clause 28. In fact he said nothing I disagreed with: he made a libertarian point about it not being the law's business to interfere with what people do in private and left it at that. No debate to speak of at all.

Got back and dozed until Hugh arrived for writing. Spent a lot of the day not writing but thinking about what I was going to say in the evening.

Jon Plowman turned up at 12.30. He and Bob Spiers, I hope, are going to produce and direct respectively the next *Fry & Laurie*.* We lunched at Langan's, once we had tracked down poor Bob Spiers who was lost and wandering desperately around St James's. I think they would be perfect those two and I believe Hugh thinks so too. Highly amiable and capable of delivering much higher production values. Lunch was fine and fun. Mostly gossip, but we agreed that we should proceed.

Sir Ian McKellen (or Serena McKellen as Kim told me he should more properly be addressed) showed up at about half-four, as did Michael Bywater who is on the opposition benches, opposing the motion 'This House Believes in an Equal Age of Consent for Homosexual

---

* Indeed they did. Bob Spiers, now deceased sadly, was an old hand from the Golden Age who had directed dozens of episodes of *Dad's Army*, *Are You Being Served?*, *It Ain't Half Hot, Mum* and, crucially, the second series of *Fawlty Towers*, which rendered him holy. Jon Plowman: an old friend from Granada *Alfresco* days who would go on to be probably the BBC's longest-serving head of comedy, ushering in *Ab Fab*, *The Office*, *Little Britain*, etc.

and Heterosexual Acts'. Poor old Michael agreed to do the debate without knowing that he was going to oppose. Claims he can't think of anything to say against the idea.

Drove to Cambridge, traffic in London bad, arrived a little late for the pre-debate drinks and dinner. There was already a hell of a queue leading into the union building.

Dinner was fine: not a culinary excitement, but fine. The President was an elegant girl called Lucy Frazer and to my left was a sporting chappie called something or other, he was from King's and reading Theology. Why have I forgotten his name already? Also there was Tristram Hunt, who is the son of the Hunts who live plumb spang next door to Hugh and Jo Laurie. Simply a poppet, he was speaking on our behalf.*

Anyway, eventually time to debate: we marched into the chamber, with *Newsnight* cameras on our heels. HUGE cheer for me. They just wouldn't stop, it was awfully sweet. Felt like blubbing. The President got things off to some kind of start, and Tristram Hunt opened the debate for us. Four speakers on each side, Tristram, Serena McKellen, Angela Mason (of Stonewall Group) and self proposing, and two undergraduates (including the one whose name I've forgotten), Stephen Green of the Conservative Family Campaign and Michael Bywater opposing.

Tristram put the case pretty ably, bless him. Our first undergraduate opposer was a cheery Scottish conservative,

---

* Now a Labour MP and dashing broadcaster who makes fine documentaries on history.

classic stout gingery politico. He was an indication of things to come, for it was clear that he did not believe in the position he had to take up at all. Serena then spoke, quite wonderfully, very moving indeed, ending up with a recitation from Housman's poem about the laws of God and man. Then the student whose name I can't remember: he was so disrespectful to the idea of the motion that Stephen Green got up and walked out! 'I'll come back when he's finished' he said. Highly entertaining.

Angela Mason next, she's the very extraordinary lesbotic campaigner who runs Stonewall. Used to be a member of the Angry Brigade, narrowly escaped conviction at some bombing trial. Oo-er. She was, as you would expect, dull and uninspired as a debater.

Then Stephen Green. What a ghastly and unfortunate specimen. Simply HOPELESS performance. Witless, graceless and useless. Didn't even try and present his real point of view, which is that he abominates anything to do with whoopsidom. Instead he tried to make some feeble, pettyfogging legal point about the age of consent which made no sense at all. He presented his book *The Sexual Dead End* some magisterial work, we are given to believe, outlining the dreadfulness of being a bottomite. Poor man. Sat down to, at the most, polite splatters of applause.

Then it was time for the floor debate. Oh yes, Stephen as usual, has to wait and wait and wait before he can speak. Undergraduates on this side and that spoke. Finally it was my turn. I had jotted a few things down on the back of an envelope as it were during the debate, but otherwise entirely busked, which is definitely the best way of doing things I think. Told them all about Cambridge and what kind of a place they were attending, the history of its alumni and what they stood for: contrasted this with the adulterers, closet cases and corrupt canters who get up at Tory Party Conferences and dare presume to talk about 'family values'.

The long and the short of it was that I got a standing ovation, which made me all trembly. They just wouldn't stop applauding me and cheering and all the rest. Very exciting. Michael Bywater spoke next and said he opposed the motion because he believed that the age of consent should not be equal: *hetero*sexual love was far too complex and difficult a thing to allow 16 year olds to engage in it. Homosexual love was fine: it was a matter for equals and those who know each other and should happily be set at 16. He ended by saying 'I'm sitting with the faggots' . . . crossed the bench and sat with us.

Well, as you can imagine, we carried the day. 693 votes to 30. Of the 30 it was mostly those who found the queue into the Aye door too long and voted by filing through the No. Was kept for at least an hour signing autographs in a great crush of undergraduacy. For the large part not the most bouncily charming bunch: 'Rory', 'Nicole', 'John' would be shouted at me as an order paper was put under my nose to be signed. Very few pleases or thank yous. One can overlook a lot by imagining that they were shy or nervous, but generally speaking a disappointing set. There is no point in being shiny, attractive, intelligent and young unless you beam it out, whatever your gender, to those older than you.

Eventually managed to get through to the room where drinks were supposed to be served. Bar had closed by that time, natch. No bad thing, since I was driving home. This we did once Serena, Michael and a couple of others could be prised away. I got home and to bed by about two-thirty. Long day. Little sleep lately.

Friday, 15 October 1993

Woke up early enough to do a Voice Over at 9.00 ... really that's so many late nights now, I'm beginning to think all the work of Grayshott is being undone. Pretty feeble ads for Croft sherry. Got back in time for Hugh to come round and we stuck at it all day. Anthony Goff (my lit. agent) rang to say that he really loved *The Hippo*, which was a huge relief. I do honestly think he meant it.

Robin Hardy came round at 5.30 and we chewed the fat on the subj. of *Bachelors Anonymous*. I told him that Thierry Lhermitte was my certain favourite for the lead. He seemed to think this was a good idea and promised to try and see if he could book him. At 7.00 I biffed to the Groucho to see if I could spot a dealer of any kind. BW introduced me to a chap called Jethro who sold me a gram. Then I loped off to Hugh's and Jo's for dinner. Alastair and Kim were there and we had a jolly dinner before I ripped off home again, by way of the Grouch. I am back to my bad old ways with a vengeance.

Saturday, 16 October 1993

Signing tour. Up early for a car to Euston station, where I met Rebecca Salt of Mandarin books and we got on the train for Chester. Late, unfortunately, trouble at Watford. This meant we were late for Chester and only just arrived in time for my 'performance'. This involved a reading and chat on stage at the Gateway theatre. Read the Sherlock Holmes story from *Paperweight** and then took questions. Very good fun, really: seemed to go well. Then we grabbed a late lunch and signed some stock in a couple of book-shops in the Chester 'Rows'. Beautiful city, quite entrancing. Car from Chester to Liverpool where we signed again and leapt on a train for London. Did some fatuous IQ test for *Esquire* magazine on the way.

Went straight to the Groucho and hung around for a while. Jethro showed up and I bought 2 grams. Finally fell into bed in some kind of a state at 3.00.

Sunday, 17 October 1993

Lunch with Ferdy Fairfax† in Clapham. Charles Sturridge

---

* An earlier book of mine, a salmagundi of writings that you are sure to find delightful and a perfect gift too, for a hated one.
† Director of two series of *Jeeves and Wooster*, also now sadly no longer with us.

and Phoebe* showed up, Robert Fox† those sort of people. Rather fine affair, hearty Sunday lunch food, lots of children, very bright sunny autumn day, splendid.

Home at 6.00 watched telly and went to bed sober and early.

Monday, 18 October 1993

Press launch of *Stalag Luft*, screening and photo-call and all that. Took place at the Imperial War Museum. Watched it. *Think* it's alright. Hard to tell. It's a good story, so it should work well. I was fat, naturally. Nick Lyndhurst and I had to fend questions from the press. They were all dead keen to know about the Elton John musical, much to the distress of the poor popsy from the press office. Tore myself away at one thirty, just in time to get home before Hugh showed up at 2.00 for writing.

Met Chris Pye of Anglia and Anthony Horowitz, the writer, for drinks and a chat about a new detective series they want me to do. At the Groucho, naturally. Who was there but David Reynolds, the producer of *Stalag Luft* and some colleagues? They had been there since the screening finished. TV people, crumbs. Meeting went okay, then John Sessions showed up with some actress who plays a nurse in *Casualty*.

Home a bit pissed and fell into bed. What a week.

* Charles directed *Brideshead Revisited* at some preposterously young age and married Phoebe Nicholls, who played Cordelia (quite brilliantly).
† Producer brother of actors James and Edward.

Tuesday, 19 October 1993

Up and just about capable when Hugh came round. Jo (sister) popped over from Huntingdon to lunch with me and James Penny, my 'personal banker'. They use some phrase like 'wealth management' that makes me so embarrassed I could scream. We lunched there. Dear, dear. Have you really come to this, Stephen? All very flattering. You are ushered in by Jeeves-dressed Messengers, all striped trousers and tail-coats. There was Bruce, the manager of the Langham Street branch where I had banked before, and there was James Penny, who looks about 10, but knows his financial onions and his commercial shallots.

Downstairs in one of the dining rooms we lunched and supped burgundy while Penny told me that my money was useless as cash and that I really should do things with it. Gilts, he felt. I have always been dodgy about all this. If I earn the money I don't see why I then have to make money out of money. But you know what it's like, they look at you as if you're mad. So I suppose I'll sink something into shares, something into gilts. The good thing is that I can afford to stop working and travel the world for a couple of years or whatever, if I felt like it, without worrying about taxes for the previous years.

The private bank is open from 8.00–8.00 and can make any 'arrangements'. If I want cash they bring it to me on a salver . . .

Came back to write with Hugh. He's written a couple of fabulous songs lately. He left and I toddled to the Groucho for a meeting with Alex Hippisley-Cox (sic) a girl who will be doing the publicity for *The Hippo*. She likes the book, which is great. People at Hutchinson who've read it seem to think it's better than *The Liar*, which is wonderful – if they're right. Stayed on upstairs to watch Norwich beat Bayern Munich 2-1 . . . unbelievable. Wonderful stuff. A goal from Jeremy Goss that will live long in legend and song. Spike Denton, the Radio London film critic was there, and Rory McGrath and Charles Fontaine the owner chef of the Quality Chop House. Spotted Jethro and nipped off to do some rather decent coke I'm sorry to say. This is going to have to stop soon. Home at 2.00.

Wednesday, 20 October 1993

Up reasonably early to go to Doug Hayward, the tailor, for another fitting. The blue whistle and flute is emerging. Hugh was round a bit late, looking at new cars and tiles for my kitchen with his wife Jo who's designing it, bless her from crown to toe.

Wrote during the day as usual, then stayed in till 10.00. Watched a video of Bill Humble's *Royal Celebration*, which was directed by Ferdy Fairfax. Very good performance from Rupert Graves. Watched a vid. of Monday's episode of *Cracker*, Robbie really is giving the performance of his life. Fabulous.

At 10.00 off to the Groucho, I'd agreed to play Perudo with Keith Allen for some programme he's making in which he's being followed around London for a day. Silly but fun. The cameras whizzed about us: God knows what they saw.

Thursday, 21 October 1993

Voice Over at 9.30. With John Gordon Sinclair. He seems in fine shape. More writing with Hugh all morning and then at 7.00 I arrived at the Tallow Chandlers' Hall for a Bowyer's Dinner, guest of old John Perkins. Most extraordinary evening. Never been at a Livery Dinner before. A lot of City figures in ermine and gowns. Fairly clear that they would never otherwise have been able to earn the right to such accoutrements, for these were bears, so far as I could see, of very little brain. A lot of pompous people in spectacles for the most part. Simply dreadful. But Perkins is such a nice man. There was the whole business of the Loving Cup and so forth, and a load of exceptionally bad oratory.

Perkins had to be back in Norfolk, so we left round about tennish and I got dropped at the Groucho for a card game. Played poker with Griff and Rory and others for about three hours and ingested rather a lot of the old Bolivian marching powder.

Friday, 22 October 1993

Writing in the morning and afternoon. Quick pop off to the Grouch for supper. Had a long chat with Bob Mortimer of Reeves and Mortimer fame. Turns out they've got a signing gig tomorrow as well, also to Leeds, but at a different time. Bumped into Z, who is worried that his C habit has been going on for too long. Takes it during the day. Bad idea. Got home reasonably early a little chastened by the thought of Z, but cheered too, to think that I wasn't in such a parlous state as he was.

Saturday, 23 October 1993

Up earlyish for King's X station. Train to Leeds, signing. Car to Sheffield, signing. Car to Nottingham, signing. The latter had such a big queue that it was as well that it hadn't been the first or I would have been late for all the others. Lots of people, all very friendly. Think *Paperweight* in paperback is doing really well, which is so heartening. Home by half past nine. Watched a bit of telly, fell into bed sober and knackered after a heavy week.

Sunday, 24 October 1993

Up at 11.00, which was really 12.00 because the clocks went back today. Spent the day preparing for the Palladium gig. This is a benefit for the Stonewall Group, part of the age of consent campaign which the Cambridge Union had been about as well.

Got to the Palladium round about half past six. Ian McKellen was organizing the affair and the usual suspects turned up, Jo Brand, Julian Clary, Pet Shop Boys and so forth. I had invited Christian Hodell to come along and mix with the merry throng. He seemed to enjoy himself mightily.

At the end of the show, walking to the party, I discovered my cab had gone from the street where it had been parked. Christ I hope it was towed away, not stolen. We strolled on Christian and I to the Edge in Soho Square. I took about an hour of it before the press of people finally wore me out and I walked home and tumbled into bed after a couple more lines and some diet coke. What an arse I am.*

Monday, 25 October 1993

Before I go any further, I must register Gary Wilkinson's 71 clearance to beat Steve James to a quarter final place in the Skoda Classic. I know this looks naff, but it was one of the great sporting contests. You, dear reader, will wonder why on earth I am going on about such a strange thing as snooker, but as the old saying has it, 'you had to be there'. Four incredible hard final reds and an on-their-

*Just the Diet Coke would now keep me awake for hours, let alone the Naughty Coke.

spot-clearance to follow. I was happy to witness such a moment.

Work with Hugh then lunch with Max Hastings at Wilton's. Max arrived late, and at the neighbouring table while waiting I bumped into Don Black* who was meeting John Barry, to whom I was introduced. Barry happens to be something of a hero, so I was v. excited to meet him. He turns out to be a very down-the-line Yorkshireman, weirdly thin fingers and hands, and very charming. Lots of gossip about Saltzman and Broccoli from the Bond days.

Max arrived and told me that if I demanded 200,000 a year he would happily pay me to provide a column. This is a strange position to be in. I could say 'yes' and 200 grand would be mine. We nattered about the Tories and he said that Major, whom he fairly regularly sees, is a paranoid figure who believes his current unpopularity is entirely down to a conspiracy of a) Thatcherite mavericks and renegades and b) media enemies. Even if Major is *right* this attitude should be hidden. A real leader would surely kick arse and establish himself? We also chatted about Lamont's bitterness over his sacking. When it was time to leave the restaurant we discovered that Lamont was sitting at the neighbouring booth. Whoops! Don't *think* he was listening. Max turns out to be genuinely anti-Murdoch. He thinks him a completely evil and appalling man. Why isn't this made more plain in the

* Astoundingly prolific and successful lyricist, often in collaboration with John Barry.

pages of the *Telegraph*? Murdoch has announced his intention to destroy the *Telegraph* within the next five years.

Got back to the flat at 2.40 and wrote some more stuff, then Hugh left. Slept for an hour before driving off to Fulham for dinner with Matthew Rice and Emma Bridgewater, his wife. Chap called Jonathan Cavendish was my neighbour at table, he produced *Into the West* and *The Severed Bride* and so forth. Turns out he's doing an Oscar Wilde movie with Alfred Molina. Bollocks. Home in time to watch video *Cracker* and *Film '93*. Barry Norman wonderfully vituperative about *Dirty Weekend*, which is clearly drivel like every Winner movie. Time for bed.

Tuesday, 26 October 1993

Voice Over in the morning, just redoing the old Croft LBV port thing. Hugh and I worked again during the day and then at 8.00 I toddled over to the House of Commons to dine with an MP.

This man had written to me last month telling me how much he loved *The Liar* and inviting me to dine with him. Intrigued I accepted. But . . .

If this is the quality of MP that the Tory party is relying on then I am happy to say that they are not long for this world. Absurd looking man with the oddest manner you've ever seen. Sounds very ungracious after I have eaten his bread, but truly . . . Very right wing in a thought-less, 'I made it by the sweat of my brow' kind of way. Anyway, went and had a line in the loo.*

Wednesday, 27 October 1993

Spent the morning being painted again by Maggi H. Not too clever at 8.30, but I warmed up and started to enjoy it. She finished off by doing two drawings of me asleep, which was wonderful! She is the most extraordinary woman. Her company is more stimulating than cocaine, but her gruffness of manner and hard glare are apt to frighten off those who don't know that she has a heart of marshmallow. She would probably retch at me saying that. Being painted by a true artist is an extraordinary experience. She's so *athletic*: all the time I heard the snap of breaking charcoal or the sweep of it on cartridge paper and the stamp of her feet constantly (and uncon-sciously it seems) readjusting her stance as, like an athlete or a cheetah, her body moved while her eyes and head kept deadly still.

Home via the Groucho, where I was supposed to meet Jethro. Unfortunately he was late, so I left without him or any C. Back at the flat Jo and Charlie were there, Charlie typed out a message for me on the computer and was generally a poppet. He's five now. Weird to think that

* See earlier.

unless I top myself, OD or get run over by a bus, I'll live to see him make 25.*

Tried to sketch up† after they went, not easy. Went off to the Groucho again to meet Jethro . . . missed him *again* as I had to get back in time to meet Anthony and Sue F. for a dinner party to celebrate the delivery of *The Hippo*, which they really seem to like. I felt a bit odd, wine and ciggies tasted strange in the mouth.

They were interested in the planning and structure of the novel and I told them that I had been writing this diary through some of it and that it would show how late certain key ideas came to me . . . Simon's role for instance and lots else besides. They genuinely didn't believe me. 'It must have all been in your head . . .' Perhaps it was, but I was buggered if I could get it out, as a glance through September will show.

Bed at half past one. Too many armagnacs.

Thursday, 28 October 1993

Up feeling v. queer. Simply not well at all. Fluey and peculiar. Lurched over to Gresse Street for a VO. Managed it somehow and then staggered back to receive Hugh for a day's work. Not very capable for most of the day, but I managed to bang down a couple of sketches: slept for

---

*Which he has comfortably done. Well on his way to thirty now. Still a poppet.
†i.e. Write a sketch.

two hours on the sofa round about mid-day. That helped a little I suppose.

At six thirty I trotted over to the Paris theatre (just two minutes walk, God bless where I live) for the *News Quiz*. Me and Alan Coren v. Richard Ingrams and Peter Cook. Alan and I won convincingly, the biggest win of the series, 20 points to 6. Quite a lark really, I managed to say the word clitoris a number of times, which is always pleasing. Then struggled over to the Groucho to see if some poker and coke wouldn't help push me out of my flu. Funnily enough it did. Won convincingly and we broke up at 12.30-ish, highly civilized. Met a fellow called, intriguingly and very Soho 50sly Nick the Basque. Home and asleep by 1.00.

Friday, 29 October 1993

Felt very bouncy and much improved by the time Hugh came round at 10.30. Worked and fiddled at sketches and then, at 6.00 Robin Hardy came round to go through the script of *Bachelors Anonymous*, the idea being to see if there was any chance of working out a rough and ready schedule. How many days shooting in France, how many in studio, how many on location, that kind of thing. Pleasant enough time chatting it through until 9.00. Then I bunged myself over to 2 Brydges Place for a dinner with Ian Brown,* Alfredo† and

* Ian Brown, film producer friend.
† Alfredo Fernandino, Peruvian founder of the club situated in the almost unbelievably narrow passageway next to the Coliseum Theatre in

Cosmo Fry. Turned out that on Booker night Roddy Doyle and party had come over after the award to continue their celebrations. Then who turned up but Salman Rushdie? *On his own.* Highly risky you'd've thought.*

Pleasant dinner, followed by two rounds of Perudo. Then, bother it, it was 2.00 suddenly. And I have to be up at the crack tomorrow to take a train to Bath. Poo.

Saturday, 30 October 1993

Struggled out of bed at 7.30 after three hours sleep, into a car driven by some maniac who wanted to tell me about his idea for a novel, 'I asked if I could be given this job specially . . .' I dare say I'll hear from him again some time.

Was being towed around by a girl called Alex Lankester, who seemed very sweet; the usual pretty leggy thing that they employ for these gigs. That sounds very sexist but it can't be a coincidence, surely? We arrived in Bristol and were met by a charming Reed Publishers rep called Andrew Whitaker. Snatched a cup of coffee in the Bristol Waterstone's and went out to meet the queue. A lot of signing, but very friendly. The manager said it was a record

---

London's St Martin's Lane. From a powerful Peruvian family, he introduced Perudo to Britain and marketed it with his friend Cosmo Fry. Cosmo Fry, elegant playboy, distant cousin, chocolate heir.

*The fatwa still very much in place then.

attendance, most books sold in such a session ever.* Gratifying. Then we went off to another Waterstone's in Bristol
where I was interviewed by a TV crew and signed some
stock.

Then we drove off to Bath where the queue was *astronomical*, really wore my hand out. Two very strange
psycho-fans turned up. Trembling, barely able to speak,
one of them said 'oh my God, I'm coming, I'm *coming*.'
Whoops. Finally got through it all, biffed off to W. H.
Smith's to sign some stock and then back to London.

Arrived at 7.00 in time to snadge over to 2 Brydges
Place again for Kim's birthday party. Highly agreeable.
Chatted to Shawn Slovo† a lot and to Jo Laurie and Kim
and lots of other poppets. Greg was on excellent form
and Hugh left at one point to pick up his nephew Hugh
Lassen from the airport and bring him back on his motorbike. Rather snazzy for a 17 year old, I should imagine,
being whisked through town on the pillion of a Triumph
by your famous uncle. Left at 1.00-ish and tumbled tired
but stupid, into bed.

---

*I think I'm right in saying that the student Derren Brown was in this
  queue and that I encouraged him to work hard at practising his magic.
  Oh dear. Condescending or what?
†The screenwriter daughter of Joe Slovo, a leading anti-apartheid
  voice. As a Communist Jew, Joe Slovo was one of the Afrikaner right
  wing's most hated figures. He became a minister under Mandela and died
  in 1995.

The American *Peter's Friends* poster.

Peter's Friends publicity shot. From left: Emma, self, Hugh, Rita, Alphonsia – it's clear I'm thinking about the *Time Out* critic.

Full cast of *Peter's Friends*, 1992. From left: Rita Rudner, Ken Branagh, Alex Lowe, Emma Thompson, self, Alphonsia Emmanuel, Imelda Staunton, Tony Slattery, Hugh, Phyllida Law.

Publicity still for *Hysteria*, 1992. I have no words.

Self.

Labour Party fundraising gala. Next to Dickie Attenborough and Melvyn Bragg.

Sir Paul Fox, the
Prince of Wales,
self, Alyce Faye
Cleese: premiere
of *The Man
Without a Face*.

With Alyce
Faye Cleese at
*The Man Without
a Face* premiere.

Publicity for Comic Relief, April 1991 – m'colleague, Hugh Laurie and Emma Freud, self,
Jennifer Saunders, Tony Slattery.

Note where I'm playing from.
Total duffer. Inverness, 1994.

Jo and my third nephew,
the most excellent George.

Carla Powell checking to see if my beard is real. It is.

I can't quite explain why I'm sitting like that: I'm going to say in order to keep
the jacket smooth . . .

Sunday, 31 October 1993

It was all going to fizzle out into a placido domingo* . . .
got up very late, shopped a little, got the papers and the
New Avenger's tapes and snuggled in for the day.

Then Kim rang to remind me that I had left a bag
behind at Brydges Place. He and Al would pop round
some time to deliver it to me. Fair enough. Then of
course, it gets later and later in the afternoon, so Kim
and Al suggest we meet at Joe Allen's for the handing
over of the bag.

No sooner sat down at Joe's than the waiter brings me
an enormous Armagnac, courtesy of a rather cute young
boy sitting elsewhere. Kim and Al very amused. We chat,
we chew the fat, we nibble dinner and time passes. The
little chap comes over to our table. About eighteen I suppose and very sweet.

'I'm sorry to be gauche,' he says . . . pronouncing it
'gorsh' rather divinely. We've all done that with words
we've only seen written down: mīsl'd and ímpious for
example instead of misléd and impīous. He hands me a
note and trots out. The note gives his name; he admires
my writings and stance on the age of consent and gives a
telephone number. Do call. Oh my.

Alastair drove me home and I invited them in for a
drink. Alastair didn't want to but Kim did so we cheerfully

---

*Spanish for a quiet Sunday, but you knew that.

bade him farewell and stayed up for hours and hours. We can talk forever, which is so happy-making.

And so the month ends.

Monday, 1 November 1993

Up in time for a Voice Over. Sanatogen Multivitamins 'Do you feel all right?' Good bloody question. Struggled back in time for work with Hugh only to discover that the *Spectator* needed my copy for the diary today. Had completely forgotten the whole damned thing. Agreed months ago during a *Spectator* lunch that I would do the Diary column for a couple of weeks. Therefore spent most of the day writing that instead of a sketch. I'm a bad bunny. Got it done anyway. Think it's OK.

Dreadful news broke about River Phoenix dying. Mortifying. So adored him. I remember changing a line in *Peter's Friends* to make a mention of him. When Emma's character in the movie tries to seduce me I tell her that I'm sort of bisexual but that I don't do anything with anyone at the moment, but if I did, she would be 'right there at the top of my wish-list along with Michelle Pfeiffer and River Phoenix'. Always got a huge laugh. Such a sweet boy. Looks as if his death might be drug-related, which is bizarre because I always thought he was a terribly straight sort of chap, all environmental concern and poppety prudishness. Oh cripes. I remember choosing him as a pin-up for the *Oldie*. 'Yum yum' I had written

... And there on the wall is a photograph of him, just above the desk where Hugh works when we're sketch writing. I'm looking at him now, so earnestly beautiful. *Running on Empty* my favourite film of his. I love all Sidney Lumet's work and he brought out the absolute best in the Phoenix who will never rise from the ashes. Oh dear, I'm actually a bit damp eyed. Bit like when Bobby Moore died earlier this year.

In the evening hastened to the Garrick for a dinner given by Lord Alexander, the chairman of the Nat West Bank. This had been arranged courtesy of Charles Powell. Arrived in good time to be greeted by Lord A, Bob as he is known to his chums. Thoroughly charming fellow: his wife Marie I had sat next to at Charles and Carla's wedding, or rather the wedding of their son Hugh. She's a lawyer with a lovely soft Irish voice and nice soft views to go with them. Then Dennis Thatcher turned up and a strange woman called Bishoff, very nice, but oddly shy or neurotic or something.

Dennis, I have to confess I took to enormously. Right wing, natch, but very wonderful. Much better read than I had ever imagined. Loves history, knows a great deal about it too and was, I think, pleased to talk to someone of my age who wasn't pig ignorant. Went so far as to describe me as a 'brilliant conversationalist'. Lumme.

Home reasonably early. Few lines, bed.

Tuesday, 2 November 1993

Up early and round to the Lauries'. We are to drive off and inspect the kitchen of my house in Norfolk. Jo has been superintendent in charge of a massive rebuilding project, of a kind that would make a Pharaoh think twice.

Hugh accompanies and we drive through a grey day to West Bilney. Amazing job has been done so far, I just didn't recognize anything. The carpentry, the roof lowering, the floor. Incredible. Simply incredible.

Spent a few hours there chatting to Brendan the builder. The architect Nigel Harding hasn't made provision for facilities for rubbish. Stupid little details, but fantastically important. I compile what I'm told is a 'snagging list'. Cannot believe Jo L's skill, commitment and kindness in giving me all this time and talent. Wound our way back, via A.J.'s family restaurant and an enormous burger.

Back at the flat waited for Sam Mendes to come round and talk about the Elton John musical. He likes the script but wouldn't want to work on anything unless it was much more interesting and dangerous and sharp. Quite right and makes me feel a prune for being involved in the thing as it stands. He'll talk to John Reid. If I had a couple of months to make it far more original then he would have loved to have done it. The swine is absolutely right. Not a swine of course. Thoroughly good man. Still only 28 and one of our best directors. Handsome too and brilliant at cricket. Tchah! Some people.

Went with him to the Groucho and we bumped into Griff there. Griff and I proposed and seconded him for the Grouch and we wandered in for sustenance. Old Jim Moir was there (aka Vic Reeves) and he joined us for merriment. Bought a couple of grams from Jethro and wandered home in rather a wired condition to watch *Stalag Luft* as it aired. Then bedness and blankness.

Wednesday, 3 November 1993

Hugh called in early this morning to report sick: or rather Jo did on his behalf. Flu, sinus, that kind of nonsense. This has left me with the day to myself. A chance to 'clear my desk' of plenty of correspondence and other dribble. A sketch didn't come though, so I biked off a mock sketch to Hugh detailing how difficult it is to write a sketch.

A car came at sevenish to take me to Alyce Faye Cleese's. We're off together to The Canteen, the Marco Pierre White restaurant, as guests of Michael and Shakira Caine. Arrive in time for a glass of wine with A F. Cleese himself is 'tired' as always and not up for fun and larks . . . hence my role as walker to A F.

We arrive at Chelsea Harbour and I watch glued at the bar as Norwich keep Bayern M. to a 1-1 draw and go through 3-2 on aggregate. Yippee. Michael and Shakira join us . . . Michael grew up in North Runcton, near King's Lynn so he harbours a secret love of Norwich City. Then David and Carina Frost turn up and we watch until the match is over. David was a fine footballer as a youth and trialled for Norwich, so he supports them too. Good dinner. I sat between Carina and Shakira. The latter is absolutely delightful, and almost impossibly beautiful. Carina is just as delightful in a quite splendidly batty way. Terribly enthusiastic about all her friends. Get quietly sozzled. Just one line in the bog, otherwise full behaviour. Tomasz Starzewski* was at another table and full of beans. Told him to be sure and turn up to the Perudo evening. Home at one-ish and straight to bed.

Thursday, 4 November 1993

Up fit and ready for the day thanks to the previous night's moderation. Jo phoned in to say that Hugh would be staying in bed most of the morning and joining me for an afternoon's Alliance and Leicester VO.

So I had to face Chris and Jeff from the Labour Party on my own. H. and I have agreed to do a Party Political broadcast for Walworth Road.† Jeff Stark is the director. We're doing it because it's actually rather a fun script. Jeff wants us to play all the parts in it, but I think it's best if we don't. For a start it'll be less work on the day and there is also the extra element of comedy to be considered that some good and unexpected luvvies will be able to add.

---

* Polish-born but British couturier, whose frocks were much favoured by Princess Diana.
† Where the headquarters of the Labour Party were then situated.

Brimped off for the VO. Hugh looking a bit pale and yucky, a bit drawn and wobbly. All went okay and I returned to the flat to climb into my best bib and tucker. Zimmed round to Emma's house. I am her date for the preview of *Remains of the Day* which also opens the London Film Festival. Em being made up by some private m/u artist, so I drink and chat to her. She then climbs into the most *stunning* top I've ever seen. Its quality is somewhat shat on by the news that it is Armani and costs £6,000. Not even a dress, for the lord's sake. Em hasn't *bought* it, you understand, they've *lent* it to her. This is what happens when you win an Oscar. Into the limo and ho for the Odeon Leicester Square. Huge crowds as always, somewhat amused to see me instead of Ken dismounting. Em, like Princess Di, leaps for the crash barriers and chats to the waiting throng. I stand on one leg looking like an arse until she joins me. Bit of posing for the paps, and then inside. Em has to wait downstairs because she'll be appearing on stage for the opening speeches and so on. I go up and find myself next to Jenny Hopkins, wife of Tony (also starring in the movie) and Greta Scacchi. Film highly enjoyable, perhaps a leeetle too long, but some stunning performances from Em and Tony. Then we trot off to the Café Royal for the party. Manage to get a line in the loo before joining the table where Kim and Shawn Slovo are already there. Slovo *hated* it, natch and Kim was less than thrilled I think. Hugh Grant and his ravishing lady are present. I quiz him on *Four Weddings and a Funeral* which he has just made. He loathed doing it, thinks he's crap in it and wanted to punch Mike Newell most of the time. Bet he's brilliant though. Also asked him about the rumour that Madonna wanted to shag him. Turns out it's true. James Fox also present: what an absolute *sweetie*. Adorable chap. Very good in the film too, in that wonderful mournful weak way he has.

Sir Dickie (Lord Dickie, I beg his pardon) came up and took both my arms and gazed lovingly into my eyes in that way he has and told me I must see *Shadowlands* . . . usual suspects also present included Kenith Trodd,* Ben Kingsley and assorted baggages. Walked home pissed but reasonably cheerful round about the two o'clock mark.

Friday, 5 November 1993

Voice Over at 10.00 for Biactol, followed by writing with Hugh all day until biffing off to the Garrick for a drink with Robin Bailey.† He had rung me up with some story about a taxi driver whose first wife had been a waitress at the Chelsea Arts Club: a painting of her hung in the bar. Would I as a member take Robin to see if it was there? I said yes, let's dine there. He suggested meet-

---

*BBC producer (yes he does spell his forename like that) best known for his collaborations with Dennis Potter and Simon Gray.
†The actor who played Uncle Mort in *I Didn't Know You Cared*, way back before you were born. Also the narrator in *Tales from the Long Room*. We had both been in the happy West End flop *Look, Look!* the year before.

ing first at the Garrick for a snort.* He turned up over an hour late. I think he's gone a bit potty. Incapable of anything other than weird conversation, acting out pretend bitterness at his career. Bit sad. We dribbled off to the Chelsea Arts and awaited Johnny Sessions who was to join us. He arrived, thank God and injected some sanity and wit into the proceedings. Drunken dinner which I hated: had forgotten what a ridiculous place the C.A.C. is. Good initials. Home late.

Saturday, 6 November 1993

Robin Hardy came round at 10.30 and we worked for hours on the script of *Bachelors Anonymous*. Ended up feeling more cheerful about it than I had for weeks. Managed to persuade him to cut a number of dodgy scenes and take a more serious view of the love story. Then shopped a bit at Fortnum's and spent the evening in front of the telly. Mm. Sober and sweet at bed-time.

Sunday, 7 November 1993

Up at 11.15 just in time to climb into a suit for Sir Charles and Lady Powell to pop round and pick me up. We were all going to a lunch at Josephine (*née* Hart)† and Maurice

---

* In its old-fashioned sense of 'gargle' or 'snifter'. A drink in other words.

† Novelist wife of Maurice Saatchi, now sadly deceased. Known for powerful, rather shocking short novels with one word titles: *Damage, Sin, Oblivion* ...

Saatchi's house in Sussex. *Very* grand. The world and his wife were there. Nicholas Soames, bless him, and his intended, Serena, Melvyn Bragg, Simon Callow and his friend Christopher,* Sir Norman Fowler, Michael Howard the Home Sec., John and Jane Birt, Alan Yentob, Christopher Bland,† Paul Johnson, Simon Jenkins, Gayle Hunnicutt, Alastair Goodlad, Grey Gowrie, Pamela Harlech and others too splendid to mention. Wine and chat flowed, all rather good fun. Signed a copy of *Paperweight* for the Saatchi child, Edmund, who is eight and very bright clearly. Josephine told me she had gone into his room last night and found him reading *P'weight*. He asked 'Mummy, what does "biopsy" mean?' Sweet.

Rode back with the Powells again and home in time for telly and bed. Without coke again. That's two nights in a row. It's becoming a habit.

Monday, 8 November 1993

Hugh couldn't come round today: meetings for his advert next week. I messed around doing correspondence and sorting things out generally. Voice Over in the morning, followed by a researcher popping round for the Clive Anderson I'm doing on Thursday. While chatting to her Alyce Faye

---

* Christopher Wood, designer. Now attached to Johnnie Shand Kydd, the photographer.
† BT chief, chairman of endless boards – BBC Governors, Royal Shakespeare Company, etc. Good egg.

rang up and asked me whether I would like her tickets for *The Meistersingers* currently wowing them at the ROH. I squeaked *Yes!* with great excitement, said to be a great production. Immediately rang up Johnny Sessions to see if he could come. Starts at 5.00 of course. He replied with equal alacrity and I spent the rest of the day in a fever waiting for the tickets to be biked round. Bathed and climbed into a suit and Johnny appeared at 4.00. We cabbed in to the Garden and ordered our first interval drinks. Sir Kenneth Bloomfield (Bromfield?) was there: a governor of the BBC, Ulster Civil Servant. I'd met him at Birt evenings, proms that kind of thing. Simon Hornby* also present.

Then the music drama itself. An absolutely knock-out production by Graham Vick, with Bernard Haitink on unbelievable form in the pit. Just sensational. Thomas Allen a fabulous Beckmesser, possibly the best acting performance in London at the moment, never mind the singing. And John Tomlinson a sensationally dignified and wonderfully voiced Sachs. Oh, I can't tell you Daisy dear, the best evening I've had in years and years. One forgets just what a great man Wagner was. This was Art, this was total magical real uncompromising Art. Genius is, I'm afraid, the only word. Unparalleled genius.

We stumbled out into the light and headed for Orso for our dinner. Ned Sherrin was there, natch, chatted to him awhile and chewed the fat. I tried to explain to Hegel

* Head honcho at W. H. Smith as mentioned earlier: the last family member to lead the company.

to Johnny: he said it was fascinating but that he knew he would forget every detail of it the moment I had stopped speaking. I know what he means. That's why I love talking and teaching: the act of reproducing ideas out loud reinforces them in the head. If, every time you read a complex book or idea, you had to explain it to someone else, you'd never forget it.

We shogged back to my place a little drunk and stayed up for hours. Johnny stayed in the spare room and I fell into bed, unable to sleep till way past four.

Tuesday, 9 November 1993

Woke Johnny at 8.15 and fell back to slumber. Dimly remember J. bidding me farewell. Jo forwarded me a letter to tell me that a set had become available in Albany. Then other Jo, Jo Laurie, rang to say that I had to go round a bed shop in Chelsea with her to choose 5 new beds for West Bilney. She turned up in a cab with Hugh. Hugh went in to work and I zipped off with Jo.

In an hour I spent £11,750 odd quid on some beautiful beds and six hundred quid on material to upholster one of them. Stunning stuff though.

Then back, through terrible traffic (State visit of TM the King and Queen of Malaysia or somesuch) to the flat. Hugh stayed for a while and then went off to interview a headmaster for the boys' prep school. I rang the secretary of the Albany trustees and arranged to see it this afternoon. Set up a meeting too with Jethro at the Grouch at 5.00.

Messed about, then the copy-edited proofs of *The Hippo* arrived and I went through them. Off to the Albany next. I think the set has great potential. I'd need to redecorate quite substantially. Definitely an exciting prospect. No children, no dogs, no noise, no publicity are their rules.

Then to the Groucho for an hour or so: scored a couple of grams off Jethro and popped upstairs for a wine-tasting, which was charming. Back home to meet one Sir Peter Ratcliffe, who is in charge of the charity for which I'm speaking at the premiere of *The Man Without a Face* next week. He told me all the stuff about the evening and when I was to make my address. 'The Prince of Wales is *delighted* that you are speaking . . .' all that sort of thing. I'm going to have to be rather good I fear.

Then to the Groucho again, bit more wine-tasting and down Old Compton Street to the Ivy, where I was due to have dinner with Tomasz Starzewski. There was a sign on his doorbell which said '9.10 Stephen . . . gone to the Ivy.' This rather confused me as my watch assured me that it was only 8.30.

Toddled to the Ivy, no sign of the man. Then he turned up. The sign was left over from yesterday . . . doh! He thought he had arranged to see me on Monday . . . in fact it was definitely Tuesday. Anyway, no harm done. Charming evening, all well. He lent me *The Witkiewicz Reader*. Back home by one ish. Read in bed.

Wednesday, 10 November 1993

Somehow an incredibly busy day on the phone. Sorting out the Perudo evening on the 17th, who's to be on my table, that kind of thing. Also, I have taken the more or less momentous decision to go for the Albany set that I saw yesterday. A lot of work needed: forward Jo Laurie and her team, but it could be something, I think.

Rang around the place trying to get references for the Albany Trustees. Banker plus two personal. Tried to get hold of Charles Powell, but he's all over the place, obviously. Managed to get John Birt's secretary: she said he'd ring back . . . which he did pretty quickly. Frankly, whatever else they say about him, he's always been an absolute poppy to me. Spoke to Carla and she invited me to a black tie dinner she's holding in honour of Colin Powell, the US Chief of Staff during the Gulf War. She's a firm friend and is inviting just about everyone in the world, so I'm *rather* honoured. What a couple.

She told me an *extraordinary* thing. Paul Johnson, whom I've only met twice (and on both occasions he has been rather scowly), and Carla were in their Catholic church this morning, Carla to pray for Nicky her son, who's having a brain scan ('too much bonking, darling. I know it. He's my beautiful son, but he does bonk too many girls.') and Paul because he's *always* in there apparently. Paul said that his wife Marigold, who was with him at the Saatchi's lunch on Sunday, is a great fan of mine and would love to get to know me better. Paul, on the other hand, when Carla told *him* that she liked me too, growled 'But he's a socialist, isn't he?' To which Carla promptly replied, 'but so were you darling, when you were his age!' Paul then agreed and said that they should pray for my deliverance from socialism. So. Carla and Paul Johnson get down in a Catholic church in London and pray for me to be converted to Conservatism. Most peculiar.

Carla was howling with laughter as she told me: well, she's Italian and has a splendid attitude to everything. Dear me, however.

Anyway, she thought Charles would be delighted to write a reference for me. He's a busy man however, so I might get a back up reference from Max Hastings.

Managed to write a small sketch: Hugh was away all day on a recce for his commercial. Then I turned to the copy-edited version of *The Hippo*. This has to be in today in order to get the thing fully done in time for proof copies to be out in December. The copy editor (Hugo de Klee . . . splendid name) has done an excellent job I think. Somewhat pernickity about the shooting scene, but very attentive. So I spent three or four hours going through that and reminding myself of it.

Six o'clock and off to the Savoy to meet Kim before the first night of *Eurovision*.* We sat and supped Old Fashioneds, said 'hi' to Neil Tennant and Julian Lloyd-

---

* A stage musical, not the peculiar television event.

Webber and others who were there then toddled to the theatre. Jo in attendance, waiting for Hugh, whom she hadn't seen all day. He fetched up at last, having forgotten all about it and only realized when he had got home and found Melissa their nanny baby-sitting.

The show was about the campest thing you could ever imagine. In fact, not very good. Made tolerable only by one astonishing performance from an actor called Julian Dreyfus.* One to watch without question. The whole 'drama' was incredibly amateurish and lumpen in structure. Some excellent farce scenes involving, of all things, the ghosts of Hadrian and Antinoüs, but somehow it was all a bit stupid. It won't appeal that much to gay audiences because they will have seen it all before at Madame Jo Jo's and a million nightclubs and gay theatre happenings up and down the country. The person in our party who enjoyed it most, as it happens, was Jo Laurie. She didn't like it when it started going on about love in the second act, however.

The Ivy afterwards for dinz. I coked up in the loo, which I have no doubt Hugh and Jo noticed. Oh dear I am an arse. I expect there'll be what I believe is called an 'intervention' soon. I keep picturing it. All my friends bearing down on me and me denying everything until my pockets are emptied. Oh the shame. Lots of wine and coffee and home by quarter to one. Then stupidly sat and gazed at the

*I meant James Dreyfus, unless he subsequently changed his name. Later to achieve fame in the immortal *Gimme Gimme Gimme*.

TV while doing the crossword and chopping more lines. Bed by half past two. Stupid. Stupid, stupid, stupid.

Thursday, 11 November 1993

Poppy day, seventy fifth anniversary thereof. A day for sitting at home and working. Bad news popped in. The legal secretary of TVS who own the lease on the set in Albany rang up to say that there was a first-comer who has now definitely expressed an interest and she feels duty bound to give him first crack of the whip. Poo. I've amassed a startling collection of references, however. One from Sir Charles Powell, one from John Birt and one from Max Hastings. All very splendid. Charles begins his with the typically, but lovably, pompous 'Gentlemen . . .' Heigh ho. Unless this chap pulls out at the last moment or can't get the right references, it looks as though I shall have to wait more.

Car came at sevenish to take me to the studios for a *Clive Anderson Talks Back*. Bamber Gascoigne was another guest, plus a chap who gives (and is a walking example of) body piercing. He had studs in his tongue, a massive spike through his septum, one through his lower lip, nipple rings, and, though this was never shown, a Prince Albert. Crumbs. I think I was alright. A very startling reception from the audience, who appeared to be delighted to see me. Much whooping and cheering. Very gratifying, but I should imagine intensely irritating to the TV audience.

Spoke a bit about the horse scene in *The Hippo* and about politics. Did my 'family values' stuff, rather hard-hitting but well received from the audience.

Shifted it from the London Studios to the Groucho for a poker game. Griff and Bob (Ringo) and an actress called Caroline. She was very sweet but introduced a game called Anaconda which all but wiped me out. First time I've lost that heavily for years. That'll teach me. Much of cocaine. Bed at Two.

Friday, 12 November 1993

Up very early for a voice over. It was in Oxford Street so I shopped at M&S afterwards. Back for Hugh, some sketch writing and normal business and then I popped at seven round to Quaglino's for dinner with Alfredo and Patrick Kinmonth an old school chum whom I've only seen twice in the last twenty years. He's a splendour, however. Painter and now theatre designer. Very talented, very sweet. Had a good dinner, courtesy of Patrick who has Quag's luncheon vouchers, part payment for decorating one of the pillars in the main dining area.

Back to my place for chat. I disappeared into the loo every ten minutes but they didn't seem to notice and popped off at 3.00; I knew it was okay because for the first time in ages I could sleep in on Saturday as much as I liked.

Saturday, 13 November 1993

Awoke at 12.20 feeling much refreshed. Went out and bought some videos at Tower Records, shopped a little at Fortnum's and then came back to eat and watch telly. Bliss. First time in ages. At six thirty off to the Lauries' for dinz. Kim and Al and Nick and Sarah. Good fun. I eschewed coking up in their loo, I know they know and I know it upsets them. Home at half past one.

Sunday, 14 November 1993

A very busy day spent completing the *Spectator* diary for next week and writing the speech for the film premiere on Tuesday. Eventually got it all done and then watched a bit of telly before packing and cabbing it to Euston station for the sleeper to Dundee.* Drank a bit of Scotch and ate a couple of sandwiches. *Huge* mistake. For some reason it gave me the horriblesty pangs of indigestion you can imagine. Bloody nuisance, acid gnawing inside me and the train hammering through the night. Very little sleep.

Monday, 15 November 1993

Next stop Dundee station at five minutes to six. Abso-

---

*I was Rector of Dundee University: by this time I think I was partway through my second three-year tenure. The honorary post, unique to the ancient Scottish universities, involves looking after the interests of the students, who vote for their rector. I would come up by train to attend meetings of the University Court and hold 'surgeries'.

lutely bloody freezing on the platform and the train was ten minutes early, so I had to hang around until my welcoming party arrived to take me off to breakfast. The w.p. consisted of Jim Duncan (the Rector's Assessor), Ayesha the President of the Student's Association (DUSA) and Dougie the Senior Vice President. Amiable people. Ayesha is actually rather stylish and splendid, the best of the three I've known so far. I'm sure she could *walk* into any job as a researcher for Clive Anderson/J. Ross that kind of thing. Sweet and bubbly. Not a fool either.

Back to Jim's house, as is traditional, to consume a large breakfast cooked by his dear wife Hilda. Lots of orange juice, black pudding, bacon and so forth. Then there was the usual hour or so of sitting and chatting, catching up with whatever issues are prevalent in the University (none really at the moment, thank God) before our first 'visit'. I've instituted this custom whereby I'm shown round a couple of different departments of the university every Court day. Bit Prince of Walesey, but they all seem to like it, and I find it 'absolutely *fascinating*'.

Actually we stopped off at Ayesha's digs on the way because she had promised her flatmates that I would pop round. They were still in bed as it happened: a couple, blond and gorgeous and tousled and studenty. So sweet. Had a coffee while they degrogged. First port of call was the Accountancy and Business School. Not very exciting you might think, but Bob Lyon the dep. head was amiable and so were all the staff. Met a gang of absurdly UN international graduates: from Sri Lanka, Saudi, Bangladesh, that sort of thing. The computer whizz, a splendid hairy faced wonderment called Roz showed me the computers and we did some internetting, trying to chase a Douglas Adams thread. Coffee in the staff room and more chatting before we slid over to the school of Politics and Social Policy. Very amiable bunch of people. Nothing actually to *see* there, unlike visits on previous occasions to other departments where one can goggle at medical equipment, labs and so forth, but nonetheless a charming group of people. Rather left-leaning which is rare for Dundee. Charles Kennedy and George Roberston both products of that school, I believe. They weighed me down with books and pamphlets.

Midday now and time to visit the Principal, Michael Hamlin. Not looking too good: bit of fluid retention under the chin and puffiness about the eyes. Not a well man, I fancy. He's retiring at the end of the year. We chatted for three quarters of an hour, he calling me 'Simon' as usual.

Time for the pre-court lunch. Sat next to a bit of an ass, can't remember his name, usual rubber chicken and split mayonnaise. Bless them. Then, at 2.00, it couldn't be put off any longer, time for Court. I dropped off three times: the first time Jim Duncan, by my side woke me up; the next two times I was awoken by a change of voice or something else. There really is nothing on earth so arse-paralysingly drear as a committee of academics discussing university business. The only time I really perked up was to repudiate a letter written by an oncologist asking how the University could morally justify the setting aside of smoking rooms to 'feed student addictions'. Per-lease.

The court wound up in record time after two hours, and I had an hour to kill before my appointment at 5.00 to address the freshers. We went to 'Pete's Bar' upstairs in the association building and drank some scotch. Lots of studes clustering round: all very charming. Then at 5.00 in I went to the 'Dead Club' where hundreds of little freshers had assembled to hear their rector speak. I had only been told this was to happen this morning, so no chance to prepare: all busk therefore. I told them that there was nothing on earth less appealing than a young person putting on a hard cynical face and trying to look as if they saw through everything and knew the world for what it was. I told them it was their duty every morning to check their faces in the mirror and to make sure that they looked lovely and open and kind and smiley.

A full hour of talking: think it went all right. Then another hour in the bar before the dinner that had sweetly been laid on in my honour by the students themselves. They had drawn lots to see who could attend, because they wanted to keep the numbers manageable. As always there seemed to be some deep desire amongst the *corpus studenti* to get me completely hammered. It was my job to circulate around the table so that I sat with every group for a fair length of time. They were all very sweet actually and welcoming. At last, tottering and with the help of a couple of lines in the bog, I was escorted by Jim and Dougie (Ayesha being off her face by this time) to the station. Another huge whisky and then the train pulled in. We're talking 10.55 pm by this time. Managed to sleep straight away, which despite the lines (both railway and stimulant) is something of a miracle.

Tuesday, 16 November 1993

Woke up in Euston at 7.00. Cab to St James's and bed for two hours before struggling up again for a Voice Over. What a business. Got back at eleven, time for opening post and a cup of coffee before a cab to Whitfield Street for a four hour photography session for *The Hippo* cover and publicity materials.

Not too bad: charming snapper called Colin Thomas and Mark McCullum and Sue F.* were present, all old chums. Tried various poses, emerging from a bath with suds, that kind of thing. Hope it isn't all too vulgar. The book is not entirely of that nature, after all. At least *I* don't think it is . . .

Left at half-three-ish, me desperate to get back to the flat and prepare my speech. In the cab back to St James's I realize I've left my coat at the studio: it contains my keys. *Arse.*

I borrow the wonderful local barber's phone and we ask Colin T. to shove it all in a cab instanter. Sue and

---

*PR and editor respectively at Heinemann, publishers of *The Hippo*.

Mark and self then repair to the Red Lion pub for a half of Guinness and so forth. Cab turns up, I'm back in business.

The speech is all right I think. I don't have time to learn it, however, so I'll read. Not ideal, but suck it. At six forty-five-ish Alyce Faye turns up looking absolutely *stunning* in a Starzewski frock of limitless elegance and beauty. We have a gin and tonic and then pop in the car for the Odeon Leicester Square. Big crowds, natch. We are welcomed by a very charming old biddy called Shirley who takes me and Alyce F. round backstage. A lot of pacing about behind the screen from me as the trumpeter heralds warm up their instruments and the screen in front of us shows the celebs and eventually, the royal party arriving.

After the fanfare and national anthem I go out on stage and make my speech of welcome. Talk about the Cinema and Television Benevolent fund and their 'work'. Seems to go well. Then escorted round to my seat in the royal box for the film itself, which I have to say I liked a great deal. Very *written*, but none the poorer for that. Intelligent and humane for the most part and containing quite simply the best child performance I have ever seen. Really a brilliant boy called Nick Stahl: quite remarkable, as good as Jodie F. in *Taxi D*. Mel Gibson too, a fine performance and well directed. Not a big film, or a possible cult film, but a *good* film: to be proud of.

As soon as it was over I was whisked downstairs to

meet the P.o.W. He was very matey and said to me 'You *did* write that speech didn't you?' I said, 'indeed I did, sir.' He said, 'Mel Gibson asked me if you had written it yourself, and I said indignantly, "of *course* he did!"' Introduced him to Alyce Faye and they chatted a bit about Cleese and *Frankenstein*.

We got in the car after HRH had gone and went all the way to Planet Hollywood where the party was. Stayed for a voddie and then to the Ivy for dinz. Parties are so ghastly at Planet H. really. Nice dinner in fact. Chatted for a while. Alyce Faye said that she (and John) thought my short writings were better than my novels. I was very stung by this. I sensed that *The Liar* was just the sort of thing that Cleese would not like, because, despite, or perhaps because of, his comic genius he does not seem to understand the profound truth that comic things are more serious than serious things. More serious and truer. It's part of his guilt at being a comedian, and reflected in his absurdly high doctrine of abstract spiritualist writing like the *Tibetan Book of the Dead*, Gurdjieff, Coelho and that kind of bogus baloney. If he had ever read a true mystic like the Author of *The Cloud* or Mother Julian he would know that abstraction and unearthed thinking are foreign to true spirituality. I tried to get some of this across. I don't know if she understood. Annoyed with myself for being so stung, however. Bed lateish.

Wednesday, 17 November 1993

What a strange day. It began early. Horribly early. It began with *The Big Breakfast* for Channel 4. I had agreed that I would go on to help plug Perudo. Cosmo Fry had asked and I, softy that I am, had consented. Felt a bit grumpy on the way to . . . god rot it . . . *Bow*. I knew that when it was over I would have to charge off in another car to go all the way over to Wandsworth for another sitting with Maggi.

Once we arrived though, the frantic and friendly spirit of the programme cast all gloom away. You'd have to be very churlish not to be engaged and charmed by the silliness of the show's spirit. I played a little Perudo with Chris Evans the presenter and did some links. I gave a 'Showbiz Tip' about how to speak in cold weather without steam or vapour coming from your mouth. The technique is to suck an ice cube. They liked this very much and for the next link I was shown sucking some ice. I took it out of my mouth and – you'd better believe it – lots of vapour streamed out. Very stupid I felt.

Car took only fifty minutes to get to Maggi's in the end. Pretty good session in fact, probably the last this year. Maggi told me an amusing story about Margi Kinmonth, cousin of old schoolfriend Patrick Kinmonth. (This is going to be confusing: a Margi and a Maggi . . .) I'd met Margi at Ferdy Fairfax's* lunch not so long ago,

*Director of series 3 and 4 of *Jeeves and Wooster*, sadly snatched from the world way before his time.

anyway it turns out she's doing some kind of documentary with Dawn French. The purpose of this doc. is to show how wonderful it is to be fat. This will help Dawn sell her collection of clothes for the larger woman, as well as pushing this idea that being overweight should not be seen to be a stigma. Patrick had had a bit of a tiff with Margi about this previously: he had ventured the opinion that fatness is not wholly desirable and that there are sound reasons why we usually find it unpleasant to behold in both others and ourselves. Margi wouldn't hear this and trotted out all the usual 'Fat Is A Feminist Issue' arguments. Anyway, that's by the by. Margi yesterday approached Maggi Hambling and asked if Maggi H. would allow herself to be filmed while painting Dawn as part of this fatumentary.

Maggi, who is an artist and not like others, replied that a) she never allowed cameras to shoot over her shoulder while she worked and b) she usually paints women nude, but that presumably that would be what Dawn wanted? Well, slight ums and ahs from Margi K. at this. Nude? Um, as in *naked*? Well, says, Maggi, not deliberately trying to rootle out hypocrisy, surely the whole idea of this is that it's a celebration of *flesh* and plenty of it? Great gulps of embarrassment from Margi K. Poor old Dawn: if she refuses to be painted nude with her tummy spread out like a pool of lava she will look as if she doesn't really mean what she is saying. On the other hand, one can't really blame her for preferring to keep her clothes on, can one?

I, being far less beautiful than Dawn, kept my clothes very firmly on and we spent a merry four hours together.

At one o'clock a car came containing Rebecca Salt to take me off on a signing tour around town. What a week.

First port of c. was Waterstone's in the Charing X Rd. Good queue, not too many mad people, fairly amiable. Then across the road to Books Etc. for an informal stock signing. Round to Hatchard's in Piccadilly for more stock signing. *P'weight* is actually number one of all sellers in Hatchard's at the moment, which is rather pleasing. Afterwards we went off to the Strand: there was a shop there to sign at round about the 5.00 o'clock mark. It being 4.00 Rebecca (and Lynne Drew from Mandarin who had joined us) suggested we pop into the Waldorf for tea. They'd booked a table, knowing there would be this hour gap. I was secretly a bit miffed that they hadn't got the timing better and indeed the locations. Why not Hatchard's last so that I could just walk to the flat? Heigh ho.

Curiously the table we were shown to was for six. 'Ha ha,' I thinks, 'plots'. 'Is this the right table?' I wondered. 'Well, you never know who might turn up when you have tea at the Waldorf,' Rebecca said. Something definitely *up* I reasoned. Sure enough John Potter suddenly walks in, the *capo di tutti capi* at Reed Books. Followed by Helen Fraser, head of Heinemann, and Angela, managing editor. Well, well, well.

It was very sweet: they wanted to feast me for sales of *The Liar* passing the half million mark. I was very touched.

But then . . . *then* . . . Sister Jo walks in too! Quite wonderful and v. touching. They presented me with a leather bound, gold tooled, head and tail-banded, edition of *The Liar.* Very sweet: nearly cried. Gorged on tea and cakes and then Jo and I cabbed it to the flat. Just time to change and bath for the walk to Northumberland Street where the Perudo tournament was taking place. Hugh arrived at seven and off we trotted.

The Royal Commonwealth Hall or Institute or somesuch was the venue. It slowly filled up with all the usual suspects. Plenty of the cool and splendid crowd. Actually mostly sweet. It was in fact round about 8.30 before I could get to the microphone and address the company in the guise of The Gamesmaster. Fairly complicated tournament rules, but everyone playing with great spirit and dash and splendour. I was at a table with Peter Cook and Carla Powell and Alyce Faye and (hurrah!) Jethro, Spike and Jo and Hugh. H. was busy cutting his commercial in his head and went fairly soon. We played informally as we had a bye into the next round.

After nearly two and a half hours half the teams had lost and I was able to announce the pairings for the next round. But by this time it was half past eleven and frankly time to leave with Peter and Lin Cook and Alyce Faye and Tomasz and David Wilkinson and others for Peter's birthday party dinner, which was in Gran' Paradiso, Pimlico. Actually, a hell of a shame to have to leave: I would much rather have stayed. I scored a couple of grams from

Jethro and B. and would have happily remained. Not to be, however.

The Cook party was fine. Alyce Faye and I talked a bit about J. Cleese, a subject I can never tire of, him being such a comic hero and all. He had not come because he'd just completed a day's filming with Robert de Niro at Shepperton and felt he'd done badly.

'Ken was disappointed in me,' was his verdict. I tried to explain to A F that this was unlikely. Left at 1.15 and bed after the crossword.

Phew! It's been a strange old time. From the Big Breakfast to the Big Tea, to the Big Dinner. Non-stop since the sleeper to Dundee really.

Thursday, 18 November 1993

Not quite such a frantic day. Stayed in most of the morning: Hugh still editing his commercial. At 12.15 Mother popped round to take me out to Fortnum's for lunch. She is doing something in the House of Commons at 1.45. Something to do with Harriet Harman and a women's thing. Never quite got to the bottom of it. The state opening today, so traffic in London ghastly.

We had a very pleasant lunch and I put her in a cab at one thirty. Back to the flat: Hugh not able to come round because of editing and so forth. I rang Christie's because I had heard that a couple of Oscar Wilde letters were coming up for auction: put in a bid of five thousand for the first and fifteen for the second. Couldn't turn up for the sale itself. Stayed in till six and decided to pop round to the Groucho to see if there would be any poker. Keith Allen and Simon Bell were present so I sat and drank with them for a while, joined by Jim Moir (Vic Reeves) and a couple of others. At eight o'clock Keith, Liam, Simon and I went up to play. Keith's agent, known as T. kibbitzed happily. I won a fair bit, we all ingested a goodly quantity of white powder and I stayed sensible enough to bed myself at 1.00.

Friday, 19 November 1993

Car at 7.00 to take me to Shepperton. Hugh and I had agreed to film a Labour Party Political Broadcast. We play a couple of shady tax advisers, Weaver and Dodge who advise a procession of fat cats how to avoid tax. There was Roger Brierley (Glossop in the first two *Jeeves and Woosters*), Robin Bailey, Jeremy Child and Tim West. The idea was to demonstrate that Tory tax loopholes for the rich could save billions for the exchequer.

At lunchtime Robin Bailey, who hadn't shot yet, was in a foully cantankerous temper. A cuntankerous cuntmudgeon, in fact . . . ordering the producer's assistant and first AD around as if they were skivvies. Hugh took against this hugely and was (rightly) rather curt when Bailey tried to communicate with him. Bailey extremely sensitive to this and not pleased at all. He's barely sane at the moment and the whole thing was somewhat embarrassing. At last he went. By this time it was apparent that we would be shooting until late. Jo and Hugh had invited Greg, Kim and Alastair round for dinner and Hugh felt put upon, simply because he hadn't been warned that shooting would take so long. If the Labour Party is as inefficient as this when it comes to running the country, we're all for the basket as Georgette Heyer characters would say.

At three in the afternoon I learnt that my bid had been successful for the Oscar letters . . . asked to remain anonymous. Four thousand for the first, thirteen for the second. All told a total of £18,700 with commish. Gulp!

The filming dragged on and on. Jeremy Child a charming fellow, *seems* to be the absolute archetype of an Etonian baronet, which he is, but clearly – by volunteering for this gig – he does not vote along with most of his class. He told an amusing Jimbo Villiers* story. Jimbo had been talking about Simon Williams who had been having a ghastly time in a play and filming and visiting his mother (since died) in hospital. Driving about four hundred miles a day. 'I hope he isn't energizing himself with the ingestion

---

* The magnificent James Villiers (pronounced the smart way to rhyme with 'millers'). In the 1960s he was apparently twenty-somethingth in line of succession. John Osborne was said to have produced a typed list of the nineteen from the Queen downwards who came between Villiers and the throne. He had this list mimeographed and distributed to friends: 'If you meet anyone on it,' he ordered, 'kill them and before we know it Jimbo will be King and it will be Gin and Tonics for everyone for ever.'

of some kind of comical pastille,' Jimbo said. Splendid phrase. The time wore on and on: eventually we were released by 11.00. Hugh not best pleased, partly brought on by the knowledge that he had made himself look grouchy. 'Twenty people now hate me,' he said. Oh dear. Made me feel guilty for being by and large cheerful all day. Of course nobody hates Hugh. Can't be done.

Got to Tufnell Park, where Kim, Al and MU* were there and Jo. We stayed about an hour and then MU took us in his car back to my place where we stayed up drinking and coking till 5.15. Naughty.

Saturday, 20 November 1993

Up at 1.15, slightly hung over and feeling like a piece of shit. Just time to do one or two things before making it over to the Coliseum to join Kim and Al for the first night of *Lohengrin* by the ENO.†

They had borne up splendidly after the ravages of the night. The show itself was excellent. Not up to the *Meistersingers* at the ROH, but still excellent. Fascinating design by Hildegard Bechtler. Worked especially well in the First Act. Slight embarrassment in the third, when the front white curtain wouldn't fly out and they had to stop.

---

*Made Up (to protect identity).
†English National Opera Company, resident at the Coliseum Theatre, when not on tour with their English-language productions of the great opera repertoire.

Audience naturally laughed and sniggered. Still, fine night and excellent performances. Very cute young man played Gottfried (or Godfrey as they rather oddly called him). Still don't really go for the translations.

Supper afterwards at 2 Brydges Place, which was very pleasanty. Had sausages and fried camembert in front of the fire and Rod, owner with Alfredo, gave me a form to become a member, since (embarrassingly) I've never actually belonged.

Bed at midnight and a long, long, long, long sleep.

Sunday, 21 November 1993

A very very quiet Sunday. As placido a domingo as you could wish. Up round about one-ish: lots and lots of correspondence to sort out and plenty of television to watch. Retired early (well, twelve) and gazed at *The Parallax View* in bed. Part of BBC2's 'it was thirty years ago today ...' Kennedy celebrations. Um, not sure celebrations is the word. Memorial. Oddly, C. S. Lewis died on the same day, but naturally his death was somewhat overshadowed. Interesting idea for a TV play or story: someone whose death, or achievement, or whatever, is completely cast in the shade by a massive, earth-shattering world event.

Monday, 22 November 1993

Voice Over this morning. Some training film with Griff as a manager. Only took fifteen minutes and then I taxied myself to South Kensington to pick up the Oscar letters. Marie Helene, the leading books and autographs popsy, was very friendly, as well she might be after being written a cheque for 18,997 bleeding quid. She also showed me Henry Blofeld's collection of P. G. Wodehouse firsts and unusuals. Simply wonderful. Simply, simply wonderful. But rather terrifying. They're going to be sold singly, rather than as a lot, which is a bore, since some of them will go for rather an amount I fancy. Poor old love has come unstuck as a result of Lloyd's* I gather. A lot of Names must be selling stuff: good for people like me and for Christie's and Sotheby's.

Back in time to do some writing with Hugh and then, at three thirty, off to Cambridge for a dinner. Paul Hartle's idea this. Paul was a young don at St Catharine's when I was at Cambridge: he's now Director of Studies in English there. Me, Nigel Huckstep (old chum from Cambridge, but a few generations older), Rob Wyke (ditto: currently housemaster at Winchester), Emma Thompson, Annabel Arden and Simon McBurney† all gathered to reminisce

---

*Lloyd's, the insurance organization, had suffered catastrophic losses, which were passed on to the Names who subscribed to various underwriting benches, in their jargon. Henry Blofield the cricket commentator (brother of the man after whom Ian Fleming named his most infamous Bond villain) sadly came out a loser.

†Simon is the much-praised founder and leading light of Théâtre de Complicité, a hugely successful company that has won more awards than any other of its kind all over the world. Annabel now mostly directs opera but collaborated many times with Simon McB.

and eat a good dinner in a private room in Cats. Partly to celebrate the fact that Annabel is spending this year as Judith E. Wilson Fellow at Cats. What a Judith E. Wilson Fellow is I never quite understood, but she teaches and lectures and seems to be enjoying herself enormously. Anyway, wonderful dinner, lots of wine and drink, in quantities that only academics know. Glen Cavaliero* showed up in Paul's rooms for the preprandials. Everyone cheery and on good form. Emma wearing her severely anti-glam Posy Simmonds round spectacles. Got highly squiffed and fell into bed in Paul's rooms at one thirty. Tomorrow I have to do this Camp Christmas thingy. Yuk.

Tuesday, 23 November 1993

Up at nine-thirty, a little hung over. Then I struggled over to Queens' to pop into an undergraduate's room for coffee. She had written disconsolately that I had done the Cambridge Union debate, but failed to do something or other for BATS† that she had asked me to turn up for. She and a knot of fresher friends stood around goggling at me while I tried to be cheerful and fun. Odd occasion. So squeaky clean and non-smoking and bright-eyed and lecture-attending. Escaped at ten-thirty and headed for

---

* Adorable old-fashioned English don at Cambridge. Great expert on those marvellous Powys siblings, John Cowper, Llewelyn, Philippa and T. F.
† Queens' College's drama club.

London. Was back by midday, where Hugh awaited. We wrote for most of the day and then I cabbed it to LWT (or *The London Studios* as the place now calls itself) for this Camp Christmas. Oh dear, oh dear, oh dear, oh dear. Horrid idea, why did I ever consent? Had to dress up as Santa and make up all my own lines, without rehearsal. Ghastly and under-rehearsed. Absolutely hopeless. Julian Clary sensibly an off stage voice. Everyone connected with it was gay. Lie Delaria was excellent doing her dyke act, but otherwise it was grim. Good Australian doing a Queen's Speech, Quentin Crisp filmed in New York, Martina Navratilova phoned in to say hi, Simon Callow and Antony Sher did something strange and then, at the end, I came on being dreadful. Completely hidden in a beard, so no one knew who the hell I was anyway. Lost steam and was simply very very bad. Christ, how embarrassing.

Zoomed straight off to the Groucho to recover. Bumped into Tim Roth of all people. Very fun to see him: he's over here filming something for the Beeb. Hung around chatting with him and his new wife. Don Boyd and Hilary turned up with Rufus Sewell and I was able to congratulate him on his excellent performance in *Arcadia*. Seemed a nice bloke, freakily handsome. Played some Perudo and escaped by 1.30. A highly drunken young man in a covert coat kept sitting too close to me . . . turns out he is the editor of the *Sunday Times* magazine or somesuch. Also the director Roger Pomfrey kept trying to score coke off me, which I find discomfiting. Relief to escape. On the way out, Greg from Channel 4 (can't think of his surname) told me that I had really opened a can of worms by writing in the *Spectator* and then saying on Clive Anderson that there were two gay men in the Cabinet. John Junor had written an article in the *Mail on Sunday* saying why didn't I have the guts to name them? This ignored the thrust of my argument, which was not to accuse them of a crime but to accuse them of hypocrisy in their insistence on telling us how to live 'core value', 'back to basics' lives. And in the *Standard* someone had written an article pointing out that Rory Bremner had done a sketch which had himself as John Major saying 'Portillo, Lilley* . . . don't think I can't see what you're doing at the back there.' On my return to the flat I wrote a note to Sir John Junor, but probably won't post it. No point really.

Wednesday, 24 November 1993

A day of quiet achievement. Ho, bloody ho. Started with a voice over for Intel processors. Stopped off at Fortnum's to buy sister Jo her birthday present for the day after tomorrow. Then round to Berry Bros and Rudd to order wine for Christmas. Simon Berry was in and I had a nice chat with him. Ordered some excellent stuff.

Back at the flat by lunchtime. Hugh was late: had a press screening of his series *All Or Nothing At All*. He was char-

*Who turned out not to be gay at all, for the record.

ismatic as ever, but I didn't especially like the script. One day Hugh will find the right material and emerge either as James Bond or something that will make him a world star. He has that star quality that I so noticeably lack. I just hope that people won't think I'm jealous when the day comes. Back to the flat at four-thirty in time only for an hour or so's writing and then he puddled off. He had time however, to speak to me man to man, as besto chummo, about *Bachelors Anonymous*. He put it to me as delicately as he could: 'Stephen,' he said, 'are you *sure* you want to have anything to do with it?' No sooner were the words out of his mouth (my *God* he is wise, that one) than I knew he was right. Secretly, inside (haven't even confided in you, Daisy Diary, dear) I have felt that a) the script is absolutely unrescuable tosh and b) Robin Hardy is not a man I can spend months and months with comfortably. Hugh pointed out that I was too modest or too flattered to realize that he had asked me to direct the movie simply because that put him in a position to be able to raise money for it. I should be aware of that and proceed only if it was the *right* project, not simply out of gratitude to a nice man who wanted me involved.

Heartrending conversation with Lo, who was wonderful and promised to ring him and pull me out. She rang back an hour later to say that she had succeeded, but that he was deeply distressed and angry. Gulp! So much easier to apply the surgeon's knife at the *inception* of these projects. Why am I such an arse?

Hugh said 'if you want to direct a film, then write one yourself: let it be as personal and as wonderful as you want it to be. If it's halfway decent an idea, money can be raised. Be aware that your name does mean something.' This has inspired me to be careful of Other People's Projects. About bloody time, Stephen.

Hugh popped off at 5.30 and I messed around till eight-ish, driving my own cab to Battersea/Wandsworth/ Clapham, where Ian Hislop and his wife Victoria live. Quiet dinner *à trois*: strangely and comfortingly bourgeois house, rather like Dan Patterson's. Modish stencilled wall-paper and perhaps over-tidy faux antique chairs. No books that I could see or any life or mess or splendour. Odd compared to Ian's thrillingly disorganized *Private Eye* office, especially given how literary both Ian and Tori are. But a delightful dinner. I think Ian is all right, not untrustworthy: I think he knows the difference between a private dinner and usable gossip. For some reason I shot my mouth off about knowing Tristan Garel-Jones and talking to him about the age of consent and meeting Ken Clarke and all that. Hope he doesn't publish or I'll feel an arse. Back home by about twelveish. Crosswords and coke, then bed. Idiot.

Thursday, 25 November 1993

Just a plain old writing day. Hugh round at the usual hour and then a lot of chat, hysterical laughter and trying to get sketches out.

In the evening went off to the Groucho and played poker. Won a heap, snorted a heap. Also present Rory McGrath, Griff, Keith Allen. All the usual suspects. Bed at three. Twice damned villain. Watched the recordings of the Labour Party broadcast which had gone out at nine and ten. Seemed okay in my haze.

Friday, 26 November 1993

Hugh and I did a spot of work before zipping over to Holland Park for lunch with David Liddiment at the new Joe Allen/Orso restaurant, Orsino's. Liddiment is the man who's replaced Jim Moir* as head of Light Entertainment at the BBC. Tall, thin, glasses, Mancunian accent: seemed wildly unfriendly at very first glance. Turned out to be shyness, rather a decent sort really. Good that we touched base with him, I think. Decent grub.

Back home for me, and off to the dubbing studio for Hugh. More work on his Cellnet commersh. At seven-thirty I walked over to the Paris studios to record a couple of *Just a Minutes*. Think they went alright. I was against Peter Jones and Paul Merton. The first one had Pete McCarthy† as a guest, the second had Jan Ravens.‡ Jan excelled at her silly voices and impressions. Merton

---

*Not the same person as Vic Reeves.
†Comedian and writer, sadly taken from the world by cancer in 2004.
‡Fellow Cantabrigian: she directed our 1981 Footlights show *The Cellar Tapes*, voiced for *Spitting Image* and starred in *Dead Ringers*.

and Jones were splendid as ever. I my usual self, I suppose. In any case I won both games, for what little that is worth.

Then I had to walk very fast indeed to Le Caprice, for dinner with the Cleeses, Marilyn Lownes,* the Lauries and Bill Goldman. I had said I would be through recording by about eight thirty: it was actually 9.45 by the time I got there. Still, everyone on good form and enjoying the chance to use me as a friendly butt. Bill Goldman, as ever, spilling over with rich advice on how to proceed with the film business. I wish I had his *huevos*. Chucked it in at about twelve-ish. Ended on a sour note, though. There was a cluster of paparazzi outside the restaurant, Hugh did the sensible thing and zoomed out through the kitchens. I went ahead on my own and left John C. to do the same.

Saturday, 27 November 1993

Stayed in cheerfully most of the day, emerging at seven to cab it to Hammersmith. Ben (Elton) on at the Apollo. Saw him backstage first: Phil McIntyre† very sweetly had arranged a free bar backstage. Lots of dahlings present. Em and Ken, Hugh, Ade and Jenny, Bob Mortimer, Rik

---

*Better known as Marilyn Coles. Highly intelligent and deeply charming, she married Victor Lownes, the American boss of *Playboy*'s British operation.

†Ben's long-time manager. Still 'in post'.

Mayall . . . all sorts. Ben on stunning form. Christ, those arseholes in the press who go on about him as if he is the quintessence of modern PC evil . . . they haven't the faintest idea, they really haven't. If it weren't enough that he is the gentlest, kindest poppet in the world, he is also so much funnier and cleverer than they realize.

The party afterwards was just absurd. Too much voddie for the undersigned. And a whole deal too much of the old Bolivian marching powder too. X at one point, wanted a line, so I chopped him one in the loo. Y fully on the stuff too. I left at two and the joint was still jumping.

Sunday, 28 November 1993

Sunday papers and coffee. Norman Fowler is 'consulting his lawyers' after the Labour Party Broadcast had suggested that he had gone from privatizing National Freight to being on the board of the new company. 'They never mentioned that nine years passed between the two acts,' he (perhaps rather justifiably) complained. Oh dear, oh dear, oh dear. I feel a bit sorry about this as he's one of the few of that generation of Thatcher's cabinet I really admire. The AIDS epidemic landed in his lap when he was Health Secretary and, since retiring, he has continued to work and proselytize in the sector when he has no reason to other than moral decency.

To the Cleese's for Alyce Faye's son's wedding. A lot of the Nile holiday crowd were there. Peter Cook, Bill

Goldman, Ian and Mo Johnstone, Tomasz Starzewski etc. etc. Wedding went all right, rather chilly in the garden grotto. Good food and wine and, afterwards I made a small speech, as requested by Alyce Faye. Then a few rounds of Perudo with Peter C., Tomasz, Martin and Brian King. I skipped at three-ish, having arranged that Bill Goldman would come round at eight to examine my computer.

This he duly did. He's just bought a Mac and wanted to know how they worked. Not what you would call technophile, Bill, but he gasped and wowed appropriately when shown what a Mac can do. We then trotted off to Le Caprice again for dinz. I still have to rub my eyes and pinch myself to believe that I know the man who wrote *Butch Cassidy* and *Marathon Man* and who inspired me so much with *Adventures in the Screen Trade*.

Monday, 29 November 1993

A day working with Hugh, rather thrown off course by Emma Thompson arriving at twelve to have her script rescued. She had been writing her screenplay of *Sense and Sensibility* on a Mac, using Final Draft. Somehow it had all got corrupted. They saved it all, but lost the formatting and so on. I managed to get it all back in shape for her, but the defragging and so on took a very, very long time.

She is rather keen for Hugh to play Colonel Brandon and equally keen, so far as I can see, for me to play no one at all. Heigh ho, quite right, no doubt.

Off to Chris Beetles gallery at six. They were holding some kind of party and sale of illustrations on behalf of the NSPCC. All the usual suspects present, Cleese, Terry Jones, Terry Gilliam, Lord Archer, Frank Thornton* (all right, he's not really a usual suspect) and many others. Stayed for a while, signing T-shirts before the Terrys persuaded me out for a bite to eat. We decided on Groucho's.

Got very blasted on a lot of wine. The Terrys left and then I stayed behind, getting even drunker with Griff and Helen Mirren. Home at one.

Tuesday, 30 November 1993

An exciting day. I knew it would be my first evening in for ages. Galleys of *The Hippo* arrived. I *hate* the type-face they have chosen. What can I do? It's a Palatino, the most annoying feature being really irritating 'inverted commas' not curly like 'these', but naffly straight and horrid. In fact the type-face I'm using here is much better. Theirs is stark and clunky and just plain foul. Bollocks.

Hugh and I didn't manage to write much: we watched the Budget instead and started reading Emma's screen-play, which I had printed out for Hugh at her request. She's actually done a smashing job. It really reads well: I was in floods of tears, absolutely loving it. Such a great story, of course. Hugh would be excellent as Brandon.

---

*The immortal Captain Peacock in *Are You Being Served?*, of course.

But top marks to Emma, really brilliant work. The cunt of it is that she's right, there is absolutely *nothing* in it for me. Boo hoo. It could make Hugh a star, which he thoroughly deserves,* but yours truly is going to be a bit of a stay-at-home naffness, while Hugh jets off to Hollywood as Mr Big. I have always known that this will happen, but what will come hard will be everyone's sympathy for me . . .

Bed reasonably early and totally sober.

End of month, daisy, time for a print out.

And there, for good or ill, that passage of the diary comes to an abrupt end. At least it doesn't, but I seem to have lost the rest of it for the time being. Perhaps it is best to have offered you that excerpt and leave the rest to be published, when extricated from corrupted hard drives and no longer readable Zip and Jaz drives and floppy disks, after my death. No need then to protect the identities or habits of those I have protected here.

I have to be honest and say that reading the preceding pages gave me quite a turn. I have felt rather like someone groping forwards barefoot in an unlit attic, forever treading on unexpected lego bricks. Only twenty-one years have passed, but I feel as though I am peering into a wholly different world. I had no idea I was quite so busy, quite so debauched, quite so energetic, quite so irremediably foolish. To live that life and each day so studiously to

---

* Alan Rickman was cast as Colonel Brandon, and Hugh made do, hilariously, with Mr Palmer.

record it is something I do not even recall doing. I cannot even be certain who I was then. If I went back into the Groucho Club of 1993 and watched myself playing a game of snooker and disappearing every ten minutes to the gents, I am not sure I'd be able to hold back from massacring myself. How I managed to do so much working and so much playing without keeling over stone dead I cannot imagine. Believe me when I say, if you are younger than me, that you will not make it if you think you can imitate my wicked, wicked ways. Hold fast to the belief that I am a genetic freak who survived and that you are not. Do not test this assertion. *Verb sap.* as my old Latin master used to tell me – not that I listened. *Verbum sapienti sat est* – a word to the wise will do.

I have a very clear black-and-white memory of Michael Ramsey, Archbishop of Canterbury during my childhood, being sycophantically interviewed on a BBC Sunday-night programme.

'Your Grace, you are considered, I believe, by those who know you to be very wise.'

'Am I? Am I? Oh my goodness. I wonder if that is true.'

'Well, perhaps you can tell us what you think wisdom is?'

'Wisdom? Wisdom? Well now. I think perhaps wisdom is the ability to cope, don't you?'

I have never heard a better definition of wisdom since.

Certainly wisdom is nothing to do with knowledge or intellectual force. There are brilliant minds who can't sit the right way on a lavatory, and wholly uneducated people whose fortitude and humour in coping with lives that we would find unendurable shames us all.

The opposite of wisdom is generally considered to be folly, not a word much in use today. There are different kinds of fool of course. I fooled for a living in comedy shows on television, stage and radio. I became something of a licensed fool in palaces and private houses. I was a fool to my body – most especially to my brain and the linings of my nostrils, almost daring them to wave the white flag of surrender.

I often lie awake now, not for the old reason, not because my bloodstream is filled with that noxious, insinuating and wickedly compulsive stimulant, but because my mind is churning around and around wondering how as a young man I could ever have got myself into such a state. Where might my life have led me if I had not all but thrown away the prime of it as I partied like one determined to test its limits?

I do not remember that an unconscious whispered command to self-destruct drove me on, but looking back across the decades, reading the diary for the first time in twenty years, shaking my head in wonder at the reckless, impulsive, stupid, vain, arrogant and narcissistic headlong rush into oblivion that I seemed determined upon, I have to believe that a death wish was some part of the story.

374

And what possible excuse could I have to throw away the abundance of good fortune that at the time I could not believe I had lucked into and which today I still find unbelievable? Maybe that is where the answer lies.

It is such gimcrack armchair psychology that it may make you groan in dismay, but it is possible that I did not think myself worthy of that incredible luck and did all I could to dispose of it. Which takes me back to the world of my first book of memoirs, *Moab is My Washpot*, where I describe what I must hope and trust is a common feeling amongst many children: that of being watched and judged. When our race was young all humans felt it and called it God. Now, most of us call it conscience, guilt, shame, self-disgust, low self-esteem, moral awareness ... there are plenty of words and phrases that dance around the rim of that boiling psychic volcano.

This very shame might paradoxically explain my bravado, in the way that the defenders of a crass, brash boor might explain that their friend acts in the way he does because he is 'so terribly shy'. It wasn't difficult for me to come out as gay, or later to be open about being afflicted with a mental condition that has led to attempts at suicide. I continue to this day unthinkingly to blurt out things which will get me slammed in the tabloids and cause embarrassment to my friends and family. A part of me truly believes that honesty is, as schoolteachers used to say, 'the best policy' in every way. It saves being 'found out', but it also – if this doesn't sound too self-regarding and sanctimonious – helps those who are in less of a position to feel comfortable about who they are or the situation they find themselves in. Without diverting ourselves about the nature of altruism and whether it really exists, I know that I write more or less the books that I wish I could have read when I was – oh, between fourteen and thirty I suppose.

Memoir, the act of literary remembering, for me seems to take the form of a kind of dialogue with my former self. What are you doing? Why are you behaving like that? Who do you think you are fooling? Stop it! Don't do that! Look out!

Books, too, can take the form of a dialogue. I flatter myself, vainly perhaps, that I have been having a dialogue with you. You might think this madness. I am delivering a monologue and you are either paying attention or wearily zipping through the paragraphs until you reach the end. But truly I do hear what I consider to be the voice of the reader, *your* voice. Yes, yours. Hundreds of thousands of you, wincing, pursing your lips, laughing here, hissing there, nodding, tutting, comparing your life to mine with as much objective honesty as you can. The chances are that you have not been as lucky with the material things in life as I have, but the chances are (and you may find this hard to believe, but I beg that you would) that you are happier, more adjusted and simply a better person.

If there's one thing that most irks my most loyal and regular readers it is the spectacle of me beating myself up in public. I try to fight it, but it is part of who I am. I am still a fool, but I have greater faith in the healing force of time. It is possible that age brings wisdom. The spectacle of many of our politicians and other citizens of middle age and beyond gives one leave to doubt that hope.

There is a fine legend concerning King Solomon, the wisest of all the Kings of Israel. You may know the story in another way. It hardly matters. It is a good story and worth remembering.

King Solomon was being visited by a great Persian king. During their conversation the Persian king said, 'You have much wealth and power and wisdom here, Solomon. I wonder if you have heard of the magical golden ring?'

'Of which ring?'

'They say that if you are happy it will make you sad, but if you are sad it will make you happy.'

Solomon thought for a second before clapping his hands for an attendant. He whispered into the attendant's ear. The attendant disappeared with a bow and the king clapped his hands again and called for dates and sherbets.

After the dates and sherbets had been consumed it was not long before the attendant had returned, bringing with him a goldsmith in a leather apron. The goldsmith bowed before both the kings and passed to Solomon a golden ring.

Solomon turned to his visitor. 'I have the ring that will make you happy if you are sad and sad if you are happy.'

'But that is not possible!' cried his guest. 'The ring is a

legend. It is not something you can command to have made in the twinkling of an eye.'

'Read it,' said Solomon.

The visiting king took the ring, still warm from the forge, and read upon it the words: 'This too shall pass.'

If days be good, they shall pass, which is a lowering thought. If they be bad, they shall pass, which is cheering. I suppose it is enough to know this and cling on to it for some small comfort when confronted by the irredeemable and senseless folly of the world; to be a little like Rafael Sabatini's Scaramouche who was 'born with a gift of laughter and a sense that the world was mad'.

But I know enough of myself and the instability that seems to be my birthright to be sure that I have not yet learned this lesson.

More fool me.

Postarse

Since there is no preface there must be a postarse. I have many people to thank. Literary parturition can be as messy and bloody a business as the obstetric kind. This book would not have been possible without all those who expend so much thought and energy clearing the thicket of my engagements and commitments in order to give me enough time to write. They include but are not limited to my writing agent Anthony Goff and my dramatic agent Christian Hodell. Most especially, of course, I owe everything to the book's dedicatee, my patient, efficient, kind and wonderful Personal Assister, Jo.

Everyone at Penguin Books has been sublimely professional, useful, wise, understanding and fun: above all my epically perfect editor Louise Moore and her stellar team: Hana Osman, Katya Shipster, Kimberley Atkins, Beatrix McIntyre, Roy McMillan and so many others. Once again David Johnson has taken on the task of organizing the author tour events, cinema streamings and those other oddities that constitute a book launch in the twenty-first century. His skill and experience have made that sluttish side of selling so much more enjoyable than it would otherwise have been.

Thanks to everyone mentioned in this book: some of you have read the manuscript and kindly corrected my memory, others have used the Search facility to jump from one mention of their name to the next and then 'signed off'.

It was the best of times, it was the worst of times.

Illustrations

Chelsea. Oh dear.

Chelsea – seems a waste of time to take trouble over tying a bow tie but neglecting to shave properly.

Kim Harris, Chelsea.

Kim in Draycott Place, taken by self (I solved that Rubik's Cube too but months after my father cracked it).

Kim Harris in our Chelsea flat.

My beloved parents . . .

My personal AsSister doing what she does better than anyone.

In 1986, I spotted a house for sale in classic west Norfolk brick. Reader, I bought it.

From P.G Wodehouse.

From P.G Wodehouse.

Chelsea: Pipes are hard work. P.G Wodehouse signed photograph evident. As is Rubik's Calendar, which is just showing off.

Chelsea flat, at work on something. You can just see the signed photograph of P.G Wodehouse on the left.

(All author's collection)

Rowan's inexplicable ability to find something more interesting than me.

Attempting a carol. Christmas Day, Norfolk, 1987.

(From the collection of Jo Laurie)

Chelsea – damn, I wish I still had that pullover.

(Author's collection)

All the details are on the clapperboard.

(Author's collection)

Quiet, dignified downtime. Eilean Aigas, Inverness-shire, 1995.

Everyone always anxious to sit next to me on the *Jeeves and Wooster* set.

(Author's collection)

Hugh, perfectionist as he is, always stays within his character: a drivelling poltroon from dawn to dusk while *Jeeves and Wooster* was being filmed . . .

(From the collection of Jo Laurie)

Official publicity still for *Jeeves and Wooster*. I remember it as if it were twenty-five years ago. (BBC photo library)

Filming *Jeeves and Wooster* at Farnham, 1989. Sister Jo visiting the set.

Giving Charlie Laurie his daily vodka and yoghurt smoothie. Christmas, 1988.

It's that butch look again. Christmas, 1988.
Newborn Charlie Laurie, adoring godparent, 1988.
My butch look, 1987.
My butch look, 1987.
(All from the collection on Jo Laurie)

Hysteria publicity show, 1991. (ITV/Rex Features)

Backstage at *Hysteria* benefit show. Sadler's Wells, 1989. (From
    the collection of Jo Laurie)
Reading at, I think, a *Hysteria* show. (Author's collection)

(*See over*) I know what you're thinking, and you're to stop it,
    January 1991. (Getty Images)

Self, Ben Elton, Robbie Coltrane, Griff Rhys Jones, Mel Smith,
    Rowan Atkinson. (Getty Images)

An idiot and an imbecile.
Ready to lay down their lives for my country.
A blithering idiot and a gibbering imbecile.
(All BBC Photo Library)

Radio Times 1988 Christmas edition: *Saturday-Night Fry* fea-
    ture. (Immediate Media)

Hugh, Jo and I. (From the collection of Jo Laurie)

With sister, Jo. (Getty Images)

A signing at a Dillons bookshop. London, 1991. (ITV/Rex Features)
Hugh's warmest, most approving look, 1991. (ITV/Rex Features)

A profile of a liar for the publication of *The Liar,* 1991, with sister Jo. (Tatler Condé Nast)

Tourrettes-sur-Loup – my best audience. (From the collection of Jo Laurie)
Tourrettes-sur-Loup – picking on someone my own size. (From the collection of Jo Laurie)

Hugh and I revealing our weekend recreational identities. (BBC Photo Library)

Mandela Birthday Concert, Wembley Stadium, 1988. About to perform in front of 80,000 people. Not in the least nervous. Oh no. (Getty Images)

I felt comfortable and ALIVE.
Incredibly, I still have that shirt. Haven't burnt it or anything . . . (BBC Photo Library)

Self and Hugh wining, dining and pointing at Sunetra Atkinson. (From the collection of Jo Laurie)

A bit more Fry and Laurie. (BBC Photo Library)

Cap Ferrat with Mrs Laurie.

Cap Ferrat, 1991 – Charlie Laurie, by this time, rightly, bored of my attempts to amuse.

Stripey me.

(All from the collection of Jo Laurie)

Self and self the National Portrait Gallery. Maggi Hambling's completed work.

Next to Maggi Hambling charcoal portrait of me commissioned by the National Portrait Gallery. Do NOT mention the hair.

(Author's collection)

Maggi Hambling's National Portrait Gallery picture of me.

(National Portrait Gallery, London)

Taking pleasure in red wellies: life gets no better, 1990. (From the collection of Jo Laurie)

The American *Peter's Friends* poster.

Peter's Friends publicity shot. From left: Emma, self, Hugh, Rita, Alphonsia – it's clear I'm thinking about the *Time Out* critic.

Full cast of *Peter's Friends*, 1992. From left: Rita Rudner, Ken Branagh, Alex Lowe, Emma Thompson, self, Alphonsia Emmanuel, Imelda Staunton, Tony Slattery, Hugh, Phyllida Law.

(ITV/Rex Features)

Publicity still for *Hysteria,* 1992. I have no words. (ITV/Rex Features)

Self. (Getty Images)

Labour Party fundraising gala. Beside Dickie Attenborough and Melvyn Bragg.
Sir Paul Fox, the Prince of Wales, self, Alyce Faye Cleese: premiere of *The Man Without a Face.*
With Alyce Faye Cleese at *The Man Without a Face* premiere. (Author's collection)

Publicity for Comic Relief, April 1991 – m'colleague, Hugh Laurie and Emma Freud, self, Jennifer Saunders, Tony Slattery. (Getty Images)

Note where I'm playing from. Total duffer. Inverness, 1994. (From the collection of Jo Lauire)

Jo and my third nephew, the most excellent George.
Carla Powell checking to see if my beard is real. It is. (Author's collection)

I can't quite explain why I'm sitting like that: I'm going to say in order to keep the jacket smooth . . . (Getty Images)

Richard Stirling trained at the Royal Academy of Dramatic Art, and has appeared on film, television and the West End and American stage. He has written for *Harpers and Queen, the Evening Standard, The Scotsman, Yours* and *The Lady*, all of which have carried his features on Dame Julie Andrews. Richard was also curator of her seventieth birthday film retrospective at the National Film Theatre in 2005. He lives in London.

JULIE ANDREWS
AN INTIMATE BIOGRAPHY

The last of the great Hollywood musical stars, Julie Andrews was possessed of a remarkable vocal talent even as a child, singing for the then Queen Elizabeth at the age of eleven. Winning an Academy Award for the title role in *Mary Poppins*, she shot to international fame as Maria in *The Sound of Music*. Though *Victor/Victoria* successfully reinvented her screen image, her performance in its long-running stage version contributed to the loss of her singing voice. Undaunted, she has forged her way back into performance with leading roles in *The Princess Diaries* and *Shrek 2*. This is a frank portrait of an enduring icon of stage and screen who was made a Dame in the Millennium Honours. But who was Dame Julie, and who is she now?

RICHARD STIRLING

JULIE ANDREWS AN INTIMATE BIOGRAPHY

Complete and Unabridged

CHARNWOOD
Leicester

First published in Great Britain in 2007 by
Portrait
an imprint of Piatkus Books Ltd
London

First Charnwood Edition
published 2008
by arrangement with Piatkus Books Ltd
London

The moral right of the author has been asserted

British Library CIP Data

Stirling, Richard
    Julie Andrews: an intimate biography.—Large
    print ed.—
    Charnwood library series
    1. Andrews, Julie 2. Motion picture actors
    and actresses—Great Britain—Biography
    3. Large type books
    I. Title
    791.4'3'028'092

    ISBN 978–1–84782–162–1

Published by
F. A. Thorpe (Publishing)
Anstey, Leicestershire

Set by Words & Graphics Ltd.
Anstey, Leicestershire
Printed and bound in Great Britain by
T. J. International Ltd., Padstow, Cornwall

This book is printed on acid-free paper

CONTENTS

Acknowledgements

I suppose I started this book as a student, when I first met Julie Andrews at the National Film Theatre in London in 1986. Almost two decades later, I was curator of the 2005 National Film Theatre season of Dame Julie's films, to mark both her seventieth birthday and the fortieth anniversary of *The Sound of Music*. In the intervening years, I had met the star several times, in a group and by myself, and had written about her extraordinary life and career for *Harpers & Queen*, the *Evening Standard*, the *Scotsman*, *Yours* and *The Lady*. This book, however, would not have been possible without the recollections, personal and professional, of the following people, to whom I extend grateful thanks:

Tony Adams, Tancred Agius, Jenny Agutter, Elva Allen (née Wiltshire), Donald Andrews, Richard Aylott, Richard Bentine, Giles Brearley, Kitty Carlisle Hart, Carol Channing, Greg Cruttwell, Bruce Forsyth, Stephen Fry, John Hewer, Trevor Hill, Michael Jeffries-Harris, Valerie Lawson, Dilys Laye, Tonia Lee, Samuel 'Biff' Liff, Gillian Lynne, Ian McKellen, Christopher Milburn, Nancy Olson, Anne Rogers, Eric Sykes, Hugo Vickers, Ann Wakefield, Sandy Wilson, Robert Wise.

I have also been extremely well served by many libraries at home and abroad, including:

British Library, Victoria and Albert Museum Theatre Archive, Westminster Reference Library, Westminster Archives Centre, Kensington Central Library, British Film Institute, Swinton Community Library (Yorkshire), Walton Library (Walton-on-Thames), Margaret Herrick Library (Academy of Motion Picture Arts and Sciences), UCLA Arts Library Special Collections, Twentieth Century Fox Studio Library.

In addition, I have drawn from six decades of reportage and interviews, in publications including:

(US) *Boston Globe, Chicago Sun-Times, Hollywood Reporter, Lear's, Los Angeles Examiner, Los Angeles Times, New York Daily News, New York Post, New York Times, Newsday, USA Today, Variety, Wall Street Journal, Washington Post.*

(UK) *Daily Express, Daily Mail, Daily Telegraph, Guardian, Independent, Observer, Sunday Telegraph, Sunday Times, The Times.*

AARP magazine, *Advocate, Cherry Lane Music, Coronet, Cosmopolitan, Empire,* Films Illustrated (UK), *Good Housekeeping, Irish Times, Life, Look, New Yorker, Parade, People, Photoplay, Playbill, Playboy, Premiere, Radio Times* (UK), *Redbook, McCall's, Saturday Evening Post, Theater Week, Time, TV Guide, TV Times* (UK), *Woman* (UK), *Woman's Own* (UK).

I have also drawn from reportage and interviews from television stations (US and UK), including:

ABC, NBC, PBS, CNN, Arts and Entertainment Channel, Biography Channel, BBC, ITV.

And I offer my sincere thanks to any whose names I may have inadvertently omitted.

'The Sound of Music'
Words by Oscar Hammerstein II, music by Richard Rodgers © 1959 Williamson Music International, USA
Reproduced by permission of EMI Music Publishing Ltd
London WC2H 0QY

I wish to thank Robin Baker for his information on *Sing-a-long-a Sound of Music*, Neil Macpherson (special events) at the National Film Theatre, Jean O'Hara for her help with research, and Simon Moss for his excellent website and selling collection of memorabilia of Julie Andrews: www.c20th.com/JulieAndrews.htm.

I also wish to thank my agent Sara Fisher at A.M. Heath and my editors Alan Brooke and Denise Dwyer at Piatkus for all their help and encouragement with this book.

Finally, I wish to pay particular credit to John Cottrell, whose biography *Julie Andrews: The Story of a Star* (Arthur Barker, London, 1969) was invaluable in providing much of the background material on Julie Andrews' early years for this current book.

Richard Stirling, London, January 2007

INTRODUCTION

THE ONCE AND FUTURE STAR

'Two roads diverged in a wood, and I —
I took the one less travelled by,
And that has made all the difference.'

— Robert Frost, 'The Road Not Taken', 1915

On a June day in 1997, at Manhattan's Mount Sinai Hospital, Scott M. Kessler MD started surgery on his patient's throat. Removing a cyst seemed a relatively ordinary procedure, but there was nothing ordinary about the patient and everything extraordinary about the throat. For fifty years, the voice produced therein had given billions of people the sound of music.

Then suddenly, the rest was silence. Julie Andrews, the singing nun, would sing no more.

The vocal gift that had guided a bandy-legged little English girl from Walton-on-Thames on to the cinema screens of the world was gone for ever. And, in fighting back, the former Queen of Hollywood would need every scrap of the determination that had inspired one colleague to label her 'a nun with a switchblade'.

'I've got a good right hook,' she once told me. I believed her.

★   ★   ★

1

'Julie Andrews', said Moss Hart, the director of her colossal stage hit *My Fair Lady*, 'has that terrible English strength that makes you wonder why they lost India'. There can never be another career like hers. The music halls from which she sprang have disappeared. There are precious few screen musicals. And the values that shaped her talents are dead and gone.

It fell to Julie, by timing as much as talent, to buttress Old Hollywood against the winds of change. If the studio moguls saw her as their salvation, it was not long before they were dis-abused. In 1965, *The Sound of Music* rescued Twentieth Century Fox from bankruptcy. Three years later, *Star!* almost put the studio back under, and the leading lady of both films fell as spec-tacularly as she had risen. But, as a child of the London Blitz, this most unlikely film legend was always going to survive — and, in 2000, like a respectable London store, she was granted a royal badge of honour to stick on her front. As Dame Julie, she now had the best role of her career.

The critic David Thomson once called Julie's career 'evidence that people go to the cinema for reasons that escape me'. According to Sir Richard Attenborough, however, the reasons were obvious: 'Julie Andrews is, quite simply, a phenomenon. She has probably brought more joy to more people than any other star of her generation.' In the BBC's 2002 line-up of *The 100 Greatest Britons*, she was voted into the top sixty, the only actress in the list. At the same time, the success of *The Princess Diaries* and *Shrek 2* unexpectedly restored her as a serious commercial prospect — not bad for a lady whose film career was declared moribund thirty-five years earlier.

Wearing her three score years and ten lightly, Julie Andrews still convinces as a show-business Peter Pan. She has kept the figure of her salad days, standing 5ft 7in and weighing about one hundred and twenty pounds. Never a sex symbol (except perhaps to superannuated schoolboys), her long legs have always been rather too slim, her jaw slightly too strong, her size eight feet somewhat too large. Somewhere, too, is the very faintest hint of the gawky kid with the boss eye and teeth her mother once called 'the sort that could be cleaned with her mouth shut'.

Yet she has always had a rare, vital beauty of her own. The retroussé nose still surprises, and the blue, blue eyes are as clear as ever. There are lines around them now, suiting her; otherwise, her skin is as smooth as her explanation for ageing so well: 'I don't think I'd get up in the morning and give an interview without being a little prepared. I wouldn't want to frighten people . . . this business is all about image.'

And her image is as a triptych: Eliza Doolittle, Mary Poppins and Maria von Trapp in, respectively, the biggest Broadway hit of its day, an Oscar-winning screen debut and the most profitable movie then made. But, marvellous though the parts were, they only ever showed one side of Julie. There was still a long, long way to run.

★　★　★

Julie Andrews left the stage door of the Marquis Theatre on Sunday 8 June 1997, ending a seventeen-month run in *Victor/Victoria*, the Broadway version of her last film hit. Unknowingly, she had also ended her musical career.

During her final months, the star had missed more than thirty performances, suffering from bouts of bronchitis and pneumonia. The most persistent of her troubles, despite repeated medication from the well-reputed Dr Kessler, nephew by marriage to the opera star Beverly Sills, related to her throat. Half a century of singing had inevitably taken its toll. As far back as 1956, triumphant in *My Fair Lady*, Julie had been 'in a ragged state from night after night of belting'. In 1960, her tonsils had been removed, which seemed to stand her in good stead for decades to come. But, even at the zenith of her fame, she admitted, 'singing has never been particularly easy for me.'

By the opening of *Victor/Victoria* on 25 October 1995, days after her sixtieth birthday, the long-term prospects for Julie's voice had been depreciating for some while. And after almost six hundred performances of the show, she was in deep trouble. A cyst had appeared on the left side of her throat. And, very soon after the subsequent operation at Mount Sinai Hospital, Julie sensed something else was wrong. During the procedure, she later told Larry King on CNN, 'a piece of my vocal cords was taken away . . . I get a kind of fried sound, and there are certain notes that just don't appear. They don't come.'

Over the next year, everyone was quiet. Everyone waited. At the end of 1998, the star and her husband of three decades, Blake Edwards, appeared to be at odds over the issue. 'I don't think she'll sing again — it's an absolute tragedy,' he told *Parade* magazine in November. 'She was told she'd be OK in six weeks, the voice would actually be better. It's over a year, and if you heard it, you'd weep.'

The tabloid press said she was furious with him — a charge that Barbara Walters later put to her on ABC television. 'I guess because I'm private, a very private person,' said Julie, surprising nobody. 'Blake is completely the opposite and he just says what he feels.'

Her friends were more circumspect. Robert Wise, the director of her greatest film success, confined himself to quoting publicly from a letter she had written him: 'As always, the wretched press have overblown facts to such an extent that everybody thinks I'm practically at death's door. So, dear friend . . . I think you know that I did have an operation on my vocal cords and certainly recovery has been very slow . . .

'With time and perseverance,' she hoped to sing again, 'though perhaps not *The Sound of Music.*'

But, to Barbara Walters, Julie let the mask slip: 'to *not* sing with an orchestra, to *not* be able to communicate through my voice which I have done all my life . . . I think I would be totally devastated.' And, if things stayed that way, 'I think it will change something inside of me for ever.'

She went to therapy — but also bared her teeth. On 15 May 1999, the *Guardian* newspaper in England reported that Julie was considering action against the American *Globe* magazine, for publishing what her publicist Gene Schwam called the 'blatantly false headline' that she had checked in to the Sierra Tucson clinic in Arizona to combat a drug dependency problem.

In fact, declared her lawyers, the treatment in May 1999 had been for 'guidance and management of emotional issues' over problems with her voice and the recent death of 'a beloved aunt who played a pivotal role in her childhood and professional development'. Aunt Joan, her mother's younger sister, had lived to the end in the leafy London suburb of Walton-on-Thames. It was Joan who had given her dance lessons in the studio in the grounds of their house. And it was Joan who, with Julie's mother, had climbed out of poverty: just how far would shortly be discovered.

By August, Julie was still 'in some kind of denial' — which is as I found her, on the Isle of Man, filming Noël Coward's comedy *Relative Values*. As slender as ever, and invigorated by her first big-screen project for many years, she confirmed she was not giving up the struggle: 'It's been — difficult; a major tragedy for me because I so adore singing, and came to adore it in the later part of my career. I don't think I'll get back to the coloratura, which I don't need anyway, but I'm optimistic that a certain part of it will return.'

But her frustration was evident. I asked if she

would ever really sing again — even in private. 'I'll make the *decision* in private,' she said sharply, her famously blue eyes glinting, and not with tears.

Later that August, on the island in the middle of the Irish Sea, she witnessed the total solar eclipse that travelled over Europe. Never a visibly religious woman, she admitted sensing 'forces, way, way out there mysteriously keeping the world in a kind of balance. I thought, 'Ah, there must be a God.'' As filming went on, she became more and more introspective: 'The thing with the voice was very devastating — is very devastating . . . It has been my stock-in-trade, something I could always go back to. And now I'm asking, 'Who am I? What do I do?''

Four months later, she had decided. On 14 December 1999, days from her appointment as a Dame of the British Empire, the sixty-four-year-old star filed a malpractice suit against Dr Kessler, his assistant, Jeffrey D. Libin and Mount Sinai Hospital, claiming she was 'precluded from practising her profession as a musical performer' and reportedly asking for substantial damages, to compensate for loss of earnings. She had not been warned of 'irreversible loss of vocal quality', claimed the lawsuit, which also accused the doctor of operating on both sides of her vocal cords, when the right side had not required it.

On Tuesday 12 September 2000, the case was scheduled for the Federal District Court, Manhattan. An out-of-court settlement, reached in August, specified that terms should not be disclosed. However, at the end of October, the

London *Evening Standard* declared that Julie Andrews had won up to £20 million in compensation. But no amount of money could restore the voice.

While her voice had guaranteed success on stage, on screen it was her personality that shone, as Robert Wise described it, 'right through the camera, on to the film and out to the audience'. The results had been sensational. In 1964, *Mary Poppins* became Walt Disney's biggest-ever hit. A year later, *The Sound of Music* became the biggest hit of all time. Two years after that, *Thoroughly Modern Millie* completed a hat-trick of musical success. But, unlike the voice, the 'squeaky-clean image' would prove indestructible.

Battling vainly against that image, the world's top star jumped into bed with Paul Newman in *Torn Curtain*, gave agonising birth in *Hawaii* — and knocked back the gin, using what one critic called a 'mule-skinner vocabulary', in *Star!*. 'Being wholesome can sometimes be a pest,' she mused on the set of the latter film, almost anticipating its disaster, 'but I'm stuck with it, I'm afraid.' Even a strip-tease routine in *Darling Lili*, her first film for Blake Edwards, could not prevent it opening in 1970 to appalling business, putting a temporary halt to their Hollywood careers.

In Swiss exile, festering from the fallout, Blake wrote *S.O.B. (Standard Operating Bullshit*, 'a phrase Blake and I use all the time', said Julie, in case her fan base was not disheartened enough already). A decade later, they filmed it: Blake's autobiographical picture of a scabrous, vindictive Hollywood, in which a film director, ostracised for making a colossal musical flop with his adorable wife, turns it into a piece of soft-core erotica. 'I've got to show my boobies,' breathes Julie's character, parting her gown rather like a countess opening her stately home. 'Are they worth showing?'

The answer, irrespective of her assets, was in the lacklustre returns of *S.O.B.* at the box office. The plot to kill the singing nun had been made in earnest, but, to paraphrase Mark Twain, reports of her death were greatly exaggerated. Reviewing *S.O.B.* on the *Tonight* show, Johnny Carson thanked Julie for 'showing us that the hills are still alive'.

'This quality she has got, call it wholesomeness if you like, was born in her; she'll never lose it,' Julie's childhood agent Charles Tucker once said. 'There's an indefinable something about her personality that makes her unlike any other girl in the world. The remarkable thing is that it comes out on the screen. Julie's no character actress. She will always play Julie Andrews. But no one can come within fifty million miles of her in a musical.'

Finally, by the dawn of the year 2001, it seemed that Julie Andrews had made peace with her image. Going back to Disney Studios, where she had filmed *Mary Poppins*, she made her most successful film in a very long time. *The Princess Diaries* proved to be the sleeper hit of the year, grossing over $100 million. But her principal trademark, the voice of mountain

9

spring purity, was gone, as astonishingly as it had first appeared.

'The fact that they discovered that I could sing was a miracle,' said Julie, 'because I didn't inherit my voice from my stepfather and my real father didn't sing, so we wondered where it came from.' She would find out more — eventually.

1

WEATHER AND TIDE PERMITTING

'You could call it tradition. You could call it good manners. You could call it knowing how to work hard, but I call it discipline. If you have that, you can really take off'

— Julie Andrews, 2000

Julia Elizabeth Wells entered the world at six o'clock in the morning of Tuesday 1 October 1935, at Rodney House Maternity Home, Walton-on-Thames, Surrey. The healthy eight-pound baby, named after her grandmothers Julia Morris and Elizabeth Wells, was born under the star sign of the Balancing Scales, indicating what she later defined to me as her 'typically Libran' ambivalence. Other characteristics — ruthless objectivity, a horror of confrontation, maintaining a positive outlook — would not be long in developing. Given the childhood in store for her, baby Julia would need them all.

At the height of Julie worship in the 1960s, an astrologer for the London *Daily Express*, given only the time and date of her birth, concluded of the mystery subject:

This woman is a fundamentally an idealistic person, and one who has a basic compulsion for harmony. She will perpetually strive to 'strike a balance' — in her activities, relationships, aspirations.

She will have a streak of reserve, due to shyness and lack of complete self-confidence; thus, she will assume a mask of apparent self-assurance which she does not actually possess . . . The personality she reveals to the world at large will be charming, friendly and seemingly rather naïve, but there is a part of herself which she never reveals — not so much because of a desire to deceive others, but due to her shyness and sensitivity.

Blake Edwards later confirmed this aspect of his wife: 'She's still finding out about herself. She's a good lady. But she's shy.'

In one of the most negative articles ever written about Julie, *Esquire* journalist Helen Lawrenson thought otherwise, defining her as having 'a background not customarily compatible with reticence and timidity'. But there was never anything remotely customary about Julie Andrews, in personality or circumstance. Her abilities came not from her stars, but from the widely disparate natures of her parents: practical common sense from her father, and — more than she knew — artistic brilliance through her mother's line.

Her father, Ted Wells, the son of a carpenter, was a handicrafts schoolteacher, a quiet romantic with a deep love of poetry and the English countryside — passions he would pass on to his daughter. Winning a scholarship to Tiffin School in Kingston-upon-Thames, Ted had gained an excellent basic education, but could ill afford further study. After six years, he took up an apprenticeship with a local construction company, specialising in the production of transformers: there, he fell in love with a vivacious redhead of seventeen named Barbara Morris.

In complete contrast to Ted, Barbara was a larger-than-life show-business personality, helping her sister Joan run a local dance Academy while pursuing a career as a popular pianist. Julie was taught to sing and dance — 'almost from the time I could toddle' — but Barbara would play even more of a key role in her daughter's career after marrying her second husband, Julie's stepfather Ted Andrews.

This much was well-documented family history, to which Julie had always had a characteristically well-versed set of responses. Yet her lineage was more disturbing, so well hidden that she was sixty-seven before she learned the story of her maternal grandparents. Only then could she fully understand her mother's frustration and later alcoholism — and, perhaps, know herself rather better too.

On Saturday 3 July 1976, a letter appeared in the *South Yorkshire Times*. Jim MacFarlane, of the University of Sheffield, had tried to research an almost forgotten local hero, commonly known as 'The Pitman's Poet'. He knew the best-known examples of the writer's work but little else, merely that the poet had left South Yorkshire in the interwar years and that his daughter Barbara had, he said, been 'a very good piano player' — just as Julie would later describe her mother as 'a fine pianist'.

MacFarlane made the connection for himself. 'Arthur Morris, our Celebrated Colliery 'Deputy' Artiste,' he wrote, 'had another claim to fame — as the grandfather of Julie Andrews, actress.'

At the time nobody seemed very interested. In 1976, Julie Andrews had been absent from the big screen for six years (with the exception of a low-budget thriller made by Blake Edwards — himself at a low ebb — two years earlier). Her much-vaunted television series had been axed after only one season. Even so, there was a remarkable lack of effort to contact the coal miner's granddaughter.

Then, over a quarter of a century later, came sensational revelations from the research of a Yorkshire solicitor, Giles Brearley, into the history of his coal-mining community. A keen historian in his spare time, Brearley had happened upon the same pieces of Morris's poetry. He recognised them as exceptional, capturing the desperate dignity of the coal mining towns in the early decades of the twentieth century. Brearley was determined to piece together the life of Arthur Morris. After endless hours spent trawling through archives, he succeeded, and in 2004 published his fascinating book *The Pitman's Poet*.

Morris, a gregarious fellow with a fine speaking voice, had been a popular character in the mining villages of South Yorkshire, going from door to door, enveloped in a black cloak, to recite his poems. A book of his early work

— containing 'The Miner's ABC', a definition of the collier's lot — was sent to King George V. In 1924, one of his poems, 'Wembley Colliery', exposed the resentment felt by many pit families at the sanitised model colliery built for the British Empire Exhibition:

Then hats off to our miners all and hats off
to their wives,
They never know from day to day, 'ere they
may lose their lives.
And do not think our collieries are quite so
danger free
As the perfect ideal pit you've seen called
Wembley Colliery.

When, in 2003, Brearley wrote to Julie with the new-found information, she sent her half-brother up to Yorkshire to 'make sure' of him. 'You know what sisters are like,' Christopher Andrews explained.

'It was amazing that Julie knew nothing of Arthur's achievements,' Brearley told me later. 'I was astounded, when Chris came to visit, that the school where his mother had had so much happiness was unknown to him. He did not even know where she was schooled.'

I asked Julie's other half-brother Donald if the news made sense of unexplained family issues. 'I can't be specific,' he replied, slowly, 'but some pieces of the jigsaw would certainly fit into place.'

On a Christmas trip to London, Julie hosted a family gathering at the Dorchester Hotel. So voluble was she about the discovery that

Christopher had to remind her, 'Remember, Jules, he's my grandfather too.'

Previously, all that Julie knew of her grandfather was that he had served in the army. In a magazine article of 1958, she had written of him as 'a fine musician . . . a drum major in the Grenadier Guards' — but 'never on the stage'. But Giles Brearley's real discovery had less to do with Morris's work than with his life — a dramatically chequered existence, culminating in a tragic and sordid end. Barbara had died in 1984, Joan fifteen years later, keeping the full, unexpurgated story to themselves. 'Obviously the trauma felt by her mother and aunt was very deep indeed,' Brearley told me. 'Their formative years were just blotted out from memory.' Their father had been a convict and — as I confirmed for myself — both parents had died horrible deaths.

William Arthur Morris was born in 1886, possibly illegitimate, to a working-class family in the railway town of Wolverton, Buckinghamshire. Quitting his first job as a barber, he joined the Army as a volunteer in 1909 and was posted to Caterham Barracks in Surrey, where he completed training as a guardsman. The tall, handsome young soldier became friendly with a twenty-two-year-old maid from north-west Surrey. Julia Mary Ward was the daughter of a gardener from Stratford-upon-Avon, whose family had moved shortly after her birth to Hersham (then a village, later a suburb of Walton-on-Thames) to live next door to the local laundry, at Gable Cottage in Rydens Grove.

Julia, susceptible to Arthur's easy way with words, soon fell pregnant. The couple were married on 28 February 1910, one month after Arthur decided to extend his military service for another seven years, and one month before he was promoted to lance corporal. On 25 July, their first daughter, Barbara, was born.

According to Giles Brearley, five days later, Arthur Morris and his new family disappeared, absent without leave. It was over a year before the Army caught up with him. At a local Bonfire Night gathering on 5 November 1912, he was spotted and arrested. Branded a deserter, he faced a court martial, and on 18 November was thrown into the cells of Caterham Barracks, where his military career had commenced with such promise.

After a month behind bars, he was discharged on compassionate grounds, to provide for his wife and baby. Starting anew, Arthur joined the Shakespeare Colliery near Canterbury and rose remarkably quickly to the position of pit deputy, thus being exempt from the First World War call-to-arms. A second daughter, Joan, was born in 1915 — and Arthur, clearly uncomfortable with parental responsibility, disappeared once more.

In his book, Brearley traces Arthur's path north, where he took up work as a pit deputy in the more profitable coal mines of South Yorkshire. His family joined him at Denaby Colliery, outside Doncaster, where they integrated well. Joan was more reserved than her vivacious elder sister Barbara, who was, by all accounts, a happy and confident child, highly proficient at the school piano.

Arthur became a key member of the local charitable lodges. Taking part in their concerts, he performed his own poems, which he had started to compose around 1920. One of the best received of these was 'A Pit Pony's Memory of the Strike', during the industrial action of early 1921:

At last I'm on the surface; from the cage I'm
led away,
They take the cover off my eyes; I see the
light of day.
Later on my mates come up and then it
came to pass,
They took us down into a field and turned
us out to grass.
We held a meeting in that field, 'twas just
beside a dyke
And we came to the conclusion that the pit
must be on strike.

As Arthur's reputation grew, he abandoned the secure existence at the colliery for a precarious living as a poet. Moving to the more cosmopolitan town of Swinton, he continued to sell his poems, and hosted local dances at which his elder daughter played the piano; sometimes he accompanied her on drums.

Barbara's reputation was threatening to outstrip that of her father: she had by now performed in many of the towns of South Yorkshire, and twice at the BBC studio in

Sheffield. In January 1926, passing her London College of Music examination, she seemed set for a career as a concert pianist. And then the family broke up.

Arthur's success in his new occupation was in part achieved thanks to the attentions of higher-born ladies, to whose houses he was now invited — and at which his wife Julia was hopelessly ill at ease. At what point he succumbed to temptation is unclear, but he almost certainly contracted syphilis before Julia decided to leave him. In February 1927, she and her daughters went back south to her family home in Hersham.

The biggest casualty of the arrangement was Barbara, whose musical ambitions were utterly ruined. At the age of eighteen, having to support an ailing mother and thirteen-year-old sister, she found work in a Surrey factory, making transformers. It was there that she met Ted Wells, an apprentice who, eager to better himself, was attending night school after a day's work.

To boost her family's meagre income and pay for Joan's dancing lessons, Barbara taught the piano. By the turn of 1928, she had an extra burden to bear. Her wayward father, unable to look after himself any longer, turned up at Hersham. Riddled with syphilis and rendered almost insane, he brought into the house another disease to shadow his elder daughter for the latter part of her life: alcoholism.

He found work for a while as a metal polisher, but it was a hopeless case. On 31 August 1929, Arthur Morris died at Brookwood Mental

Hospital, Woking, aged forty-two. The cause of death was given as 'General Paralysis of the Insane', which he had suffered for some 'considerable duration'. Two years later, on 22 June 1931, Julia also died, only forty-four years old. The death certificate listed the horrors her husband had inflicted upon her, including tabes dorsalis: congenital syphilis. He had destroyed her, in more ways than one — but her Christian name would live on in the next generation.

Lack of money forced Barbara and Joan to move again and again, to ever-cheaper apartments. For each move, Ted Wells lent a helping hand, borrowing a builder's handcart to carry their one valuable possession: a piano. At one stage, times were so hard for Barbara and her younger sister that Ted sold his motorcycle for £12 to help pay their rent. It was an enormous sacrifice: as a newly qualified handicrafts teacher, he needed to travel as much as forty miles to give lessons at schools in five different villages. He now had to cover the daily route by bicycle, his only consolation being that he rode through some of the most picturesque scenery in Surrey.

After Ted's first term as an itinerant teacher, he and Barbara decided to wait no longer. On Boxing Day 1932, they were married at St Peter's Church, Hersham, witnessed by Barbara's maternal grandfather William Ward, and Ted's mother Elizabeth Wells. On their joint earnings, they could just manage a rental of £1 a week for a prefabricated asbestos bungalow on the outskirts of town.

Joan's dance training had begun to pay

20

dividends, in the form of a small dance school in Walton, with half-hour lessons costing only a shilling. These were held in the evening at a local preparatory school, and the enterprise was very much a team effort. Joan taught, Barbara provided piano accompaniment and Ted built the props and scenery. Often working until the early hours of the morning, he created pieces such as a twenty-four-foot model of the liner *Queen Mary* or an elaborate roundabout, his expertise bringing a touch of professionalism to the school shows.

Ted and Barbara Wells had now been married for over two years of grinding poverty. By living with Joan, they could just afford to support a family, so they moved to a three-bedroom, semi-detached brick house in the more fashionable Westcar Lane, Walton-on-Thames. They named the house 'Threesome'.

Then, on 1 October 1935, Threesome became Foursome. The future Julie Andrews had arrived.

* * *

Born in a trunk Julia Elizabeth Wells may not have been — but the other hallmarks of a show-business childhood were all too apparent. A stage mother, for instance. Barbara Wells's life revolved around the Joan Morris School of Dancing, and it was only a matter of time before the shows featured the proprietor's little niece, who made her stage debut aged two, as a tiny fairy waving a wand.

In 1986, I met Julie Andrews for the first time

at London's National Film Theatre, where she spoke of her mother and aunt's endeavours. 'Between them, with my dad's help, they used to put on these shows in my home town of Walton-on-Thames. One of my earliest memories is of peeing my pants on stage. I was about three.'

Her assurance, even at that age, was remarkable. At the local Walton Playhouse, performing a gavotte with another little girl, Julie took control of the dance when the top hat slipped over her partner's eyes. The following year, wardrobe problems blighted her solo routine in the pageant *Winkin', Blinkin' and Nod*. Co-starring as Nod, Julie wore a white pyjama suit. At a climactic moment, the buttons burst open — exposing bright pink underpants. But, totally immersed in her song, she finished to huge applause.

'Julie lived in a world peopled with fabulous, storybook characters,' Barbara recalled. 'She'd stand outside the door and cry, 'Now close your eyes — I'm coming in. Guess who I am.' And in would walk Queen Bess or a pixie or a tough little boy. We always kept a prop box with stage clothes and accessories. It was Julie's paradise.'

The precocious little girl did not attend an ordinary school. The decision was only partly to do with Barbara's stage ambitions for her daughter. Although Ted Wells was employed by traditional schools, he was progressive in his attitude to education, believing in a more individual approach. He decided to teach his daughter at home.

It seemed to work. By the age of three, Julie could already read and write, and had started to acquire, from his reading to her each night, a love of poetry. Ted also introduced her to Père Castor's whimsical adventure stories of animals and birds. These and *The Little Grey Men*, by an author known only as 'BB', a simple nature story of the last four gnomes left in England, set over the four seasons of the year, became lasting favourites.

The family belonged, nominally, to the Church of England, but was not particularly observant. In her seventieth year, Julie remembered her father as believing in nature more than anything, 'that religion resides inside of you'. Above all, Ted shared with her his love and knowledge of natural history, teaching her the leaves of the trees and the songs of the birds, sailing with her in a hired boat on the nearby River Thames. At that stage of their lives both she and her brother John David, two and a half years younger, enjoyed a normal English childhood. 'Cosy years,' is how Julie later described them, 'and all my memories of them are cosy.'

There was a time and a place for everything in Walton-on-Thames. On screen at the local Capitol Cinema good triumphed over evil, couples kept one foot on the ground when embracing and everyone went happily home to supper (a particular favourite of Julie's being boiled potato sandwiches — 'all squashy and dribbling butter'). Late in life, his daughter now one of the most famous women on the planet,

Ted Wells retained a plaintive story she wrote at this time, of a mother's longing for a little girl and boy: 'It was Chrisms, the night Santer Claus hee came to bring the two babis.' Naturally, the family lives 'hapleevrovter'. Reality would prove otherwise. The Wells family would soon be split in two, and the happy little girl would suffer considerable torment — to what extent, she would do her best to ignore for over two decades.

★ ★ ★

In the long, hot summer of 1939, talk of war was everywhere. Yet, for little Julia Wells, there was no indication that the suburban security of her childhood was almost at an end. Ironically, the catalyst was a trip to the seaside. Barbara had been engaged for the season as pianist to the Dazzle Company, a music-hall variety troupe, in the south coast resort of Bognor Regis. In July, Ted joined Barbara and Joan and his children, to make it a complete family holiday. It would be their last. Precipitously, a member of the Dazzle Company was injured and had to leave the show. The replacement was a burly, ginger-haired, thirty-two-year-old tenor, styled 'The Canadian Troubadour: Songs and a Guitar'. His name was Ted Andrews.

Each night, he was accompanied by attractive, flame-haired Barbara, three years his junior. But, before their professional relationship could become anything else, war with Germany was declared on Sunday 3 September, and the troupe was disbanded. The Wells family returned to Walton-on-Thames. Ted volunteered for the Royal Air Force, Barbara joined ENSA, the Entertainments National Service Association (known colloquially as 'Every Night Something Awful'), and Britain faced the eerie days of the phoney war, of gas masks and panicky air-raid alerts.

A rush to evacuate schoolchildren to the countryside convulsed the country. Ted, waiting to hear from the RAF, was delegated to transfer evacuees from Surrey. While Barbara performed her initial concerts for ENSA, Julie and John were tended by Aunt Joan. Then, along with thousands of others, they were displaced from their home, evacuated to a riding school in Kent, where Julie had what she remembered as 'a glorious time'.

ENSA, meanwhile, had also recruited the Canadian Troubadour. By accident or design, Barbara found herself in the same unit as her Dazzle Company colleague. This time, the inevitable happened, and the seven-year marriage of Mr and Mrs Wells was shattered.

As the injured party, Ted was awarded custody of both his children — but, in the most agonising decision of his life, he waived the right over Julie. One reason was his failure to be accepted for RAF aircrew. His war effort would be in running a factory at Hinchley Wood in Surrey, working for up to seventy-two hours at a stretch — on one occasion, arriving home so tired that he fell asleep with his head in a bowl of porridge. 'With the war work taking up so much of my time,' he

25

later wrote, 'I could not do my duty to both of them as a father.'

Ted felt that 'a growing girl needed a mother's influence', but it was a second factor that had decided him. He recognised that Julie's talent, if not her happiness, would be served by a career in show business, for which his wife and her lover were equipped to prepare her. Many years later, though, he revealed his doubts as to whether he had made the right decision, however unselfish: 'I know separation from me and her brother John caused her a lot of suffering.'

In 1944, Ted Wells would remarry. His second wife, Winifred Birkhead, a former hairdresser and the widow of an RAF bomb-disposal expert, had come to his factory as a trainee lathe operator. A year later, they would have a daughter of their own, Celia.

Having lost two members of her family, Julia Elizabeth Wells also lost her home. The thin little five-year-old girl was now to live at 1 Mornington Crescent, in Camden Town, north London. Thirty years earlier, the brilliant artist Walter Sickert (suspected of having been Jack the Ripper) had lived at No 6. Even then, the street had been in decline. By the time Ted Andrews and Barbara took rooms in the corner building, backing on to the railway tracks from Euston Station, it was a grimy, unfashionable location.

Instead of the leafy views of Walton-on-Thames, Julie now looked out at a mammoth, quasi-Egyptian temple, the entrance flanked by two seven-foot bronze cats: the Carreras Factory, home of the famous Craven 'A' ('for your throat's sake') cigarettes. While her stepfather was still alive, Julie laid her ambivalence aside to recall 'the bleak turn of events: I hated my new house and the man who seemed to fill it.'

Compared to the quiet, thoughtful Ted Wells, the other Ted, 'with a personality as colourful and noisy as show business itself', seemed an unbearable substitute. Even his singing 'made the tooth-mugs jump on the bathroom shelves'. Barbara suggested that she call him 'Uncle Ted', but Julie remained stubbornly determined to resist him.

The lovers had formed a variety act, with which they would eventually tour the country from Brighton to Aberdeen. As Barbara later described it, 'We were never top of the bill. After all, we were musical and not comedy, and the comedians got the best billing. But we were the second feature, a good supporting act with a drawing-room set and ballads — nice, family-type entertainment.'

For the moment, their work for ENSA was very badly paid. And there would soon be another mouth to feed. In July 1942, Barbara gave birth to a son, Donald Edward, in the comparative haven of Rodney House, Walton-on-Thames, where her elder two children had been born.

Although Ted and Barbara marketed themselves as a respectable family couple, they were not yet married. Clearly, Ted Wells had not pursued the issue of divorce until Barbara's new baby meant the separation was irreparable. On

27

25 October 1942, he petitioned against her, naming Ted Andrews as co-respondent. It was usual in those days for the woman to petition, but Wells had been too much of a gentleman already. While unmarried mothers in the Second World War were common enough, at thirty-two Barbara was older than most. With no legal commitment from Ted Andrews, she was in a very uncertain position indeed — as was her daughter, who was fast learning the need for self-reliance.

As if to illustrate the point, the Blitz lit up the skies on a nightly basis. Whenever the sirens moaned, Barbara and 'Uncle Ted', with baby Donald and Julie in tow, would dash across to Mornington Crescent station. 'Incendiaries were dropping all over the place,' Julie told me, 'and I do have fairly good memories of going down into the Underground and witnessing some of the scenes that Henry Moore depicted so brilliantly in his graphics of the time.'

Down in the bowels of London, they would sometimes remain all night on the platform with dozens of other Londoners. As the small hours edged towards morning, Ted would entertain the huddled crowd with songs on his guitar. During one air raid, he realised he had left his instrument behind. Before anyone could stop him, he ran out of the shelter, Barbara rushing behind. Julie was left alone in the crowd with baby Donald in his carry-cot, listening to the bombs thundering above, fearing the worst. Then the couple reappeared, the Canadian Troubadour provided songs and a guitar, and

Julie buried yet another bad scare — for the time being.

When Ted and Barbara were away on tour with ENSA, a nanny would look after the two children, on occasion sneaking them into the famous old Bedford Theatre in Camden High Street. The rowdy music-hall atmosphere would be part of Julie's own life all too soon. In 1942, as the war began to tilt in the Allies' favour, she took a step closer to her destiny, with classes at the Cone Ripman (later Arts Educational) stage school in Upper Grosvenor Street, Mayfair.

The following year, Ted and Barbara were at last earning enough to rent a ground-floor flat (with its own basement air-raid shelter) at 29 Clarendon Street, Pimlico. Julie's mother still registered herself as Barbara Wells, but on 25 November 1943, only three days after her divorce was made final, she and Edward Vernon Andrews were finally married, in Westminster City Register Office. The ceremony was witnessed by Barbara's sister Joan, herself now married, although her husband, Bill Wilby, was at that time an RAF prisoner-of-war. Joan lived in a small flat nearby, where Julie and Donald stayed whenever ENSA concerts kept their parents out of town.

Ted and Barbara Andrews were frantically busy, saving as much as they could to buy a home of their own. By the end of 1943, they had scraped together enough to put down a deposit on 15 Cromwell Road, Beckenham, ten miles south-east of central London, on the edge of Kent. Money now also stretched — just — to pay for Julie's fees at the private Woodbrook Girls' School in Hayne Road, where for two years she received what she would call 'some of the best schooling in my life'. But even as she became used to this more stable environment, the threat of bombing proved greater than ever, as she told me: 'The doodlebugs began arriving while we lived in Beckenham, and it was terrifying to look up into the sky and see and *hear* one of those rockets coming down.' The droning sound would be followed by a sudden, fearful silence, as the missile plummeted to earth.

Beckenham lay directly under one of the main air routes into London. 'Julie, then eight, would arm herself with a whistle, stand on the mound and keep a look out,' said her mother. 'She'd blow at the sight of a doodlebug and we'd run for cover.' One day, Julie was staring into the sky so fixedly that she forgot to sound the alert; the flying bomb landed a matter of yards from the house.

Ted's guitar sessions in the air-raid shelter were more welcome than ever. And it was beneath the onslaught of the doodlebugs, when a group of neighbours started singing 'Strawberry Fair', that one of the most famous voices in the world is said to have been discovered, rising up above all the others. 'I ended,' said Julie, 'an octave higher.'

According to legend, the eight-year-old acted as if nothing unusual had occurred, while Barbara stared in amazement at Ted. Closer attention revealed her range to be truly remarkable, as Barbara noted: 'Over three octaves, there was this unbroken line of voice.'

'I sounded like an immature Yma Sumac,' Julie told me, referring to the Peruvian soprano with the stratospheric four-octave range. But in the general amazement at the power of her voice, there was one person who was less than surprised: the vast personality who, in Julie's own words, 'thundered across my childhood', Ted Andrews. In fact, it was not long after Barbara had left Ted Wells in Walton-on-Thames that the Canadian Troubadour had first sensed the little girl's musical gift. Consequently, on an early ENSA tour, he had written a letter that was to have a profound impact on every aspect of Julie's life.

Madame Lilian Stiles-Allen was one of Britain's great sopranos. Famous in the oratorio repertoire, she had performed in *Hiawatha* at the Royal Albert Hall in the 1920s, Vaughan-Williams' *Serenade to Music* in 1938 and over a thousand BBC broadcasts. Her music master once described her as having 'a throat of gold . . . her speaking voice and her singing voice are so much alike'. They were words that might equally have applied to Lilian Stiles-Allen's own most famous pupil.

A highly gifted teacher, Madame had given lessons to Ted Andrews a few years earlier, and had, she said, 'saved his voice'. She abhorred the practice of singing on the open vowel. 'I call that gargling. I *will* have perfect diction . . . In the Bible, it says, 'In the beginning was the Word.' I thought, if it's enough for God, it's enough for me.'

Replying to Ted's letter, Madame agreed to hear Julie sing. But bombing forced the retired opera singer to leave London and move more than two hundred miles north to Yorkshire, making her home in a beautiful seventeenth-century farm house in Headingley, just outside Leeds. It was not until 1943 that Ted was finally to take Julie to meet her prospective singing teacher.

Madame Stiles-Allen died in 1982, aged ninety-one. She left behind a personal memoir, *Julie Andrews — My Star Pupil*, in which she vividly recalled the first of many meetings with the seven-year-old prodigy:

Julie was then the plainest child imaginable. She wore a brace for her buck teeth, and she had a slight cast in her right eye and two flying pigtails. Her parents could not really afford the expense of lessons, but that did not matter. Even then, as a skinny seven-year-old, she had a special magic. She radiated personality.

In my big book-lined music room with the piano in the corner she sang for me, unaccompanied, Waldteufel's 'Skater's Waltz'. She sang it beautifully, but I felt she was rather young to begin lessons or to concentrate on the work I should want to give her. 'Thank you, Julie; that was lovely,' I said. Then, when she had left the room, I told Ted, 'Let her play with her toys and dolls for the present. But bring her here again.'

'Oh gosh,' Julie told me. 'The early years were such a mixture of pain and joy. I wasn't very happy. It was hard for me to embrace my stepfather because I still adored my dad. I felt that I would be disloyal to him if I cared too much about performing. I began studying when I was about seven or eight with my stepfather. It was an effort to get close to me that made him start giving me singing lessons.'

Despite her hostility, Julie would grudgingly follow Ted into the piano room, and listen as he taught. But when it came to practical demonstration, she turned to stone. He was asking her to feel his back as he breathed into it. There seemed nothing untoward about this — except that she could not bear the idea of touching him. 'I just stood there, silently defying him,' she later said. But Ted, for all his brashness, genuinely wanted to make her understand the importance of technique. 'Come on now, Julie,' he coaxed. 'If you don't want to do it for me, do it for Mummy.' Sensing that he spoke in good faith, Julie started to learn from his example.

At the same time, Barbara was determined to correct her daughter's 'lazy' right eye, buying Dr William H. Bates's manual *Better Sight Without Glasses*. To Julie, it all seemed a huge bore. It had been one thing singing for fun in the air-raid shelter, quite another having to practise breathing and scales every day — let alone beastly eye exercises. Realising how much she hated the routine, Ted bought Julie *The Art of Seeing* by Aldous Huxley. Inside the front cover was the message, 'Dear Julie, this is for you, and I hope, when we read it together, it will help you. With love from Pop.'

Slowly, Julie began to be more trusting of him. In the summer of 1944, she followed 'Pop' and Barbara on tour. Performing in Leeds, Ted remembered Madame Stiles-Allen's open invitation. The family paid the Old Farm another visit, during which Julie sang again.

But Madame was still mindful of the dangers in training such a young talent: 'I explained these to her parents. I could see that she had a most remarkable voice, already possessing adult power and range. What I feared was that this phenomenon might not last, or that training might do permanent damage to her growing vocal cords.' She explained that she would require medical opinion before accepting Julie as a pupil. A series of examinations by throat specialists ensued — and it was then that Ted and Barbara discovered Julie's secret: she had a fully developed adult larynx. 'Yes,' said Madame, finally convinced. 'I *will* take her.'

With the end of the war in 1945, Ted and Barbara Andrews transferred their act from ENSA to the music halls. But money was still tight. Madame Stiles-Allen agreed to let them pay for the lessons when they could afford it, a mark of faith in her newest pupil.

Twice a month, Julie now faced the alarming prospect of making the long train journey on her own. Even when she arrived at Leeds, to be met by Madame's husband, Sydney Jeffries-Harris ('Uncle Jeff'), her fears were not over. As Madame recalled, Julie was over-sensitive to the

34

Old Farm: 'Its long corridors, dimly lit and strangely shadowed by gas brackets, gave her a feeling of eeriness, until she got used to it. The old timbers creaked at night and she began to think the old place was haunted.' But soon, Julie came to regard it as a second home; the dreaded train journeys also became less traumatic, building her incipient self-reliance.

The youngest pupil at the Old Farm, Julie was also the most conscientious. Next to the huge studio, which had once been a hay barn, was the little study where, at nine o'clock each morning, she would be the first at work. 'Apart from her singing,' said Madame, 'I paid a lot of attention to the clarity of her diction, which has always been a fetish of mine. I always made a point with her that singing is musical speech. 'They are not two things apart,' I told her. 'If you can't hear a singer's words, it is like a body moving without legs to carry it.''

As classes progressed, Madame saw Julie blossoming.

Her singing was coming alive; even the exercises were becoming exciting for her. She also had a very keen ear for languages and very quickly learned to sing the aria '*Je suis Titania*' in fluent French. Yet she had no sophistication, no illusions, no inflated ideas that she was anything outstanding — only a genuine love of singing.

The range, accuracy and tone of Julie's voice amazed me. All her life, I discovered, she had possessed the rare gift of absolute pitch. I make it a rule as a singing teacher to get three octaves in all voices. Julie, as a little girl and right up to the age of fourteen, had a most unusual four-octave range, from two Cs above Alt. right down to two Cs below middle C. She had absolute confidence in her voice, and in me.

Above all, Madame impressed on Julie a lesson that would carry her to future triumph: 'A voice is a gift, given in trust, given to be used and treated with care. And, in doing so, you yourself will gain great joy.'

Hard work, brightness of delivery, eagerness to please: lessons like these would permanently define Julie's image. There was another discipline: control over the audience. 'You are like a fisherman,' said Madame, 'you have to get them on a hook.'

'I never had another teacher,' Julie said later. 'She was wonderful.'

Back at Woodbrook School, the other girls were unimpressed. The budding prodigy still had bandy legs and a face covered in freckles — still needed a tooth brace and eye exercises. 'I was', she told me over fifty years later, 'a pretty hideous child.' She was particularly aware that, unlike her friends, she did not have a regulated home life. One week she would be boating on the Thames with her father; the next, she would be out on tour with Ted and Barbara Andrews, by now well-known entertainers on the wireless as well as on stage.

The bond between mother and daughter

remained very close. But, in late 1945, Barbara found herself pregnant with her fourth child. Self-conscious in all but her singing, Julie desperately wanted to retain her 'very important privilege', to be the only girl in the family — even though she knew that Barbara wanted another daughter. 'Please God,' she prayed hard each night, 'let the new baby be a boy.' In May 1946, a boy, Christopher Stuart, was born, and Julie felt a rush of remorse — the desperate insecurity of a young girl still craving for the certainty of love.

Soon after Christopher was born, the family moved back to Walton-on-Thames, where Ted and Barbara had bought a rambling, five-bedroom house on West Grove Road. It was called The Old Meuse. There, for the rest of Julie's childhood, they were to remain.

Madame Stiles-Allen also moved, to Kent. She now taught from a cottage in the village of West Kingsdown, where Julie resumed her training, on more than one occasion giving a recital at the local hall. Madame would eventually hand over the Old Farm to the Yorkshire College of Music and Drama, where the hay barn in which she taught Julie Andrews to sing remains the principal studio to this day.

Julie seemed ready to try her wings professionally. Further training at RADA, the Royal Academy of Dramatic Art, was considered; instead, as Barbara later explained, 'We decided that a little toughening up as far as the theatre world was concerned would be good, and so we took Julie into our act. Let's face it — it didn't hurt the act either.' With hindsight, RADA would have stood Julie in good stead for the huge challenges that lay ahead. Financial necessity, however, put practice ahead of theory; but despite the delight she had known in Madame's lessons, little Julia Wells was mortified by the idea of performing with Ted Andrews.

★   ★   ★

'I loathed singing, and resented my stepfather. He embarrassed and upset me by asking me to perform.' So would Julie remember her professional beginnings, supporting Ted and Barbara Andrews in the immediate post-war years. 'It must have been ghastly, but it went down all right,' she said. 'They performed by the sea; underneath the times of the performances would be written 'weather and tide permitting'.'

From Blackpool to Bridlington, the routine, as she described it to me, was always the same: 'Occasionally, they would have to get permission from the front-of-house manager: 'Our daughter sings and would you mind . . . ' I would stand on a beer crate beside my stepfather, so we could both reach the microphone together. I had a very pure, white, thin voice, a four-octave range — dogs would come for miles around.'

Despite the freak-show element, her acrobatic coloratura soon proved the highlight of the act. But when I asked her if a legitimate opera career had been a serious option, she answered from the heart: 'Madame was sure that I could do

Mozart and Rossini, but — to be honest — I never was.'

Nevertheless, it was clear to Ted Andrews the way the wind was blowing. Finding it awkward to introduce his stepdaughter as Julia Wells, he proposed to change her name by deed poll. 'I eventually took his name', said Julie, 'for the convenience of it. I believe my mum decided it would be easier.' Ted Wells bowed once again, in the interests of his daughter's career; thus, officially, was Julie Andrews born.

Making her debut for the BBC, she performed with Ted and Barbara in the popular wireless programme *Monday Night at Eight*. Julie realised, with a sickening attack of stage fright, that from now on she would be judged strictly as a professional. Never was this more evident than on Thursday 5 December 1946, when she created her first real impact. At the Stage Door Canteen for servicemen in Piccadilly, where Ted and Barbara had often appeared during the war, the audience included the Queen (later the Queen Mother) and Princess Margaret. For Julie, it was almost too much. Nevertheless, coupling the technique she had acquired with the iron focus that had always been hers, she sang the 'Polonaise' ('*Je suis Titania*') from Ambroise Thomas's opera *Mignon*.

Afterwards, on hearing that she was to be presented to the Queen, her nerves resurfaced. She need not have worried. For the first time, she received royal benediction. 'You sang beautifully, Julie,' beamed Her Majesty. 'We enjoyed it very much.' The following day, she was besieged by the other girls at school, all wanting to know about her royal presentation. For once, it was they who envied her.

The boost to her confidence came at exactly the right moment. 'I had three huge building blocks in my life,' she told me in 1999. 'The early years and vaudeville, then Broadway and then movies.' The first of the three was about to be set in place.

★   ★   ★

The following year, 1947, was a happy one for Julie Andrews. Ted and Barbara were still getting good bookings, and the family had settled down at The Old Meuse. The 'darling, shabby old house', as Julie described it, was five minutes' walk from the railway station, set in extensive if unkempt grounds. The garden seemed a paradise for Julie and her young stepbrothers, with a large stretch of lawn and plenty of trees to climb, yet it was only just over twenty miles from the West End of London.

Strangely, the name Barbara Wells appears on the electoral roll for 29 Clarendon Street until the end of 1948, some two years after they had moved to Walton-on-Thames. It is likely that, for a reasonable rent, Barbara retained it to use when she returned to London late at night from touring — but a mystery remains as to why she did so in the surname of her former husband, when she was now known as Barbara Andrews. It is just possible that a seed of discord between Ted and her had already taken root.

40

In Garrick Close, Walton-on-Thames, lived the family of Lieutenant Colonel A.V.Agius. His son Tancred vividly remembered his neighbours to me, more than half a century after he had played in the garden of The Old Meuse with the Andrews children: 'After the Second World War, people were short of houses. My parents had a huge eight-bedroom house and we had a lady staying with us. She was a choreographer in London and the suburbs — Joan Morris — and she lived with us for about a year. Then, in the big house called The Old Meuse, above what was the stables, she set up a dance studio. Joan Morris taught me, my sister and many of our friends ballroom dancing. This would be 1947, that awful winter when the whole Thames froze up.'

Elsewhere in the grounds of The Old Meuse was a prefabricated bungalow (known by Julie as 'Dinglebell'), where Aunt Joan and her husband Bill would stay. Julie loved spending time there with her aunt, discussing the future. Her ambitions varied wildly. At one point, she wanted to be a florist. Then, like so many girls of her age, she became mad about ponies, spending her spare time at the nearby stables: 'I always imagined myself as a rancher,' she said, 'married to Roddy McDowall in *My Friend Flicka*.' She also enjoyed playing a role she would one day recreate on screen: acting as nanny to five-year-old Donald and baby Christopher. But it was always going to be Julie's voice that would support her — and, indeed, her whole family.

One afternoon in May, she and Donald were

sitting high in a tree, when they heard Barbara calling from the house. 'Julie! Some friends of Pop would like to hear you sing.'

'I was absolutely covered with filth,' said Julie, 'just a dirty, repulsive child.' She went inside, washed and changed, then entered the music room. She had often sung for visitors before, and she recognised two of the three men present from an earlier occasion. The portly one with white hair was Mr Charles Tucker, an agent. The American, who knew Ted Andrews from the local golf club, was Mr Ben Goetz, head of Metro-Goldwyn-Mayer British Film Corporation. The third, a stranger to her, was Val Parnell, general manager of Moss Empire, Britain's largest theatre circuit.

Unaware of the stakes, Julie was about to perform her first serious audition. As usual, she sang the 'Polonaise' from *Mignon*, and — as usual — effortlessly reached an incredible F above top C. 'Thank you, Julie,' her mother said with a nod of pleasure, signalling that she was free to run back to the garden to play with Donald.

The five adults remained in the music room, shaping Julie's entire future in a matter of minutes. Ben Goetz had acted as instigator, introducing Ted to Charles Tucker — who, it was decided, should be Julie's manager. 'Uncle Charles' had, in turn, introduced Val Parnell, who was considering Julie for *Starlight Roof*, his forthcoming West End revue. Before this, Julie was to appear at the armed forces' Burma Reunion at the Royal Albert Hall. The opening act, in a show that boasted the talents of Noël Coward and Vera Lynn, was clearly billed as 'Ted and Barbara Andrews with Julie', marking a step up from her arbitrary appearances on tour.

On 1 October 1947, whatever semblance of a normal childhood Julie had retained was finally discarded. The London County Council, which prohibited any child under twelve from working in a West End theatre, could no longer restrict the career of Julie Andrews. The timing — as so often in her story — was immaculate. A week later, she made her television debut in the BBC *Radiolympia Showtime*, featuring Stanley Holloway. Two weeks after that, Val Parnell's revue was scheduled to open at the London Hippodrome, Leicester Square.

Starlight Roof presented a daunting challenge for a twelve-year-old, boasting as much Broadway-style glamour as the West End could manage, with a line-up headed by Vic Oliver (the divorced son-in-law of Winston Churchill) and Pat Kirkwood. Julie could, however, relax in the conceit that she was not officially part of the show, and not listed in the programme. All she had to do was emerge from the audience in her little frock and big white dancing pumps, chat to Vic Oliver and, at his invitation, sing. After two rehearsals, Julie was ready for the premiere on Thursday 23 October.

Then, arriving at the theatre for the dress rehearsal, with only two days to go, she learnt that she had been dropped from the show. Val Parnell had had second thoughts. What might look like a child amateur stunt had no place in his sophisticated revue.

Julie was in despair. 'At which point,' she later recalled, 'my mother and my agent stormed the producer's office and said, 'You can't deny this kid her big chance. For God's sake, let her go on.'' Parnell agreed to let her sing at the dress rehearsal, after which he would make his final decision.

'Uncle Charles' Tucker told Julie to pray for success. Remembering everything she had learned from Madame Stiles-Allen, the twelve-year-old sang from the bottom of her heart. When she had finished, the cast of *Starlight Roof* burst into sustained applause. Bowing to sentiment, Parnell put her back in the show.

On Thursday afternoon, Julie and Barbara Andrews walked up Charing Cross Road to the London Hippodrome. Julie would always remember what happened next: 'My mother was leading me through the stage door, and she stopped to buy me a bunch of violets, 'for luck,' she said. 'And what does she need luck for?' asked the flower lady. And my mother said, 'She's singing here tonight.' And the flower lady said, 'Well, you're not buying nothing — these are from me, love.' And she gave me three beautiful bunches of violets and wished me all the luck in the world.'

Julie's memory of this seemed as sharp as anything else she would ever recount. She tilted her head back, closed her eyes and told me, 'I can see her face even now.'

Whether or not because of the flower seller's wishes, *Starlight Roof* was a smash hit. The *Daily Express* heralded it as 'the complete answer to

the gloom-merchants who say England cannot produce a musical. It has luxury, glamour, speed.' Yet the greatest ovation went to a little girl not even named in the programme.

Early in the show, the American comedian Wally Boag twisted balloons into animal shapes, finally asking if any girl or boy would like to come up and get one. 'Yes, please,' piped a voice, and a child rushed forward from the back stalls, in party frock and pigtails. 'Hello, little girl. How old are you?' asked Vic Oliver, coming on stage.

'I'm twelve. How old are you?' said Julie.

'What are you going to sing for us?'

'I'd like to sing the 'Polonaise' from *Mignon*.'

'Oh, lovely, just the kind of junk I like,' said Oliver. And that night, as on the hundreds that followed, the child proceeded to electrify the audience with the 'Polonaise'. At the end of the aria, effortlessly transcending the top F, she received five full minutes of applause. 'I absolutely stopped the show cold. The audience went crazy,' she would remember. Julie Andrews had made her first appearance on a West End stage.

Added to her extraordinary voice, the 'mystery singer' angle ensured a barrage of publicity — all favourable. Typical was Lionel Hale of the *Daily Mail*: 'Miss Julie Andrews sings with the prodigious assurance of an infant prodigy.' The only cavil was about the toll such a nightly aria would take. 'Her voice was put under a terrific strain, and we all thought it would be ruined,' said Pat Kirkwood, but Julie was not a pupil of Lilian Stiles-Allen for nothing. 'She could sing all day without strain,' said Ted Andrews. Three weeks later, on her free Sunday night, she appeared in the BBC's *Jubilee Variety Gala*, broadcast live from His Majesty's Theatre. Julie Andrews was now a star.

2

THE OTHER SIDE OF THE TRACKS

'Try your hardest and do your best'

— Uncle Charles Tucker

In December 1947, at the Borehamwood studios of Metro-Goldwyn-Mayer British, Julie Andrews made her one and only screen test. It was for the famous musical producer Joe Pasternak, who had made stars out of Deanna Durbin, Kathryn Grayson and Jane Powell. Yet if Ted, Barbara and Uncle Charles saw in Julie the chance to create something similar, their plans would prove stillborn.

Dressed in a tiny frock that cruelly exposed her long, thin arms and legs, her hair in sausage curls, she was led in front of the camera like a lamb to the slaughter. As she later expressed it, 'They tried to make this bandy-legged, bucktoothed girl look like an English Shirley Temple. I was really hideously ugly and seemed to have been put together with all the wrong bits and pieces.'

The test was prefaced by a card, listing her vital statistics:

Height: 4'10½" Weight: 79lbs Age: 12
Experience: Stage and Radio

47

Accompanied by her mother at the piano, Julie sang her number and endured a brief question session, betraying her nerves with clutched hands and the slight slackening of her 'lazy' eye. It was, she remembered, 'a disaster'. Having endured years of eye exercises, posture classes and braces to straighten her teeth, Julie was rejected in a manner guaranteed only to hurt. Rumours that she was non-photogenic would later stalk her reputation, reaching even the ears of Robert Wise the film director who was to turn her into the biggest star in the world.

So it was back to the Hippodrome, where her voice alone seemed enough to please the public. In recognition of her success, the cast list for *Starlight Roof* now ended: 'And Julie Andrews, the Youthful Prima Donna.'

Her pay packet was estimated at £50 a week. 'But, so far as she is concerned,' said her stepfather, 'success means a rise in her pocket money from two shillings to five shillings a week.'

For all Julie's triumph, she was denied a final curtain call, the law demanding that performers younger than fifteen leave the theatre by ten o'clock. The law also stipulated a minimum of three hours with a governess every day, and homework for her dressing room. 'I detest lessons. I really do,' she said at the time. But later, her lack of a formal education would cause her to remark, 'I bitterly regret not having had more.'

A long West End run at least meant a period of stability at home. Though no one could pretend that she was an ordinary child, she was never in any danger of being spoiled, as she explained to me: 'My mum and stepfather were very good — they said, just don't get a big head, because you could be out as quickly as you were in.' In the summer, Julie spent an idyllic week with her father, his wife Win and her brother John. 'When I was with him,' she later said of her father, 'everything was forgotten except the outdoor life.'

Julie remained with the show for a year, singing with what one critic described as 'a true, sweet soprano of surprising range'. In that time, she made friends with nearly every one of the fifty-strong cast — including another newcomer, Michael Bentine. 'She was so polite,' said the future member of the Goons. 'You couldn't help liking her. She was so natural; no airs at all.' According to one report, however, she occasionally compromised the spontaneity of her entrance by elbowing her way on stage. 'Sometimes she'd be beaten by an eager kid,' Wally Boag the balloon artist recalled. 'She usually made it first.'

The 'Polonaise' served for Julie's initial gramophone recording, made at the Hippodrome as part of an album of the show. A few months later, she recorded 'Come to the Fair', joined for posterity by Ted Andrews, in an echo of their seaside engagements, and a coloratura version of 'Twinkle, Twinkle, Little Star' with her mother at the piano.

Three weeks after her thirteenth birthday, Julie completed her year in *Starlight Roof*. At that point, bureaucracy once again intervened. London County Council restrictions prevented a juvenile from working for longer without a break — but the 'Polonaise' would be heard again only a few days later.

Julie had been drilled to hand over all her fan mail to her mother. One morning, towards the end of the run, she remembered some letters given to her a few days earlier. One of these sent Barbara into an instant frenzy: an invitation to appear in that year's Royal Variety Performance at the London Palladium. There was only a day left before the deadline for acceptance expired. Julie had very nearly missed the opportunity to be the youngest artiste ever to appear by royal command — in the company of Danny Kaye, the Nicholas Brothers and the popular male impersonator Ella Shields, who was to perform her trademark number 'Burlington Bertie from Bow'.

The decision to include the Youthful Prima Donna in such exalted company was vindicated. On Monday 1 November 1948, Julie sang the ubiquitous 'Polonaise' and, at the end of the night, led the cast in 'God Save the King', clasping her hands as if her life depended on it. Only thirteen years old, and already a veteran of two official performances before the royal family, Julie Andrews once again stopped the show.

★ ★ ★

Two days after the Royal Variety Performance, Julie took a front-page advertisement in the trade paper *Show World*, signalling that she was ready, willing and able:

To all my friends

Mummy and Daddy join me in a big 'Thank You' for your great help and guidance, and especially to dear Madame Stiles-Allen for her patience and loving care during my lessons.

Julie Andrews

Ted and Barbara Andrews were now confident in what they had, but the little girl whom even her ambitious mother had once considered 'plain to the point of ugliness' was struggling to balance the Libran scales between calm professional determination and chronic private insecurity. She told me: 'It helped enormously at school — what little schooling I did have — to be able to show off and sing before the Queen, but I thought it was a flash in the pan. Although I had this enormous range, and phenomenal coloratura ability, I didn't feel confident: I felt I was trying to obtain the unobtainable.'

Few in the theatre world shared her doubts. In December 1948, two months after leaving *Starlight Roof*, she was to be reunited with Pat Kirkwood and Vic Oliver in her first traditional pantomime, *Humpty Dumpty* at the London Casino. The producer, Emile Littler, made the offer conditional on being able to hide her size-six feet. He ordered a pair of gnome's shoes with curled-up toes, and Julie was given her first title role in the West End — as well as, from Ted and Barbara, a corgi puppy named Humpty.

Notwithstanding Pat Kirkwood as the Principal Boy and Richard ('Mr Pastry') Hearne as the Dame, one critic wrote, 'It was the 'Humpty Dumpty' of Julie Andrews who stopped the show, proving she can act as spiritedly as she sings.' For the first time, Julie was regarded as more than just the child with the freak voice. She was also looking rather more attractive. Her teeth were straighter, thanks to Charles Tucker's proprietary interest and expenditure, and sessions in Aunt Joan's studio had helped correct her posture and bandy legs — made bandier from too much pony riding.

'She was a funny-looking kid but she always had beautiful skin,' said Pat Kirkwood, who noticed that Julie was more controlled now than in *Starlight Roof*. Then, despite looking natural from the front, she had knitted her fingers furiously behind her back: 'She seemed very highly strung. But it was rather different in panto. There were long intervals between appearances on stage and we had much more chance to get to know one another. However nervous Julie may have been in *Humpty Dumpty*, she seemed to have a certain inner strength: she always knew what she wanted to do and did it.'

Before the end of the pantomime, Miss Kirkwood gave Julie a ring, set with a huge black opal. 'I'd been told that it was a very unlucky ring for anyone except a person born in October and, though it was ridiculously large for Julie's fingers, I like to think that it helped her. For, after that show, she went up and up — whoosh!'

One night, sitting on her wall as the eponymous egg, Julie noticed two schoolboys in the front row of the stalls, who seemed totally caught up in the show. Exactly fifty years later, the younger boy recalled his impression: 'When the egg fell from the wall, there was this enchanting little girl with some kind of chocolate make-up all over her legs — which I found extremely seductive.'

The same two boys were standing in the train corridor outside her compartment when Julie travelled back to The Old Meuse that night. Tony Walton and his younger brother Richard were accompanied by their mother, who entered the compartment, explaining that her sons had enjoyed the show but were too bashful to speak for themselves. Julie giggled girlishly; Tony looked sheepish, later recalling, 'When we all got out at the station at Walton-on-Thames, I asked where she lived, and she said, 'The other side of the tracks.''

In more than one way, this was correct. Tony's home at 10 Ashley Road, less than ten minutes from The Old Meuse, was on the opposite side of the railway line, and the two children came from very different backgrounds. By the standards of Walton-on-Thames, Julie's mother and, particularly, her stepfather led a rackety, itinerant existence, cheerfully announcing themselves in the telephone directory as 'Ted and

Barbara Andrews, Radio Artistes'. Ted's colourful air of *bonhomie* was as much a part of his act as his guitar. And when the act wore a little thin — and the engagement diary a little sparse — there was a growing tendency to resort to the bottle.

It was all very unlike the home life of Lancelot H.F. Walton, orthopaedic surgeon with a practice in Harley Street, whose four children (Jennifer, Tony, Richard and Carol) had lived in the area for most of their lives. But Anthony John Walton (his surname only coincidentally the same as that of his home town) was captivated by the girl from inside the eggshell.

'And the next thing I knew,' said Julie, 'Tony and his brother were around at the house.' They had come to ask for a publicity photograph. Her stepfather was the first to spot the boys coming up the drive. He was in no mood for uninvited guests: when Julie explained that they were friends, he growled, 'They're not coming in here; entertain them somewhere else.'

Nonetheless, Tony kept in touch. After he returned to boarding school — Radley College in Oxfordshire — he sent Julie what she called 'such sweet and lovely letters with wonderful drawings' — telling her that he too saw a career in the theatre, as a designer.

Tony, aged fourteen, was a year older than her. His birthday fell in the same month, but critically (to those interested in such matters) not under the same star sign. He was born a Scorpio, on 24 October, a day after the end of Libra. 'One of those goons from home, gawking from the front row,' Julie recalled her first impression, yet within three years, 'we became boyfriend and girlfriend and went through our teens together.'

★　★　★

For the moment at least, boyfriends were a secondary consideration. After three months in pantomime, Humpty Dumpty found herself sharing the bill at the Lyceum Theatre with Sir Laurence Olivier and Paul Robeson, in a fundraiser for the Royal Academy of Dramatic Art, where Barbara Andrews had considered sending her daughter.

Television, which a decade later was to start making the impact in Britain it already had in America, was still a minority luxury. Variety theatre — seaside seasons in summer, pantomimes in winter — remained the working man's entertainment. And for Julie, the offers were plentiful. 'I must have gone around England three or four times — completely around,' she once estimated, 'playing every major vaudeville theatre.' And plenty of minor ones as well. The Andrews family act travelled continually, changing trains on a Sunday at Crewe railway junction, waving to other touring acts heading in the opposite direction. According to Michael Bentine, Julie's fellow cast member from *Starlight Roof*, Ted and Barbara 'used to drag poor Julie around with them, and she didn't mind doing it'.

She was not given much choice. Beryl Reid,

55

appearing on some of the same variety bills as Julie, considered that she had never seen a more dedicated theatre child. 'She had a very strict upbringing, practised her singing for hours every day, and was always taught to address everyone as Mr So-and-So and Miss So-and-So. It seemed tough on her at the time, but I have seen the same thing in circus families where children are worked terribly hard at an early age. It pays off in the end.'

'A voice is a gift,' Madame Stiles-Allen had said, 'to be treated with care.' Sometimes, it was a hard lesson to remember. 'I had not a clue what I was in for,' said Julie when I saw her in 1986. 'The terrifying part of it was playing the music halls, which in those days were all over England, and second house Saturday night in places like Liverpool or Glasgow was frightening — bottles were flying, they had to turn all the house lights on.' The child survived. 'Miraculously, I think I was so young, nobody hurts a young kitten — which is sort of what I was in those days.'

Her mother and stepfather were faring less well, off stage as well as on. All too soon, the billing changed, from 'Ted and Barbara Andrews with Julie' to 'Julie Andrews with Ted and Barbara'. 'Not terribly good for my stepfather's ego,' Julie would later remark, starkly assessing the evidence. 'He was an alcoholic — a nightmare for the whole family.'

According to Tony Walton, her diaries at the time were 'filled with fanciful images of what a beautiful, happy life she had and what a glamorous existence she led, when in reality it was pretty seedy'. The fiction extended to a couple of children's stories they wrote together, Julie providing the words, Tony the pictures. 'Peter Piccolo's Great Idea' and 'Conceited Mr Concerto' were published that summer in a newspaper in Blackpool, where the Andrews family had found work — at different venues. While Ted and Barbara were playing the Central Pier, Julie was at the more prestigious Hippodrome — billed as 'Melody of Youth' in *Coconut Grove*, a musical revue starring Josef Locke the Irish tenor, and Jean Carson.

The difference in status was abundantly clear. Monica Avis, a dancer in *Coconut Grove*, remembered that a 'very polite' Julie would arrive by chauffeur-driven car, ten minutes before she was due on stage: 'She would sing a couple of numbers and then return by car to her parents who were performing at the Pier.'

Although Julie was, in Barbara's own admission, 'really a step above us', the family was at least together, renting a house at nearby Lytham St Annes. But this was not to be a happy summer for any of them. The money that Ted and Barbara had made after the war, on stage and on the airwaves, belied their long-term prospects. With changing tastes, their 'nice, family-type entertainment' was not going to sustain the family for long.

In Blackpool, Julie became acutely aware of 'some strange atmosphere' between her mother and stepfather, which was liable to break out in sudden acrimony. Quietly, she confided her fears to Barbara, who admitted their financial insecurity. The issue hung uneasily in the air for the rest of the season and in the following months on tour. Julie felt certain that, once again, her family was about to fall apart — and that they would lose their one real asset, The Old Meuse, the only place she had ever really considered as home.

The answer, if one existed, lay in her ability to earn good money. For Julie Andrews, singing was no easy pleasure: 'As my mother said, I never sprang out of bed with a glad shout.' But she had been taught that most British of lessons — to 'get on with it'. 'From the age of thirteen, Julie was head of the family,' said Tony Walton, 'and it was a Grade-B movie existence.'

★ ★ ★

Just after the war, BBC Radio made a star of another child singer from Surrey. 'Petula Clark and I were childhood contemporaries,' Julie would recall, 'and I remember how we used to walk round each other with great respect . . . '

Petula's many broadcasts, culminating in her own series, had turned her into a more prominent name — but Julie soon caught up. In late 1949, she made her first real impact on the airwaves as one of the 'Outstanding Young Artists' on BBC *Children's Hour*, for which her fee was ten shillings and sixpence. Travelling to the studios in Manchester, Julie was met by producer Trevor Hill, who told me of his lasting impression. 'I made it a rule that parents, teachers, tutors went out of the studio,' he remembered. But Barbara, he discovered, had other plans: 'To my surprise, Julie's mother came bouncing in, carrying this enormous teddy bear, which she plonked down on top of the piano. Mrs Andrews turned to me and said, 'I do like Julie to be like other children,' and Julie was so embarrassed; I can see the case with a child of five, but she was fourteen.'

If Barbara had wanted to accompany Julie, she had met her match. At the piano sat the redoubtable Violet Carson, later famous as Ena Sharples in the long-running soap opera *Coronation Street*. The objective, said Hill, was to 'get rid of Mum'.

Back in Walton-on-Thames, Tancred Agius, still attending Aunt Joan's dance classes, would see the rising young star 'hanging around during the day' at The Old Meuse: 'I thought that was pretty strange, because most people of that age were supposed to be at school.' Julie, he discovered, had a governess, and was working for the BBC. 'She was appearing on the old Home Service . . . on a show with a ventriloquist called Peter Brough, *Entertaining Archie*. Only in those days could you have a radio show starring a ventriloquist.'

Educating Archie — the British equivalent of America's hugely popular Edgar Bergen and Charlie McCarthy show — was named after Peter Brough's cheeky schoolboy dummy Archie Andrews. 'They all thought I was Archie's sister,' said Julie, who filled the musical interval with such pieces as 'The Blue Danube', 'Cherry Ripe' or a dazzling 'Love Is Where You Find It'. 'I guess it was an odd conception, but it worked.'

'I used to call her the cherry on our cake of humour; we looked upon her as giving us class,' the comedian Eric Sykes, who created the series, told me. 'What was so attractive about Julie was her age. She had such a beautiful voice, and she was very ordinary as a person. I'm sure she would have loved to join in all the frolics, but she had a very serious outlook.'

As would so often be the case in Julie's career, she was in the company of first-rate comedians. *Educating Archie* featured almost more talent than it could handle, including Tony Hancock as Archie's tutor, Hattie Jacques as Agatha Danglebody, Alfred Marks, Harry Secombe and Max Bygraves ('I've arrived and to prove it — I'm 'ere!'). The show, launched on 6 June 1950, was recorded on a Sunday at the BBC Paris Cinema in the West End and broadcast a few days later. The pace was rapid, but Eric Sykes could always rely on Julie: 'I was editing even then, while she was singing.'

Within a few weeks, the show had over twelve million listeners. Later, it was judged Best Comedy of the Year, and, with two repeats a week, became BBC Radio's most popular programme. Immortalised in wax at Madame Tussaud's, Archie was one of the first stars to have his image marketed on books, sweets and toys. When he was kidnapped in 1951, the press treated the story as if he were a real child (he was traced to the lost property office at King's Cross Station). By November 2005, the puppet could

60

still command £34,000 at auction, his three spare heads reaching £3,000 apiece.

'People always said: 'Why a ventriloquist on the radio?'' said Peter Brough. 'I always used to say 'Why not?' ' As for Julie, 'she was perhaps a little shy and self-conscious before going on stage, but once a show had started she was always confident and professional. She was a very determined girl, but she was extremely polite and never threw a tantrum or gave any difficulties at all.'

'She wasn't running around like a normal little girl,' said Eric Sykes. 'She knew that she was going places.'

Between her two seasons with the show, those places were confined to the theatre circuit. In *Music for the Millions*, Julie toured for one of Britain's best-known impresarios, Harold Fielding. She was still attended by a governess, Miss Gladys Knight, 'a wonderful old lady who took no nonsense'. But her childhood, such as it was, was almost over. On Sunday 1 October 1950, at a birthday party in the *Educating Archie* studio, fifteen-year-old Julie Andrews announced, 'At last I am free from the London County Council.'

No longer classed as a juvenile, she could now work on the stage without restriction. Yet she continued to be presented like a child, to her frustration: 'Most of the time, I was kept in short, short dresses, patent leather shoes and ankle socks, trying desperately to look ten years younger than I really was, growing a bosom and feeling wretched about that.'

Resuming pantomime duty, she played another

little girl (albeit the title role) in *Red Riding Hood*, which opened two days before Christmas at the Theatre Royal, Nottingham. Starring opposite her, as Jolly Jenkins, was a giant of British comedy, her *Educating Archie* colleague Tony Hancock, whose lugubrious manner affected her less than her own mishaps: 'I remember two awful moments. One, I was so busy reading some Enid Blyton children's story that I forgot to go on. And the other, I finally did get on, and started to sing 'The Gypsy and the Bird' and the audience started to giggle. I couldn't think why, and it got worse. In fact, one of the flying cables with the great weighted sack on it — there was a flying ballet in the pantomime — was missing my head by about an inch.'

The three-month run of *Red Riding Hood* meant Julie spending her first Christmas away from Walton-on-Thames. For her pains, she was rumoured to be earning £200 a week, but still received only ten shillings in pocket money. The rest was placed in a trust, the details of which she would not know until she was seventeen.

After that, it was back on the road, belting out what she called 'my bastardised versions of operatic arias'. The billing now changed to 'Julie Andrews, the Phenomenal Singing Star, accompanied by Barbara Andrews'. Three had become two. 'And what I did was get on with it,' the star admitted, at a distance of over fifty years. 'It's the way it was.'

Like a montage sequence in a Hollywood musical, the towns once more flashed by: Stockton, Jersey, Leicester, Aberdeen, the Isle of

Wight, Manchester, Margate, More[...] [...] to London for a charity show at th[e] [...] Theatre with Max Wall, Adelaide Hall, [...] Lillie — Southampton, Belfast. In Bournem[...] her father and brother paid her a visit. To [...] Wells, wherever his daughter's career led, she would always be 'naturally a country girl'. The three of them went boating, recapturing one of the pleasures of Julie's early childhood, but it was all too brief and rare a moment.

'I had not too many friends,' she said later, at the apex of her stardom. 'Mostly I was alone. I think I protested endlessly that I was the happiest girl in the world. I think I protested too much. Actually, it was pretty bad, the nasty digs, the bad trains, the grubby theatres, but it proved to be the best training I could have had.'

She needed to believe it.

★   ★   ★

Shortly after Julie's sixteenth birthday, Charles Tucker took her to the Theatre Royal, Drury Lane, to see the most glamorous American musical in the West End: Rodgers and Hammerstein's *South Pacific*. 'Wonderful!' Julie exclaimed about the show and its star Mary Martin. Uncle Charles smiled down at her shining face, but spoke seriously. 'One day, Julie, you will be on that stage. And one day Rodgers and Hammerstein will write a show for you.'

If Julie entertained such thoughts, she kept them to herself. She was, however, about to appear in the West End, after a gap of nearly two

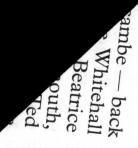

wn-up role.

ulbadour in the pantomime
ned to the London Casino
mpty producer Emile Littler,
no adverse comment about
ight have been excused for
her height. The skinny young
up like a beanpole, making it
necessary ... r friend Jean Carson, as
Principal Boy, to don four-inch heels.

Aladdin was, unsurprisingly, a hit — so much
so, that Julie rather disingenuously told her
friends, 'Please don't think I'm getting a
big-shot.' She had her half-brothers to prevent
that, pelting her with buns when she started
singing at home. Her pet corgi was not much
better in the confines of a BBC recording studio:
'As soon as I started to sing, Humpty just lifted
his nose to the sky and gave a most melancholy
howl. The recording was ruined and we had to
start all over again.'

During the run of *Aladdin*, Julie was first out
of the stage door each night, rushing over the
river to Waterloo to catch the train back to
Walton the town — and Walton the boyfriend,
home for the holidays in his last year at Radley.
Over the last few terms, their letters had become
progressively more intimate in tone. Julie had
written that, should the stage not sustain her, she
would be happy on a farm, or a stables. This
seemed an unlikely event. Tony, however, looked
set to follow his father into a medical career,
until the results of his science exams told him
otherwise. A subsequent foray into Latin and

Greek made him realise the futility of concentrating on anything other than his artistic talent.

'Lots of love,' Tony would end his letters. Julie was guarded enough to send him her best wishes. Then, after Christmas, for the first — and not the last — time, she cooled on him altogether. She had met someone else, the antithesis of the polite public schoolboy with the eager smile, and the contrast was exhilarating.

'Freddie', as she named him later, was 'a Danish acrobat in the show', but neither the programme for *Aladdin* nor the flyer for her next job, the touring revue *Look In*, lists any performer by that name. *Look In*, presented by Uncle Charles in the spring of 1952, did however feature the acrobatic troupe 'The Four Fredianis'.

The Frediani dynasty, one of the most revered in European circuses, became famous in eighteenth-century Italy, and exists to the present day. It is likely that it was one of the spirited quartet on that very English revue who put Tony out of Julie's mind. Whatever his identity, the newcomer was good-looking, athletic, with a seductive foreign accent. It was a casebook example of a schoolgirl crush, and Julie brought him home to Mother.

Julie's friends, having long regarded her as 'Tony's girl', were unimpressed. And they were especially shocked one day, when a group of them was debating how to spend the evening. 'Well, Freddie,' said Mrs Andrews, 'what would you like to do?'

'Joost coodle Joolie,' answered the young acrobat, effectively sealing his reputation. Shortly afterwards, he left to join his family act on tour in Europe, and Julie had little to remember him by, other than the foreign stamps from his occasional letters.

Meanwhile, on another provincial trek to Birmingham, Blackpool and all points north, Julie began to think once more of the neglected Tony. Missing both him and news of home, she started writing to him again. Soon, they were exchanging letters as of old, the 'Freddie' interlude forgotten — although Julie's way of expressing the reconciliation was less than romantic: 'I was one of the gang again.'

Tony was shortly to commence a two-year period of National Service, but his plans to be a stage designer were now in earnest. During the final years at Radley, he had taken art classes in Oxford. The artist John Piper had seen his designs for a puppet version of *The Magic Flute* and encouraged him to apply for the Slade School of Art in London.

On Sunday 11 May, Julie had quietly closed a chapter in her life, performing with Ted and Barbara for the last time. The show was the Rats Revel Society gala *Calling All Ages*, at the Victoria Palace Theatre. The family act could at least be said to have gone out at the top, joining an extraordinary line-up of red-hot Sophie Tucker, a very young Joan Collins and Norman Wisdom.

'My idyllic summer', Julie called the two months' respite she was allowed from touring. Much of it was spent with Tony in Walton-on-Thames, and it was on one of their riverside picnics that he kissed her for the first time. She allowed herself to think of settling down. Her husband would preferably bear 'a strong resemblance to Tony'. She might have four children, or five. But her career and its burgeoning impact were never far from her mind.

A few months later, after her seventeenth birthday, Uncle Charles informed Julie she was to work with Wisdom again, in *Jack and the Beanstalk* at the Coventry Hippodrome. Her salary would be an astronomic £250 a week — the highest price ever for a pantomime Principal Girl, and over ten times the average national wage. Ted Andrews could only watch as the little girl, whom he had taught to sing as a means of getting closer, shot ever further out of his orbit, propelled by the talent and opportunities that had never been his. Finally, bitterly, he gave up show business altogether, taking a job as a travelling salesman. In a direct parallel with the play that would become *My Fair Lady*, Pygmalion was vanquished.

The situation was to have serious consequences for all the family in the following years, and would never be forgotten. In 2004, giving an interview to the *Guardian*, Julie Andrews spoke of her continuing ambivalence: 'I have great compassion for him, because he had a tough life himself . . . but his demons got in the way. He'd go sometimes for two years if we were lucky, and be completely sober, and then fall right off the wagon again.'

By now, he was not drinking alone. Barbara,

whose own early life had been blighted by her father's addiction, was finding similar solace, becoming what Julie would later haltingly call 'eventually, probably, a co-dependent alcoholic'. The family neighbour Tancred Agius put it more bluntly: 'Her mother and stepfather were always drunk, on liquor that Julie had paid for. It was sad.'

It was no wonder that she was paying rather more attention to Charles Tucker, on her visits to his office at 17 Shaftesbury Avenue: 'Often I'd forget what Mummy said, but not when Uncle Charles said it.' In particular, he delivered lectures on the need to look like a star, as well as sound like one. 'Sometimes,' she recalled, 'as we walked down Piccadilly, I would point to a beautiful car or a lovely frock, and Uncle Charles would say, 'You'll be able to buy things like that one day. You're going to be a big star.' And I would giggle, 'Don't be silly, Uncle.''

★　★　★

Contrary to popular belief, Julie Andrews' screen career did not begin with *Mary Poppins* in 1964. She was first heard, if not seen, in British cinemas back in 1952.

La Rosa di Bagdad was made in 1949 by Anton Domeneghini, in a style similar to Walt Disney's *Snow White and the Seven Dwarfs*. The first full-length Italian animated film, it won the Grand Prize at the International Children's Film Festival. For its English-language release, the adventure story was dubbed as *The Rose of*

Baghdad, using Patricia Hayes for the voice of the minstrel boy Amin. As Princess Zeila, the rose of the title, Julie amply demonstrated her coloratura range in songs like 'Who Is Queen of All the Garden?' and her sincerity in lines such as 'You saved me — you are my hero — I shall sing your lovely songs again.' The final narration captures both the innocence of the period and the appeal of its leading lady: 'Once more, love had triumphed over hate, right over wrong and good over evil.' The film enjoyed warm praise, but would not receive American distribution until, fifteen years later, the owners realised that the world's biggest star was to be heard on their soundtrack, and hastily re-released it as *The Singing Princess*.

It was as the singing Princess Bettina that Julie opened at Coventry in *Jack and the Beanstalk*, two days before Christmas Day, 1952. Having worked with a number of top-line comedians, Julie was by now a remarkably adept comic foil. She was quite able to hold her own against Norman Wisdom, playing to type as Simple Simon, who had to carry Julie off stage on his back. During the run of the show, he noticed that she was jumping higher before landing on him, until one night he buckled and collapsed under her: 'After that, Julie was as light as a feather — though a little bird told me later that she had a bet with another member of the cast that she would get me on my knees.'

What stayed in his mind, though, was her eye on the future, as he recounted in his autobiography *My Turn*: 'Julie was down to earth, full of fun — and *determined* to be a star. People have called her both an English Rose and an Iron Butterfly, and both descriptions fit.'

For the first time, Julie was enjoying the trappings of stardom. Her dressing room at the Hippodrome was filled with flowers, and her wages allowed the purchase of her first car, a 1948 Hillman Minx, which she named Bettina after her pantomime character. Charles Tucker wanted to take the process one step further. Aware that his prize client lacked the demeanour of a true leading lady, he asked Pauline Grant, the ballet director of the show, to curtail Julie's somewhat tomboyish habits.

For the best part of the next two years, Miss Grant was in charge of the final, most delicate stage of Julie's training, giving her advice on dance, deportment and dress. 'While it was my job to give her a West End polish, I simply developed what was already there by precept and suggestion,' she said. 'I may have helped Julie, but I am convinced that she would have reached the top anyway. She was a born star and I believed in her absolutely.'

In 1953, as Britain's appetite for television surged with the approaching coronation of its young Queen, the more run-down variety theatres were starting to close for good, making way for road expansion schemes and office blocks. But Julie Andrews, able to command the best of the major venues, embarked on her longest bout of touring yet. *Cap and Belles*, a new revue presented by Uncle Charles, starred the great British jester Max Wall, who also wrote the songs. Julie, second-billed as 'Britain's Youngest Prima Donna', performed 'My Heart is Singing' and (in case the audience had missed the point) 'I Feel Like Singing', twice nightly at quarter past six and half past eight, six nights a week for six months. Travelling from Nottingham to Southport, Glasgow to Manchester, Birmingham to Edinburgh, the tour also took in almost twenty other provincial dates.

It was on this tour that Julie wore her first off-the-shoulder dress and finally unravelled her pigtails. Women's magazines started to feature the ingénue in the odd article on clothing and make-up, and audiences appreciated her new sophistication. She was on the verge of becoming a woman now, and Pauline Grant's assistance was making her a most attractive one — yet she was not sure who she really was.

The manager of the Finsbury Park Empire wrote, 'She is no longer a child singer but a young lady of considerable charm and good looks. Her excellent numbers give full scope to a lovely voice.' But the Liverpool Empire report suggested there was still some way to go: 'Will soon cease to be a child prodigy, when she will have to take a more mature line in presenting herself.'

Julie was now earning between £100 and £150 a week, and old enough to spend it as she wished. It did not quite work out like that. By her eighteenth birthday, she was paying towards the mortgage on The Old Meuse, the school fees for her younger half-brother Chris, and an increasing drinks bill for Mr and Mrs Andrews.

'It's only in retrospect that one realises one was ever unhappy or uncomfortable,' she later reflected. 'If I hadn't been around, I suppose they'd have found a way to support themselves. But actually, the ability to be a breadwinner and things like that came pretty naturally — we needed money and I was able to manage it and keep us going.'

* * *

Christmas was approaching, and Uncle Charles had the most splendid booking of all. Val Parnell, the taciturn gentleman who had first heard Julie in her parents' music room — and nearly dismissed her from her West End debut — had now requested her for the 1953 winter season at the London Palladium, in the title role of *Cinderella*.

This was as good as pantomime could get. To be playing in Britain's most prestigious variety theatre, in the most famous fairy tale of all, seemed a dream. After all the touring, she would have three months at home. While her weekly wage broke no records, it was still substantially above the national average. And she would once again be working with the cream of British comic talent.

The script was written by her radio mentor Eric Sykes and a virtually unknown comedian named Spike Milligan. Friends in the cast included Max Bygraves as the kindly Buttons,

Richard Hearne as Baron Pastry and Jon Pertwee (known to a later generation of British children for BBC's *Doctor Who*) as Dandelion, one of the Ugly Sisters. The glittering production opened on Christmas Eve and was a glorious success. Julie, it seemed, had everything she could want: a marvellous job, a healthy wage, and a lengthy period at home.

On 14 January 1954, another show had its West End premiere. *The Boy Friend*, Sandy Wilson's musical pastiche of the 1920s, starred the lovely Anne Rogers (like Julie, a youthful veteran of pantomime) as the guileless heroine Polly Browne. Both show and star became the talk of the town, and a Broadway transfer seemed inevitable. The producers, however, decided to keep the original actors in London and cast afresh. With this in mind, Vida Hope, the plump, vibrant director, went to see *Cinderella*. Afterwards, she knocked on Julie Andrews' dressing-room door and enthused about her performance, adding, 'We're taking *The Boy Friend* to New York — and I think you'd be perfect for Polly.'

Julie was astounded: she knew how many girls were after the role. But her initial pleasure turned to a thumping sense of panic. Vida Hope was talking about a two-year contract — two whole years away, 3,500 miles from her home, her mother, her friends . . .

'No! Really, thank you, but — no.' With that, Julie Andrews turned down as good a chance of fame and fortune as any actress could expect to have. A startled Miss Hope left the dressing room — but not before persuading Julie to meet the author of the show, Sandy Wilson, at the London Coliseum.

On the appointed day, Julie reluctantly walked on to the Coliseum stage, accompanied, said Wilson, by 'a rather forceful lady with red hair', who sat in the pit to play the piano. 'We asked her to dance,' said John Heawood, the choreographer, 'and Barbara stood up and said, 'Go on, Julie, show them your tap.''

Julie demurred, but Barbara insisted. When she had finished her bashful dance, not knowing how perfect it made her for the role of Polly, Vida Hope turned to Sandy Wilson and said emphatically, 'We've found her.'

It was a golden opportunity. But there was nothing Barbara — or Uncle Charles — could say to persuade her. Julie listened, wavered, agreed that in principle the only sensible thing to do was say yes. Yet her every instinct militated against doing so.

Cinderella ended in early March. The cast of *The Boy Friend* was scheduled to leave in less than six months' time. For the moment, the eighteen-year-old tried to ignore the issue. Accepting a week's concert engagement on the blustery Lincolnshire coast, she and her mother packed their bags and went to Cleethorpes.

* * *

On Saturday 17 April 1954, Julie Andrews stared out of the hotel window at the North Sea. Her concerts, at the New Café Dansant on the seafront, finished that evening. But the performance was the last thing on her mind.

In the middle of the afternoon, the telephone rang. 'Julie,' said Uncle Charles, 'you have to decide. Now. They won't wait any longer.'

Julie burst into tears — no longer able to hold out against the thing she wanted least. 'All right, Uncle,' she blurted out, dashing the tears from her eyes with the back of her hand, 'I'll go.' Then, trying to salvage something from defeat: 'But only for one year — not two.'

She hung the telephone back on its receiver, and forced herself to think of her evening concert. In London, Charles L. Tucker made a call to Feuer and Martin, the production company due to present The Boy Friend on Broadway. The one-year clause was agreed.

That, in any case, was how Julie recalled it, writing in Woman magazine four years later. In reality, the situation was a little more protracted. She had not given up hope of another contract in England, one that would render her unavailable for America. So, when she was offered a dramatic role — something she had never attempted before — she accepted it almost wilfully, hoping that its promised journey to the West End would knock The Boy Friend out of the equation.

Mountain Fire was by the Americans Howard Richardson and William Berney, whose previous play Dark of the Moon had been a Broadway success and would become a repertory favourite across the United States. By contrast, the British run of their latest effort was its first and last.

The company of nineteen was led by 'Singing Cowboy' Jerry Wayne, Andrew Cruickshank and Julie Andrews as Becky Dunbar, 'a pretty girl in her teens' from the Ozarks, Tennessee. 'It was an absolute disaster,' was her verdict. 'The story was all about Sodom and Gomorrah and bootleg whiskey and Lot's wife turning into a pillar of salt. I can't tell you what went on. You've never heard a worse accent than mine. I got pregnant by a travelling salesman — in the play, of course — and thank God, the miserable thing closed before we got to London.'

Bad as it sounds, on the page it looks worse: an incredible choice for Uncle Charles to have made for his young client. The three-act play — originally entitled *Sodom, Tennessee* — opens with a blast of thunder, and runs to incest, religious fervour and the lynching of a Negro by the Ku Klux Klan; there are appearances by Lucifer and the Archangel Gabriel, while three songs for Julie are thrown in for good measure. Act Three concludes on a mountainside, with Becky turning back to gaze at her lover: 'The lights dim, then rise again. Becky has become salt.'

The audiences at the Royal Court Theatre in Liverpool, where *Mountain Fire* opened on 18 May, were bemused, as were their counterparts in Leeds, Bournemouth and Birmingham. One critic summed up the proceedings as 'a piece of muddled brilliance', and for once Julie's singing was understandably judged as out of place.

The cast included a young dancer named Gillian Lynne, later the choreographic genius of

76

Cats and *The Phantom of the Opera*. 'It was the first straight play that either of us had done,' she told me. 'I was the sexy murderess and she played the heroine.' There were moments of unintentional hilarity, particularly during the Ku Klux Klan parade. 'We marched across the stage in those dreadful pointed hats; then we had to rush round the back and come on again from the other side — to make it look like one long procession.' Miss Lynne also recalled the seventy-eight-year-old Esmé Beringer declaiming one line 'in that marvellous way the older actors all had: 'The hoooot of doooom . . . ' Julie and I would watch this in the wings, and just fall about.'

Julie considered her own contribution to have been an 'unbelievably appalling job of acting'. But the critics were kind to her, the *Yorkshire Evening News* opining, 'Even in this strange and sombre piece, she gives a remarkable performance for a girl whose stage work has been confined to singing.' In the *Yorkshire Evening Post*, Ernest Bradbury wrote: 'Julie Andrews gives a beautiful and moving performance . . . proving her undisputed musicianship by taking one song on high E flat, solus, and in perfect tune.' And one day, at the Leeds Grand Theatre, Julie's unaccompanied musical entry caused a stir in the half-empty auditorium.

Vida Hope had refused to take no for an answer. Unbeknown to Julie, she had travelled from London, bringing with her Cy Feuer, one half of Feuer and Martin. The short, excitable, cigar-smoking American found *Mountain Fire* 'hilarious, in a horrifying way'. But the young actress, who was proving so obdurate about appearing in his show, was something else. 'The first thing I noticed was that she had perfect pitch. The music followed her. That was pretty amazing. But even more impressive was her voice.' On top of that, 'she was cute'. Feuer and Vida Hope took Julie to supper, and appeared to reassure her about the New York offer. But once they left, Julie dropped the mask, her doubts and fears all too visible. She just did not want to go.

She had reckoned without Cy Feuer's tenacity: 'When you run across raw talent like that, it sorta takes your breath away, and you make whatever accommodations have to be made to get them to participate in your show.'

Mountain Fire did not look like proving an obstacle. A West End transfer to the Strand Theatre had been scheduled for 16 June, straight after the tour. Posters had been printed, but the dreadful reviews killed its chances. At the Theatre Royal, Birmingham, the show was put out of its misery on Saturday 12 June.

Julie was back where she had started. In desperation, she blurted out her dilemma to various friends and colleagues. One of her confidants was Michael Bentine: 'She'd been crying. 'I'm off to America with the boyfriend.' And I said, 'The swine, taking this young child to America,' and she said, '*The Boy Friend* — the show.' I said, 'Oh my God, yes, well, why are you crying? It'll be a big success.' 'Oh, I'm frightened and I don't want to leave home.''

In fact, there was a real boyfriend in Julie's life. She dreaded leaving him as much as she did her family. But the young man was no longer Tony Walton.

Billed eleventh in *Mountain Fire* had been a handsome, quiet-spoken actor from Lake Ontario named Neil McCallum. Like her mother, Julie found herself attracted to a personable Canadian, but that is where the similarity ended. Born on a prairie farm in Saskatchewan and originally headed for the ministry, Neil seemed quite unlike Ted — or Tony. Gillian Lynne recalled the serious twenty-four-year-old as 'something neither Julie nor I had come up against in our life, that sort of performer'. He was also the first man with whom Julie had fallen truly in love.

Ironically, Tony had himself been living in Canada for much of the previous two years on National Service, describing himself as 'almost certainly one of the worst pilots ever foisted on to reluctant Air Force instructors'. He had taken the opportunity to make lightning visits to New York, where his eyes had been opened to the extraordinary quality of Broadway theatre of the time. This was the world that his former girlfriend was resisting so strongly — but not because of him.

Coming home to England, Tony visited Julie twice during the tour of *Mountain Fire*, only to find her smitten with a new love — and this time, it was far more serious than her crush on Freddie-the-acrobat. A young man of integrity and charm, Neil McCallum had already been invited back to The Old Meuse. However, not even he could help Julie solve the conundrum of *The Boy Friend*.

'I not only paused, I very nearly did myself out of it altogether,' Julie remembered. 'Because I had toured England so much, I had an inordinate desire to stay home, of all silly things, and I had a sort of separation anxiety . . . being away from the family.'

Finally, when her agent, family, friends and colleagues had worn her down without convincing her, Julie turned to her father, 'the wisest and dearest man I know'. Ted Wells, who lived some miles away in the village of Ockley, came over to Walton-on-Thames to help her reach a decision once and for all.

But as they walked in the garden of The Old Meuse, discussing the situation, the central problem remained. She could not bear the idea of being away from home. 'That's when I distinctly remember him saying, 'Well, it could only last three weeks or three months. Why don't you go and open up your head and it'll do you good.''

Finally, Julie gave in. She would go to Broadway — for one year only. But her life would change for ever.

3

AMERICA

'I owe a great deal to the Americans. In fact, I owe everything to them. They, and not my own people, made me a star. Had I remained in London and not appeared in the Broadway production of The Boy Friend, who knows, I might be starving in some chorus line today'

— Julie Andrews, 1968

The most momentous step in the career of Julie Andrews was taken on the overcast evening of Monday 23 August 1954, when, in the pouring rain, she mounted a gangway at London Airport, bound for New York.

As Julie explained in 1999, this was the second of the 'three huge building blocks' in her life. 'I began to be known by radio and what I was doing in England, but it was nothing compared to the big world out there — it was a small pond.' Yet it was against a background of appalling emotional pressure that she reluctantly made her first journey abroad. And it is a mark of her extraordinary resolve that, as an unworldly eighteen-year-old, she persevered in the face of agonising events on both sides of the Atlantic — having just suffered the most traumatic weekend of her life.

It had begun when Tony Walton arrived on the doorstep of The Old Meuse to wish her every success in New York. Blurting out his true feelings, the nineteen-year-old declared how much he still loved her.

The response was withering. Julie told him not to be so serious, that he was far too young to know whether he was truly in love — that they were both too young to make any long-term commitment. Arguably, she was right, but her summary dismissal shook him to the core. Tony stormed from the house — and ran straight into a flowerpot. Julie watched as he bent down to put it upright, wishing he had saved face by leaving it on its side, yet knowing he was not that sort of chap.

His feelings were too deep to vanish overnight. The following day, he swallowed his pride and made one last telephone call. 'I really do love you, Julie. But I promise to be over it by the time you come back.'

'Yes, Tony,' she replied. 'Do try.'

But the row between Julie and Tony paled in comparison to another at The Old Meuse, where an horrific domestic storm was set to break.

Ever since the summer of 1949, Julie had been aware of mounting discord between her mother and stepfather. The bickering had become more and more frequent, based on the usual underlying concern: lack of money. Ted Andrews' self-esteem had hardly been buoyed by Julie's support of the family for the last five years. That he had played such a key role in developing her career made it even more galling:

he was no longer the main breadwinner, no longer in control of the family — worst of all, no longer performing in his own right. Show business was in Ted's blood. By now a beefy, red-faced man, somewhat eccentric in dress with a penchant for baseball caps, he was patently not cut out to be a suburban salesman.

On Sunday 22 August, while Barbara was organising a luncheon party to mark her daughter's imminent departure, Ted escaped to a midday drinking session at the local pub, the Ashley Arms, where his pent-up resentment came to the boil. As Julie later recalled, her stepfather 'mostly got belligerent when he was drinking'. She never saw him more so than on that Sunday, when he arrived home to find the extended family already gathered for lunch. Almost immediately, he got into an argument with his wife; as the others joined in, matters escalated alarmingly.

No one — not even a calm, collected Julie — could reason with him. He launched a bitter verbal attack on Aunt Joan and physically threatened her husband, Bill — becoming so violent that they escaped from the room, running for refuge to the bungalow at the bottom of the garden. Totally out of control, Ted roared after them and proceeded to smash the bungalow windows, threatening to 'murder the lot'.

At this point, as she later testified, Barbara was in 'a state of terror'. She and her children fled The Old Meuse there and then; nine days later she would file a petition for divorce.

Such was the background to Julie's departure

for New York. The following evening, when her mother and friends gathered at London Airport to see her off, there was the semblance of a happy scene. But in reality, as she later remembered, Julie was 'moving in a nightmare from which I couldn't wake up', in despair at the thought of being a year away from her friends and the man she really loved, Neil McCallum. Above all, she wanted to stay and support her family. She feared that, for the second time, she was destined to become the daughter of a broken home.

The other actors were gathering on the tarmac; Julie knew none of them. The Boy Friend on Broadway was to be played by a young English comedian, John Hewer, who gave me his memory of the airport — and of Barbara Andrews: 'We got into this bus to go out to the aircraft; there were a lot of girls I'd never set eyes on before. Julie's mother came up to me: 'Look after my little girl.' And I've often thought since, I wish her little girl had looked after me!'

Another player delegated to look after the little girl was diminutive, dark-haired Dilys Laye. Like Julie, she had started in pantomime at the age of thirteen, thereafter appearing in plays and variety tours, and on the wireless. Barbara had telephoned Mrs Laye to ask if Dilys, eighteen months older, would take Julie under her wing. As she told me: 'It was arranged that Julie and I should share a room. It was our first time out of England and away from home . . . I think the mothers were very frightened.'

The rest of the company, including an

ex-chorus girl from *Guys and Dolls* named Millicent Martin, were boarding the aeroplane. After kissing her mother one last time, Julie walked up the gangway and forced a smile as she turned to wave goodbye.

Finding her seat on board, Julie cut a curiously isolated figure. She felt 'the plainest, drabbest girl in the whole bunch. As the plane took off, I left all my heart behind. I sat through the flight all night, numb with misery.' While the others laughed and chattered into the early hours of the morning, eagerly anticipating the adventure ahead, the star of the show — and the youngest in the company — sat in silence, brooding on the situation she was leaving behind, far below.

Unbeknown to her, the hard-won battle for a year's contract would prove redundant. She would never quite come home again.

★   ★   ★

The Boy Friend was born in the summer of 1952, when the small Players' Theatre Club, lodged in the tunnels under Charing Cross Station, decided to vary its usual programme of Victorian music-hall songs. A young Oxford graduate, Alexander Galbraith (Sandy) Wilson, was asked to write a *divertissement* for £50, payable in two instalments. Wilson obliged with a pastiche of 1920s musical comedies, such as Rodgers and Hart's *The Girl Friend*. 'Well,' said the Players' management, 'we've commissioned it; we'd better do it' — and staged it for £850.

The Cinderella story of *The Boy Friend* has been documented elsewhere, notably in its author's autobiography *I Could Be Happy* (the title of the show's main ballad). The disaster of the dress rehearsal, when the leading lady collapsed, and the eleventh-hour emergence of the pretty young understudy Anne Rogers, is its best-known legend.

Opening in the spring of coronation year, 1953, the show was an instant sensation. Much credit went to its director Vida Hope, who insisted that the cast play the period with sincerity. After some uncertainty, a West End venue was made available, and *The Boy Friend* transferred to Wyndham's Theatre in January 1954, for a near-record run of over two thousand performances. It had a rapturous press, sparked a revival in 1920s fashion, and made a star of Miss Rogers as Polly Browne, the poor little rich girl who longs for the eponymous hero to make her dreams come true.

The last British musical to have had any success on Broadway was Noël Coward's *Bitter Sweet* in 1929. But *The Boy Friend* looked a contender to crack the twenty-five-year jinx. The New York management of Cy Feuer and Ernest Martin, whose biggest hit *Guys and Dolls* was currently playing on both sides of the Atlantic, made enquiries. As Sandy Wilson recalled to me, fifty years later, 'There were Americans other than Feuer and Martin, but they were the ones who said they wanted to do it exactly as it was.' He twisted his lips, bitter still at the memory of subsequent events.

A ciné-film was taken of the London production; copies were made of the set. The simple orchestrations were augmented to Broadway proportions, under the musical directorship of Anton Coppola (uncle of fifteen-year-old Francis Ford). Money was no object, as Sandy Wilson told me: 'It cost about fifty times as much on Broadway as in London.'

Most of the Broadway cast was to be English, a rare occurrence even then. *The Boy Friend* was scheduled for early 1955, by which time Feuer and Martin confidently expected the Players' to release the Wyndham's company. But when a revival of the 1920s college musical *Good News* threatened to precede them on Broadway, Feuer and Martin moved the opening forward to 30 September 1954. (They also asked Sandy Wilson to rewrite the climactic dance number 'The Riviera', as its tune shadowed too closely the *Good News* anthem 'The Varsity Drag'.)

Wyndham's Theatre had no intention of letting the other actors go so quickly, so Vida Hope started to recast. The principal concern was to find a leading lady, as Anne Rogers remembered ruefully: 'The Americans wanted me to leave the London show and open it for them on Broadway. But the management wouldn't let me go. I couldn't get out of it. So they had to find someone else to play Polly Browne on Broadway. They auditioned over three hundred girls and they couldn't find anyone.'

One evening, at the Players' Theatre bar, Vida

Hope mentioned her problem to the comedienne Hattie Jacques. Hattie remembered the little girl with whom she had worked on *Educating Archie*. 'She's in *Cinderella* at the Palladium. Why don't you see her?'

Sandy Wilson found his mind stretching back further than *Educating Archie*: 'I first saw her at the Hippodrome in *Starlight Roof*; she was a huge success, with an incredible voice and — like girls used to wear — big white shoes.' In impact and voice, Julie was 'rather like Deanna Durbin, but I didn't know she could do anything else . . . I never saw her on stage again, until she did *Cinderella*.'

'And so,' according to Anne Rogers, 'at the last minute, along came a girl called Julie Andrews. I wonder what happened to her!'

Before the cast of *The Boy Friend* left for New York, Wilson took his new leading lady and her real-life boyfriend out to dinner. 'Throughout the evening I was struck again by Julie's perfect behaviour: a combination of school-girlish innocence and a control and poise far in advance of her years,' Wilson later wrote, continuing:

As I watched her and listened to her, I wondered if we might be about to assist at the birth of a new star, someone as remark-able in her way as Gertrude Lawrence. Then, in a moment of insight unusual for me, I realised that this girl would be a star anyway, with or without our assistance. It was nothing that she said or did, and she certainly betrayed no symptoms of egotism or ambition; she simply had about her an unmistakable air of cool, clear-cut determination. For Julie, I could tell, it was going to be the top or nothing. She knew, in fact, exactly where she was going.

Eighteen years after the event, launching her television series in Britain, the star gave the *TV Times* a rather different story: 'I felt behind other people in sophistication, knowledge of the world and of myself. Coming to America was the best decision I ever made in my life, but I thought it was the end of the world at the time . . . I had no idea even of how to send clothes to the cleaners or go about finding a laundry.'

'Her parents had to sign her over to us because of her age,' wrote Cy Feuer, a stocky, freckle-faced American of exceptional drive and energy, 'but I was struck by her maturity. Most performers at that age are very amateurish, but even then she had great equanimity and poise. She didn't rattle . . . she was an instinctive actress.'

It was vital indeed not to rattle. Whatever the problems Julie had left behind in England, she was to discover that she had merely exchanged one war zone for another.

★ ★ ★

At seven o'clock in the morning of Tuesday 24 August, the cast of *The Boy Friend* landed, tired and cramped, at Idlewild (later John F. Kennedy) Airport, in the middle of a New York heat wave. The contrast with London was an assault on the senses. 'Oh dear Lord, I was a green little thing,' the star said half a century later.

The scrum of reporters shocked even the bubbly Dilys Laye: 'I was a bit thrown when we got off the plane and they said, 'Show us your legs.'' Coyly, the girls inched their calf-length skirts up to knee level.

'Breathe in, girls,' John Hewer recalled them shouting. 'That was our first experience of the American press — bazooms.'

Dilys, the joker in the pack, had a fit of the giggles on being asked by Customs if she had any narcotics to declare. Her extrovert good humour was infectious, and Julie was feeling marginally better when they were met by Lou Wilson, a small, dark, thickset American delegated to look after their welfare in New York. Wilson drove them over the bridge to Manhattan, to the rather seedy Piccadilly Hotel at West 45th Street and Broadway, across the road from the Royale Theatre where *The Boy Friend* was due to open. Julie and Dilys were installed in a stuffy room on the thirtieth floor, 'with a shaft that looked up to the sky', said Julie. 'I could stick my head out to check the weather.' Thoroughly tired and depressed in the sweltering August heat, only Dilys's cheerfulness prevented her from sinking into deeper gloom.

They had little time to rest. The management was throwing a welcome party for the cast that evening at Broadway's most famous restaurant — Sardi's. There, the English contingent met the American members of the company, including

Angela Lansbury's mother Moyna MacGill, cast as the dragonish Lady Brockhurst. The next morning, there were fittings with the dressmakers, followed by a meeting of the company at the Imperial Theatre, where rehearsals were to take place. Vida Hope outlined the plot and Sandy Wilson played his tunes in America for the first time.

Later, at a press photo-call in Times Square, Julie was given a pale reminder of Trafalgar Square back home, as the girls were pictured feeding breadcrumbs to the pigeons. They were joined by Ann Wakefield, who had created the role of Maisie, the heroine's best friend, in the Players' Theatre run. An English pantomime contract had precluded her transfer to the West End — which ironically left her free for Broadway.

After a thoroughly uncomfortable outing to Coney Island in the fierce heat wave, rehearsals began on what Miss Wakefield told me was 'a very humid hot Monday at the Imperial Theatre. Julie was a pal on and off stage. She had salt — a good sense of humour that helped us through some very difficult periods before the end of September.'

The first incident had nothing to do with the company. Ann was perturbed at Cy Feuer's habit of bringing stars from his other shows to view rehearsals, including Gwen Verdon from *Can Can* and Don Ameche from the forthcoming *Silk Stockings*, 'but most of us just assumed it was the American way. It would never have happened in England.'

A major bone of contention was the degree to which *The Boy Friend* was gentle pastiche or outright send-up. Dilys was aware that it was 'such a stylised show, you had to stick within the parameters of the period. So you couldn't do 'your own thing'.' Sandy Wilson's specification had been for the American management to replicate the London production. But, said Dilys, Feuer and Martin now wanted a bigger show: 'A bigger orchestra, and also Cy Feuer wanted it much more precise.'

'We all knew Vida: we were all happy with things,' John Hewer said, 'but then they did start to want to push it — push it — push it, and I think most of the cast quite liked that; I'm not sure about Sandy or Vida . . . '

Julie, however, was turning out to be 'a director's dream,' Wilson later remembered in the *Sunday Times*, 'cool, obedient and totally professional, reproducing, as soon as she was given it, each nuance . . . There were all sorts of pressures to contend with, but Julie remained unflustered throughout, and also, it must be admitted, a little remote.'

For five weeks they rehearsed, for eight hours a day at first, then twelve. 'Julie never had a chance to feel like the star of the show,' recalled Dilys. 'She was never pampered, never treated differently from anyone else. We were all worked like racehorses, drilled and bullied into a performance rather than coaxed. It was terribly hard work but, by golly, it paid off.'

The two girls had by now moved from the Piccadilly Hotel into what Julie called 'a modest suite in the modest Park Chambers Hotel' on the Avenue of the Americas. Their small, air-conditioned service apartment on the fourteenth floor was an improvement — but as the first preview drew close, things took a major turn for the worse. 'Vida rehearsed them up to the dress rehearsal,' the show's author told me. 'At the end, we were summoned to the smoking lounge in the theatre, and they said, 'Where's the magic it had in London?'

Wilson protested vigorously that the changes demanded would only damage the show, at which point the producers lost patience. 'I was forcibly removed from the theatre. I wasn't allowed back until the first night, and even then I couldn't go backstage to see them all. Later on, I was allowed, but by then . . . '

A detective was stationed at the theatre to prevent both author and producer returning. Cy Feuer and Ernest Martin had taken complete control.

Vida Hope made her version of events clear: 'Sandy and I have been asked to stay away from the theatre because we have been behaving like a couple of spoilt babies. The management call us 'the problem pair', who refuse to listen to any advice. My name is still officially on the bills as the producer, and financially our contracts are being scrupulously honoured. Otherwise we are being edged right out. They tell me the show is not working up the same here as it did in London. Well, how can it with a different cast?'

'Cy Feuer took over the directing,' said John Hewer, 'and everybody was very impressed with

Cy.' While he thought Vida's original direction was 'so delightful, it didn't need jazzing up', he recognised Feuer's instinct as being right for New York. 'We were all terrified — but we knew we were going to have to expose ourselves.'

The hiring and firing extended to the cast. The lucky ones were reinstalled, but Ann Wakefield's dancing partner was dismissed outright. Ann herself was demoted to Millicent Martin's role for a day. 'We didn't know whether we were going to stay or not, did we?' said Dilys. There had been an earlier instance, when Eileen Murphy arrived from England to play the role of sophisticated Mme Dubonnet. 'She got off the plane to be told she was no longer required for the part. They were giving it to a woman called Ruth Altman, who was an American . . . But the Americans have always been more ruthless, haven't they?'

Nobody was immune, according to Sandy Wilson: 'At one point there was even talk of replacing Julie.' Choreographer John Heawood recalled her understudy as 'a woman of about thirty-five, who sang very nicely and moved like a Churchill tank'.

Despite the problems, the homesick little girl from Walton-on-Thames was proving her mettle, as Ann Wakefield observed: 'I thought Julie was just perfect as Polly. Her voice had a tender quality of the twenties, a joy to listen to. And a natural comedy sense . . . A wonderful moment was in Act One, when Polly and Tony sing 'I Could Be Happy'. She stepped up on a tuffet and whistled, while Tony tap-danced around her.'

'Julie had been trained to dance,' John Hewer said, 'but I don't think it was her favourite sport.' So Julie whistled instead — marking out for the future a further small corner of her talent.

On most evenings Julie returned to the apartment to write letters home. On rehearsal pay of $100 a week, she could not do much else; in any event she was invariably far too tired on most nights to want to go out on the town. 'How they work you on Broadway. It's detail, detail all the way. Every gesture, every line is gone over again and again. But,' she added, with desperate cheer, 'it's fun and terrific experience.'

The city, however, still overawed her. 'I was reeling,' she would remember. 'I would literally huddle in Manhattan doorways to get my bearings and stop my mind from spinning out of control.' And, all too often, her mind dwelt on what was happening back in Walton-on-Thames — where her mother and stepfather were still in bitter conflict.

Just one week before the Broadway opening of *The Boy Friend*, Barbara Andrews appeared in London's Vacation Court, seeking an injunction to restrain Ted from continuing to occupy The Old Meuse.

Three days before the court hearing, a British television programme, *Limelight*, had featured Julie happily engaged in a transatlantic telephone conversation with her mother and stepfather — with no hint of discord. But now, the true situation was made public as Barbara and her sister Joan recounted the 'terrifying' events of Sunday 22 August. Julie's mother testified, 'I am

95

afraid to return to my house as long as he is in it'; Joan, referring to the assault on her husband, stated that Ted had 'a ferocious temper'.

In an affidavit, Barbara declared that they had bought the house in 1946, transferring it to her name in 1950. It was valued at £6,000, with about £2,500 outstanding on the mortgage; she claimed that the furniture belonged to her. Ted, for his part, denied cruelty and disputed his wife's claim to be the owner of the house. Having heard the evidence, Mr Justice Sachs ordered him to vacate The Old Meuse by six o'clock the following evening and not to molest his wife in any way. At the same time, Julie's mother gave an undertaking not to dispose of any property, pending the hearing of the divorce suit.

Julie's name was kept out of the proceedings. Patently, it was necessary to shield her as far as possible. She needed to bring all the focus and purpose acquired in the last eight years — not least from the man who had now made her mother's life untenable — to show her talent to its best advantage, on stage at the Royale Theatre, New York.

Previews were due to begin on Monday 20 September. As if the cast were not under enough strain, the final dress rehearsal started at ten o'clock the next morning and lasted eighteen hours. Vida Hope and Sandy Wilson, relieved of their duties but still in New York, could only surmise at events from occasional sheepish meetings with cast members at their hotel, but their worries were no less intense than those of

96

the leading lady, preparing for the greatest challenge of her career.

Dilys saw Julie's growth in terms of her role: 'Suddenly, she's being asked to play a girl . . . who's lost, lonely, who thinks nobody loves her for anything but her money, who falls in love. It's a long journey she was asked to make at the age of eighteen.' So it was a huge disappointment that, when previews began, the lack of magic, as Feuer saw it, emanated principally from the leading lady. Instead of delivering the fresh, innocent quality he required, Julie came across as stilted, glib — and dead.

Throughout the fortnight of previews, she was beset with self-doubt. Her singing was fine, and in the Marcel-waved wig and short skirts she looked every inch the flapper of the 1920s. But somehow she did not feel she was Polly. 'I was green, frightened and inadequate,' Julie remembered much later. 'I would try one thing one night and then another thing the next. I was floundering.'

The situation worsened until, on Thursday 30 September, the eve of her nineteenth birthday, Cy Feuer took Julie out on to the fire escape of the Royale Theatre, and told her just how far she was falling short. 'Julie,' he said quietly, 'you can't feel that part until you really *believe* in it. You've got to *be* Polly Browne.'

The Boy Friend was supposed to be a light-hearted romp, a joyous skit: 'The most exciting news to reach the USA since the *Mayflower* landed!' promised the handbill. Yet, as an extraordinarily glamorous audience — including Claudette

Colbert, society hostess Elsa Maxwell and the British Prime Minister's daughter Sarah Churchill — started to fill the theatre, two distinctly unhappy people took their seats in the stalls: Sandy Wilson and Vida Hope, barred from the theatre during previews, there to see the American version of their creation for the first time.

The author was bitterly angry: 'The Americans told us we were both amateurs, incapable of completing the show to American standards. In the opinion of our lawyer here, and of the Dramatists' Guild of America, great injustice has been done to both Vida and myself. If the show succeeds, I shall be glad. And I shall earn dollars. But that is small compensation for the fact that we shall never know whether our *Boy Friend* — as we originally created it — would have succeeded on Broadway. I'm heartbroken. The show makes its bow without my blessing . . . We are all keen to go home.'

In her drab little dressing room, Julie put on her blonde wig and heavy eye make-up, all the time concentrating on Cy Feuer's words, which she would come to appreciate as 'maybe the most valuable piece of advice anyone ever gave me'.

A long way away, she could hear the overture played by Paul McGrane and his Bearcats, the pit band hired for the show. There was a riff in the middle of the overture, where the musicians stood up and played their banjos — and the audience burst into applause. Backstage, members of the cast waiting in the wings had their first intimation of what was to come. 'I think the overture stopped the show,' said Dilys.

'I was amazed at how well it was going, you could tell that,' said John Hewer, but not everyone was happy: 'I am told Sandy was walking around, saying 'It's not my show!''

In 2005, as he prepared to travel to Connecticut to see a major touring revival of *The Boy Friend*, staged by Julie in her directorial debut, Sandy Wilson's mind was still on the anger he had felt at its Broadway premiere: 'I've never quite got over it. Even now.' As fond as he was of his leading lady, he viewed one of her recollections askance. Julie, ever ambivalent, had alluded in a press interview to both Vida Hope and Cy Feuer: 'She was protective, but Cy knew what audiences here wanted. Both parties were right.'

'That's *impossible*,' said Wilson. But his view of Julie's assurance remained constant: 'Well, she's extraordinary — she can do practically anything you tell her to. She'll just do it, almost like a performing animal.'

Backstage at the Royale Theatre on that sultry September evening, Julie left the dressing room in her pale blue sailor-suit dress and walked towards the stage. The first song, 'Perfect Young Ladies', had just ended to howls of delight. How dreadful, she thought, if she were now a complete flop.

Her cue line was approaching, squeaked by Dilys: '*Cave*, chaps — here comes Polly!'

Julie Andrews took a deep breath and walked on stage, to face a first night audience of stars and socialites — and that septic critical septet, the Seven Butchers of Broadway.

'Polly Browne — Polly Browne — Polly Browne!' As the roar of enthusiasm swept across the footlights, any doubt that Julie Andrews would succeed in her international debut was silenced for ever. But there was no sign of her. 'I had to race to the dressing room,' said Dilys Laye, 'and I grabbed her and said, 'Come on, they're calling for you — come back on stage.''

Not even Julie could deny the reaction to the show. During the performance, each song had won an ovation, from Ann Wakefield's tap dance *en pointe* in 'Safety in Numbers' and Dilys's 'It's Never Too Late to Fall in Love' to Julie's duets with John Hewer, 'I Could Be Happy' and 'A Room in Bloomsbury'. As far as her actual acting was concerned, Julie was less sure, only knowing 'Everything I did, I did from the heart.' She just prayed it had come across that way.

It certainly looked like it. The capacity audience was refusing to leave the theatre. Some were doing the Charleston in the aisles, actress Hermione Gingold was wiping away tears of mirth, and Elsa Maxwell was so transported that she was dancing in her seat.

Not everybody was so ecstatic. 'The author-composer-lyric writer Sandy Wilson and producer Vida Hope slipped out looking anything but happy, and vanished into the night,' reported the London *Evening News* next day. Wilson later voiced his frustration: 'It isn't our *Boy Friend*. It stumbled into burlesque from the start. They underline and exaggerate everything they can.'

Yet the echoing cheers appeared to justify the approach. After the noise had died down, Julie and Dilys returned to their dressing room to meet the news reporters, most of them British, most remarking on the brisk tempo compared to the gentler London production. Then, in accordance with Broadway tribal ritual, the girls went to the first night party at Sardi's. As Julie entered the restaurant, the crowd of theatre folk, backers and hangers-on put down their champagne glasses and broke into warm applause. It was past midnight, the morning of 1 October 1954. Julie Andrews was nineteen years old.

The first editions of the morning newspapers had also just arrived. The birthday girl steeled herself. So did John Hewer — for whom the reviews had an added importance. 'I had it in my contract that if the show ran more than ten weeks, they would pay to bring my wife and kids over; when the notices came out I went down to the Gents, and Cy Feuer came in and stood beside me and said, 'John, bring your wife over.'' *The Boy Friend* had passed the test, like no other British musical in decades.

'And, to my total surprise, it threw me up into some kind of stardom,' said Julie, 'because the notices were wonderful.' All the critics praised her, one of them vindicating Cy Feuer's lecture on the fire escape earlier that evening — a lifetime ago — crediting her with playing Polly Browne as if 'she believed each word'. Julie searched out Feuer and showed him the notice,

101

calling it 'the most wonderful birthday present I've ever had'.

The Seven Butchers had sheathed their blades that night. The leader of the pack, Brooks Atkinson of the *New York Times*, declared *The Boy Friend* 'a delightful burlesque . . . extremely well done in manuscript as well as on the stage'. Referring obliquely to the backstage altercations, he praised 'someone' for directing with 'great ironic skill', but ultimately found that it was 'probably Julie Andrews who gives *The Boy Friend* its special quality'. In particular, 'She keeps the romance very sad. Her hesitating gestures and her wistful, shy mannerisms are very comic. But by golly, there is more than irony in her performance. There is something genuine in it, too.'

Elsewhere, Walter Kerr in the *Herald Tribune* wrote that Julie was perfect: 'With a blonde Marcel, the largest amount of blue eye-shadow I have seen anywhere, and hands clasped winsomely just above her right knee, she breathes lunatic sincerity.' And Woolcott Gibbs of the *New Yorker* found that Julie's 'unvarying expression of lofty imbecility is the season's dramatic highlight'.

In England, the *Daily Express*, within a page, showed how journalistic coverage had gone from one extreme to another within twenty-four hours. 'It was a first night full of strife, cruel gossip, and bitterness,' ran the main article, sent to press while the show was still playing. But then, just before the paper left the building, a last-minute bulletin was inserted: '4.30 a.m.

latest — New York, Thursday — Clapping, stamping, shouting and whistling told cast of *The Boy Friend* that the show was a hit with New Yorkers.' Later that afternoon, the *Evening Standard* informed Londoners, 'Blonde, lanky Julie Andrews from Walton-on-Thames has a handsome present for her nineteenth birthday today. She is acclaimed as a Broadway star.'

The following day, Britain could read more of the same. '*Boy Friend* makes Julie Andrews a star at nineteen,' ran the *Daily Mail* headline, '*Boy Friend* is smash hit on Broadway,' declared the *Daily Telegraph*, and the New York critics' response was detailed in *The Times*: 'They had good words for the performance as well as for the play itself, and for Miss Julie Andrews, in particular, their praise was without any restraint.'

Sometime in the early hours, Cy Feuer made his young star a special promise. She stole into a corner to telephone her mother with the news — that outside the theatre, the name of Julie Andrews was now to be in lights.

4

THE FAIREST LADY

*'I thought, what are these Americans going to do
to poor George Bernard Shaw?'*

— Julie Andrews, 1973

'I can't do it — it's all too much!' wailed
Broadway's newest star.

A pack of pressmen, photographers and
advertising gurus had invaded Park Chambers,
all making strident demands on her time and
energy. 'This is America, Julie,' said her New
York manager Lou Wilson. 'You *have* to cash in
on success.'

For Julie Andrews, success was relative. 'The
mink-and-diamond stage of stardom is still a
million miles away,' she said. 'I used to phone
home nearly every day, thinking dollars were just
pieces of paper. I changed my mind when I got
the first bill.'

'Rent, agent, health insurance policies,' said
Dilys Laye. 'Equity automatically took a
withholding tax. We were always short of
pennies, I can tell you.'

And often short of a decent meal. The girls'
one-bedroom apartment, costing a hefty $275 a
month, boasted little more than a cupboard
kitchen — which Julie had little inclination to

use. 'She couldn't cook an egg,' Dilys told me, looking back at their time together. 'I'm not quite sure what she did, I just know that I did the cooking. We ate out an awful lot.'

More often than not, Lou Wilson picked up the bill. One Sunday, when the girls decided to return the favour, they found they could manage only thirty-five cents between them. Two tins of stew cooked on their hot-ring had to suffice. The next day, Wilson sent them a rotisserie cooker. Even then, Julie let Dilys take charge, joking, 'I'm the muggins who does the washing-up.'

Later, she remembered the relationship as 'the oddest but ultimately most satisfying coupling. Where I was absolutely painfully shy and wouldn't have dared venture out, she was this wonderful extrovert that wasn't frightened of anything.'

Dilys agreed. 'I effervesced off in all directions, Heaven knows, I don't think I went to bed for four months. Julie did. Her heart was always in England.'

At least Julie had a substitute for Humpty, her corgi (whom she would hear barking down the transatlantic telephone line, prompted by a kick from her half-brother Donald). Walking along Sixth Avenue, the girls had fallen in love with a dachshund puppy pressing its nose to a pet shop window. The dog, which they bought as a Christmas present to each other, they named Melody. She was anything but harmonious, yet in spite of her snapping — and worse — the girls took her everywhere, letting her sleep in the dressing room during the show.

After the trauma of rehearsals, the mock-1920s charm of *The Boy Friend* was a pleasure to perform, and had become a big enough hit to attract Hollywood royalty, including Cary Grant and Gloria Swanson. In early 1955, Julie met the girl of the hour, Grace Kelly, who said how much she had enjoyed her performance. 'I don't know why she bothered with me at all,' gushed Julie. 'She's so *very* well known.' And there was plenty of opportunity during the run to socialise with other young actors on Broadway. These included three of Julie's future co-stars: Christopher Plummer in *The Dark Is Light Enough*, Robert Preston in *The Tender Trap* and, making a non-speaking debut (under the name of James Baumgarner) in *The Caine Mutiny Court Martial*, James Garner.

'Florence Henderson was one's great friend,' said Dilys Laye. 'She was doing *Fanny* in the next theatre, which our stage door backed on to, and we all used to sit out there. It was a very exciting time. Bob Fosse and Gwen Verdon were doing *Can Can*, and *Damn Yankees* opened . . . Julie and I would be phoned up on a Sunday morning by one of the American kids in the show, saying, 'What are you girls doing today?' We'd say, 'Well, nothing much.' 'Come on, we're all down at Ezio Pinza's house' — and the whole of Broadway would be there . . . It was wonderful.'

In lots of ways, Julie agreed. Broadway had taken her to its heart, awarding her the Donaldson Award for her debut in a musical play. She loved many aspects of the city: its drugstores, milk shakes, cream cheese and jelly sandwiches and fashionable clothes. According to her fellow cast member Millicent Martin, the girls regularly enjoyed 'takeout Chinese food at midnight and watching television until five a.m.'

Yet Julie still pined for Walton-on-Thames, 'the long talks with Auntie on Sunday mornings, the long walks with Daddy through the Surrey woods, the fun with my brothers'. And more than anything, she longed to earn enough money to fly her family over to see her, whenever she felt like it.

John Hewer was more fortunate. As promised, his family arrived for the duration, taking a house on Fire Island outside New York: 'Julie came out and stayed with us for a weekend, a Sunday, and got herself severely sunburned — I was very worried about her.'

So was Dilys: 'Julie is very fair-skinned, and she fell asleep in the sun. She arrived back in New York lobster-red and in some pain. A large washing-up bowl was procured: we filled it with tea and ice cubes, and, stripping ourselves and rolling the carpet back, proceeded to lay great wads of cotton wool, soaked in cold tea, all over her — rubbing was out of the question. I finished up as wet as she was, but we still managed to laugh.'

All the while, Julie was bombarded with invitations from admirers but, for all her newfound fame, she was still the girl from Walton-on-Thames, the opposite of Broadway's erstwhile English darling, Gertrude Lawrence, to whom she was inexactly compared. 'Mummy would box my ears if I ever went in for that sort of thing,' said Julie, at the thought of living it up like Gertie. But she did have one gentleman caller who still meant a great deal to her, as Dilys confirmed: 'Neil McCallum came down from Canada and spent the odd weekend with us in New York. And of course he and Julie were together — very, very much together . . .'

Neil, now pursuing acting work in his home country, made lightning trips from Toronto, or, when this was impractical, expensive telephone calls running into the early hours. 'It became too much,' said the long-suffering Dilys, 'when Julie was under the bedclothes with the telephone at three o'clock in the morning and talking about visions of green fields. I called out, 'Yes, and I've got bloody visions of getting some sleep.''

But gradually the gaps between Neil's visits grew longer, and Julie once more fell back on her faithful swain, Tony Walton, now studying at London's Slade School of Art. Her first letter ended formally, 'All the best, Julie'; it was some weeks before Tony replied, in the same manner. Soon, though, they were back to their old relaxed style with each other. Later on, their letters would be replaced by Dictaphone tapes as the favoured means of correspondence. It was a habit Tony and Julie would maintain throughout their relationship, long after both the habit and the relationship had lost spontaneity.

Hankering for England, Julie also started a tradition she would maintain in her future shows. 'Whenever I passed her dressing room,' Ann Wakefield recalled, 'I'd hear her cry 'Cup

— of tea!' It was almost a password. There was a pot of tea waiting for us.' And, almost like a prisoner marking time on a cell wall, Julie started to cross the weeks off the calendar at the stage door — each Saturday night bringing her closer to home.

Two incidents, however, suggested that New York might hold her for longer than she cared to admit. The first was the elevation of her name, already in lights, above the title of *The Boy Friend*. The second was a brief article in the London *Evening Standard* on 16 March, confirming that Julie Andrews was coming home that September, but adding, 'she may not stay'. The young English star had been approached about starring in another show — 'the Broadway musical version of *Pygmalion*'.

★　★　★

Back in 1952, Alan Jay Lerner (words) and Frederick Loewe (music) had been approached by maverick Hungarian film producer Gabriel Pascal to turn George Bernard Shaw's most commercial play into a stage musical. Pascal had already made the classic 1938 film of *Pygmalion*, starring Leslie Howard as the professor of phonetics and Wendy Hiller as the Cockney flower girl he passes off as a duchess. In principle, Lerner was enthusiastic — but in practice, the piece proved resistant to song. 'It can't be done,' his fellow lyricist Oscar Hammerstein told him. 'Dick Rodgers and I worked on it for a year and gave it up.' So Lerner and Loewe in turn gave it up.

Then, in July 1954, Pascal died, just as the writers decided to try again. This time, they found it less daunting, though still more challenging than their previous hits, *Brigadoon* and *Paint Your Wagon*. With a leap of faith, they started to work speculatively — while the stage rights, complicated by Pascal's death, were being settled — on what was variously titled *Lady Liza*, *London Pride*, *Promenade*, *Fanfaroon* (Loewe's favourite) and *Come to the Ball*.

It is said that most stories fall into one of two categories, *Faust* or *Cinderella*. While the character of Professor Henry Higgins appropriates some elements of the first, Eliza Doolittle is a full-blooded, twentieth-century manifestation of the second. And in creating musical identities for these two protagonists, Lerner and Loewe needed to have specific actors in mind.

The role of Higgins was first offered to Michael Redgrave, who boasted a pleasing singing voice but refused to play the part for more than six months. Noël Coward and George Sanders were also approached — before fate smiled on Reginald Carey Harrison, who seized what would be the defining role of his career.

Mrs Patrick Campbell was almost fifty years old when she played Eliza on the London stage in 1914. Gertrude Lawrence triumphed on Broadway in 1945, aged forty-seven. Shaw had specified a girl of eighteen. 'We began to think,' said Lerner, 'how refreshing it might be if, for the first time since the play was written, a girl of precisely that age played the role.'

Despite this, some interest was evinced from forty-year-old Mary Martin, physically and critically flying high as Peter Pan in the same Broadway season as *The Boy Friend*. Although the writers thought her unsuitable, they remembered the edict of another lyricist, Lorenz Hart: 'If a star is interested, do not say no for twenty-four hours.' They played the first few songs for Miss Martin and her husband, theatre producer Richard Halliday. But the reaction to the 'Ascot Gavotte' and 'Just You Wait, ('enry 'iggins)' was stunningly negative. 'How could it have happened?' Mary exclaimed after they had left. 'Those dear boys have lost their talent!'

'Well, I guess they didn't like it,' said 'Fritz' Loewe, with Viennese nonchalance, and the team looked elsewhere. The gutsy, glamorous Dolores Gray was suggested, but Lerner had another idea, personally contacting Deanna Durbin, who had retired from Hollywood at the ripe old age of twenty-seven to marry a Frenchman. Although tempted, Miss Durbin declined to leave her farm outside Paris.

By this time, Broadway had a new star at the Royale Theatre. Lerner and Loewe, accompanied by their producer Herman Levin, went to see the young English import. Lerner found himself almost embarrassingly touched by the lovelorn Polly Browne, his assessment of the actress the same as Cy Feuer's a year earlier: her diction was superb, her movement charming, her manner sincere — 'and physically, she was as pretty as any eye might decide her to be'.

So it was that in March 1955 (not six weeks

before the end of *The Boy Friend*, as she later stated) Julie Andrews received the most important telephone call of her career. The caller was a Mr Dick Lamarr: whatever Julie's confusion over the date, she would always remember the conversation.

'He said, 'I represent some people called Lerner and Loewe — would you just tell me how long a contract you have in *The Boy Friend?*' I said, 'Oh, I'm going home in a few weeks.' He said, 'My God, I *told* them it would only cost ten cents to call — I thought you had a two-year contract like everybody else. Will you come and audition for *My Fair Lady?*' It was an enormous stroke of luck.'

Two days later, Julie was being interviewed for the most coveted theatre role of the day, singing 'Getting to Know You' and reading some of *Pygmalion* in a Cockney accent. Fritz Loewe then played her some of his music for the show, including 'Wouldn't It Be Loverly?' 'I Could Have Danced All Night' and 'Say a Prayer for Me Tonight'. Julie, finding the tunes irresistible, joined in as much as she could.

In a subsequent session with Alan Jay Lerner, she worked on the script in more detail, concentrating on the transformation of Eliza from Cockney flower seller to gracious lady. 'I vividly remember,' Lerner wrote in his autobiography *The Street Where I Live*, 'an occasional, unexpected flash of fire and, at one point, a sudden downpour of tears. I reported to Fritz and Herman that quite possibly there was a lot more to Julie Andrews than met the eye and ear.'

For the moment, she was given the standard response, 'We'll let you know.' Lerner did, however, indicate his excitement by asking her not to commit to anything until they had spoken to her again ('and — please God — acquired the rights').

Suddenly, it was all happening. Lou Wilson came bounding into her singing class a few mornings later, telling her that Richard Rodgers wanted to meet her about his new show, *Pipe Dream*. Julie thought of her trip, less than four years ago, to see *South Pacific* in London, and of Charles Tucker's prophecy that one day she would sing Rodgers' music.

Fifty years on, Julie recalled her meeting with the great composer: 'I belted out an operatic aria. Afterwards, Dick said, 'That was absolutely adequate.''

He then enquired if she had been seen by anyone else; Julie told him about the audition for Lerner and Loewe. Rodgers looked at her for a moment and said, 'If they ask you, I think you should accept. If they don't, let me know, because I would also like to use you. But do take Eliza if they ask you.' The composer was being generous — and somewhat prescient. *Pipe Dream*, based on John Steinbeck's novel *Sweet Thursday*, opened at the end of 1955 and ran for only seven months, a flop by Rodgers and Hammerstein's epic standards.

Meanwhile, Lerner, Loewe and Levin had been granted the rights on which they had gambled their time and effort. They were not long in pinning down a superlative production team, helmed by Moss Hart, one of the most dazzlingly multi-faceted men in American theatre, as director. Lerner and Loewe's long-time designer Oliver Smith was booked to provide the elegant settings and Cecil Beaton the even more elegant costumes. Eliza's father, the dustman Alfred P. Doolittle, would be portrayed by the English character actor Stanley Holloway, Colonel Pickering by Robert Coote, and Higgins' mother by the veteran Cathleen Nesbitt.

As for Julie, the role of Eliza Doolittle was ideally suited to her talents. And her timing was immaculate. In the summer of 1955, she accepted the role that would dominate her life for the next three and a half years. This time, there could be no vacillation about the length of her contract. She knew the importance of what she had been offered.

On Saturday 1 October, a year after her first appearance on the New York stage, Julie kissed Dilys and Melody goodbye and passed her share of the apartment over to Millicent Martin. Clutching the copy of *Pygmalion* which Lerner had told her to study before rehearsals began in the New Year, she flew home to England with the contract for one of the most exciting musical roles of all time. It was her twentieth birthday.

★   ★   ★

England lay far below, in the pink glow of dawn. Julie Andrews was almost home. But at London Airport, she was forced to stay on board the

BOAC airliner until the other passengers had disembarked, because of the phalanx of pressmen waiting for her. Barbara Andrews pushed through to embrace her daughter after a year's absence. But little Julie was gone for ever. 'Whatever have you done to your hair?' Barbara exclaimed, hugging the sleek young woman who had replaced the gawky teenager.

Her father Ted Wells was there, as was Aunt Joan, and even Joan and Barbara's grandmother, eighty-eight-year-old Emily Ward. Driving back to Walton-on-Thames, Julie marvelled at the relatively tiny English roads, cars, houses — all of which she had missed so much — finding everything 'near and dear and within reach again'.

At The Old Meuse, Julie hugged her stepbrothers, Humpty the corgi — and Tony Walton. But, reported the *Daily Mail*, she was still talking about Neil McCallum: 'I want to make it quite clear that he is a boy friend . . . We are not engaged and have no definite plans about marriage. I have lots of friends — but let us say that he is rather special.' Yet that, strangely, was the last time she was quoted as mentioning Neil's name in print.

Julie had only been back a fortnight when she received a telephone call from Uncle Charles. What he had to offer — a CBS television musical with Bing Crosby in Hollywood — was far from welcome news. All that Julie wanted was to be with her family. 'Someone should have shaken me,' she later remarked. Her first trip to California would be to film *High Tor*, Maxwell

Anderson's tale of love across the centuries, opposite the biggest star of the previous decade.

Once more crossing the Atlantic, Julie was met at Idlewild by Lou Wilson. The following day, she flew on to Los Angeles, where homesickness again hit her, until the excitement of being in the film capital — at the former RKO Studios — took hold.

Julie had been cast as Lise, a seventeenth-century girl from High Tor in Dutch-settled New York State, whose ghost is idealised by the present-day Crosby. The contemporary rival for his affections was played by Nancy Olson, in real life, Mrs Alan Jay Lerner.

High Tor would air across America on 10 March 1956, just five days before the Broadway premiere of *My Fair Lady*. It was the first musical ever made for television, and, with its studio-bound papier-mâché mountain, looked like it. But Julie, singing Arthur Schwartz's 'The Life of a Sailor's Wife' and 'Once Upon a Long Ago', acquitted herself well enough. In Bing Crosby, she had a leading man sympathetic on screen and off — so much so, it was rumoured he had proposed to her. When filming ended, he presented her with a gold and pearl ring, inscribed 'Julie, thanks. Bing'.

As fast as she could manage, Julie was back at The Old Meuse for Christmas, determined to make the most of her time with her family. 'New York and rehearsals,' she would recall, 'still seemed a long way off.' So she closed her mind to what lay ahead.

'Julie had no sense of being a star,' Alan Jay

Lerner noted, 'none of that sense of obligation that a star has toward a play. Rex Harrison had. He returned from London a week or two before rehearsals started, to talk over his part. So did Stanley Holloway. But not Julie. She sent us a letter saying she would arrive on the day rehearsals began — not before — because she had promised to take her two little brothers to the pantomime. It was so different, so unbelievably unprofessional, that we were amused rather than annoyed.'

★   ★   ★

'It's absolutely unknown. It will probably be a terrible flop. We've got this little girl called Julie Andrews. I mean, nobody knows anything about her at all. Nobody knows whether she is any damn good or not.' Thus Rex Harrison confided to colleagues in the hit London comedy *Bell, Book and Candle*, from which he extricated himself to join the cast of *My Fair Lady*. In return for his release, impresario Hugh 'Binkie' Beaumont, for H.M. Tennent Ltd, shrewdly secured the rights to present the musical, as and when it ever came to the West End.

On Tuesday 3 January 1956, the company congregated at the New Amsterdam Theatre on 42nd Street. 'Downright squalid,' recalled Harrison of the former home of the Ziegfeld Follies. 'We worked cheek-by-jowl with the blue movies and the strip-tease shows.' Up on the third floor, in what had once been the theatre's supper club, the cast read through the script,

Loewe playing the piano and Lerner singing the score. Almost immediately, Rex Harrison started complaining. Henry Higgins had little to do between the start of Act Two and his final song of self-revelation, 'I've Grown Accustomed to Her Face'. A new song was written to plug the gap: 'Why Can't a Woman Be More Like a Man?' It was but one of Harrison's many cavils: 'a martyr to indecisions and doubts', Cecil Beaton called him.

'At the beginning, he was very difficult,' the stage manager, Samuel 'Biff' Liff, told me. 'He was going to uphold the Shaw *Pygmalion* against the American colonials.' By Harrison at all times was a Penguin edition of *Pygmalion*. Each day he would yell, 'Where's my Penguin?' to check that Shaw's genius was not being defiled. Eventually, Lerner bought a stuffed penguin from a taxidermist and threw it at him. For once, the irascible actor laughed; he kept it as a mascot throughout the run of the show.

He was less amused by his leading lady's habit of walking into rehearsals practising her scales, or nervously giggling in the middle of their dramatic scenes. 'I always asked her why she laughed,' he later recalled, 'and she never did tell me.' The answer, to the other members of the cast, was obvious. She was completely out of her depth.

'Julie, who had done such an extraordinary audition,' said Biff Liff, 'retreated during the first part of rehearsals . . . she didn't have the confidence.' In less than a week, Harrison, Stanley Holloway and Robert Coote, even

Cathleen Nesbitt, all had a strong grip on their roles. Julie, having done no preparation, was even more lifeless than she had been in her early days as Polly Browne — signally failing to capture the stages of Eliza's metamorphosis, from guttersnipe to model pupil to independent spirit. She thought she knew what her director wanted, but whenever she tried to do it, she felt, in her own words, 'like a crab clawing at a glass wall, with Moss on the other side'.

After three weeks, things could hardly have been worse. Harrison stormed out of rehearsals, declaring, 'If that bitch is here on Monday, I'm quitting the show.'

Moss Hart described himself as 'terrified that she was not going to make it'. He voiced his alarm to his wife, the actress Kitty Carlisle; as she told me: 'Moss and I were in a taxi, and he turned to me and said, 'Is she as bad as I think she is?' And because women are meaner than men, I said, 'She's worse.' He said, 'If I was Belasco, I should take her away and paste the part on her.' I said, 'Why don't you?''

The Victorian showman David Belasco had been famous for dragging his leading lady across the floor by the hair, to get what he wanted. By 1956, even a verbal haranguing was, said Hart, 'the sort of thing you couldn't do in front of a company without destroying a human being'. He dismissed the rest of the cast on Friday evening, turning his energies to pulling the performance the show demanded from Julie, having insisted that she watch the 1938 film over and over again — to absorb the grime and glitter of Wendy

Hiller's definitive portrayal.

What they both later termed the Weekend of Terror began at two o'clock on Saturday afternoon. In the dark, empty cavern of the New Amsterdam Theatre stood director, actress and stage manager. 'Julie,' the tall, cadaverous Hart said quietly, 'this is stolen time — time I can't really afford. So you mustn't take offence, because there aren't any second chances in the theatre. There isn't time to sit down and do the whole Actors' Studio bit. We have to start from the first line, and go over the play, line by line.'

In a direct parallel with her role, Julie faced a tortuous transformation — but in this instance, so much more was at stake: the fate of a supremely gifted (and expensive) company of artists. At first, the director was patient. But, gradually, he toughened his approach. 'If Julie wavered at all,' said Biff Liff, 'he brought her back sharply. He certainly wasn't cruel, but there was no time for politeness. He missed nothing and he spared her nothing.'

Until six o'clock they worked, and then, after a two-hour break, until eleven. On Sunday, the schedule was repeated — but went on even longer, making Henry Higgins' words to Eliza speak for themselves: 'I know your head aches. I know your nerves are as raw as meat in a butcher's window. But think what you're trying to accomplish.'

'You're not thinking,' Hart would insist, 'you're just oozing out of the scene . . . you're gabbling . . . you're playing this like a Girl Guide.'

120

'It was like going to the dentist to have a tooth pulled, when you know there will be a lot of pain but you hope it will be better after it's done,' Julie much later admitted. 'He bullied, cajoled and pleaded to pull my character into shape.'

'That's what you set yourself to conquer, Eliza,' says Higgins. 'And conquer it, you will.' And, finally, in the early hours of Monday morning, Julie started to achieve her own victory, comparable to Eliza's musical triumph in 'The Rain in Spain'. 'Talk about Pygmalion and Galatea,' said Julie. 'Moss was my Svengali.'

Her director made his famous assessment. 'She was neither affronted nor hurt. She was delighted. We were both absolutely done in. But she made it. She has that terrible English strength that makes you wonder why they lost India.'

'She came back to rehearsal that Monday a changed woman,' Biff Liff told me. 'A changed actress, not completely — but she made a big leap over that weekend.' The day went smoothly. 'My goodness, Julie, you *have* improved,' exclaimed Harrison, and for the first time, Julie Andrews felt 'as though I were an actress — a *real* actress'.

There was still much ground to make up. Kitty Carlisle Hart found that listening to her after ten days, 'I could hear every inflection of Moss's.' But, as rehearsals drew to a climax, 'I couldn't take my eyes off her. She mowed everything down with her charm.'

It now looked possible that Julie could indeed become the Fair Lady of the show's belatedly

121

confirmed title. She was certainly going to look the part, as dressed by Cecil Beaton, of whom Lerner said, 'It is difficult to know whether he designed the Edwardian era or the Edwardian era designed him.' The designer found Julie to be 'almost unbelievably naïve. And simple. She was angelically patient at the many fittings of her clothes and never expressed an opinion.' By the end of rehearsals, she was too exhausted to do so. One day, trying on her resplendent ball gown, she suddenly keeled over in a dead faint. As she came to, she murmured over and over, 'Oh, Mummy, what a silly girl I am . . . '

On another occasion, Beaton made a passing comment on how important the show was to her career. Julie stared at him, the weekend of terror still fresh in her mind, and said, 'The only thing that matters is if I do it right.' Doing it right also meant subjecting herself to Alfred Dixon, an American phonetician, whose job it was to get her to speak Cockney in a way that New York audiences would understand.

With so much energy devoted to creating a credible Eliza, and keeping Higgins on an even keel, Stanley Holloway was feeling distinctly ignored — until Moss Hart pointed out that this was an oblique compliment to his abilities, notably in what would be his two show stoppers, 'With a Little Bit of Luck' and 'Get Me to the Church on Time'. Less easy to please was Harrison, who now refused to stay on stage during Julie's final song, 'Without You', informing Moss Hart with his usual tact that he was not 'going to stand up there and make a cunt of

122

myself, while this young girl sings at me'. Accordingly, Lerner and Loewe revised the number to end with an interjection of Harrison's earlier 'You Did It'. With the focus diverted from Eliza back to Higgins, Harrison was happy once again.

At the run-through, Biff Liff caught a sense of what they had: 'I can pinpoint it: after the conservatory scene with Mrs Higgins, and as Rex came to do 'Accustomed to Her Face', there was something about the momentum of the play and the performance . . . I thought, my God, this is going to be something special.'

On the Sunday after rehearsals ended, the company regrouped at Grand Central Station and caught the Connecticut train to New Haven. There, at the Shubert Theatre (where so many successes — and disasters — had been born) the first preview was scheduled, after a week of technical rehearsals, for Saturday 4 February.

'Late that afternoon,' Lerner remembered, 'with the house sold out and a fierce blizzard blowing, Rex announced that under no circumstances would he go on that night. He needed more time to rehearse with those thirty-two interlopers in the pit.'

'Wait until you get the orchestra,' Julie had blithely assured him, 'it's like a marvellous sort of eiderdown.' But Lerner's wife Nancy Olson recalled that Harrison 'just went to pieces and locked himself up in the dressing room'. Radio bulletins announced the performance as cancelled due to 'technical difficulties'. Even so, by six o'clock, hundreds of people had lined up in the snow outside the theatre. With the house manager threatening reprisals, and even the star's agent bellowing 'You'll never work again!' through the door, Rex Harrison eventually, reluctantly, appeared, and the show began only ten minutes late.

'From the moment the curtain rose, I felt that we were on a winner,' said Stanley Holloway. 'You could sense the cordiality coming up from the audience in waves. There was an electricity in the atmosphere. You realised that everything was falling into place.'

Moss Hart had shown himself a political as well as artistic genius, bringing a group of phenomenally talented people to the peak of their game. As for his gauche young leading lady, her core of steel, which had sustained the brutal exposure of rehearsals, was not about to buckle under her co-star's tantrums.

Biff Liff saw how things had changed. 'They finished the song 'The Rain in Spain', and the audience went wild. There were Robert Coote and Rex Harrison, the so-called experienced professionals, lying on the sofa — and they didn't quite know what to do.' Julie stuck an elbow into each of them, grabbed their hands and made them take a bow, to stop the applause. 'So it was Julie who then became the really big professional.'

A further sensation was caused by the 'Ascot Gavotte'. According to Cecil Beaton's biographer Hugo Vickers, 'when the lights went up on that frieze of black and white ladies, there was an absolute gasp of delight, because he did have this extraordinary capacity for designing costumes which were elegant and funny at the same time.'

In Act Two, Holloway, listening in the wings to the reprise of 'On the Street Where You Live', felt even more certain that the show 'was going to be a world wonder'. Only Beaton was unhappy, rushing backstage after Julie's spirited rendition of 'Show Me', fuming 'That bitch! I told her that hat had to be pulled forward!' But it was a trivial issue that could not detract from her triumph. Julie looked stunning, she sounded amazing — and she had brought Eliza to life.

The preview ran for over three and a half hours, finishing well after midnight, but the audience was transfixed. Afterwards, the previously traumatised Harrison stood in his dressing room, surrounded by rapturous friends and colleagues.

There was one further week in New Haven and four at the Erlanger Theatre in Philadelphia before the Broadway opening. During the try-out tour, the show was shortened: a ballet sequence was excised, as was Higgins' exhortation to Eliza, 'Come to the Ball'. Eliza's song, 'Say a Prayer for Me Tonight', showing her lack of confidence, was also cut, resurfacing in Lerner and Loewe's Oscar-winning film *Gigi*.

The response in Philadelphia was, if anything, more ecstatic, and rumours intensified that a hit of sizeable proportions was heading to Broadway. The $400,000 put up by the Columbia Broadcasting System to cover the show's budget looked like a spectacular investment. Goddard Lieberson, who had fixed the deal, would soon become company president. Few wondered why.

Back in New York, on the morning of Thursday 15 March, Julie arrived at the Mark Hellinger Theatre. She could see the queue for standing-room tickets stretching down the block. In her dressing room, the signs of first night frenzy — bouquets of flowers, bundles of telegrams — were already starting to appear. Like a talisman, the basket of violets for her first entrance sat on the table. It was less than a decade ago, and a whole world away, that Julie had been given violets by a London flower seller on the night of her West End debut. Her mother had been with her then — and was with her now, 3,500 miles from home, to witness what was confidently expected to be a huge triumph.

Julie attended an early orchestra call for conductor Franz Allers and then returned to her apartment to rest before the show. With the performance only hours away, she thought back to an exercise her father, Ted Wells, had taught her as a little girl. One by one, she emptied her head of random thoughts, gradually bringing her mind to a gentle standstill. There was a final prayer: that she might do well that night. Then Julie fell asleep.

'When I woke,' she later recalled, 'I had the extraordinary calm strength that would carry me through the evening.' Everything in her life, 'the singing lessons, the exercises, the work', not to mention the sacrifice and separation, 'all fell into place, pointing clearly toward this night'.

Had she allowed her mind to wander, she might have pondered the real-life manifestations of Pygmalion that had brought her to this moment: Moss Hart's insistent, bullying belief in her talent, Cy Feuer's lecture on the fire escape, Uncle Charles promising her the luxuries of a shop window, her stepfather showing her how to sing and, not least, Madame Stiles-Allen, tutoring her in the study in Leeds, telling her, 'One day you will bring pleasure to many people. And, in doing so, you yourself will gain great joy.'

As daylight started to fade, extra police were called out to 51st Street and Broadway, to cope with the surging crowds around the Mark Hellinger Theatre. Inside the auditorium — one of the most ornate in New York — the audience comprised the great, the good and the glamorous, sporting white ties and jewels in profusion, making this the grandest Broadway premiere since the end of the war. Somewhere in the swirling throng, in the Dior gown her daughter had bought her, was Barbara Andrews.

In a few minutes, the curtain would rise, and Rex Harrison would ask, in the rhetorical *Sprechgesang* he had made his own, 'Why Can't the English Teach Their Children How to Speak?' As if to prove his point, a bedraggled flower girl would pick herself out of the gutter, yelp a long, agonised 'Aaaooowww!' and, turning her sooty face into the light, start to sing 'Wouldn't It Be Loverly?'

At the age of twenty, in the aptly named *My Fair Lady*, Julie Andrews was on the brink of major stardom.

5

TONY

'Julie has one career — and I have another'

— Tony Walton, 1958

As the lights went up on *My Fair Lady*, revealing Oliver Smith's depiction of 'a cold March night' in Covent Garden, the atmosphere inside the Mark Hellinger Theatre suddenly caught a chill of its own. During the first scene, the audience was concentrating too hard, staring glassy-eyed at the much-vaunted activity. For a horrid moment, it looked as if failure was being dragged from the jaws of success.

'I felt,' wrote Alan Jay Lerner, 'as if they had gathered for the second coming of Christ and he was late.' Even Moss Hart's composure started to crack. 'I knew it,' he hissed. 'It's a New Haven hit. Just a New Haven hit.'

'My dear Moss,' smiled Frederick Loewe, 'if you can't see that this is the biggest hit ever seen on Broadway, we had better go and get a drink.'

By the time they returned from the bar, Stanley Holloway was raising the roof with his dustman's dance in 'With a Little Bit of Luck', a feat consolidated minutes later by Rex Harrison's masterly performance of Henry Higgins' aria 'I'm an Ordinary Man'. Even so,

128

Lerner and Hart could not completely relax until the middle of Act One, when the vociferous reaction to 'The Rain in Spain' proved that the magic from New Haven and Philadelphia truly had arrived on the Great White Way. In the *New Yorker*, Walter Gibbs would regard the number as 'just about the most brilliantly successful' of any musical: 'It is a moment that has practically everything — charm, style, wit, gaiety — and I will cherish it as long as I live.'

Above all, the audience's imagination was caught anew, that night of 15 March 1956, by the story of Eliza Doolittle, each step of her journey marked in song. Whether plaintive ('Wouldn't It Be Loverly'), vengeful ('Just You Wait'), desperate ('Show Me') or liberated ('Without You'), Julie Andrews received one burst of applause after another.

But it was following 'The Rain in Spain' that *My Fair Lady* reached its lyrical climax, with Eliza, tired but too happy to sleep, singing the rapturous 'I Could Have Danced All Night' — and, as Julie later recalled, she felt exhilarated enough to have done just that. Halfway through the show, after Eliza's triumph at the ball, Julie went to her dressing room and gulped down two cups of strong English tea. She was in her corner between rounds, with the energy and confidence of a prize fighter, of Eliza Doolittle herself.

As the final curtain slowly fell on Henry Higgins' study — his demand for his slippers betraying an aching plea for Eliza, something Shaw had deliberately avoided, but which Lerner had made his masterstroke — it was obvious that

129

Broadway had a palpable hit. The stampede towards the orchestra pit, ten curtain calls and a riot of cheering marked the greatest first night reception of any show since *Oklahoma!* thirteen years earlier.

Backstage, Julie embraced her mother and the three wise men who had kept faith in her: Hart, Lerner and Loewe. Amid her mass of floral bouquets, one bore the message, 'To Julie, from Marlene Dietrich, with love.' In Harrison's dressing room, admirers included T.S. Eliot, who declared, 'I must say, Bernard Shaw is greatly improved by music.'

Despite the euphoria, there was no official first night party: Alan Jay Lerner believed that such occasions tempted fate. He, Moss Hart and Rex Harrison went to dinner at the '21' Club, while Julie retraced the path to Sardi's that she had made after the premiere of *The Boy Friend*. She was joined by her mother and Uncle Charles Tucker — and 'Fritz' Loewe, less superstitious than his nervous colleague.

Sardi's was packed, people she hardly knew mixing with friends and colleagues — all of whom jumped up when they saw her, clapping, cheering, calling her name. Someone gave her a glass of champagne, spilling a little on her new dress, yet she hardly noticed. A big sheaf of newspapers was distributed and, for a moment, Julie's spirit faltered. But a line or two, from the flurry of pages thrust at her, told her all she needed to know.

The critics who had welcomed Julie Andrews's debut eighteen months earlier now outdid themselves in praise. In the *New York Times*, Brooks Atkinson found the show 'wonderful' and considered Julie to have done a magnificent job: 'The transformation from streetcorner drab to lady is both touching and beautiful. Out of the muck of Covent Garden something glorious blossoms. Miss Andrews acts her part triumphantly.'

The legendary writer George Jean Nathan acclaimed it as 'a fine, handsome, melodious, witty and beautifully acted show', in which, according to Richard Watts Jr of the *New York Post*, it was 'difficult to say too much in praise of Rex Harrison and Julie Andrews, who have the leading roles. They would be first rate if they were appearing in a straight *Pygmalion*, and they have, in addition, a brilliant skill for musical-comedy playing.'

'A miraculous musical', Walter Kerr declared in the *Herald Tribune*, writing of Julie, 'She is funny, she is pathetic, she is savagely true. Miss Andrews descended a staircase looking like all the glamour of the theatre summed up in an instant.' All of which was music to the ears of the star's mother. 'Opening night of *My Fair Lady* in New York,' said Barbara Andrews, 'was the greatest night of my life.'

On the other side of the Atlantic, daylight was starting to break over Walton-on-Thames. In a couple of hours, Julie Andrews would place a telephone call to the young art student who had been pacing the floor for most of the night, waiting for news. 'It's three o'clock in the morning,' she would tell him. 'We've had the reviews. I think it's a success.'

131

One month later, at eleven o'clock on a dank April morning, the mournful siren of the *Queen Elizabeth* heralded the huge liner's arrival in dock on the West River. A quarter of an hour after berthing, Tony Walton stepped on shore.

His parents had given him the last few pounds he needed to travel to see his girlfriend, who was there, waving excitedly. They celebrated their first day together in exactly the way Julie's friends (and detractors) would have anticipated: chatting over cups of tea at her small patio apartment on the Upper East Side, into which she had recently moved.

There was a practical as well as a personal reason for Tony's trip. He had left the Slade School of Art in London, where he had been an occasional fine art student from October 1955 to March 1956, to pursue a more active route into theatre design in New York.

Alongside his embryo plans, Julie's achievements seemed daunting. As he later admitted: 'For the first few months, I did feel rather an appendage. You know, being introduced at parties as some vague boyfriend who didn't seem to be doing anything in particular. But gradually work came along: commercial art book and magazine illustrations, murals, caricatures.' One commission he refused: a caricature of Julie, which he knew had only been requested so that the caption might read 'Julie, by her boyfriend'.

While he was finding his feet in New York, Tony would call for her at the stage door after the evening show. Sometimes they would stop for a soda at the Windsor Pharmacy on 58th Street, but long nights out on the town were few. As always, Julie resisted excess, getting as much sleep as she could. Tony may have been staying in her block, but she shared her apartment only with 'Mr Pocket', a canary named after Alec Guinness's character in the film of *Great Expectations*.

Julie was nevertheless more sociable than during her previous year in New York. Sadly, Dilys Laye was no longer in town: *The Boy Friend* had closed on Broadway, and gone out on a national tour. But Julie had made some new friends — notably a young Maggie Smith, making her American debut in the revue *New Faces of 1956*.

Meanwhile, as the months started to slip by, with no sign of Tony returning home, gossip-mongers pursued the couple with an endless line of enquiry: were they engaged? were they already married? who paid for whom? The last question was particularly infuriating. It was all too easy to concoct a story about the $1,500 a week star 'keeping' her penniless boyfriend. Tony's mind was made up: any thought of marriage would have to wait until he had established himself on his own terms, no matter how long that took.

★ ★ ★

'At twenty, this wistful new star appropriates the attention of all telescopes.' Writing his 1957 book *The Face of the World*, Cecil Beaton tried to make up his mind about Broadway's latest comet. Praising her ability to 'belt a ballad across with a vaudevillian authority', he peppered his opinion by noting (as had so many others) Julie Andrews's eye on the future, reiterating a comparison that was beginning to haunt her:

> *The Boy Friend* put her forward, and *My Fair Lady*, in which we watch the metamorphosis from *gamine* to lady of poise, has clinched the promise of a theatrical personality who has all the talent and drive, but hardly the innate grace and elegance, to make her into a Gertrude Lawrence of her day.

For the moment, however, all that mattered to Julie was getting Eliza under control. 'The impact of what had happened — what we had and the effect on the public — really didn't hit me until about three months after we opened,' she said later.

Demand for seats was reaching four thousand requests a day, and the queue for return tickets continued to grow. Mark Hellinger, the show's landlord, gave Julie a brooch of diamond and sapphire forget-me-nots as 'a small memento of the good fortune you have brought my theatre', and offered to have her dressing room painted in any colour she chose, even 'decked out in pure gold'.

For the unlucky, there was some consolation in the cast album, recorded over fourteen hours on a Sunday, ten days after the premiere, in a converted church at East 30th Street. Columbia would not start recording in stereo until November of that year, but, even in mono, the artists conveyed the thrill of being in what the papers were already proclaiming 'the most successful musical comedy this century'.

With Al Hirschfeld's brilliant sleeve illustration of Shaw-manipulating-Higgins-manipulating-Eliza, the $5 album was rushed into release before the month was out. It proved an instant sensation, heading the *Billboard* charts for fifteen weeks (and would last lower down the list for almost three hundred). With a million copies sold in its first year, orders would eventually top the three million mark in America alone, making it the best-selling cast recording of its time.

English law forbade its sale until midnight after the first theatre performance in the United Kingdom — whenever that might be — but in 1956 and 1957, every transatlantic aeroplane and liner seemed to be carrying the contraband.

Over half a century later, the album remains a classic, more so than the stereo version made after the London opening. Never was the fluidity of Julie's voice, the brightness of her diction, heard in higher definition: raging like wildfire through 'Show Me', floating over 'I Could Have Danced All Night', exulting in 'The Rain in Spain', in which she, Rex Harrison and Robert Coote performed extempore footwork as they sang.

The recording session had ended at midnight with Julie singing 'Just You Wait', shrieking the last ' *'enry 'iggins'* in a rare moment of risk to her vocal cords. She had then been briefly interviewed by Goddard Lieberson, who produced the album for CBS as part of the deal to bankroll the show. The conversation, not released until 1994, captures her rather too persuasive good humour. 'I shall be twenty-one in Hoctober,' she says, echoing Eliza's observation that ''urricanes 'ardly *hever* 'appen'.

On 1 October 1956, Julie Andrews' twenty-first birthday and Stanley Holloway's sixty-sixth, Rex Harrison led the audience in singing 'Happy Birthday' to both his co-stars, through six curtain calls. As had always been her dream, Julie could now afford to fly friends across to visit her. Two girlfriends from Walton-on-Thames made the trip, as did Barbara Andrews. Joined by Lou Wilson and Maggie Smith, the group celebrated her birthday with cocktails at the Waldorf Astoria, and a trip to the aptly named '21' Club.

Tony gave his girlfriend a brooch, in the shape of a tiny gold laurel leaf; she would wear it constantly. Observers wondered if it was in place of an engagement ring, because at last Tony was achieving some recognition in his own right.

In late November, his first New York show opened: a revival of Noël Coward's operetta *Conversation Piece*, at the off-Broadway Barbizon Plaza Theatre. An infinitely smaller project than *My Fair Lady*, it was just as exclusive. Coward was on hand to give advice, the young rehearsal pianist was John Kander (future composer of *Cabaret* and *Chicago*) and the leading lady was Joan Copeland, who invited her brother Arthur Miller, and his new wife Marilyn

Monroe, to watch the proceedings.

Late at night, during the technical rehearsals, a young woman would appear, stitching the front curtain, generally making herself useful. 'Keep up the good work — whoever you are!' piped Coward, fully aware that it was the designer's girlfriend, just arrived from her nightly triumph at the Mark Hellinger Theatre.

★ ★ ★

There exists, somewhere in the United States, a ciné-film of Julie as Eliza, made for the perusal of her understudy, Lola Fisher. Those few who have seen it claim to be astounded by Julie's brilliance. To the general public, her performance would remain in memory only, other than in television excerpts, such as when she sang 'I Could Have Danced All Night' on *The Ed Sullivan Show*. But television would preserve the whole of her next role — one with certain similarities to Eliza.

In 1955, Mary Martin had enjoyed a spectacular success with the NBC television transcript of her stage hit, *Peter Pan*, the first time a Broadway musical had been brought into living rooms across America. The impact prompted NBC to approach Rodgers and Hammerstein to adapt the world's best-loved fairy tale, *Cinderella*. The writers knew exactly who they wanted in the title role. But Julie Andrews was under contract to CBS, as a bonus for their backing of *My Fair Lady*: as a result, the project switched from one network to the other.

Television's most ambitious spectacular was, at $370,000, the most expensive. It was treated like a stage musical, and there was one gutwrenching similarity. Unlike Julie's previous television musical *High Tor* (which had taken six months to edit), *Cinderella* was to be shown live, from CBS Color Studio 72 on Broadway and 81st Street.

The sponsors, Shulton and Pepsi Cola, embarked on a mammoth publicity campaign: five million *Cinderella* booklets were inserted in six-packs of Pepsi, Julie's photograph adorned almost every television magazine in the country, and, the Sunday prior to the telecast, Rodgers and Hammerstein sang the show's praises on *The Ed Sullivan Show*, which would be replaced by *Cinderella* the following week.

The score, surprisingly, was below par for the team. Richard Rodgers was depressed with the recent failure of *Pipe Dream* and suffering the onslaught of alcoholism. Nevertheless, 'In My Own Little Corner' with its major-minor tones (sung by Julie), 'Do I Love You Because You're Beautiful?', 'A Lovely Night' and 'Impossible' were better than average for Broadway, and light years above the standard of usual television fare.

Cinderella featured Broadway veterans Dorothy Stickney and Howard Lindsay (the latter was also librettist for Rodgers and Hammerstein's next show, which was to be called *The Sound of Music*), with Alice Ghostley and Kaye Ballard as the Ugly Sisters. Five years after finishing the pantomime at the London Palladium, Julie found herself back in her old role. This time, Cinderella was no two-dimensional comic foil, but a girl with plenty of Doolittle spirit. Julie rehearsed between performances of *My Fair Lady*, with so little opportunity to learn her lines that she recited them while waiting for her cues as Eliza.

On Sunday 31 March 1957, *Cinderella* went live at eight o'clock eastern time, in colour. In the Pacific zone, it was aired later, as a black and white kinescope. It was the fourteenth anniversary of the opening of *Oklahoma!*, Rodgers and Hammerstein's first work together, with which they had redefined American musical theatre.

'Just before we went on,' said Julie, 'somebody said, rather foolishly, 'Do you know that more people will see this show tonight than could see *My Fair Lady* in a generation?'' Added to this was the grim knowledge that live television offered no second chances. Edie Adams, delightful as the Fairy Godmother, later remarked, 'I just thought it was going to be the biggest train wreck in the history of show business.'

But the girl from Walton-on-Thames got on with it, admitting later, 'It was a bit of a scuffle.' She found herself changing costumes during her dialogue: while the camera was on her (size eight) glass slippers in the transformation scene, someone was placing a tiara on her head. The lack of space meant the technical crew was crammed behind the scenery, dangerously close to view. The magic effects were planned elaborately, but in the event refused to work. Firework sparklers sufficed, and nobody complained.

'Given the things that could go wrong,' said Edie Adams, 'nothing went wrong.' Viewed with

139

hindsight, *Cinderella* is raw, jerky, badly recorded — but glowing with charm. Especially touching is Julie's burning sincerity, a quality that Middle America took to its bosom. A quite extraordinary 107 million people watched the ninety-minute broadcast, extraordinary even by latter-day standards. Outside the studio, the streets of Manhattan were deserted. Jon Cypher, playing the Prince, felt 'it was almost as though they had dropped a neutron bomb. Everybody was inside watching the show.'

Julie had again scored a triumph, one that would net her an Emmy Award nomination. The critics lavished her with praise, calling her 'freshly beautiful . . . captivatingly lovely . . . a lark at Heaven's gate'. The *New York Times* described her as 'the best reason yet to buy a colour set'. She had achieved an almost impossible task: performing one record-breaking show by night, preparing another by day — both to a first-rate standard. As ever, there was little time to reflect on her success. The following day, Julie reported for duty on *My Fair Lady*. 'It was kind of business as usual and going back to my day job.'

★ ★ ★

In May 1957, a frayed rope sent a forty-foot piece of scenery, weighing several tons, hurtling to the stage behind the drop cloth, in front of which Rex Harrison was singing 'I've Grown Accustomed to Her Face'. Had the accident happened a few minutes earlier, on the full stage set, both he and Julie would have been seriously injured, if not killed.

Less traumatic, but more embarrassing, was the night one of the ballroom chandeliers hooked on to Harrison's toupee and lifted it into the flies at the end of Act One. Julie was well equipped, from her days in variety, to keep a straight face, but even she found it difficult to restrain herself when Harrison broke wind in the middle of the conservatory scene, just as Mrs Higgins said 'Henry, dear, please don't grind your teeth.' Somehow, Julie kept herself together, but when she came to 'Without You', with its lyric 'No, my reverberating friend', she fell apart, as did most of the audience.

Julie's relationship with Harrison had settled into something surprisingly amicable: 'He was quirky, selfish, charming, dashing and brilliant — and I would learn so much, just by standing on stage and watching him. However mad one got at him for the odd bit of selfishness, he cut the mustard every single night so brilliantly that one forgave him.'

Rex Harrison returned the compliment: 'She is marvellously even, her performance doesn't vary; it is highly professional from the word Go. Julie always was — a very boring old word — a good trouper.'

One perennial problem, ill health, asserted itself in the first August of the run, when a Saturday show was cancelled less than halfway through, with both Harrison and his understudy stricken by laryngitis. Julie also had her throat trouble. The official diagnosis was tonsillitis, but it was symptomatic of another issue. Despite the nightly eulogies, she remained less than confident of her ability, admitting, 'I still feel unsure sometimes, as though I've tackled something miles above me.'

Whatever her doubts, she was the toast of Broadway. Among the famous paying court was Ingrid Bergman, on her first visit to America after a decade of exile from Hollywood censure; Danny Kaye also came backstage, recalling the little girl who had sat on his lap during rehearsals for the 1948 Royal Variety Performance. The show was less than six months old when one of Hollywood's brightest stars paid a visit, and was clearly enchanted: on 8 August 1956, the *Los Angeles Times* ran a piece entitled 'Audrey Hepburn aims at *My Fair Lady*'. For fortune-tellers, it was a straw in the wind.

In his diaries, Noël Coward bestowed his benison: 'Rex Harrison and Julie Andrews are wonderful, the score and lyrics excellent, the decor and dresses lovely and the whole thing beautifully presented.' *My Fair Lady* had become and would remain Broadway's benchmark of quality. The most literary, and literate, musical of its period, it was the only one with no proper love story. 'Lerner didn't make *Pygmalion* into a musical,' wrote Ethan Mordden in *Coming up Roses*, his essay on 1950s Broadway. 'He made a musical into *Pygmalion*.'

Records were shattered in the show's wake. On 29 September 1962, it ended a six-and-a-half-year Broadway tenure, having played for

2,717 performances — at the time, the longest run of any musical in history (it would later be overtaken by *Hello, Dolly!* and *Fiddler on the Roof*, before the advent of Andrew Lloyd Webber). For the two years in which its original stars appeared in the show, not one seat was left unsold. The advance waiting list eventually settled down to an average of six months, and the gross earnings from the New York run alone exceeded a record $10 million.

My Fair Lady won almost every award on offer: the New York Drama Critics Circle, the Outer Critics Circle, and the Antoinette Perry, or Tony, which was also awarded to Rex Harrison, Moss Hart, Cecil Beaton, Oliver Smith and conductor Franz Allers. Julie was pipped at the post by Judy Holliday in *Bells Are Ringing* — a notable feat for Miss Holliday since, as the legendary songwriter Irving Berlin told Moss Hart, *My Fair Lady* was making it 'awfully difficult for anyone writing a musical this season'.

A year after the premiere, a national touring company was formed, starring Brian Aherne and Anne Rogers, from the London production of *The Boy Friend*. Miss Rogers proved such a feisty Eliza that she won the Sarah Siddons Award in Chicago, a reminder that, brilliant though Julie was in the role, it was not hers by right.

In the autumn of 1957, the thoughts of the principal Broadway players started to turn towards the West End production, scheduled for April the following year at the most glorious of all London playhouses, the Theatre Royal, Drury Lane.

Rex Harrison was the first of the principals to leave the Broadway cast, succeeded in November by Edward Mulhare (later famous in another Harrison hand-me-down, the television version of the film hit *The Ghost and Mrs Muir*). On the star's final night, in the ballroom scene, the Queen of Transylvania seemed more beautiful than usual. It was Mrs Harrison, the actress Kay Kendall, making her only appearance on Broadway.

With the end of her Broadway contract in sight, Julie felt a mixture of emotions. Alan Jay Lerner summed up the situation: 'This is only the start for Julie. She can be anything she wants in the theatre, the same kind of star that Gertrude Lawrence was. Only I'm not sure that's what she wants.' On one hand, she still eagerly awaited her family's Dictaphone tapes and dreamed of returning to England and reigning supreme at Drury Lane. On the other, she had Tony to alleviate any pangs of homesickness and recognised that she was going to miss New York.

On Saturday 1 February 1958, after more than six hundred shows, Julie Andrews gave her last Broadway performance as Eliza, receiving from the company a pendant of diamonds and pearls. She was replaced by another British child star, Sally Ann Howes, who acquitted herself extremely well (on a slightly higher salary). Julie had two whole months free before the London opening. But relaxing in her apartment on the

Upper East Side was quite impossible. Great things were expected — demanded — of her. When the box office at Drury Lane had opened the previous October, twelve extra people were engaged to cope with the rush. By the beginning of March, two months before the premiere, the show was already into profit. 'It's a bit frightening,' said Julie. 'They must be expecting paradise or something. I hope that people won't be disappointed . . . it's just a musical.'

For the first time, financial considerations dictated her agenda. With her wage in New York at $1,500 a week, she had become, as she put it, 'comparatively rich' — so wealthy, in fact, that for tax reasons her return to England, after such a long absence, needed to be delayed until the start of the financial year.

Thus, from New York, she flew to Paris, the first time she had ever been to mainland Europe. There, the press winkled her out almost immediately. Was she going to marry Tony? Had they quarrelled? When would she see him again? Rather too emphatically, she replied, 'Not tomorrow, or ever. I have at the moment no intention of getting engaged to anyone.'

Julie's father and his family joined her in Paris for a few days, the first time Ted Wells had seen his daughter in over two years. When they left, their place was taken by Julie's mentor from pantomime days, Pauline Grant, with whom she travelled to Switzerland. Tony then flew in from New York to spend a fortnight with Julie in the ski resort of Klosters. For all their protestations, it was expected that their engagement would be announced soon after Julie began rehearsals for *My Fair Lady* at Drury Lane.

★ ★ ★

Julie Andrews flew into London Airport with 260 pounds of excess baggage, another seven trunks following her by sea. It was a far cry from the two old suitcases she had forlornly carried to New York for *The Boy Friend*, or the slightly larger set with which she had set off for *My Fair Lady*. Her manner was smarter, too. 'I'd have come to London earlier,' she told one reporter, 'but I've dodged the tax-man.'

Back at The Old Meuse, almost a hundred friends and relatives were waiting to welcome her home. But Walton-on-Thames' most famous inhabitant stayed only a night in her old bedroom before following another jet-set habit, checking into a £112 a week suite at the Savoy Hotel, ready for the first rehearsal on Monday 7 April.

Eliza's Cockney accent underwent re-evaluation for London, becoming more authentic than that prescribed for New York (though still not authentic enough for some critics). Rex Harrison, however, declined to be re-evaluated, stating that he was not going to rehearse a show he had been performing for the last two years. Binkie Beaumont, the London producer, threatened to replace him with Michael Redgrave, the original suggestion for Higgins. Harrison backed down.

There was trouble in another quarter. The night before the first preview, Beaumont unceremoniously dismissed the young Peter Gilmore, as being unsuitable as foppish Freddy Eynsford-Hill. 'Eliza's boy friend sacked', screamed the *Daily Express*, which also ran a daily banner: 'Five more days . . . four more days . . . three more days . . . ' until 30 April 1958, when it simply read 'Tonight'.

That evening, the scene outside the Theatre Royal, Drury Lane was chaotic, a mass of camera bulbs exploding at one of the most exclusive audiences in memory. If it could not match the 'Ascot Gavotte' quota of every duke and earl and peer, it did at least provide a bevy of diplomats, politicians and tycoons, not to mention Dirk Bogarde, Kay Kendall and Ingrid Bergman, revisiting the show she had enjoyed so much in New York.

'No play in the history of the West End was ever awaited with more anticipation,' stated Alan Jay Lerner, bracing himself for an anticlimax. But, like New York, the ovation at the end of 'The Rain in Spain' brought events to a standstill — and the show ended triumphantly with eight curtain calls, as Julie Andrews took possession of the stage from which Mary Martin had once held her enraptured in *South Pacific*.

Unlike New York, caution was thrown to the wind with an orgy of entertaining. Jock Whitney, the American Ambassador, held a huge reception at his official residence in Regent's Park, Binkie Beaumont hosted a party at his house, and Julie gave a dinner at the Savoy Hotel, attended by Tony, her mother, Maggie Smith and Uncle Charles Tucker, who had predicted her Drury Lane glory eight years before.

Over the next few days, the papers judged that

147

the massive expectations had been met: 'Still the great Cinderella story of the century', said the *Sunday Express*. 'A spirited and beautiful Eliza', said *The Times*, while the *Daily Telegraph* affirmed, 'Julie Andrews' Eliza seems to me to have gained in fire and force.' Even the normally caustic Kenneth Tynan in the *Observer* seemed won over: 'Nothing in Julie Andrews' Cockney becomes her like the leaving of it, but she blossoms, once she has shed her fraudulent accent, into a first-rate Eliza, with a voice as limpid as outer space.'

On Monday 5 May, Queen Elizabeth II, accompanied by Prince Philip and Princess Alexandra, attended a gala performance. Afterwards, at yet another Savoy reception, Julie turned to Moss Hart and whispered, 'We've done it. We're engaged.' It was supposed to be a secret: Tony Walton had proposed on the Sunday, and only a few close friends and relatives knew. But Moss Hart's pleasure was uncontained. 'I blurted it out,' he admitted afterwards. 'I couldn't help myself.'

The press had a field day — and, unusually, some of the background colour came from Julie herself. She had been persuaded to write her life story for *Woman* magazine, which was published on 3 May, the day before Tony's proposal. Under the heading 'So Much to Sing About', it gave a romanticised account of her years up to the opening night at the Mark Hellinger Theatre, ending with a homily and some wishful thinking: 'If I am blessed with lots of children, which is one of my dearest dreams, I will wish nothing more for them than they shall know the same strength of family love which has been given to me . . . impossible things *can* happen, all the time.'

They would be engaged for a full year, in which time playing Eliza would become less a matter of art than one of endurance. 'It was overwhelming,' Julie told me, forty years later. 'All one could think about was the doing.' Nonetheless, she made time for a number of charities, particularly the Imperial Cancer Research Fund. She also spoke at the Woman of the Year luncheon, appeared in her second Royal Variety Performance, and was immortalised in wax in the actresses' gallery of Madame Tussaud's.

Then, in August, tonsillitis returned to plague her, as it did Rex Harrison and Robert Coote. Eight songs a night, eight times a week, with only one row of float microphones to help her reach the back of the cavernous Theatre Royal, were taking a toll. And on 1 October, she celebrated her twenty-third birthday in the London Clinic having her wisdom teeth removed, allowing her understudy Tonia Lee a share of the limelight.

By the end of that month, Julie had recovered enough to announce, at long last, the plans for her future. She would marry Tony after finishing her eighteen-month stint in *My Fair Lady*, and they would live, initially, in Belgravia, where she had leased an exclusive two-bedroom flat at 70 Eaton Square.

Since returning to England, Tony's career had taken off. His break, like Julie's, came with a

Sandy Wilson musical. *Valmouth*, a brilliant adaptation of the epicene novels of Ronald Firbank, was caviar to the general, lasting in the West End only a matter of weeks. But Tony's decadent designs attracted great praise. He now looked less likely to be known as Mr Julie Andrews. So it was a good time to get married, particularly as Julie's producers had offered her a honeymoon period during the run. The wedding date was moved back to Sunday 10 May.

Tony's best man was, by coincidence, Rex Harrison's son Noël, who had been with him at Radley; Julie's bridesmaids were her thirteen-year-old half-sister Celia Wells and Tony's fourteen-year-old sister Carol. Naturally, Ted Wells was to give the bride away — but not forgotten in the mêlée was the man who had taught Julie to sing. On the eve of her daughter's wedding, Barbara allowed Ted Andrews back into her life — and the family home — almost five years after a judge had ordered him to leave.

The former 'radio artiste', now paunchy, his ginger hair fast vanishing, was a commercial traveller for a firm of china wholesalers. It seemed that he had found a way of living with 'his demons', as his stepdaughter would later call them. 'I came back because I wanted to and because I knew I should be happy,' he told reporters. 'You'd better ask Mrs A. for the details.' But Mrs A. was too busy to answer press questions. 'Julie and Tony didn't give us much time,' said Aunt Joan, matron of honour. 'We are all working overtime.'

The week before the wedding was just about

the busiest Julie had ever known. All thoughts of resting between shows at Drury Lane were abandoned — at times, she was lucky to make it on stage in the right costume, such was the rush to get everything organised. 'Poor Julie,' said her future mother-in-law, Hilda Walton. 'She has fifty million things on her mind.' To add to the pressure, the bride-to-be was sitting for the most fashionable portrait painter of the day, Pietro Annigoni. Charles Tucker had commissioned the artist, famous for his coronation likeness of the Queen, to paint the star of *My Fair Lady* in flower girl attire.

Later that week, Julie had a final fitting of her wedding dress, designed by her fiancé but made by Madame de Rachelle, a theatrical dressmaker in Soho. She and Celia Wells then visited a Mayfair hairdresser. Their father sat on an upturned wheelbarrow, getting a shilling haircut from the local gardener at his home in Ockley.

★　★　★

Sunday 10 May 1959 dawned a perfect English summer's day. The sun shone brightly, as yet not too hot for comfort. But the couple's slim hopes for a 'quiet family country wedding' evaporated as a crowd started to build, stretching a mile along the peaceful Surrey lanes leading to the Victorian church of St Mary's, Oatlands in Weybridge.

By noon, there were over two thousand spectators, many of them Walton and Weybridge locals, recalling the skinny young girl who had gone up to London to sing for the BBC long before she became the most lionised musical lady on the West End stage. The groom, rather dark-eyed from his stag night party, was shocked at the crush. 'Our wedding was kind of a zoo. I certainly wasn't expecting it. Noël, my best man, was using his top hat to smash people aside to try and get us through into the church.'

Sixty photographers and cameramen delayed the arrival of the bride and her father. As their car pulled up, the crowd surged forward. The police tried in vain to hold it back, but the tide was so strong that Julie's dress was caught up in the stampede. Newsreel footage of the wedding was accompanied, inevitably, by 'Get Me to the Church on Time', yet the word on everyone's lips, as the bride emerged from the scrimmage, was, equally inevitably, 'Loverly'. Julie was stunning in her £350 dress — which Tony could now see properly for the first time — of embroidered white silk organza, overlaid with tulle. Her veil and train were similarly diaphanous, and her father knew she had never looked more beautiful.

Inside the church, thirteen-year-old Richard Aylott was preparing to sing 'The Lord's my Shepherd' as a duet. In fact, he told me, 'I did it as a solo, because the other choirboy just mimed the words.' Three hundred invited guests squashed up against two hundred gatecrashers, and the temperature rapidly escalated. The vicar referred to the half-hour ceremony as 'a homely affair' — even though the thrum of the huge crowd outside was clearly audible. 'I preferred the first night at Drury Lane to this,' Julie said afterwards. 'There was at least more room to move about there.'

It took the couple fifteen minutes to reach their car, after leaving the church to the Mendelssohn wedding march. They finally drove off, liberally sprinkled with confetti, to the three-hundred-year-old Mitre Hotel on the Thames at Hampton Court, where Julie and her father had once used to dock their boat. During the reception, the bride and groom tried to slip away to the riverbank, to seek some respite from the humid afternoon — and were instantly pursued by photographers. The press were also having a field day snapping the guests, who included Sandy Wilson, Maggie Smith, Svetlana Beriosova from the Royal Ballet and Stanley Holloway and Robert Coote from *My Fair Lady*. Noël Harrison did his best to convince reporters that his father's absence was due to filming in Paris.

Despite the excessive heat, the reception went with a swing. Tony Walton's fair lady was remembered as a 'long-legged, pig-tailed, buck-toothed girl'; and of course, the band played excerpts from a well-known musical. The three-tiered cake was topped by two miniature figures, one in a flower girl costume, the other in an artist's smock, and the general mood of jollity was set by Julie's brother John Wells, who rolled up in a vintage Austin with pink footprints running across the roof, blowing an antique post horn.

Ten years after their chance meeting on a train

journey and a few ups and downs, the childhood sweethearts were man and wife. 'At least we can't be accused of rushing into this,' quipped the groom. Then, to the cheers of their guests, Mr and Mrs Tony Walton set off to London Airport, in a Rolls-Royce with tin cans tied to the back, for a two-week honeymoon before Julie's last few months in *My Fair Lady*.

As they took their seats on the TWA aeroplane, it seemed that the two young people, who knew each other so well and had so many common interests — not to mention sharing a lively sense of humour and a love of family — stood a much better chance of marital bliss than most theatre couples. It was no doubt only incidental that they were flying that night to Hollywood . . .

Landing in Los Angeles, Julie alighted first, to be greeted by the hugely popular comedian Jack Benny, on whose television show she had agreed to appear. Tony stood behind his wife on the tarmac, bleary in the Californian sun. The honeymoon was obviously going to be Mrs Walton's pleasure mixed with Miss Andrews's business. It remained to be seen if this was the shape of things to come.

6

TIPTOE THROUGH THE CUT GLASS

*'Julie works just as hard at her life as in
her profession'*

— Svetlana Beriosova

On Saturday 8 August 1959, Julie Andrews played
Eliza Doolittle for the last time. Stepping off the
stage at Drury Lane, with the farewell audience
still cheering her to the rafters, she rushed into
her dressing room and burst into tears.

She likened the feeling to leaving school
(although this was hardly from her own experience). 'One week you think it can never happen,
and suddenly you find yourself saying goodbye
and going out into another world. It's sad and
a little unsettling.' The following Monday, she
was succeeded as Eliza by her friendly rival Anne
Rogers.

In reality, Julie had been looking forward to
leaving *My Fair Lady* ever since returning from
her fortnight's honeymoon — most of which had
been spent rehearsing with Phil Silvers for *The
Jack Benny Hour*, on which she performed 'I'm
Just Wild About Harry' and 'Ain't We Got Fun?'
(her husband certainly had little) on Saturday 23
May, before flying back to England.

The London run would leave her with a

155

kaleidoscope of memories: the gala performance for delegates of the 1959 Congress of NATO; Stanley Holloway warbling 'I've Thrown a Custard in Her Face' backstage; Julie's wax effigy being unveiled at Madame Tussaud's. And the night she gave a lift to the elderly actress Margaret Halstan, whose one line as the Queen of Transylvania, 'Charming, charming', was addressed to Eliza in the ball scene. Miss Halstan explained how tiring she found getting home after the show. 'Yes, I know,' said Julie. 'I'm in *My Fair Lady*, too.'

'Really, my dear,' exclaimed Miss Halstan, 'and what part do you play?'

Julie's last weeks as Eliza had required all her strength of will. For three and a half years, she had sung eight songs a show, eight shows a week. 'I was becoming an automaton,' she later revealed. When I asked her about the strain of repetition, she told me: 'Alan Jay Lerner once said that a very good role in a long-running play was probably better than a great deal of repertoire in a short run.' But she had explored Eliza's many facets as much as she was able. 'Doing it for two years on Broadway and eighteen months in London was so exhausting that when it was over I felt like I'd come out of a long, dark tunnel.'

She remained her own harshest critic: 'You know, I never did get that part completely under control, but I came very close sometimes.'

That autumn, Julie Walton played the little wife quite convincingly, redecorating the third-floor apartment at 70 Eaton Square, but setting her mind on finding a bigger home where she and Tony could balance work with a traditional family life. Contemplating her first real break for over five years, she mused: 'Sometimes, I think my success has come too soon. I feel that I'm continually running to catch up. Now *My Fair Lady* is over for me — and in some ways it's really the beginning.'

In terms of her public image, this was certainly the case. Magazine advertisements captured a young woman with a creamy complexion, clear eyes, nearly always a smile about her lips, claiming that by brushing for one minute with Vitapointe conditioner her hair gained 'a wonderfully healthy shine' and that there were 'One, two, three, four reasons!' why Julie Andrews ate Ryvita biscuits.

She was now dressing the way she would for another thirty years: pale slacks, well-made shirts and pale sweaters (often tied around her shoulders). With her slim figure and short hair, she looked, remarked one female journalist, 'like a young boy about to play Shakespeare'. Her Soho dressmaker was still called upon for fitted gowns, sometimes designed by Tony, but Julie had no great interest in jewellery, and stayed loyal to her favourite scent, 'Carnet du Bal' from Revillon.

'We've been able to entertain all our chums,' she chirped, declaring a newfound skill: 'I've done all the cooking!' Her inner circle now included the tall, dazzling Svetlana Beriosova — a prima ballerina at the Royal Ballet, Covent Garden, around the corner from *My Fair Lady* at Drury Lane.

Beriosova's husband was the Pakistani psycho-analyst Mohammed Masud Raza Khan, a proponent of Freudian theory. The handsome and charismatic Khan was the antithesis of the self-effacing shrink: genius, bully or both, he was to have some long-term influence on Mr and Mrs Walton. Julie would later tell Linda Hopkins, author of *False Self*, the definitive study of Khan, about the games they played, including guessing the names of their future biographies: 'Masud said to me, 'I know yours, Julie: *Tiptoe through the Cut Glass*.' That seemed then and still seems utterly right for me. I am a very careful person . . . '

Another confidante was the theatre and ballet photographer Zoë Dominic. 'I'm closer to Zoë and Svetlana than with anyone,' said Julie. 'We three could chat for centuries, about children and love, audiences and work.'

Tony, meanwhile, was branching out from design into management. In September, he joined Philip Wiseman (with whom he had worked in New York on *Conversation Piece*) in producing the West End drama *The Ginger Man*, starring Richard Harris. At the opening was the brilliant, wayward film director Michael Powell, casting what would be the most notorious film in British cinema to date, the 1960 thriller *Peeping Tom*, about a homicidal cameraman who films women at their moment of death. Powell noticed Julie in the audience. As he wrote in his memoirs, *Million-Dollar Movie*, he added her to his shortlist for the principal victim, adding his thoughts on their qualities:

Julie Andrews ('too famous')
Moira Shearer ('too glamorous')
Joan Plowright ('too sympathetic') . . .

Ultimately, he decided on Moira Shearer, the star of his triumphant ballet film *The Red Shoes* — and cinemagoers lost the chance of seeing Julie making her first big screen appearance at the hands of a homicidal scopophiliac, in a film considered more insidious than Alfred Hitchcock's *Psycho* of the same year.

During her eighteen months at Drury Lane, there had also been some interest expressed in Julie for the film of another George Bernard Shaw play, *The Devil's Disciple*, starring Kirk Douglas and Burt Lancaster. Whether the part or the fee was too small, nothing transpired. Julie, of course, hoped to make her onscreen debut as Eliza Doolittle. For the moment, though, her Pygmalion was Tony. 'She has no conception of her capabilities,' he said. 'It's all there — just needs a bit of dragging out.' In the hope of doing this on television, Julie signed a contract with the BBC for a short, fortnightly series, *The Julie Andrews Show*. Her guests were a mix of old acquaintances and new names, with (as would so often be the case now) less than six degrees of separation between them.

The first show, with décor by Tony, aired on 12 November, featuring Vic Oliver from *Starlight Roof*, Pietro Annigoni, whose portrait of Julie was now completed, and Kenneth Williams, star of the West End revue *One Over the Eight* (also designed by Tony). Another chum, Pauline

Grant, worked with the choreographer Kenneth Macmillan to stage the show. But it all ended up static, stilted and dull. 'Julie is a singer and an actress, but she can never aspire to the curious status of TV personality,' wrote the *Daily Express* critic. 'The girl is superbly genuine and unspoiled — not an ounce of phoney in her. And it is a pity that such sterling and unusual qualities merely give her, on TV, the impression of being very, very cold.'

In the next two episodes Julie interviewed Ted and Barbara Andrews — whether through tact or catharsis — as well as Stanley Holloway and Michael Bentine. The fourth (and last) show, broadcast on Christmas Eve, was Julie's third (and least memorable) television musical, *The Gentle Flame*, based on Hans Christian Andersen's 'The Little Match Girl'. One of the more noteworthy guests on an earlier episode was the reclusive author Terence Hanbury White, who had travelled from his Channel Islands sanctuary on Alderney to talk about Julie's next production — one that would dominate her life for the next two years.

* * *

While *My Fair Lady* was settling into its London run, Alan Jay Lerner and Frederick Loewe had been fishing around for their next venture. By September 1958 they hooked on to T.H. White's *The Once and Future King*, a composite of four books, inspired by the legends of King Arthur, his love for Guenevere and hers for Sir Lancelot.

160

Somewhat over-confidently, the writing team, together with Moss Hart, decided to produce the show themselves, buying the rights to the last three books of White's quartet. The first volume, *The Sword in the Stone*, the tale of Arthur's childhood, was already appropriated by Walt Disney.

In late 1959, 'Tim' White wrote to friends, 'If only those buggers Lerner & Loewe would give me lots of money at once,' but the buggers would take more than twenty months and twenty thousand miles of travelling to complete their first draft. Earlier that year, with only a third of the material, tentatively entitled *Jenny Kissed Me*, they approached their only choice for Guenevere — and Julie Andrews had become the first cast member to commit to the new musical.

To play King Arthur, Moss Hart suggested Richard Burton. Aged thirty-four, the Welshman was considered one of the half-dozen finest classical actors in the world, enjoying spectacular success at the Old Vic Theatre in London. His star quality was almost mythical, his magnificent speaking voice the anchor for much of his success. The rest of the sixty-strong cast would include Robert Coote (Colonel Pickering himself) as King Pellinore and Roddy McDowall as Arthur's bastard son, the evil Mordred. In the role of Sir Lancelot, the producers cast a handsome young baritone of French-Canadian stock, who turned up on the last day of auditions in blue jeans: Robert Goulet.

The production team was, unsurprisingly, something of a *My Fair Lady* reunion. Once again, CBS committed the entire budget ($480,000 this time). Moss Hart directed, Franz Allers conducted and Oliver Smith created the sets. The Arthurian legends were not, however, considered natural Cecil Beaton territory, so the costumes were delegated to the designer Adrian, whose work went back to the glory days of MGM.

In January 1960, Julie Andrews flew to New York to appear on television in *The Fabulous Fifties* for CBS (paired with Rex Harrison in the inevitable *My Fair Lady* medley) — and to finalise the biggest contract she had yet signed, with a fee not far short of Richard Burton's stupendous $4,000 a week, for what was now named *Camelot*.

One of her first appointments after her return to London Airport on 14 February was as godmother at the christening of Michael Bentine's baby son, Richard — a duty she would also assume for Madame Lilian Stiles-Allen's grandson, Michael Jeffries-Harris. Then, with Tony concentrating on the West End production of *The Most Happy Fella*, she went back into the London Clinic.

The problem remained her throat, which Julie described as being 'in a ragged state from night after night of belting'. With the rigours of *My Fair Lady* behind her, but with *Camelot* still to explore, she had her tonsils removed. 'I thought I would never sing again. I very tentatively and timidly took on *Camelot*. It was an enormous period of anxiety about my voice. The next eighteen months were a miracle to me — I got my voice back.' She would not always be so lucky.

Her recuperation meant missing Princess Margaret's wedding to Anthony Armstrong-Jones in Westminster Abbey that May. Julie's disappointment was somewhat assuaged by a visit to Tim White on Alderney, where the brisk Channel air reinvigorated her. Big, bearded and outwardly friendly, the author was a complex man, but had taken to Julie immediately, finding her 'plainly a darling person'. The feeling was obviously mutual. 'Julie and her husband want to adopt me — my age is equivalent to theirs put together,' he wrote (he was then fifty-four). Their friendship would continue until his death in 1964.

On Saturday 20 August, accompanied by Shy, their French poodle, Julie and Tony flew to New York. Before they left Britain, the Waltons had been interviewed on television, very much playing to type. Tony sat quietly, looking down; Julie, bright, light and tight as ever, admitted being 'very nervous' of meeting Richard Burton, whose Lothario reputation preceded him, but was positive that *Camelot* was going to be 'fabulous'. For her third extended period in Manhattan, Julie had taken a seventeenth-floor apartment with a glorious view of the East River. While she prepared for work, he oversaw his designs for the off-Broadway production of Sandy Wilson's *Valmouth*. After their difficult experience on *The Boy Friend*, Wilson and his director Vida Hope were finally working in New York without interference (the show was, however, short-lived).

Over a Sunday dinner of roast lamb, something Julie could always cook, Vida felt bold enough to ask the newlyweds if they had enjoyed their honeymoon. Tony said not, *The Jack Benny Hour* still a sore subject. 'But since then,' said Julie, giving Tony a meaningful look, 'we haven't done too badly, have we darling?' The comment was in keeping with her previously stated plans: 'What I really want to do is to settle down and be plain Mrs Walton. That's why I've insisted that my contract in New York should be for only eighteen months. After that, I want to start a family.'

She sounded sincere. She had had a blissful year of semi-retirement, and had started to make a circle of London friends who were fashionable, interesting — and not all actors. But her creative muscles would always tug, demanding exercise, work. It was more than a challenge. It was, as her husband later said, 'the only thing she knew'.

★   ★   ★

Rehearsals for *Camelot* commenced on Saturday 3 September 1960. After the read-through, Julie somewhat self-consciously reprised her habit of brewing tea for the company. 'Everyone knocked off for the customary bit of old England,' said Alan Jay Lerner; 'everyone, that is, but Richard, who retired to his dressing room for more stimulating refreshment.' Moss Hart toasted his new company, promising the *My Fair Lady* veterans a less back-breaking experience. 'From that moment,' said Tony Walton, 'everything went wrong.'

The problems had actually started eighteen months earlier, just as *My Fair Lady* was setting up shop at Drury Lane, when Fritz Loewe had suffered a massive heart attack. He decamped to Palm Springs for much of the writing process, but even as he recovered, coronary failure claimed the life of the costume designer, Adrian.

Ironically for Julie Andrews, in a reversal of her previous Broadway experiences, she was secure from the start, whereas all around her was chaos. The songs were lovely, including 'I Loved You Once in Silence' for Julie and 'How to Handle a Woman' for Richard Burton — but the script came across as badly structured and interminable.

After four weeks of rehearsals, the company packed its bags and crossed the border to Toronto, where *Camelot* was due to open on Julie's twenty-fifth birthday. The show was then to move to Boston, before its scheduled Broadway opening at the Majestic Theatre in late November — with a colossal $3 million in advance bookings.

No less than $12 million had gone into building the gargantuan O'Keefe Centre in Toronto, which was officially opened on Saturday 1 October as the curtain went up on *Camelot*. Four and a half hours later, the curtain came down. 'Only *Tristan und Isolde* rivalled it as a bladder contest,' said Lerner, and one critic dubbed it '*Götterdämmerung* without the laughs'.

Words like 'jinx' and 'curse' started to gain currency as a string of backstage accidents occurred. An electrician was nearly killed when a plugging-box fell on him. A wardrobe mistress's husband was found dead in their apartment. A chorus girl ran a needle through her foot on stage. 'We will all be replaced tomorrow by hospital orderlies,' said a technician. Gallows humour had suddenly pervaded the Broadway-bound epic.

Then — disaster. Alan Jay Lerner collapsed from internal bleeding caused by ulcers. A fortnight later, as he was being discharged from the Toronto hospital, he saw a trolley wheeling another invalid into the very same room. It was Moss Hart, felled by a coronary thrombosis. 'It went on and on, until it was a riderless horse,' said Tony Walton, hearing the bush telegraph loud and clear in New York. 'There was nobody in charge of it, and it was Richard and Julie who kind of held it together.'

In late October, the show and its huge amount of scenery wended its way to Boston — where, at the Shubert Theatre, a young reporter appeared for the first but not the last time in Julie's life, compiling a cover story for *Time* magazine on 14 November. The journalist, by name of Joyce Haber, suggested that Lerner's directorship in Moss Hart's absence was lessening the show's chances of success by the minute. She had done her homework on the heart attacks and ulcers, itemising the troubles 'that had very nearly turned *Camelot* from a musical into a medical'.

Anything like Rex Harrison's fractiousness in

My Fair Lady would have been fatal for the musical. But Richard Burton showed himself to be a prince among men, driving the company forward when morale was at its lowest, even accepting a new second act a fortnight before the Broadway opening — which was now delayed by a week. In his foreword to the published libretto, Alan Jay Lerner credited him as the main reason 'that *Camelot* stayed together in one piece and did not disintegrate like a decayed tooth'.

Desperately hacking away at the running time, Lerner condensed a long scene between Guenevere and Lancelot into a new song, 'Before I Gaze at You Again', writing the lyrics even as the company travelled back from Boston to New York. With only two previews, it was too much to expect anyone to assimilate it before the premiere. Nevertheless, Lerner asked Julie to try. 'Of course, darling,' came the answer, 'but do try to get it to me the night before.'

'There is no star in theatre today, nor perhaps has there ever been one, who would have agreed to that outrageous request, but Julie Andrews,' said Lerner. Roddy McDowall watched as they rehearsed the new number. 'I said to Alan, 'It's *impossible* to do it — what if she can't?' and he said, 'She will,' and of course she did, and it looked like she'd been rehearsing it for months . . . '

Thus, *Camelot* — or *Costalot*, as wags would have it — came to town, opening on Saturday 3 December 1960. The Majestic Theatre lay directly across 44th Street from the Royale Theatre, where Julie had made her first theatrical impact in New York. But this time she was carrying the responsibility for her colleagues more than for herself.

The auditorium was ablaze with starlight: Rock Hudson, Myrna Loy and many who had applauded Julie's previous Broadway outings, including Gloria Swanson, Marlene Dietrich, Noël Coward and Robert Preston. The impossibility of living up to *My Fair Lady* was acknowledged in the respectable but far from electric response. 'There was', said Lerner, 'no excitement in the house'.

The lyricist ignored his own superstition and attended the first night party at Lüchow's Restaurant. Within moments of the papers arriving, it was evident that *My Fair Lady* had not passed on her winning ways. 'Beneath unfailing splendour,' said Walter Kerr for the *Herald Tribune*, 'the pulse stops.' Richard Burton was judged superb, but the moment 'in which Guenevere's unwilling passion leaps towards Lancelot is missing', though the finger was pointed neither at writer nor at actress.

In the *New York Times*, Howard Taubman found Julie to be 'regal and girlish, cool and eager'. *Camelot* itself, however, he found 'a city only partly enchanted' and of the writers, 'it cannot be denied that they miss their late collaborator George Bernard Shaw.' The *Daily News* reported, '*Camelot* is magnificent', in an unqualified rave, but the *Post* found it too much of a good thing: 'All its elements contain lovely and imaginative things, but they are seldom fused successfully, and it often seems that several fine musical plays are fighting for recognition.'

But in London, writing for the *Observer*, Kenneth Tynan paid tribute to the stars. 'Since we last saw her, Julie Andrews has matured, with no loss of tenderness,' while Richard Burton was 'a peerless king'.

Tim White had arrived in Boston and stayed on for the Broadway opening, writing: 'I have pretended to everybody that I am perfectly satisfied with this new version of my book . . . Julie is as always enchanting beyond words.'

The cast album became the best conduit for the ravishing score, obviating the hours of clumsy plot. It reached No 1 in the spring of 1961, and stayed in the Top 40 for almost three years. Warner Brothers made an early bid for the film rights, and won them for $1 million. But it was all rather different from the frenzy over *My Fair Lady*. In the New Year, up to two hundred people were leaving the theatre before the end of the show each night. Analysts at CBS forecast a six-month run, at most. Tim White wrote to Richard Burton, telling him to ignore his author's sensibility: 'I want *Camelot* to succeed. Put in bubble dancers, if you want.'

Thankfully, it did not come to that. In March, having traded on Burton's inspiration for so long, the show finally had its miracle. Moss Hart had sufficiently recovered from his thrombosis to rehearse yet more cuts, finally bringing *Camelot* down to size — at exactly the point that Ed Sullivan offered to mark the fifth anniversary of *My Fair Lady* on his CBS show with a special tribute to Lerner and Loewe.

The team saw a golden opportunity to succour their ailing child. In a generous selection from the show, Julie sang 'Where Are the Simple Joys of Maidenhood?' and joined Burton in the standout item of the evening, 'What Do the Simple Folk Do?' in which Arthur and Guenevere sing, dance and whistle to banish their impending sense of doom.

The next morning, there was a queue along 44th Street. *Camelot* was finally, officially, a hit. Backstage, the Old Vic actor became even more the life and soul of the party, his dressing room known to visitors as 'Burton's Bar'. One night, he accepted a bet from his friend Robert Preston that he could down a bottle of vodka during the matinee and another during the evening show — without Julie being aware of it. 'How was I today, love?' he asked her at the end of the day. 'A bit better than usual,' came the answer.

'Actually, I *was* aware of it,' Julie revealed, over forty years later, on BBC Radio. 'He probably started drinking the night before, didn't sleep that night, and then went through the matinee and the evening performance . . . He was such a consummate actor, devil that he was, that he was able to use that fatigue and he suddenly became the most tired king, and he could hardly lift the sword — very vulnerable.'

Although his wife Sybil was in New York, Burton found time, in between work and drinking, to cast his eyes around the ladies of the company. At first, they fell on M'el Dowd, who played the sprite Morgan le Fey, but she did not have a monopoly. The opening number, 'I

Wonder What the King is Doing Tonight', was often ghosted by the chorus as 'I wonder who the King is screwing tonight'.

Of the other two players in the onstage triangle, Guenevere would watch Lancelot singing the show's big ballad, 'If Ever I Would Leave You' each night. 'And,' said Julie, 'all I could think was, 'The backs of his knees are just great.' His voice was pretty good, too.' That was as far as it went for Mrs Walton, but, according to Alan Jay Lerner, Goulet 'developed a wild crush on his leading lady', and turned to Burton for advice. Burton had none to give. After Goulet left the room, he asked Lerner, 'Why did he come to me? I couldn't get anywhere either.'

When I met Julie, she laughingly told me a sequel to the story: 'Richard rang me up and said, 'Do you know, you're the only leading lady I've never slept with.' I said 'Well, don't *tell* everybody; it's the worst thing for my squeaky-clean image.''

After a while, Julie began to tire of his stream of anecdotes, brilliant though they were: 'He can entertain you non-stop for three weeks with his conversation, but in the fourth week he starts to repeat himself.' Ultimately, however, she would remember him as 'probably the most charismatic man I ever met . . . I have to confess that if he had wooed me at first, I probably would have succumbed . . . '

Burton's point of view remained one of healthy respect, especially after the large shaggy dog in the show discharged itself on stage as Julie was singing 'The Lusty Month of May'.

'The look she gave on the next line, 'I think there's a hint of summer in the air', had me and the audience in hysterics,' he said. 'She's as wicked as a street Arab.' Pushed further, about her air of purity, he cautioned, 'Don't muck about with her — you'll see nature red in eye and tongue.' He waxed lyrical over the emblems of her appeal. 'Radiance, shafts of gold, bars of light — all that stuff. Every man I know who knows her is a little bit in love with her.'

At the Tony Awards that season, Burton became Julie's second leading man to win as Best Actor in a Musical, although *Camelot* was beaten as Best Musical by the up-tempo *Bye Bye Birdie*. Julie was nominated again as Best Actress, and lost again, to Elizabeth Seal for *Irma la Douce*.

★ ★ ★

During the first six months of *Camelot*, Julie met one of the great friends of her life. But, as was so often the case, she had to drop her Libran ambivalence to do so.

A year before King Arthur pitched camp, there had been another medieval kingdom on another part of Broadway, ruled by Princess Winnifred the Woebegone. *Once Upon a Mattress*, written by Richard Rodgers' daughter Mary, had made a star of Carol Burnett. Julie had seen the show, and Carol had seen Julie in *My Fair Lady*. 'I think you two can hit it off,' Julie's manager Lou Wilson told her, saying the same to Carol. 'I'm not sure if I want to meet anybody new,' said

Queen Guenevere. 'Me and Julie Andrews?' panicked Princess Winnifred. 'Why not?' said Wilson. 'You're both kinda nutsy.'

'We met at Ruby Foo's,' Carol remembered. 'Julie thinks that Chinese food, like the Statue of Liberty, is one of the glories of American civilisation.' Wilson was there as well, with a representative of the popular CBS variety programme *The Garry Moore Show*. 'But they never got in five words edgewise,' said Carol, likening it to two new kids on the block discovering each other. Julie later put it more bluntly to the *New York Daily News*: 'We came from alcoholic families, and we both had been caretakers . . .'

The spark between them was so immediate that the usual half-promises to work together came to fruition within a few months. *The Garry Moore Show*, on which Carol was a regular, booked Julie for four slots, starting with a double act on 2 May 1961.

Finally, after all the early years of touring the halls with the great and not-so-good of Britain's comedians, Julie was being given a chance to see if she could make people laugh. The two girls chose the cowboy duet 'Big D', from *The Most Happy Fella*, which Julie had seen, designed by Tony, in London. It went down better than any previous guest appearance on *The Garry Moore Show*; the next day, Julie had a flurry of telephone calls from colleagues, adamant that she and Carol should have their own show.

At that point, a smash-hit revue was playing on the next street to the Majestic Theatre. Both performers in *An Evening with Mike Nichols and Elaine May* were occasional imbibers at 'Burton's Bar', and Nichols, who was to become another of Julie's closest friends, offered to write a television revue for the two girls. The networks were uninterested. 'I wasn't yet under contract to CBS,' said Carol, 'and nobody had heard of Julie west of New Jersey. We went everywhere trying to sell the idea — to NBC, ABC, and XYZ.' They would have to wait.

In the summer of 1961, the eyes of Hollywood and much of the world were on Rome, where Elizabeth Taylor was trying to launch her cinematic barge in *Cleopatra*, having almost died in the attempt the previous year in England. When the call came from Twentieth Century Fox for Richard Burton to 'don a breastplate to play opposite Miss Tits' — words that would haunt him — Lerner and Loewe gracefully agreed: they owed him the favour. Burton quit *Camelot* on 23 September, handing the crown to William Squire, and went to meet his destiny.

The following month, Julie was also flying across the Atlantic, on a three-week holiday. 'My next production', she told reporters, 'will definitely be a baby.' In London, met by Tony, she sounded more circumspect. 'You might say we're not hurrying, but we hope it will happen very soon.' They then set off for Alderney, to see Tim White — and to look over 'Patmos', the tiny cottage they had bought. The peace of the island had entranced Julie from her first visit, as had the stone house, one of a row of three and 'roughly the size of a matchbox', with its fireplace, chintz-covered chairs and painted wooden table.

In White, there was something of her father: like Ted Wells, he had a passion for boating, swimming and bird watching. The writer had started to identify in Julie an elusive Helen of Troy figure he had sought for years. In a privately published book of poetry, two verses entitled 'Julie Andrews' captured what he had seen of her in *Camelot*:

Helen, whose face was fatal, must have wept
Many long nights alone
And every night men died, she cried
And happy Paris kept sweet Helen.
Julie, the thousand prows aimed at her heart,
The tragic queen, comedian and clown,
Keeps Troy together, not apart
Nor lets one tower fall down.

In their determination to stay together, Tony had kept himself free to stay in New York during the early months of *Camelot*. During the run, he had made as many as a dozen crossings from New York to London, designing shows in both cities. Now he was concentrating on his biggest assignment yet, creating the sets and costumes for Stephen Sondheim's brilliant musical *A Funny Thing Happened on the Way to the Forum*, starring Zero Mostel and Milton Berle.

Despite the prestige, there was still a vast disparity in the couple's wages. Julie, in the manner of the time, played down her advantage:

'I get mine in chunks; he gets his regularly, and I expect he'll work far longer than I will.' By mutual agreement, money was seldom discussed. 'If Tony minds my being Julie Andrews he certainly doesn't let me know it,' she said.

Then, five days before Christmas, the company of *Camelot* suffered its biggest-ever tragedy: Moss Hart fell down dead of a heart attack at home, aged fifty-seven. Coming after the recent announcement of Fritz Loewe's retirement, it marked the end of an era.

As if in epitaph, on 6 February 1962, Warner Brothers won the rights to film *My Fair Lady* for $5.5 million. Arthur Freed, Hollywood's finest producer of musicals, had been hungry to buy the property for MGM, but was outbid by Jack L. Warner, whose record offer served ominous notice that any casting decision was going to be brutally commercial.

Despite this, it was axiomatic to many that Julie would recreate her role. On 11 February she reinforced her claim, starring in *The Broadway of Lerner and Loewe*, a rapturously received colour tribute on NBC. Alongside her were Maurice Chevalier, Stanley Holloway, Robert Goulet and Richard Burton, on leave from Rome.

Julie was also moonlighting for the rival network. Refusing to give up on the idea of a television showcase for the pair of them, Carol Burnett had persuaded James Aubrey, president of CBS, that they were a good risk. The two girls rehearsed solidly throughout February, working through the athletic dance routines. 'Julie lost weight,' said Carol, 'and I gained it, mostly in the bags under my eyes . . . Working opposite her is like having Winston Churchill for your co-pilot.'

'I talk dirty with Carol Burnett,' was how Julie described the show, taking a night off from *Camelot* to record it on Monday 5 March, for transmission three months later. No matter how daunting the venue — former home of the New York Philharmonic and scene of Judy Garland's 1960 concert triumph — the pair were on a mission to debunk, marked by Carol's opening belter, 'There'll Be No Mozart Tonight at Carnegie Hall'. The Texan comedienne and the English miss were then contrasted in 'You're So London' ('you're so Kensington Gardens, and I'm so — San Antone'), and a ten-minute history of the American musical, in which Carol sang 'Wouldn't It Be Loverly?' and Julie parodied 'I Cain't Say No' from *Oklahoma!* ('How can I be what I ain't? I cahn't say cain't.')

'Big D' was reprised from *The Garry Moore Show*, but the high points were Mike Nichols' brilliant spoofs, 'The Nausiev Ballet' (touching on the current obsession with Rudolf Nureyev) and 'The Pratt Family of Switzerland'. The latter parodied a show which, a year before *Camelot*, had hit Broadway like a tidal wave: Rodgers and Hammerstein's *The Sound of Music*. Dividing the critics from the start, it nonetheless enraptured audiences with the story of the Austrian nun (a Tony-winning turn from Mary Martin) who tends seven motherless children, marries the father, and helps them all escape the Nazis. As if this was not enough, its box-office power surged anew on the death of Oscar Hammerstein in August 1960. 'It became', said Sandy Wilson, who saw the show at the time, 'like a sell-out Requiem Mass.'

Mike Nichols was having none of it. His Pratt Family boasted nineteen sons, Carol as the only daughter, and Julie as Mama Pratt, chirping, 'We bring you a happy song that I used to sing when I was a happy nun back home in Switzerland.' The song, echoing 'My Favourite Things', ended, 'The things we like best are these: pigs' feet and cheese.' 'We were always putting *The Sound of Music* down,' Carol remarked, 'and Julie always made fun of that happy nun.'

'I love to dress up in mad get-ups, camp around, to horse around,' said Julie. 'Tony says he married me because I did a good impersonation of Stan Laurel.' The high spirits that had been kept for private were now to be revealed at large. At ten in the evening, Monday 11 June 1962, *Julie and Carol at Carnegie Hall* aired nationwide — to excellent ratings and subsequent reviews, *Variety* hailing 'this expert fusion of talent and virtuosity'.

The show would win the 1963 Rose d'Or at Montreux, the first American television programme to do so. Julie won plaudits for her comedy as well as her singing. But it was Carol who did best of all, scooping an Emmy Award — as did the show's producer Joe Hamilton, who married her the following year. 'I got through that show with the help of God and Carol,' said Julie. 'Mostly Carol.'

By then, she had already departed *Camelot*. In

his memoirs, Alan Jay Lerner pondered the Julie Andrews enigma: 'I cannot remember one moment in the almost seven years we worked together that was anything but joy. Nevertheless, I cannot say in all honesty that I knew her any better at the end of those seven years than I did at the beginning . . . '

Whatever the agonies of its inception, Julie told me that *Camelot*, while 'not as huge as *Fair Lady* — but then very little could be — was a *loved* show'. On another occasion, she pondered which of her Broadway outings was the most special: 'I think *Camelot* was the most fun, and probably I was more mature by then and it was my size and weight; it wasn't too hefty. Obviously, *My Fair Lady* was the most wonderful show to be in, because it was so perfect in every way, the role was so lovely, the look of it was so lovely . . . but, I suppose . . . ' She paused for a second, and smiled warmly. 'Well, Richard Burton was just dishy, that's all.'

When the Queen of Broadway left *Camelot* in 14 April 1962, she could never have imagined that her theatre career had effectively ended for another three decades. But she did know that the next several months were already decided for her.

One small moment during the performance at Carnegie Hall gave a clue why. At the end of 'The Pratts', Carol, in character, had thumped Julie in the stomach during the bow — then, out of character, had registered panic. She was one of the few to know the news. 'Julie was about ten minutes pregnant,' Carol joked, some forty years on. 'Her husband had just come out of the dressing room after having wished her luck . . . ' But anyone who imagined that marriage and motherhood had finally caught up with her was wrong: there was already another challenge ahead of her — the last and biggest of the 'three huge building blocks' in her life.

It had all happened during a matinee performance of *Camelot* in the spring of 1962, when the audience included the owner of the rights to *The Sword in the Stone* — Walt Disney. He came with a professional interest in seeing what had been made of the rest of *The Once and Future King*. But never far from his mind was the *grand projet* on his production slate: the celluloid version of P.L. Travers's classic *Mary Poppins* books, about the magical, flying nanny.

By the interval of *Camelot*, Disney was impressed enough with the leading lady to send her a note, alerting her to his presence. But during the second act, he sat bolt upright (just as producer Cy Feuer had done eight years earlier). It was Julie's whistling in 'What Do the Simple Folk Do?' that decided him. He had found his Mary Poppins.

'I went backstage,' he said, 'and tried to convince her I was capable of making a picture with live actors as well as cartoons.' Out of nowhere, Julie Andrews was being handed the chance to star in a Hollywood musical — something that, no matter how hard Alan Jay Lerner was angling on her behalf, had not yet come through *My Fair Lady*.

'It was quite amazing,' Julie reflected. 'He just

made up his mind that that's what he wanted.' But, with the caution inherent in her star sign, she held back from enthusing too much — let alone accepting. 'Do you think I should do it?' she asked Carol Burnett. 'Work for Disney? The cartoon person?'

Walt Disney's name was enough to override the need for major stars in his films: even with his famous cartoon characters, the biggest star was always Disney himself. But the non-photogenic label from all those years ago haunted her still. 'I think Julie felt she wasn't made for the movies,' said Tony, 'so she was kind of hesitant.'

In May, *A Funny Thing Happened on the Way to the Forum* opened on Broadway to glowing notices. Disney took note of the designer, whose stylish work was one of the reasons for the success, and further baited the hook. He invited Tony to accompany his wife to California to see the preliminary work on *Mary Poppins*, adding, quite casually, 'You know, you can work on the costumes too.'

The Waltons delayed their journey back to London and flew to Hollywood. There, Disney personally escorted them through his dream factory, introducing the producers of the film, Bill Walsh and Don DaGradi, whose third-floor offices were strewn with a myriad of sketches. The film was to utilise the talents of every artist, craftsman and technician on the Disney lot. For Tony, as an artist, the degree of imagination and detail was enticing, but for Julie, the matter was not quite decided.

Then, meeting the songwriting team of brothers Richard M. and Robert B. Sherman, Julie listened to some of their compositions for *Mary Poppins* — and knew. The numbers had a certain redolence of her childhood days on the halls, 'a kind of vaudeville quality, and I instantly connected with them. I thought, my gosh, I can really contribute to that.' Yet her most fervent professional wish remained to play Eliza on screen. When Disney repeated his offer, Julie finally accepted — with the caveat that she be allowed out, should Warner Brothers offer her the film of *My Fair Lady*.

That same month, in a Swiss chalet above Lake Lucerne, one of the great stars of the world was waiting for the telephone to ring. When it did, Audrey Hepburn received the news with joy. And so erupted the biggest casting controversy in motion picture history.

Still in Hollywood, Julie and Tony were visiting her West Coast representative's office when the door burst open and several younger agents burst in, chorusing, 'We did it, we did it — we got the part for Audrey!'

'They had no idea that this was Julie sitting in the room,' remembered Tony. 'It was a truly macabre moment.'

The decision to cast her as Eliza Doolittle never sat completely easily with Audrey Hepburn. 'Julie made that role her own, and for that reason I didn't want to do the film when it was first offered.' she said. She would later come to know Julie as a good friend, telling her: 'Julie, you should have done the movie, but I didn't have the guts to turn it down.' But, as she revealed to Barbara Walters in 1989, she was informed that her refusal would result in the role going to another cinematic icon. 'I thought I was entitled to do it as much as the third girl, so then I did accept.'

The other contender was Audrey's friend Elizabeth Taylor, currently earning her keep as the Queen of the Nile — and who would badger her then husband Eddie Fisher with the urgent pillow talk, 'Get me *My Fair Lady!*' even after the choice was made official. Miss Taylor was a client of Kurt Frings, who had negotiated the first ever $1 million contract for a female star on *Cleopatra*; he would secure another for Miss Hepburn, another client, to play Eliza.

Julie, meanwhile, put a brave face on her $150,000 contract with Disney. Tony, signing on to create the costumes, was under no misapprehension about his place in the scheme of things, but a film offer was a film offer. With shooting not due to begin until May 1963, Mr and Mrs Walton flew back to England.

7

FLYING

'Someone, somewhere, made the decision to include Andrews out of the movie version of My Fair Lady. There is an evil and rampantly lunatic force at loose in the world and it must be destroyed'

— *Time* magazine, 1963

'My Paradise' was how Julie described 'Patmos', her cottage in La Trigale, Alderney, where she escaped for much of her pregnancy. For seven months, she 'kept a diary, cooked roasts and stews on the old-fashioned stove, waxed the woodwork, shopped . . . ' She also, as she told her friend Carol Burnett, lay on the beach with her 'big belly stuck in the sand', running off lewd limericks (sadly, never for print).

Here she was able to forget the theatre, Jack Warner — even Walt Disney — and spend uninterrupted days with her husband. Occasional visitors included the composer Stephen Sondheim, with whom Tony was working; and, in due course, it was Tony who was called back to London, while Julie remained looking out over 'windblown meadows of maroon and yellow tulips, blue irises and daffodils dancing on the hills'.

184

With the abundance of botany and wildlife, it was not surprising that her nature-loving father came to visit in August, bringing his wife Win, their daughter Celia and Julie's brother John. Six months pregnant, Julie managed to join them in swimming off the coast of Telegraph Bay, and when Tony rejoined her, she was able fully to enjoy her first family holiday in years. She could not have guessed it would be her last.

Half a universe away, on Saturday 29 September 1962, *My Fair Lady* came to the end of its Broadway run. The last performance was front-page news both in America and in Europe, and immediately escalated Jack L. Warner's plans for the film version. Shortly after came the announcement that Julie Andrews would make her first big screen appearance in Walt Disney's $6 million fantasy *Mary Poppins*. 'It should be tremendous fun,' said the star determinedly, back in London by the third week of November.

Four days after this, and a fortnight overdue, she was taken to the London Clinic. There, at one o'clock in the morning of Tuesday 27 November 1962, she gave birth to a 7lb 12oz baby girl.

Later that day Julie Walton posed for the cameras, telling reporters rather over-brightly that this was only the beginning. 'I'd like a family of three or five boys, weather and tide permitting, as we say in England. Tony wants girls. I just want a family of little Tonies.' One of the keenest photographers was the father himself, dropping in between rehearsals of his newest show. In New York, Carol Burnett received a telegram:

SHES HERE KNOWN OFFICIALLY AS EMMA STOP START LEADING A GOOD CLEAN LIFE STOP YOURE HER GODMOTHER

Emma Kate Walton was to have been called Sarah, but, said Julie, 'she didn't look like a Sarah: she was chubby and comfy,' with dark blonde hair, big blue eyes, and more than a touch of her father's eager smile. Present at the hospital was Julie's close friend, the ballerina Svetlana Beriosova, who became Emma's other godmother.

The day after the birth, Julie had a telephone call from the author of *Mary Poppins*. 'This strange woman's voice came on the phone and said, 'Hello, talk to me; P.L. Travers here. I want to hear your voice.' And I said, 'Oh, dear, what can I say?' 'When can we meet?' she said. And I replied, 'Well, I'm feeling rather weak at the moment,' and asked her if we could leave it for a while.'

They met shortly afterwards. The somewhat hawkish author took one look at Julie and remarked, 'You've got the nose for it.' As she was written, Mary Poppins resembled a Dutch doll, with black shiny hair, small blue eyes and large feet. Apart from her size eight feet, Julie was physically unsuited to the part, being really too pretty. But Pamela Travers was captivated, declaring, 'I hadn't spoken to her for five minutes before I realised she had the inner integrity for the part.'

From her hospital bed, Julie fielded another professional visitor. Sandy Wilson had an idea for a show: 'I said, 'Have you ever read Christopher Isherwood's *Berlin Diaries*?' I gave her the book, and she liked it very much ... I asked her to play Sally Bowles and she was interested.' But it was not meant to be. A new pair of writers, John Kander and Fred Ebb, had their own plan: in 1966, this became *Cabaret*.

On 10 December, mother and child left the London Clinic for their first Christmas as a family. Julie found to her chagrin that the American pram she and Tony had bought for Emma did not fit in the lift at Eaton Square. As with so many of their wedding presents, it would require a bigger house. So would Mr and Mrs Walton.

In the last few months before leaving for Hollywood, Julie balanced motherhood with the company of her friends, particularly Beriosova and her husband Masud Khan, who lived up the road, at the back of Harrods. Khan, a social scalp-hunter, was only too pleased to mix with the leading lights of the Waltons' world, from both sides of the Atlantic: Mike Nichols, Stephen Sondheim, Richard Burton, T.H. White — as well as Beriosova's occasional ballet partner Rudolf Nureyev and the balletomane Princess Margaret.

Beriosova was an avid dancer at nightclubs as well as at Covent Garden, but the Waltons loathed 'making Entrances', preferring to play party games at home. One such game, symptomatic of the Cold War years in which they were living, was describing one's last minutes in the event of an atomic bomb. Masud Khan declared he would climb a mountain and scream at God. 'I'd climb into bed and cuddle,' said Julie.

For all their homely instincts, Julie and Tony had come a long way from the bourgeois certainties of Walton-on-Thames. At the end of January, Tony left for Hollywood to begin work as design consultant on *Mary Poppins*, and to set up temporary home for the family in the San Fernando Valley. One month later, en route with her baby daughter, Julie told reporters that she was excited at the prospect of working for Disney — 'but also terribly nervous'.

Then, like Mary Poppins, she flew off into the sky. Mary Poppins, of course, made no promise to come back again.

★ ★ ★

The Mouse House, as Disney Studios is nicknamed after its most famous cartoon character, sits on South Buena Vista Street, Burbank, one block from Warner Boulevard. 'I *did* shout some obscenities at Jack Warner, without him knowing it, when I passed by,' admitted Julie Andrews, reporting for duty on *Mary Poppins*. Otherwise, she tried not to think of the upset over *My Fair Lady*, which recalled a furore of the previous year, when — also at Warner Brothers — Ethel Merman had lost the film of her stage hit *Gypsy* to Rosalind Russell.

Despite Alan Jay Lerner's persistent lobbying on Julie's behalf, the old star system — by which Warners might have built her up, as they did with Doris Day in the late 1940s — was not so much on its last legs as flat on its back. Yet, even after *My Fair Lady* was released, Jack Warner still felt obliged to justify himself. 'There was nothing mysterious or complicated about that decision,' he wrote in his 1965 autobiography *My First Hundred Years in Hollywood*. 'With all her charm and ability, Julie Andrews was just a Broadway name known primarily to those who saw the play . . . In my business I have to know who brings people and their money to a movie theatre box office. I knew Audrey Hepburn had never made a financial flop.'

'At the time, I really did understand,' said Julie, when I saw her at London's National Film Theatre. 'They needed a big name and it was an important movie.' And the idea that she might have stuck pins in an Audrey Hepburn doll made her laugh. 'No, it's only in later years that I wish that I had put my own stamp on *Fair Lady* once and for all . . . '

To make it all the more galling, her stage co-stars had won the opportunity to do just that. Cary Grant tartly informed Jack Warner that he was not only declining the role of Professor Higgins on screen, but would refuse to see the film unless Rex Harrison was in it. And when James Cagney made it plain that he was not going to break his retirement by playing a Cockney coalman, it was the little bit of luck that

Stanley Holloway needed — releasing him from *Mary Poppins*, where he had conditionally accepted the small role of Admiral Boom.

It has since transpired that Warner did in fact offer Julie Andrews a screen test — which she turned down, whether because of its half-hearted nature or through fear that the MGM experience of 1947 might be repeated. By contrast, the instinctive, outright nature of Disney's offer was almost as pleasing to her as *Mary Poppins* itself.

Strangely, for a little girl who had once been such a bookworm, Julie had not read the P.L. Travers books, even though they were almost contemporaneous with her childhood, the first volume having been published in 1934. 'Out of the sky she had come, back to the sky she had gone.' Thus the flying nanny, borne through the air by her parrot-headed umbrella, starts and ends her employment at 17 Cherry Tree Lane, where George Banks is at a midlife crossroads, his wife is losing control and his children are running amok. Mary Poppins is controlling ('Spit-spot!'), vain (constantly checking her daisy-sprigged straw hat in shop windows) and magical. She slides up banisters, produces a cornucopia of wonders from her bottomless carpet-bag — and, above all, knows how to fly, imbued with P.L. Travers' interest in the occult.

To Disney, the existential dimension was superfluous: audiences demanded of him simply that the values of Main Street, America, be paramount. As in the books, the crisis-ridden Banks family would be brought closer together by the anarchic nanny — but the overall tone would be more benign, augmenting its live action with cartoon animation.

Sensing this, Pamela Travers ('A pretty crisp lady, in many ways,' Julie recalled) had long resisted the overtures of Disney, who, knowing how popular the stories were with his daughters, had been interested in acquiring the film rights for almost twenty years. Eventually, in 1960, he made her an offer that was too good to refuse. There had, however, been other interested parties along the way.

Shortly after the war, Anna Neagle, British cinema's queen of rectitude, and her producer husband Herbert Wilcox had considered the subject, and decided against it. 'I still think our decision was right,' Wilcox wrote later. 'What Walt Disney produced was a delightful soufflé. In my hands it would have been a Yorkshire pudding.' A young Stephen Sondheim had spent almost a year speculatively writing a stage adaptation, before abandoning it in 1950. And, in the early 1960s, Maureen O'Hara, star of the Disney comedy *The Parent Trap*, pitched her own concept for *Mary Poppins* to him. 'His people called a few days later,' said Miss O'Hara, 'and told us that Mr Disney thought our idea was a heap of rubbish.' The eventual film, she averred, was exactly as she had pitched it.

Leaving aside an early idea that Bette Davis should play the title role, Walt Disney knew exactly who, and what, he wanted. He started with the composer-lyricist brothers Richard M. and Robert B. Sherman, who wrote over thirty numbers, fourteen of which made it to the final cut. Most, like 'Supercalifragilisticexpialidocious', were destined to enter the collective consciousness almost on first hearing.

Inspiration came from many quarters — 'A Spoonful of Sugar' from Robert Sherman's son Jeff, arriving home from school, having just been given the polio vaccine on a cube of sugar. Robert Sherman also recalled co-producer Don DaGradi showing him a sketch of 'a little chimney sweep, carrying his brooms and whistling, and I said, 'This is a song.'' An Academy Award-winning one at that: 'Chim Chim Cher-ee'.

The principal cast was predominantly British. An excellent David Tomlinson and Glynis Johns, stalwarts of many English films, played George and Winifred Banks, the starchy banker and his daffy proto-suffragette wife. Karen Dotrice and Matthew Garber, both aged seven, were Jane and Michael Banks. Stanley Holloway's departure for Warner Brothers resulted in Reginald Owen playing the Admiral, and Elsa Lanchester and Hermione Baddeley took minor roles in the Banks household.

Bert — chimney sweep, pavement artist and Mary's respectful admirer — was played by all-American Dick Van Dyke, at the peak of his television popularity. His persuasive charm and talents as a singer and dancer stopped short at his Cockney accent — which England would never, ever allow him to forget. 'I know,' Julie laughed, interviewed on BBC Radio over forty years later, 'and he's the first person to say, 'I wish I could have done it better' . . . He's such a sweet man, and he agonised over it — but he managed to transcend it even so.' A more serious issue was his incipient alcoholism. 'I think he was struggling with it,' said Julie, 'but he very, Very carefully kept it under control; I never saw any sign of it.'

For the Bird Woman on the steps of St Paul's a non-speaking cameo, Julie suggested her old singing teacher Madame Lilian Stiles-Allen, but Disney persuaded the retired Oscar winner Jane Darwell to make one final film. 'Feed the Birds', which underscored the scene, was Disney's favourite song. On Friday afternoons, he would call the Sherman brothers into his office and ask them to play it. 'He'd look outside,' said Richard Sherman, 'and get a little misty-eyed.' Robert Sherman regarded the song as 'the heartbeat of the entire movie', and it held echoes for Julie of the flower seller giving her the bunch of violets outside the London Hippodrome, all those years ago.

The score, arranged and conducted by Irwin Kostal, was recorded early on. Strangely, the most difficult song for Julie was the simple lullaby 'Stay Awake', which took her almost fifty attempts to capture. On the other hand, Madame Stiles-Allen's lectures on diction made the tongue-twisting 'Supercalifragilisticexpiali-docious' a breeze — even when her husband suggested she sing it backwards: 'Dociousaliexpi-isticfragilcalirepus'.

Large sets were being constructed on every soundstage in the studio. Choreographers Marc Breaux and Dee Dee Wood were meanwhile left to rehearse 'Step in Time', the chimney sweeps' rooftop dance, under a black tarpaulin on the back lot, in the searing heat of the San Fernando Valley.

The concept was for every frame of film to be shot indoors, conjuring up a consistently stylised London. The delicate panoramas of the city, lighting up at night, dimming with smog, were painted on glass by Peter Ellenshaw, known as the master of the matte shot. And the expertise of the studio art department was perfectly complemented by Tony Walton, who chose a spun-sugar palate of colour for his costumes, particularly in the 'Jolly Holiday' sequence, where the action was to be superimposed with animation.

The cartoon figures, the province of Frank Thomas and the inner circle of Disney animators known as the Nine Old Men, would be overlaid long after live photography had ended. 'One was dancing with imaginary penguins and things like that, which was all very difficult,' said Julie. 'It took such an age that one was sitting around and thinking, gosh, is this how they make movies?'

On the first day of shooting, Bert the chimney sweep — his pavement drawing having turned into a life-size fantasy landscape — declared, 'Mary Poppins, you look beautiful.' To which the nanny twirled her parasol, dipped her pink and white bonnet and replied, 'Do you really think so?' The dialogue could hardly have been more apposite. Julie Andrews had started, as Mary Poppins would have done, with best foot forward.

'What you have in Julie is a pro,' said the

kindly English director Robert Stevenson, who had had little involvement in her casting. 'She does her work, minds her own business, appears to be completely without malice or hostility, which is rather rare in film circles. When she comes on, she brings the sun with her.'

Dick Van Dyke later marvelled at his co-star's assurance: 'You would never have known that she had never done a movie before; she seemed to know exactly where the camera was and exactly what she was doing.'

She even found a way to work in her pitch-perfect whistling, the very thing that had caught Walt Disney's imagination in *Camelot*, by providing the birdsong for the electronic robin during 'A Spoonful of Sugar'. And, already confident enough to play the clown, she joined Van Dyke as they each mimed to the other's voice during one take of 'Chim Chim Cher-ee'. As the lyrics to the song would have it, she was in 'glad company'.

'I never saw a sad face around the studio,' remarked Disney of the high morale. 'This made me nervous . . . then a horrible thought struck me: suppose the staff had finally conceded that I knew what I was doing?'

Robert Sherman certainly thought so: 'When we'd come up with a great idea, he'd make it greater.' But P.L. Travers demurred. Her position as consultant, it had been made clear, was in name only. For the duration of the filming, she would remain in London, at her little house in Chelsea.

Julie assumed responsibility for keeping Mrs

Travers in the picture, metaphorically at least. 'It's all very exciting and new — but oh, so slow!' she wrote. 'If we manage to get forty seconds worth of film at the end of the day, we are doing pretty well — and it's hard to practise my singing . . . ' They had filmed the tea party in the air. Ed Wynn was 'delightful as Uncle Albert — very dear'. Karen Dotrice was 'quite a good little actress'. Matthew Garber, however, hated heights (and was paid a dime in compensation for each take). 'We've had tears once or twice,' she said, but, having looked after her two half-brothers, Julie Andrews was well equipped to comfort a frightened little boy.

Dick Van Dyke was 'grand' as Bert, her letter continued. 'He's extremely winning — and I like to think that he and I look well together on the screen.' She was 'so proud' to wear Tony's costumes, and particularly admired his work on the set for Cherry Tree Lane. Then, ever the peacemaker, she ended: 'Please don't worry about anything — I really do think that on the whole you'd be pleased with the way things are going.'

★ ★ ★

According to the *Los Angeles Times*, the Waltons' rented home had 'a British accent'. In fact it was furnished like a Disney repository for Hayley Mills, with a sofa from *The Parent Trap*, curtains from *Pollyanna*, paintings from *Summer Magic* and a chair from *In Search of the Castaways*.

Each evening, Julie would rush back home from the studio to be with her baby daughter. Once, having filmed the chimney sweeps' dance in 'Step in Time', she arrived home with soot all her face. 'She was working so hard, she didn't really have time to play with Emma, but she *made* time,' said her friend Anne Rogers, staying for a few weeks. Occasionally, Emma would come on set. 'And I'd do some feeding,' said Julie. 'It was dear. It was a very happy time.' At home, she tied a rope across the swimming pool, marking out a safe area in which the baby could splash about.

Just as Julie had learnt, despite herself, to appreciate New York, so she was starting to enjoy her place in the sun — especially when old friends paid a visit. On a rare day off, she was sitting by the pool with Sybil Burton, who was now resigned to the banner headlines of her husband's affair with Elizabeth Taylor. Julie jumped up, draped a towel over her body, wrapped another around her head like a turban, and paraded up and down like Cleopatra — much to Sybil's amusement.

Another visitor from London was Svetlana Beriosova, in town with the Royal Ballet. One night, they sat up until late, listening to Benjamin Britten's recently composed *War Requiem* twice through on the gramophone. Julie had what Beriosova called 'a great love and understanding of music and dance', which Tony was keen to show he shared. He later admitted to having been 'a terrible theatre snob' in his attitude to Hollywood, where most of his work on *Mary Poppins* was completed by the time shooting began. He did not need reminding that his job had only been proffered as an incentive for Julie to make the film. 'I used to get up in the wee, wee hours and design *The Love of Three Oranges* for Sadler's Wells and *The Rape of Lucretia* for Britten's English Opera Group, then go to the studio and mail them off from the Disney post office and think, that's my work for the day. Then I'd treat the place as an exotic candy factory . . .'

Before Tony returned to England, Carol Burnett came to call, visiting Disneyland with them and riding on the roller coasters. Julie was still talking of balancing the scales, of taking a year to do a film, then another to have a child — then repeating the pattern. It still seemed possible. Just.

★ ★ ★

In August, three months into the schedule at Disney, *My Fair Lady* started filming at the neighbouring Warner Brothers Studio. Julie denied that she had been tempted to peep over the wall. 'It would have been a little tactless, don't you think?' She was not, however, averse to meeting Audrey Hepburn socially. 'Not that there's any ill-feeling on either side, but each of us seems to think the other might be terribly upset.'

Then, suddenly, the embers of the casting conflagration burst back into flame. Marni Nixon, who had dubbed Deborah Kerr's songs in *The King and I* and Natalie Wood's in *West Side Story*, was discovered to be doing the same for Audrey. Once again, quite unsolicited, the press bayed on Julie's behalf that the best musical role of recent times had been appropriated by someone who could not sing.

'We've been doing this for years,' said Jack Warner. 'We even dubbed Rin-Tin-Tin.'

Julie gave short shrift to the idea that she had been offered the dubbing job: 'I had a very unprintable reply ready. But they didn't ask. Just as well . . . ' It went more or less unnoticed that Miss Nixon (nicknamed the Ghostess with the Mostes') had managed to squeeze in a recording session for Walt Disney, providing, with Julie, the voices for the animated geese in 'Jolly Holiday'.

Towards the end of September, filming of *Mary Poppins* wound up with the final flying scenes. 'They saved all the really dangerous stuff till the end of the film, just in case I had a horrible accident and they lost me,' Julie recalled. On the very last day, high up in the grid and wearing the flying harness, she felt the support wire give way by about a foot: 'I got very anxious, and I said, 'When you let me down, would you be very careful . . . ' so the message went all the way to the back of the studio, 'Let her down easy, Joe.' At which point, I *fell* like a rocket — and there was this awful pregnant silence, and a voice at the end of the studio said, 'Is she down yet?' I was very nearly through the floorboards. But luckily, I was weighted and I didn't do myself much damage.' She did, however, regain her equilibrium with 'a few

Anglo-Saxon words, which I don't often say'.

'She swears like a Marine,' vouched Karen Dotrice on television in 2006, 'and I don't mean to be rude to the Marines. She's got quite a foul mouth; you can be standing in a line-up with her, and she'll pinch your bum. Somehow or other, that camera would turn, and on would come this perfect person, the perfect nanny.'

Forty years after the film's premiere, Julie attempted to explain the gleam in Mary Poppins' eye: 'First of all, she is magic and she makes it happen. Secondly, she puts it away all the time. She is special and she's kind of wicked underneath. But there's that wonderful rigid safety about her.'

Some of the impetus had come from Tony. 'Notice the colour of her petticoats,' Julie pointed out. Tony had told his wife, 'I think Mary Poppins has a secret life,' and designed a riot of red, orange and violet underpinnings beneath the sedate outer garments. Carol Burnett, of course, knew the actress had a similar flair for fun, as she wrote for *Good Housekeeping* magazine in a 1964 article, 'My Friend Julie Andrews': 'Julie Andrews is not Queen Victoria; she's an irrepressible British kook ... Julie Walton can't fake anything, including friendship.' And Carol shared Karen Dotrice's opinion of Julie's vocabulary: 'Some of her best lines are better not in print, but those pear-shaped British inflections make them sound like pure poetry.'

'She has sex appeal with dignity — subtle but glowing,' said Bill Walsh, the film's co-producer and scriptwriter, delighted at the way that the filming had gone. As at the end of Uncle Albert's tea party, the cast and crew drifted slowly back to earth. With more regret at leaving Hollywood than she could ever have imagined, Julie flew home with her baby daughter.

★ ★ ★

Back in London, it was Tony's turn in the spotlight. The West End version of Stephen Sondheim's *A Funny Thing Happened on the Way to the Forum* opened successfully on 3 October 1963. Not only had Tony recreated his New York sets and costumes, he was also producing the show with his friend Richard Pilbrow.

One night, Larry Gelbart and Bert Shevelove, Sondheim's librettists, dined with the Waltons. Julie skipped pudding and, following the fashion of the time, started to breast-feed Emma at the table. The next night, the writers dined with Richard Pilbrow, whose wife repeated the process during dinner. The following evening, Gelbart called Shevelove and asked, 'Bert, are we booked in for any good breast-feedings tonight?'

But things would not remain so domestic for Julie. During the latter stages of the filming, Walt Disney had taken the highly unusual step of showing forty minutes' rough-cut footage to other directors — so keen was he to show off his new star, who looked set to eclipse the vastly more expensive fair lady currently filming for Jack Warner. Sitting in the projection room was the Oscar-winning director of *West Side Story*, Robert Wise, currently preparing Twentieth Century Fox's film of the derided but popular Broadway musical, *The Sound of Music*. One of his major concerns was to find a star to play the lead role of Maria, the singing nun. From what he had heard, Julie Andrews — whom he had never seen on stage — sounded ideal. But there were doubts, as he told me when I met him at his home in Hollywood in April 2005, five months before his death:

'There was some unfounded rumour around town that she wasn't as photogenic as she might be. That gave us pause. So we called Bill Walsh, the producer of *Mary Poppins* over at Disney. He OK'd my coming over, with Saul Chaplin my associate, to see some pieces — they were still in the cutting room — and when she came on the screen, we went, 'Ah, boy, that's it!' So we went right back to the studio and said, 'That's our girl — sign her.' Then I went off to Austria, with Sollie Chaplin and Boris Leven, my art director, to check set locations. We left word at the studio to send us a cable.'

Meanwhile, his choice of leading lady pondered the offer with misgivings. She had not cared for *The Sound of Music* when she saw it on stage. And, considering the general lack of industry enthusiasm about its chances on the screen, it looked as if she was right. Just as in 1954, when she had resisted her life-changing move to New York, so a full decade later, she hesitated to take the step that would seal her cinematic fate. For ten weeks her Libran instinct pulled one way, then another. 'I thought it was too mushy,' she later admitted. 'Luckily, I changed my mind.'

In early November, Wise came back to his Salzburg hotel to find a telegram from Fox: 'I said, 'We've got her!'' For better or worse, Julie Andrews had signed (the first member of the cast to do so) for a comparatively meagre fee of $225,000.

'The gods were on our side,' Wise told me. 'If we had not been able to get Julie, we might have ended up with Doris Day — but, thank goodness, we didn't have to.'

Robert Wise was not the only one to be shown advance footage of *Mary Poppins* — or to make Julie an offer. The independent producer Marty Ransohoff, dubbed 'the Messiah of the New Hollywood' by writer Budd Schulberg, was similarly enthused, offering Julie the chance of a straight film drama before her new musical started in March 1964. It cannot have escaped her attention that Ransohoff and his associate producer John Calley were to make and release their film under the auspices of Metro-Goldwyn-Mayer, shooting it at the MGM British Studios in Borehamwood, where sixteen years earlier she had taken the wretched screen test. It would at least mean she could live at home.

Julie, who had never officially had an acting lesson in her life, was 'very timid about doing anything 'legit', as they say'. Her previous film had been scripted almost as a means of joining one song to another. Now she was being asked to cut her dramatic teeth on the work of Paddy

Chayefsky, whose track record included an Oscar-winning script for *Marty*, the low-budget drama that had changed the direction of Hollywood in 1955. Taking a deep breath, she agreed to play Emily Barham, a young English war widow in love with an American officer, in *The Americanization of Emily*.

Thus, far from finding a family house and settling down with Tony, Julie Andrews faced almost a whole year of film work, with not only the pressure on her marriage to ponder, but also the demands of her next role.

For a moment, it looked as if *The Americanization of Emily* might be helmed by William Wyler, thrice an Oscar winner for *Mrs Miniver, The Best Years of Our Lives* and *Ben Hur* — but the great director, who had made a star of Audrey Hepburn in *Roman Holiday*, demanded too many changes to Chayefsky's script. He was let go, and replaced with the relative newcomer Arthur Hiller.

On another soundstage at Borehamwood, *A Shot in the Dark* was shooting, starring Peter Sellers as Inspector Clouseau. Marty Ransohoff asked the opinion of its director about the suitability of the actress he had chosen for the title role of his own film. 'No,' said Blake Edwards, who had met Julie but once, socially. 'I'm not sure she's right . . . '

The star of the film had no such qualms. As the self-confessed coward Lieutenant-Commander Charles E. Madison, James Garner not only had the best role of his career, but the right to veto his leading lady. He recalled Julie from his early days in New York, when, as a supernumerary in *The Caine Mutiny Court Martial*, he had mixed with the young English girls from *The Boy Friend*. He had subsequently seen her in *My Fair Lady*. 'And that', he said, 'was good enough for me.'

The Americanization of Emily was shot in black and white, the only such film Julie Andrews would ever make. A sardonic anti-war comedy, it takes place in 1944 London, during the build-up to D-Day, when Britain played host to thousands of American soldiers, 'over-sexed, overpaid, and over here'. As aide-de-camp to a schizophrenic admiral, Charlie Madison is a 'dog-robber', arranging every creature comfort for his boss and, naturally, himself.

'Don't show me how profitable it will be to fall in love with you, Charlie. Don't Americanize me,' says Emily, his smart, priggish ATS driver, who has lost her husband, father and brother in combat. She falls for him anyway: 'It is your most important asset, being a coward. Every man I ever loved was a hero and all he got was death.'

'We had a love scene on the bed — a very passionate one,' Julie remarked, 'and I thought, I'm going to be hugely professional and I'm not going to let it affect me at all, and we did take after take, and I began to get slightly dizzy and I got up thinking, snap, there's nothing to this, and my legs buckled — and I *really* mean that they did . . . '

A few days into its schedule in October, the production abruptly closed down. The actress Liz Fraser, who played Julie's ATS colleague, told me that she came in one day to be told 'Pack your bags': because of trouble with the 'obstreperous' unions, the unit was to decamp to the MGM Studios at Culver City. Julie and Tony were destined, it seemed, never to enjoy home and work together; once again she left him for work in Los Angeles. Filming took place until the end of November, Julie playing opposite the English comedienne Joyce Grenfell in a darker than usual role as her delusional mother, James Coburn as Charlie's gung-ho friend, and Melvyn Douglas as the Admiral, whose order 'The first dead man on Omaha Beach must be a sailor!' initiates the film's climax.

The most demanding scene was the inevitable big row with James Garner, at an aircraft hangar in the pouring rain. Wisely avoiding any attempt at great acting, Julie played off her own sincerity, and produced something of real truth. 'I admire Julie the way I admire Audrey Hepburn,' said Garner. Having just filmed *The Children's Hour* with Audrey (ironically, directed by William Wyler) he was one of the few who could accurately compare the actresses. 'They don't give to anybody past a certain line, but they give to everybody up to that line.'

In her first real acting challenge, Julie was robust and sexy, holding her own opposite three Hollywood leading men, in this the most surprising and invigorating of all her early films. Arthur Hiller and Marty Ransohoff (who, with uncharacteristic sweetness, would call her 'my angel dream girl') seemed genuinely pleased at her progress. And Julie had good reason to be pleased too: it looked as if she might be breaking free of typecasting before it had even become a problem.

At the beginning of November, a footnote from her past unexpectedly jumped back into prominence. At a press event at Disneyland to promote the release of *Mary Poppins*, Julie sang 'By the Light of the Silvery Moon'. Her partner was the very balloon artist who had called for her to hop on stage at the London Hippodrome in *Starlight Roof*, half a lifetime ago: Wally Boag, a featured attraction at the theme park since its inauguration in 1955.

Three weeks later, on Friday 22 November 1963, just as Julie's work at MGM was finishing, news from Dallas flashed that President John F. Kennedy had been assassinated. At Warner Brothers, where *My Fair Lady* still had another month of filming, production came to a standstill for the day: Audrey Hepburn had been the last actress to sing 'Happy Birthday' to the President, just before beginning work as Eliza that summer.

Poignantly for Julie, she too had been scheduled to sing for Kennedy at the White House. And *Camelot*, the show she remembered so fondly, was to gain its own mythical status by association with the President. He had been elected a week before the show's Broadway premiere; his assassination was followed by an interview with Jacqueline Kennedy in *Life* magazine, in which she likened her husband's period in office to the reign of King Arthur: 'When Jack quoted something, it was usually classical, but I'm so ashamed of myself — all I keep thinking of is this line from a musical comedy. At night, before we'd go to sleep, Jack liked to play some records; and the song he loved most came at the very end of this record . . . ' And she quoted the final lines of Lerner and Loewe's title song, of the 'One brief shining moment that was known as Camelot'.

★ ★ ★

While filming *The Americanization of Emily*, Julie's worries over the saccharine nature of her next commitment lingered. On his return to Hollywood from Austria, Robert Wise went to see her on the MGM lot, and realised that Twentieth Century Fox still had some work to do on their star: 'I set up a luncheon date in the private dining room. Outside the door, she grabbed my hand and said 'Bob — how are we going to get the sweetness out of this thing?' I was concerned about that same thing.'

At the end of the luncheon with vice-president Richard Zanuck and other executives, Wise played his trump card. 'I pointed out that *The Sound of Music* would be playing on the opposite side of the street to *My Fair Lady* — and watched the reaction. She looked at each of us in turn without speaking. Then she threw back her head and laughed. 'All right then, let's show'em, eh fellows?' That, sir, was the new Julie Andrews talking.'

Feeling somewhat more confident, but frustrated that she would have to shoot her third film before she knew the fate of the first two, Julie returned to Tony in London — where, that winter, Mr and Mrs Walton finally found their family home. 'We really wanted something right in London,' Julie admitted, but she had seen nothing suitable. For just over £20,000, they purchased Worsley House, a three-storey, five-bedroom wing of a splendid Victorian pile at 4 West Side, Wimbledon Common, which the three of them would share with Emma's nanny. 'There's no doubt that you know straight away,' said Julie. 'A house speaks to you, I think.'

From the leafy south-west suburbs of Wimbledon, it was a quick drive to Walton-on-Thames, where unopened wedding presents were still waiting for them. After the cramped London flat, the priority was space: 'Both Tony and I want as much empty feeling as possible . . . We both like simple décor and furnishings — white walls, textured carpets, lots of natural wood. This is going to be our first real home.'

Yet husband and wife were destined to have precious little time together there — far less than they had spent at Flat 4, 70 Eaton Square, which Julie Andrews had only taken as a temporary measure, but maintained for the last four years as Mrs Tony Walton.

Similarly, opportunities to catch their breath at 'Patmos' on Alderney would become ever rarer. And, indeed, on one of their last visits to the cottage as man and wife, there had been a bad moment. Tony had too much talent and confidence to worry about being seen as the consort of a star. But, on the island, he expected their lives to be in some way more conventional

— and there, at a dinner party, someone called him 'Mr Julie Andrews' at just the wrong moment. 'And I completely lost it. I went ballistic. The poor bugger came round the next day with handfuls of flowers. He was abject. I behaved completely inappropriately.' But he could not rely on it not happening again.

★ ★ ★

In early 1964, Julie flew back to Hollywood with Emma, ready to start dance rehearsals and wardrobe tests for *The Sound of Music* on Thursday 20 February.

It seemed that the only space she and Tony were to enjoy for the foreseeable future was apart. And, with painful irony, just as she prepared to play the role that would define her in the eyes of the world as surrogate mother *par excellence*, Julie Andrews was handing over her infant daughter to a real-life nanny. Since the age of thirteen, she had worked, both as a means to pay her family's way and to focus on something other than domestic trouble. It was not so very different now.

'I lost myself in work, work, work,' Julie later recalled. 'As long as someone was telling me what to do — 'Stand here, say this, do that' — I didn't have time to think. But at night, when I would go home, I would hug Emma Kate, and I would think — what am I doing here? What kind of life is this for you? A father thousands of miles away and a mother who's locked in a studio all day.'

She could, of course, have turned the work down and gone back to being Mrs Walton of Wimbledon Common. But Julie was not at all sure she wanted to go back anywhere. Even before she left London to start work on *The Sound of Music*, she stated, 'I thrive best on challenge, and I feel my life is completely free for two reasons: I love what I'm doing and seven times out of ten I can choose what show or film I want to do.'

The current film, of course, was one that had chosen her. The singing nun was waiting in the wings — or, rather, on the mountainside.

8

THE SOUND OF STARDOM

'I felt as if I were pushing a load of treacle up a hill'

— Julie Andrews, quoted by
Cathleen Nesbitt, 1975

High in the Alpine meadows, a young woman runs into the sunlight, throwing her arms wide and singing from her heart. A helicopter bursts out of the clouds, roaring towards her. The young woman's outstretched hands start waving, first in jest then in panic, her smile changing from joy to fear to fury, as the helicopter swings over her head and turns on its tail. The young woman lies blasted to the ground — her language proof, contrary to her appearance, that she is certainly not a nun.

'I will never forget it,' said Julie Andrews in 2005, on the fortieth anniversary of *The Sound of Music*'s release. 'We shot the scene many times, and at the end of each take, the helicopter would circle round. The downdraft nailed me flat on to the grass, and I bit the dust. At first it was funny, but after several times I began to get very angry.'

A feisty star spitting out grass, dirt and the odd expletive was the least of the director's worries. Robert Wise was on borrowed time. With two months of studio filming still ahead of him, he was more than three weeks behind schedule — and Twentieth Century Fox had ordered the unit back to Hollywood. 'One more day,' Wise had pleaded for the title song sequence, the last to be filmed on location. But Thursday 2 July 1964 had dawned like the previous three mornings, with the crew huddled under a tarpaulin against the bitter rain. Nearby, the star shivered in her fur coat. Then, in mid-afternoon, the clouds parted and the Bavarian mountain of Mellweg, just over the Austrian border with Germany, was suddenly bathed in sunshine.

Julie Andrews ran out on the hillside to do battle with the rising helicopter jets, as Robert Wise grasped his chance to film the most famous opening shot in cinema history.

* * *

The Sound of Music has, for over forty years, been such a dazzlingly successful film that it is hard to appreciate how ill-starred its beginning really was. At one point, it seemed unlikely that the story of the Trapp Family Singers would come to the screen at all.

Just as the film opened with an aerial shot, so it closed with the family crossing the Alps from Nazi Austria to neutral Switzerland — rather than, as actually happened, catching a train to Italy. It was on another train, during a night journey to Vienna, that Maria von Trapp had been born Maria Augusta Kutschera, in 1905. An orphan by the age of six, she was raised an atheist by an elderly male relative, but found her calling when a Jesuit priest preached at her school.

Entering the Nonnberg Benedictine Convent in Salzburg, the tomboyish Maria was — more than *The Sound of Music* showed — the black sheep of the abbey. The story of her exile as governess to the sevenfold brood of Baron Georg von Trapp, her inevitable marriage to the boss (a widowed First World War captain) and the family's escape from the Nazis combined some elements of the Bible and rather more of *Cinderella*. Over the next decade, the Trapp Family Choir toured America, finally settling on a large, quasi-Alpine farm in Stowe, Vermont, where Maria died in 1987, aged eighty-two.

In 1949, at a friend's insistence, she had published her memoirs, *The Story of the Trapp Family Singers*. Wolfgang Reinhardt, son of the famous stage director Max Reinhardt, bought the rights to film her story for just $9,000: *Die Trapp-Familie* and its sequel *Die Trapp-Familie in Amerika* became the biggest hits of 1950s German cinema.

Paramount Pictures, looking at properties for Audrey Hepburn, bought an option in 1956, but did nothing with it. However, Richard Halliday, husband of *My Fair Lady* refusenik Mary Martin, recognised the story as a stage vehicle for his wife, and acquired the rights. The score was originally to comprise songs from the Trapp repertoire, but Miss Martin contacted her *South Pacific* creators, Richard Rodgers and Oscar

Hammerstein, to write one extra number. Rodgers and Hammerstein preferred to write a full show afresh, and the team for one of Broadway's biggest hits was formed.

The Sound of Music opened at the Lunt-Fontanne Theatre in November 1959, playing for 1,443 performances — second only to *My Fair Lady* as the most popular show of its day. Winning Tony Awards for Best Musical and Best Actress, the show sold more than three million cast albums, defying the many critics who deplored its sentimentality.

Among the opening-night audience was Spyros Skouras, president of Twentieth Century Fox, which had first call on the screen transfer of any Rodgers and Hammerstein musical. In June 1960, the studio bought the property for $1,250,000 — a comparative bargain, weighed against the $5,500,000 *My Fair Lady* had cost Jack Warner.

The contract, however, stipulated that any film version could not be released until the closure of the Broadway show. In the long interval, Twentieth Century Fox experienced the most turbulent period in its history, brought on by the $44 million calamity of *Cleopatra*. The film started shooting in London in 1960, before Elizabeth Taylor's pneumonia shut it down. The following year, it regrouped in Rome, now co-starring Julie Andrews' two Broadway leading men: Rex Harrison as Caesar and — arriving by way of *Camelot* — Richard Burton as Marc Antony. *Cleopatra* was finally exposed to public view on 12 June 1963 (three days before *The*

Sound of Music finished its Broadway run), having brought Fox to the brink of bankruptcy. Even the explosive Taylor-Burton love affair could not yield a profit on the most expensive film ever made.

During this appalling time, Darryl F. Zanuck, Twentieth Century Fox's founder, wrested back control of the studio, installing as vice-president in charge of production his son Richard — who promptly decided to give the green light to the stage property purchased three years earlier.

In Hollywood, and within Fox itself, there were many who felt that *The Sound of Music* was a cinematic loser (later, they would insist they had known it would be a smash hit all along). Yet Richard Zanuck considered a family musical to be the perfect way to herald a new epoch for the studio. In December 1962, he announced that the highly respected Ernest Lehman would adapt *The Sound of Music* for the screen. Fox was back in business — but only just.

Arriving in early 1963, Lehman (whose adaptations of *The King and I* and *West Side Story* were less characteristic than his scripts for *Sweet Smell of Success* and Hitchcock's *North by Northwest*) found the once mighty Hollywood studio looking like a ghost town. 'Where's my office?' he asked. 'Where would you like it to be?' came the reply. In the reopened studio commissary one lunchtime, Burt Lancaster — Lehman's colleague from the pungent *Sweet Smell of Success* — came over to ask him what he was doing.

'*The Sound of Music*,' replied Lehman.

'Jesus,' said Lancaster, 'you must need the money.'

The attitude was typical. Though the show had an enormous public, its reputation within the industry was lethal. No director wanted to touch it. Robert Wise (*West Side Story*), Stanley Donen (*Funny Face*) and Gene Kelly had all turned down the job, Kelly calling it 'this kind of shit'. Then, after weeks of dogged persuasion from Lehman, William Wyler agreed to take it on, despite his distaste for the material.

In May 1963, he flew to the Alps, accompanied by Roger Edens (associate producer on many a Judy Garland musical at MGM) to scout for locations. These included Berchtesgaden, tersely summed up in Edens' notes: 'Hitler's hideaway. This was purely a tourist call.' Then, in Salzburg, Wyler 'quite easily charmed' the Bürgermeister, who 'even indicated that he was not averse to showing scenes of the *Anschluss*'.

As Wyler wrote in his autobiography, 'I had a tendency to want to make it, if not an anti-Nazi movie, at least say a few things.' Indeed, according to Richard Zanuck, 'He wanted tanks. He wanted a real invasion, blowing up the town and everything. I didn't see any need for all this right in the middle of a musical.'

One night, Wyler and Lehman were playing gin rummy at Glenn Ford's house, when a mind reader invited guests into a bedroom for specific consultations. Wyler asked him the question still preying on his mind: should he direct *The Sound of Music*?

'Let me hold the screenplay in my hands,' said the mind reader.

'There is no screenplay,' replied the director, 'but the writer is in the living room. Maybe you could hold him in your hands.'

Wyler found a way out with the adaptation of John Fowles' macabre *The Collector*. As with *The Americanization of Emily*, he abandoned the chance to direct Julie Andrews — although later, when iconolatry of Julie/Maria had taken hold, he made his own claim for casting her from rushes of *Mary Poppins*: 'I went over to the studio and met her on the set. Walt showed me some rushes, and she was signed.'

Lehman, anticipating Wyler's departure, had reverted to his original choice, Robert Wise, whose versatile career encompassed most genres, from the science fiction classic *The Day the Earth Stood Still* to the serious drama *I Want to Live!* By a stroke of luck, contingency made the director available. The Mirisch Corporation, for which he had directed *West Side Story*, had gone cold on his new project, *The Sand Pebbles*. Wise had moved it across to Fox, but was stalled by its logistical problems.

'I got a call from the studio, saying, 'Would you be interested in taking a look at the script of *The Sound of Music*?' It had been done by a good friend of mine, Ernie Lehman.' Though he had disliked the stage show, Wise was impressed with the screenplay; he talked to Saul Chaplin, his associate producer on *West Side Story*, and finally signed on in October, admitting, 'I do feel a definite sense of embarrassment for having laughed at one point about Ernie doing *Music* and now finding myself on it too.'

In early 2005, when I met Robert Wise in Hollywood, he made it clear that his experience in musicals went back much further than his Oscar for *West Side Story*: 'I worked on a lot of Astaire-Rogers films at RKO — in editing — so from that I knew the whole form. It wasn't like I was going into something cold.'

He moved fast, taking Saul Chaplin to New York to see Richard Rodgers. Popular though the score was, it was not without its drawbacks, and Wise needed a new love duet for Maria and the Captain: 'They had another song in the original stage show, a kind of negative title — 'An Ordinary Couple'. We got hold of Rodgers. He said, 'They're not really ordinary.' We said, 'It's not a good song.' He said 'OK, I'll get you one.' A couple of weeks later, that became 'Something Good'.'

Ernest Lehman had previously met Rodgers, and the question of casting had arisen. 'I suppose,' remarked the composer, 'you'll be putting Doris Day in the picture?'

'There's one girl I'd love to see play Maria,' answered Lehman. 'Julie Andrews.'

Rodgers, for whom 'The Pratt Family of Switzerland' at Carnegie Hall was fresh in the mind, regarded Lehman at length. 'So what else is new?' he said finally.

'I *was* a bit nervous about it when they started to consider me,' Julie laughingly remembered of the possible conflict caused by her television performance. 'I knew it would come back to haunt me. At the time, we all felt it was just so twee, and far too sweet. Once the film version came around, and I found out that Robert Wise was directing, well, let's just say I changed my tune.'

Before backing out, William Wyler had suggested the ubiquitous Audrey Hepburn or Austrian-born Romy Schneider for the lead role — but Robert Wise, interested in the actress who had so publicly missed recreating her biggest stage triumph on screen, made his fateful trip to Walt Disney Studios, and immediately knew he had found his girl.

His ideas for the supporting characters centred on Victor Borge and Noël Coward for the rakish Max Dettweiler, eventually played by the rakish Richard Haydn, and a glittering array of suggestions (Cyd Charisse, Eva Gabor, even Grace Kelly) for the worldly Baroness, from which the glamorous Eleanor Parker was chosen. The shortlist for the Mother Abbess was headed by Irene Dunne, to whom Julie Andrews would at times be compared. Jeanette MacDonald was another suggestion, in a nod to the musical's operetta qualities, but Peggy Wood, from the television version of *I Remember Mama*, was finally offered the role.

As the stereotypically brusque Captain, two possibilities were Bing Crosby and Yul Brynner, whose Oscar for *The King and I* did not hurt his chances. Wise also considered Peter Finch and Sean Connery, but was keenest on a Shakespearean actor he had seen on Broadway, Christopher

Plummer: 'It was my wife's idea . . . I think he was marvellous in the role. He gave a kind of dark edge to it, which I felt was very helpful.'

The Canadian actor, fearful that the part would harm his classical theatre profile, was nonetheless coerced by his agent Kurt Frings (who had also snared Eliza Doolittle for Audrey Hepburn) to make the film. Then he found out that his songs, including the beautiful ballad 'Edelweiss', were to be dubbed. Unlike Miss Hepburn, he was not prepared 'to play a part in which I am to be castrated' — and he jumped ship.

He came back on board, begrudgingly. A classical pianist as well as an actor, he had enough musicality to know the limitations of his voice, and Bill Lee took the job of dubbing him. With Peggy Wood moving into the shadows to mime to 'Climb Ev'ry Mountain', an indignant Jack L. Warner was among the first to point out that there was as much ghosting on *The Sound of Music* as on *My Fair Lady*.

Ironically, Marni Nixon was cast in her first onscreen credit as Sister Sophia. But if her presence rekindled Julie's disappointment over Eliza Doolittle, there was no sign of it at Miss Nixon's first rehearsal, as she recalled in her autobiography *I Could Have Sung All Night*: 'Julie stood up and strode over to me . . . 'Marni,' she said, in that delicious English accent, 'I'm such a fan of yours!' There was a collective sigh of relief throughout the room.'

For the seven Trapp children, unsuccessful applicants included the Osmond Brothers, Kurt

Russell and Richard Dreyfuss, whose lack of dancing ability let him down. Of those chosen, Nicholas Hammond (Friedrich) and Angela Cartwright (Brigitta) would sustain the most visible show-business success, in *Batman* and *Lost in Space* on television.

Auditioning in London, Robert Wise considered Charles Chaplin's daughter Geraldine for the role of the lovelorn Liesl. Her competition in Hollywood comprised Sharon Tate, Lesley Ann Warren and an unknown Mia Farrow. But it was the beauteous Charmian Carr who was cast, in mid-February 1964, prior to six weeks of rehearsals with choreographers Marc Breaux and Dee Dee Wood and conductor Irwin Kostal, all three repeating their *Mary Poppins* duties.

Filming commenced on Thursday 26 March, on Stage 15 of the Fox lot, with one of the brightest numbers, 'My Favourite Things', sung by Maria as she calms the children during a thunderstorm. It was a perfect way for Julie, sporting a blonde bobbed haircut for her role, to establish a relationship with her young charges, helping them over their initial nerves by joking between takes. Far from irritating her director, 'she made them easier to work with'. And, almost from the start, Julie was relaxed enough to portray Maria as spirited rather than sweet.

In the third week of April, the company flew to Austria. The Trapp family house was recreated from two locations, some miles from each other outside Salzburg. Most of the scenes were filmed at the lakeside Schloss Leopoldskron, requisitioned by the Nazis after the takeover of March

1938, a matter that local residents were only too keen to forget. Jettisoning William Wyler's brutalist concept, the film would take a fairytale tone from its introductory subtitle, 'Salzburg, Austria, in the last golden days of the 1930s'.

Nonetheless, Robert Wise managed to suggest enough Nazi infiltration in the latter stages of the plot — such as the peal of Maria's wedding bells turning to one dull toll, as a straight line of storm troopers march across the square — to make the city entirely resistant to the eventual film. 'That was really rather nasty of them', remarked Julie, given that *The Sound of Music* tours would prove Salzburg's biggest tourist attraction, other than the local Mozart heritage trail.

Spring in the Austrian Alps, however, was not as idyllic as it eventually looked on screen. Robert Wise had scheduled just six weeks on location, which eventually stretched to eleven. The unplanned element was the weather. 'Nobody happened to mention that Salzburg has Europe's seventh-highest annual rainfall,' said Julie, but she credited it for some of the film's texture: 'It wasn't just bland, funny picture-postcard skies. It was huge, towering cumulus at times . . . I think the weather gave it that drama.'

The endless downpour turned the mountain tracks into mud ditches. The truck carrying the camera was abandoned in favour of an ox-drawn cart, in which Julie, trouper to the last, rode in her mink coat, using her umbrella to keep the equipment dry.

With cast and crew clustered on the

mountainside for days on end, unable to film sequences such as the famous 'Do-Re-Mi' montage, Julie kept spirits as buoyant as possible. During gaps in the schedule, still dressed as the postulant nun, she launched into repertoire amassed from her early years, singing anything from 'Hawaiian War Chant' to 'Knock 'em in the Old Kent Road'. At other times, she joined up with Saul Chaplin and Marc Breaux, singing old standards to such good effect that Julie named the trio 'The Vocalzones', after the well-known throat pastilles. She also organised and financed a sixty-mile coach outing for the cast to the State Opera House in Munich, where Svetlana Beriosova was on tour with the Royal Ballet, regaling her guests on the journey as a self-styled Cockney 'bus mother'.

Julie's grounding in vaudeville had equipped her no less for the role itself. One of Saul Chaplin's anonymous contributions to the film was 'I Have Confidence', Maria's transition from nervous nun to gungho governess, in which he had combined fragments of Richard Rodgers' music. During the number, Julie incorporated comic gags not used since her touring days with Ted and Barbara — catching her guitar sideways in a doorway, tripping herself up on the road to the Trapp home. 'She must have eight thousand bits of business,' said one technician, and Robert Wise was more impressed than ever: 'It convinced me more than anything else that she could really clown.'

'I Have Confidence' was also notable for a glimpse of the real Maria von Trapp, who had assumed that Twentieth Century Fox would consult her over the film. But, as P.L. Travers had discovered with *Mary Poppins*, Hollywood could not have cared less. 'We were in Salzburg for a visit,' remembered her daughter Rosemarie von Trapp. 'My mother asked if we could take part in the scene and she was told, 'You can pass by across the street, behind Julie Andrews.' And that's what we did . . . It was all very nice, but we had to do it at least twenty times. Being in that one small scene was enough for us.' Maria greeted Christopher Plummer with a kiss on the lips, exclaiming, 'My God, darling, I wish my husband had looked as good as you.'

Julie confessed she had been warned that Plummer was cold and aloof but, perhaps surprisingly, they got on well together. 'I have found him a dear,' she said. 'He is introspective, keeps to himself, and people confuse this with unfriendliness.' In return Plummer could only manage a backhanded compliment, 'Working with her was like getting hit over the head with a Hallmark card.' That quote — like his reference to the film as 'The Sound of Mucus' — would haunt him for decades.

The younger children were certainly scared of him, reflecting Captain von Trapp's onscreen relationship with his offspring. By contrast, Julie continued to bond with them, off camera as well as on, as if playing with her half-brothers in Walton-on-Thames. It made a song like 'The Lonely Goatherd' not only less cloying but even joyous.

'She has tremendous strength, and when you

give her a challenge, great determination,' Saul Chaplin remarked of her resilience, similar to that displayed by Maria on screen. For some, it was all a little too calculated, a little too relentless: one, sadly nameless, crew member described her as 'a nun, all right. But she's a nun with a switchblade.'

Yet she was as tough on herself, knowing instinctively what she wanted to achieve, no longer the raw recruit who needed Moss Hart to compensate for her lack of preparation. At the beginning of the year, Julie had run through the score with her old singing teacher, Lilian Stiles-Allen, before leaving London for Hollywood. Her major difficulty had been to find a visual image for the film's panoramic opening sequence. The veteran opera singer had reiterated what she always taught. 'You must see the picture clearly and take the public into your confidence, so that they will see that same picture . . . When you really want peace and quiet, you go to the hills because you find nature there — but this time you find something special.' And when she finally saw *The Sound of Music*, Madame Stiles-Allen knew that her pupil had taken her advice.

For Julie, work was both a blessing and a curse, taking her mind off the very problem it had caused. Five years into her marriage, Mrs Tony Walton was seeing almost nothing of her husband. 'I realise the dangers of being apart only too well,' she admitted. 'But what can you do? Surely it would be much worse if one of us gave up a career to sit at home and mope. That could lead to dreadful resentment.'

She was also worried that baby Emma might forget her father. 'So I talk a lot about him, and he sends her presents and tape messages and they have chats on the phone. It seems to work,' she ended, somewhat plaintively.

Throughout the Salzburg shoot, the eighteen-month-old toddler stayed in the palatial Österreichischer Hof Hotel with her mother, who was determined to spend as much time with her as possible. 'I never want to have that horrible feeling that Nanny's taken over for good,' she explained. But, sacrificing married life for a tough filming schedule, Julie was bound to doubt her judgement, as she returned to Hollywood on Friday 3 July.

The next day, the company resumed interior work at the studio, finishing the twenty-three-week shoot at the end of August — by which time it was apparent, even to Christopher Plummer, that a combination of masterly direction, stunning photography and unforgettable songs had yielded something extraordinary. Only once towards the end, 'so tired and nervous that I couldn't keep going', did Julie's concentration fail her. While singing 'Something Good' with Plummer, the groans from the hot arc lamps made the couple giggle unremittingly; an unusually exasperated Robert Wise had to light them in silhouette to hide their mirth. But this was the sole lapse of the professionalism that had invigorated the film's fragile fortunes from the start.

The genial yet canny director had allowed 'the

Rock of Gibraltar', as he called his star, free rein: 'She just had such a range of emotions and talent, far beyond what I had somehow expected.' And, if she had sometimes seemed too single-minded on location, the results justified her persistence. 'Julie Andrews didn't go to Salzburg to make friends,' wrote Charmian Carr in her astute memoir *Forever Liesl*. 'She went there to make a movie. And she made a great one.'

Whether or not the piece still force-fed more than a spoonful of sugar, Julie made it possible to believe in Maria. As Robert Wise put it to me, 'I just happened to be the director: she was just right for the part.' A part she was born to play.

* * *

From the Twentieth Century Fox set of *The Sound of Music*, Julie Andrews was dragooned into an extensive round of publicity for Walt Disney. Upwards of $20 million had been spent on her first three films; the entire sum remained speculative. But, at long last, the backlog was ready to be released.

On the evening of 27 August 1964, *Mary Poppins* was unveiled at Grauman's Chinese Theatre, Hollywood Boulevard. In the cinema forecourt, where stars since the silent days had planted their hand-and footprints, a group of Pearly Kings and Queens set the scene, and Dick Van Dyke danced with a *corps de ballet* of oversize penguins. Several London 'bobbies' acted as security for the celebrity audience, which included Van Dyke's television wife Mary Tyler Moore, Maureen O'Hara and Roddy McDowall, and several of the Hollywood old guard. Slipping by almost unnoticed was Tony Walton, as Julie stopped to talk to Walt Disney for the cameras before the film began.

From the second that the magical nanny appeared above the rooftops of London, carried by the east wind on a cloud, powdering her *retroussé* nose, it was clear that there was a new star in the Hollywood heavens, one whose graceful appearance caused the audience to ponder why anyone would have thought Julie Andrews non-photogenic. But there was something more than prettiness coming from the screen. There was star quality. As the audience emerged enraptured, the critics took their cue, the *Hollywood Reporter* instantly recognising it as 'the kind of film that creates not fans but evangelists'. The remark was echoed across America after the East Coast opening one month later.

'In case you are a Mary Poppins zealot who dotes on her just as she is, don't let the intrusion of Mr Disney and his myrmidons worry you one bit,' raved Bosley Crowther in the *New York Times*. 'Be thankful for it and praise heaven there are such as they still making films.' As for the title character: 'It is she, played superbly by Miss Andrews . . . with her unrelenting discipline and her disarmingly angelic face, who fills this film with a sense of wholesome substance and the serenity of self-confidence.'

Judith Crist of the *Herald Tribune* called the

film 'a charming, imaginative and technically superb movie musical', and *Time* magazine found it hard to distinguish character from actress: 'All speeches and cream, with a voice like polished crystal, she seems the very image of a prim young governess who might spend her free Tuesdays skittering off to Oz.'

The Wizard of Oz was a point of reference for several critics: what the MGM classic had done in 1939 for Judy Garland, *Mary Poppins* looked like doing now for Julie Andrews. Within days, there were queues of families forming outside Radio City Music Hall in New York, just as they would across America, and beyond.

In London, where *Mary Poppins* had its royal premiere the week before Christmas (Princess Margaret and Lord Snowdon compensating for the absence of the stars), the critics were more puritanical, harping on the liberties that had been taken with the books — even though, strangely, the stories were more popular in America than in Britain. 'Oh dear,' ran *The Times*; 'another example of looking gift horses in the mouth. The latest production from Mr Walt Disney's studios has colour, cartoon interludes . . . just about everything you could ask for to make up a splendid Christmas entertainment. Except charm.' But even the anonymous critic admired 'the charming Miss Julie Andrews' — and the film quickly enjoyed sell-out business.

Julie's success, however, could not overshadow the biggest production of the year. *My Fair Lady* had its world premiere in New York on 21

October. For Rex Harrison and the film, there was nothing but praise. And, to Bosley Crowther, 'Audrey Hepburn superbly justifies the decision of Jack Warner to play the title role.' Other reviews, while taking exception to her unconvincing Cockney scenes, were respectful of her stunning transformation and truthful playing in the second half of the film. But veteran gossipmonger Hedda Hopper could not resist an open goal: 'With Marni Nixon doing the singing, Audrey Hepburn gives only half a performance.'

Audrey herself was battle-weary. At the New York opening, asked yet again about the dubbing, she smiled bravely, 'I take my hat off to those marvellous people in Hollywood who twiddle all the knobs and make one voice out of two.' Then she wilted, admitting what had been obvious all along, 'I'm not a soprano — I'm not a singer.'

The perceived underdog, however, did not have it in her nature to gloat. In any case, she had worries of her own. In early September, the *New York Times* had run an article, 'The Hollywoodization of Julie', in which the up-and-coming star, despite all the excitement, seemed to have reverted to Walton-on-Thames:

'What I am thinking about is a vacation and a chance to work on the new home my husband and I have just bought outside London,' said Miss Andrews, whose sentences spill out in sudden terse outbursts. Miss Andrews is a restrained, perhaps bland young woman who has always been content

231

to offer pre-packaged replies to interviewers' questions.

The terse outbursts betrayed her problem: the first tendrils of global fame that clawed remorselessly at any hope of solidifying her marriage. In New York, Julie recorded an episode of *The Andy Williams Show*. Singing 'Supercalifragilisticexpialidocious' with the Osmonds, she seemed relaxed and happy. But Tony, in town to design the Broadway musical *Golden Boy*, found himself just one of many with claims on her time. As Julie remarked, 'Finally, Tony said, 'I'll tell you what, love, I'll check into another hotel. At least we'll be able to phone each other.''

On 28 October, however, they were very much a couple, appearing at the New York world premiere of *The Americanization of Emily*. 'If you can stand watching Julie Andrews playing a role in which she doesn't sing, but in which she does make some beautiful music with a delightfully un-heroic man,' said Bosley Crowther in the *New York Times*, 'then nothing should deter you from going as swiftly as you can to see *The Americanization of Emily*.' He regarded the film as 'a spinning comedy that says more for basic pacifism than a fistful of intellectual tracts'.

Elsewhere, it received a mixed press, Pauline Kael remarking, 'Julie Andrews could play a promiscuous girl and shine with virtue.' Six years before the not entirely dissimilar *Catch-22* and *M*A*S*H*, the film was something of an anti-heroic vanguard, despite asking more questions than it could answer, and running away with (or from) itself at the end. At the box office, it proved a solid commercial success, earning almost twice its $2,700,000 cost. Moreover, there were Academy Award nominations for its cinematography and art direction as well as Johnny Mandel's musical score, the theme of which was recorded as a song by Frank Sinatra and Barbra Streisand, but never by the actress playing Emily.

The Americanization of Emily was not released in London until April 1965. With the censors having accorded it an adult X certificate, there would be no royal premiere, but it received strong reviews. *The Times* called it a 'ruthless film comedy', likening it to the contemporaneous *Dr Strangelove* in its willingness to offend, and finding it 'blessed with three ideal principals' — James Garner, Melvyn Douglas and Julie Andrews.

For one brief shining moment, it looked as if Julie had indeed broken free of typecasting, serving notice that there was more to her than a pretty set of pipes, even as her Disney musical piled up the grosses. 'At the age of twenty-nine,' shouted *Newsweek*, 'Julie Andrews suddenly finds herself transformed into a full-fledged movie star.'

★ ★ ★

With the first blush of spring, as Alan Jay Lerner put it, 'the voice of the Oscar is heard in the land.' The awards season proper actually begins rather earlier, with the nominations for the Golden Globes, and from then on, madness reigns.

233

At the end of 1964, it came as little surprise that Julie received a Golden Globe nomination for Best Actress in a musical or comedy film, and on 8 February 1965, she beat fellow nominee Audrey Hepburn to win her first major award. Her speech, however, was what made the news, ending with a guileless smile: 'And finally, my thanks to a man who made all this possible in the first place: Mr Jack Warner.'

There was a short silence — then a burst of laughter and applause. The movie mogul who had rejected her as the screen Eliza was sitting directly in front of her. It was 'grand fun', Julie said afterwards, adding the next day, 'I hope I didn't sound too bitchy'. Perhaps not, but she had started to slough off her diffident chrysalis, already beginning to metamorphose into what the columnist Sheilah Graham would call 'the Iron Butterfly'.

Back in London, Julie was nominated by the British Film Academy as Most Promising Newcomer, against the biggest sensation in contemporary culture, the Beatles, nominated collectively for *A Hard Day's Night*. They lost to the star of *Mary Poppins*.

In the third week of February 1965, two quite disparate events, one on either side of America, reflected parallel universes within the country. In New York, the civil rights activist Malcolm X was shot dead by three members of the Nation of Islam. And in Los Angeles, the Academy Award nominations for the previous year were announced, with all eyes on the girl who seemed to offer a panacea for the nation's discord.

Sensationally, Julie Andrews was nominated as Best Actress — while Audrey Hepburn was ignored altogether. Julie, the immediate favourite to win, only needed to be patient. The result would not be known until April. In her new hacienda-style home in Hidden Valley Road, off Coldwater Canyon in Hollywood, the white furniture and tiled floors were covered in bouquets and telegrams. Julie did her best to relax with Emma, as the calls poured in. 'I'm very thrilled — though it's rather sad that Audrey didn't get named,' she said. 'Anyway, why should anyone blame Audrey because I didn't get the part? It wasn't Audrey who passed me over when they cast the film. It was you-know-who.'

Further down the list of nominations, almost unnoticed, was Tony Walton, for his costume designs. *Mary Poppins* was also short-listed as Best Film, along with *Dr Strangelove, Becket, Zorba the Greek* and *My Fair Lady* (nominated in every major category except that of Best Actress). It did indeed look as if 'when the Lord closes a door, somewhere He opens a window.' The quote, however, came not from *Mary Poppins*, but from the next and even more important musical landmark in her career.

On 15 January 1965, rumours of Julie's sensational performance as Maria von Trapp had received confirmation at the Mann Theatre, Minneapolis, where *The Sound of Music* had its first preview. 'The weather was miserable, and we thought nobody would show up,' Richard Zanuck remembered, 'but the theatre was full, and at intermission, the whole audience stood up and applauded for five minutes. They did it again at the end — and these were people who had paid to see it. Bobby Wise and I looked at each other, shell-shocked.'

The following evening in Tulsa, the situation was repeated. With a New York premiere scheduled for Easter, followed by a premium priced, reserved-seating road show release, Julie's latest film started to build up over a million dollars in advance bookings. In the *Hollywood Reporter*, the veteran columnist Radie Harris placed her bets:

> Had Julie recreated 'Eliza' for the screen, there is no doubt that she would have been nominated and won the 'Oscar' . . . Now, if by a twist of fate, compounded by talent, she wins for *Mary Poppins*, it is also safe to predict on this second day of March 1965, that no one will come along in the coming year to top her performance as Maria in *The Sound of Music* . . . Again, she dominates a film that will shatter world records as entertainment for adults and children alike.

On Tuesday 2 March 1965, *The Sound of Music* burst onto the screen at the Rivoli Theatre, Broadway, in front of a wildly cheering audience — including Richard Rodgers, Beatrice Lillie, Bette Davis, Salvador Dali and Adlai Stevenson. Oscar Hammerstein's widow Dorothy called it 'as close to perfection as any movie musical I've ever seen'.

Tony, who had been in New York for the last few months, escorted Julie, who flew from Los Angeles with Emma. At the cinema, she was asked if the screaming hordes outside had unnerved her. 'No, not really,' said the girl who had always been so shy, as her husband looked on quietly; 'all of this is very important to me now, you know.'

After the screening, at a magnificent March of Dimes banquet in the Americana Hotel, the star was applauded once more by the glittering crowd. 'Julie Andrews is that rare thing — a lady!' exclaimed an unusually effusive Bette Davis, telling Julie, 'You are just beautiful . . . the motion picture business is in love with you!'

Wearing a stone-coloured silk jersey dress and a huge topaz pendant she called 'my television set', Julie seemed slightly bemused by the euphoria. 'Her nose is a little wobbly, a little baffled, tonight,' said Tony Walton. 'It's a little like a ski-slide,' agreed his wife, who also described her haircut as that of 'a female Beatle'. From that evening, Julie Andrews was every bit as famous as the Fab Four, eulogised by the likes of James Powers, who went into raptures in the *Hollywood Reporter*:

This lady is not just a great star; she is a whole whirling dazzling constellation. She is not just an ordinary movie personality, she is a phenomenon. Once there was Mary Pickford, then there was Garbo, now there is Julie. She is very likely going to be the object of one of the most intense and sustained love affairs between moviegoers and a star in the history of motion pictures.

And yet . . . for all her brilliance, most major reviewers considered Julie's performance as Maria as a flower blossoming in ordure. Five years earlier, the Butchers of Broadway had savaged the stage production, to the thunderous disagreement of the paying public. Now, possibly realising their words would be to no avail, the film critics went for broke.

In the *New York Times*, Bosley Crowther paid tribute to 'Julie with her air of radiant vigour, her appearance of Plain Jane wholesomeness and her ability to make her dialogue as vivid and appealing as she makes her songs', but had no time for the film itself: 'The whole thing is staged by Mr Wise in a cosy-come-corny fashion that even theatre people know is old hat . . . ' Other than Julie, he found the adults 'fairly horrendous', especially Christopher Plummer who 'acts the hard-jawed, stiff-backed fellow artificially'.

Judith Crist of the *Herald Tribune* opened by praising Julie Andrews as 'the most enchanting and compleat performer to come to the screen in years', but lined up her ammunition against what she called '*The Sound of Marshmallows*':

One star and much scenery do not a two-hour-and-fifty-five-minutes-plus-intermission entertainment make, and the issue itself must be faced . . . This last, most remunerative and least inspired, let alone sophisticated, of the Rodgers and Hammerstein collaborations is square and solid sugar. Calorie-counters, diabetics and grown-ups from eight to eighty had best beware . . .

For Robert Wise and Ernest Lehman, surreptitiously reading the reviews in a corner of the Americana ballroom, the party had just turned into a wake.

There was some comfort in the trade papers and the tabloids. *Variety* called it a 'warmly pulsating, captivating drama' and the *Hollywood Reporter* forecast that it would be one of the 'all time hits . . . it restores your faith in movies. If you sit quietly and let it take, it may also restore your faith in humanity.' The *New York Daily News* gave the movie its top rating and described it as 'A magical film in which Julie Andrews gives an endearing performance', and the *Journal American* chanced its arm by saying Julie was 'in line for the Oscar again'.

As if in response, the unmistakable signs of public enthusiasm were already starting to make themselves manifest. Sensing this, Pauline Kael, America's most feared critic, threw everything she could into her review for *McCall's* magazine, reckoning that '*The Sound of Money*' was 'probably going to be the single most repressive influence on artistic freedom in movies for the next few years':

The success of a movie like *The Sound of Music* makes it even more difficult for

239

anyone to try to do anything worth doing, anything relevant to the modern world, anything inventive or expressive . . .

Whom could it offend? Only those of us who, *despite the fact that we may respond,* loathe being manipulated in this way and are aware of how self-indulgent and cheap and ready-made are the responses we are made to feel . . . It's the big lie, the sugarcoated lie that people seem to want to eat . . .

And this is the sort of attitude that makes a critic feel that maybe it's all hopeless. Why not just send the director, Robert Wise, a wire: 'You win, I give up,' or, rather, 'We both lose, we all lose.'

As the public, manipulated or otherwise, began to fill long-empty cinemas, a group of fans, incensed at the review, successfully demanded that *McCall's* dismiss Miss Kael.

Something similar happened at the end of March in London, where *The Sound of Music* had its European premiere — Princess Margaret and Lord Snowdon again cutting the ribbon — and Derek Malcolm grabbed his chance to become the film critic for the *Guardian*: 'My predecessor was sacked when he filed a review, which read '*The Sound of Music*, Odeon, Leicester Square: No.''

Fergus Cashin, for the *Daily Sketch*, snored his way through the press showing. 'Sleep is a form of criticism,' he would maintain, concluding that the film might just make it as a good effort. *The Times* opined that 'sheer professional know-how can do wonders, and that is what we get'.

But Kenneth Tynan demonstrated that the qualities that made him the leading critic of his generation included his ability to surprise. For the screen transposition of the show he had labelled 'The case for Trappism', he found himself 'mostly bored but intermittently, unexpectedly touched'. His approbation was particularly for the young actress who had disarmed him, not for the first time: 'It is Julie Andrews of the soaring voice and thrice-scrubbed innocence who makes me, even in guarded moments, catch my breath.'

Elsewhere, the film divided opinion as before — either an 'almighty egg laid by a dodo' or 'the best screen musical ever'. Yet there was nothing but praise for Julie Andrews, to whom it was conceded that *Mary Poppins* had been no lucky accident.

That same March, she found herself on the front of *Life* magazine, smiling from ear to ear. The previous week's cover had been given over to the murder of Malcolm X — but if there was any doubt that America had found an antidote to its nascent troubles, it was quashed by the magazine's panegyric: 'Julie's radiance floods the screen, warms the heart and brings back the golden age of the Hollywood musical with a film destined to be one of the biggest hits ever.'

And yet . . . 'How do you solve a problem like Maria?' ran one of its songs, summing up the star's own feelings. Whither Julie Andrews? She needed some answers — and not only about her career.

9

ON THE COUCH

'Someday, I am going to lose my temper. I've never done it, and I'm determined'

— Julie Andrews, 1964

The coronation of Julie Andrews took place on Monday 5 April 1965 in the Santa Monica Civic Auditorium, at the thirty-seventh awards presentation of the Academy of Motion Picture Arts and Sciences. It was the climax of a night of glory, particularly for the British contingent, of whom English-born master of ceremonies Bob Hope quipped, 'There'll always be an England — even if it is in Hollywood. Winners will go to the Oscar Ball. Losers will join hands and march on the British Embassy.'

The pattern had been set early on, with Cecil Beaton winning Best Costume Design for *My Fair Lady*, his screen creations for Audrey Hepburn having edged out Tony Walton's work on his wife's first major film. At that point, Julie turned to her husband, who had arrived from New York on a flying visit, and murmured a word of sympathy. She was carefully watched by the phalanx of reporters, who had recently begun to remark on his long absences from her side.

As the evening wore on, *Mary Poppins* began

to give its rival a run for its money, winning four of the awards, including Best Song for the Sherman Brothers' 'Chim Chim Cher-ee' and Best Special Visual Effects. But all the while, the duel of the Elizas remained uppermost in people's minds, if not on the ballot paper.

Audrey Hepburn silenced her detractors by turning up, stunning in white Givenchy, to present Rex Harrison with his heavily predicted Oscar. 'I have to thank *two* fair ladies, I think,' said Harrison, and Audrey smiled gracefully. Then, seconds later, came the picture story for which every editor was waiting. Despite a strong field of Anne Bancroft (*The Pumpkin Eater*), Sophia Loren (*Marriage, Italian Style*), Debbie Reynolds (*The Unsinkable Molly Brown*) and Kim Stanley (*Seance on a Wet Afternoon*), Sidney Poitier opened the envelope and announced that Julie Andrews had been chosen as Best Actress for *Mary Poppins.*

For her first appearance on the big screen, Julie had won the most glamorous prize in the world. Walking quickly on to the stage, in lemon-yellow chiffon, crystal necklace and long white gloves, she looked radiant. 'Oh, this is lovely,' she said. 'You Americans are famous for your hospitality, but this is ridiculous.'

This time, there was no crack at the expense of Jack Warner, who could feel quite happy with *My Fair Lady*'s haul of eight Oscars, culminating in his own for Best Film and George Cukor's as Best Director. But on the front pages the following morning, it was Julie Andrews who stood next to her former Broadway co-star, clutching the twenty-four-carat gold-plated statuette — intrinsic value sixty dollars, prestige incalculable.

Asked if her victory had come from sympathy votes against Warner, a flicker of concern crossed her eyes. 'I hope it didn't; I like to think I won it for good reasons rather than for those.' But, in years to come, Julie would be more circumspect: 'When I saw the people around me that year, I was absolutely sure that Anne Bancroft should have had it.' She would also quote a scene from *The Pumpkin Eater* that had affected her deeply, where Anne Bancroft and Peter Finch, after a blazing row, become aware that their young son has been listening. They call out to him, but there is a long, dead silence. Then a little figure tears past the door. 'It's a wonderful moment,' Julie would say, her own memories of parental strife at The Old Meuse still clear.

Penelope Mortimer, author of *The Pumpkin Eater*, was sadly unable to return the compliment, later writing in the London *Observer*: 'Miss Andrews depresses me. If she were a flower baby or a transcendental meditator, I would understand her better. If her vowel sounds weren't quite so pure, and her expression was less totally confident, I might be able to feel a twinge of sympathy for her. I do not understand what makes her the world's sweetheart; or, if I do, it's better not thought about.'

Strangely, Julie might have understood this opinion, in her hour of glory. The pressure of putting a smile on every situation, of projecting herself as the girl who liked to be known as Mrs Walton, masked the fact that she and Tony were

244

now deeply concerned about the way their careers were keeping them apart.

Yet, late the previous year, with her house on Wimbledon Common still standing empty, Julie Andrews had made a decision of some significance. Before she walked through the gates of 9531 Hidden Valley Road, Coldwater Canyon, she could still have regarded herself as a visitor to the film capital. But after she had looked around the Spanish villa, her mind was made up: Beverly Hills 90210 would now be home.

The garden with its rocky-edged swimming pool was overgrown, and paint was peeling from the walls of the house — but its eight main rooms were large and airy, and the neighbourhood, close to many of the studios, was peaceful. Julie took the property, calling it 'perfectly smashing'. At that moment, she became a citizen of Los Angeles more than of any other town, no matter what her passport said. 'London is my home and it will remain my home,' she stressed to reporters, but it was not where the work was. And, as Tony knew, where Julie's work lay, her heart lay too.

A 'husbandless house', one of Julie's friends described the new address. And Julie too would be absent for long stretches of time. 'They may think of me as the girl next door,' she said, shortly before departing for her next film location, 'but I'm never there.'

For Tony, this was true of their entire marriage. Unless by chance they were working in the same place, as when *Camelot* and *A Funny Thing Happened on the Way to the Forum* had overlapped on Broadway, or on the same project, as with *Mary Poppins*, it seemed that the childhood sweethearts were fated to be apart.

When they did make a joint appearance, it only served to emphasise the gulf between them: for every picture of the Waltons dancing the Frug at a Manhattan nightclub (such as Sybil Burton's 'Arthur') there was a report that they were about to split up. 'Beastly', Julie called the rumours, but they had intensified following the news that Tony had not been with her for Christmas 1964. Building on his burgeoning reputation, he was now busy in New York, designing Verdi's *Otello* for the Spoleto Festival in Italy.

Less than six years married, Mr and Mrs Walton found themselves on either side of the country, working ever harder, as if to forget the toll such work was taking. Yet, as producers and directors lined up to pitch their ideas to her, Julie Andrews felt distincly ambivalent about what she had to offer. It was ambivalence that made her box up Oscar and stick him in her attic. 'I just didn't feel worthy,' she later remarked. 'When I got to know more about film, I felt safe trotting him out.'

Perhaps not joking, she was reported as saying she would play a prostitute if the script was strong enough — worrying, according to her friend Carol Burnett, that she was 'doomed always to be the governess, never the mistress'.

'Never work with animals or children,' ran the old W.C. Fields adage; Julie had comprehensively demolished it. Not only had she coped with a defecating dog on stage in *Camelot*, she had proved immune to the second danger on screen — rather too much so. Julie had no illusions about her histrionic abilities. In England, her father Ted Wells commented on the *Mary Poppins* prize, 'I don't think she was acting when she got that' — and she knew what he meant. Similarly, Barbara Andrews had watched her as Maria von Trapp and thought of 'the way she behaved with her kid brothers at home'.

Six months short of her thirtieth birthday, with only three films to her credit, Julie Andrews nevertheless stood at the apogee of Hollywood's firmament. Walt Disney, so thrilled with his protégée, could only rue not signing her for another picture while she was cheap.

That option had been cannily taken up by Robert Wise, whose story editor was already researching an idea to reunite the star and director of *The Sound of Music*. At the end of 1964, under the headline 'Julie Andrews Just Right for Gertie — This Biography May Click', the *Los Angeles Times* reported that Wise was preparing a screen adaptation of *Gertrude Lawrence as Mrs A*, the biography by the late actress's husband Richard Stoddard Aldrich: 'How perfect . . . Miss Andrews has that same lovely quality, that same delightful British voice, so gay, so titilizing . . . '

Meanwhile, Jack L. Warner was turning his mind's eye to Spain, where his mammoth production of *Camelot* was scheduled to film. This time, he determined, in tacit reversal of his earlier position, there would be no doubt as to the singing ability of the leading lady (if she ever took his telephone call). But Julie had other plans, in which she would follow the advice of a new agent, Arthur L. Park. The Chasin-Park-Citron Agency on Wilshire Boulevard, created from what had been Music Corporation of America, spelt big men, big offices, big money — light years from the friendly, faded muddle of Charles L. Tucker's Enterprises Ltd, with its well-worn list of music and variety artistes.

Despite a choice of almost every musical film in embryo, the mission was to develop Julie Andrews as a non-singing dramatic actress. 'I just hoped to do as much that was as varied as possible,' she recalled. 'Also, at the time, the people who were representing me in Hollywood encouraged very much that I do that kind of film, and I'm awfully glad they did.' Yet the kudos earned from *The Americanization of Emily* had not conquered Julie's doubts about her dramatic ability: 'I thought of myself, because of the early vaudeville days, as being a singer and a singer only.'

Gone, then, was faithful Uncle Charles, who had first heard her piping voice one distant May afternoon at The Old Meuse. Julie had retained him for longer than she might, with more than usual loyalty. But the plump English manager was completely out of his depth in the tumultuous waters of Hollywood. In early 1965, he was quietly sidelined, with the vague agreement that he would be consulted from time to time; in Britain, Julie would list him in her

Who's Who entry until 1970, in an increasingly tenuous link with her past.

★ ★ ★

Only a few months old, 1965 was already, clearly, Julie Andrews's miracle year. Even before the release of *The Sound of Music*, the girl who had once been the youngest to sing at a Royal Variety Performance had been invited to perform at President Lyndon B. Johnson's Inaugural Gala, on 18 January, at the National Armoury in Washington DC. Reviving 'Big D' from their Carnegie Hall concert, she and Carol Burnett had joined a line-up that read like Julie's Christmas card list now and to come: Mike Nichols, Carol Channing, Harry Belafonte, Barbra Streisand, Rudolf Nureyev, Alfred Hitchcock.

Many years later, Julie would still say that Carol 'seems to bring out some devil in me'. Never more so than on the night before the Presidential Gala, when the two girls were waiting outside their hotel elevator for Mike Nichols to arrive, trying to think of something to make him laugh. 'I suddenly said, 'Let's be kissing.' At that moment, the elevator went 'ping', and I bent Carol across my knee in a deep embrace. The doors opened, and it was packed with Secret Service men. Not one of them got out, and you could see the stunned look on their faces as the doors closed.' Someone got out the next time, however. Carol swore it was the President's wife, Lady Bird Johnson. And when

Mike Nichols finally arrived, he walked nonchalantly by the couple's fond embrace with nothing more than 'Hi, girls!'

But such frivolous episodes would now become all too rare for Julie. Returning to Hollywood, she threw herself into her first solo television special, *The Julie Andrews Show* for NBC, recorded around Oscar time. Her guest star was Gene Kelly, with whom she sported umbrellas in publicity pictures, calling to mind his classic routine in *Singin' in the Rain* and her airborne entrance into *Mary Poppins.*

The Programme would be aired in colour on Thanksgiving Sunday, 28 November 1965. As Julie was keen to tell everyone, television was her least favoured medium, a prejudice compounded by her diffidence at having a vehicle of her own: 'It seems not right, a little cheeky, to come in from left field to be the star.'

Nonetheless, she would register another hit — one hour of song, dance and comedy, using every scrap of her training at the hands of Madame Stiles-Allen and Aunt Joan Morris. A highlight was the 'Family Tree' segment, in which Julie summoned up the supposed ghosts of her clan, including a figure reminiscent of Queen Boudicca, a knight in not-so-shining armour singing 'Camelot' through his helmet, and a lusty music-hall girl.

She also danced to 'Just in Time' with Gene Kelly, showing for once an easy grace, rather than mere determination to do her job well. Solo, she sang 'Auld Lang Syne', 'Try to Remember' and, of course, 'The Sound of

Music'. The songs were arranged and conducted by Irwin Kostal, who had performed the same duties on her musical films.

Winner of the Silver Rose at Montreux, a Peabody Award and two Emmys, *The Julie Andrews Show* was artistically among the best of its kind, attracting an audience of over thirty-five million, more than the other two major specials that year, *Frank Sinatra: A Man and His Music* and Barbra Streisand's acclaimed *My Name is Barbra*.

So good was the response that the programme was repeated the following March, by which time Julie was deep into her next trio of films — like the earlier three, shot almost back-to-back — keeping her mind off a little thing called marriage.

The first of the batch was the $12 million epic *Hawaii*. It was adapted from the best-selling novel by James A. Michener, whose *Tales from the South Pacific* had yielded the musical that had so enthralled Julie all those years ago. In over eleven hundred pages, *Hawaii* mixed fact and fiction, plotting the islands' prehistoric geology, the Polynesian settlement of the early ninth century, Captain Cook's arrival a millennium later — and the influx of New England missionaries in the 1820s.

Buying the rights for $600,000 on publication in 1959, producer Walter Mirisch, with screenwriter Daniel Taradash, had long envisaged two full-length feature films. For practical reasons, this was eventually reduced to one. While still covering love, hate, desire and twenty-three forms of incest, the story was now of Reverend Abner Hale's ocean voyage in 1819, and his mission to convert the Hawaiians to Christianity over the ensuing fifteen years.

The scheduled director had been the legendary Fred Zinnemann, whose award-winning work included *The Nun's Story*, in which he had guided Audrey Hepburn to arguably the finest performance of her career. As if her name had not crossed Julie's path enough over the last couple of years, Audrey had been his initial choice for the role of the missionary's wife, Jerusha. But, late in 1964, after four years of preparation, Zinnemann had resigned from *Hawaii* over conflicts with the shortened script, telling *Cinema* magazine, 'I'm out of that. George Roy Hill is going to direct it.'

Hill, a former Yale music student and Marine pilot, had only three film credits to his name; his directing background was in television drama, at the other end of the scale from the mammoth logistics of *Hawaii*. He was not the only late recruit. The screenplay was completed by Dalton Trumbo, one of the Hollywood Ten blacklisted by the post-war House Un-American Activities Committee, but now back in the fold.

As Jerusha, the New England maiden who gives up her love for a rugged sea captain to marry the humourless Abner Hale, Julie received a hefty $700,000 and top billing, despite the secondary nature of her role. The production centred on the great Swedish actor Max von Sydow, who would achieve the impossible by making the audience feel a modicum of sympathy for the fundamentalist preacher. Sydow was no stranger to religious debate. His previous role, as Jesus Christ in *The Greatest Story Ever Told*, had hit the cinema screen one month before Julie's apotheosis as Maria von Trapp.

'Marvellous publicity: Mary Poppins marries Jesus,' Julie chuckled. 'She must have flown up to him and said, 'Listen, with my magic and your talent, we'd make a great team. I can fly — you can walk on water — what more do we need?''

In the early New England scenes, her father was played by Carroll O'Connor (before his television fame as Archie Bunker in *All in the Family*), while Dorothy Jeakins, the costume designer on *Hawaii* as on *The Sound of Music*, made her acting debut as Julie's mother. Other cast members included Gene Hackman, in his first featured role as the doctor, and, in a bit part, a young Hawaiian-born actress by the name of Bette Midler.

Unlike most films, shot out of sequence and pieced together later, *Hawaii* was to be made chronologically and almost entirely away from Hollywood. Principal photography began in March 1965 and was completed in October, $3 million over its already large budget.

George Roy Hill started work with the actors in Sturbridge Village, Massachusetts, a superior form of theme park that recreated the post-Colonial era as closely as possible. 'That little place,' said William Buell, Julie's make-up man and general factotum, 'that's where she learned what she was.' On 19 April, Patriots' Day in

Massachusetts, the entire compound was besieged with holiday tourists and film fans, all converging on the star as she walked to her private trailer.

Despite some 'rather nice husky policemen' sectioning off the film unit, Julie was terrified: 'They didn't mean any harm, it was a lark for them, but then I got into the trailer and I was alone in eight square feet of space, alone in this island. You could hear them outside giggling and joshing and pushing. And the trailer was swaying. They were scratching at the walls. I pulled down the shades and sat there alone. I thought, my God, how alone I am. I can't send for anybody. I can't get out.'

Max von Sydow could only marvel at her ability to handle the pressure. 'I can't imagine what I'd do if people came screaming at me the way they do Rock Hudson,' he said. 'I'd probably be afraid to go out of my house.' Regarded as Ingmar Bergman's muse, Sydow had made the best part of a dozen major films for the Swedish director, including *The Seventh Seal* and *The Virgin Spring*, yet was known mainly to diehard *cinéastes*. He represented the most daunting acting partner Julie Andrews had yet faced — but, to her delight, he turned out to be a considerate colleague and a sympathetic friend.

The company moved briefly back to Holly-wood for interior scenes at the Samuel Goldwyn Studio — where the prolific Blake Edwards happened to be setting up his next comedy for the Mirisch Corporation, *What Did You Do in the War, Daddy?* Thence, in April, they travelled to Hawaii, for more than five months' work on Oahu. South of Honolulu, near Waikiki Beach, Julie took a house with Emma Kate, Kay the nanny and 'Daddy Bill' Buell. From there, it was ninety minutes up the coast to Makua Beach, where a settlement had been recreated on a five-hundred-acre stretch of sand, providing a glorious background to the film's action. 'What beautiful scenery to chew!' Julie exclaimed, on seeing it for the first time.

The missionaries' odyssey through the Strait of Magellan was filmed on board the *Grethe*, a thirty-year-old Danish trader converted into a square-sailed 1820s brigantine. For three weeks, cast and crew battled against chronic seasickness. Julie was able to write to her father with the proud boast that she had not been among the invalids.

As on *The Sound of Music*, the weather wrought daily havoc, the area of the world's heaviest average rainfall also attracting some of the fiercest sunshine. But there was another problem. Rather as Stanley Holloway had felt neglected in rehearsals for *My Fair Lady* while the director had lavished his attention on his co-stars, now Julie was less than overjoyed to see Hill spending so much time on the Hawaiian and Polynesian players, mostly amateur, who played the native characters.

One Friday afternoon in July, the director picked up the unit telephone — to be told he was fired. His replacement was none other than Arthur Hiller, who had won Julie's confidence on *The Americanization of Emily*. The natives mutinied, led by the six-foot-tall Tahitian Jocelyn LaGarde, making her only screen appearance as the Hawaiian Queen Malama. She and Manu Tupou, who played her son and heir, announced that they would not work unless Hill was reinstated.

The following Monday, he got his job back. But matters improved on his return, as he devoted time to modifying the qualities Julie had shown in her previous films. 'She's always doing something, bubbling and bouncing,' said Hill, 'but the part of Jerusha was very still, so I had to put her in a vice and tell her, 'When in doubt, do nothing.''

Julie's nervous energy betrayed her commitment to getting the role right: 'Because I'm the sort of person I am, it can be very hard for me to say 'Good morning' and keep my expression immobile at the same time. And Jerusha was that type of person.' Mary Poppins, Emily Barham and Maria von Trapp all had a lot more to say for themselves than Mrs Hale — who accepts religious dogma, poor diet, agonising childbirth and death as her lot. The only time Julie had covered similar territory had been in the awful *Mountain Fire* a decade earlier. The actress who was so focused on her career found it difficult to sympathise with Jerusha's marital commitment: 'I had reservations. She has left a man she loves to marry a missionary, and when the lover returns and offers her another chance, she stays with the missionary. I don't know that I would have done that.'

The third person in the romantic triangle is

Rafer Hoxworth, the libidinous captain of a whaling vessel. The role was taken by Richard Harris who, like Max von Sydow, came to *Hawaii* from a Hollywood slice of religion, portraying Cain in John Huston's idea of *The Bible*. But it was his reputation for raising Cain off screen that preceded him. The Irish actor saw something of his own disregard for danger in Hoxworth. 'I like him for his tremendous conceit,' he said. 'Live to the fullest, because you only have it once.'

Hoxworth brings death, disease and disaster, the last of which was almost duplicated during filming. For the pivotal conflagration, where the sailors torch Hale's church, Julie dispensed with her stand-in — and suffered rather more than singed eyebrows: 'I could distinctly feel the heat, and I was muttering under my breath, 'George, isn't it time we put me out?' Finally, everybody realised the flames had gone a *little* too high. I don't think I have ever been more scared in my life; I went totally silent.'

But the scene that made the most impression was of Jerusha's confinement, as she gives breech birth without anything to lessen her pain. There was a real doctor counselling Julie behind the camera — and, if agonised screaming was any indication of artistic integrity, she was on course to prove herself in material almost wilfully the reverse of her musical work. When Ted Wells finally saw the film, he would pay his daughter tribute, saying, 'This was the first time I could tell her, 'Now you're an actress.' '

Julie credited the support she had received

from her co-star, placing Sydow at the top of her list: 'He was the unqualified front runner, the most generous man I've ever met. And he had such a lovely light sense of humour. These qualities really lay you flat out. I consider it a privilege to have worked with him.'

Of Richard Harris, she made no comment. 'I was dealing with an unknown quantity,' said George Roy Hill, 'because these were two very 'opposite' type performers, and I had no idea how they would blend.' The answer was, not at all. Julie had worked with a hell-raiser before, on *Camelot*, but the other Richard had balanced bar-room bingeing with backstage camaraderie. With Harris, things were almost internecine. By night, he would fuel himself with Mai Tai, the island rum cocktail, and go out looking for trouble, smashing his fists against the windows of oncoming traffic on Diamond Head Road.

By day, the roistering Irishman, who six years earlier had starred in Tony Walton's production of *The Ginger Man*, took against his old boss's wife in no uncertain terms, as he told his biographer Michael Feeney Callan in *Sex, Death & the Movies*:

I hated her. She was condescending and mean . . . I wasn't any role model, and I'm sure she saw how much I was enjoying myself, and I thought that annoyed her. My patience wasn't great in those days, so there was a lot of cussing. She would say something, all quiet and conspiratorial, to the director. And I would shout, 'Did you say something, *Jules?*' — which just pissed her.

It was in Hawaii that he heard of Warner Brothers' plans to film *Camelot*: 'It took me about fifteen seconds to say, 'I want that.' The only hesitation for me was Julie Andrews, who'd played it with Burton on stage. I thought, if it's her, forget it.'

Few would have begrudged Julie her chance to sting Jack Warner for her loss of Eliza Doolittle on screen, but tit-for-tat was not her game, as she told me when I first met her: 'Guenevere I did hear about, and felt that having passed on' — she corrected herself — 'having not done *My Fair Lady*, it would be perhaps compared in some way . . . For some reason, I said I'd rather not do it.'

In a generally sylvan landscape of admiration for Julie Andrews, Richard Harris's vehemence falls like a douse of acid rain. He had, he told Michael Feeney Callan, 'rarely if ever experienced such hatred for a person'. Finishing his work on *Hawaii* before either of his co-stars, he flew back to Hollywood, to begin a successful campaign for the role of King Arthur. Warner then signed Franco Nero as Lancelot, who would succeed where Robert Goulet had failed, and bed the Queen — in the guise of Vanessa Redgrave. 'I'm sure if Julie Andrews had wanted to play this part, she'd be playing it,' Miss Redgrave would allow.

'Can you see two men and two armies going to war over Julie Andrews?' the director Joshua

Logan added, ignoring the fact that audiences had paid to see just that for two seasons on Broadway.

★ ★ ★

Even in Paradise, the outside world made its presence felt. The 25th Infantry Division on Oahu was in training prior to leaving for Vietnam, and Julie joined them for a day as they prepared for combat. 'It sounds silly,' she said, as the jet bombers carrying the 'Tropic Lightning' boys streamed overhead, 'but you become much more aware of human lives in Hawaii. The war is closer than ever before. In all this beauty . . . '

Sometimes, Julie gazed out from her house across the shimmering sands of Waikiki Beach, with the surf hissing on the shore and the trade winds sighing through the coconut palms, and tried to set down in diary form her feelings about the past, her hopes and fears for the future. With the vast expanse of the Hawaiian sky glowing down nightly upon her, she had become interested in stargazing, buying a telescope in Honolulu, and studying Walter Mirisch's present to her, a map of the heavens.

In the more temporal Hollywood firmament, Julie's position now seemed secure. So much had happened in the last few months: the new house, the television show, the Oscar. But behind everything was the thunderous presence of *The Sound of Music*, which, while she was filming in the fiftieth state, had been embraced like no other film since *Gone With the Wind*.

'The happiest sound in all the world', ran the slogan; but not even Mike Kaplan — Fox's publicist and chief optimist, who had thought it up — could have anticipated the results. Indeed, analysing the appeal of a film that had now topped the box-office charts for six consecutive months formed the major topic of conversation in Hollywood.

'As you start to watch this movie,' said Richard Rodgers at the time, 'you can tell right away that it did *not* come from a sausage factory!' And yet, in a sense, it did — the ultimate product of the Hollywood dream machine, the whole rather greater than the sum of its perfectly constructed parts.

From coast to coast, *The Sound of Music* had captivated the country's heart, omitting no possible ingredient of popularity: music, scenery, pathos, religion, and — like a fairy on top of the Christmas tree — Julie Andrews. But, with a generation of young Americans entering the hills of the Viet Cong, the lure of the film's escapism was matched by its primal story. 'There isn't anyone on earth,' said Ernest Lehman, 'who hasn't felt, at one time or another, a wistful yearning for more love.'

In Europe, *The Sound of Music* was a hit in Spain (*Sonrisas y Lagrimas*) and Italy (*Tutti Insieme Appassionatamente*). Even France, normally indifferent to the American musical, welcomed *La Mélodie du Bonheur*. In Britain, the film was an outright sensation, taking more than double the gross of any film ever released. Only in Germany and Austria did *Meine Lieder*

— *Meine Träume* find disfavour, with one cinema projectionist in Munich being sacked for cutting out the scenes of the Nazi *Anschluss*.

In South America, *La Novicia Rebelde* made millions of fans and, in Tokyo, サウンド・オブ・ミュージック initiated the Japanese cult of Julie Andrews. Elsewhere, it served like a United Nations cultural ambassador, transcending race, caste and creed — from Egypt (*Love and Tenderness*) and Hong Kong (*Fairy Music Blow Fragrant Place, Place Hear*) to Thailand (*Charms of the Heaven Sound*) where, at the Bangkok premiere, King Bhumibol played 'Do Re Mi' on his clarinet.

From the money that flooded the coffers of Twentieth Century Fox, replenishing the pillage of *Cleopatra*, Julie saw little more than her basic $225,000 fee, while others — such as Robert Wise, who received ten per cent of the gross profits — collected somewhat on her strength. Julie's financial rewards came from the soundtrack album, which like her Broadway cast albums was a team effort.

Julie's solo efforts, such as *The Lass with the Delicate Air* (1958) and the vaudeville flavoured *Don't Go in the Lion's Cage Tonight* (1962), had been released at various points during her Broadway years, but — unlike the *My Fair Lady* and *Camelot* recordings, which had both gone gold — they sold unremarkably. It was the one area of show business in which Julie was never to score individual success. Barbra Streisand, without a film to her name, had already won two Grammys in her own right. Petula Clark, whose childhood career she had shadowed for a while in England, had also triumphed in the charts and at the Grammys. Whatever Julie's success on stage and on the cinema screen, being one-to-one with her voice in the semi-dark of a living room was obviously not where the money lay.

As if to rub it in, the *Mary Poppins* soundtrack had just received a Grammy Award for Best Recording for Children — something for which she would never be nominated as a soloist. The album remained at No 1 on the *Billboard* charts for fourteen consecutive weeks — longer than anything produced by Elvis Presley, the Beatles or the Rolling Stones at that time.

The Sound of Music, however, trampled all other titles underfoot. Royalties from it earned Julie considerably more than her part in the film itself. Beautifully produced by RCA Victor, it leapt to the top of the charts worldwide, with over nine million copies sold by 1969, in America remaining in the Top 100 for over five and a half years. Astonishingly, the essay on Rodgers and Hammerstein that formed part of the album's picture booklet was written by Judith Crist ('rhymes with 'hissed' ', observed a *Time* reporter), the very critic who had given the film such a withering review in the *Herald Tribune*.

It was all academic. The film was selling, as was the album, and for the latter, Julie was well on the way to becoming a millionairess.

Only when Julie returned to California would

she appreciate fully the titanic proportions of her success. But she had seen the news stands in Honolulu — seen how the press, bored with the Cinderella aspect of her story, had started to concentrate on her private life.

The May edition of *Pageant* had promised to reveal 'The man Julie Andrews can never forgive', but rehashed little more than the fuss over Jack Warner and *My Fair Lady*. By August, the tone had hardened considerably. *Photoplay* bore the cover story 'The woman who broke up Julie Andrews' home'. The woman turned out to be Julie Andrews herself, the article focusing on her driven nature towards her career, allegedly putting her family happiness at risk.

And Tony Walton, coming through an airport terminal, saw his wife sharing the cover of a magazine with Elizabeth Taylor: 'It had one of those headlines which was absolutely full of excitement and promise — 'Will Liz be breaking *Julie's* heart next?' I hurtled through it in case it was something terribly thrilling about Liz Taylor and me, but alas, it turned out to be something about a film part they were allegedly competing for . . . '

In response, Julie had already started to harden her own attitude to the press, closing down enquiries with a chilly, efficient smile and a vocabulary of pleasantries as tough as any fortress wall. Yet the fact remained that she had not seen Tony properly for months. The forces piling up against the couple were starting to seem insuperable.

One drastic solution, for Julie to give up her

career altogether, might have been an option on Broadway, where glamour was soon exhausted by the rigour of a long run. But Julie was too much at home in front of the camera. A good take was caught on celluloid for ever: she no longer had to worry nightly that she might be found wanting. 'This confidence is the most marvellous and valuable thing about her success,' Tony would allow, 'and I wouldn't want to be responsible for taking that away from her.'

They were still exchanging Dictaphone messages of determined good cheer, but Tony was coming to see these as yet another performance: 'Every day out went the tapes, Julie saying how frightened she was of acting, how unreal the whole thing was. But we got too good at the tapes and a bit too tricky. Every once in a while I'd get one from Julie saying, 'It's midnight and I'm just dragging in from rehearsal,' and I would hear the birds singing in the background.'

Away from work, the world's brightest, busiest star was in fact 'desperately unhappy'. The pressures had been a long time building. The need to be in control, the feeling she was anything but, a latent aggression — these had all been aspects of her personality since the day she had gone to live with Ted Andrews in Mornington Crescent. She had always managed to channel them into her career: 'I always get upset when people don't get on with the job at hand. I always feel like saying, 'Let's get on with it; it's the piece that matters, not our own personal thing.'' But one day soon, she promised herself, she was going to break out.

Right from the start, the traits characteristic of Julie's birth sign had been both her strength and her limitation — 'one hundred per cent ambivalent' was the oxymoron by which she defined herself to me. At certain points in her career, this had come close to cold-bloodedness. Through the angry rehearsals for *The Boy Friend*, noted Sandy Wilson, 'Julie, not unexpectedly, survived.' During the temporary dismissal of George Roy Hill on *Hawaii*, Julie held her counsel, not so much balancing the scales as sitting on the fence.

But ambivalence could only carry her so far. She had demanded so much of herself for so long, through duty, discipline, compulsion — never joy. With the dimensions of her fame as yet uncontained, sooner or later she would have to commit to finding what she wanted, what she felt, and who she really was.

Organised religion was not going to answer her questions, despite the sincerity she brought to her playing of Maria von Trapp. One month before the release of *The Sound of Music*, the Beatles had given an interview to *Playboy* magazine, discussing their own scepticism. 'We're not quite sure 'what' we are,' John Lennon reflected, 'but I know that we're more agnostic than atheistic.'

'Well, I'm afraid I'll have to go along with the Beatles on that,' Julie concurred to the Los Angeles *Herald Examiner* in mid-September, as she finished her role of Jerusha, the missionary's wife. 'The only time I pray is the first night of a show. I say 'Dear God, don't let me die in this one.' But this doesn't mean I'm anti-religion . . . ' And she returned to the matter that she had pondered in Hawaii, and even earlier in Salzburg: 'Rather than just sort of waffling on, believing something you've been told to believe, I'd rather know what I am. I need to find out more.'

Julie cast her mind back to the evenings in Eaton Square which she and Tony had so enjoyed with their group of clever friends — disparate talents epitomised by the marriage of ballerina Svetlana Beriosova and psychoanalyst Masud Khan. And now, knowing she needed some outside guidance, Julie focused on what Khan, a disciple of the Freudian analyst and theorist Donald Winnicott, did for a living.

To Khan's biographer Linda Hopkins, Tony revealed that he had already begun the same journey. 'It was during my break-up with Julie and I was totally raw.' Their mutual friend Mike Nichols had recommended a New York analyst to whom, 'in a stiff-upper-lipped way', Tony had described his situation. 'But then he asked me something about my baby daughter, and I completely came to pieces.'

The analyst recommended that he see Donald Winnicott, Masud Khan's guru. In London, he did so. 'I don't know the girl,' said Winnicott. 'I've only seen her in movies. But from what you say, you were quite happy with her?' Tony nodded. 'Well,' Winnicott responded, judging his words to appeal to Tony's evident zest for life, 'count your blessings, cut your losses, and cheer up!'

The advice apparently worked. Travelling to Spain, to design the film of *A Funny Thing Happened on the Way to the Forum*, Tony started to see the way forward, even as his wife was pondering her own leap of faith.

'One day, I just did it,' she said. 'I rang up everybody who had a psychiatrist and asked who would be good.' Her advisors included John Calley, Marty Ransohoff's associate producer on *The Americanization of Emily*, with whom she had remained close. Various names were given, such as Gerald J. Aronson, a veteran Hollywood psychiatrist who had treated Marlon Brando and Anthony Perkins. 'It is the only decision I have ever made totally, one hundred per cent. It was also the wisest,' Julie would state.

Her mother, of course, had a very Walton-on-Thames attitude to digging about in one's inner self. 'My Ju?' she scoffed. 'Bloody nonsense. Of course, you understand we still look on them as quacks in England.' Yet her father, writing later in the British magazine *Woman's Own*, clearly understood what had made Julie take the step: 'As a young girl she had bottled up her feelings and got on with the business of living. But the separation of her mother and me caused her great grief and now nearly a quarter of a century later, all the pent-up unhappiness of that period had suddenly caught up with her.'

Julie's close friend Carol Burnett, whose own childhood had been riven by alcoholism, empathised completely: 'As adults, Julie and I both try to control situations, because as children we were trying to cope with what was essentially an uncontrollable problem. Being a caretaker is a positive manifestation of that. We also understood the negative part — that we were sometimes too controlling, too perfectionist, too organised, because we so much want everything to go right. We grew up trying to make everything perfect because we thought it might be our fault if it wasn't.'

And an apparently perfect career had made the stakes impossibly high. 'When Hollywood hit big, that swept me off my feet for a while,' Julie told me, choosing her words with care. 'There were just so many interviews and appearances — it was very heady stuff and quite dizzymaking. It's so wobbly up there, you're trying to please everybody and you get too careful and it's an insanity.' The situation was clear: 'I had a lot of garbage I was carrying around with me at the time. I needed some answers, and I think I'd have been a pretty rotten mother without them.'

Coming to and from her sessions at the analyst's office on Roxbury Drive in Beverly Hills, Julie had begun to notice another car, always travelling in the opposite direction. The other driver had noticed her too. 'I met Julie in a wonderfully kind of Hollywood movie story kind of way,' he recalled. 'I kept looking over and three or four mornings a week, there she would be.'

One day, caught in traffic in the middle lane on Sunset Boulevard, he wound down his window. 'I said 'Are you going where I think you're going?' She said, 'Where do you think I'm going?' I said, 'I suspect you're going to your analyst' — and she said, 'You're right and I suspect you're coming from yours' — and that was our meeting.'

She knew who he was, of course: Blake Edwards.

10

BLAKE

'Hollywood is the most malicious place in the world, and poor Ju's life has been made a misery there. It seems because her image is so wholesome, her private life must be just the opposite. The scandal-mongers go out of their way to try to smear her name'

— Barbara Andrews, 1966

'Of course I know Julie Andrews,' said Paul Newman, meeting the star in late 1963, at a party during her first bout of film-making. 'She's the last of the really great broads.'

'Nobody has ever called me that before,' Julie laughed. 'I wouldn't mind having that as my epitaph.' But Maria von Trapp put paid to that.

Eighteen months later, at another Hollywood party, film director Blake Edwards was discussing various cases of stardom. When Julie's name came up, he took aim and fired: 'I know exactly what that's about. She has lilacs for pubic hairs.' The following day, Joan Crawford, who had been present, telephoned to tell him that it was the funniest thing she had ever heard.

Blake had recently been to visit Julie in her new house, to discuss a film idea that would eventually become *Darling Lili*. Julie had been quite taken, with both idea and director: 'It was like — gosh, I wish I could ask him to dinner, I hope I get to see him again.' A few weeks later, she paid a call to his house in Rising Glen Road, above Sunset Boulevard. 'I've just bought three lilac bushes,' she said. 'Would you like one?'

Blake viewed her askance. 'You're having me on,' he said, 'aren't you?' Julie looked blank. So he repeated what Joan Crawford had found so amusing at the party.

The singing nun roared with delight. 'However did you know?'

He omitted to tell her the comment of another party guest: 'With your luck, Blake, you'll marry her.'

★ ★ ★

William Blake Crump was born in Tulsa, Oklahoma, on 26 July 1922. When he was four, his mother, whom his father had abandoned while she was pregnant, moved to Los Angeles and married Jack McEdward, an assistant director at Twentieth Century Fox. Somewhat overlooked is that Blake's family was connected to Hollywood already, his uncle Owen Crump being married to the niece of Douglas Fairbanks and Mary Pickford.

After attending Beverly Hills High School, Blake found studio work through his stepfather — whose name he took in abbreviated form — delivering scripts and appearing as an extra. 'We lived practically with Fox Studios in our back yard,' he recalled. 'I used to climb over the fence . . . walk through the sets and imagine things.' He was a neglected and isolated youth, already forming his defence against the world: a dark, depressive sense of humour that would lead his second wife to call him 'Blackie'.

Maintaining a body-building regime from late boyhood, he served in the Coast Guard during the early years of the war, but eventually left because of a back injury. 'You never could finish anything,' said his mother — a phrase that would haunt him.

'I always got the impression that he was hugely precocious and talented,' said Julie. 'They probably didn't know how to handle that, or couldn't in those days.'

With his athletic build, thatch of dark hair and wide smile, the good-looking youngster (who had some Native American blood) continued to work as a bit-part actor at Fox and elsewhere. He was almost always in uniform, appearing in films such as *Thirty Seconds Over Tokyo* or William Wyler's seminal *The Best Years of Our Lives*.

What he really wanted to be was a writer. In 1951, after various radio assignments, he signed a contract with Columbia Pictures, where he wrote and directed several low-budget films with Richard Quine. One of the first featured a young English actress, Patricia Walker, whom Blake married in 1953. 'All of my life,' he would later say, 'the bottom line was to have a family.' A daughter, Jennifer, was born on New Year's Day 1959; a son, Geoffrey, followed two years later.

In 1958, he had created the NBC detective

series *Peter Gunn*, one of the first television shows with an original music score — bringing him into contact with composer Henry Mancini. A year later, he directed his breakthrough big screen hit *Operation Petticoat*, a Second World War comedy with Cary Grant and Tony Curtis.

Blake then enjoyed a run of his best-received and remembered films, starting in 1961 with *Breakfast at Tiffany's*, in which a ravishing Audrey Hepburn — without the help of Marni Nixon — sang Mancini's Oscar-winning 'Moon River'. The following year, Mancini won another Oscar, for the title song of Blake's *Days of Wine and Roses*, starring Jack Lemmon and Lee Remick. A savage drama about alcoholism, it brought much praise from those who had considered its director a lightweight. Most popular of all, however, was *The Pink Panther* in 1963. Starring Peter Sellers in the role of his life, utilising a battery of deadpan mispronunciations and pratfall routines as the inept Inspector Jacques Clouseau, the film was to define the rest of Blake's career.

A year later came a hit sequel. Blake's reputation seemed assured, although he swore never to work again with Sellers. 'Midway through *A Shot in the Dark*, Peter became a monster — bored, angry, sullen and unprofessional,' he said in 1980, two years after the star's premature death. 'He began looking for anyone and everyone to blame.'

But Blake's decline — as so often in Hollywood — was brought on by his first big budget. *The Great Race*, a multi-starred car-chase comedy with the most custard pies (2,357) ever thrown, was fuelled to the figure of $12 million — and crawled at the box office. His next escapade, *What Did You Do in the War, Daddy?* (shot during Julie's Hawaiian expedition), therefore bore added pressure in advance of its August 1966 opening.

Bullish, acerbic, philandering, he already knew his marriage was over. By 1965, his wife Patricia had had enough, decamping to England with their two children. And Blake, even as he got to know Julie, was dealing with his problems as she was — on the couch.

Having become a zealous convert to Freud, Julie would now fit in up to five visits a week to her own psychoanalyst, Dr Gerald Aronson, whenever her schedule allowed. Much later, she explained: 'If it hadn't been for therapy, Blake and I would have had the most terrible rocky road. Even though we might have gotten together for the wrong reasons — hooking into things that we had tried to conquer as children — we certainly found out what they were. There's great reassurance in that.'

She was too responsible to explore other, equally fashionable, avenues, much as the idea might have appealed to her friends' imaginations. Mike Nichols, newly arrived in Hollywood to direct his first film, stuck a bumper sticker on her new black Ford Falcon: 'Mary Poppins is a Junkie'. He dared her to take it off.

'So I can't, of course,' said Julie, happily.

* ★ ★ ★

275

At the end of October 1965, two years after their social introduction, Julie Andrews met Paul Newman again, on the back lot of Universal Studios, as his co-star in Alfred Hitchcock's fiftieth film, the cold war thriller *Torn Curtain*.

It had been back in April, two days before the Oscar ceremony at which she was expected to triumph, that Julie had first discussed with Hitchcock a project that would allow her, for the first time, to play a contemporary woman — with contemporary morals. The story was based on one that had convulsed Britain for over a decade, as Hitchcock explained to his greatest fan, film director François Truffaut: 'I got the idea from the disappearance of the two British diplomats Burgess and MacLean who deserted their country and went to Russia. I said, 'What did *Mrs* MacLean think of the whole thing?''

The woman's angle was one at which Hitchcock had previously excelled, getting defining performances out of a bevy of female protagonists, from Joan Fontaine to Janet Leigh. Of Julie Andrews, however, he was unsure, saying, 'The audience will be waiting for her to start singing.' Fair haired, cool of aspect, beautifully spoken, she epitomised his ideal of the lady in the drawing room. But it was harder for him to envisage her as the whore in the boudoir, as he had Grace Kelly in *Rear Window* and *To Catch a Thief*.

Hitchcock was also disenchanted with Paul Newman, who, over dinner at the epicurean director's house, had not endeared himself by spurning the fine wine on offer and grabbing a can of beer from the refrigerator. To Truffaut, he revealed that he had capitulated to the front office's demand for stars, of whom there was 'such a shortage that these 'cattle' are demanding astronomical figures'. But, just as Jack Warner had stubbornly resisted using Julie, so Universal head Lew Wasserman was no less determined to book her, at whatever cost.

Her agent's advice and the director's incredible track record kept Julie interested, script unseen. By August, author Brian Moore submitted his third draft, telling the director, 'If it were a book I were writing, I'd scrap it, or do a complete rewrite.' Yet it was this version that winged its way to Julie in Hawaii.

She disliked it very much. Her role, Dr Sarah Sherman, was neither as exciting nor as involving as she had been led to believe. Indeed, the lady scientist was reduced to a cipher. 'East Berlin? But — but — that's behind *the Iron Curtain!*' she gasps at the supposed treachery of her boyfriend, American rocket physicist Michael Armstrong — long after the film indicates that his defection to Eastern Europe is a bluff. But Arthur Park of Chasin-Park-Citron remained persuasive, not least because of his percentage. The Oscar for *Mary Poppins* and the response to *The Sound of Music* had pushed his client's price up to $750,000 against ten per cent of gross — more than that of the top-billed Paul Newman, the most important star with whom Julie had yet worked.

The timing was tight, however. The following spring, she was committed to making the comedy *The Public Eye*, to be directed by Mike Nichols. To have his final script by October, Alfred Hitchcock turned to the Yorkshire-born team of Keith Waterhouse and Willis Hall, whose work included the play and film *Billy Liar* and the BBC satire *That Was the Week That Was* (which featured Millicent Martin, late of *The Boy Friend*). 'For this piece of celluloid play-doctoring', wrote Keith Waterhouse in his memoir *Streets Ahead*, 'we were paid huge sums by Universal — little did they know that we would almost have paid them for the privilege of working with 'the Master'.'

By the time they arrived, principal photography was drawing perilously close, 'so that we often found ourselves revising scenes only hours before they were to be shot'. The experience reminded them of their early days as newspaper hacks in the north of England. It reminded the stars they were in trouble.

Back from Hawaii, Julie had barely had a week in which to make any sense of her confused private life before being pushed centre stage to receive the Star of the Year Award from the Theatre Owners of America — and thence to Universal. *Torn Curtain* was her first film since *Mary Poppins* to be shot entirely in Hollywood, with some dubious back projections masquerading as East Germany.

Leaving Coldwater Canyon in the semi-dark each morning, Julie now drove to work in the brand new, bright red Mustang that Universal had provided, along with a private dressing-room house on the studio compound. As on her previous two films, the queen had her faithful courtiers: hairdresser Lorraine 'Mom' Roberson and make-up man Willard 'Daddy Bill' Buell.

Behind the camera stood the Buddha-like Hitchcock, in his rumpled blue suit, white shirt and tie, directing from the rough cut he had already decided in his head. 'The first day of production,' Julie later told Dick Cavett on PBS television, 'he announced that for him the fun was over — the creative part was finished with the script and storyboard preparation — and now, the rest was a bore. You can imagine how that made us feel.'

Even so, she set to work with brisk, gung-ho humour. Filming one shot, Hitchcock called out to a crew member, 'That light is making a hell of a line over her head.' Julie put her hands on her hips. 'That's my halo,' she quipped demurely. Ostensibly, she would hold polite memories of her director. 'Funny, possessive, very endearing,' she recalled, two decades on, yet she had also remembered a 'certain fear' of women.

He was certainly circumspect with her. She learnt her lines, turned up on time, delivered the goods. But the fires of passion burned low. In one scene, where Sarah Sherman is described as beautiful, he requested a script change. 'Not that I wish to cast any aspersions on Miss Andrews' physiognomy,' Hitch noted to Waterhouse and Hall, 'but do you think 'beautiful' is perhaps too much, and cannot we say 'lovely' instead?'

Julie's first onscreen bedroom action, in which Michael and Sarah jump the gun on their wedding vows, presented less embarrassment than discomfort. 'It was a boiling hot day,' she explained, 'and what you couldn't see was that the sheets and blankets off-camera were rolled back and there was a fan blowing underneath . . . Instead of being amorous it would have been much easier for us just to slither away in the heat.' Needless to say, this was not the scene observed by Princess Margaret and Lord Snowdon, visiting Hollywood during their state visit to America that November, when they stopped by Universal Studios to chat to Britain's most famous film director and the actress they had both known for the best part of a decade.

The amount of press coverage the below-blanket sequence attracted only betrayed the paucity of interest in the rest of the story. One scene alone impressed: a farmhouse sequence, where Michael Armstrong kills the Stasi agent (before he himself gets killed) by bludgeoning him with a spade, strangling him with his bare hands and finally forcing his head inside a gas oven. It had nothing to do with Julie's character.

No effort had been spared to make her look glamorous: her hair, having grown back to its natural mouse colour in Hawaii, was highlighted and bouffant, and her slender figure was costumed by Hollywood's most famous designer, Edith Head. But clothes could not disguise her skeletal role, and she knew it.

Shooting finished in February 1966; at a cost of $6 million, *Torn Curtain* was Hitchcock's most expensive ever feature, but far below his best. 'It's a bad film,' said Brian Moore, the original writer. 'And if you know Hitchcock, you know he's simply ransacked his bag of tricks here.'

'We all knew we had a loser on our hands in this picture,' Newman told author Donald Spoto, in *Alfred Hitchcock: The Dark Side of Genius*. 'When Hitchcock first asked me to his house and described the story in detail, it sounded exciting, so I agreed to do it. But somehow the story didn't turn out the way he'd told it, and all during the shooting we all wished we didn't have to make it.'

★   ★   ★

Acting the party girl was hardly Julie's style but, with her husband long absent, she had now become rather more visible on the Hollywood scene. She was seen around town on the arm of producer John Calley, with whom she had stayed close since *The Americanization of Emily*, having flown back to visit him on odd weekends from Hawaii.

She also acted as hostess for Mike Nichols at a party he threw at the achingly trendy Beverly Hills nightclub The Daisy. Among the guests were Rock Hudson and Lana Turner, both of whom lived near her in Coldwater Canyon, the ubiquitous Burtons, and Sean Connery — whom she was chasing in the Top Ten popularity index.

Her friend Roddy McDowall, the safest date that Hollywood had to offer, had squired her often, taking Tony's place at the Golden Globes and the Los Angeles premiere of *The Sound of Music*. 'To be with her was overwhelming,' he recalled later; 'everybody reacted to her like she was part of their family, they owned her . . . That sort of fame requires one has the guts to overcome it.'

Julie had learnt this the hard way. 'I need order, desperately. But I can't have it,' she admitted. 'And then there is this very great loneliness.' As always, the trouper spirit pulled her through. 'If one can manage, stand still, work out proportions, work off the excesses,' she said, 'then someday it will all be just wonderful.'

More and more, it was the film director, thirteen years older, with his mordant sense of humour, who occupied her thoughts — and who was increasingly to occupy her heart. She and Blake Edwards were spotted at the fashionable restaurant La Scala, and on his seventy-foot yacht, the *Tempest*. 'Most people would suppose that it might be a little difficult to make it with Mary Poppins,' she later said. 'Blake has been unmercifully teased, as you can imagine.'

But it was blue-eyed Emma Kate, resembling Tony more than Julie, who remained the most important person in her life — although it was sometimes hard for Julie to offer her normality, as Roddy McDowall remembered: 'She would come to the beach with Emma, and people would come up with Mary Poppins dolls. Life for her was like being on a personal appearance tour.'

Matters came to a head at Christmas 1965, when Emma was three. 'I did a terrible thing,' Julie remembered almost forty years later. 'I allowed *Look* magazine to take a picture of her, and it turned out to be on the cover. I suddenly saw it in every bookstore and was mortified. I thought, my God, what am I doing?' From then on, she determined, there would be no more such pictures — but the threat of stalkers or even kidnappers now preyed on the mind of the young single mother in her daughter's early years at school and at home.

Mother and daughter were finally settling down at the house in Hidden Valley Road, with Kay the nanny, Covington (or 'Cov') the butler, and Q-Tip, her little white poodle with one black eye. The place had remained almost unfurnished since Julie had bought it, packing cases still piled in the main rooms. After a long day's filming, the star had sometimes eaten her supper while propped up on cushions, using the stairs as a table. Gradually, though, it was starting to be a home.

As with her sadly vacant house in England, Julie favoured space and light — and this was easy to achieve. A huge set of French windows flooded the lofty sitting room with sunshine, and a black Steinway grand piano contrasted with the predominantly white and beige furniture. An open staircase led up to the bedroom floor, where Julie's room occupied much of the space. There was a large fireplace in the sitting room, and another in the corner of a sun porch which served as the dining room, a refectory table stretching along the red tiled floor.

Outside, the terrace was edged with greenery. Apple and pear trees ringed the property; and the grounds, with their overgrown flowerbeds and rock pool, offered Julie the chance to develop an interest that would grow stronger with the years: gardening.

Inside, her interests included a growing art collection, including a primitive Polish wood carving above the fireplace and a sculpture of her head, created by the artist Anna Mahler, a friend. Her taste in music — Ravel, Debussy and Britten — was echoed in her love of the Impressionist and Fauve schools of painting. If her sober business manager Guy Gadbois, middle aged and thoroughly conservative, would allow it, Julie planned to make plenty of acquisitions, one of the few perks of stardom she was ready to embrace. She also had her eye on a grey Mercedes 190, but, for the moment, her Ford Falcon station wagon stood in the courtyard by the oak front door — not unlike the walnut door of The Old Meuse back in Surrey.

With her commitment to her career, there seemed little likelihood of England's golden girl returning home for some time. But, midway through the filming of *Torn Curtain*, Barbara and Ted Andrews came to visit, seeing just how glorious was the world of the girl Ted had first spotted as a future star. Some of the tension from her childhood relationship with him appeared to have been addressed. Analysis was proving to be of help. He was also on her territory: she was in control.

Barbara relished the time with Emma Kate, who was about to start nursery school — but the visit was abruptly cut short, when Ted suffered a mild stroke, and had to be taken home to

Walton-on-Thames.

Tony was also in England, working on a new film. Tax penalties were given as the reason he avoided the house on Wimbledon Common (just as they were used to explain Julie's staying away entirely) but the fact that young Mr Walton was back home with his mother in Walton-on-Thames was not lost on a hungry press. On 20 February, the *Sunday Mirror* quoted Hollywood rumours that the marriage had hit the rocks.

'I haven't read the reports, although I've heard about them,' Julie told an interviewer at Universal, 'but until Tony and I make any kind of announcement, people will have to believe what they want to believe.' And she was less than enchanted to be compared with actor Laurence Harvey, who had flown from London for a one-day tryst with his future wife Joan, the widow of Columbia Studios boss Harry Cohn. 'Maybe Laurence Harvey hasn't got to get up at six a.m. on a Monday morning,' Julie snapped.

Shortly afterwards, in the London *Daily Express*, Tony gave Ann Leslie a remarkably frank interview on the subject. 'It's the problem of who at any one time is going to be the support. I don't mean financial, but emotional.' And the constant switching of roles, which they had managed reasonably effectively during Julie's Broadway days, no longer seemed satisfactory to him — or, he suspected, his busy wife: 'I think it's very hard for many women to feel really happy about it. They're grateful that this is possible so that they can work and be independent, but ultimately they resent a man easing up on his dominance for a second.' Then, almost unwittingly, Tony acknowledged the possibility of defeat for the first time: 'They're always trying to succeed on this double wavelength — and it's hard to imagine anyone who can.'

Consciously or not, he had never seen the Coldwater Canyon house. He had hardly seen his daughter either. 'I feel I'm missing some of the best of her growing-up,' he said sadly. 'She's nearly three, and I've seen her for about a third of that time . . .'

Barbara Andrews was one who thought the problem would be solved if Tony moved to Hollywood, where Julie was now so much at home. He disagreed. 'The few times I have been there and not been able to get on with the work I find satisfying, I've just become impossible to be with. And that's as dangerous as not being there at all.' If he had not settled in Hollywood as his own man, he was certainly not going to do so as Mr Julie Andrews. 'Some husbands of stars can fit into the 'agent-manager' role,' he said. He was certainly not one of them.

* * *

A new year had begun during the filming of *Torn Curtain*. On 5 January 1966, Quigley's *Motion Picture Herald*, in its annual survey of United States cinema exhibitors, listed Julie Andrews as the fourth biggest money-making star of the previous year, behind Sean Connery, John Wayne and Doris Day.

Almost a year after its release, *The Sound of Music* was still defying gravity, with grosses now expected to approach — if not beat — the record total attained by *Gone With the Wind*. On 21 February, the Academy of Motion Picture Arts and Sciences rewarded the musical with Oscar nominations in ten categories, including those for Best Film, Best Director, Best Supporting Actress (Peggy Wood) and, of course, Best Actress, giving Julie a shot at retaining the title she had won the year before.

Internationally as well as domestically, she could do no wrong. It was no surprise that, on 28 February, *The Sound of Music* and Julie, favourites in their categories, won Hollywood Foreign Press Association Golden Globes, for Best Musical/Comedy Film and Best Actress, Julie doing so for the second year running. In London, she received a rare double citation from the British Film Academy, with nominations as Best British Actress for both Emily and Maria. In the event, she lost to another shooting star, Julie Christie in *Darling*. The biggest accolade of all came on Saturday 26 March 1966, a month after *Torn Curtain* finished filming, when Julie Andrews wrote her name and placed her hands and shoes in wet cement (her large white shoes got stuck) outside Grauman's Chinese Theatre on Hollywood Boulevard, becoming celebrity no 131 to do so.

Julie's stock had soared to fantastic heights — and would only go higher, as *The Sound of Music* continued to sweep all before it. Having cost $8,200,000 to make, the film (now known simply as 'the Mint' by its studio) had earned over $1 million a week in its first year, from a strictly limited road show release. Fox, which had sustained a $40 million loss in 1962, was heading towards a $20 million pre-tax profit for 1966.

Then, in August, *The Sound of Music* finally achieved the impossible, stripping *Gone With the Wind* of its box-office championship. Even allowing for inflation, its achievement was enormous, having taken more in eighteen months than the 1939 Selznick-MGM epic had managed in twenty-seven years.

In November, the record breaker was the subject of a large article in the *New York Times*: 'Biggest Money-Making Movie of All Time — How Come?' Reactions from the public ranged from 'I kept thinking of Red China' to 'It's cheaper than therapy.'

'In any of the twenty-nine countries where it has broken all previous box-office records,' ran the article, 'it's the crisply gratifying sound of money.' Fox executives were now said to estimate an eventual gross of $200 million, taking into account bookings at neighbourhood cinemas, drive-ins and what one newspaper called 'the prospect of re-release until the last vestige of recorded time'.

In Salt Lake City, over half a million people had attended in eighteen months, almost three times the local population. Similar figures had been recorded from Cedar Rapids to Atlanta, Syracuse to Colorado Springs. And in Moorhead, Minnesota, college students were protesting under the name POOIE (People's Organisation of Intelligent Educatees) at the film's relentless, year-long run at the local cinema.

There were plenty who had attended more than a dozen times, including Julie's mother. Travelling into London, Barbara Andrews would see 'an *enormous* poster of Julie alongside the tracks' as the train passed Clapham Junction — an incentive to see the film yet again at the cavernous Dominion Cinema, where it had taken up long-term residence. And then there were the diehards who managed over a hundred visits. By the time of its fortieth anniversary in 2005, the Guinness World Record for multiple viewings of any film was still held by Mrs Myra Franklin of Wales, who saw *The Sound of Music* at the Capitol Cinema in Cardiff an incredible 940 times, 'because it makes me feel happy'.

It was this sheer pleasure that was emphasised by audiences worldwide. 'They find themselves smiling back at the screen,' Robert Wise explained, confirming the catalyst as Julie Andrews: 'She goes right through the camera on to film and out to the audience. Julie seems to have been born with that magic gene that comes through on screen.'

Decades after the event, the star, who attributed the success to 'a quality of joyousness', denied that she might have seen Maria von Trapp as a dangerous career move: 'No, simply because I'd such a good time being Emily, and that seemed like such a different role, and I hoped it would suffice.' But, for all the Alpine vistas of *The Sound of Music*, Julie would find the horizon shrinking in the light of how others now saw her.

Occasionally, also, a golden chance would slip away — as the star clearly recalled when I first met her: 'You asked about the nanny image, and there was talk at one time of my going to do *The Prime of Miss Jean Brodie* — which would win Maggie Smith the wonderful Oscar — and I said, 'I *cannot* play another teacher or nanny or governess.'' In making this decision, she overlooked the fact that Miss Jean Brodie used her magnetism as a teacher for pernicious ends. But it seemed that Julie was now so antipathetic to any subject to do with children, no matter how strong the context, that she was never going to be interested.

She was, however, greatly looking forward to *The Public Eye*, Peter Shaffer's comedy, which had been a West End hit. The screen version for Universal Studios promised three advantages: it was to be made in England; it was to be directed by her friend Mike Nichols; and Julie's role as an errant young wife (ironically, played on stage by Maggie Smith) would give her the sort of challenge she craved. Nichols had arrived in Hollywood just as Julie was leaving for Hawaii; like his friend, he would achieve global fame with his first film, *Who's Afraid of Virgina Woolf*, starring Julie's *Camelot* co-star Richard Burton and Elizabeth Taylor.

Alas, plans did not work out. Mike Nichols would never work with Julie again, no matter how much they both wanted it to happen. He was scheduled to direct the Broadway musical

The Apple Tree, which Julie had been offered, but turned down — whether or not because Tony Walton was the designer. As for *The Public Eye*, Universal lost faith in the small-scale marital comedy — leaving Julie Andrews with a commitment to work for them, for a fee of $750,000.

Ross Hunter, the studio's most commercial producer, had been a fan of Julie's since he had seen her in *The Boy Friend* on Broadway. His first wish had been to transfer the camp delights of the stage show, including its star, to the big screen. The rights were, however, owned by MGM, a studio with its own ideas for Julie. Instead, Hunter turned his attention to a spoof of the Jazz Age by Richard Morris, which bore a strong resemblance to Sandy Wilson's pastiche. 'I do know I recognised some similarities when I read the script, which was enchanting,' said Julie.

Thoroughly Modern Millie was the story of a smalltown girl who travels to the big city to become a flapper, get a job and marry her boss — escaping the clutches of Chinese white slave traffickers in the process. Julie felt an immediate enthusiasm for the role, which allowed her to revisit the comedy territory she so much enjoyed, after the deeply frustrating time with Hitchcock. And so, with the Gertrude Lawrence story still in embryo, she committed the summer of 1966 to going back to the 1920s.

Hunter concentrated on turning the piece into a flat-out musical. His instinct for his audience had revitalised the careers of female stars such as Lana Turner (*Imitation of Life*) and Doris Day

(*Pillow Talk*). With Julie, however, he was keen not to reinvent, but to capitalise on what he knew her strengths to be. In this, he was rather too successful. The slender story was, Julie said later, 'puffed up into an enormously big film, and it was meant to be a little, tiny sort of hatbox of delight'. Surprisingly, given the stormy experiences of *Hawaii*, Julie recommended that Universal sign George Roy Hill to direct what was obviously going to be a very commercial enterprise.

The supporting cast, as ever with Ross Hunter, was dominated by *les girls*. Mary Tyler Moore made her film debut as Millie's poor-little-rich-girl best friend Miss Dorothy. At first, she found the coy wide-eyed innocence of the WASP heiress hard to capture, until Hill told her to keep her eyes on her shoes and speak only in a whisper — 'and within a few hours,' declared Mary, 'I nailed the bitch!'

As madcap heiress Muzzy Van Hossmere, Carol Channing hit Hollywood with her trademark manic energy and mop of peroxide hair, direct from the tour of *Hello, Dolly!* from which she had — at a cost — been extracted. In 2006, speaking to me from her home in Modesto, California, Miss Channing remembered Julie as 'the finest star to work with — she just helped me all she could'.

After playing in vast auditoria across the country, she would always recall her first film scene, a close-up. 'George Roy Hill said, 'Now, we're shooting from your eyebrows to your lower lip, so don't move because you'll go right out of the camera, and don't breathe, but give me energy . . . ' And Julie walked in, in her jeans and no make-up, and took both my hands . . . I said, 'Julie, I wouldn't have talked the same way to your stand-in as I would to you.' And she said, 'I know that; that's why I'm here.''

For the men, square-jawed John Gavin (Ronald Reagan's future ambassador to Mexico) put his stamp on square-jawed Trevor Graydon, Millie's boss — while the handsome young English actor James Fox played Jimmy, the asinine hero. With most of his scenes opposite Julie, Fox could see how much ruthless dedication she was capable of giving her work. 'She is a dominating performer but a generous one,' he reflected later. 'I thought it would be in character if I did a bit of juggling with the plates . . . Julie looked sideways at me. After all, we had lines to say and it was a scene where there wasn't a lot of hanging about. Nevertheless she said 'OK.''

Like Julie, he had to contend with a public image of niceness, and made his attempt to escape it. 'People think it was the film *Performance* that was my undoing,' he said of his later role of a psychopathic gangster opposite Mick Jagger. 'But I have to tell you, it was *Thoroughly Modern Millie* — for I had to impersonate Julie Andrews in drag.'

This and other labyrinthine shenanigans culminate in Muzzy knocking seven bells out of two Chinese laundrymen, henchmen to the dragonish villainess Mrs Meers — in which role Beatrice Lillie (dubbed 'the funniest woman in the world' as far back as the real 1920s) was threatening to walk away with the film. Aged seventy-two, Bea had enjoyed a spectacular theatre career on both sides of the Atlantic. But by the time she arrived at Universal, her genius was challenged by the first shadow of Alzheimer's disease, which would darken the last two decades of her life. Oblivious to this, she made up many of her own lines; miraculously, the role was the better for it. She did, however, keep asking the name of the girl who did the singing.

The songs, with the notable exception of Sammy Cahn and Jimmy Van Heusen's highly catchy title tune and a dance number entitled 'The Tapioca', were drawn from the 1920s back catalogue, including 'Baby Face' and 'Poor Butterfly' for Julie and 'Jazz Baby' for Carol Channing. Bizarrely, the scoring and arranging were taken by not one but two of Hollywood's most talented musicians. Elmer Bernstein, whose rugged work on *The Magnificent Seven* could hardly have prepared him for 1920s camp, split the duties with André Previn, former maestro of the MGM orchestra — and film conductor of *My Fair Lady*.

André and his then wife, lyricist Dory Previn, were already Julie's friends from her early days in Hollywood, part of a group, including Blake Edwards, who admired the star's performances more than they did her films. According to Dory, Julie's new agents were commercial but unadventurous, preventing her from developing areas in which she had expressed an interest: film adaptations of oddball books or plays, or working with *nouvelle vague* directors like François Truffaut.

In fact, while Julie had just completed filming for Hitchcock, Truffaut's hero, her estranged husband Tony was working with the French auteur himself, designing *Fahrenheit 451* in England. The film co-starred Julie Christie, who looked like providing Julie with her biggest challenge on Monday 18 April, at the Academy Awards.

Heading for a direct showdown with *The Sound of Music* was the year's other blockbuster, *Doctor Zhivago*, directed by David Lean. MGM's all-or-nothing attempt to claw back some of its former glory had attracted its share of critical bile, Pauline Kael calling it 'stately, respectable and dead'. But the sweep and beauty of its transition from Boris Pasternak's epic novel had touched a nerve with audiences around the world, and its huge success was acknowledged with eleven Oscar nominations.

Julie Christie, who played Lara, Zhivago's luminous mistress, was nominated as Best Actress — but for another film, the satire *Darling*, for which she had already won the New York Film Critics' Award as the brittle London model. The two Julies were joined by a third English girl, Samantha Eggar, for *The Collector* (the film that William Wyler had abandoned *The Sound of Music* to direct), as well as Elizabeth Hartman in *A Patch of Blue* and Simone Signoret in *Ship of Fools*.

If the curse of Oscar was to be believed, Julie Andrews faced a double danger. Only one actress had won consecutive awards: Luise Rainer in 1936 for *The Great Ziegfeld* and 1937 for *The Good Earth*. A year after her second win, she was forgotten.

On the big night, the Julies, whose contrasting images — respectively sweet and sexy — made easy magazine coverage, had planned to confound the equally easy rumours of bitchy rivalry by arriving together from Miss Andrews' house, where Ms Christie was to be a houseguest. The idea came to nothing; rival production representatives saw to that. 'Our schedules for the weekend were both so hectic,' said Julie Christie, with political tact. Instead, Julie Andrews walked up the red carpet at the Santa Monica Civic Auditorium on the arm of Saul Chaplin, associate producer of *The Sound of Music*. With her hair still bouffant from *Torn Curtain*, she wore a kimono-style dress in flame-coloured jersey wool, designed by her friend Dorothy Jeakins (whose costumes for *The Sound of Music* were also nominated) and a white fur stole against the unusually cold Los Angeles weather, smiling radiantly through the roar of recognition that greeted her arrival.

It was the first time the Academy Awards had been broadcast in colour. Otherwise, the proceedings were as on any other year, with Bob Hope again leavening the dough. Julie's duties were threefold: on her own behalf as Best Actress nominee, as presenter of the Best Actor award, and to represent Robert Wise, whose prolonged activities on the Yangtze River with *The Sand Pebbles* prevented him from discovering in person if he had been chosen as Best Director.

The Sound of Music claimed its first victory with William Reynolds, whose award for Best Editing was tribute to sequences such as 'Do-Re-Mi'. 'When in doubt, cut to Julie Andrews,' said Reynolds, voicing the thoughts of almost every businessman in town. Having announced and presented the statuette as Best Actor to Lee Marvin for the spoof Western *Cat Ballou*, Julie betrayed her nerves by yelping with pleasure at the news that Robert Wise had been chosen as Best Director. Walking off stage with his award, she crossed Rex Harrison, who walked on, holding the Oscar for a lucky actress.

With characteristic pomposity, Harrison tore open the envelope. 'Julie — ' he said, and paused for a long moment — 'Christie, for *Darling*.' As the victor, wearing a gold lamé pantsuit, rushed on stage, Julie Andrews applauded bravely, comforted at least that Luise Rainer's tortuous record was left intact.

Elsewhere, *Doctor Zhivago* won Best Adapted Screenplay and a clutch of technical awards. But *The Sound of Music* more than held its own, with wins for Irwin Kostal's arrangements and its sound department — and finally, most important of all, as the Academy Award winner for Best Film of 1965. 'We did it!' exclaimed Julie Andrews, beaming with pleasure and relief. 'Isn't that great?'

The next day, having resumed rehearsals on *Thoroughly Modern Millie*, she pronounced on the ceremony with typical sportsmanship: 'You know, it's almost a relief not to win again.

It's a little difficult to live up to that kind of image.'

'At the time, I didn't think of anybody but myself,' said Julie Christie. 'I can't say I'm sorry, of course. She won it last year, after all!' Of all the floral tributes she received, the one that impressed her most was the huge paper rose sent by Julie Andrews.

When the dust had settled, one thing was obvious. *The Sound of Music*, its five Oscars giving it an impetus it hardly needed, remained, like its star, at its zenith.

★　★　★

On 1 June 1966, a small item appeared in the *Hollywood Reporter*:

> Julie Andrews to London today, to attend funeral of her stepfather, musician-singer Ted Andrews, who launched Miss Andrews on her career at age of ten.

The previous Sunday, Ted Andrews had suffered another stroke in Walton-on-Thames. He was taken unconscious to nearby Weybridge Hospital, where he died, only fifty-nine years of age. 'He packed an awful lot into that life,' said Barbara Andrews, reflecting on the excitement and misery — never boredom — of their life together.

At Los Angeles Airport, Julie's flight home was delayed at the last moment. 'As she only had a twenty-four-hour leave of absence from the studio, I phoned to tell her not to come,' said her mother. 'She was really heartbroken as she loved her dad very much.'

If Julie's sessions with the analyst had addressed anything, it was her childhood. For all the resentment and anger she had felt for Ted Andrews, she had started to put his place in her life into perspective, as she revealed to the *Sunday Telegraph* as late as 2004: 'This was a man who certainly had his demons. But he is the man who taught me how to sing, built me a Wendy House in the garden, bought me my first puppy. He tried very hard — and I resented the hell out of him.' In particular, she recognised the irony of her early public and financial success: 'My stepfather must have been castrated by that.'

For Julie, work was a perfect antidote to her introspection. Quite apart from her stepfather's death, she had arrived at an impasse with Tony, with whom channels of communication had almost dried up. As she pushed herself ever harder, rehearsing the dance routines each evening after a long day's filming, she demonstrated, not for the first time, that her career offered its own therapy. 'When she's turned on — wow!' said George Roy Hill. 'It's a delight in *Millie* to see her just let go.' But it came at a price.

The world premiere of *Torn Curtain* took place in mid-July, at the Metropolitan Theatre in Boston, New England's largest cinema. Hitchcock cut a fifty-layer cake in honour of his fiftieth film but, not surprisingly, the stars stayed away — the only one of her world premieres that Julie had yet missed. She could legitimately cite her work schedule as an excuse, but it leaked out that she had quietly advised her friends not to see the film. 'I don't feel that the part demanded much of me,' she admitted, 'other than to look glamorous, which Mr Hitchcock can always arrange better than anyone.'

A few days later, *Torn Curtain* opened in New York and London. The reviews were chilly at best, one critic judging the sight of Miss Andrews in bed with Mr Newman to be 'as shocking as seeing Shirley Temple kicking the cat'.

In the *New York Times*, Bosley Crowther, up till now a Julie cheerleader, was scathing: 'A pathetically undistinguished spy picture . . . a collection of clichés'. The *New York Post* listed Julie's three previous screen characters as reason enough why she was unsuitable as Sarah Sherman, and *Life* magazine found 'a distracted air about much of the film', as if Hitchcock 'were not really paying attention to what he was doing'.

'We'd have done much better without Julie Andrews or Paul Newman,' said the director, with a distinct lack of grace. 'Bad chemistry, that was. Up front they said, 'Oh, she's so hot.' The two of them, with overhead, cost us $1.8 million which was to me a disgrace, spending all that money — and miscasting, at that!' However, in Charlotte Chandler's book *It's Only a Movie: Alfred Hitchcock*, Newman was gentlemanly in support of his co-star: 'I think he owed it to us not to say we were miscast after he had approved us . . . We were stars, and we brought in fans at the box office.'

Indeed so. Despite, or thanks to, the National Roman Catholic Office for Motion Pictures, which lambasted the 'gratuitous introduction of pre-marital sex between its sympathetic protagonists', the combined heft of Julie Andrews, Paul Newman and Alfred Hitchcock made *Torn Curtain* the biggest money maker in the history of Universal Studios.

Hawaii, meanwhile, was still being edited, George Roy Hill having balanced shooting *Thoroughly Modern Millie* with post-production on his first Julie Andrews film. It was finally released in October as a road show engagement, to justify its $15 million cost and whopping length of three hours nine minutes. 'As big and familiar as Diamond Head, and ultimately almost as heavy,' wrote Vincent Canby in the *New York Times*. 'Mr von Sydow and Miss Andrews, however, do contribute the film's few moments of genuine emotion.' And, remarkably, Pauline Kael's opinion was far from damning: 'As they say in the South, this movie sticks to your bones.'

Flying to New York for the world premiere, Julie also joined her husband at a private screening of *A Funny Thing Happened on the Way to the Forum*, the transcription of the stage hit with which, in happier times, Tony had maintained some degree of parity with his wife's achievements. On 10 October, at the opening of *Hawaii* at the DeMille Theatre, New York, Mr and Mrs Walton made their last public appearance as man and wife. Tony looked hunted, morose; Julie stood remote, in a long

301

white gown and gloves, the inches between them suddenly cavern-wide. The next morning, she flew back to Hollywood.

Ten days later, it was announced that they had formally split up. 'We have been separated for about a year now,' Julie was reported as admitting. 'There is no question of divorce. But there's no thought at present of getting back together again.'

Back in England, at The Old Meuse, Julie's widowed mother put a brave face on the situation. Julie had rung her, she said, saying 'that she and Tony were still 'wacky' about each other' — but that their work had come between them. 'But I'm not all that broken-hearted,' said Barbara, 'because, after all, a separation isn't as final as a divorce, is it? I have no doubt in my mind that Julie will do what's right for her and Tony.' She regarded Blake as a marvellous fellow. 'But as for romance, that's a lot of rot. At least, I think it is.'

Only four days after the New York premiere of *Hawaii*, Julie Andrews had attended the Hollywood opening, wearing exactly the same long white dress as before — but with her new companion by her side.

11

THE RHINESTONE FOLLIES

'Jesus, it was embarrassing'

— Twentieth Century Fox executive, 1968

One of the more specious fables about Julie Andrews is that everything she made after *The Sound of Music* turned to ashes. Nothing could be further from the truth. On 21 December 1966, the *Motion Picture Herald* announced her as the top star of the year, toppling another British export, Sean Connery, from his omnipotence as 007. *Torn Curtain* was breaking all records for Universal Studios. And *Hawaii* would become the highest grossing film of the season, even though the bulk of its $15.6 million take was devoured by its excessive budget — making 1967 the third year running that Julie Andrews had starred in the film that sold the most tickets at the box office.

Of her first five films, the only one not to achieve a record of some sort contained, ironically, her strongest performance. But *The Americanization of Emily* had more than paid its way, and — given that the public was interested in Julie plain and simple — was now about to be re-released, as *Emily*, plain and simple.

Meanwhile, somewhere in Italy, someone had

woken up to the fact that the world's biggest star could be heard singing, free of royalties, on the soundtrack of the 1952 dubbed version of *The Singing Princess*. The production company had no trouble in finding a distributor, TransNational Films, to issue it in America, where it opened in November 1967 with the tagline, 'It's joy . . . it's magic . . . it's Julie Andrews!' Before that, however, came *Thoroughly Modern Millie*, Hollywood's last original film musical of the decade — and, for Julie, yet another blockbuster from the start.

In New York, it opened at the Criterion Theatre on 22 March 1967, following what Bosley Crowther in the *New York Times* called 'a big, bang-up benefit premiere for all the swingers who could make the scene the night before'. Crowther's review betrayed his pleasure in old-fashioned star vehicles, of which *Millie* was one of a dying breed, calling it 'a joyously syncopated frolic'. Julie was 'absolutely darling — deliciously spirited and dry'. Beatrice Lillie was 'jimdandy' as the white slave racketeer. Carol Channing had the edge, he thought. 'But why try to make comparisons? All three are wonderful fun.' On the debit side, he found that 'the whole thing's too long. If they'll just cut out some of those needless things . . . it'll be a joy all the way.'

The star herself, who attended the Hollywood opening on 13 April, privately agreed. The road show era — propagated to win back to the cinema as many defectors to the television screen as possible — was now at its height. But whereas separate performances, reserved seats and inflated prices had suited the Broadway-to-Hollywood *The Sound of Music*, the more whimsical *Thoroughly Modern Millie* threatened to outstay its welcome.

George Roy Hill also felt strongly about the issue, but he and Julie were unable to persuade Universal to wield the scissors. As far as studio head Lew Wasserman was concerned, almost all the filmed footage would be included in the 153-minute final cut, to justify an intermission — one of the hallmarks of a road show release.

Judith Crist was succinct: 'What a nice 65-minute movie is buried therein!' And Pauline Kael in the *New Yorker* lost patience, calling it 'desperately with-it . . . the players work so hard that one begins to suffer for them and, finally, to feel numb.'

Initially, the film was, as Millie would have said, 'terrif'. The problem came with the incessant gags and references to the days of silent films (caption frames, wipes between scenes, camera irises). The title song — featuring Millie turning from bumpkin into flapper — Millie and Miss Dorothy tap-dancing in the lift, and Beatrice Lillie in all she did, worked. The Harold Lloyd tribute with Millie and Jimmy balanced on a skyscraper window ledge, the circus scene with Muzzy being shot from a cannon, and the *faux*-fight finale, did not. But, for every nonintegrated, action-halting sequence like the 'Jewish Wedding Song', there were 'delish' delights like 'Baby Face' with Millie swooning over her new boss to a soundtrack of the 'Hallelujah' chorus — in which Julie's dazzling assurance and technique showed more than ever why her stardom was no accident.

A strange theme, though, could now be traced through her musical films. Once again, she played a lovable character with no hinterland. Nobody knows much about Millie, and her English accent in an American town remains unexplained. Like Mary Poppins coming out of the sky, or Maria von Trapp coming down from the mountains, Julie's new incarnation was as another Little Miss Fix-It, existing only within the action of the film.

'Julie as you love her — singing, dancing, delighting', trilled the marketing campaign. She also appeared her best in the designs of Jean Louis, which could have come from a boutique in Beverly Hills. 'We looked at our flapper gowns,' said producer Ross Hunter, 'and we knew: the 'Millie Look' is back.' *Thoroughly Modern Millie* became the highest-ever earner for Universal Studios — knocking *Torn Curtain* into second place — with worldwide grosses of $40 million by the end of its initial release, making it the third Julie Andrews musical in succession to top the fortunes of a Hollywood studio.

The film had its London premiere on 12 October 1967, opening the new Odeon, St Martin's Lane, where it played for almost a year. It had found a champion in John Russell Taylor of *The Times*: 'It is about as near to guaranteeing a hit in advance as the cinema can get nowadays to put Julie Andrews in a musical.

Easy, therefore to be superior about the result. Easy, but in this instance, quite unnecessary . . . it makes a thoroughly delightful evening in the cinema.'

And Sandy Wilson recognised the debt it owed to *The Boy Friend*, calling it 'a top-heavy but intermittently amusing film, in which I was touched to see Julie employing many of the nuances of expression and posture which she had learned from Vida during rehearsals in that troubled summer of 1954'. Vida Hope had not lived to see Julie's screen triumphs. At Christmas 1963, her car had crashed into a lorry in the English countryside, killing her instantly. But her legacy stretched out across the years as Julie, whose ingénue days were almost over, infused her role with the sweetness and light she had earlier brought to Polly Browne on stage.

In February 1968, the film received seven Academy Award nominations, as had *Hawaii* the previous year (predominantly for technical and craft achievements). Elmer Bernstein, nominated for Best Original Music Score both times, was successful for *Thoroughly Modern Millie* — the film's sole winner. Repeating the pattern set by *Hawaii* was an unsuccessful nomination for Best Supporting Actress, in this case Carol Channing. Like Jocelyn LaGarde a year earlier, she was compensated by winning at the Golden Globes, where Julie was also honoured, picking up the first of two consecutive Henrietta Awards as World Film Favourite.

Back in London, John Russell Taylor lamented the lack of modern-day cinema legends — but made an exception for Julie. He wrote: 'In a musical, it really seems that she cannot go wrong.' Reiterating the success of her new film, he stated what was no more than popular wisdom: 'If the forthcoming *Star!*, a film biography of Gertrude Lawrence with Julie Andrews in the title role, does not follow suit, it will be a miracle.'

The Sound of Music, meanwhile, had led to a derivative cult — for the most part only showing how inspired Robert Wise, Ernest Lehman and Julie Andrews had been. MGM's convent entrant was *The Singing Nun*, produced by Joe Pasternak, for whom twelve-year-old Julie had made her wretched screen test. The romanticised story of the Belgian nun Soeur Sourire, it featured a Maria clone (Debbie Reynolds), a hit song ('Dominique') and a bevy of kids and nuns. These included Julie's colleague from *The Boy Friend*, Ann Wakefield, who told me, 'Debbie wanted to have a go, but it didn't measure up.' It was, nonetheless, one of the highest grossing films of 1966.

Columbia led the other acolytes with *The Trouble with Angels*, starring Rosalind Russell as a Mother Superior and Disney *alumna* Hayley Mills as the trouble, yielding good enough box-office results to inflict a sequel, *Where Angels Go . . . Trouble Follows*.

But to Richard Zanuck, the critical element in *The Sound of Music* was music rather than prayer. With this in mind, Twentieth Century Fox would conceive its most expensive singing triplets ever: Rex Harrison in *Doctor Doolittle*,

Ernest Lehman's production of *Hello, Dolly!* and, sandwiched between the two, *Star!* — the most demanding film yet for the actress Sandy Wilson now described as 'the superstar she had always planned to be'.

★ ★ ★

At Christmas 1966, Julie Andrews had joined the select band of individuals to grace the cover of *Time* magazine. 'They don't make them that way in show business much any more, and Americans seem to sense it,' ran the inside panegyric.

> She is everybody's tomboy tennis partner and their daughter, their sister, their mum. To grown men, she is a lady; to housewives, the gal next door; to little children, the most huggable aunt of all. She is Christmas carols in the snow, a companion by the fire, a laughing clown at charades, a girl to read poetry to on a cold winter's night.

But, tellingly, neither a wife nor a lover.

The demands of stardom had left Julie without time to spare even on her thousand-strong Christmas card list. Everything was geared to work — even the festive season itself, with her recording of *A Christmas Treasure*, a $1 Firestone album of carols accompanied by her friend André Previn. It achieved better than average sales for an Andrews recording, appealing as it did to addicts of Maria von Trapp.

In a determinedly cheerful article, 'Why This is My Favourite Time of All', for *Good Housekeeping* magazine that same December, Julie recalled other Christmases with her family in England: coming home from pantomime engagements to The Old Meuse, walking up the curved driveway, opening the door to see a big tree in the hall.

She remembered the previous Yuletide in Beverly Hills, picking out a tree with Emma Kate. 'My husband, Tony Walton, has decorated some of the most stunning Christmas trees I've ever seen,' she told the magazine. But, in reality, Tony had not been with them then, nor was he now. Instead, she and Emma had another family member living with them — Julie's younger half-brother Chris, now nineteen, who had started to study photography at Los Angeles Art Centre, and to whom, in Tony's absence, four-year-old Emma had become very much attached.

Julie imagined her ideal Christmas 'in a snowy country', in a log cabin high in the mountains. For the moment, in Hidden Valley Road, she would have to be content with her select group of friends — the Previns, Carol Burnett, Joe Hamilton and Mike Nichols — who were treated, whether they liked it or not, to the tradition Julie had continued from England of mulled wine, 'all icky and sticky'. And there was one other guest this year: Blake Edwards.

From now on, Julie was constantly reported in the same breath as the forty-four-year-old film director. Knowing this, she reacted less defensively than in the past: 'I don't think anybody goes out of her way to be a scarlet woman, but then there's very little I can do about it if that's what they want to make of it.'

In early 1967, she met her husband on one of the rare occasions his work brought him to Hollywood. Tony had started to see Genevieve Melia, the estranged wife of Warner LeRoy (son of Mervyn, the prolific film director). One of Norman Rockwell's former models for the *Saturday Evening Post* front covers, Gen was also an artist in her own right. For Julie and Tony, there was now no real chance of reconciliation.

Julie was painfully aware that when she had been Emma's age — almost to the month — she had suffered the break-up of her own parents' marriage, been parted from her beloved father, and been obliged to accept her mother's lover as her new parent. She had 'got on with it' — worked through it — reconciled herself to two fathers. It was, of course, impossible to do so with two husbands.

* * *

In April 1964, during a wet, chilly lull between takes on *The Sound of Music*, Robert Wise had made it clear how much he wanted to work with Julie again. Though not alone in predicting she would become a major star, he was the first to back his hunch, as he revealed to me in Hollywood, shortly before his death in 2005: 'When we said we want to sign Julie for *The Sound of Music*, they got her for a two-picture deal. When we heard that, we said, 'Oh boy'; we rang the front office and said, 'We want to put dibs on Julie.' We had to come up with a story.'

Yet, when he and co-producer Saul Chaplin mentioned the name Gertrud Alexandra Dagmar Lawrence-Klasen to their leading lady, her reaction was, 'Here we go again.'

Julie had been in *My Fair Lady* when colleagues first touted Gertrude Lawrence as a suitable role. Born in 1898, the London minstrel's daughter known as Gertie had risen from the back streets of Clapham to become Noël Coward's favourite stage partner, beloved on both sides of the Atlantic. When she died suddenly of cancer during the run of *The King and I* in 1952, the lights of Broadway were dimmed in her honour. Alan Jay Lerner, while recognising 'the indefinable substance that is the difference between talent and star', noted that 'the substance is not always the same. Gertrude Lawrence was electric: Julie was all that is endearing.'

Gertie and Julie had each conquered a generation of theatregoers, but Eliza Doolittle was their only role in common, Gertie's 1945 *Pygmalion* being the longest Broadway run of the play until the advent of *My Fair Lady*. Sophisticated, decadent Gertie — of whom Cecil Beaton wrote, 'She smoked a cigarette in a way that suggested she had just got out of bed and wished to return to it' — seemed the antithesis of Julie, who had never seen her on stage. But Robert Wise knew which element of the story would resonate with his star: 'Saul Chaplin and I began telling her the facts of Gertie's beginnings in music hall with her father, that she came from a split home, and that she eventually became known all over the world. Julie smiled and said, 'This is so much like my story, it's crazy!''

High on a hill, shrouded in the mist that threatened the filming of Maria von Trapp's stunning entrance in *The Sound of Music*, the fifty-year-old director had consolidated a remarkable working relationship. For a straight $225,000 fee, no more than her price for Maria, Julie agreed to play Gertrude Lawrence on screen.

Unusually for one so ambivalent, she committed herself without seeing a script — a mark of naïveté in the film world, but testament to the trust she placed in her director. Wise and his story editor Max Lamb then bought the rights to Gertie's autobiography, *A Star Danced*, and the tribute by her husband Richard Aldrich, *Gertrude Lawrence as Mrs A*.

During almost three years of preparation, working titles ranged from *Mrs A* to *Gertie was a Lady*. Finally, in April 1967, *Variety* confirmed that, 'despite earlier objections from some studio quarters', the year's most ambitious musical was to be called — *Star!*.

The English playwright William Fairchild was signed to write the screenplay. One problem he and Robert Wise encountered almost immediately was in portraying those of Gertie's fellow luminaries who were still alive. They began by approaching Beatrice Lillie, shortly before the filming of *Thoroughly Modern Millie*.

'We thought it would be nice if Bea let us do

her role, except that she insisted on playing herself,' Wise told me. 'Ridiculous! Maybe thirty or forty years ago ... Her manager felt, 'You guys have thick lenses.' We offered her thirty, forty thousand dollars to let someone else portray her, but she wouldn't hear of it.' So Miss Lillie was removed from the screenplay. But the next person approached was a great deal more important, said Wise: 'There was no way we could do Gertrude Lawrence without Noël Coward, no way.'

Coward had first worked with Gertie in pantomime, in 1910. Twenty years later, in his comedy *Private Lives* (its balcony scene used almost complete in *Star!*), they had made theatrical magic. 'The Master' remained her closest confidant; the last letter she ever wrote to him ended, 'It's always *you* I want to impress more than anyone.'

Nervously, Robert Wise travelled to London: 'Saul Chaplin, Bill Fairchild and I made a date to see him one Sunday morning at the Savoy Hotel. Noël was stretched out on the chaise-longue in a robe. The first thing he said was 'Well, fellows, who's to play me?' We really hadn't known if he had ideas of doing a Bea Lillie. We said, 'We could almost kiss your hand.' He went, 'Fine, fine.''

The smiles belied Coward's true feelings, which he confided to his diary after Fairchild visited him again, at his home in Switzerland:

Saturday 17 July 1965
On Tuesday Bill Fairchild came ... to

discuss *The Gertrude Lawrence Story*, a project of which I heartily disapprove . . . We argued back and forth. Julie Andrews is to play Gertie, about as suitable as casting the late Princess Royal as Dubarry. However, she's a clever girl and will at least be charming and sing well.

He then isolated the point which, had it been equally obvious to Twentieth Century Fox, might have saved the studio a fortune — and its reputation:

Why they are doing the film I shall never know. There isn't any real story beyond the fact that she started young in the theatre, became an understudy, then a star, lived with Philip Astley, married Richard Aldrich and died. I really do think that the Hollywood film mentality is worse than ever.

But to Saul Chaplin, Coward seemed 'most co-operative', his only condition being the right to approve his screen likeness. Candidates included comedian Peter Cook and Robert Stephens, whom Coward thought 'a bit toothy'. A young classical actor named Ian McKellen also made a screen test. Forty years later, Sir Ian told me: 'I had to learn any Noël Coward song and I chose 'Parisian Pierrot'. When I'd finished, the whole studio burst into applause. William Fairchild said he had never known anything like it . . . I'd got the part, I was perfect.'

What McKellen did not know was that Daniel Massey (whose father Raymond had played Higgins to Gertie's Eliza on Broadway) had also given a stellar audition — and was Coward's godson. 'Robert Wise just said. 'No, no, we go with Daniel.''

Coward's memories of Gertie summed up her contradictory character: 'She could wear rags and look ravishingly beautiful . . . She was irresponsible . . . Magical but quite mad . . . Exaggerated her humble beginnings . . . She had affairs with just about everybody . . . Treated her beaux abominably. Made everything around her seem platinum-plated.' All of which made the casting of Julie Andrews highly questionable. But, Wise maintained to me, the biggest star of the day was 'the one, the only one' to play her predecessor, albeit not as a carbon copy: 'Julie had this marvellous voice; Gertrude didn't have anything like that. The aim was to celebrate Julie — with whatever feeling of Gertrude she could get into it.'

Wise's proposed filming schedule nearly caused Julie's agent to cancel the deal. Arthur Park made clear to Twentieth Century Fox chief Richard Zanuck just how far his client had come in the fifteen months since her discussion in the Alpine rain.

As early as August 1965, Park emphasised how beneficial it would be to channel what was left of the studio system into the service of Julie's biggest film, and how much faith the star had in the Hollywood way of doing things. And, very smoothly, he indicated that she might have to withdraw unless plans were changed.

The real reason, of course, was financial. A shooting schedule conservatively estimated as lasting six months or longer meant that filming in England would render the star liable for double taxation — and it was becoming increasingly obvious how large the sums could now be for her.

With Julie calling the shots, the production was specified as a Hollywood-based enterprise, and her original fee was drastically revised. On the eve-of-shoot budget, dated 7 April 1967, Julie's name now commanded $625,500.

For all its expenditure, the film only followed Gertie up to her 1941 triumph in Kurt Weill's 'psychoanalysis musical' *Lady in the Dark* (which had been directed by Moss Hart). Audiences would again be denied the chance to see Julie as Eliza on screen, through the perspective of Gertie's 1945 performance, and would miss her reinterpretation of Rodgers and Hammerstein's great 1951 score, *The King and I*. 'We didn't think we were making the entire, definitive biography of Gertrude Lawrence; we'd tell the most interesting part,' said Saul Chaplin. 'There was no reason to get involved with matters leading up to her death.'

Chaplin had bought the rights to almost everything ever sung in public by Gertie, including 'Someone to Watch Over Me', 'My Ship', 'Someday I'll Find You' and a dozen others used in the film. Even with a plethora of Gershwin, Weill and Coward standards, there was room for Jimmy Van Heusen and Sammy

Cahn to reprise their *Thoroughly Modern Millie* duties, writing a lively title number serenading 'A genuine, positive, totally marvellous, perfectly wonderful *Star!*'

The cast contained forty-four speaking roles, 345 bit-part players (including an unknown Roy Scheider) and 10,000 extras, but even co-star Richard Crenna had no illusions about his place in the scheme of things. 'The rest of us are window dressing,' he said of his role as Gertie's husband, Richard Aldrich. Costume designer Donald Brooks added further cinematic records, creating the largest, most lavish wardrobe ever for an actress (125 outfits for $347,000) and hiring the most costly jewellery (a $3.4 million Cartier treasure trove, guarded by a private detective).

Robert Wise would call *Star!* the most complicated of his thirty-two films to date — more so than *The Sand Pebbles*, which had just taken him eighteen months to shoot in Taipei. Reporting to the set on 12 April 1967 for the first day of shooting, he received nervous word from Richard Zanuck, who had been exercising considerable thought on how to trim the $14 million budget. One economy was to incorporate more of the social background into the film-within-a-film format, cutting from Gertie watching documentary footage of her life to her actual living of it. Echoes of a similar framing device in *Citizen Kane* were not surprising. The editor of Orson Welles' 1941 masterpiece was Robert Wise.

But there were limits to what this could

achieve without making the historical perspective look cursory (which it eventually did). It also seemed rather late to be cutting corners. The most anticipated star vehicle of the year was about to start filming.

★　★　★

Star! began as it continued, with the Wise/Chaplin/Andrews triumvirate gladly reunited. 'It was a very happy shoot,' said Wise. 'We tried not to anticipate the problems down the line.'

Michael Kidd had been hired to recreate Gertie's dance routines — 'from intimate presentations of Julie Andrews done with class to raucous, riotous routines'. Nowhere was the routine more raucous than on the first day, in the simulated Brixton Music Hall, where Julie, as a rather matronly teenage Gertie, joined the family act alongside Bruce Forsyth as her father and Beryl Reid as his common-law wife. 'In the Los Angeles sunshine, they recreated the music hall as it was,' Forsyth, one of Britain's best-loved variety performers, told me of his film debut. 'They were always making up the crowd, putting in the smoke. I knew it was a very big undertaking.'

He and Beryl Reid worked for the best part of a week with Kidd, 'who was incredible'. So, apparently, was the girl playing his daughter. 'Julie is a perfectionist,' said Forsyth. 'She is constantly analysing her performance to see if she can make it better. If she needs to do another take, she'll make sure she does it until she gets it right.'

Most of the vaudeville numbers were filmed early on. Dressed as a tramp, singing 'Burlington Bertie from Bow', Julie came as close to her theatrical roots as she had done since leaving England. Beryl Reid had appeared on the same variety bills as the Andrews family, when Julie was thirteen years old. 'She hadn't changed so very much. She was still a tremendous worker,' said Miss Reid, noting that she retained 'a great sense of economy, rarely talking to anyone unless it served some useful purpose'.

Robert Wise had prepared a file, 'Impressions of Gertrude Lawrence: Confidential', to help his star with the huge challenges that lay ahead. 'It's like going into training,' Julie said. 'I must take care of myself or I'd be dead.' And when Ted and Win Wells came to California to stay for a month, she had her father encourage her fitness regime by running with her in the early morning sun on Malibu beach.

Julie also took delight in reading poetry with Ted, keeping alive an interest that, together with their love of wildlife, had been an early bond. One of her favourite writers had long been Robert Frost, whose poem 'The Road Not Taken' held a special resonance:

Two roads diverged in a yellow wood,
And sorry I could not travel both
And be one traveller, long I stood
And looked down one as far as I could
To where it bent in the undergrowth . . .

It had ever been thus for Julie. But compounding her natural ambivalence was the certain knowledge that, where two roads had diverged, taking what Frost called 'the one less travelled by' had grown ever harder — and threatened to continue so.

★　★　★

On 13 May, the company of *Star!* flew to New York to begin location work. The most authentic element of the final film was the use of several Broadway theatres, such as the Cort, Lyceum and Music Box. The last sat next to the Piccadilly Hotel, where, fourteen years earlier, Julie Andrews had spent her first night on American soil.

A temporary hoarding, 'Gertrude Lawrence in *Skylark*', masked the Music Box's current attraction: Harold Pinter's *The Homecoming*. One of the play's English cast, Michael Craig, was to appear in *Star!* as Sir Anthony Spencer, a rather stiff amalgam of Gertie's upper-class boyfriends. Craig, a glutton for punishment, had already marked time as a similar feed to Barbra Streisand, in the London run of *Funny Girl*.

At the start of June, Wise moved from Manhattan to Dennis, Massachusetts, filming at the Cape Cod Playhouse, owned by Gertie's widower Richard Aldrich. The distinguished sixty-six-year-old watched avidly, coming up to Richard Crenna on the first day: 'How do you do? I'm so glad to meet me.' Then, voicing what few others would later echo, he murmured, 'How much Miss Andrews reminds me of Gertrude.'

Flying to the South of France a week later, cast and crew regrouped at the Hotel Negresco in Nice — where the Mediterranean summer let them down. Waiting for the sea to calm, the Julie of old joked with technicians, clowning on a motorcycle belonging to one of the French crew, emulating biker chic in swimming costume and leather helmet.

Not everyone saw such moments as spontaneous. One crew member remarked, 'It's very important to her that people believe she is sublimely happy. Julie is quite incapable of admitting there's so much as one dark cloud on the horizon. I've seen Julie go to any extremes to preserve an illusion of sunny bliss. There's a gnawing restlessness in her, which won't allow her to relax — she has a perfect horror of admitting any failure.'

At a villa overlooking Cap Ferrat, Julie filmed opposite fifteen-year-old Jenny Agutter, playing Gertie's estranged daughter Pamela. 'Did you leave Daddy or did Daddy leave you?' Pamela asks her mother — who explains that they left each other. Watching from the sidelines for much of the French filming was little Emma Kate. And, with the separation from Tony still very raw, the parallel was obvious to Julie: 'I think I understand many of Gertie's problems,' she said. 'She was terribly insecure and, for much of her life, I think she was very lonely.'

Barbara Andrews came to visit in Nice — mother enough to criticise her daughter's hair, back to its natural 'country mouse', as Julie described it, under the wigs. At night, Barbara entertained the crew with music-hall songs on the piano, the closest link to home Julie would have for a while. Because of her tax situation, Robert Wise was using her stand-in during background filming in England, while she returned to Hollywood at the end of June to prepare for the major dramatic sequences.

'I never worked so hard in my life,' she later declared of the schedule. But, as Pauline Kael would write, 'Hard work is the opposite of glamour.' Ominously, the gulf between the wholesome image of one and the extravagant nature of the other remained, summarised by the cheery notice above Julie's dressing-room mirror: 'Keep Smiling'.

In private, Julie, like Gertie, had been known to swear like a trooper; but, for public consumption, the script went as far as it dared with 'bloody', 'bastard' and the rather inauthentic 'cripes'. Gertie's debauchery, on the other hand, was epitomised by the scene that would ultimately cause most comment: a show-business party, with the star ranting, drinking and ending in a heap on the floor.

'I doubt if Julie's ever been drunk,' said Wise. 'I don't know if she did any research.' Whether or not memories of Ted Andrews' alcoholism came to mind, the star stood silently for some minutes before a mirror — then played the most intense acting scene of her career with surprising abandon. Pleased at having acquitted herself so well, Julie was dismayed to learn there had been a flaw in the film. The next day, summoning her 'terrible British strength', she did it again — against all odds, even better.

During this period, Blake Edwards — who, despite his pledge never again to collaborate with Peter Sellers, was shooting *The Party* with the recalcitrant star — would turn up regularly to accompany Julie home from the studio. For Blake's forty-fifth birthday, Julie's chauffeur arrived with a 'fun present' she had bought for him: a three-foot model of a railway engine. As she left to meet him for lunch, Michael Kidd joked, 'How does it feel to be in love, Julie?' There was an embarrassing silence. Quietly, the star replied, 'I know how it feels when I'm not.'

To a film journalist from London's *Daily Mirror*, she was a good deal more expansive. 'It's queer. I've only known Blake two and a half years, and I knew Tony most of my life. Yet Blake is the one who's actually watched me grow up. I was still a frightened little girl when I was married to Tony, but Blake knows me as a woman.'

It was only a matter of time before the world's media would be able to judge them side-by-side. It happened, naturally enough, on a film set, during one of the climactic (and bloated) musical numbers on *Star!* — on which Julie's years of self-discipline came to the fore. The massive finale, 'Jenny' from *Lady in The Dark*, was the latest, most determined, attempt to dynamite Julie's *Mary Poppins* image. 'If anything can wreck that, this song will do it,' said Saul Chaplin.

'Jenny' was set in a dream circus, in which

Julie, clad in a black sequinned body stocking, was to slide down a cable, burst through a hoop of fire and perform a 'Risley act', balancing on the feet of circus jugglers, eight feet above the stage. Typically, she refused a double for the acrobatics, training for five weeks with the troupe. After shooting the frenetic routine to the applause of cast and crew, Julie cleared an altogether different hurdle. She hurried over to Blake and introduced him to a second visitor to the set, whom she kissed. It was Tony Walton, in California to design the film *Petulia*, starring the 'other' Julie, Miss Christie. He and Blake shook hands, the first time the men in Julie's life had met in public.

A few days later, on 14 November, a year of speculation about her marital situation was ended. Julie, accompanied by her attorney Allen E. Sussman, filed for divorce at Santa Monica Superior Court. Her petition stated: 'The various demands of our careers have kept Tony and me apart for long periods of time, thus placing obvious strains upon our marriage. It has therefore become clear that a divorce will be in the best interests of all concerned.'

Two months earlier, Blake's fourteen-year marriage had also ended at the Santa Monica court. On 20 September, his estranged wife Patricia had come to get an interlocutory divorce decree — telling the judge that, as long ago as 1965, Blake had told her that 'he didn't want to be married any more'. His freedom came at a hefty price: monthly alimony of $5,000 for Patricia and child support of $1,000 for Jennifer and Geoffrey, who would continue to live with their mother in England.

Once Julie's own divorce proceedings were set in motion, there was a frenzy of conjecture that she would soon follow Gertrude Lawrence's example by marrying an American. First, however, there was a film to finish. So 'unbelievably rigorous' was Julie's workload that she hardly had time to read the newspapers, let alone make marriage plans. Yet even she could sense how the world — and the industry — was changing.

On 13 August 1967, *Bonnie and Clyde* had opened, championed by Pauline Kael as the greatest American film for years. Among Julie's former colleagues, Paul Newman was about to star opposite newcomer Robert Redford in *Butch Cassidy and the Sundance Kid*. Its director, hot from *Hawaii* and *Thoroughly Modern Millie*, was George Roy Hill. And one of Julie's closest friends, Mike Nichols, had just directed *The Graduate*, which opened to ecstatic business in New York, four days before Christmas.

A week earlier, on Friday 15 December, *Star!* finally ended its epic 149-day filming schedule with the production number 'Limehouse Blues'. Exhausted but radiant, Julie appeared at the end-of-shoot party on Fox Soundstage 14, sporting a new piece of jewellery: a nine-carat diamond 'friendship ring' given to her by Blake, who would be joining her for Christmas in Switzerland.

In the New Year, they would be working

together on *Darling Lili*, the big-budget espionage picture which they had discussed, somewhat prosaically, on their first date. For the moment, however, all Julie wanted was to see her new Alpine chalet in Gstaad, and start living the winterland fantasy she had imagined the year before.

★ ★ ★

On 9 January 1968, having seen the rough cut of Julie's latest vehicle, Doc Merman, the studio chief of staff, wrote to Robert Wise that picking a hole in *Star!* was 'like trying to pick a hole in the Koh-i-noor Diamond . . . the greatest yet'. But even the screenplay suggested otherwise. 'Isn't this kind of thing a little out of date?' an ageing Gertie is asked in one scene. *Star!* provided its own answer.

The marketing office went through obvious indecision in designing the promotional material. Concepts ranged from art deco to a Warhol-inspired face shot. The final design, a close-up of Julie with a star over one side of her face, caused one exhibitor to ask, 'What's with the black eye?'

In the weeks prior to the London world premiere, every major British magazine carried an extensive feature on the three-hour film. Donald Brooks' lavish inter-war costumes provided dream copy for the female market: 'For women who do not want to follow the hippie road or slick moon-blast trail to fashion, here is salvation.'

The Royal Charity Gala on Thursday 4 July, at

the Dominion Theatre, Tottenham Court Road, where *The Sound of Music* had enjoyed its incredible success, seemed set to be one of the most spectacular nights in the life of Julie Andrews. London had waited to give her a proper homecoming for nearly four years — a period in which she had become the world's top star, yet had never attended a British premiere of one of her own films.

At the Dominion, two generations of Zanucks, Darryl and Richard, gathered with Robert Wise, Saul Chaplin and Fox's vice-president David Gurley Brown to welcome the Duke and Duchess of Kent. The audience included Earl Mountbatten of Burma, Gertie's daughter Pamela Clatworthy and her children and, of course, Noël Coward. But there was only one person the crowds were interested in seeing — and she had not arrived. Walking up the red carpet, the Duchess of Kent looked around the foyer and asked, 'Where's Julie?'

The answer was, two hundred miles away, in Brussels, filming *Darling Lili*. The Rank Film Organisation had had a jet standing by all day at Heathrow Airport, doomed, like the flower-decked suite at the Dorchester Hotel, to go unused. With the Paramount picture running frighteningly behind schedule, Julie could not be spared.

Robert Wise put a brave face on it: 'They just had to film all night. We appreciate the situation — we are film-makers ourselves.' This did not stop press officers at Fox telephoning their Paramount counterparts, in a futile effort to beg her release. According to Sheilah Graham, whose days as a gossip columnist were preceded by a stint in the chorus with the real Gertrude Lawrence, 'I heard resentment on all sides towards the star who wasn't there. It makes you wonder if Julie, who loathes crowds, had really wanted to come.'

Noël Coward wrote in his diary: 'Quite a lot has happened during the last two weeks, but nothing of world-shattering importance. Unless you call the movie of *Star!* world-shattering. Julie Andrews was talented, charming, efficient and very pretty but *not* very like Gertie.'

Amazingly, most London critics were upbeat, possibly wary of castigating another Julie Andrews film when they had been so out of step with the public on *The Sound of Music*. The *Evening Standard* rhapsodised: 'Only one thing worries me: when they come to make *The Julie Andrews Story* years from now — possibly entitled *Superstar* — who on earth will they find to play Julie Andrews?' Even the left-leaning *Guardian*, never part of Julie's fan base, considered it 'a totally enjoyable triumph of popular entertainment'.

More probing was the *Sun*: 'It is still possible, despite all the lovers she takes . . . to accuse Julie Andrews of being wholesome.' In the same vein was the judgement of the *Daily Express*: 'It didn't tell me much about Gertrude Lawrence, but it told me quite a lot about Julie Andrews. Rather more than I wanted to know, in fact.'

In sharp contrast, the *Daily Mail* spoke aloud the prayers of Twentieth Century Fox: 'Well, that's it. Say goodbye to the Dominion Cinema for another five years ... the unmistakable sound of another hit — and its name is *Star!*. If Julie Andrews is unique at the present moment, this film is likely to make her immortal.'

It was a false dawn. On general release, the sight of Julie as a drunken harpy caused hilarity among the younger customers, outrage among the matrons. And when Gertie started to 'damn' the 'bastards', vacated seats snapped up like gunfire. By early August, the production manager at Twentieth Century Fox admitted, 'We certainly have some problems here.' Back in May 1967, an advertisement in the *New York Times* had invited readers to join an advance reservation list for *Star!*. Over fifteen thousand letters had flooded in. But, with interim reports suggesting Julie was not adhering to the 'Doris Day formula for the sweetest-girl', less than a hundred correspondents had actually bought tickets.

The New York premiere was held at the Rivoli Theatre on 22 October 1968. Julie was again absent, filming *Darling Lili* in Hollywood — and this time the vultures descended.

The most damning review was the shortest. Renata Adler in the *New York Times* led off with 'Miss Andrews is not at her best here ... Miss Lawrence is portrayed as a kind of monster', and ended four terse paragraphs with 'People who liked Gertrude Lawrence had better stick with their record collections and memories.' That a hugely expensive, highly touted film should be dismissed with such brevity appalled the studio. Miss Adler shrugged, 'I took one look at the silly thing and thought, what the hell.'

Almost as bad were Bosley Crowther and Judith Crist, while Pauline Kael's scorn was evident from the top: '*Cripes!* Julie Andrews does her duties efficiently but mechanically, like an airline stewardess . . . a nasty Girl Guide.' Fairchild and Wise's attempts to get beneath Gertie's surface were dismissed outright: 'They go rummaging about . . . trying to find a social 'statement' when the best demonstration of integrity would be to make a decent musical.'

Underlying the scabrous notices was a gleeful certainty that, unlike *The Sound of Music*, the film was 174 minutes of commercial dead weight. 'We were all so hyped up about the possibility of another sizeable hit, at least, with *Star!*,' its director told me in 2005, 'we were absolutely devastated when we saw some of the reviews — you spend a year on something, and then . . . '

The trade papers were better. But even an exhibitors' magazine sounded nervous, detailing its 'Exploitip' for the release: 'Stress the reteaming of the creative elements which made *The Sound of Music* so successful.' The catch-line echoed the title song: 'A Totally Wonderful Musical Entertainment!' It fooled no one. At the Rivoli, where Maria von Trapp had been deified, tiny audiences (bigger at midweek matinees than on Saturday nights) regarded Julie's new image as akin to public betrayal.

By the end of the month, at the Hollywood opening — attended by Julie and Blake — a gala dinner for six hundred at the Fox studio could not disguise the feeling of galloping disaster. Jan Versaw, a student from Diablo Valley, California, who had previously been bounced from two studios trying to meet her idol, arrived early at the Fox Wilshire Theatre. 'I thought it would be crowded like the Rose Parade,' she commented. There was not a soul in sight. Die-hard fans aside, *Star!* was fast becoming what Richard Zanuck called 'my Edsel', a reference to the 1950s wonder car that no one bought.

'I was shocked, yeah,' Robert Wise told me. 'I didn't expect that at all. I said, right, what happened here? You misjudge your audience sometimes . . . I think it's a damn' fine film, and it deserved better than it got. Julie did some of her best work in it; she told me she worked harder on that film than on *The Sound of Music*. I always thought *Funny Girl* took the edge off us, had a negative influence on our reception.'

A new star had announced her presence from the tarmac of John F. Kennedy airport: 'To me, being a star is being a movie star.' With this, Barbra Joan Streisand of Flatbush Avenue, Brooklyn, stepped on to the aeroplane for Los Angeles. Pauline Kael led the welcoming chorus, with oblique reference to the current box-office queen: 'Barbra Streisand arrives on the screen in *Funny Girl*, when movies are in desperate need of her. The timing is perfect. There's hardly a star in American movies today . . . Barbra Streisand is much more beautiful than 'pretty' people.'

Bitter words for Fox — triply so for Julie. As 1920s comedienne Fanny Brice, Barbra was given the chance, denied Julie, to recreate her most famous stage role on screen. The subject matter of *Funny Girl* was dangerously similar to *Star!* but better written. And its genius director had declined two of Julie's own films.

William Wyler, who had abandoned *The Americanization of Emily* and *The Sound of Music*, knew enough of the latter's grosses to regard *Funny Girl* as a good thing. At the Academy Awards of 1968, Barbra won the Oscar, as had Julie, for her screen debut. Columbia, her studio, also produced the year's Best Film, *Oliver!* — like *Star!* sporting an exclamation mark, but in exuberance rather than desperation.

And Twentieth Century Fox was desperate. Hastily conducted surveys indicated there might still be a market for Julie Andrews, but certainly not as Gertrude Lawrence.

Teenagers, whose parents had happily sat through *West Side Story*, and who had themselves been taken to *The Sound of Music*, were in no mood to neck in the back row to Gershwin's 'Do Do Do (what you done done done)', trilled by an actress they regarded as a square, portraying a woman of whom they had never heard. Many of their parents were ending the habit of moviegoing for good. *Torn Curtain* had attracted many, goaded by Roman Catholic censure, to see how Mary Poppins was making out under the blanket, and enough housewives had dragooned their husbands into seeing

333

Thoroughly Modern Millie to make it more than a camp cult. But the American Midwest which had so embraced Maria von Trapp knew Gertie little and cared less.

A smokescreen of high production values seemed poor exchange for plot and character — like being force-fed a whole box of chocolates after ordering a three-course meal. And of the lavish wardrobe, which made Julie appear at times like an embalmed transvestite, she remarked, 'I think it put me off rhinestones forever.' Seven Oscar nominations (with no wins) did nothing to help *Star!*. At the end of 1968, *Variety* posted a gross of $1.3 million: even drive-in quickies like *The Savage Seven* and *The Miniskirt Mob* had done better.

Final cost: $14 million. Final yield: $4 million. 'I'll be haunted by its failure forever,' said Saul Chaplin.

12

FROM BAD TO WORSE

*'I always knew that one day the bubble
would burst'*

—Julie Andrews, 1994

It began with a rumble and built to a roar: before
1968 was half over nothing short of cultural
revolution had raged through the free world,
storming over broken idols like a tornado. In
almost every Western capital, there was some
form of rebellion: civil rights marches, student
riots, anti-war demonstrations, the trampling
into the ground of age-old taboos. Somewhere,
caught in the detritus — the tatters of what
Alfred P. Doolittle knew as middle-class morality
— was the career of Julie Andrews.

Nobody could foresee how quickly all would
be lost. At the start of the year, the Queen of
Hollywood ruled absolute. By the end, following
the first abysmal returns for *Star!*, her enemies
would be at the gate.

The screen biography of Gertrude Lawrence
could scarcely have been worse timed. With a
fraction of the budget and Ginger Rogers singing
the ditties, it might have turned a nice profit in
1948. Twenty years on, the public was dancing to
a very different rhythm. In June alone, Noël

Harrison, the best man at Julie's wedding to Tony Walton, was heard singing 'The Windmills of Your Mind' in the hit film *The Thomas Crown Affair* — while her Hawaiian nemesis Richard Harris reached second place in the *Billboard* Hot 100 with 'MacArthur Park'.

On 26 September 1968, two months after the world premiere of *Star!*, the Lord Chamberlain of England finally lost his 230-year-old power of stage censorship. The very next day, the 'Tribal Love-Rock' musical *Hair* opened in London's West End, the dawning of the Age of Aquarius heralded by the cast emerging naked from a blanket. During its four-year run, fans included Princess Anne, seen dancing on stage in a purple trouser suit after the show, clearly untroubled by its four-lettered freedom. Elsewhere, the Beatles were growing out their mop-top hair, under increasing challenge from the Rolling Stones: as Mick Jagger and Keith Richards had recently learned, being busted for drugs meant no dip in sales.

What then for Mary Poppins, Maria von Trapp or not-so-Thoroughly Modern Millie?

★ ★ ★

Professionally, in January there seemed little sign of danger. Once again, Julie Andrews headed the *Motion Picture Herald* poll as the world's greatest attraction (the last time an actress would so do until Julia Roberts in 1999, thirty-one years later).

For the moment, it was Julie's private life that

was seriously in question. Divorce proceedings having been set in motion, a ravenous press was feverishly speculating not if she would marry Blake Edwards, but when. Only Sheilah Graham, thinking of Julie's ambivalence, was sceptical. 'She'll wait for her California decree to be final and, even then, I'll be surprised if they marry.'

The little girl who had once longed so much for home had not made a lengthy visit to England for four years, kept away by that most worldly of excuses: tax exile. But on her way back from Switzerland, the superstar paid a remarkably low-key trip to London, with none but her closest family and friends knowing about it.

Staying at the Dorchester Hotel, Julie took her daughter, now five years old, to meet her mother and her half-brother Donald in Walton-on-Thames. Emma also had tea with her other grandmother, Mrs Lancelot Walton, who put a brave face on the break-up of her son's marriage: 'We are all very good friends in spite of everything. It's a very unfortunate and unhappy situation — but there you are . . . '

As it happened, Tony was in London, to work on the opera *The Midsummer Marriage* at Covent Garden. The choreographer was Julie's co-star from the dismal 1954 tour of *Mountain Fire*, Gillian Lynne. And, just as in 1954 Tony had worn his heart on his sleeve, only to have Julie spurn him, so fourteen years later he appeared to be suffering more visibly from the separation. Meeting to discuss the opera, Gillian

Lynne found him 'very sad ... He said 'I'm trying to make an appointment to meet my wife.' He felt he was kept away from his wife.'

Later that January, Emma flew to Stockholm with her father. Tony, designing the film of Chekhov's *The Seagull*, admitted that the impending divorce was 'the least surprising thing that could have happened', given the 'lunatic additional pressures' on Julie: 'I suppose we've both changed. I've got older, anyway. Julie says she's changed — she says she'd have been horrified if she hadn't.'

Remembering the fun of their early days, he explained how she was not 'at all like her image — there's much more of the clown in her than people realise. There's probably a lot of her in *The Sound of Music*.' A major factor in the breakdown of their relationship had been his dislike of Hollywood: 'It's very disjointed ... I'm just not geared to it.'

Of Blake Edwards, he would only say, 'I've met him once, but not for long enough to form an opinion. I can't say whether I get jealous when I read about him and Julie — I'm concerned that she should be happy.' Asked how things might have been had his spouse been a housewife, tiredness overtook him. 'It's pointless to speculate. Whatever happens, happens.'

Julie seemed to agree. 'I can't be what I was before I came to Hollywood,' she told one reporter sadly. 'You can't be bending over backwards to show everybody you haven't changed. I'm growing up late, that's all, desperately late.'

Meanwhile, it looked like business as usual. On 22 January, MGM announced that, in 1969, Julie would star in one of the 'biggest and most important musicals' in the company's history. *Say It With Music* — featuring the songs, old and new, of Irving Berlin — was to be produced by Arthur Freed, whose fabulous track record at MGM included the Judy Garland canon, *Singin' in the Rain* and Lerner and Loewe's Oscar-laden *Gigi*.

The film had been planned as Arthur Freed's swan-song as far back as late 1963. In the flurry of interest in her during the making of *Mary Poppins*, Julie had been offered a role, along with Robert Goulet, Ann-Margret and even (it was rumoured) Sophia Loren. *Say It With Music* had then gone through various permutations, with Frank Sinatra attached to it at one point. It was to be directed by Hollywood's greatest maker of musicals, Vincente Minnelli, who planned it as 'the bang-up musical to end them all'. But, as with George Cukor and William Wyler, Minnelli was not to work his Academy Award-winning magic on Julie Andrews. Internal politics at MGM meant, he said, that 'the whole project fizzled out' — other than for the star. 'Everything Julie wants, Julie gets,' said columnist Dorothy Manners, with the news that Blake Edwards had been appointed as director — and co-producer — of the revivified film.

The concept was also overhauled. The original script, by the *Singin' in the Rain* team of Adolph Comden and Betty Green, had simply been the story of Berlin's life. Blake now enlisted playwright George Axelrod, with whom he had turned *Breakfast at Tiffany's* into Audrey Hepburn's signature hit. The new *Say It With Music*, Axelrod declared, would 'not be like the image one would have of an Irving Berlin-Julie Andrews musical'.

Then, a couple of months later, MGM made a sudden series of cutbacks, just as the first reports of musicals doing less than Julie-size business started to filter through Hollywood. *Say It With Music* was one of the titles to be cancelled.

But MGM was hardly the centre of attention. In April, all eyes turned from Twentieth Century Fox, where *Star!* was being frantically edited, to Paramount, where Julie Andrews faced her lover for the first time on the other side of the camera, on the set of *Darling Lili*.

★   ★   ★

In 1966, Gulf & Western, one of America's biggest conglomerates, had taken control of Paramount Pictures. But Gulf's founder, Austrian-born Charles Bluhdorn, had no real passion for movie making. He delegated a charming, persuasive young head of production named Robert Evans to oversee the studio's hugely optimistic raft of blockbusters, of which the Andrews-Edwards title demanded the most attention.

With a massive budget, necessitated by such period trappings as aeroplane battles and martial parades, *Darling Lili* had been approved on 11 March 1967 on the strength of Julie rather than Blake — whose work, of late, had been decidedly off-form. Even *The Party*, his latest film with Peter Sellers (and reputedly Elvis Presley's favourite), had failed to restore his status as the man to whom everybody sent their comedy script.

That position was now occupied by one of Julie's closest friends, Mike Nichols. *The Graduate*, only his second film, had turned the eager-beaver sketch writer into the hottest director in town. With a laugh quotient far higher than any of Blake's recent efforts, it was set — after only three months — to become second to *The Sound of Music* as the decade's biggest industry earner. Everyone wanted to work with Mike.

Everyone, that is, apart from Doris Day, America's other girl-next-door screen heroine. Ross Hunter, who prior to *Thoroughly Modern Millie* had produced many of Miss Day's hits, compared the two stars: 'They're similar, only Julie has had bigger films.' Doris had only herself to blame: in 1966, she turned down the role of *The Graduate*'s seducer, Mrs Robinson, later writing that it 'offended my sense of values'.

Quite what value there was in her latest offering *Where Were You When the Lights Went Out?* was known only to Doris and God. Playing an actress constantly cast as a virgin, it suggested she was (like Julie) keen to smudge her pristine image — but only within her own brand of 'sex comedy'. Public lack of interest was summed up by the review in *Time*: 'Doris Day's fans, if there are any left . . . '

In April 1968, the sudden death of her profligate husband and manager, Marty Melcher, from a heart attack, meant at least she would be signed to no more dud pictures. But Doris discovered that the millions she had earned in a twenty-year film career had been squandered — and that Marty had committed her to CBS for a television series without her knowledge. The most popular star of the 1950s and early 1960s quit the big screen — just as her successor started work with her most famous former co-star. In *Darling Lili*, Julie was to make screen love to one of America's top hunks — associated with Doris since their 1959 hit *Pillow Talk* — Rock Hudson.

It was the fourth time that Doris and Julie had shared a leading man. Rex Harrison had left the London stage production of *My Fair Lady* to terrorise Doris in the thriller *Midnight Lace*. In *The Americanization of Emily*, Julie had jumped into bed with James Garner one year after his 1963 romps with Doris in *The Thrill of It All* and *Move Over Darling*. And Richard Harris went from spitting about Julie in *Hawaii*, to gushing over Doris ('She was fine — she was a ball') in *Caprice*.

Darling Lili, a First World War story to be filmed in Hollywood, Ireland, Belgium and France, starred Julie as Lili Smith, an English musical star — in reality, Lili Schmidt, a Mata-Hari clone. The latest attempt to defrock Maria von Trapp was in a shower scene with Hudson's American air ace Major Larrabee, whom Lili seduces in the cause of the Kaiser's victory. The screenplay was principally written by Blake's collaborator on *A Shot in the Dark*: William Peter Blatty, two years away from the publishing phenomenon of *The Exorcist*.

Finally, Julie's agent Arthur Park was able to win his client a proper market wage. The days of off-the-cuff picture deals with Robert Wise long over, Julie was guaranteed $1,100,000 against ten per cent of receipts, and a whole suite of dressing rooms at Paramount (remodelled for $70,000) whether she needed them or not. There was rather less of Jolly Jules: the pressures of *Star!* had put paid to that. Julie had gone native. Like Barbara Streisand and Elizabeth Taylor, she would no longer run to meet the demands of publicists and photographers, behaving, if she pleased, as remotely as Greta Garbo.

On set, however, she was among friends. 'Mom' Roberson attended to her hair and 'Daddy Bill' Buell to her make-up. A third confidante Dorothy Drake looked after her wardrobe — which, as with *Star!*, was a vast and lavish collection designed by Donald Brooks. For Blake, the unit was almost incestuous. The production manager was his stepfather Jack McEdward, the executive producer his uncle Owen Crump. Geoffrey Productions, named after Blake's young son, was the nominal production company.

A strong supporting cast was headed by Jeremy Kemp (as Lili's German mentor Colonel von Ruger). It was rumoured that Blake wanted comedian Benny Hill to play a cameo role: what he got was one of Hill's ex-showgirls, Gloria Paul, as the nightclub stripper Crêpe Suzette. But it was Lance Percival's drunken air officer 'TC', cowardly and brave by turns, who proved, in his few scenes, the most interesting character.

The shower sequence, filmed early in the schedule on a closed set, was Julie's first nude scene. Opposite her, forty-two-year-old Rock Hudson remained covered up — in more ways than one. Despite the advance in permissiveness, the word 'gay' was still used to describe Julie's sunny demeanour rather than her co-star's sexual proclivities. But exposure was now the order of the day. And a certain reporter decided that this was the moment to destroy not one legend, but two.

Hollywood's legendary gossip queens were long gone: Louella Parsons was retired from Hearst Newspapers and Hedda Hopper, on the rival *Los Angeles Times*, had died in 1966. Miss Hopper's successor, however, was the *Time* reporter who had compiled what Julie called 'the most vicious thing imaginable about all the trouble we were in' during the Boston try-out of *Camelot* eight years earlier, none other than Joyce Haber.

At the *Los Angeles Times*, Miss Haber did not take long to make her mark, referring to celebrities by the initials of their most salient characteristics. While almost impossible to sue, she regularly came as close to libel as any mainstream show-business journalist of the period. It was all depressingly popular: after two years, Joyce Haber was syndicated across America. In April 1968, she went to work on Julie.

Her coded message reported that Miss P & P (Prim & Proper), a well-known leading lady, was enjoying an affair with Mr X, her director on a major movie. The co-star, Mr VV (Visually Virile), was allegedly mocked by the other pair for his 'less than manly behaviour', Miss P & P telling him, 'Remember, *I'm* the leading lady.'

Over a decade later, Blake recalled Haber's other conjecture, 'that Rock Hudson, Julie and I were a sexual threesome. She also implied Rock and I had spent a lot of time together in San Francisco leather bars,' — more specifically, that Mr VV had walked into a favourite Frisco haunt, to find Mr X preening at the bar.

To Blake, Hudson quipped, 'How in hell did she find out so quick?' When the *Los Angeles Times* hit the stands, however, he held his counsel — for reasons that would become tragically obvious to the world with his death seventeen years later.

But Julie and Blake, with whom Hudson had a genuinely warm platonic relationship, were incandescent. Blake had for years been followed by rumours about his own sexuality. Julie, whose defensive armour had prompted similar speculation about her femininity, was in no mood to explain. For the first time, Miss P & P dropped her mask, with a piece of home-spun philosophy that rocketed around Hollywood: 'They should give Haber open-heart surgery, and go in through the feet.' Declaring that Blake had been elsewhere at the time of the leather bar allegations, they considered legal action, but backed off later that year, claiming, rather lamely, that 'suing her would dignify her'.

Unfortunately, Joyce Haber was not alone. A

345

pack of press bloodhounds were construing Julie's jealously guarded privacy as evidence that the girl next door was in personal crisis. And, indeed, she was feeling far from her best, sleeping only fitfully, kept awake by severe headaches and brooding over her forthcoming divorce.

Granting an interview to the London *Daily Mail*, Julie spoke for the first time of failure, professional and personal: 'My nightmare is not being able to adjust to the pit if all this happiness that I have at the moment should end.' Her dream, by contrast, was of being 'a little old lady in a cottage with roses round the door, and rubies round my neck'. Despite, or because of, the rate at which she pushed herself, she longed for time. 'Especially time. There is never enough time.'

★ ★ ★

Before leaving for Europe, where the bulk of *Darling Lili* was to be shot, Julie arranged that Worsley House, Wimbledon Common — the home for which she and Tony had once hoped so much — be put on the market for £25,000. And at eleven o'clock on Tuesday 7 May 1968, she entered Santa Monica Superior Court, to be granted her divorce. Wearing a black and white hound's-tooth coat, white silk scarf and gloves, her crystalline voice softer than usual, she testified that Tony had always been a devoted father to their daughter, but went on, 'When I did see him, he was very hostile to me and my friends, and unsympathetic to the demands of my career.' Guy Gadbois, her business manager, confirmed that Tony's attitude had made his client 'unhappy and extremely depressed'.

The suit was uncontested. Julie waived her right to alimony and child support, and was awarded custody of Emma. With that, the five-minute hearing brought the nine-year marriage to an end, almost two decades since the childhood sweethearts' chance meeting on a suburban London train.

Under Californian law, Julie was free to marry again from 14 November 1968, one year after she had filed the divorce action. But, even now, work took precedence. The weekend after her divorce, she flew to the Republic of Ireland, to continue filming *Darling Lili* — followed closely by the press. Thirty miles south of Dublin, in the palatial expanses of Carton House, Blake and Julie threw caution to the wind, living openly together for the first time. 'It seemed dumb not to admit we were in love,' said Blake.

Carton's stunning classical interiors also served as the setting for the film's War Office scenes. Julie found the house and its grounds 'simply glorious, especially for the kids'. Jennifer and Geoffrey Edwards, aged nine and six, were visiting from London. Emma Walton joined them, flying into Dublin by private jet. 'On location, our families kind of moved together as a group,' said Julie.

She had plenty of time to prove that Mary Poppins was no wicked stepmother. Outside the peaceful, wooded grounds of Carton, filming had stalled with a vengeance — for many of the reasons faced in Ireland by David Lean two years later, on *Ryan's Daughter*.

The weather veered from the unpredictable to the atrocious, making Blake dread editing the aerial battle shots. 'For the most part, Ireland's just a bad place to shoot a movie,' he said later. 'I wanted to shoot the aircraft sequences in South Carolina, which can be made to look like German or French countryside, but Paramount stuck to its decision to shoot in Ireland, so off we went'.

On top of this, the local crew members were proving unequal to the technical demands of the enormous aero-drama/musical/romance/spy caper. In the confusion over what type of film Blake was trying to make, there would be another unhappy parallel with David Lean's Irish epic: a small story was drowning in an oceanic budget. There was worse to come.

★   ★   ★

Nowhere, in the high noon of 1968, was Western anarchy more evident than in Paris. The *haut bourgeois* paternalism of President Charles de Gaulle was submerged in a quicksand of student protest, the like of which had not been seen in the City of Light since the end of the Second Empire a century earlier.

In May, following months of conflict with the students, the police shut down the University of Paris. A general strike was called, over a million people marched through the city — and, with spectacular bad timing, Blake arrived to shoot *Darling Lili*. The following month, de Gaulle won a hastily convened general election and the crisis abated, but not soon enough for Blake and his production team, who had moved to Belgium to finish the 'Paris' scenes in Brussels.

There, Blake transformed the ground floor of the Palais de Justice into the Paris Gare du Nord. But Belgian bureaucracy over the use of public buildings slowed everything down. The revised film budget was now edging towards a hideous $20 million.

Further weather problems made Blake's job of matching close-ups of Julie and Rock with long-shot footage from Ireland almost impossible. 'Everything that could have gone wrong, went wrong,' said Julie. Worst of all, the collapse of morale indirectly caused her absence at the London premiere of *Star!* — the point at which the real-life star began to fall, first in lustre, then in grace, out of the Hollywood constellation. 'I almost cried my heart out,' she said. 'All my family are attending the premiere. I had a special dress made in Dublin for the occasion . . . I can't tell you how sad I feel.' But then defensiveness took over: 'It's not my fault. Work must go on.'

Blake and Paramount locked uneasy ranks. 'How could anyone doubt that she wanted to go?' said Blake. 'It would have been good for Paramount and for us too. But it was just impossible.' Micky McCardle, his assistant director, stated, 'Filming here is costing $70,000 a day.'

In August, the *Darling Lili* crew wended their

way back to France to film at Diane de Poitiers' Château d'Anet, where Julie took stock. Despite all the problems — and their apprehension about working together — she was enjoying being directed by 'Blackie'. Yet the nervous, chatty energy evident on her previous film sets was gone. Something harder had taken its place, an attitude her mother might have called bloody-mindedness.

'Fame didn't happen to me overnight,' she told Clive Hirschhorn, in a frank interview for the *Sunday Express*, 'I've been an ambitious girl ever since I was twelve. I've worked bloody hard to get where I am today.' The big challenge for her was now to live as normal a life as possible. But, she added, 'I'm less naïve and much wiser than I was — maybe even a bit cynical.' The one thing that made her react violently was 'the invasion of my private life. I'm on display to the public enough in the cinema.'

Referring to the trip to see her family back in January, she revealed: 'I feel resentful I haven't been around to experience it . . . the whole new swinging London bit.' She had 'got a look at the King's Road. It made me homesick . . . made me feel like a total stranger, which is sad.' But Los Angeles and its people were, she said, 'smashing'. As were most Americans, to whom she paid generous tribute: 'They and not my own people made me a star.'

From the château in the Loire, Blake returned to a now calm Paris. Staying in the Hotel Bristol, he had an uncomfortable meeting with Charles Bluhdorn about the perceived lack of budgetary control. 'There's only one thing that's important,' said the studio owner. 'If this film is a success, you're a hero. If it isn't, you're finished.'

As if to emphasise how long *Darling Lili* was taking, Jennifer and Geoffrey showed up again, this time in their summer holidays. Like a real-life Jane and Michael Banks, they were apt to run amok, leaving their clothes all over the floor and not brushing their teeth. Julie suggested a game of forfeits. In return, Jennifer insisted that her stepmother-to-be stop her liberal use of 'healthy Anglo-Saxon swear words', or write a story.

Inevitably, Julie lost in the first hour, and found herself returning to her childhood pastime of writing. The result became her first children's book, *Mandy*. Dedicated 'To Jenny, because I promised', it is the story of a little orphan girl, with all that the subject suggests. Published in 1970, it sold well, but *Time* summed up the critical reaction: 'Julie Andrews has fondly read *The Secret Garden* and deserves every success as a singer and film-actress.'

The film unit then pitched up at the home of the Duke and Duchess of Windsor, in the Bois de Boulogne. The Duke, who had agreed for a 'very substantial' fee to allow the façade of the house to be used, watched from the roadside. Standing beside him was the Duchess who had cost him the crown of England. And, just as the Duke and the former Wallis Simpson had done many years ago, Julie and Blake decided that personal happiness meant more than a good press.

As Julie later said: 'When we came back to California, it would have been too painful and quite ridiculous to go back to our separate houses, so almost without saying too much about it, we just moved in together and kind of pooled our lives and our children.'

* * *

In late summer, when the unit returned to Paramount to complete shooting, alarmed executives viewed what one of them called '$15 million of film and no picture'. With taxes and post-production costs, the final tally was expected to be in the region of $25 million, making the accountants mutter the dread word 'Cleopatra' under their breath.

There seemed only one reliable element: Julie as Darling Lili — the singer. But even the songs seemed a long way from those of Maria, the goatherd puppeteer. And why Hermes Pan, Fred Astaire's great choreographer of the 1930s, was needed was unclear — until it came to the one number that needed (and got) plenty of attention: Julie's strip-tease.

Suspecting Larrabee of philandering, Lili decides to show him the kind of lady she is, breaking into a full bump'n'grind routine in front of the Allies, discarding her gown, thrusting her hips and letting it all hang out (all under bizarre 1970s disco lighting). In September, Abe Greenberg wrote in the Los Angeles *Citizen News* of his trip to the set: 'Minus her robe the actress was yet clad in flesh-colored bra and briefs . . . No totally in-the-buff scenes involving the super-personality of *Mary Poppins* and *The Sound of Music* were being done that day . . . But the power of suggestion serves well enough . . . '

Meanwhile, filming ran on — and on. Unbelievably, Blake wanted to shoot still more material in Europe. But Paramount had had enough. According to one source close to Robert Evans, Charles Bluhdorn tried, unsuccessfully, to sell a half-interest in *Darling Lili* to the self-styled Vatican banker Michele Sindona.

The studio had other worries: *On a Clear Day You Can See Forever* and *Paint Your Wagon* (both by Alan Jay Lerner) were guzzling credit. One afternoon, Paramount's publicity department, desperate to parade the expenditure, gathered its unusually strong roster of stars for a group photograph, the like of which had not been seen since MGM's silver jubilee of 1949. Joining Rock Hudson were John Wayne (*True Grit*), Barbra Streisand and Yves Montand (*On a Clear Day*) and Lee Marvin, Jean Seberg and Clint Eastwood (*Paint Your Wagon*).

Julie failed to make the line-up. As with the premieres of *Star!* in London and New York, her director had first call. The rest of Hollywood's finest — including Streisand — were all, unbelievably, prompt, and less than happy to wait for her. Robert Evans personally went to ask Blake to move things along; Blake replied he would not hurry for a publicity shot.

'Are you going to furnish chairs while we wait for the queen?' asked 'Duke' Wayne, the oldest member in the group shot — and the only one whose film would yield a profit. His drawing power was confirmed the following year, when *True Grit* won him a not altogether sentimental Oscar for Best Actor. Standing next to him was Maggie Smith, Best Actress for *The Prime of Miss Jean Brodie*, in the role Julie had refused a couple of years earlier.

At long last, *Darling Lili* wound up in November, nicknamed by those with no patience for Blake or his girlfriend 'the $24 million Valentine'. Many journalists treated it as a joke. Abe Greenberg, who finally saw a rough cut of the strip-tease, commented: 'Julie, ol' gal, if you ever decide to give up the cinema arts, I can guarantee you billing as the world's top torso tosser! Wheee! That girl is good . . . '

★　★　★

For the second year running, Julie and Blake escaped to Gstaad for Christmas, in relief. Early box-office returns on *Star!* suggested a flop: just how big, remained to be seen. *Darling Lili* had been exhausting.

On New Year's Day 1969, Julie was declared the top female star for the previous year. But she had slipped two places to third, behind Sidney Poitier and Paul Newman, and, if her press coverage had any bearing on public opinion, it seemed unlikely that she would even be in the top ten in twelve months' time.

The year was barely under way when *Screenland* headlined the 'revelation' that Julie was having a clandestine interracial affair, 'Julie Andrews defends her intimate dates with Sidney Poitier'. The 'evidence' rested on comments falsely attributed to Julie, and a photograph of Poitier bestowing her Academy Award four years earlier. Another picture showed Julie presenting the 1967 Best Picture Oscar to Walter Mirisch (her producer on *Hawaii*) for *In the Heat of the Night* — except that Mirisch was cropped, showing Poitier, the film's star, standing alone with his alleged *inamorata*.

More dangerously, her daughter was now caught in the field of fire. Julie had always been at great pains to shield Emma, even from appearing in joint photographs, so when *Modern Movies* appeared, she was beside herself. The front cover, purporting that Emma had been ill with anxiety over her future stepfather, screamed: 'Julie Andrews; the sentence that almost stopped her marriage! 'I don't want that man for a daddy!''

From her Swiss chalet, Julie took immediate action. On 7 January, her lawyer filed simultaneous libel suits, totalling $6 million against the two magazines, 'for impairment to her professional and personal reputation'. The suits were subsequently settled out of court a year later, by which time Julie had grown immune to the worst diatribes, including the continual shrapnel from Joyce Haber.

At the end of January came even worse, and from a 'respectable' publication. Helen Lawrenson's demolition job in *Esquire* magazine had been compiled over the last year, from meetings in Cap Ferrat during the making of *Star!* and in

Paris, when filming on *Darling Lili* was at its most stressful. Lawrenson had taken umbrage — to put it mildly — at not having the star answerable to her call. The article, 'Sweet Julie', was subtitled 'Sweet, sweet, sweet, sweet, sweet, sweet, sweet, sweet poison for the age's tooth'.

The following six pages contained the most destructive written assault on any star of the decade — one that captured the impotent fury of almost all 'serious' critics that 'Hollywood's prime purveyor of delusory pap' should have proved so unassailable. Lawrenson charged Julie with maintaining 'artificial strictures', then refused to find anything funny in the star's music-hall sense of humour. (An assistant had offered her a box lunch, apologising because it had been left in the sun. 'Nothing like a hot banana — as the actress said to the bishop,' said Julie.)

Everything about the subject was viewed askance: her voice ('lightweight'), her appearance ('as sexy as a petunia'), her acting ('circumscribed') — and yet 'the public will flock to see her in *anything*, a display of undiscriminating devotion that hasn't been equalled in decades'. The clouds had closed in on the star long before the piece appeared, but the writer was obviously leaving nothing to chance.

At the end of their second Swiss holiday, the endless gossip had it that Julie had married Blake over Christmas, was pregnant (presumably by Blake) or had had an abortion. The pregnancy story found its way on to ABC television, but by early February, the *Hollywood*

Reporter declared the wedding rumours to be 'just that — rumours'.

The ever-dependable Radie Harris, also writing in the *Hollywood Reporter*, received a 'sweet note' from Julie for being a lone voice in her defence: 'Julie Andrews is dead! Long live Barbra Streisand! This seems to be the new slogan in Hollywood these days. Without detracting from Barbra's superstar appeal, this hostility towards Julie seems highly unjustified . . . Like most Britishers, she doesn't enjoy sharing her private life with strangers.' Unfortunately, any good this did was quickly undone.

A gala benefit had been planned on Sunday 9 February at the Waldorf-Astoria Hotel, New York, honouring Alan Jay Lerner's first twenty-five years as 'a lyrist' (his term). Promising the onstage reunion of Rex Harrison and Julie, it quickly assumed the proportions of a medium-scale Broadway production. Despite a fierce snowstorm that Sunday, most of the audience managed to fight their way to the Waldorf, having paid highly to hear the original stars of *My Fair Lady* recreate something of their glory. But it was not to be. Rex had flown in from Italy just before the blizzards started, on Friday — around the same time that Julie had telephoned from California and pleaded sickness, both hers and Blake's.

Nothing that Mrs Alan Jay Lerner (the fifth) or their mutual friend André Previn could say would persuade Julie to make the journey. On the night, Rex Harrison sang 'I've Grown Accustomed to Her Face', but the only sign of

Julie was in the famous *My Fair Lady* cartoon by Al Hirschfeld. The following week, Joyce Haber hammered another nail in the coffin: 'Poor Julie will soon run out of excuses, and what will her fans, her public defenders, say then? (I assure you, she has few important defenders in the industry).'

Meanwhile, back in the Paramount editing suite, Blake had the studio boss breathing down the back of his neck. As he recounted on the Biography Channel profile of his life and work, 'I challenged Bob Evans to step outside. I said, 'You have done everything possible that you could do to embarrass me and insult me, and you leave me no alternative but to act like a cave-man. If you're going to hire me, then you hire me — not you telling me what to do.''

What Robert Evans wanted — needed — was to turn *Darling Lili* into that safest of commodities: a Julie Andrews musical road show. More precisely, as Blake would recall in an exclusive 1982 interview for *Playboy* magazine: 'Because we'd spent so much money on those second units, the studio decided to leave in as much of the aerial footage as possible just to show the money that was spent. So stupid! That film was a product of people's taking over a motion-picture company without having any credentials at all. By that, I mean Charlie Bluhdorn's giving directives and Bob Evans, who'd hardly made a movie before, being head of the studio.'

Blake would enjoy his revenge. His weapon was his future wife.

13

OUT IN THE COLD ·

'My husband says he swears by the eleventh Commandment: Thou shalt not give up'

— Julie Andrews Edwards

On 8 May 1969, a little film that Peter Fonda had shot in New Mexico and Louisiana opened at the Cannes Film Festival. Costing $340,000 — less than the costume bill for Julie as Gertrude Lawrence — *Easy Rider* would turn more than $30 million in profit. Meanwhile, at Twentieth Century Fox, Richard Zanuck was still pondering *Star!*

Twenty-seven years earlier, as a lowly editor for RKO, Robert Wise had hastily re-cut Orson Welles' *The Magnificent Ambersons*, after, as he told me, 'the audiences started laughing' at the original. For this, he had faced the wrath of *cinéastes* who, bemoaning a lost masterpiece, would now see the fate of his monumental *Star!* as poetic justice.

In early 1969, Fox had withdrawn *Star!* from road show release and edited it down to two and a half hours. It was reissued at normal prices, as the more titillating *Loves of a Star* — in complete denial of what the public seemed to want from Julie Andrews. The posters even included one of the photographs of Julie astride a motorbike, taken while larking about in Nice — the closest that she would ever get to *Easy Rider*.

Undeterred at the continued audience apathy, Zanuck pulled the prints in for a second time on 1 July 1969, and brought back the editor William Reynolds (who, in 1981, would attempt similar surgery on Michael Cimino's calamitous *Heaven's Gate*) to hack it down further to two hours, under the title *Those Were the Happy Times*. By now, Robert Wise had had enough, removing his director's credit, though not, he told me, without a certain degree of understanding: 'I said, 'I recognise there's a problem there; I know it needs cutting, but I'm so close to it. It needs someone from outside.''

The two-hour version — obliged to carry a public safety warning, 'Formerly entitled *Star!*' — staked its fortunes on exhorting what was left of the family market:

Be Glad they still make films like this!
Julie Andrews sings in *Those Were the Happy Times*

Reissued in October 1969, it failed once again.

On 6 January 1970, at his estate in San Clemente, California, President Richard Nixon faced a new decade with a private screening of the mutant musical. But if so-called Tricky Dicky enjoyed *Those Were the Happy Times*, it was hardly the message that Fox needed to attract the audience that all polls now showed as ruling supreme: the eighteen-to twenty-five-year-olds.

The titanic misfortune of *Doctor Dolittle* adding to its woes, the studio was heading into such dire straits that Richard Zanuck would be ousted as president by the end of the following year. '*The Sound of Music* was the worst thing that could have happened to us or the industry,' he said, shortly before packing his bags. 'We tried to copy it, to make big musical smashes, and we all made costly flops.'

★ ★ ★

Gold fever might have abated at Twentieth Century Fox, but other sections of Hollywood were still under quarantine. For every vibrant *Oliver!* (which was anyway made in England) there was a moribund *Sweet Charity*, which not even an established star like Shirley Maclaine and an inventive director like Bob Fosse could resuscitate.

Even with *Oliver!*, the outcome — and the cast — could have been very different. Back on Sunday 29 May 1966, Albert 'Cubby' Broccoli (producer of the James Bond franchise) had sat in the Beverly Hills Hotel, waiting to meet English producer James Woolf, who owned the screen rights to the musical. Among his ideas to play the leading roles were Laurence Harvey as Fagin and Julie Andrews as Nancy. Woolf, however, had failed to appear; in fact, he had died in his bed (coincidentally, on the same day that Ted Andrews succumbed to a stroke back in England). His casting suggestions died with him.

From mid-1967, there had been reports that

Julie's name was about to enter the *Hello, Dolly!* stakes (joining that of Elizabeth Taylor) but, in reality, she was never a serious contender. The unhappy precedent of *My Fair Lady* was, however, repeated when Carol Channing lost the chance to recreate her stage triumph to Barbra Streisand, who was fast overtaking Julie in both critical and popular estimation.

Meanwhile, the Disney Studio had been second-guessing Uncle Walt's unfinished plans ever since his sudden death, at sixty-five, in December 1966. There had long been mention of a *Mary Poppins* sequel but Julie's attitude was always the one she expressed when I first saw her: 'My instincts are, I would walk away from it very fast . . . because I don't see how you could repeat such a joyous, lovely thing, and if it failed, it would be such an awful follow-up.'

Nonetheless, Julie had been offered a chance to reunite with the *Mary Poppins* team — albeit for Cubby Broccoli, not Disney — on *Chitty Chitty Bang Bang*, adapted from the children's book by Ian Fleming, creator of James Bond. Disney cohorts transferring for duty included Dick Van Dyke and the songwriting Sherman brothers. It was only natural that Julie should have been asked to play the heroine Truly Scrumptious — and just as obvious that the name of the part alone disqualified it from her career plan.

More than one other former Eliza Doolittle was alerted to take Julie's place. Anne Rogers was reported as 'one of the principal contenders'. But it was Julie's Broadway successor as

Eliza, Sally Ann Howes, who eventually played the role.

When *Chitty Chitty Bang Bang* finally opened in December of 1968, it did reasonably good business, particularly in Britain, and over the years developed its own legend. A year earlier, however, another children's fantasy, *Doctor Dolittle*, had had a wretched Christmas opening. Its producer, Arthur P. Jacobs, was now preparing a musical remake of *Goodbye, Mr Chips* for MGM. His dream to pair Rex Harrison with Julie Andrews on screen fell apart at Harrison's lack of interest and Julie's apparent wage demands, which led one studio wag to remark, 'We'd have to change the title to *Hello, Mrs Chips*.'

Metro-Goldwyn-Mayer had other plans for Julie. Fredric Molnar's play *The Shop Around the Corner* had first been served up on screen in 1939, then reheated for Judy Garland as *In the Good Old Summertime* ten years later. Recycled as a Broadway musical under the title *She Loves Me*, it had achieved qualified success on Broadway in 1963, starring Barbara Cook, and in London the following year — produced by Tony Walton and starring Anne Rogers. MGM now transferred Julie and Blake to its screen transcription, in place of *Say It With Music*, the Irving Berlin extravaganza which had come to naught.

* * *

If proof were needed that the Hollywood Dream Factory was now Nightmare Alley, it came on 9

August 1969. In Bel Air, at the former home of Doris Day's record producer son Terry Melcher, the pregnant young actress Sharon Tate was murdered, a victim of the bloodbath initiated by Charles Manson for grievances against Melcher.

To the audience that had made Julie a star, the face of modern Hollywood was now symbolic of a more violent age, best avoided by staying at home in front of the television set. Stanley Kubrick's 2001: *A Space Odyssey* was a continuing cinema hit with younger audiences — but the small screen trumped even that, for free. On 20 July, three weeks before the Bel Air massacre, America had allowed itself a moment of glory, watching television footage of Neil Armstrong and Buzz Aldrin landing on the moon.

A remnant of confidence exuded from President Nixon on 3 November, when he addressed his fellow Americans on television, defending his decision to keep US forces in Vietnam and appealing to what he termed 'the silent majority' who did not join in the large demonstrations against the war, did not engage in riots, did not embrace the counterculture. Unfortunately, nor did they queue at the cinema box office.

On television, Julie could still find favour, although it remained her least favourite medium — 'rushed and different', she called it. She recorded her new one-hour television special, co-starring Harry Belafonte, with the superlative team of Gower Champion as director and Michel Legrand in charge of the music. Material

364

came from contemporary sources, such as 'Scarborough Fair' from *The Graduate* (sung almost romantically with Belafonte), but also included a finale of Julie's standards from *My Fair Lady* and *Mary Poppins*. She had agreed to perform these after seeing Lena Horne singing 'Stormy Weather' on television, and realising that she could not easily cheat the public of what they obviously most wanted to hear her sing.

An Evening with Julie Andrews and Harry Belafonte, transmitted on 9 November 1969, was well received by press and public — despite the still sensitive issue of a mixed-race pairing of attractive young performers. Only the year before, Petula Clark's own television special with Belafonte had been plagued by controversy, when she had merely touched his arm. Belafonte found the show with Julie to be less contentious: 'There was no network censorship and Gower never pulled back because of colour. We cavort around the stage holding hands, dance and sing cheek to cheek — it could have been Frank Sinatra or Robert Goulet instead of me, or Lena Horne instead of her.'

A week later, Julie was upstaged by Blake Edwards' ten-year-old daughter Jennifer, who made an even bigger impact on NBC — for reasons beyond her control. In the title role of the Swiss children's story *Heidi*, blonde-haired Jenny proved just as able to act her way up an Alp as Maria von Trapp. Unfortunately, she did so at the expense of a football game between the Oakland Raiders and the New York Jets — which was cut off before the final whistle, to let *Heidi* begin. The uproar over what was dubbed 'the *Heidi* Bowl' led to subsequent over-running football games being shown in their entirety.

For a while Jennifer became what she called 'the most hated little girl in America'. The press gave her the same scrutiny as was currently being meted out to her father's lover — who, three days after her own broadcast, was to become Mrs Blake Edwards.

★ ★ ★

On Julie's second wedding day, the absence of any Andrews family members highlighted just how far apart they had drifted from her recently — none more so than her half-brother Christopher, who had been living under her roof for almost three years. Midway through 1969, the twenty-two-year-old moved out. His photography course at Los Angeles Art Center was ending, and he had started to forge his own identity away from Julie's world. Her contemporaries were a decade older than him, his prospective brother-in-law double his age.

At college, Chris had found himself becoming an honorary member of a generation of young Americans who were challenging and exploding the very values his sister's films, even the non-musical ones, seemed to perpetuate. Among his group was Ron Raffaelli, later known for his photographs of rock musicians such as Jimi Hendrix. Writing of his student days, he remembered: 'On a number of occasions I was with Chris when someone introduced him as Julie Andrews' brother, not mentioning his given name at all. I always felt that had diminished him as an individual. Chris had his own unique talent and personality that were completely ignored when someone introduced him as a sibling of a famous personality.'

Julie's other siblings, pillars of rectitude, had almost entirely escaped such pressures. John Wells, the younger brother from whom she had been so abruptly parted in childhood, had recently married. A jet pilot in the Royal Air Force, stationed in Nigeria, he had seen Julie only a handful of times in the last decade, but she thought of him with nothing but fondness: 'John is dark and handsome, droll and funny . . . Years pass, yet when we see each other, it seems as though we were together only yesterday.'

Celia Wells, Ted's younger daughter by his second wife Win, shared her father's love of nature and her sister's love of riding. Now twenty-four, she had married radar expert John Mackey, who worked at the daunting Fylingdales Early Warning System on the North Yorkshire Moors, responsible for alerting Britain to impending nuclear attack.

Donald Andrews, like his half-brother John, had worked abroad as a pilot, in Rhodesia. Now, at the age of twenty-seven, he was a British bobby, pounding the beat around his home town in Walton-on-Thames, where his mother still lived.

In her widowhood, Barbara Andrews had

taken stock of The Old Meuse, where she had lived for almost a quarter of a century, and which held, on balance, many more happy memories than sad. The rambling house with its leaded bay windows and tall chimneys stood on too valuable a stretch of land to justify its presence, in the less conservationist days of the late 1960s. A decision had already been made to demolish it and build a development of flats and houses in its grounds. Barbara would shortly move to a detached house, plaintively named Little Meuse, in what had been the rhododendron-fringed copse — where, before the great tall trees came crashing down, it was still possible to remember Julie and Donald playing with their baby brother Chris.

And it was Chris for whom Julie had always felt most responsibility — acting as unofficial nanny, paying his school fees and now seeing him through college. But Julie was now about to enter an entirely new phase of her life. As she started to look for a new home, in which Blake and she could raise their children together, it seemed an appropriate time to clear her life of those who had taken her largesse for granted for perhaps too long.

Contact between brother and sister was less close than it had been. Chris was enjoying the hedonistic lifestyle of late 1960s Los Angeles, in a manner far removed from how Julie chose to conduct herself. In the month of her wedding to Blake Edwards, she cut off Chris's $500 monthly allowance. But it would not be the end of the story.

★ ★ ★

At eight o'clock on the morning of Wednesday 12 November 1969, Blake and Julie were on the road, driving south to Orange County, avoiding any possibility of attracting the Los Angeles press. The previous day, their statutory State blood tests had been carried out by their family doctor Herb Tanney in Los Angeles, but only Blake's secretary and Julie's cook and staff knew of the ceremony planned for the following afternoon. Nobody else had been told, not even the children, who were all at school. 'Otherwise, they'll all want to take the day off,' said Blake.

The wedding was to be held privately at Julie's Hidden Valley home, attended only by Ken Wales (Blake's production associate and best man), his wife Karen (Julie's matron of honour) and Dr Tanney. In the biggest possible contrast with the Sunday afternoon in May, ten years earlier in Surrey, there was no press and no family.

Blake had once said Julie would be late for her own wedding, and so it proved. On the way back from Orange County, the girl who had once been so fond of boiled potato sandwiches wanted to stop to eat a doughnut. At a quarter to one, the intended couple finally appeared, leaving Julie fifteen minutes to change into a white and coral short-sleeved outfit. While she was doing so, Blake (unusually formal in a double-breasted suit) set up a camera to film the service for Jennifer, Geoffrey and Emma to watch later. Just after one o'clock, in the glorious Californian sunshine, Blake Edwards and Julie Andrews were

369

married by the splashing waterfall, Julie's favourite place in the garden. Despite the low-key atmosphere, the bride's cheeks were flushed, betraying her emotion.

After the ceremony, Blake asked to see a replay of the service. Nothing came up on the screen. Dr Tanney had accidentally disconnected the cable. Blake turned to his wife. 'How about another take, darling?' he said.

'Of course, Blackie,' said Julie, anxious as ever to do her job properly.

'Looks like we're going over schedule on this one as well.' remarked Blake, dryly.

That afternoon, he and Julie watched the rough cut of their $24 million opus *Darling Lili*. As they sat in the private screening room at Paramount, word of their nuptials was already circulating around Hollywood, started by a diligent Orange County reporter. By eleven o'clock that night, the headline was official: 'Actress Julie Andrews married film director Blake Edwards this afternoon.'

The marriage was founded, Julie later stated, on two mutual points of agreement: 'We would not set any goals, and we would just literally take it a day at a time.'

'And work together whenever possible,' added Blake.

For the moment, this seemed viable. Mr and Mrs Edwards had emerged from their first viewing of *Darling Lili* far from dispirited. How much of this was surprise that anything of value should have been extricated from the morass was unclear — but Paramount's plans for yet another

Julie Andrews road show release were kept in place.

Over in Culver City, however, Metro-Goldwyn-Mayer had appointed a new president on 21 October 1969. James T. Aubrey was one of the CBS executives who had sanctioned *Julie and Carol at Carnegie Hall* in 1962 — but that was now a long time ago. The man called 'The Smiling Cobra' had no intention of letting the film star dubbed 'The Iron Butterfly' do to MGM what some said she had done to Twentieth Century Fox — and what her husband was rumoured to be doing to Paramount.

The new reality of Hollywood was spelt out in *Time* magazine on 9 February 1970:

The nub of the problem is that TV is not going away and people are not going to the movies. Since the 1940s, the population has increased 30%; admission prices have doubled since 1959. Yet last year the box-office gross was 24% less than in 1946 . . .

Though his $20 million *Hello, Dolly!* may nose into the black eventually, Fox Board Chairman Darryl F. Zanuck confesses that he would be some kind of nut to launch such an extravagant film today . . . The *Easy Rider* belt is tightening around the necks of prima donna producers and directors with a record of bringing pictures in late and over budget. Blake Edwards, whose *The Great Race* came in at 100% over, and his wife

Julie Andrews, no longer sure fire box office since *Star!*, are reportedly being paid a $1 million settlement by MGM not to shoot their previously committed film, *She Loves Me*.

James Aubrey had cut his losses. The Queen of Hollywood was paid to get off the lot.

If the decade had not dawned rudely enough, on the day after the *Time* analysis, Julie's new yacht ran aground off the coast of the Bahamas. The crew and passengers of *Impulse*, a $500,000, eighty-seven-foot vessel chartered through Geoffrey Productions (Blake's company for *Darling Lili*), were evacuated by what the press described as 'a huge Air Force helicopter'. As an analogy for Julie's career, it took some beating.

★   ★   ★

In the run-up to the summer release of *Darling Lili*, Paramount was in no mood to chop out the very commodity that might enable it to recoup its huge investment. The picture was to be sold, whatever Blake's opinion, as a Julie Andrews songfest. A week before its New York world premiere, *Time* magazine wrote: 'The role seems precisely tailored for Dietrich. Instead it will be played by Mary Poppins. Julie Andrews has in fact gone the English dance-hall route before — and flopped miserably — in one of Hollywood's most expensive bombs, a multimillion-dollar loser called *Star!* On looks, anyway, *Darling*

Lili figures to do better.'

'Everyone loves *Darling Lili*: so will you — you and your family!' promised the posters. 'She sizzles, she dances, she spies.' Thus, on Wednesday 24 June 1970, *Darling Lili* opened at Radio City Music Hall. The reviews were mixed: some critics were happy to be treated to an old-fashioned romantic comedy — others were sad not to get it.

Vincent Canby for the *New York Times* had a foot in both camps:

> It is big, long, overproduced, but it has a lot of perverse charm and real cinematic beauty ... Although Miss Andrews has always struck me as a very mitigated delight ... her angular, aggressive profile, combined with her coolness and precision as a comedienne and a singer, give the immediate, comic lie to the adventures of a supposedly irresistible *femme fatale* ... When you take the clothes off a Girl Guide, you've got a very naked Girl Guide.

If the package had been pitched to Julie as an opportunity to strip (for the first time), say 'bastard' (again) or take a shower with hunky Rock Hudson (knocking her image but perpetuating his), she had seized her chance — but the film straddled at least four different genres: spy caper, romance, aero-drama and period piece. That it should contain elegiac passages was not surprising. It was both far too much, and not enough. A curious metropolitan public, admiring the aerial displays and willing to give Julie one more chance after *Star!*, helped *Darling Lili* to break the house record for its first weeks at Radio City. For a month or so, it looked as if Paramount had yanked success from the jaws of disaster. But, on general release, the public stayed away in droves.

In London, John Russell Taylor in *The Times*, having expected 'Thoroughly Modern Mata-Hari', was dismayed to find 'the most upsetting sort of misfire — the sort which could so easily have been put right with a little more thought (or a little less worry), a little more confidence in hitting the right tone and sticking to it'. Julie remained philosophical, as she told me twenty-five years later: 'The truth is, if you survive in any way in this business, you're going to see enormous roller-coaster ups and downs. I remember Mike Nichols said to me, after he'd gotten bad notices for *Catch-22*, that it was almost a relief to start at the bottom again; it's so wobbly up there, you're trying to please everybody and you get too careful and it's an insanity.'

Ironically, *Catch-22*, adapted from Joseph Heller's seminal novel, had opened in New York on the very same day as *Darling Lili*. With a huge cast, extravagant budget and lavish aerial footage, its fate was identical. It sank like a stone, demystifying its *Wunderkind* director Nichols. Not that this made Blake feel better. 'I felt very responsible,' he said later, of his wife's second consecutive unpopular film.

Vincent Canby had signed off his review with

some pertinence: 'I doubt that Hollywood, now practically broke and trying desperately to make a connection with the youth market, will ever again indulge itself in this sort of splendidly extravagant, quite frivolous enterprise.' The shortfall between expenditure and revenue on *Darling Lili* only continued to yawn throughout 1970, leading to a loss for Paramount Pictures of more than $18 million. This time, there was no hedging of bets. Julie Andrews was now officially box-office poison — a liability with whom few could afford any association. 'There's an unwritten law in Hollywood that says, once you're on a pedestal, let's throw some rocks and knock her off it,' said Julie, as if anybody needed telling.

But the star was not alone. Alan Jay Lerner's screen versions of *Paint Your Wagon* and *On a Clear Day You Can See Forever* added to Paramount's horrors, proving, respectively, that a lyricist had no business producing films of his own work, and that Hollywood's new diva, Barbra Streisand, was as ill-equipped as Julie to extend the goodwill of the public towards the musical form. Twenty-eight-year-old Michael Campus, a Young Turk from CBS television, said, 'Young people are saying that it's a crime to spend $20 million on *Paint Your Wagon*. That amount could remake a city.' Even at MGM, the spiritual home of the Hollywood musical, the genre was dead. *Goodbye, Mr Chips*, now starring Peter O'Toole and none other than Julie's childhood contemporary Petula Clark, had opened — and closed.

One last song and dance title remained on the studio slate — perversely, the property that had escalated Julie to stardom in the first place. *The Boy Friend*, which MGM had resolutely refused to sell to Ross Hunter, was now scheduled to be directed by Ken Russell, for whom the words *enfant terrible* could have been trademarked. Even more perversely, the designer was Tony Walton. But his difficulty in having to face the spectre of Julie was lessened by Russell's concept for the whole film, to be shot in England, starring the super-model of the day, Twiggy.

Set as a show-within-a-show, the film depicted a down-at-heel 1930s theatre company, touring a 1920s musical called *The Boy Friend*. The musical is seen, one desultory matinee, by a Hollywood director — in whose eye the tacky dances become phenomenal routines. It had nothing to do with *The Boy Friend* and everything to do with Ken Russell. Its author Sandy Wilson sneaked into a midnight preview. 'Twiggy was the only sort of human being in it,' he told me. 'It wasn't painful. It was just astonishing.'

While *The Boy Friend* was filming, Julie was given her biggest temptation yet to return whence she came. Disney Studios wanted her for another Sherman brothers musical based on a British children's book: *Bedknobs and Broomsticks*. Julie was asked to play the benevolent witch, Eglantine Price, whose hocus-pocus in wartime England transports the evacuated children in her care to the bottom of the animated 'Beautiful Briny Sea', echoing 'Jolly

Holiday' from *Mary Poppins*.

The similarities did not stop there. Julie would be reunited with the same director, Robert Stevenson, and Mr George Banks himself, David Tomlinson — along with Bruce Forsyth, her father from *Star!*. The whole package was rather too neat for the woman who so badly wanted to leave all this behind. But the team was persuasive and, although Uncle Walt was no longer around, Julie was assured of a warm return to the studio that had made her a global star.

She hesitated a moment too long. By the time she had wrestled with her ambivalence, producer Bill Walsh had called on Angela Lansbury, and Eglantine Price was cast.

At MGM, even though Julie had been paid off, James Aubrey still had a commitment to work with Blake. There was a script kicking around the studio, in which nobody had much interest, a Western called *Wild Rovers*. With Paramount's accountants sticking pins into his likeness, Blake knew it was the best offer he was going to get.

Starring two genuinely important names, William Holden and Ryan O'Neal, it looked promising, the plot summarised by the eventual tagline on the poster: 'They were damned good cowboys, until they robbed a bank.' But, shooting in Utah and Arizona, the director was incensed to hear that Aubrey was personally cutting the film back in Hollywood.

Blake had an enormous, widely reported tantrum (*Time* magazine referred to his 'career-long addiction to anger'), telling the *New York Times*: 'Cuts? He doesn't know as much as a first-year cinema student.' Later, he lamented that Aubrey 'personally destroyed *Wild Rovers*, cutting out forty minutes and changing the ending and a lot of the relationships. Then he suckered me into directing another film for him, *The Carey Treatment*, by Michael Crichton. I said I'd do it only if I could make certain changes, and Aubrey agreed. Then he simply reneged. I found out Aubrey was cutting the movie even before I finished shooting it.'

Where the outside world was concerned, only one thing mattered. Both films were flops. Both Mr and Mrs Edwards were now unemployable.

* * *

Less than a month after her wedding, Julie's lingering worries about stalkers (and worse) were realised. On 1 December 1969, she called for police protection, claiming that she was 'being hounded' at Hidden Valley Road by a strange man in his mid-forties, just over six foot tall and two hundred pounds in weight. 'Police Guard at home of movie star,' ran the *Hollywood Citizen* headline on 9 December. 'She had been twice visited,' said the police, 'by a big man who drove up to the house in a taxi.'

The stranger, who had appeared the previous Wednesday and returned on Saturday, was sandy haired and wore a dark suit, dark hat and horn-rimmed glasses. Edwards answered the door, told him he could not see Julie and asked him to leave, warning: 'You'd better not come back.' The man replied, 'You'd better not be here when I come back.'

The police established no link with the Sharon Tate case, but it was nonetheless something of a relief for Julie to leave Coldwater Canyon for an elegant mansion in Beverly Hills — her first home as Blake's wife. At the front of 813 Greenway Drive was a large circular courtyard, leading to a formal rose garden, swimming pool and terrace, beyond which was the vista of the Los Angeles Country Club. The couple also acquired a beach house at Paradise Cove, 27944 Pacific Coast Highway, Malibu. An hour's drive from Beverly Hills, the property sat on a cliff, surrounded by orange and eucalyptus trees, overlooking the ocean.

If Julie had become a Californian housewife, Blake was learning to moderate his own lifestyle. Their preferred way of spending the evening now, 'with a few select friends' over dinner, was close to that of the stockbroker belt in Walton-on-Thames. As far as their children were concerned, Blake had established a bond with Emma, and Julie was learning to be a diplomat with the first Mrs Edwards in matters concerning Jennifer and Geoffrey's visits. 'It is not an easy thing,' she said carefully. 'Blake and I are doing our very best to make this family arrangement less difficult for everyone. But we must work at it. Naturally, there are flare-ups and misunderstandings . . .'

She also coped with the children's menagerie, including Duffy (a Scottie), Moose (a spaniel) and Beatle (an enormous Great Dane), as well as two cats, a hamster and Niven the canary, named after David of that ilk, who lived in a cage by the kitchen telephone.

There was one other inhabitant. Tony Adams, a young Irishman who had been co-opted by Blake as a production assistant, had come to stay with them in Los Angeles, attending a film course at Pepperdine University. He would never really leave them — becoming, said Julie later, 'our second son'.

Things were not going so well for another young man. It was a nasty shock for Julie — and the cause of great worry to Barbara Andrews — that, on Tuesday 25 May 1971, having just turned twenty-five, Christopher Stuart Andrews was arrested with his new wife Sherry Lynne in Laguna Beach, Orange County, when hashish and heroin were discovered in their car.

The couple were living in West Los Angeles on welfare assistance at the time. Their daughter Julie Lynne was only three months old. Chris, unable to post bail of $2,500, was thrown in jail, where he languished for almost two months pending court action. His half-sister refused to put up the money; the probation officer was later reported as saying, 'Miss Andrews did not want anything more to do with her brother.'

On 15 July, Chris and Sherry Lynne appeared in court at Santa Ana, pleading guilty to possessing dangerous drugs. The Superior Court judge gave Chris a choice: going to jail for a year, or returning to his mother's home in London with sentence suspended. Chris chose to leave

America immediately, but press reports stated he had to remain in a cell until his wife disposed of their home. Julie now agreed to pay the air fares for her brother and sister-in-law to travel to England, where Barbara Andrews would vouch for them at Little Meuse.

'Julie Andrews' kin deported for drugs' ran an article in the *Los Angeles Herald Examiner* the following day. The star's concern, as so often, was for her mother.

Back in Surrey, Tancred Agius, who had grown up near The Old Meuse, was now living further up the Thames at Shepperton, where he visited a local pub: 'And who was playing the piano? Barbara Andrews. A terrible fall from grace. I thought, my God, that's Julie Andrews' mother . . . nobody else knew who she was. I think she was playing more for alcohol than for money.'

But Julie had only compassion for Barbara: 'I've never lost the closeness I had to my mother,' she would say. 'There's usually a reason for people being the way they are.' In later years, she would remain adamant in her defence: 'I am not going to criticise my mother. She was far more alive and vivacious than I will ever be.' And she would always see Barbara's life in perspective. 'She had a lot on her plate. She had some guilt. She was an extremely creative lady and I think she wasn't meant to be a housewife.'

Mrs Edwards, on the other hand, was content in the role. As one journalist described it, 'a family for Julie is the most desirable of all possible groups'. In the eighteen months since finishing *Darling Lili*, the workaholic star had been idle professionally, except for her NBC television special. 'When you have three children around, each with their own dog, and a husband who does most of his pre-production work at home, well, there's plenty to do.' Julie laughed, then admitted: 'I would have been very restless if I had known there was to be no end to this leisure: I have worked hard all my life. I am a working woman.'

And, in the world of Disney at least, still a star. On Friday 29 October 1971, she led the NBC broadcast of the opening of Walt Disney World in Orlando, Florida. Glen Campbell, Buddy Hackett and Bob Hope were featured, but it was Julie who dominated proceedings, singing 'When You Wish Upon a Star' and 'Zip-A-Dee-Doo-Dah', accompanied by one thousand instrumentalists. Finally, she joined a huge choir of children in 'It's a Small World', written by the ubiquitous Sherman brothers. It was just what the public wanted.

On 7 December, Julie further retraced past glories, in *Julie and Carol at Lincoln Center*. The CBS show had been taped earlier that year on 1 July, without retakes, before a New York audience. Carol Burnett's husband Joe Hamilton again produced, and Ken Welch, who had helped Mike Nichols script the first show at Carnegie Hall, provided much of the dialogue. The songs echoed the earlier triumph. 'Our Classy Classical Show' kicked things off in the manner of 'There'll Be No Mozart Tonight', and the finale brought back memories of 'Big D' as the two girls cavorted in bright yellow mackintoshes and sou'westers to 'Wait Till the Sun Shines, Nellie'.

The audience enjoyed it, and so, just about, did the press. An article in the *Los Angeles Times* was headed, 'Another romp for Julie, Carol. Can lightning strike twice?' The answer was 'almost':

> Never mind, though, since the bolt misses by about two inches and the results are appropriately devastating. What caused the lightning to go two inches off its mark, I think, is that Carol and Julie have grown up, lost some of that joyful, uninhibited quality they once had. But then so has television and so have we all.

The show's purpose, however, had been served. There still seemed to be a public out there for Julie, a fact not lost on the nearest thing Britain ever had to Louis B. Mayer or Jack L. Warner — the cigar-chomping commercial television tycoon Sir Lew Grade.

The chief supplier of popular British fare (from Tom Jones to *The Saint*) for American television, Sir Lew had first met Julie when she was six and he was a variety agent in partnership with Joe Collins, father of Joan and Jackie. 'I had to wait until she was fourteen before I could sign her,' he said, 'and in that time somebody else stepped in.' But now he was about to outdo Uncle Charles Tucker.

He contacted her current agent, Arthur Park, and flew to Los Angeles to work his awesome powers of persuasion. 'Everybody had tried to get her for TV without success,' he recalled. 'I kept persevering, promised her the best of everything and don't worry about the budget. It was a challenge, I said. She bent a little.'

The deal by which Grade finally persuaded Julie to drop her antipathy was to make twenty-four episodes of a variety television show, with the option to extend to five years, for a reported fee of $2 million for the first two years alone. As added bait, he also guaranteed a feature film to be shot in Europe for each year of the series, to be directed by Blake. And this was where Julie Andrews, who had never really accepted that her cinema career was over, responded. 'It's the biggest deal of my TV career,' Sir Lew declared. 'It's taken me three years to pull it off.'

In America, the series was to be broadcast by ABC. The producer Nick Vanoff, a former dancer at the Hollywood Palace, was charged with delivering each week 'what would take three months on film' — with a rumoured budget of $240,000 an episode.

'When I was doing the show, Blake and I swapped roles completely,' Julie remembered of the schedule. Each morning, she was picked up by helicopter and flown to the ABC studios on the outskirts of Hollywood — leaving her husband at home with the children. 'For the first two months, I felt relieved that he was taking care of everything, but then I began feeling left out. He had to cook on the servants' day off. Blackie cooks like a dream — the best I can manage is scrambled eggs and a pot of tea.' The fact remained that there was nothing else for Blake to do.

Thursday and Friday were the recording days. Before each show, Julie's doctor gave her a vitamin shot, and the taping went on through the early hours. By three in the morning, it would generally be over — and Julie would start to think about the next episode. 'TV has always scared me,' she told reporters, 'but I had not worked for two years. If I waited any longer I would be too old and tired — I certainly couldn't have the energy I have now.'

The Julie Andrews Hour aired on 13 September 1972. It was nostalgic from the outset, the first episode featuring numbers from *The Boy Friend* and *Camelot*. Now that both film versions had been released to less than stellar business, Julie could be said to have reclaimed the material for herself — but reprising 'Burlington Bertie From Bow' from *Star!* seemed an odd reminder of her own box-office mortality.

Comedy was supplied by Alice Ghostley, her stepsister in the 1957 CBS telecast of *Cinderella*, as her sidekick throughout the series. In an effort to pre-empt hostility towards Julie's sugary reputation, Miss Ghostley turned to the audience after one song and quipped, 'Isn't she perfect? Don't you hate her?' It was tempting fate.

Carl Reiner, creator of *The Dick Van Dyke Show*, headed her line-up of guest stars on the second show, which also featured Cass Elliot from the Mamas and the Papas. Julie joined her in 'Dream a Little Dream of Me' and 'Make Your Own Kind of Music (even if nobody else sings along)' — a rather poignant lyric for Miss Andrews at that moment.

'I came not prepared to like her,' admitted Mama Cass. 'One night it got to be four o'clock in the morning and the actors were ready to kill each other; Julie was putting out on every take as if it were the last one she'd ever make. I dunno, but there is something very special there, which you grow to love. If she could just free it up a little, I mean — groovy!' Being groovy, of course, ignored the point of Julie Andrews in the first place.

The third week Julie performed a compendium of love songs in three-part harmony with Jack Cassidy and Ken Berry. From then on, there were a series of reasonably big household favourites on the show, no more than two a week, including Sammy Davis Jr, Robert Goulet, Angela Lansbury, Steve Lawrence, Peggy Lee, Henry Mancini — and the real Maria von Trapp.

But ABC had clearly made a tactical error in programming the show for ten o'clock Eastern Time on a Wednesday night, too late to capitalise on the middle-market family audience. The first results from the Nielsen survey were ominous proof of a further disappointment for America's former golden girl, with a low 17.3 rating. 'A slow starter', was ABC's cautious explanation, but the following week, the rating slipped catastrophically by a third. It recovered — but not by enough.

Producer Nick Vanoff blamed the late slot,

adding 'Julie's fans are all asleep.' The star put a characteristically brave face on things. 'The jury's still out,' she said. 'I think people want to see something joyous and pleasant and filled with emotion.'

Two months in, the show was shifted to an hour earlier on a Saturday night, to 'maximise her audience potential', something that should have been obvious all along. And, if hard work alone could have guaranteed success, the series would have been a winner all the way. Julie continued to work for up to eighteen hours a day, with unflagging good spirits against the dispiriting forecast. 'Endurance is absent among many performers today,' she stated. 'I think it's an attribute we should all strive to attain.' Despite this commendable zeal, the last episode was broadcast on 28 April 1973.

'It was the most ambitious show — musically — on television,' said Nelson Riddle, whose presence as conductor and music arranger was indicative of its quality. 'I'm not saying it was the best show, but they spent a lot of time, a lot of money. I think it's laudable.'

The Julie Andrews Hour was awarded the Silver Rose at the International Television Festival in Montreux. And on 20 May, the show won five Emmy Awards, for Art Direction, Costume Design, Lighting and Technical Direction — and as Outstanding Variety Musical Series of 1973. Julie Andrews had made a spectacular return to the awards roster with her first Emmy, as star of the show.

In an interview to *McCall's* magazine earlier

in the year, Julie had been waiting to hear if the series had made it to its next twenty-four episodes. 'Of all the people who will know, they tell me I'll be first,' she said, with a degree of scepticism. 'Which, it seems to me, would only be good manners.' In reality, by the time of the awards, the decision to axe *The Julie Andrews Hour* had already been taken. 'That hurt for a long time,' admitted its star. 'I found out we'd been cancelled at the same time the general public did. There was no personal message, no politeness about it.' But that was show business. 'It was a very good series,' she considered later, 'with a lot of content, and someone wrote that, because it was me, people felt they had to put a suit and tie on to watch.'

More bluntly, she recalled facing the writers of the series, who shared something of the same sentiment: 'It seemed I was still coming across a bit icy and a bit too polite. The writers told me they wanted to show people how I really am, so I thought about it for a second and said, 'Well, I could ball the band.' And there was this awful silence. Nobody thought that was funny at all — and I got so depressed about it, because if they didn't get it, then sure as hell my show was absolutely doomed. Which turned out to be the case.'

Back at home, her husband had had 'enough of women's lib'. And so, perhaps, had Julie. 'I'd come home,' she said, 'and he'd start to tell me something that had happened, and I'd grab my head and say, 'Please, darling, I've had such a day . . . '' She had invested endless time and energy in the series — to the exclusion of her newly established family life — even writing the theme song, the melodious 'Time Is My Friend', with English composer-lyricist Leslie Bricusse. So when it all ended, despite Lew Grade's commitment to make two feature films with her (whatever their commercial worth) there was an emptiness for the first time in many a year in her life.

The previous year, Julie had mused on the possibility of 'a modest home in Switzerland, to enjoy winter sports and for a change of scenery — but that's the extent of it'. Now, there seemed less and less reason to stay in her adopted country. In London, a small notice appeared in *The Times* on Thursday 7 June:

Spring Fever: Miss Julie Andrews, the entertainer who has been living in America for the past ten years, said yesterday that she is returning with her family to live in Britain, chiefly because she missed the English spring.

A decade after she had flown to Hollywood to begin rehearsals for *Mary Poppins*, Julie Andrews was travelling back in the opposite direction.

14

SINGING FOR HER SUPPER

'If you sit by the river long enough, you will see the body of your enemy float by'

— Japanese proverb, quoted to Blake Edwards by William Holden

When Julie Andrews arrived back in the land of her birth, it was hardly to the sound of trumpets. If she and Blake Edwards had expected to find more generosity of spirit than they had left behind in Hollywood, they needed only to have read the reaction of *The Times* to the first episode of *The Julie Andrews Hour*. 'The inference we were invited to draw,' wrote the television critic, 'was that Miss Andrews is to show business as Mr Hoover was to the vacuum cleaner, Mr Birdseye to the frozen pea, and Mr Kellogg to the cornflake . . . The mind keeps returning to those twenty-three weeks ahead — not so much a spoonful of sugar, more like a couple of hundredweight.'

Nowhere, it seemed, could Julie escape the legacy of her early film roles — or the musical madness they had engendered, from which only Bob Fosse and Liza Minnelli had emerged with credit, with their Oscar-winning 1972 master-piece *Cabaret*. Two offers with which Julie had left Hollywood encapsulated the barrel-scrapings of the genre.

The first came from Ross Hunter, her producer on *Thoroughly Modern Millie*, who was preparing to remake the 1937 classic *Lost Horizon* with a Burt Bacharach score. Julie passed. The role of the singing schoolteacher who crash-lands into Shangri-La was finally crash-landed on to Liv Ullmann; the ensuing flop, known by some as *Lost Investment*, led comedienne Bette Midler to quip, 'I never miss a Liv Ullmann musical.'

Warner Brothers had made the second approach, their screen version of the Broadway hit *Mame*, but the idea of Julie in the title role was not pursued very far. The studio, repeating the mistake of *My Fair Lady* ten years earlier, overlooked the stage Mame, Angela Lansbury, in favour of an infinitely miscast Lucille Ball. It would be the last such case of casting, and almost (but not quite) the last film musical for decades to come.

Julie's husband, meanwhile, had spent the last few months in Hollywood writing their next film. 'Blake agrees that it would be wise of me to appear in a modern story,' she had told *Photoplay* magazine during the recording of her television series. She added plaintively, 'It's quite difficult today to judge what audiences expect of a film, isn't it?'

'A lot of people characterise our leaving Hollywood and going to London as running away,' Blake later protested. 'It's not true at all.' Even though *The Julie Andrews Hour* had been cancelled, the television contract with ATV still called, by default, for a number of one-off television specials to be made in England. Before that, however, was the feature film to which Sir Lew Grade had agreed at a time when prospects were rosier.

The Tamarind Seed, a 1971 romantic spy novel by Evelyn Anthony, contained the contemporary role in which Blake saw his wife: Judith Farrow, a British Foreign Office employee who, holidaying in Barbados, falls in love with a Soviet military attaché to Paris. Reprising his *Doctor Zhivago* function as Hollywood's favourite Russian, Egyptian-born Omar Sharif was cast opposite Julie as the male romantic lead. If the subplots of British, French and Russian espionage appeared to edge in the direction of *Darling Lili*, there were three main differences: it had no songs, no comedy, and not much in the way of budget.

Julie had already filmed her scenes in Barbados in May, prior to flying to London where the production would continue. The locations included Eaton Place, Belgravia — just around the corner from where Julie had spent the early years of her first marriage, and close to Chester Square, where the Edwards family took up residency in a six-floor Regency house. 'It is inevitable that Julie and I discuss the film at home in the evening,' Blake confided to *Films Illustrated*. 'We continue our conversation in the bedroom — because it is more convenient.'

Julie appeared to be enjoying their first work together since their marriage. She was delighted to be costumed by Dior, and pleased with her co-star. 'Just delicious,' she would later describe him. 'Omar is adored by all ladies; I can see why.' The film's juiciest roles were commandeered by Oscar Homolka (in his last screen appearance) as the villain, the sterling Anthony Quayle as Julie Andrews's boss, Daniel O'Herlihy as Britain's treacherous ambassador to France — and Sylvia Syms, chewing the scenery as his Lady Macbeth-like wife.

From London, the crew moved to Paris and, finally, Switzerland — close to the chalet that Mr and Mrs Edwards had bought in Gstaad, which Julie considered the ideal base for the family. 'In winter, the hills are pink, and the trees are navy-blue,' she had mused, shortly before leaving Hollywood. As for work: 'There are plenty of film studios around. And if worse came to worst, we could hole up and write.' For the little girl who had once kept a defiantly happy diary, who had been so eager to see the Alps on her first European trip, and whose biggest career success had been forged in the mountains, the chance to surround herself in a fairytale landscape promised a degree of peace she was not finding in London.

The workplace had completely invaded her home, the basement of their tall, narrow townhouse entirely given over to Blake's production office. One day, with secretaries, house staff and acolytes all milling around, it suddenly became too much for her. As Blake remembered it, 'She just said, 'I've had it,' and I'd never heard that come out of her before. She said, 'I want to live in Switzerland, I want to get away from all this madness.''

'I needed to do that — really do it,' Julie later told me, of her desire to concentrate on her family, to 'put my arms around them' away from the pressures of work.

Blake felt that she was right, as he explained nearly a decade later, in his 1982 interview for *Playboy* magazine. 'But I also had to tell her, 'Listen, you're fantasising that little Swiss village. It's not going to work unless we clean up whatever prompts us to live in this mad way. Otherwise, we'll just take the madness into Gstaad.' In my view, that's exactly what we did for a while.'

In the same interview, Julie recalled the outcome: 'Blake exploded, my daughter got mononucleosis, Blake's son Geoff resisted the governess like you couldn't believe, and I was utterly miserable because my idea to stand still and be quiet for a bit just fell to pieces. But when you move away to a quiet spot, people don't come to visit as often, the phone doesn't ring quite so much, things calm down and you learn to live with yourself.'

Her husband agreed, in his way. 'If Julie asked me why I was so upset, I couldn't very well say, 'Well, I had a fucking hard day at the office . . .' I was home all day.' Home, and locked in his study, writing furiously. 'He wrote his demons out,' said Julie. In the winter of 1973, he would break only for meals, even then bringing his writing to the table. Twelve-year-old Geoffrey would subsequently recall, on the Biography

394

Channel television tribute to his father, the blank expression on Blake's face: 'I knew the gears were working on something.' He understood enough just to 'leave him alone and let him eat and disappear back into his bedroom and write some more'.

With his recent troubles in Hollywood, Blake, who would always consider himself 'not a director but a writer first', was bound to be in autobiographical mood. But when Julie saw how one particular script was shaping up, even his nickname Blackie seemed tame. The title was *S.O.B.* — or *Standard Operating Bullshit*, a phrase that had an active currency in his — and her — recent professional life.

The protagonist was a film director, ostracised and driven to the edge of insanity after the failure of a big-budget family musical — the star of which, his wife, is then persuaded by him to remake it as a porn flick. 'At first,' remembered the real-life wife, 'it was kind of, my God — what is he writing here? The whole piece was so far out in those days, and seemed a little horrifying.'

Despite his spurt of creativity, Blake was still prone to cast a pall over the household with fits of savage depression. 'I used to take it personally,' Julie reflected to *Lear's* magazine almost twenty years later, 'and think, oh my God, what can I do to put it right? But it never had anything to do with me. It was mostly an airing of feelings — a frustration with himself, a need for attention, who knows?' Her most effective way of dealing with it was in the brisk rejoinder, 'Bullshit, Blackie, all you have to do is make another hit.' But, for the moment, this seemed wishful thinking.

Blake was not the only writer in the household, of course. Julie's second children's book was about to be published, under her *nom de plume*, Julie Edwards. *The Last of the Really Great Whangdoodles* told of three children travelling into Whangdoodleland, in search of the last of the native breed: an antlered creature that grows its own bedroom slippers. Strange characters such as the High-Behind Splintercat try to discourage them, but the children hold true to the Whangdoodle motto '*Pax, amor et lepos in iocando*' ('Peace, love and a sense of fun').

If not quite Narnia or Oz, the fantasy sold well and would continue to do so, giving the lie to the *New York Times* review: 'Edwards is more committed to improving her young readers than she is in entertaining them, and her book is sunk by an overload of virtue.' It was, inevitably, too much to expect critics to ignore the image of the author whose identity, despite the use of her married name, was plain to all.

Meanwhile, Julie continued to make periodic trips to London to fulfil her ATV contract — out of which five television specials would appear in dogged succession from Elstree Studios over the next two years. *Julie on Sesame Street* co-starred Perry Como and Jim Henson's Muppets, with Julie singing 'Bein' Green' to Kermit the Frog. It aired on ABC in America on 23 November 1973, followed three weeks later by *Julie's*

Christmas Special, in which the star in a white fur-trimmed coat sang well-known carols alongside the stalwart Peter Ustinov, and breezed through a medley of 'Just in Time' and 'Sentimental Journey' with Peggy Lee.

She also joined her conductor friend André Previn to perform a Christmas concert in the vast Royal Albert Hall on 4 December that year. Accompanied by the London Symphony Orchestra and Chorus, she consummately delivered to an enraptured audience, making her first official stage appearance in her native country since *Mountain Fire* in 1954.

Previn had taken up the baton at the LSO in late 1968. In doing so, he had marked a key change in his personal life: he and Dory, who had both been good friends to Julie since her early days in Hollywood, were divorced in the summer of 1970. Later the same year, Previn married one of America's most publicised young actresses, Mia Farrow. They were now living in London, with a growing brood of children both natural and adopted — an arrangement that Julie watched with growing interest.

⋆ ⋆ ⋆

1974 began with *Julie and Dick in Covent Garden*, an ATV special reuniting Julie with Dick Van Dyke, alongside the creator of *The Dick Van Dyke Show*, Carl Reiner. It was directed in workaday fashion by Blake who, in February, gave a dispirited interview to Barry Norman in *The Times*: 'I guess that working on

397

a television show, as opposed to working on a film, is like having an abortion rather than having a baby. It may be possible to have a creative abortion, but I don't quite see how.'

With that, he looked back at the carnage of his last Hollywood film, *The Carey Treatment*, the 1972 thriller that James Aubrey at MGM had recut in his absence. 'I was strung up, hanged, drawn and quartered and thrown to the wolves. I'd been an opponent of the Hollywood system for many years. I was very aggressive, too aggressive perhaps. I don't regret the things I said, but there may well have been better ways to say them . . . It's been a long, hard struggle back.'

Julie and Dick in Covent Garden was hardly enough to restore his reputation. The show depicted Julie giving her co-star a crash course in Cockney rhyming slang (sadly, ten years too late for his performance in *Mary Poppins*). Included also was a potted version of *Cinderella*, with Dick Van Dyke and Carl Reiner dragging up as the Ugly Sisters, and Julie doubling as Cinders and the Prince in a pale reminder of her days in pantomime.

Next off the ATV conveyor belt was *Julie and Jackie — How Sweet It Is*, for which American comedian Jackie Gleason travelled by air for the first time in twenty years to record the show in London. This time, Blake was not behind the camera. He had, however, announced: 'I have a Trilby and Svengali comedy for Julie, which I hope to make in London following my next film.' To some observers, Svengali had exacted enough penance from Trilby already.

On 11 July 1974, *The Tamarind Seed* had its premiere in New York, where it found little favour — or circulation. It managed better in Europe, although the critical consensus in London was one of polite boredom. In *The Times*, David Robinson found the plot's intrigue compromised by a script heavy with 'schoolgirl debate on political philosophy', and the sight of 'cucumber-cool Mary Poppins (alias Mrs Blake Edwards, alias Julie Andrews)' as a cold war pawn. He did allow that, with 'such a hankering these days for a return to a less permissive cinema', it seemed churlish to criticise.

That October, after the film had been pulled from its limited number of American screens, and as its release was petering out in Europe, a perceptive analysis appeared in England in *Photoplay* magazine:

One big question does arise out of *The Tamarind Seed* and that is the one regarding the future career of Julie Andrews. It proves once and for all that she is more at ease in a musical film than in a dramatic one. Pictures like *Mary Poppins, The Sound of Music* and *Thoroughly Modern Millie* all brought out her star quality and marvellous musical talent. So, too, do her excellent TV shows, in which she can dominate the screen rather than share it with leading men . . . Perhaps next time her husband Blake Edwards will allow her to return to what she really does best.

But what she really wanted was a return to motherhood. As she explained many years later: 'We were hoping to get pregnant while I was working with Blake in London. We were trying and trying for a number of years and not getting lucky for some reason.' In California, the couple had been members of the Committee of Responsibility, a group made up of ordinary citizens and doctors that brought to America wounded or orphaned Vietnamese children for medical aid and long-term care at the height of their country's misery. 'André Previn and Mia Farrow are close friends of ours and they adopted such a child,' Julie said at the time. 'We are also friends of the Yul Brynners who adopted two Vietnamese children. So we decided to go through the same agency in Saigon that helped them.'

Amelia Leigh had been sent to them in early August. 'We have good reason to believe little Amy was an abandoned child,' Julie explained. Both she and Blake, in London when the telegram arrived from Saigon, drove to Heath-row to watch the aeroplane land. When the baby was placed in Julie's arms, it was, she later said, like a miracle. 'That night back at our home in London, when Blake and I knew there was another little life asleep in the next room, I'm afraid we got a bit sticky. It was a gloriously happy moment for us both.'

She had two further television specials to make, but they paled into insignificance. 'Right now,' she said, 'I prefer to think of home, Emma, Geoff and Amy. After that we will see what happens ... If I'm smiling a great deal it's because I'm a mother again.' The following April, Julie was smiling once more, at a new arrival: Joanna Lynn, again from Vietnam, joined her adoptive sister and family at the chalet in Gstaad.

The star still made visits to Hollywood but, more and more, only for family matters, such as registering the adopted girls as naturalised American citizens. 'I am in the fortunate position to be able to work if and when I want, and I do work at some point every year,' she told Linda Gross of the *Los Angeles Times*. 'When I finish a job, I come back to being a mom. Mostly, I've been Mrs Blake Edwards.'

'She submits to an interview like a Victorian wife submits to sex: dutifully,' wrote Miss Gross. 'She is polite, not spontaneous. Ironically, at an age when many women strike out on their own, she clings to her husband and family.' Judging Julie's appeal to be of no relevance to the age, the article finished with a striking prophecy: 'But who knows, she may be rediscovered in the future. She could be smashing playing grandmothers.'

★ ★ ★

While his wife immersed herself in domesticity, Blake had started to flex his muscles once again. He later admitted to feeling let down by the way *The Tamarind Seed* had been marketed — and pre-sold to ABC television in America — but he understood why Lew Grade should have let it happen that way. 'At that time, I wasn't terribly successful,' said Blake, 'and I don't think he had a great deal of confidence in me.'

He and Julie had already started planning their next film: a remake of the 1948 hit *Rachel and the Stranger*. The original had starred William Holden as an Ohio widower during the pioneer days, who takes Loretta Young, an indentured servant, as his bride, but fails to appreciate her until Robert Mitchum comes along. 'I disliked the idea intensely,' wrote Lew Grade in his autobiography *Still Dancing*. 'I had a meeting with Blake in London and told him I didn't want to make *Rachel*, and that I'd buy off the remainder of his contract.' But Blake knew that another cancellation would be the end of his career. 'My future is at stake,' he said. 'People will think I went heavily over-budget on *The Tamarind Seed*.'

Both producer and director later claimed credit for what followed. According to Sir Lew, he told Blake, 'You own the rights to the *Pink Panther* films. So, why don't we make a film called *The Return of the Pink Panther?*' He then picked up the telephone to contact the star of the original films, Peter Sellers — 'and two hours later, I'd persuaded him'.

According to Blake, Sir Lew envisaged the idea as another television series, and — if it was going to be a film — demanded to know how much it was going to sting. Blake took the biggest gamble of his career. 'Lew,' he said, 'Peter and I won't take a nickel. All we each want is expenses and ten per cent of the gross from the first dollar on.' It was a deal.

Despite the old friction between director and actor, Blake stated: 'I still wanted Peter for *The Return of the Pink Panther*, and I had high hopes for the movie.' In April 1974, it started shooting at Shepperton Studios, just a few miles up river from Walton-on-Thames. Blake's young production assistant Tony Adams could see the synergy between his boss and Peter Sellers. 'When it worked, and it really worked, it was amazing,' he would recall on the Biography Channel. 'It was like watching great musicians play a great score.'

An almost unrecognisable Julie Andrews popped her head into the film, in 'a very stupid, silly bit', she remembered when I first met her. 'I played a silly German maid who came in with a vacuum cleaner and curlers and that kind of thing. Great fun to do, and it was simply appalling when it was shown, so I'm *very* glad it ended up on the cutting-room floor.'

The premiere, as gala as all get out, was held in Gstaad, where some of the film's action took place. It was attended by Julie and Blake's Swiss neighbours, Richard Burton and Elizabeth Taylor, now married to each other for the second time. When *The Return of the Pink Panther* went on general release in the summer of 1975, it was a runaway hit. 'The box-office figures were incredible,' said Sir Lew Grade. Somewhat to his surprise, he had become the producer of a serious cinema success.

The return of Blake Edwards now a reality, the director started to plan the next in the *Pink*

Panther series, remarking of the film that had turned his fortunes around: 'While it was in the making I had no idea that it was going to be such a hit and would be challenging *Jaws* for America's money. But that is the way it has happened . . . '

The following year, the team would regroup on *The Pink Panther Strikes Again*, which would take even more money and, as with its predecessor, go on to win the London *Evening Standard* film award for Best Comedy. During the opening credits, a cartoon pink panther, parodying several classic films, twirls in a nun's garb on a mountainside. The real Julie would make her presence felt elsewhere in the film. Henry Mancini's song 'Until You Love Me' appears to be sung by a drag artist in a club scene, but the ghost vocalist is credited as Ainsley Jarvis. The singer's initials, inverted, reveal the director's wife, happy to be of service.

★ ★ ★

On 1 October 1975, Julie Andrews was forty years old. She remained as fresh faced and clear skinned as ever, drinking Evian or Perrier bottled water instead of tap, spending ten minutes each morning exercising her famously slim figure, and keeping her hair to a longer version of her 1960s bob, styled by Hal Saunders of Hollywood or René of London, Princess Margaret's coiffeur. As if to emphasise her Peter Pan credentials, the Annigoni portrait of Eliza Doolittle came up for sale at Sotheby's in London the following month, selling for £7,000 to an anonymous bidder. It turned out to be Blake, acquiring a memento of his wife's finest hour on stage.

And Julie found herself turning back to the talent with which she had made her name. The girl once described by *Time* magazine as symbolising 'Christmas carols in the snow' recorded an album, *The Secret of Christmas*. Released in 1975 in Britain, it would not surface until 1982 in America, under the title *Christmas with Julie Andrews*.

She also taped her last special for Lew Grade, sentimentally titled *My Favourite Things*, and the second to be directed by Blake. It featured the Muppets, a ballet with a troupe of Pink Panthers, Julie's daughter Emma, now fourteen, on a unicycle — and a spoof of the Fred Astaire and Ginger Rogers musicals of the 1930s, 'Flying Down to Brighton', with Peter Sellers in Busby Berkeley guise as producer Binkie Barclay.

Then, on Thursday 1 April 1976, *The Times* made a parish announcement to please the faithful: 'Julie Andrews is returning to the London stage, and will give fourteen special performances at the London Palladium starting on June 9.' The last official performance she had given in the West End had been more than twenty years earlier, on Saturday 6 March 1954 in the title role of *Cinderella* on the same stage.

For her new show, she secured the services of British musical director Ian Fraser, who came to her from working with actor Anthony Newley and composer-lyricist Leslie Bricusse, and who would remain one of her most loyal colleagues in the following years. At Shepperton Studios, on a soundstage next to where Blake was shooting *The Pink Panther Strikes Again*, Julie rehearsed with her chorus boys and the young variety artist Bobby Crush. There was some new material, but what she called 'the show's vanilla moments' predominated, as her public expected they would.

Julie's original notion for a support act had been the zany Monty Python team. In late 1976, Michael Palin wrote in his diary: 'Julie Andrews is, believe it or not, a Python freak. She wanted us to co-star with her at the Palladium earlier this year.' Sadly, the team was unavailable, but the star was compensated in being joined by her friend of almost thirty years, Michael Bentine.

Julie's appreciation of the Pythons was not so surprising, given the wealth of comic talent with which she had grown up, and which continued to surround her through her husband's films. Monty Python had largely assumed the profile of *Beyond the Fringe* (stage) and *That Was the Week That Was* (television) — which, in turn, had taken over where the Goons had dominated. And Julie had worked with most of them.

Julie Andrews at the London Palladium opened to solid, appreciative audiences of rather more than teenage vintage. In *The Times*, Geoffrey Wansell considered 'the universal aunt, that kindly English nanny, the nice girl next door everyone should have married but never quite did'. He then isolated what it was that left him cold:

She may have all the fame, happiness and money she wished for but the Fairy Godmother somehow denied her a personality to call her own ... So the audience were left to admire the elegant, perfectly staged spectacular and mourn the glimpse of what might have been made of the chance for a performer embalmed in the aspic of her own talent to emerge.

During her fortnight's run, Julie had evinced surprise at her ever-increasing homosexual appeal, when asked by *Woman* magazine whether she thought that her songs could be considered as high camp. 'What', asked Julie, with a chill in her voice, 'is high camp?' Whether the mainstay of her audience was gay, middle-aged or infantile, the London *Evening News* obviously thought her day was done. On 21 June, the Monday after she finished at the Palladium, the paper ran an article suggesting that her engagement had not been financially successful — and that she was not expected to be invited back to the Palladium for a very long time.

In response, Julie made a return to litigation, after a gap of seven years. At the end of February 1977 in the High Court, she was represented by Leon Brittan, barrister, Conservative Member of Parliament and future European Commissioner. 'The article is both inaccurate and damaging,' Brittan informed the judge, 'and has caused Miss Andrews great distress.' He added that the newspaper now admitted the statement to be unfounded and without basis in fact — and that the theatre management had said they would gladly have Julie back in future. On 3 March, Julie Andrews won an apology and what were described as 'substantial libel damages'. They were not her first and they would not be her last.

Two months after her London appearances, Julie had accepted the offer of eight weeks' engagement at Caesar's Palace, Las Vegas, for a reported $250,000 a week. It sounded too good to be true, and it probably was. After a week, the engagement was curtailed. Although she was drawing the crowds, Julie's audience was not the sort to gamble a life's savings away on the slot machines. And, outside her loyal following, it appeared that resistance to the star remained as trenchant as ever.

★   ★   ★

On Easter Monday 1977, Mrs Winifred Wells, Julie's fifty-eight-year-old stepmother, set out on a bicycle ride from the family home in Ockley, Surrey. She did not return. During the next three days and nights, forty volunteers from the village joined the police and their dogs to comb an area within a radius of five miles from Ted and Win's house. Frogmen even searched a local lake; the British press carried picture stories of the search.

By Thursday, the hunt was still on. Julie had flown in from Switzerland, staying at the Dorchester Hotel, but driving down to Ockley to be with her father. 'Julie Andrews joins search for stepmother' ran a piece in *The Times*, with a picture of the star in her customary large sunglasses, all the more apparent over her drawn face. Blake, accompanying her, knew how distraught she was, calling her 'OK, but emotionally unglued at the moment . . . Her father is not well.'

Julie's brother John, now a pilot with an industrial firm, spoke of the general bewilderment: 'If you had to pick out a level-headed couple in the village, they would come out top of the list.' And Ted, now sixty-nine, responded to suggestions that she might have walked out on him: 'Since we have had thirty-five years of devoted marriage, I don't see why she should have done.'

That evening, at half-past nine, Winifred Wells was spotted by a passing motorist, sitting on a grass verge next to the road in Hitch Hurst, near Ockley. To the family's relief, she seemed not to be seriously harmed, though she was treated at hospital for exposure. She had spent the last three days wandering about in the local woods, having 'snapped under stress' brought about by her husband's recent health problems. Despite his daily fitness regime, Ted Wells was reported to be suffering from high blood pressure, although this did not seem to account fully for his wife's reaction.

Julie was said by Blake to be 'greatly relieved' at her stepmother's safety. But, inevitably, the episode heightened her concerns for the wellbeing of her beloved father.

★ ★ ★

That August, Julie returned to America to pursue her concert career, with a week of performances in Westchester, New York, and one night at the New Greek Theatre in Los Angeles. But the bulk of her energy was reserved for a tour of Japan, taking in Tokyo, Osaka, Sapporo and Fukuoka in the second half of September and early October. The Japanese had remained among her fastest supporters, young and old — although, on one occasion, on holiday in Switzerland, a group of their compatriots was taken by surprise.

'I was getting ready for a big concert,' Julie told me. 'I'd taken some walks for several days and not met a soul. So I thought, I can now start vocalising a little; Richard Burton used to tell me he went to the mountains in Wales to do some of the Shakespearean speeches. So I was singing away, 'The hills are alive . . . ' just as this huge crowd of Japanese tourists came over the ridge with cameras. They looked so stunned — convinced that I did that sort of thing every day of my life. I felt a real twerp.'

In November, Julie returned for one night only to the London Palladium, joining many of her peers, including Sir Lew (now Lord) Grade, Shirley Maclaine, Harry Belafonte, Carol Burnett, Rudolf Nureyev and the Muppets, at the Royal Variety Performance to mark the Silver Jubilee of Her Majesty Queen Elizabeth II. It was the first such show in which Julie had appeared since piping the 'Polonaise' and 'God Save the King' to the Queen's father George VI, alongside Danny Kaye on the same stage almost thirty years before.

Throughout the autumn, there had been rumours of another reunion with destiny — a Broadway musical of George Bernard Shaw's *Major Barbara*. 'It was Blake Edwards who first saw her tambourine-playing potential,' said one English newspaper, 'and Leslie Bricusse is producing a Broadway score.' Julie would take the title role of the munitions tycoon's daughter who joins the Salvation Army.

And over at what was now MGM/EMI Studios at Borehamwood, Bryan Forbes was putting together a sequel to the 1944 smash hit *National Velvet*, the film that had catapulted twelve-year-old Elizabeth Taylor to international stardom. It was with *International Velvet*, bringing the story of the young girl jockey up to date, that Forbes, keeper of the flame for what was left of the British film industry, hoped to reactivate the family film.

Julie was offered $500,000 to take up the reins of Velvet, now aunt to Tatum O'Neal — and wife to Christopher Plummer. Whether the latter casting made the prospect seem a retrogression, or whether motherhood and Switzerland were calling, she turned it down. Bryan Forbes' previous film, a British musical version of *Cinderella* entitled *The Slipper and the Rose*, with songs by the Sherman brothers, had failed to make the expected impact. *International Velvet* would not do much better. Disney Studios had also had a mediocre response to *Pete's Dragon*, a fantasy mixing live action with animation, in which the singing star Helen

411

Reddy was heralded by headlines such as 'Reddy for the new Julie Andrews?' The answer was inconclusive.

By contrast, the world premiere of *Star Wars* had taken place in Hollywood on 25 May 1977 — and its mammoth ambitions were quickly vindicated at box offices worldwide. Twentieth Century Fox, in their first family hit since *The Sound of Music*, had created a franchise that would go on, and on, and on, delighting children of all ages — children who were no longer interested in the films their grandparents expected them to enjoy.

Blake, however, was comparatively immune to such market trends. His London office was setting up the *Revenge of the Pink Panther*, which he cheerfully admitted making for 'sheer greed'. He had told himself, 'One more, and I'll be able to put enough away so that I'll never have to work again. I wasn't wrong about that, either.'

The film dragged his relationship with Peter Sellers, whom he called 'schizophrenic, certifiable', to a new low. 'I want to surprise you,' the actor told him on the telephone late one night, 'but don't worry, I've talked to God, and He told me how to do it.' On set the next day his comedy routine fell flat. 'Peter, will you do me a favour?' said Blake. 'The next time God speaks to you, would you tell her to stay out of show business?' Nonetheless, the latest *Pink Panther* sequel completed a hat-trick of success for all concerned.

Meanwhile, Julie confined her work to the

small screen, appearing on *The Muppet Show* on 23 November 1977. It was four years to the day since she had featured Jim Henson's creations on *Julie on Sesame Street*, in which time they had become a television legend. Now it was Julie who was the guest star, singing 'The Lonely Goatherd' and a composition of her own, 'When You Were a Tadpole (and I was a fish)', to Kermit the Frog.

The following March, she made her last special of the decade for CBS. In *Julie Andrews — One Step into Spring*, aired in March 1978, she appeared with the elegant Leslie Uggams and the equally elegant Miss Piggy — all three ladies sporting (to Miss Piggy's chagrin) the same bonnet in the Easter Parade finale. Waiting for her cue, Julie turned to the chorus of Muppets with a sudden glimpse of her music-hall heritage, telling them brightly, 'Suck in, tuck in — and smile!' There was life in the old girl yet.

★ ★ ★

For all his triumph with the trio of *Pink Panther* sequels, Blake Edwards' reputation was still not yet quite restored. Sections of the press still carped at him, about his directing of his wife — and worse.

Consequently, like Julie, he was not averse to a spot of litigation. On 21 June 1978, *The Times* reported his High Court action against *Private Eye*. The British satirical magazine had detailed his alleged profligacy on the last *Pink Panther* film, also accusing him of malpractice over the purchase of a chalet in Switzerland.

The plaintiff — described by the magazine as 'Mr Julie Andrews, whose real name is Blake Edwards' — was reported in *The Times* 'to receive substantial damages because of offensive references to him in *Private Eye*. The magazine admitted in the High Court yesterday that the references had 'no basis whatever in fact.''

Quite apart from this, Blake had been pondering events. His career had been revitalised, but only in exile. Sooner or later, he would need to prove himself again on the Hollywood film stages where he had forged his early career. Among the scripts on his desk was one he had written during James Aubrey's tenure at MGM. 'I wrote about midlife crisis and nobody thought that it was going to make a nickel,' said Blake. Revising the screenplay in Switzerland, he experienced again the nagging feeling that he still had to make a success of directing Julie Andrews.

That decided him. They would return to Hollywood.

15

BACK WITH A VENGEANCE

'It's very difficult, when you're doing a love scene with someone and your husband says, 'I'd like you to do it better' — *and you wonder whether he really means it'*

— Julie Andrews, 1986

Dr Milton Wexler gazed around his penthouse office, observing the great and the good of Beverly Hills. The seventy-year-old psychoanalyst — something of a rule-breaker and rather more of a star-struck kid — favoured a social approach to work, presiding over one of the most prominent networking units in Los Angeles.

More than a decade before Robert Altman's film *The Player* showed a Hollywood shark cutting deals at his local Alcoholics Anonymous, Dr Wexler had built up a celebrated clientele including architect Frank Gehry, venture capitalist Max Palevsky, Oscar-winning film star Jennifer Jones, legendary director Sydney Pollack — and Blake Edwards, who, in his trademark leather jacket and dark sunglasses, returned to the group in late 1978 from his period in exile.

The family Edwards was back in town, with a new house in Beverly Hills, a new school for Amy Leigh and Joanna Lynn — and a new contract for Blake at Orion Pictures, to shoot his script about one of the most discussed issues of the day: the male menopause.

A decade earlier in Los Angeles, daydreaming at a set of traffic lights, Blake had seen a beautiful girl drive by on the way to her wedding, sparking the inspiration for what would eventually be billed as 'a contemporary comedy where you don't play by the rules — you play by the numbers'. The role of Hollywood songwriter George Webber, facing the abyss of his forty-second birthday, seemed ideal for Jack Lemmon or Peter Sellers — both of whom turned it down. Instead, George Segal was signed to play the philanderer, who spends the film searching for the fantasy female figure to live up to — or exceed — his perfect score of *10*.

Blake and his co-producer Tony Adams found their girl in the shape of twenty-two-year-old model Bo Derek. 'We were crossing our fingers,' Blake remembered later, 'and hoping: 'Let her be able to act; please let her be able to act.' She could.' Miss Derek would make a considerable impact, rising from the waves like Botticelli's Venus, her hair woven into corn-rows — providing a visual image for the film as famous as the soundtrack use of Ravel's 'Boléro' to accompany its anti-climactic sex sequence.

Julie Andrews had been cast as George Webber's long-suffering girlfriend Samantha. And it was rumoured to be script changes favouring her role that led to the sudden exit of George Segal on the eve of shooting. In some desperation, Blake recalled a short English comedian he had seen at his analyst's office. Dudley Moore, not long arrived in Hollywood, was one of the *Beyond the Fringe* team who had reinvented British comedy in the early 1960s. At five foot two inches, he had never been seen as leading man material — until he visited Dr Wexler. 'Suddenly one night,' said Blake, 'I looked over and thought, I've been sitting here all this time, and the man I'm writing about in the movie is facing me.'

'He really didn't get to know me,' Moore recalled to his biographer Douglas Thompson, 'except from chatting in group sessions, about life, death and all those things . . . someone was dealing the cards my way.'

In the 1967 British comedy film *Bedazzled*, he had played the part of timid Stanley Moon, who sells his soul to the devil — on condition that, to have his wishes granted, he utters the magic words 'Julie Andrews'. Little over a decade later, acting opposite the real thing, Dudley Moore found his breakthrough role. From *10*, he would acquire sex symbol status at forty-four years of age.

As Samantha, Julie's first film role in five years made few demands, other than to look good in maroon leather trousers and drive a silver Mercedes sports car. And if her function was to counteract the film's inherent misogyny — lecturing George to pay more attention to 'his bedroom guests' — it was but a version of the old governess routine. Nevertheless, Moore was a fan. 'There's a marvellous English ice about Julie,' he said, 'and you don't have to chip very hard to get at the fire.' And, however incidental her role, she was part of what promised to be a success of sizeable proportions.

Tagged as 'the funniest sexiest midlife crisis in movie history', *10* was released on 5 October 1979, and took off almost immediately. Capturing the spirit of the times, Blake's adult-rated comedy of middle-aged angst and impotence chimed exactly with the American public in a post-Vietnam period of introspection.

In the *New York Times*, Vincent Canby welcomed both its theme and its star, calling the film 'almost as much a celebration of the comedy talents of Dudley Moore as *Darling Lili* was a celebration of Mr Edwards's admiration for his wife, Miss Andrews'. He gave Julie what credit he could: 'Miss Andrews is onscreen for what seems like no time at all, though her no-nonsense presence is essential to much of the comedy, even when she doesn't participate in it.' But his attention, in common with that of most of his colleagues, devolved more on Bo Derek, a 'truly magnificent looking young woman'.

10 would eventually gross a remarkable $75 million, almost (but not quite) erasing memories of *Darling Lili*, enabling Blake Edwards to set his agenda for the future. His wife, however, took a big step backwards, into precisely the kind of material from which she had so long tried to distance herself: a family film — and not even a good one.

Little Miss Marker, written and directed by Walter Bernstein, was the first Julie Andrews film without Blake since *Star!* more than a dozen years earlier. The choice seemed bizarre: even with Hollywood's short memory span, most people in 1980 still associated the title with Shirley Temple, who had made it such a hit back in 1934. Since then, the picaresque story by Damon Runyon had been subject to the law of diminishing returns, Bob Hope remaking it in 1949 as *Sorrowful Jones*, and Tony Curtis starring in a pale 1962 copy, *40 Pounds of Trouble*.

When I first saw Julie, she pondered her reasons for agreeing to it. 'Mostly for the opportunity to work with Walter Matthau,' she allowed. 'It was quite a sweet screenplay and probably a very — perhaps a foolish choice . . . actually, it *wasn't* a foolish choice, because I so enjoyed working with him, but it wasn't a successful film. That's just the way it goes.' As *Sorrowful Jones*, the mordant Matthau accepts a young girl, played by Sara Stimson, as a marker for her father's gambling debts, with Julie supplying tepid romance along the way. Filmed for Universal on the same street sets as those used for *Thoroughly Modern Millie*, it had sporadic moments of charm, but made no impact whatsoever on its release in March 1980.

It looked as though the naysayers were correct, that the former No 1 star really had reached a dead end — her appearances best restricted to television specials such as *Julie Andrews' Invitation to the Dance*, presented that November as part of the somewhat worthy CBS Festival of Lively Arts for Young People. Featuring ballet superstar Rudolf Nureyev, Broadway hoofer Ann

Reinking and the Green Grass Cloggers, Julie hosted a show that demonstrated her love for the art form, an enthusiasm stretching back further than her friendship with ballerina Svetlana Beriosova, to her early classes at the Joan Morris School of Dancing.

But, if Julie appeared to be treading water professionally, there were more important matters to occupy her attention. Shortly after their return to Hollywood, she and Blake had heard of Operation California, a rapid-response relief organisation founded by Los Angeles lawyers Richard Walden and Llewellyn Werner. Its first mission in 1979 was to send an aircraft of food and medical supplies to the Vietnamese boat people in Malaysia. 'Blake and Julie gave us $10,000,' Walden revealed; a few weeks later, they donated very much more, to help charter an airlift of famine relief to Cambodia. The following year, they joined the charity's first advisory board of directors.

Quite apart from this, Julie was concentrating on family. 'I'm more contented and at peace with myself now than I was as a box-office queen,' she told the *Saturday Evening Post*. 'I certainly wouldn't compare the rewards of watching one's children grow and mature with that of money piling up at the box office. Both are pleasant, but to varying degrees. As the old saying goes, you can't take an audience home with you.'

As to future work, she was vague: 'It all depends on whether Blake is involved in the project or approves it, and whether it suits my schedule with the children.' But, in the same interview, she dropped a clue: 'I've always had a body — a rather nice one, too, but people who had only seen my movies assumed I was either sexless or puritanical.' Her next appearance on screen would mark her strongest attempt yet to prove her public wrong.

In mid-1980, with *10* now his most profitable film ever, Blake turned his attention to the vicious little tale of Hollywood that he had first drafted in Switzerland: *S.O.B.*

Twenty years later, Julie would recall on the CNN show *Larry King Live*: 'That script of Blake's went around every studio and every one of them said, 'We love it' — and then they wouldn't touch it at all.' It was hugely ironic, therefore, that the two studios to become involved were those to have instigated the internecine feud in the first place. Paramount Pictures agreed to release *S.O.B.* in America, despite the fact that the producer (played by Robert Vaughn) was clearly modelled on its ex-chief of production, Robert Evans. But the role also bore resemblance to James Aubrey, former head of MGM — the soundstages of which were used by Lorimar, producers with Blake's Geoffrey Productions on the film.

Finally, Blake was able to vent his spleen about Tinseltown, doing so through his onscreen counterpart Felix Farmer, played by Richard Mulligan (best known as Burt Campbell in *Soap*). The film's other life studies included Loretta Swit's columnist, a compendium of the bilious traits Blake and Julie ascribed to Joyce Haber of the *Los Angeles Times*, and Shelley

421

Winters' power broker Eva Brown, based on Sue Mengers, the Hollywood agent who expressed the wish that an Alp should fall on Blake's chalet. 'That would be preferable to Sue Mengers falling on it,' remarked Blake.

In the last role of his distinguished career, William Holden played Felix Farmer's executive producer, the only vaguely rational man in the film. The edges of the story were filled out by Larry Hagman and the Roberts Loggia, Webber and Preston — the last as a quack doctor (tellingly, psychoanalysts were left out of the range of fire). Blake's family doctor Herb Tanney (credited as Stiffe Tanney) was also in there somewhere as the owner of a funeral parlour, as was Blake's daughter Jennifer, now twenty-two, as a hitchhiker-cum-junkie. But all this was nothing compared to what the director had planned for his wife.

Julie Andrews was cast as Sally Miles ('Smiles'), the world's star purveyor of sweetness and light, whose latest film — directed by her husband, Felix — is the massive musical flop *Night Wind*. One of Smiles' responses to failure is to hurl her Oscar through a window. 'Good heavens, no!' Julie exclaimed, when I asked her if she had used her own award for *Mary Poppins*. 'It was a fake one — and a fake window.'

And a fake premise. The disastrous *Night Wind*, in which the befreckled star sings a sappy version of 'Polly Wolly Doodle', was not really comparable to Julie's great family hits; and it seemed to have escaped Blake's attention that he and his wife had been excommunicated from

Hollywood not for a children's musical, but for a wartime drama that had itself sought unsuccessfully to change its leading lady's image.

The decorous strip-tease of *Darling Lili*, however, was to be obliterated by a full-frontal unmasking in *S.O.B.* — showing 'America's G-rated darling in the B-U-F-F', is how one character puts it — as Sally Miles agrees to turn *Night Wind* into a cinematic sex fantasy. 'My mind says yes, but my body says no,' wails Smiles in a last-minute panic, before being drugged into acquiescence, pulling apart her bright red chiffon gown to exhibit her 'boobies', beaming fixedly like the Bride of Frankenstein.

When the pornographic version of *Night Wind* is released at the film's conclusion, it is proclaimed as 'the biggest money-making film in motion picture history'. But, again, this had no bearing on reality. If Blake thought *S.O.B.* would make back as much money as his earlier flops had lost, he was to be disappointed.

'Blake Edwards in tiff over *S.O.B.*', shouted the *New York Times*, one week before the film's launch. Alleging that the director had been up to his old tricks with 'excessive expenditures', Paramount Pictures had cancelled the film's $225,000 press junket. Blake, it was reported, had assumed financial responsibility for the 'fun weekend', including a screening in Malibu and dinner at the Beverly Hills Hotel.

Hostilities had recommenced, after a gap of a decade. 'Clearly they perceive the film first as the baring of my wife's breasts and second as a comedy,' a somewhat disingenuous Blake told *Time* magazine of the marketing campaign. 'The parallel between what is happening now and what happened on *Darling Lili* is chilling.'

On 1 July 1981, *S.O.B.* opened to delight and disgust, summed up by Vincent Canby in the *New York Times*: 'Blake Edwards's newest, most manic, most bitter farce . . . has the class consciousness of a snobbish press agent . . . It's a nasty, biased, self-serving movie that also happens to be hilarious most of the time.' And he ended with what, in the circumstances, must have been intended as a compliment: 'It's difficult to remember a film as mean-spirited as *S.O.B.* that also was so consistently funny.'

In *Time* magazine Richard Schickel wrote of Julie's efforts, 'If they gave a good-sport Oscar, she would be a shoo-in,' and considered Blake to have 'bitten the hand that feeds him — and discovered that it is soul food'.

Two days later, the film arrived in London. 'Julie Andrews is the Peter Pan star who turns Emmanuelle for the good of the grosses,' said *The Times*. 'When she finally bares her breasts, she does it with the awesome deliberation of someone who knows that this is indeed a moment of motion picture history.'

One month after Julie's attempt to demolish her image hit the cinema screen, her childhood rival Petula Clark opened in the first West End stage revival of *The Sound of Music*, with advance sales of more than £1 million. Forty-eight-year-old Petula earned rave notices from the critics and the real Maria von Trapp, with crowds hungry as ever for a musical of hope and happiness.

In *S.O.B.*, by contrast, nothing was sacred. Sex, drugs, suicide, homosexuality — love and pain and the whole damn thing — were pitched into the cauldron. From the opening shot of a dog on the beach with his master dead beside him, to Sally Miles singing over her dead husband's coffin (unaware that his body is being burnt at sea by his friends), Blake let rip with what Julie called his 'black, black sense of humour'.

In perverse tribute, he was nominated for two Razzies ('Golden Raspberry' Awards) as Worst Director and for Worst Screenplay. Fortunately, 1981 was also the year of the Joan Crawford hagiography *Mommie Dearest*, which swept the board. 'I have no regrets,' Julie told *Woman* magazine. 'I didn't feel degraded — I had a super time. It was a lovely part.'

And Tony Adams was at pains to defend his boss against charges made by the industry: 'I'm fed up hearing them make Blake out to be the bad guy, a Svengali who is now forcing Julie to take her clothes off. If she didn't want to do it she wouldn't have.'

Yet it was clear that the ghost of Mary Poppins had still not been vanquished. At La Cage Aux Folles nightclub in Los Angeles, one impressionist's act now added an element in which Sally Miles was portrayed baring her all. 'Which is rather smart,' said Julie, 'since it's played by a man . . . ' But the real joke was in seeing Nanny naked.

Shortly after the dust started to settle on *S.O.B.*, Mr and Mrs Edwards packed their bags again, and flew to London with their two small girls — to make a film that Julie's fans worldwide felt instinctively was her last real chance to reinvent herself on screen.

★ ★ ★

Victor/Victoria went back a long way, to the dying days of the Weimar Republic. If Julie Andrews had once missed the chance to play Sally Bowles, she was now to assume a contemporaneous role made famous by Renate Müller in the 1933 German film *Viktor and Viktoria*, of a woman pretending to be a man pretending to be a woman.

In 1935, high-kicking, saucer-eyed Jessie Matthews — one of the few English actresses before the advent of Julie Andrews to have had a successful career in musical films — had remade it in English as *First a Girl*. 'I think I saw maybe two seconds of it,' Julie later allowed. 'We were only able to get a clip of it — but I did see the German version.'

Although Blake focused on the 1933 film, he made two key alterations. The location would move from Berlin to Paris. And the homosexual angle, almost disregarded in the original, would form an integral part of the plot. Thus decided, Blake wrote his adaptation in a month, later claiming, 'This one came very easy.'

The film was to be produced for Metro-Goldwyn-Mayer. Strange as it was for Blake to be working for the company which had treated him so badly in the past, it was doubly so to be reactivating a genre that was generally agreed to have died a decade earlier — since when, the sole success of *Grease* in 1978 had been counteracted by the twin catastrophes of *Can't Stop the Music* and *Xanadu* in 1980. 'Musicals were passé,' Blake said later. 'They just weren't being done. I have to give all the credit to a man then in charge of MGM, David Begelman. He liked me, he thought I was talented; he felt if I was that committed to a project, it was worth doing.'

More than four decades after her abortive screen test, Julie Andrews would finally be making her first MGM musical, with Pinewood Studios, England doubling for Paris, France. This enabled Blake to create the ambiance of a 1930s Hollywood film, as Julie later described: 'All the exterior shots, every single thing about *Victor/Victoria*, were made on two soundstages that were opened up and made into one big street. The intimate look of that film was because it was actually shot under a roof.'

Compared to her previous three roles, Victoria Grant/Victor Grazinsky presented a considerable acting challenge. As a down-at-heel soprano who is persuaded to pass herself off as a man, and who then stuns Paris with her/his female impressions, Julie worried that she would not be convincing as a man, let alone a female impersonator.

Ultimately, she settled for being as still as possible, 'because men in general seem a little less busy than women'. What Julie called her 'fairly ample chest' was strapped down, and her suits made rather too big for her. Her hair was cropped most becomingly, and dyed a deep red each week by John Isaacs of Michaeljohn, who had attended to her onscreen coiffure since *10*. Physically and mentally, it was Julie's biggest stretch since *Star!* and she knew it. So did Blake, who later remarked: 'It was a wonderful role for any actress and I could give it to my wife, and that pleased me more than anything.'

Julie would look back on *Victor/Victoria* as 'probably the film we view with the most affection' — not least because of the warmth between cast members. To play the ultra-masculine gambler King Marchan, who falls worryingly in love with 'Victor', Blake turned to Julie's co-star in *The Americanization of Emily*. Eighteen years after their first onscreen affair, she was back in bed with James Garner.

Marchan's blonde moll Norma Cassidy was assigned to Lesley Ann Warren — who had made her debut in the 1965 television remake of Rodgers and Hammerstein's *Cinderella*, taking Julie's old role. And, in a role earmarked for Peter Sellers before his fatal heart attack the previous summer, Robert Preston played Victoria's gay mentor Toddy. The supporting cast included Graham Stark, who had appeared in all the recent *Pink Panther* films, as a surly waiter; Blake's son Geoffrey as a fey chorus boy; and Dr Tanney (credited this time as Sherloque Tanney) as a hapless detective. 'If he was as good a doctor as he is an actor, I'd be dead by now,' said Blake.

Surrounded though she was by trusted colleagues, Julie found *Victor/Victoria* exhausting. 'It was rather a difficult time,' she told me. 'Not too long before, we had adopted our two children, and we moved to London at the very moment I lost one of the great nannies of the world for my kids. I was so desperately weary, trying to be a good mother and show up at the end of work, that the last thing I would have time for was to study my lines. The memory of making the film was one of great joy, working with Preston, which was phenomenal — and Garner, who's a great friend — but the pressure was tremendous.'

Early in the film, there was to have been a transformation montage, of Victoria turning into Victor, having her inside leg measured — even getting a shave. But, as the film was already running on the long side, Blake abandoned the scene. The legacy of Robert Evans and James Aubrey still plagued him, the fear that the studio would rework his material behind his back. As a result, he tried to shoot as little extraneous material as possible, later claiming: 'If I gave them too much, they were liable to use it.' He nevertheless saw to it that the songs were balanced by verbal banter and slapstick, reprising gags used in his previous films: the idiotic detective on the hotel roof, an intruder's finger squashed in a wardrobe door, utter bedlam in a restaurant scene.

'We both have a love of vaudeville,' said Julie, and this informed some of her choices in the film. An obvious inspiration was the early twentieth-century male impersonator Ella Shields, whose signature tune 'Burlington Bertie from Bow' Julie had already accommodated in her career. 'You and Me', a soft-shoe duet with Robert Preston, was influenced by another music-hall turn, the Western Brothers, who, as Julie remembered from her youth, performed at the piano wearing monocles, white tie and tails.

Elsewhere, Henry Mancini and Leslie Bricusse's score conjured up both pastiche and pathos in its nightclub songs and underscoring. 'The Shady Dame from Seville' was presented as a big number for Victor, and reprised at the end of the film as knockabout farce for Toddy. And the lovely ballad 'Crazy World' — with the camera moving in one long, continuous take around Julie as Victor in white tie and tails, echoing the opening shot of *Darling Lili* — amply demonstrated Julie's still remarkable vocal purity, heard so seldom in recent years.

'Le Jazz Hot', the catchiest number, contained the pay-off-when Victoria stalls the applause by removing her wig to show that she is really Victor. The required suspension of disbelief was set against the promise that the film would create its own crazy world with its own set of values. And this it seemed to do. 'It's about love, really — all kinds of love,' Julie would say, 'and that's not a bad thing to make a film about.'

'I think it meant a lot to Julie to finally have something that really clicked with both of them,' said Geoffrey Edwards, confirming the feeling that his father and stepmother had produced something the public might actually want to see.

Victor/Victoria had its world premiere at the Plitt Century Plaza Theatre, Los Angeles on Tuesday 16 March 1982, and opened in New York three days later. In the *New York Times*, Vincent Canby came out with a review the likes of which Blake and Julie could only have dreamed a couple of years earlier: 'Get ready, get set and go — immediately — to the Ziegfeld Theater, where Blake Edwards today opens his chef d'oeuvre, his cockeyed, crowning achievement . . . ' He continued:

> Mr Edwards has never before treated Miss Andrews, his wife, with such confidence, admiration and generosity. She looks absolutely great and is at peak form both as a comedian and as a singer. Nothing she has done before, on the stage or on the screen, probably can match the exuberant charm of her switches between Victoria and Victor . . . She isn't meant to convince the movie audience she's a boy, only the characters within the film. The slightly eerie, androgynous purity of her singing voice also underscores the comedy of her masquerade.

He finished prophetically: '*Victor/Victoria* is so good, so exhilarating, that the only depressing thing about it is the suspicion that Mr Edwards is going to have a terrible time trying to top it.'

'Divine!' cried Liz Smith. 'A delight,' said *Newsweek*. And Stanley Kauffman in the *New Republic* named it 'the best American film farce since *Some Like It Hot*'. Sweet, too, was the praise from Judith Crist, who described *Victor/ Victoria* in the *Saturday Review* as 'a lavish, luscious ribald musical comedy' and said of its star: 'Julie Andrews is simply brilliant. All the gifts that sparkled in her Broadway and film musicals glitter in her maturity; she is pure enchantment as performer and as actress.'

There was, naturally, a fly in the ointment, and its name was Pauline Kael: 'The picture is at its yeastiest in the slapstick embellishments of the preparatory sequences; when the infuriatingly sane and distant Julie Andrews finally gets into men's clothes, there's nothing remotely funny about it.'

In Britain, opening at the beginning of April, the film was rather disregarded by critics, *The Times* commenting that Julie had always had 'a tomboyish appeal' and 'packs a mean right in a brawl'. But in France, *Victor/Victoria* was rated highly, picking up the 1983 César Award for Best Foreign Film (over *E.T. the Extra-Terrestrial*) — while in Italy, Julie and Blake won the David di Donatello Awards for Best Foreign Actress and Best Foreign Screenplay.

Julie would later admit to being less sure about her transgender performance than anything she had previously done. 'As someone who likes to be in control, I felt wobbly,' she said. 'There was something else, too: when you get older, you kind of get on to yourself. You know the tricks you play to get by, and you like them less and less if you care about your work. I was trying hard to get away from them.'

Back in Hollywood, however, there was nothing but praise. On 29 January 1983, Julie won the Golden Globe as Best Actress in a Motion Picture (Comedy/Musical) — her third such award — over her old friend Carol Burnett in *Annie*. A fortnight later, *Victor/Victoria* was nominated for seven Academy Awards — including Best Actress and Best Adapted Screenplay. It was Julie's third nomination and — amazingly — Blake's first. 'You appreciate it more as you go along in your career,' Julie told Army Archerd for *Variety*. 'At the beginning, if you receive it, you're primarily dazzled.'

Everywhere, there seemed to be a desire to reclaim her, to view *Victor/Victoria* as a comeback. At Harvard University on 13 February, she picked up the Hasty Pudding Award as Woman of the Year. Flanked, aptly, by drag queens, she was paraded through Harvard Square, above which a banner stretched, acclaiming 'Jazz Hot Julie'. Viewing askance the pudding pot award, she asked, 'All right if I throw up in it?'

Two months later, on 11 April 1983, the fifty-fifth Academy Awards took place at the Dorothy Chandler Pavilion, Los Angeles. It was eighteen years since Julie had last attended in competition. As the only actress of her generation in the category, she was up against Jessica Lange (as tragic 1930s film star Frances Farmer) in *Frances*, Sissy Spacek in *Missing*, Meryl Streep (the clear favourite) in *Sophie's Choice* and Debra Winger in *An Officer and a Gentleman*.

Elsewhere, it was a clash of the titans: Steven Spielberg's all-time box-office champion *E.T.* against Richard Attenborough's epic *Gandhi*. The latter hauled in the lion's share of statuettes, its star Ben Kingsley beating out Dustin Hoffman in *Tootsie*, another gender-bender success, in which Hoffman played the same role as Julie, in reverse.

As predicted, Julie lost to Meryl Streep, as did Blake to Costa-Gavras for his political thriller *Missing*. Robert Preston and Lesley Ann Warren were also outvoted in their Oscar bids — but Henry Mancini and Leslie Bricusse won for Best Original Song Score/Adaptation — making *Victor/Victoria* the first Julie Andrews film since *Thoroughly Modern Millie* to take home gold.

* * *

Towards the end of the previous year, and after some initial reservations, Mr and Mrs Edwards had granted an exhaustive interview to *Playboy* magazine, which appeared in the Christmas 1982 issue. But if the public expected to find Julie disrobed once more, across a centrespread with a staple in her midriff, they were to be disappointed: the interview was revealing in quite a different way.

Julie admitted that the failure of their first two films had made her wonder if they were ever going to know joint success: 'Once in a while, I felt that maybe I was a jinx for Blake and we shouldn't work together . . . We're way past that now. And it never really mattered, anyway, because the pleasure of doing a film with him far outweighs any other consideration.'

Blake reflected on the suggestions of homosexuality that had dogged him for years, exacerbated by the gay content of *Victor/Victoria*. 'I'm too analytically trained to let that hang me up,' he said; denying that there had ever been anything more than 'some homosexual fantasies' in his younger days, he attributed the rumours to those 'so fearful of their own sexuality that they have to snipe at others'. By implication, the sexual gossip to which *Playboy* journalist Lawrence Linderman referred also applied to Julie, but she felt no need to explain herself.

The basis of the Edwards' marriage, after more than a decade, remained that expounded in their latest film by Victor/Victoria and King Marchan: 'No secrets, no grudge collecting. If something bothers us, we say so. We don't plan past tomorrow — we just take it a day at a time.' Remarkably, it seemed to be working.

16

MATTERS OF LIFE AND DEATH

'There's a place where one says, that's for family, that's for me. It's nothing I've withdrawn from. I just don't think people need to come into the bathroom with me'

— Julie Andrews, 1999

Julie Andrews lay on an operating table, her mouth wide open, the medical appliance approaching her throat. The doctors around her spoke in low voices: 'Let me have the 'scope . . . Small granular lesion . . . When will they know?' And the answer: 'They should have this back by Monday.'

Later, the star was driven home by her doctor, ruminating on the biopsy: 'If it's benign, I'll hit a C above top C. If it's malignant, I'll hear about it soon enough anyway.' Then, a change of heart: 'I want to talk about it now — am I going to sing again?'

Meanwhile, the credits continued to come up across the screen. What had just occurred was no more than the opening shots of Blake Edwards's comedy *That's Life!*, depicting a weekend of crisis in the lives of a popular singer and her fractious husband. Shooting the film in late 1985, Blake could not possibly have seen the dreadful omen lurking in the plot — that, just over a decade later, his wife would be subject to fears frighteningly similar to those visited on her latest screen counterpart.

★ ★ ★

Four years before the release of *That's Life!*, Julie had come face to face with tragedy on a vastly more important scale. In the summer of 1982, she and Tony Adams, so long an integral part of the Edwards family, had spent twelve days in Southeast Asia, under the auspices of Operation California, visiting Ho Chi Minh City and Phnom Penh.

'I will remember this place to my dying day,' she wrote after visiting one orphan camp on the border between Thailand and Cambodia, witnessing for herself the appalling malnutrition and disease. She came back to California determined to focus media attention on the young survivors of the Vietnam War.

The following year, President Reagan presented Operation California with his Volunteer Action Award. In June 1984, the United Nations High Commissioner for Refugees included Julie in a conference on African relief. From then on, she would devote more of her energy — and, privately, her money — to relief work, recognising, as she had started to do with her family and friends, that time was no longer her friend.

On 15 July 1982, Madame Lilian Stiles-Allen died in Kent, aged ninety-one. Of all the bereavements that Julie Andrews would suffer in the decade, this was almost more significant than any that followed. It was Madame who had forged the link between talent and technique, carrying the little girl with the freak four-octave voice up to the stars — and keeping her there. Even as the range of Julie's voice had grown shorter, the sound of Lilian Stiles-Allen's teaching still rang clarion clear: the diction, the tonality, the focus — all tribute to the only vocal coach she had ever had.

Quite what Madame would have made of her pupil's next musical foray was anyone's guess. In the spring of 1983, Julie took a trip to Nashville, Tennessee, to record a collection of country and western classics, including 'Crazy', 'You Don't Bring Me Flowers' and the album's title track, 'Love Me Tender', a duet with Johnny Cash. The result, immaculate and wistful, had as much in common with country and western as Johnny Cash's solo albums had with Broadway. *Love Me Tender* was released first in Britain, Julie finding a common chord between the ballads on the album and the English songs of her youth. Few others made the same connection.

As far as her film career was concerned, Julie was back working for her husband. But after the box-office smash of *10* and the critical bouquets for *Victor/Victoria*, Blake was facing a debilitating series of setbacks in all aspects of his life.

Cobbling together outtakes of older *Pink Panther* films with new footage shot in England, he had hoped to obviate the death of Peter Sellers by keeping Inspector Clouseau alive in

Trail of the Pink Panther and *Curse of the Pink Panther*. The results were little short of a disgrace. But Blake moved on, preparing an English language remake of François Truffaut's 1977 hit, *L'Homme Qui Aimait les Femmes*. Julie had once been said by her old acquaintance Dory Previn to hanker after making a film for a European master such as Truffaut. Sadly, when she finally came to work on *The Man Who Loved Women*, it was one large step removed from its *auteur*.

The original had managed to be both sexy and funny. The remake for Columbia Pictures was doomed to failure. 'It's been my experience that any time I think I know where it's at, it's usually somewhere else,' William Holden's character had said in *S.O.B.*; Blake seemed not to take his own scripted point.

His protagonist was David Fowler, a Los Angeles Lothario, played by Burt Reynolds. His onscreen conquests included Kim Basinger and Marilu Henner, with Jennifer Edwards playing yet another slut for her father. Further down the cast list was the newest addition to the Edwards clan, Denise Crosby (granddaughter of Bing, Julie's amorous co-star from *High Tor* in 1956), who married Geoffrey in 1983.

Pervading the entire production and co-authoring the screenplay was Blake's psychoanalyst Dr Milton Wexler, now seventy-five. His onscreen alter ego, Marianna, was played by Julie, who took advantage of his continual presence on set: 'A great deal of the time we just sat and talked. He advised me on attitude, the way one would behave

439

and how still one would be. And I drew on the fact that I've had psychoanalysis myself, so I know how it feels to be in an office like that.'

What made Wexler's involvement contentious was that Blake was still in therapy with him — a huge breach of the convention that analysts and patients should keep their distance outside sessions. But while the doctor's peers (and some of his clients) were vocal in their disgust, Blake was less censorious, as he told Stephen Farber and Marc Green for their book *Hollywood on the Couch*: 'I couldn't have had a family if I hadn't gotten into therapy because I'm too fucked up. I'm a major hypochondriac.'

Shot in Los Angeles, Houston and Harris County, Texas, what emerged from the soul-searching was talkative and non-involving, although Reynolds gave an engagingly frank portrayal of the titular womaniser. As the psychoanalyst, Julie's onscreen tumble into bed with her leading man (to whom she paid the usual compliments: 'Working with him is such a joy . . . makes it easy for us ladies . . . ') seemed unprofessional rather than interesting. She did not even look very good, the streamlined contours of *Victor/Victoria* giving way to office frumpishness. Her hair, too, blonde and with a long fringe over her forehead, made her look suddenly older.

The New York premiere on 16 December 1983 was no occasion for rejoicing. For the *New York Times*, Vincent Canby tried to be polite, praising Burt Reynolds' performance as 'chief among its virtues', but adding, '*The Man Who*

Loved Women is not top-drawer Blake . . . The screenplay by Mr Edwards, Milton Wexler and Geoffrey Edwards, doesn't build to any climax. It coasts toward a known destination.' He liked Kim Basinger as an oversexed Texas millionaire's wife, and Julie, whom he considered 'awfully good at listening' — an unknowing comment on her qualities as wife as much as actress.

In *Time* magazine on 26 December, Richard Schickel added little festive cheer, accusing Blake of turning 'François Truffaut's delicious 1977 Gallic soufflé into singles' restaurant quiche'. By and large, the film was ignored; it swiftly headed to videotape release the following autumn, long before Julie's most popular films made the same journey.

Only a year after her third Oscar nomination, Julie found herself consigned to the death camp for actresses known as middle age. With 1983 the first year since 1957 in which the entire Quigley Top 10 list of money-making stars was made up of men, producers seemed interested only in booking Meryl Streep (if absolutely necessary) for Art.

Julie was in good company. Barbra Streisand had just made her own screen appearance in men's clothing with the musical *Yentl*. Like *Victor/Victoria*, it was well received, but other offers were unforthcoming. Even Shirley Maclaine, taking home an overdue Oscar for *Terms of Endearment*, would find similar roles of quality to be few and far between.

As for Blake, whether because of the negative reception of the film, or just his age, he was

441

attacked in 1983 by the worst case of illness he had ever suffered. 'He took an enormous nosedive into depression and feeling terrible,' Julie would say on the Biography Channel tribute to him. 'It was a very difficult time.'

'Everyone around him was incredibly worried,' said Tony Adams. 'He was wasting away — in deep physical and mental crisis.' There was another name for it: chronic fatigue syndrome.

Nor was Julie in the best of health. For the last couple of years, she had been prescribed a high protein, low starch diet for her longstanding low blood sugar. It had meant a reappraisal of the wartime diet that Julie had enjoyed into adulthood: boiled potato sandwiches were now off the menu.

* * *

The Edwards family continued to split the year between Gstaad, where Julie paid for the high street Christmas lights, and Malibu, where Amy and Joanna (a year apart in age, and both still short of their tenth birthdays) went to school. They, Emma and, to a lesser extent, Jennifer and Geoffrey had what many children could only imagine, Maria von Trapp as a mother — whether they liked it or not. Julie acknowledged to me that her reputation must have made her a difficult act to follow: 'I've been conscious of it all my children's lives. On the other hand, that's the way it is, and I would be a fool to deny my own abilities.'

She had always been at pains to emphasise

442

that she had five children, giving them all equal public status, but it seemed that her blood daughter was the most responsible of them all — 'always such a good sport', Julie would say. Emma had plans to be an actress herself, studying drama at the Herbert Berghoff Studio in New York.

When I saw Julie for the first time, she recounted what she called 'a real mum's story' about her daughter's early television appearance in a soap opera. Emma had said she was playing a waitress with a little green feather in her hair. Julie duly tuned in: 'All I saw were close-ups of the most important characters and this little green feather, and in typical ambitious mother fashion, I kept saying, 'There she is, Blake!' — terribly excited — and he and I started to laugh, because it was so painful and funny and sweet and I was so keen that she succeed . . . I couldn't see her face, even.'

The glossier television soap operas and mini-series were one of the few areas where ageing female stars were still in demand. Such offers that came her way, Julie turned down, preferring to wait until the work she really liked came along. In June 1984, she hosted the thirty-eighth Tony Awards in New York, part-nered by Robert Preston, her co-star from *Victor/Victoria*. And in mid-October, *The Times* of London reported that the Broadway season of 1985 was to include the premiere of *Victor/Victoria*: Julie and Blake were translating their screen hit to the stage.

That same month came news that Blake was

not only planning to resurrect old successes, but to reignite old carnage — blaming the failure of *The Curse of the Pink Panther* on Metro-Goldwyn-Mayer's marketing, and suing the studio for $180 million. MGM promptly countersued Blake for $340 million, alleging that he had 'overspent and squandered large sums on unnecessary expensive items', while making *Victor/Victoria* in England. Blake then counter-countersued MGM for $400 million for libel, playing yet another round of Russian roulette with his career in Tinseltown.

★ ★ ★

The next loss that Julie suffered was one that would affect her more deeply than perhaps even she might have expected. On 19 December 1984, Barbara Andrews died in St Peter's Hospital, Chertsey in Surrey, aged seventy-four. She had been treated at the hospital for circulation problems, and had subsequently had an operation on an aortic aneurism, from which she sadly did not recover.

The surgeon, Martin Thomas, enlisted her daughter's support to raise funds for a laboratory specialising in vascular ultrasound procedures. 'She started us off with a very nice cheque,' he told me, 'and allowed us to use her name.' In March 1986, the star would return to St Peter's Hospital to open the Julie Andrews Unit, in appreciation of the treatment her mother had received.

Memories of flame-haired Barbara and her

lust for life would stretch out across the years. Speaking to the London *Evening Standard* in 2000, Tony Walton recalled how she retained a healthily down-to-earth attitude towards her daughter's prowess: 'Julie's mum used to be really upset that she would always try to stay in the shadow, even at the peak of *My Fair Lady*. So, once in a blue moon, Julie would put on something a little tasty and go out and make her presence known — and her mother would immediately say 'Who the — do you think you are, you little tart?''

But always, Barbara's pride would shine through, as on a 1979 visit to Los Angeles. 'Of course we never dreamed of film,' she confided to journalist Jane Ardmore. 'Julie used to complain bitterly about her nose and her jaw. But for a plain little girl, I think she has . . . not necessarily beauty, but a wonderful warm quality — somehow luminous.'

The gap would long remain in Julie's life. On the British television chat show *Parkinson* in 2004, the star could not mention her mother without adding, simply, 'I miss her.'

A highly gifted pianist, with the early potential to be a serious show-business entity, Barbara's commitment to all her children was echoed in Julie's deeply felt words at the memorial service on Saturday 29 December: 'She touched us and gave us joy and made the quality of our lives a little more special.' The service at St Peter's Church, Hersham, where she was first married, was attended by Barbara's children and her quieter, younger sister Joan who continued to live in Surrey, much loved in her own right. Also paying his last respects was Barbara's first husband, Ted Wells, still proudly erect of carriage but now rather shorter than his daughter, who held his hand in the churchyard after the service, in the raw winter afternoon.

The following summer, as Julie Andrews approached her fiftieth birthday, she faced an artistic reminder of her own mortality, with the return of Dr Milton Wexler to the world of film. Serenely rising above the failure of *The Man Who Loved Women*, Wexler began work with Blake and his wife on an original, heavily autobiographical idea — *Crisis*.

The plot centres on Harvey Fairchild, an architect on the verge of both his sixtieth birthday and a nervous breakdown — and his wife Gillian, for whom still waters run deep. Blake was back in the same territory as *10*. Playing the Blake prototype was the actor who had turned down the lead role in the earlier film — Jack Lemmon. The film also attempted to probe the inner Julie Andrews. Gillian is, like Sam in *10*, a singer in public and a long-suffering partner in private. In *Crisis*, the two aspects converge in her anxious wait for the results of a biopsy on her throat, while Harvey and their three adult children remain oblivious to all but their own problems.

Much of the dialogue was improvised from a thirteen-page treatment by Dr Wexler, more than ever conjuring the image of a manipulative Shaw in Hirschfeld's cartoon for *My Fair Lady*. 'Milton would be on the set, because we didn't have a script,' said Blake. 'It was almost like group therapy. We would sit and talk about this character and what they would say.' Geoffrey Edwards, working behind the camera, could see how close the analytic process came to home: 'It was our kind of family religion. We didn't go to church, we went to group therapy.'

At the outset, the leading lady asked the director how she should play her part. 'Just be yourself,' said Blake. 'Oh, God, who is that?' Julie exclaimed. She was not alone. Jack Lemmon's son Chris played his film counterpart Josh (with possible overtones of Geoffrey Edwards), Jennifer Edwards the elder daughter Megan, and Emma Walton the youngest of the three, Kate (her middle name in real life).

There was more. Julie's doctor, who tells her the biopsy is thankfully clear, was Jordan Christopher, whom Sybil Burton had married after divorcing Julie's *Camelot* co-star in 1964. As usual, the executive producer was Jonathan D. Krane, another Wexler client. His actress wife Sally Kellerman, who had met him in therapy, also appeared in the film, as did Mrs Jack Lemmon, alias Felicia Farr, in a minor role.

That's Life! — as *Crisis* was to become known — started shooting in November 1985. Blake had put up the entire budget of $1.5 million himself, little more than the living expenses on *Darling Lili*, if inflation were taken into account. The cast and crew had been recruited to work for non-union salaries (a polite way of saying next to nothing). A lot of union people were very unhappy as a result, picketing in protest outside the gate at 27944 Pacific Coast Highway, the Edwards' Malibu house, where almost the entire film was to be shot.

The estate certainly looked handsome, the automated white front gate opening on to lush green lawns, carved in two by a long driveway. The ubiquitous Hollywood pool was there, as were the tall windows with the ocean view, the open staircase, the white-painted brick walls in the bedroom. The impression was that Blake and Julie Edwards, every bit as much as Harvey and Gillian Fairchild, had just stepped out of bed.

Julie watched her husband, now sixty-three, directing her co-star: 'And it was as if the past was coming up right in my face again, because Blake was telling Lemmon to be Blake.'

At the end of the film, Gillian lashes into Harvey for all his selfishness. How much of this resonated within the Edwards' marriage itself had been the stuff of press speculation for the previous quarter of a century — but, in reality, Blake's fragile health, which meant working hours were kept to a minimum, had made the couple closer than ever. 'Blake was deeply in love with Julie, very much counting on her,' said Milton Wexler, and Tony Adams would call it 'truly the definitive autobiographical film'.

When, many years later, I asked Julie to name her favourite film, she was coy: 'That is a little like asking, 'Which puppy in the basket do you love best?'' Pushed further, she still resisted: 'I have really enjoyed all the movies I have made, each for a different reason.' Asked a third time, she gave in: 'One of the films that is very dear is

That's Life! — a really wonderful work experience.'

★ ★ ★

Shortly after Christmas, Julie received a call from England. Faye Dunaway had quit the film *Duet for One*, claiming the script was not to her liking. When Menahem Golan and Yoram Globus of the British Cannon Group (known, a little worryingly, as the Go-Go Boys) asked Julie to take over, she was only too aware of the challenge. 'It was,' she said, 'a little bit like going to America for the first time, when Dad gave me the push; Blake said it was good and I should try to do it.'

Tom Kempinski's play had been a West End success with Frances de la Tour (and a Broadway flop with Anne Bancroft) five years earlier. Based on the life of Jacqueline du Pré, struck down at the height of her career as a cellist by multiple sclerosis, *Duet for One* depicted a virtuoso violinist named Stephanie Anderson, afflicted with the same muscle-wasting disease.

The only other role in the stage play was that of the analyst. But if Julie was wary of yet another bout of introspection, she would at least be playing opposite the actor with whom she had worked so happily on *Hawaii*, and who had already performed in *Duet for One* on Broadway, Max von Sydow.

Elsewhere, the script had been opened out, not particularly to its benefit. Liam Neeson featured as the rag-and-bone man to whom

Stephanie turns for sex pure and simple — requiring Julie, for the first time on screen, to use the F word a very great deal. Stephanie's unfaithful husband was played by Alan Bates and his mistress by Cathryn Harrison — the granddaughter of Julie's *My Fair Lady* co-star and the daughter of the best man at Julie's first wedding, as well as one of the children Robert Wise had auditioned when casting *The Sound of Music*.

In London, Julie stayed as usual at the Dorchester Hotel. She visited a multiple sclerosis clinic in Bromley, close to where she had once lived in Beckenham: 'I worried there would be a voyeuristic quality to my going and looking in on their illness . . . but far from it; they welcomed me with open arms.'

Filming commenced on Monday 10 February 1986 at the EMI Studios in Borehamwood. Julie had not only studied the bodily effects of the disease, but also learned the violin: 'It was terrifyingly difficult to learn to do. Within my first week of shooting, I made my debut at the Albert Hall in front of a symphonic orchestra.' Her interpretations of Bach and Bruch were ghosted by Nigel Kennedy, the wild child of the British classical music world. And in the film itself, there was another *enfant terrible*, albeit a more aristocratic one, Rupert Everett.

In his autobiography *Red Carpets and Other Banana Skins*, Everett would write of his nursery obsession with Julie, which stemmed from repeated visits with his real-life nanny to see *Mary Poppins*. Everett was to discover, as had so many who presumed too easily to know her, that she could be 'a hard nut to crack'. When he first met Julie, his nerves got to him, and he could only stammer, in the Dick Van Dyke Cockney accent he was adopting for his role, 'Wotcha.'

'Do you always speak like that?' asked Julie.

Come the key Royal Albert Hall sequence, however, the audience was filled with what Everett called 'queens with Julie obsessions, some of them quite freaky in wigs and flashers' Macs'. Julie looked at him and winked, just as they started shooting, and he knew he had broken through her reserve.

The acting scenes were extraordinarily daunting. As Stephanie's abilities slowly wither, she declines through denial, despair, fury, bitterness, debauchery and attempted suicide before reaching a measure of peace. Julie's work, showing a greater range of emotion than ever before, was if anything too deeply felt — possibly more unsettling than had a more battle-worn actress, such as Glenda Jackson, taken the role. Unfortunately, the Russian director Andrei Konchalovsky failed to create a cohesive framework around her, and none of the other players could deliver a satisfying performance within the limitations of the script.

Whatever the compromises of the film during the ten-week shoot, Julie was, she said, 'right royally spoiled — working with English crews is just wonderful'. Because of the tight schedule, she was unable to go to Yorkshire, where her father now lived near his son John and other daughter Celia. Instead, Ted Wells came to

London to see her, after filming had ended, at a rare question and answer session at the National Film Theatre.

Wearing a white silk shirt and a black skirt, with a coral-coloured pullover across her shoulders, she appeared the epitome of elegance, hair well cut with an auburn rinse and skin as flawless as legend had it. But, as always, what registered most to me was the blueness of her eyes.

Pertinently, asked whether she read her own reviews, she resisted the opportunity to be disingenuous. 'You do — and good friends always make sure that you do, anyway . . . ' But she had had enough rave notices in her time to rationalise any carping comments: 'Obviously, nobody sets out to make a bad picture, and everybody tries very hard and hopes that the work is well received. But the most important thing is to enjoy it while you're doing it; and if the endeavour has been honest, then the rest is just icing.'

She was shortly to be put to the test — twice. On 9 September 1986, *That's Life!* was showcased at the Toronto Festival, and released a fortnight later. 'Full of sunlight, warm feelings and wonderfully rude gags,' wrote Vincent Canby in the *New York Times*, calling the cast 'first-rate'; on the opposite coast, the *Los Angeles Times* voted it 'one of the funniest, and perhaps the most life-embracing, movies Edwards has made in the '80s', adding that 'the currents of despair give the humour a deeper bite'.

Time magazine also gave it a good report,

judging that Lemmon gave 'what is unquestionably the greatest of his portrayals of the middle-class American male at bay'. It credited Julie's strong, spirited support: 'Her tart, get-on-with-it Englishness stiffens the spine of her characterisation — and makes the one moment when she gives in to her dread all the more poignant.' Having cost so little to make, the relatively meagre income of $4 million for Columbia Pictures was enough to put *That's Life!* into the black.

In November, Julie's other film of 1986 was released — what *Variety* called 'a moving portrait of a life in turmoil'. *Duet for One* contained, said Richard Corliss of *Time* magazine, 'one of Julie Andrews' strongest performances . . . she doesn't tear a passion to tatters; she uses it to stitch a coherent soul.' But he added: 'All else is a shambles.'

Duet for One soon disappeared — but not before Julie received a notable tribute at the beginning of 1987, a double nomination at the Golden Globe Awards for Best Actress in a comedy (*That's Life!*) and drama (*Duet for One*). Neither performance won, however — nor yielded a more important nomination for the Oscars.

★ ★ ★

Before either of her films was released, one of Julie's dearest colleagues, Alan Jay Lerner, succumbed to lung cancer in New York at the age of sixty-seven, on 14 June 1986. One week later, 1,500 people congregated at the Shubert Theatre, Broadway, to pay emotional tribute. Frederick Loewe, aged eighty-five, sent a letter from his retirement home in Palm Springs: 'It won't be long before we'll be writing together again. I just hope they have a decent piano up there.' Julie sang Noël Coward's 'If Love Were All', which she had recorded many moons ago for her album *Broadway's Fair*.

Even though reports that *Victor/Victoria* was coming to Broadway had proved false, Julie's thoughts were turning back to music in general — just as they had done, in the absence of any firm film offers, a decade earlier. One musical project, mentioned as far back as 1982, had been a screen remake of *The Merry Widow*, with Julie in the title role opposite one of the world's greatest opera stars, Placido Domingo. It might have been spectacular, but Julie was said to harbour reservations about the script, and the idea never came to fruition. In 1987, however, she joined forces with Domingo to retrace her musical steps to Salzburg, in one of the last great old-style television specials for American television, *The Sound of Christmas*.

Filmed entirely in Austria, using locations from *The Sound of Music*, the pair were joined by the folk singer legend John Denver; surprisingly, the chemistry was good between all three performers. Domingo sang 'Ave Maria', Julie performed the almost obligatory 'Edelweiss' with Denver, and the trio came together for '*Stille Nacht*', at the Alpine chapel where it had been composed. The King's Singers backed Julie in various carols, and she gave solo renditions of 'In the Bleak Midwinter' and 'The Sound of Christmas'. Even her costume, consisting of an outfit akin to silver aluminium foil that made her look ready for oven roasting, could not detract from a tasteful and well-performed programme.

First televised on ABC on 16 December 1987, *The Sound of Christmas* was repeated two years later, and won all the awards for which it was nominated — its five Emmys including one for the musical direction of Julie's long-time colleague Ian Fraser.

Julie had by then made another album — intended only as a sixty-fifth birthday present for Blake. The collection of songs, recorded in 1987 with Bob Florence accompanying her on a very obvious synthesiser, included 'Come Rain or Come Shine', 'Tea for Two' and 'What Are You Doing the Rest of Your Life?' Blake was enthusiastic enough to suggest releasing the album commercially, under the title *Love, Julie* — but, on the open market, the pleasant, middle-of-the-road release went nowhere. One track in particular, 'Nobody Does It Better (baby, you're the best)', begged an uncharitable response.

Nevertheless, Julie seemed ready to deliver to the audience that had consistently needed her most: the ageing fans of her salad days — who, in the absence of any musical film or Broadway show, were more than happy to attend a retrospective concert. At the end of October 1987, the star set out on the road with a forty-piece orchestra. Her tour, which stretched into the spring of 1988, went up and down the

East Coast, from Pennsylvania and Cleveland to Florida, and travelled further into the central zone to cities including St Louis, Chicago, Detroit and Minneapolis. Self-referencing material included Noël Coward's 'Don't Put Your Daughter on the Stage, Mrs Worthington', leading into a scratchy recording of her singing the 'Polonaise' in *Starlight Roof*, and reminiscences of wartime music halls summarised by 'Burlington Bertie from Bow'.

Stephen Holden for the *New York Times* caught her performance in November, at the Westbury Music Fair on Long Island: 'If Miss Andrews' full-out lyric soprano voice isn't as lustrous as it used to be, her singing still has plenty of fibre.' And he had the grace to acknowledge that 'the resolute optimism' she still purveyed seemed not to be superficial cordiality but 'a deep-rooted and engaging character trait'.

Julie also included a new piece, 'Fifty Words or Less', running through a laundry list of the adjectives most frequently applied to her — with particular mention of 'wholesome', 'sweet' and 'cold' — before arriving at her preferred word: 'lucky'. Closing the programme was a Lerner and Loewe medley, which brought the audience to its feet in automatic delight. It was an apt tribute to Frederic Loewe, who died while Julie was on tour, on 14 February 1988.

* * *

One of the more morbid points of reference for any ageing star is honorary award status. In May

1988, Julie was host rather than recipient, at the American Film Institute Life Achievement Award to Jack Lemmon, televised on CBS. But Lemmon had his chance to return the favour later in the year, on Saturday 7 October, when Julie was honoured in her own country by the British Academy of Film and Television Arts, the first woman to be given the Lifetime Tribute Award. 'There is no one, believe me, that I respect and admire and love more than you, my dear,' Lemmon enthused. 'You have inordinate talents — all my other leading ladies sang like turkeys . . . '

At the Odeon cinema in Leicester Square, David Tomlinson, James Coburn and James Fox were among those to share their personal memories. Blake, trading his black leather jacket for black tie, also contributed to the commentary: 'According to California community property law, I'm entitled to half this award. Good on you, digger.' Calling Julie 'a tremendous ambassador for Britain', Anne, the Princess Royal, President of BAFTA, paid her own tribute: 'There is only one word for Julie Andrews: 'Supercalifragilisticexpialidocious'.'

Julie — wearing the black taffeta gown from the concert scene in *Duet for One* — replied, 'It's just across the road at the London Hippodrome that it all began for me.' She then told the story of the old flower seller who had given her the violets and wished her luck. 'I'm very proud of my British heritage,' she ended. 'I'm first and always British and I carry my country in my heart wherever I go.'

The evening had included a filmed contribution from Carol Burnett. This Julie appeared to enjoy most of all, although it finished with the thought that pervades all such ceremonies: 'You know, when they start giving you awards like this, it's almost over . . . ' But it was not, quite: the old friends had already taped their third variety show, *Julie and Carol: Together Again*, on 9 and 10 June before a live audience at the Pantages Theatre, Hollywood, for ABC telecast on 13 December.

In rehearsals, Carol had wryly noted the difference in their lives: 'Twenty-five years ago, it was 'Gosh! Golly! Let's go bowling! Let's go to the Peppermint Lounge and do the twist!' Now Julie's saying, 'Have you ever just sat in some good Epsom salts? Oooooh . . . that's so good!'' The format too was rather more arthritic, with reviewers casting up memories of the two previous outings by unflattering contrast. There were some potentially embarrassing moments, like 'Mama's Rap', in which the two 'girls' mocked the ageist attitudes of their daughters' generation — yet, when they threw away their baggy clothes, it was to reveal legs any thirty-year-old would have envied, and the sentimental, almost valedictory, appeal of the show was summed up by the final duet, Stephen Sondheim's 'Old Friend'.

Julie had not yet finished with her own solo show. After recording the special with Carol, she went back out across the country, finishing at the Wiltern Theatre, Los Angeles, in August 1989. There, *Julie Andrews in Concert* was taped by

PBS (Julie spreading her favours between the major networks) to be broadcast on 9 March 1990.

And, in the country of her birth, Julie closed out the decade with another old friend. On Monday 11 December 1989 at the Royal Festival Hall, André Previn conducted the London Symphony Orchestra, as Julie Andrews sang a selection of Christmas carols to a packed, enraptured audience. 'Most of all, we love her for her diction,' wrote Alastair Macaulay in the *Financial Times*, tongue in cheek but with a self-confessed tear in his eye. 'Her every syllable hangs — pure, firm, crisp — like an icicle in the air.'

★ ★ ★

Back in 1986, Julie had spoken of balancing motherhood with a high-profile career: 'It isn't easy. There's always guilt. I try to make quality time with my kids, rather than quantity. Who's to say, as long as they're hugged and loved a lot, some adversity doesn't strengthen them, to a degree . . . ' In February 1987, *Reader's Digest* magazine had quoted Emma's description of Julie Edwards around the house: 'She's always there to read a bedtime story or to go for a quiet walk and talk in the garden. Inevitably she is the one to clean up after a family pet. She will look up and sigh, 'I wonder if Elizabeth Taylor does this.''

And in 1989, Julie reflected how, as a child, it had been she rather than her parents who had made quality time, recalling, 'I would travel enormous distances to come home for even a few hours.' Things had not changed so much. 'I couldn't live without my career, but I also can't give up caring for my family, so I'm always balancing the two sets of needs.'

But not even the self-defined Lady Libra could control the balance for other people. Kayti Edwards, Jennifer's daughter, brought up in Blake and Julie's household, had been causing trouble for some little while, running away from home, taking Julie's keys to take the car on joy rides, clearly heading towards a stormy future. At the same time, the two adopted girls were also experiencing problems — especially Joanna. Reported as having taken drugs from the age of eleven, she was hospitalised in 1991 for alcohol and cocaine addiction.

'It wasn't such a surprise when it all unravelled,' Julie told Jan Moir for the *Guardian* in London. 'Since she is an adopted daughter from another country, she has always had a real identity problem, as to who she is and where she belongs. I imagine that having Julie Andrews as a mum and Blake Edwards as a dad is hard to deal with, although we took that into consideration . . . Mine was an odd life and hers is, too.'

At the turn of the decade, both Blake's son and Julie's daughter were also shaping their futures. Geoffrey divorced Denise Crosby, while Emma married actor Stephen Hamilton, whom she had met at the experimental Ensemble Theatre in New York.

Shortly afterwards, the newlyweds decided

that the rewards of a struggling thespian were not enough for either of them. Steve would later say, 'I was earning a living, but I felt I wasn't captain of my own ship and Emma felt the same way. My ambition was to produce and live outside New York.'

They found their ideal spot where Tony and Gen Walton had a country house, in the small East Hampton town of Sag Harbor, Long Island. There, like a latter-day Judy Garland and Mickey Rooney, Emma and Steve set about creating their own theatre, enlisting the support of Tony and one of the family's oldest friends, Sybil Christopher, who lived nearby. The Bay Street Theatre, created out of a former torpedo factory on Long Wharf, opened successfully in 1992. It could, of course, count on Mum to sing at a fundraiser and Dad to do the odd design.

* * *

After a four-year break from films, Julie had entered the 1990s making what was known severally as *A Fine Romance* (America), *Tchin-Tchin* (Northern Europe), *Cin-Cin* (Italy), *A Touch of Adultery* (Britain) and *Afternoon Tea in Bed* (Japan). Co-starring Marcello Mastroianni, and based on a boulevard comedy by François Billetdoux, it was a flop in any language.

The two stars played up to the image expected of them: tired Latin lover Cesario and starchy English lady Pamela, who realise their respective spouses are having an affair. When Cesario pushes her to admit her own private passions,

461

Pamela haltingly admits, 'I'm no different from anybody else. But I'm strait laced and I'm British and I'm very *busy*, so people think I'm cold.' Inevitably, the couple fall a little bit in love, and end up having their own affair — long after their spouses have returned to them. Julie, dressed by Versace, looked smart but not particularly elegant. She was seen riding a motorcycle, driving a Range Rover, dispensing charity to the Parisian poor and treating her twenty-two-year-old son in the film as if he were Friedrich von Trapp.

Filmed mostly in Paris, it was directed by Gene Saks, without much authority. Further marred by bad dubbing, it came out and went almost straight to videotape. And that was the end of Julie's cinema career for a very long time.

On the French film set in March 1990, Julie was told that Ted Wells, her beloved father, had died in Ryedale, Yorkshire, at the age of eighty-one. Julie, who had been the linchpin of the family as a girl, was now, other than Aunt Joan, the eldest of them all.

Death also hung over Julie's next acting role. In 1991, she made her first serious television drama, *Our Sons* — light years from her previous work. The director was John Erman, who had made the first teleplay to deal with AIDS, *An Early Frost*, in 1985. That same year, the disease had claimed the life of Julie's *Darling Lili* co-star Rock Hudson.

The title refers to two young gay men, one of whom has AIDS. The healthy partner (Hugh Grant, a couple of years from stardom) asks his mother to contact his dying lover's own estranged mother. So San Diego tyro Audrey (Julie) makes the journey to Arkansas to persuade trailer trash Luanne (Ann-Margret) to see her son (Zeljko Ivanek).

The two actresses were very good, as they should have been, playing saint and sinner respectively. 'We were such opposites,' wrote Ann-Margret in her autobiography, *My Story*. 'Julie had everything under control. She was always cheerful, prepared, well-organised, and perfectly dressed, Mary Poppins-like . . . Her dressing room was always tidy, whereas five minutes after I arrived, mine was a disaster.'

Broadcast by ABC on 19 May, *Our Sons* received respectful reviews, but the success was rather too obvious for both women. As much as the teleplay attempted to challenge conceptions about its subject matter, it happily embraced the stereotyping of its two lead actresses, Julie in particular.

★ ★ ★

On 2 June 1991, alongside Jeremy Irons, Julie co-hosted the forty-fifth Tony Awards. During the show she sang a Lerner and Loewe medley, including 'I Could Have Danced All Night'. The following season, she would herself receive an honour of sorts, when she was spoofed in the third of the knockabout *Forbidden Broadway* shows with 'I Couldn't Hit That Note'. A caustic take on her growing tendency to rely on pentimenti to get up to and out of difficult phrases, it was funnier than what came next — the most embarrassing production on which she and Blake would ever embark.

Julie, a sitcom starring the eponymous Mrs Edwards and directed by her husband, began life as a pilot made in 1991, entitled simply *Millie* — but if the idea was to make something thoroughly modern, Julie and Blake were deluding themselves. The pilot was never screened, although six episodes of the rebranded *Julie* were made for ABC and scheduled for broadcast in the summer of 1992. Co-produced by Tony Adams, with music by Henry Mancini, *Julie* was among friends but this, as she knew from the past, was no guarantee of success. And the show was a loser from the start.

Julie starred as Julie Carlyle, the star of a television variety show, who marries a veterinarian (played by James Farentino), moves to Sioux City, Iowa with her husband and his two children, and continues to shoot her series from there. First broadcast on Saturday 30 May, it was dismissed by the *Los Angeles Times* as 'perfunctory'. Other Hollywood commentators agreed on its failure to reach the level of even the average domestic sitcom, at a time when shows like *Seinfeld* and *Married . . . With Children* were redefining the genre.

Blake directed the first two episodes only, so he could be excused for the lamentable fourth instalment, when Julie was seen singing to an orang-utan. By then, the show's fate was sealed. The sixth episode aired on Saturday 4 July — and that was the end of it, an uneasy reminder of the big screen flops that Mr and Mrs Edwards had suffered in their early career together.

★ ★ ★

A failed television comedy vehicle, however, seemed very insignificant when set against the humanitarian relief work with which the star was now seriously involved. In March 1992, Julie Andrews was appointed Goodwill Ambassador for the United Nations Development Fund for Women, and presented with her diplomatic passport in New York by United Nations Secretary-General Boutros Boutros-Ghali.

I listened to her address, given in the still clear, precise, English voice, to the National Press Club, Washington DC on 11 December 1992. She described her visits that April to Senegal, where she saw how UNIFEM could empower women in developing countries with better control of their destiny. The aim, Julie vouched, could be described as 'creating many ripples from dropping one pebble in a pond'. She continued: 'I am a woman who has enjoyed privilege and good fortune. I was born in a safe and friendly place. I do have the right to vote, to travel, to be free, to explore my own potential and many other things. I take some of these things for granted. One should never do that.'

From her work with UNIFEM, Julie travelled to London, where the Julie Andrews rose was previewed at the Chelsea Flower Show, in support of her fund for arterial research. The rose was coral pink, with a bright, sweet smell: 'We sent Julie photographs and she OK'd it,' the surgeon Martin Thomas told me. But the bloom was not well suited to the star's adopted home. 'It seems to be fairly hardy,' Julie, a keen gardener, would explain in a 2001 interview with *Target* magazine, 'but it needs the kind of dampness not found here in Los Angeles.'

Thence to France, where, at the Cannes Film Festival, Blake was honoured with the Légion d'Honneur and a retrospective of his work — including his director's cut of *Darling Lili*, shorn by half an hour of extraneous musical material, refocused as a war drama with savage comedy at its heart, something he had intended all along.

* * *

Towards the end of 1992, Julie gave the loyalists who had kept the faith through fat years and lean — as well as those who had never previously been well disposed towards her — a very pleasant surprise indeed: the Philips studio cast recording of one of the great musicals of the century, Rodgers and Hammerstein's *The King and I*. Singing the role of Mrs Anna, the Welsh governess who arrives in Siam in the mid-nineteenth century and captures the hearts and minds of the royal children — and the King — Julie was tackling material she had never performed professionally, even though it was ideal for her in every way.

She was also combating the memories of two

luminous portrayals: Gertrude Lawrence, who had created the role of Mrs Anna in the 1951 Broadway production, shortly before her death, and Deborah Kerr, who — dubbed by Marni Nixon — had made the classic 1956 film. Similarly, as the King of Siam, Ben Kingsley faced daunting comparisons with Yul Brynner, whose stage and screen portrayal was indelibly etched on the minds of millions.

Miraculously, in contrast to Julie's last few projects, everything worked. With John Mauceri conducting the Hollywood Bowl Orchestra, it was the finest album Julie had made since the days of her own Broadway and Hollywood triumphs. 'One of the best creative experiences I've ever had,' she told Edward Seckerson of the London *Independent*. 'There was a kind of aura, a kind of karma about the whole enterprise.' And she revealed a more mature attitude to her public than of yore: 'I used to assume that the audience judged me the way I judged myself. And I wasn't that fond of myself in those days . . . I'm able to give so much more now.'

What all her fans wanted, of course, was a chance to see their idol bring her diamond-bright stardom back to the legitimate theatre. Then, on 28 October 1992, news broke that, after a gap of over thirty years, Julie Andrews was returning to the New York stage.

17

CURTAIN CALL

'It is a pleasure to hear Julie produce a loud, dirty laugh. A great many English women look as though they should constantly be carrying a garden basket over one arm . . . but their sense of humour is a holdover from Elizabethan days'

— André Previn, 1995

Changes were afoot in the Edwards family. In 1992, with the younger children about to leave school, Blake and Julie rationalised their living arrangements, selling their residences in Beverly Hills and Malibu and buying a house in between, on Chadbourne Avenue, Brentwood, complete with white picket fence.

The five-acre Malibu estate, with its spectacular vantage point above the ocean, would subsequently be sold again, for $7.3 million. In 1999, Julie revealed to me what had happened to it two years earlier: 'The next owners tore a great deal of it down and rebuilt it for the gentleman who was with Princess Diana.' Pondering the Princess and Dodi Fayed, Julie quietly added, 'Of course, it was never lived in . . . '

As well as moving from Malibu, Julie was changing direction with her career. Six years earlier, I had listened as she talked of a return to the stage: 'I'd love it — and this is the ultimate greed — if I could promote new musicals, rather than recreating old ones . . . I'm a great admirer of Stephen Sondheim's work, and I think if he ever asked me to do anything, I probably would rush to do it, wherever it was.'

So, when Cameron Mackintosh, Britain's most dynamic impresario, contacted her in autumn 1992 to ask her to perform the off-Broadway premiere of a Sondheim anthology he had tried out in Oxford, she listened. The title, lifted from a song in the composer's musical *Sunday in the Park with George*, was *Putting It Together*. 'Our little revue', Mackintosh later wrote, 'was an ideal way for her to flex her theatrical muscles after three decades as a film star.' Elsewhere, he described the offer as 'an irresistible $500 a week — sharing a dressing room in a basement with no star billing'.

Towards the end of the year, Mackintosh gathered with choreographer Bob Avian and director Julia McKenzie (who had helmed the show in Oxford) at Sondheim's New York brownstone, to run through the material for Julie. She sat in front of them wearing, said Miss McKenzie, 'a wonderful white shirt, and looking about twenty-two years old'.

A musical conversation piece, *Putting It Together* had the bare bones of a plot. A wealthy husband and wife (Stephen Collins and Julie Andrews) tenuously celebrate their wedding anniversary with a business associate (Michael Rupert), in the presence of a sexy maid (Rachel York) and a mystery guest (Christopher Durang)

469

who provokes the others into playing truth games — which, in turn, precipitate the songs.

The cast rehearsed for three weeks in a loft in Chelsea, during the biting New York winter. Mackintosh commented later on his leading lady's demeanour: 'Watching her ask for help and advice from everyone as she re-honed her theatrical skills, I learned more about what makes a really great star than from anyone else I have ever met.' He noted with pleasure the appearance of the ubiquitous kettle, its proprietor dispensing tea and sympathy. Gillian Lynne, who had acted with Julie almost forty years earlier on *Mountain Fire*, told me of his enthusiasm: 'I remember Cameron saying to me, 'Julie is amazing — what a brick, a trouper, always making the tea and making everyone feel good . . . ' I said, 'You don't have to tell me!''

It was, Sondheim observed, the first time Julie had played 'a contemporary character in a contemporary musical — she hasn't had a chance to do that kind of work'. He had known Julie since the early 1960s, when his first hit *A Funny Thing Happened on the Way to the Forum* had been designed by Tony Walton. 'She's an extremely versatile actress,' said the composer, 'with a lovely, warm stage presence.' Her response was equally complimentary: 'Stephen Sondheim is the reason I'm here.'

The other cast members discovered Julie to be a touchingly eager team player. Playwright and actor Christopher Durang later wrote, 'I almost don't have any good Julie Andrews stories because she's just so nice and easy to be around.

It became clear she liked being part of a small ensemble; she didn't want to think of herself starring in the show, she wanted to be in it with the rest of us.'

Rachel York was then only twenty-two. In 2005, talking to *Playbill*, she remembered the rehearsals with mixed feelings. 'I had a really hard time with the director . . . Julia McKenzie would go, 'No, no, no! What are you doing? Let's go on to Julie's number.' I felt like I never got any practice.' But she found a rock in Julie, with whom she would share a dressing room. 'I remember I had a really bad day. I was just going to mosey on out with my backpack . . . and I just started crying. She said, 'You're doing so well — let me give you a hug.' She was so lovely.'

News of the show had caused a small sensation among theatregoers. Shortly after dawn on a freezing February morning, hundreds of people started to queue outside the Manhattan Theatre Club's Stage 1, at City Center on West 55th Street. Six hours after the box office opened, the entire twelve-week run at the three-hundred-seat off-Broadway venue was sold out.

Putting It Together had its first preview on Tuesday 2 March 1993. Stepping on stage in a lavender blue jumpsuit and scything her way through songs of middle-aged pain, Julie delivered the most highly defined performance of its kind in the city. As svelte as ever at fifty-seven, she looked entirely appropriate opposite the rather younger Stephen Collins, best known for his starring roles on television.

Her dexterity with a crisply resentful number like 'Could I Leave You?' from *Follies* might have been expected. But her pyrotechnical display with the desperate 'Getting Married Today' from *Company* came almost as an electric shock. In December 2001, on BBC Radio's *Desert Island Discs*, Sir Cameron Mackintosh would pick this as one of his eight favourite recordings; the presenter Sue Lawley, normally uncommunicative about her guests' choices, exclaimed, 'Great, isn't it?'

After four weeks of previews, the show opened on Wednesday 31 March. The atmosphere was predictably euphoric, both at the theatre and at the opening night party at '21' — where Julie had gone after the premiere triumph of *My Fair Lady* in 1956. The following morning, the reviews were almost entirely favourable. In the *New York Post*, Clive Barnes called the show 'tuneful, singular, surprising and as brittle as a glass snake in a barbershop quartet' and considered that Julie's voice 'not so much gilds, as heats, the gingerbread'. For *Newsday*, Linda Winer wanted the show to go on for a further five hours, saying of Julie, 'She treats the meaning of these witty and heartbreaking songs like the grown-up literature they are. And no mikes? Bliss.'

Only Frank Rich — the latter-day Butcher of Broadway — cavilled, in the *New York Times*, at what he called Sondheim's 'knee-jerk romantic disillusionment'. But in London, the *Evening Standard* headline made glad reading for the star's British fans: 'Julie Andrews is the hottest thing in New York — again.'

Seven weeks later, on Sunday 23 May, *Putting It Together* was over, ending its limited run after ninety-six sold-out performances. The album, cut during the run and issued by RCA Victor, established that Julie's success with *The King and I* had been no accident. Happy now to return to the music that had sealed her reputation, Julie then recorded *Broadway: The Music of Richard Rodgers*, backed by Ian Fraser conducting a full symphony orchestra. The 1994 release was sumptuous — rather too much so; sweeping orchestrations surrounded Julie on lyrics ranging from Oscar Hammerstein's 'If I Loved You' to Lorenz Hart's 'I Wish I Were in Love Again'. The album caught a much warmer glow in Julie's voice than of yore, and, for the first time in her career, she was nominated for a Grammy Award in her own right.

At the end of the year, some of the same material was channelled into the PBS special *Some Enchanted Evening: Celebrating Oscar Hammerstein II*. Hosting a cast of Broadway luminaries including Mandy Patinkin and Bernadette Peters, Julie taped the special before a live audience at City Center (where she had performed *Putting It Together*) for broadcast on 6 March 1995.

But to her myriad fans, it was another PBS special that caused most excitement. *Julie Andrews: Back on Broadway* was the most comprehensive, and authorised, attempt yet made by any broadcasting company to capture Julie's public and private life on camera. With both her husbands and Emma Walton taking part, other contributors included Robert Wise, Michael Kidd, Roddy McDowall, James Garner and Michael Bentine — a reminder of just how long Julie Andrews had been at the peak of her profession.

As an adjunct, a glossy picture book of her life and times, with a foreword by Carol Burnett, was also released. But no sooner had the publication reached the shelves than it was unceremoniously pulled. Among the photographs, including many images of her young life, were one or two rumoured to have been published without permission. The star was still very much on her guard.

Disappointed acolytes were left with the television programme itself. *Julie Andrews: Back on Broadway* aired across the United States of America on Wednesday 25 October 1995. And the same night at the Marquis Theatre on Broadway, its star was making the comeback of the year.

★　★　★

Since *Putting It Together*, Julie had been preoccupied with more than her professional prospects. There was the ongoing problem of Kayti Edwards, Jennifer's daughter, who had fallen into a world of crack cocaine users, worked as a stripper in dingy Dallas bars, and had recently given birth to a daughter, Shaely — all by the age of nineteen.

The adopted girls, Amy and Joanna, had also

had their rebellious moments, although Julie would later only refer to these in general terms. 'They both had problems,' she would tell Vicky Ward for the London *Daily Mail* in 1998, 'but they are on the other side of the mountain now.' Two years earlier, Blake had been rather more specific, divulging to Charlie Rose on PBS television that the two girls had been at a drug rehabilitation hospital, in different wings — but had nonetheless managed to 'moon' each other through opposite windows.

Julie would later describe her husband on the Biography Channel as 'this odd mixture of a very tough dad as they grew older and an absolute pussycat. He's either one thing or the other.' As for herself, had there been any doubt as to her daughters' welfare, she would not have agreed to return to the Broadway stage. In October 1994, she told the *New York Times*, 'My children are old enough, almost twenty and twenty-one. And I get the feeling that if I'd said no, ten years from now, I would have regretted it.' She was ready now to be 'Mum' to a much larger family.

★ ★ ★

'I felt, as I was writing it, that this would make a terrific Broadway musical.' Thus spoke Blake Edwards in 1995 about his screenplay for *Victor/Victoria*, for which he had always seen a long-term future. Just how long, he could not have imagined. For more than a decade following the release of the film, its progress to Broadway was punctuated by frustration, false

475

hope and personal sadness — what the show's lyricist Leslie Bricusse would describe as a 'mostly comic, occasionally dramatic and at one point tragic saga'.

The first production schedule had been dated October 1984, but rights problems, availability issues and the continual upward revision of the budget — not to mention Blake's illness — meant that the initial plan never came to fruition. 'I don't know if it will again,' said Julie in 1986. 'There's still talk about it, but . . . I kind of geared myself up for it, and I'd have to think about it now.'

Then, halfway through 1993, Blake — now a far from hearty seventy-two years of age — willed himself into action, thanks largely to the zeal of his much younger co-producer and fellow theatrical novice, Tony Adams. Henry Mancini made the trip to the chalet in Gstaad in early 1994, and the team was complete. 'From February 1 till finished, we all agreed,' Bricusse wrote later. 'So, there we were — Blake, Julie, Tony, Henry and myself — the Famous Five. During two inspired weeks of all-out work, the final breakthrough we had so long needed was finally achieved.'

They retained just four songs from the film, replacing the others and adding several more. Then, wrote Bricusse, disaster struck: 'We were only a song-and-a-half away from home when Henry had to fly back to Los Angeles to conduct a couple of concerts. He was scheduled to return three days later. He never came back.'

Henry Mancini died of cancer on 14 June. The

producers would dedicate the show to his memory.

It seemed, for now, that he had left behind enough material for Bricusse and musical director Ian Fraser to finish off arranging the score. In late October, the Broadway opening was announced for 23 April 1995, following a four-week try-out in Boston. The $8.5 million capitalisation, however, was far from secure, and when partner company Polygram Diversified Entertainment pulled back, Blake was left to put up a $2 million shortfall himself. A revised itinerary was agreed. After summer engagements in Minneapolis and Chicago, the show would hit Broadway in October, at the Marquis Theatre on Times Square.

It had been Blake's original plan that Robert Preston should repeat his screen creation of Toddy, Victoria's gay mentor, but the actor had died in 1987, yet another good friend gone. Tony Roberts, Woody Allen's sidekick in so many films, assumed the role for Broadway. Taking over from James Garner as King Marchan, the gender-confused Chicago gangster, was tall, dark and handsome Michael Nouri, the possessor of a fine baritone voice. His garish moll Norma was Rachel York, from *Putting It Together*.

Although the cast was thirty strong, success or failure would be ascribed to one member alone: Julie Andrews. Not only did she want to see her husband make a success of his first Broadway show, but she also knew that most of the money had been raised on her name — and with surprising difficulty. As collateral, she had committed to the show for a year on Broadway or, if it failed to recoup its capitalisation in that time, a year and a half.

On Monday 21 August 1995, *Victor/Victoria* went on sale at the Marquis Theatre. That day, in *Theater Week*, Ken Mandelbaum analysed what had been happening on the road and reckoned, with a month between the Chicago run and Broadway previews, that the show stood a healthy chance. 'Even with only lukewarm notices, *Victor/Victoria* should be able to get by; with good reviews, it could be a box-office powerhouse.' Back in New York, the first few weeks of business suggested that this was an understatement. By mid-September, advance ticket sales for *Victor/Victoria* already totalled $13 million and bookings were reported to be coming in at the rate of $100,000 a day. The star's name was still box-office gold.

★   ★   ★

On Sunday 1 October 1995 Julie Andrews was sixty years old. In the land of her fathers, she now qualified to receive a free bus pass, free medical prescriptions and an old age pension. But the cover story of the *New York Times* magazine, part of the great wedge of newsprint that landed on doorsteps all over the city that Sunday morning, showed the star singing, dancing and japing in rehearsals for her forthcoming show, looking as blithe and bonny as in her prime.

The text was not quite so complimentary;

there were echoes of the *Time* magazine cover story on Lerner and Loewe thirty-five years earlier, when *Camelot* had seemed a city divided. It was unlikely that Julie would ever forget Joyce Haber and her poison pen, so it was surprising that journalist Philip Weiss had been allowed such free access. Under the title 'What She'll Do for Love', he described in detail the time he had spent with *Victor/Victoria* over the last four months.

Rehearsals had begun back in late March, in a fourth-floor studio at 890 Broadway, a long way down the street from where the show would eventually play. There was an even longer distance to cover artistically. 'Because I am Blake's wife,' Julie once said of filming with her husband, 'I try very hard not to pull rank . . . because I know that the entire crew the first couple of days are watching to see if I will.' In the rehearsal room, she had needed even more to balance her skills: to be one of a family, and also be there for her husband, who had left it perilously late in his career to cut his teeth on a mammoth enterprise such as a Broadway musical. 'How did we do this in the movie?' he was heard to ask.

As Weiss acidly wrote, Julie's style of 'polite indirectness', disguising the fact that she was more at ease than Blake, would generally begin with a self-apology: 'Sorry, so sorry.' 'Can I just say something?' 'Sorry. I was late on that.' Or, meaningfully: 'I'm terribly sorry, but we have to decide which lyrics are being used . . . '

At the beginning of May, the company had

flown to Minneapolis (the city that had so embraced the first public screening of *The Sound of Music*) to continue rehearsals on stage at the Orpheum Theatre. Then, after a week of previews, the official world premiere had taken place on Sunday 11 June — polite applause for the show turning into instant ovation as Julie Andrews took her final bow.

The show had run there for four weeks. The experienced choreographer Rob Marshall seemed secure. Blackie, on the other hand, sat with his cane, introspective and fierce, constantly thinking up new business, yet — in the eyes of Philip Weiss — ignoring the structural problems of pace and cohesion. And, as with *Camelot*, the show was too long.

Leslie Bricusse and a new kid on the block, composer Frank Wildhorn, supplied extra material — including, for Julie, a ballad, 'Living in the Shadows'. The new songs were nobody's favourite part of the show. The gallows humour of the chorus — again, echoing *Camelot* — was picked up by Weiss: 'A joke goes around the company: the wrong composer died.' The scenery wagons then hit the road for the Windy City.

On Sunday 23 July, three days before Blake's seventy-third birthday, *Victor/Victoria* opened at the Shubert Theatre in Chicago, where it would play until 3 September. Richard Christiansen of the *Chicago Tribune* wrote, 'nobody but Edwards would have the nerve to put in all the *Pink Panther*-type sight gags that he has worked into the proceedings.'

The party was on the top floor of Marshall Field's department store, where Philip Weiss took his leave of Blake and Julie: 'Edwards wears a terrified expression and Andrews goes around greeting everyone. It's just like what one of the dancers told me about rehearsal. If she stops to have a cough drop, she has to give everyone one. Andrews goes to great lengths both to maintain adorers and distance herself.'

* * *

By all appearances, the Broadway season of 1995 was the last bastion of the middle-aged diva. If Hollywood was obdurate about actresses over the age of forty, using the New York stage seemed to be putting them at a premium. Joining Julie Andrews in the city's best playhouses were her old friends Carols Channing (seventy-four) and Burnett (sixty-two) in, respectively, the umpteenth revival of *Hello, Dolly!* and *Moon over Buffalo*, a farce that marked Miss Burnett's Broadway debut. More serious fare was offered by Zoe Caldwell (sixty-two) as Maria Callas in *Master Class*, and Uta Hagen (seventy-six), off-Broadway in *Mrs Klein*.

Driving into Manhattan from the airport, with the glittering skyline rising up before her, Julie was suddenly terrified, as she later told Larry King on CNN: 'I said, 'Blake, are we crazy? What do we think we're doing, trying to bring something into this city?''

'I had to beat her over the head to get her to do this,' Blake told Mike Wallace on 60 *Minutes* for CBS television, three days before the opening. As the first preview on 3 October drew close, Julie was only too aware of the colossal expectation of her.

On BBC Radio in 2006, she would remember it well: 'The day we opened, we'd been in tech hell, and suddenly, in the middle of the afternoon, I found myself getting rather tearful, and I said to my husband 'I'm really feeling terribly nervous about this evening.' And he looked at me as if I was a dummy, and he said, 'Well, darling, did you really think at this point you would be feeling anything else?''

Backstage, as she slicked back her short auburn Victor haircut under the Victoria wig, Julie would not have had time to ponder one remarkable coincidence — that she was only a few feet of air space away from where her old seventeenth-storey bedroom in the Piccadilly Hotel had been. The building to which she and Dilys Laye had first came after landing in America had fallen to the wrecker's ball in 1982, when a massive development of more than fifty floors had been built along the west side of Broadway, between 45th and 46th Streets. Lodged within the concrete edifice, now operated by Marriott Hotels, was the Marquis Theatre, which was to be Julie's workplace for the foreseeable future.

★ ★ ★

Making my way into the Marquis Theatre on the evening of Wednesday 25 October, I asked

482

Barbara Walters, America's feared interviewer, what she expected from the star of the show. Miss Walters smiled dangerously. 'Julie Andrews? She's a superb performer, a very nice person — and in *Victor/Victoria*, she's going to light up the Broadway scene.'

Everyone was in good humour. With an incredible $15 million advance — Broadway's highest ever — this was always going to be more than just another show. Lauren Bacall acted like royalty, and Mary Tyler Moore, Robert Goulet, Joan Collins, Roger Moore and rock group Aerosmith — surprise investors in the show — were among those congregating for the nearest thing to an old-fashioned star vehicle in years. But the prize for chutzpah surely went to Mayor of New York Rudolph Giuliani, who — even as the lights were dimming — sprang on stage over the orchestra pit to emphasise the historic nature of the evening, urging the audience to 'welcome Julie back'.

The star's first scene came as an anti-climax. In a dim pool of light, it was hard enough to see her, let alone reconcile the deep, sombre voice with the one I knew. But on her subsequent entrance as a man, the Peter Pan simile which I among others had made before was vindicated. Tall, slender — her legs displayed to dazzling effect — with a wealth of old-style star power at her command, Julie Andrews was back.

As a show, *Victor/Victoria* won — just — on points. The new numbers, including the tacky 'Paris Makes Me Horny', sung by Rachel York, and the sub-pastiche 'Louis Seize (who cares what Louis says?)' proved that Cole Porter had no new rivals. And neither Julie's bewitching personality nor her masterly technique could disguise the fact that the script and direction were not half as sophisticated as they pretended to be.

It was now clear that Blake had failed to find a way of translating his cinematic humour into theatrical terms. The second act contained one brilliant scene in which the four main protagonists and the police chased each other up and down the stairs of the dual-level hotel set, under beds, into cupboards, out through windows. But I suspected that the credit went more to the choreographer Rob Marshall than to the director.

Towards the end of the evening, a curtain swept down to facilitate a scene change. Julie stood alone in the spotlight, singing her last solo, and everyone relaxed. 'The most valuable ingredient in the making of *Victor/Victoria* — the one which ultimately ensured its survival — is the feeling of family that is an essential part of any Blake Edwards-Julie Andrews project.' So said Leslie Bricusse — and, as if to prove his point, the finale, sung flat out by the company, radiated genuine warmth of feeling, focused on its star. A torrent of applause rose to a furious level when Julie Andrews walked on to take her curtain call — the automatic standing ovation in remembrance of times past, rather than a response to what had just been seen.

★ ★ ★

In a theatre anteroom, cameramen from every continent of the world waited. And waited. Two hours after the show had ended, Julie finally appeared, sleek in lace-encrusted black satin. Behind stood her husband, gimlet eyed, with her co-stars at the rear.

If the early editions of the newspapers were out, the artists denied having seen any reviews. Julie spent the first few minutes playing for time by organising her colleagues into position for the press call. Finally, she levelled her clear blue eyes at me. 'This is probably the most exciting first night of all for me,' she said, in a low voice. And being back on Broadway was like coming home. She rested her head on Blake's shoulder: 'A new home.'

'Not right now, no. I don't have time,' she replied, when asked if she was still in therapy. With eight performances a week for the next year, or for as long as it took to break even, few were likely to pay $55 to see the understudy. And when I asked her how she planned to cope, her answer was automatic: 'I've got a good right hook.'

Over the floor, in the grand ballroom of the Marriott Hotel, the opening-night party was in full swing. Ice sculptures melted gently, Veuve Clicquot ran freely — and there was hardly anywhere to stand. Among the guests was Biff Liff, who remembered a gauche young lady fighting for her professional life in rehearsals for *My Fair Lady*. 'There's an expression we Americans use,' he told me about Julie. 'She always "comes through".'

Julie Andrews took one look at the heaving

throng and returned home to the Upper East Side, where she had a bowl of cornflakes and went to bed.

Later, walking up the Avenue of the Americas, I saw an early placard for the *Daily News* carrying the question, 'Is Victor victorious?' I soon found out. '*Victor* spoils Julie's return' was the headline for Howard Kissel's review, which commenced with a killer: 'Edwards' half-Blaked musical drags down Andrews'. The critic had only praise for the star: 'She looks no older than she did in *Camelot* . . . her voice is still melting, her diction impeccable.' But he had no patience for what was going on around her: 'Julie Andrews' return to Broadway should have been an occasion for champagne. *Victor/Victoria* is only worth breaking out a small beer.'

For the *New York Times*, Vincent Canby, who had so eulogised the film, began his review in incredulity at the passage of time: 'As far as Julie Andrews is concerned, thirteen years is no more than the blink of an eye . . . time has made no dent in her immaculate appearance and diction, and in her grandly funny stage presence.' Lower down, the tone curdled at the mention of Blake: 'When it comes to writing and staging a multi-million-dollar Broadway show, one that's based on his own hit movie, he's still a master of film comedy.' Canby criticised the tempo ('the show comes to life as if by accident'), hated the new songs, preferred the second act, and came back to Julie: 'She's been away too long, but I suspect she will now be around as long as she wants.'

In the *New York Post*, under the headline 'Drag queen rules', Clive Barnes admired both 'the truly incredible, defiantly delightful Andrews' and her husband's script: 'You really care for the characters — something not that common in movies and rarer in musicals.' Brad Leithauser's *Time* magazine review, however, was headed 'Le Jazz not so Hot': 'Star quality is a term notoriously hard to define. But whatever it is, Julie Andrews, with her out-flung smile and crystalline enunciations, still has it.' Yet, for him, even that was compromised: 'Edwards' brain-child may flirt with naughtiness, but it really wants to be nice, which gives Andrews a chance again to play Julie Andrews.'

The day after the premiere, the company cut the cast album at the Edison Studio. Then, as the star told Patrick Pacheco for *Newsday*, 'We all sort of figured, well, we just better get on and do the show.' But over the next year and a half, for all the production's plastic charms, drama of a high order would be found more often backstage.

★   ★   ★

Once the overture started, there was no turning back. Julie had no fewer than nine songs, five of them in the second act, as well as a vast array of costume changes and a huge footprint of activity on stage — more than in *My Fair Lady*, as she also had to dance. 'Intermission,' she told me, 'is the only time one is able to return to the dressing room.'

Backstage, the star had her long-time assistant

Francine Taylor to answer her mail, and her dresser Al Annotto to tend to her needs. One of these was to regulate the temperature, which needed to be kept low for Julie's throat (and which, to the dancers, felt like the Arctic). A humidifier helped — as did a vaporiser, into which Annotto occasionally shook some drops from a bottle that had been given to Julie by a throat specialist named Scott M. Kessler.

Off stage, she socialised hardly at all, other than having Carol Burnett to dinner for Thanksgiving. At the rented Upper East Side house, she relied on the best medicine she knew: eight or nine hours' sleep a night. Blake quietly worked on the floor below her — writing, as ever, through the small hours.

Weekends were sacrosanct. After the Sunday show, Julie stepped into the chauffeur-driven four-wheel-drive Ford waiting for her at the stage door, and stretched out on the futon mattress in the back. Then she was off, down 45th Street, turning right and whizzing north, out of the city, through the night to the East End of Long Island. Mr and Mrs Edwards had bought a house at Sag Harbor, minutes from Emma and Steve Hamilton — and a few minutes more from Tony and Gen Walton.

Despite her caution, illness started to plague Julie from the beginning of 1996. One Saturday night in January, her understudy Anne Runolfsson took over during the second act. Julie had been taken ill with influenza, which kept her off for a week. The immediate result was that the capacity houses plummeted to around the sixty per cent mark, receipts dropping off by almost $250,000. She put a further chill into the backers' hearts on Wednesday 28 February, when she was taken to Lenox Hill Hospital, for emergency removal of her gall bladder. The following morning, 'Mum' was sitting up in her hospital bed, writing a long letter in verse to her *Victor/Victoria* family.

Over the following year, her absences would grow more and more regular. From the corresponding dips in revenue, it was clear that the star was the show.

★   ★   ★

Back on opening night, as the principal members of the cast were leaving the press call, one enthusiastic gentleman had shouted to Rachel York, 'See you at the Tonys!' She had laughed, shaking her head — but clearly meant to take him at his word.

On Monday 6 May 1996, the nominations were announced for the year's Antoinette Perry Awards, many observers reminding themselves in amazement that Julie Andrews had never won the prize. There was even more amazement at the omissions from the shortlist. Not only had *Victor/Victoria* failed to be nominated as Best Musical, it was conspicuous by its absence in every category — other than that of Best Actress. Julie was in the running for the award she had missed as Eliza and Guenevere. On both previous occasions, she had been nominated for a Tony along with fellow company members

— many of whom had won. Now, she was on her own.

Two days later, as the cast of *Victor/Victoria* took their bows after the midweek matinee, a phalanx of press cameramen moved swiftly down the aisles on each side of the theatre and positioned their equipment at the front of the orchestra pit. Julie Andrews stepped forward in her glittering costume and headdress, held up her right hand and read from a document. She acknowledged the nominations for the season's Tony Awards — but stated, despite being among the chosen, how sad she was to be recognised alone 'in this extraordinarily gifted company'.

Then came the bombshell. 'I have searched my conscience and my heart and I find that sadly, I cannot accept this nomination. I prefer instead to stand with the *egregiously* overlooked.'

There followed a ferocious roar of applause, and the pressmen ran to file their copy. 'We hope she changes her mind, claims what looks like her inevitable Best Actress award, and uses the opportunity to give the nominating committee a piece of her mind,' urged the *New York Times* editorial. 'Mary Poppins Hoppin' Mad!' shrieked the headline of the *New York Post*. 'Get over it,' said *Esquire*.

The story would still be hot enough by the end of the year for *Time* magazine to include it as one of the Worst Public Performances of 1996. 'Not saying thank you is one of our least favourite things,' *Time* thundered. 'Her sincerity would have played out a little better if somebody hadn't tipped off the TV news crews, who came rushing into the theatre thirty minutes before the curtain.'

'It was, on the one hand, the easiest decision I ever had to make,' the ambivalent star told the *New York Times*. 'On the other hand, I was quaking in my boots . . . It just felt right. It came from my heart, that's all I can say.' Family, as always, came first.

Some compensation came from the Drama Desk Awards, when Julie Andrews and Rachel York were announced as Best Actress and Supporting Actress in a Musical. Later that month at Sardi's, Julie was presented with the Outer Critics' Circle Award, and saw *Victor/Victoria* win as best Broadway Musical. Meanwhile, Julie Andrews's name stayed on the Tony Awards ballot. 'She's been nominated and the nomination will stand,' said spokesman Keith Sherman.

Prior to the brouhaha, she had been the runaway favourite to win in her category. But, in the fallout from her pronouncement, the voting membership declined to give themselves an even bloodier nose. On Sunday 2 June, the fiftieth Tony Awards went ahead, Julie's name being read out as a nominee. Previously considered an also-ran, however, Donna Murphy was the winner — as Mrs Anna in *The King and I*. Needless to say, Julie was not in the audience.

The major success story of the night was *Rent*, a rock version of *La Bohème*, which had barnstormed since its opening earlier that year. Adding the Pulitzer Prize to its haul at the Tonys — including the Best Musical award — *Rent* pointed the way to a future in which, it seemed, the old-fashioned qualities of *Victor/Victoria* had no place. Nevertheless, backstage at the Marquis Theatre, stagehands hung a giant replica of the Tony medallion, purloined from the previous year's awards, by the dressing-room door of the newest (and most unlikely) Broadway firebrand.

While the episode was evidence to many of the star's trouper spirit, cynics considered it to be a publicity stunt — the best thing possible for *Victor/Victoria*. Ticket sales for the show had leaped thirty per cent the week after the outburst, and jumped yet again after the televised ceremony in June. When, in August, I saw the show for the second time, I spoke to Tony Adams about the affair — particularly Julie's speech. 'It's all history now,' he laughed. 'I think the thing that really came out of it was Julie putting a word back into the vocabulary that most people had forgotten: 'egregious'. I dare say she educated America.'

Adams' Dublin accent belied the years he had spent in the United States. Twice divorced and something of a ladies' man, he was keeping a more than professional eye on Anne Runolfsson (Julie's understudy and, at thirty, exactly half the star's age), whom he would marry the following February.

As I left the theatre, I saw Julie Andrews come out of the stage door, dressed in a casual shirt and baseball cap. Smiling briefly at the crowd who would have gladly held her captive, she drove away in her Ford. Then I saw — pinned up in the stage-door office — a picture of Maria von Trapp, singing high in the hills above Salzburg.

And I realised, more than ever, Julie's dichotomy. Everybody wanted her to be perfect. And she always had been. The trouble was, not even the stage doorman seemed able to let her forget it.

★ ★ ★

In October, Emma Walton Hamilton gave birth to a little boy named Samuel. His grandmother had just turned sixty-one. One week after her birthday, Julie released what was in some ways her most personal album. Recorded two years previously, *Broadway: Here I'll Stay — The Words of Alan Jay Lerner* proved as good as her Richard Rodgers collection, with the added frisson that the original star of *My Fair Lady* and *Camelot* was singing music she could call her own.

For *My Fair Lady*, Julie had been paid $1,250 a week. For *Victor/Victoria*, she was pulling in a minimum of $50,000 a week as a guarantee against ten per cent of gross, and another five per cent of the show's net profits. By now, however, business had dropped off markedly, even when she was performing, and it looked certain that the show would require her services for the full eighteen months.

In November, Julie was off *Victor/Victoria* for a fortnight, with pneumonia. And by the end of 1996, battle weariness was taking a severe toll on her voice — which is when Liza Minnelli agreed to take over for a month. 'Julie would do the same for me, I know she would,' said Liza in *Playbill*. 'She really, really needed to rest, or she would have injured herself and done some long-range damage if she continued.'

Liza began her stint in the first week of the New Year, in a wig she said made her look 'like Tyrone Power'. In the February edition of the gay magazine *Advocate*, writer and drag artiste Charles Busch compared the two Oscar-winning stars: 'I'd say Julie has the edge in masculine swagger, but Liza has those growling low notes. The truth is, neither star is truly convincing as a man. Julie seems like an elegant nineteenth-century lesbian and Liza like a feisty Italian dyke.'

Overall, Liza performed most spiritedly — but with a certain lack of focus. Her co-star Tony Roberts was disenchanted, and made his feelings clear. It all boded ill for the time, fast approaching, when Julie would leave the show for good.

Just before returning to the show on 4 March, Julie made an appearance on the syndicated *Rosie O'Donnell Show*, in which she described her sabbatical. She had spent a few days at Emma's house with her new grandson Sam, and three weeks in Switzerland, where she had gazed out at the winter landscape, eaten out for the first time in ages and cooked bacon and egg sandwiches in the middle of the night.

'Liza's been an absolute trouper, but the company is happy that 'Mum' is back,' said Tony Adams. But now, more than ever, there was trouble in store — this time, relating to Julie's normally unimpeachable professional conduct. 'Producers of *Victor/Victoria* Sue Carriers Over

Coverage For Missed Performances', ran the heading across the front of the *Wall Street Journal* on 4 April, in an article by the aptly named Leslie Scism. With half of the $8.5 million capitalisation rumoured to be as yet unreturned, the paper spelt out the row between the producers and their nine insurance companies, which were refusing to pay for losses sustained during Julie's absences for influenza ($442,435), gall bladder surgery ($980,850), and larynx problems ($180,000).

Lexington Insurance Company claimed that Julie had not supplied enough information about her medical history when cover was arranged — answering 'no' when asked if she had ever suffered from muscular or spinal disorders, asthma or other bronchial problems. But Peter Parcher, the lawyer representing the *Victor/Victoria* camp, declared, 'Julie Andrews did absolutely nothing wrong. We expect to prove that the insurers owe us the money.'

Huge sums of money, legal proceedings and a great big star added up to a dream story. The following day, the *New York Post* enjoyed itself with 'Mary Poppins: Liar, Liar' all over its front page, surmounting a photograph of Julie as Maria von Trapp. The result was that, after playing six hundred performances, Julie's final months in *Victor/Victoria* were clouded by a lawsuit of over $1.5 million against the insurers, which would not be resolved until long after she had left the show.

On Sunday 8 June, Julie Andrews played Victor/Victoria for the last time — and was surprised and delighted at the finale by the sudden onstage appearance of Christopher Plummer. A week earlier she had made a surprise appearance of her own, at the Tony Awards that evening, the very event from which she had been so keen to distance herself the year before.

The following Tuesday, the title role of *Victor/Victoria* was physically, if not artistically, filled by the ample charms of Raquel Welch, who had signed a six-month contract to keep the show alive. 'Oh, come on!' wrote Peter Marks in the *New York Times*. 'Not for a single moment does Ms Welch, who has replaced that stay-the-distance trouper, Julie Andrews, in the long-running Broadway musical, make a remotely persuasive case for temporary manhood. With its new leading lady, the show could be re-titled, *Victoria/Victoria*.'

By any name, the show's time was up. It closed eight weeks later on 27 July 1997, after a run of 738 performances.

18

INDIAN SUMMER

'Shut up!'

— H. M. Queen Clarisse Renaldi of Genovia

At Manhattan Supreme Court on 25 March 1998, Metropolitan Opera diva Teresa Stratas initiated proceedings against the two doctors whose 'careless and unskilful' surgery on her nose at Mount Sinai Hospital in 1995 had, she said, all but ended her career. The surgeons, it was alleged, 'did not possess the requisite knowledge and skill of medical professionals in the community'. They were identified as Scott Kessler and Jeffrey Libin — the very same who, in June 1997, had operated on Julie Andrews.

In the week after leaving *Victor/Victoria*, Julie had checked into the Mount Sinai Medical Center, 1190 Fifth Avenue, overlooking the calm green expanse of Central Park. There, she met Scott M. Kessler, the doctor whose vocal drops she had taken so assiduously over the last year or so.

'I had an intracordal cyst, according to my doctor,' she explained in 2004, 'which is literally like a blister inside one vocal cord. And I was told that it could be dealt with and that the cord would return to normal.' There seemed no reason to doubt it.

Waking from the operation, however, Julie had sensed something she could not properly identify — 'just the kind of feeling that I got, from things that were said at the beginning.' She had not, of course, expected to sing straight away. 'I had to be silent for two weeks; then, after about six weeks, I thought, this is not getting any better, and I was told that maybe it was taking longer than usual.' By autumn, her doubts had grown. After six months, she was worried. 'And then after a year, no — something was very wrong.'

It was as much information as the star would ever be likely to give, talking in July 2001 to Larry King on CNN. But, however circumscribed Julie may have been — as the result of a lawsuit that had dwarfed the case of Teresa Stratas — she could at least countenance the subject that until recently had held her in the grip of denial, panic and despair.

* * *

Sag Harbor, the beautiful Long Island fishing village two hours from New York, had been Julie's home for much of the past several years, especially valuable in the months after *Victor/Victoria* on Broadway. Her husband, now in his late seventies, was there too, having made no films since the best-forgotten *Son of the Pink Panther* in 1993.

Across the broad expanses of the East Hamptons, Julie was often to be seen in her out-of-town uniform of baseball cap, loose shirt and slacks, a tall, slender figure walking her dog

498

along the shore — waiting, hoping to recuperate. Close up, her blue eyes now watered rather more easily, but her face remained as smooth and freckled as that of a young woman. She openly revealed having had cosmetic surgery, telling Vicky Ward for the London *Daily Mail* in the summer of 1998, 'my business is the art of illusion.'

Asked about the result of the other surgery, she was as yet keen to play down, to the point of rebuttal, early rumours that she might not sing again: 'I had a minor procedure, which required a small amount of surgery. It was not serious, not nodules. It was a very old injury that I've had for thirty years. It began in *My Fair Lady*.'

She described the cause: 'It's a little like a blister that fills with liquid — but it was inside one vocal cord, so occasionally I was experiencing a slight swelling, especially when I was working hard.' Having been so weary after the Broadway run, the operation had taken its toll. 'So now I'm resting, like any athlete would who's had an injury.'

Yet underneath the optimism was a dull, gnawing dread. On 19 November 1998, Julie's publicist Gene Schwam admitted that there was a 'fifty-fifty chance' that her singing voice might never return. And three days later, Blake Edwards declared in *Parade* magazine that her surgery had indeed taken an irreversible toll on her voice: 'If you heard it, you'd weep.'

The star continued to put on a brave face. 'It is taking me a while to get my voice back into shape,' she said, interviewed for a BBC Radio

Christmas broadcast, but added firmly, 'I intend to be singing by early next year.' As if to prove her point, she had already taken part in a new stage musical, recording the voice of Polynesia the Parrot in *Doctor Dolittle* at the Hammersmith Apollo in London. The £4 million show, by her *Victor/Victoria* lyricist Leslie Bricusse, was a big success — unlike the film, which in the 1960s had done for Rex Harrison what *Star!* had for Julie Andrews. Ironically, as the voice of the two-hundred-year-old parrot, she spoke-sang in a manner very similar to that of her *My Fair Lady* co-star. The results (including parts of the song 'Talk to the Animals') were placed on a computer chip, which sat in the mouth of the remote-controlled bird created by Jim Henson's Creature Shop — but actual singing, such as audiences had known from the Julie Andrews of old, it was not.

Elsewhere, Julie kept as busy as she could, desperately trying not to dwell on the subject about which she was so concerned. That winter, she made her second television drama, *One Special Night*, filming for five weeks in Montreal, where temperatures dipped to twenty-nine degrees below zero. What had decided her was the chance to be reunited with James Garner, one of her very favourite co-stars.

The script centred on Robert, a retired builder, caught in the snow while visiting his dying wife in hospital, who is given a lift home by Catherine, a widowed paediatrician. Their mutual sympathy develops into friendship, which then becomes something more. *One Special*

Night was strictly formulaic, the issues of bereavement and pride subordinate to two much-loved stars pussyfooting around each other in smart winter catalogue clothing for the senior set. It was notable mainly for the chemistry that still existed between the stars of *The Americanization of Emily* and *Victor/ Victoria*.

'These dependable performers can still generate enough sparks to warm two hours on Sunday night,' wrote Rob Wertheimer in the *New York Times*, advising cynics to keep the remote control handy. 'Everybody else; put your feet up.' And there would be plenty happy to do just that. *One Special Night* would air on CBS television on Sunday 28 November 1999, becoming the highest-rated television special of the season.

Shortly after finishing work in Montreal, Julie felt brave enough to talk to Barbara Walters on 20/20 for ABC television, about what should have been her 'routine' surgery. She had been told, she said, that 'given a certain recuperative time — and it certainly wasn't two years — I would be singing just as well or better than ever'. And, of Blake's comments in *Parade*: 'He was telling the truth, yes. Indeed he was.'

Asked whether Mr and Mrs Edwards were on the verge of a split, she crisply replied, 'The marriage is very healthy, thank you.'

'Really?' said Barbara Walters.

'Really healthy. Yes,' said Julie Andrews.

But this was a difficult, unsettling time, made more so by sad news from England. On Sunday 28 February 1999, Aunt Joan Morris died in

Walton-on-Thames, aged eighty-three. The last family member older than Julie was now gone, compounding the growing, irresolvable distress the star felt about her own health.

Flying to Arizona, she checked into the Sierra Tucson Clinic, best-known for treating celebrities for alcohol and substance abuse — leading the *Globe* tabloid to conclude, wrongly, that Julie Andrews was there for an addiction to painkillers. 'The *Globe* story is absolutely false,' thundered her lawyers in May. 'Miss Andrews did recently spend time at Sierra Tucson for guidance and management of emotional issues related to grief.' While they pressed — successfully — for a full apology, Julie forged ahead with what had always been her salvation: her work.

★ ★ ★

In July 1999, Julie Andrews returned to England — more specifically, the Isle of Man — to shoot her most typically British film ever, an adaptation of Noël Coward's 1950 West End comedy hit *Relative Values*. Other than the transient *Tchin-Tchin*, it was her first big screen venture for over a decade.

The last time Julie had filmed in her home country, she had bared body and soul in *Duet for One*. Now, she found herself at the other end of the spectrum, in a comedy of manners, playing a countess trying to save her son from unsuitable marriage to a Hollywood star — whose long-lost sister just happens to be the countess's maid.

'We're setting the film in 1954, such a pretty era,' Julie piped up when I met her on set, and I was reminded that this was the same pretty year in which she had hit America like a meteor. I also noted that *Relative Values* was only the third film in three decades in which she had been directed by someone other than Blake Edwards. 'It isn't quite as people might suppose,' she said, 'that scripts come across your desk every day of the week. When your husband offers you a beautiful role on a platter, you'd be an idiot to turn it down. But we've never been mutually exclusive.'

As Felicity, Countess of Marshwood, Julie's participation was a coup for the producer Christopher Milburn, who told me: 'I still can't quite believe she's working with us . . . she was our first choice — a legend'. He had found no trouble in signing a stellar cast to join her, headed by William Baldwin and Jeanne Tripplehorn, who called Julie 'the embodiment of the word 'lovely''. Perhaps surprisingly, the English players, including Stephen Fry, Edward Atterton, Sophie Thompson and Colin Firth, were just as much in thrall. 'Julie was fantastic,' Firth later told the London *Independent*. 'She was a company leader in the traditional sense.'

'I think Noël Coward would have loved Julie's genius for friendship,' said Stephen Fry, who played the Jeeves-like butler Cresswell. When I met him in the autumn of 2006, he recalled her first day of filming: 'The crew were a typical British camera crew, they'd worked with Steven Spielberg, everyone from Clint Eastwood downwards, but they were as nervous as kittens, and the camera operator said, 'I've got Mary Poppins in my teddy bear's arsehole' — which is the chamois leather eye piece that they use . . .

'I looked at her and I realised I knew every vein in her forehead, I knew the planes of her face because, in an unparalleled way, she was seared into the tablets of one's memory.' Referring to the iconography of Julie's early musical roles, he added, 'It is very hard to see beyond it into the real person, the person who was the child star, married to Blake Edwards and who is a Hollywood creature and who likes making fart jokes.'

To everybody's delight, she could also make fun of herself. For the party scene, a large crowd of extras had been drawn from the island. The assistant director reminded them to stay animated without making any noise, to be smiling and miming. 'And suddenly,' said Fry, 'Jules went, 'Smiling and miming, and miming and smiling' to the tune of 'My Favourite Things', and the place erupted — it was as if this volcano had been tapped.'

Under the guidance of the young English director Eric Styles, she turned in a sweet, clever and sometimes touching performance. Filming took place at a castellated stately home dating back to the thirteenth century, called The Old Nunnery. 'Which,' remarked the leading lady, before anybody could beat her to it, 'I've spent my entire fucking career trying to escape . . . '

Hearing Julie Andrews swear for the first time was always bound to cause a sensation. 'It's like seeing your mother naked,' said Stephen Fry

504

— although, he added, 'it would be pissing in the wind to try and reinvent her as the bad girl of Hollywood.'

On the Isle of Man, accompanied by her cheerful assistant Francine Taylor, Julie could take some strength from the company spirit and almost village-like atmosphere to reflect on issues other than work: those for which she had sought counselling at Sierra Tucson. As filming drew to a close, she told a reporter from the *Los Angeles Times*, 'It's been a tough two years. I can't pretend it's been easy. But I'm a very optimistic lady. I think I will sing again. I hope to.'

Back in the United States, it became clear that optimism was not going to be enough. On Tuesday 14 December, Julie Andrews filed a malpractice suit against her throat specialist in the Manhattan Federal Court. 'My inability to sing has been a devastating blow,' her statement said, to which her lawyers added, 'Julie is saddened and deeply regrets that she has to seek redress in the courts.' Neither Scott Kessler, nor his assistant Jeffrey Libin, nor the spokesman for Mount Sinai was available for comment.

By almost shockingly cheerful contrast came news from London, on Friday 31 December 1999, that Her Majesty the Queen had appointed Julie Elizabeth Andrews Dame Commander of the British Empire, for services to acting and entertainment. Prime Minister Tony Blair had used the Millennium New Year's Honours List to confer damehoods on four women from the performing arts: Dorothy Tutin, one of Britain's most brilliant Shakespearean actresses, Shirley Bassey, the epitome of show-business glamour, Elizabeth Taylor, whose life on and off screen had defined her times, and the girl from Walton-on-Thames, who entered the new century a certified living legend.

Julie's investiture was set for Tuesday morning, 16 May 2000. Elizabeth Taylor had chosen the same day to visit Buckingham Palace, and the two Oscar-winning stars sat side by side in the gilt and white ballroom, exchanging the odd word and smile as they waited for the Queen to honour them. The band played selections from the Sherman brothers' best-known films — including *Mary Poppins*.

Julie, first to receive the gold and aquamarine insignia, stepped forward smartly in her pale pink two-piece suit and bobbed a curtsey before her monarch. Elizabeth, wearing blue embroidered silk jacket and pantaloons, was less certain of step but smiled broadly at the Queen, as she was decorated for services to acting and charity. Afterwards, the two friends stood together in the central courtyard for press photographers. Dame Elizabeth then joined her four children, announcing, 'We're going to go and have roast beef and Yorkshire pudding.'

Dame Julie was accompanied by her brother John Wells and her daughter Emma. 'This is the greatest honour of my life,' she told the BBC; it appeared that she meant it.

★　★　★

High in the sky, an aeroplane was pummelled by violent turbulence, pitching the passengers almost out of their seats. Alone among them, Julie Andrews kept a stiff upper lip, undoing her seatbelt and marching up the aisle into the cockpit. 'It's all right everybody,' said Julie, into the captain's microphone. 'We'll get through this.' And she started to sing. 'Getting to know you, getting to know all about you . . . '

One passenger grabbed her husband's arm. 'Julie Andrews is in the cockpit.'

The man visibly relaxed. 'Thank God.'

If ever Julie had wanted to send up her image in public, she had a perfect opportunity to do so in P.J. Hogan's black comedy *Unconditional Love*, lip-synching to her recording of *The King and I* in a non-credited cameo as herself. The story of the devoted fan of a dead pop star, who travels from Chicago to attend his funeral in rural England, *Unconditional Love* starred Kathy Bates (the fan), Jonathan Pryce (the star) and Rupert Everett (his secret lover). Unfortunately, the film, shot in late 1999 and early 2000, was plagued with distribution problems. Its production company, New Line Cinema, delayed the American release for over three years, eventually airing it on the Starz television network in 2003, before consigning it to DVD oblivion.

The film of *Relative Values* had fared better, but not significantly so, receiving its premiere in London at the Odeon cinema, Leicester Square on 21 June 2000. The BBC review had lauded Julie for being both iron and a butterfly: 'As she

507

nudges sixty-five, she seems — even when standing motionless — to have the jolliest kind of life going on inside her and to represent an England which barely exists any more.'

Empire magazine, however, had declined to be charmed: 'Returning to the big screen for the first time since *Tchin-Tchin*, Julie Andrews remains as poised as ever. But she's spent so much time in the oh-so-clever angst-ridden chat-fests of her husband Blake Edwards that she tends to deliver her lines like an LA luvvie.' Further afield, the film was ignored, despite its cast, and frustratingly foreshadowed the fate of *Unconditional Love* by being unveiled in America on the Starz network in October 2000, denying the star a fully fledged cinematic comeback.

By way of compensation, Julie had re-emerged as a writer. *Little Bo*, about a tiny kitten looked after by a sailor, was published in October 1999, a quarter of a century after *The Last of the Great Whangdoodles*. It did well enough for her to decide not to leave such a long gap again, joining forces with her daughter Emma to create a series of storybooks. The subject matter was inspired by her three-year-old grandson, as Julie told the *New York Times*. 'I asked Emma, if she could take Sam to the library and pick any book, what would she pick. And she said, 'Mum, there's no contest, anything with trucks.''

At first, the pair worried that they might not be compatible writing partners, but what emerged, after 'a lot of giggling', were the adventures of a rejuvenated dump truck named Dumpy. The illustrations were by another resident of Sag Harbor,

Tony Walton. In September 2000, *Dumpy the Dump Truck* appeared on bookshelves to positive reviews and sales. Its flyleaf made blissful reading for genealogists: with its authors listed as Julie Andrews Edwards and Emma Walton Hamilton, nobody had cause to feel excluded. 'I thought I would always use the name Edwards when I wrote,' Julie explained, 'because, if not for Blake, I would not have had the courage to go on writing.'

★　★　★

On Wednesday 6 September 2000, the lawyers for Julie Andrews released another statement. It declared the malpractice claim against Dr Scott M. Kessler to have been settled privately, without arbitration — pre-empting a hearing in the Federal District Court the following Tuesday. It added that Julie had agreed to drop her charges against the assistant, Dr Jeffrey D. Libin, and Mount Sinai Medical Centre, and ended that she was glad 'to close this chapter on an event which was unfortunate for all concerned'.

The terms of settlement remained confidential — for a few weeks only. On 31 October, the London *Evening Standard* broke cover: '*Sound of Music* star Julie Andrews is said to have won £20 million after a bungled throat operation robbed her of her singing voice.' It was an astonishing claim — but the lady who had elsewhere been quick to instigate legal proceedings kept quiet, thus lending worldwide credence to the figure.

The same day the *Evening Standard* story appeared in London, a children's book was published in New York, for pre-teenage girls unlikely to be interested in *Dumpy the Dump Truck*. The modern-day mixture of *Cinderella* and *The Ugly Duckling*, written by Meg Cabot, was entitled *The Princess Diaries*. Disney Studios, who had taken an early option on the book, was already shooting it as a medium-budget comedy, directed by Garry Marshall, purveyor of the 1990s bonanzas *Pretty Woman* and *The Runaway Bride*. Co-produced by music legend Whitney Houston, it starred newcomer Anne Hathaway as Mia Thermopolis, unknowing Princess of Genovia — and, as her duty-conscious grandmother Queen Clarisse Renaldi, Dame Julie Andrews.

Fate had smiled on both actresses. At her audition, eighteen-year-old Anne Hathaway had fallen off her chair, making herself instantly recognisable as the klutzy Mia. And, although the role of the Dowager Queen had already been earmarked for Meryl Streep, Garry Marshall had declared a preference for Julie Andrews — who, with *The Princess Diaries*, was coming home to Walt Disney after a gap of thirty-seven years.

Interior work was shot at the Burbank lot, on Soundstage 2. 'There's a plaque on the door that says that *Mary Poppins* was filmed on this stage,' Julie told the *Los Angeles Times*, 'and that took me back a little.' And, by coincidence, director Garry Marshall was living in the same Century City house where she had stayed on arriving in Hollywood.

Many of the exteriors were filmed on the streets of San Francisco, where Queen Clarisse escapes a traffic charge by knighting the officer with a gear stick. Waving regally to a streetcar full of bemused passengers, she trills, 'Goodbye, trolley people!' — hardly Noël Coward, but enough to win Julie her biggest laugh in the film. Playing the Dowager Queen of a fictional realm between France and Spain, she enjoyed the role for what it was: 'I get to wear all of those Armani and Valentino clothes . . . and get to play it all tongue-in-cheek. What could be nicer?'

Reversing the pattern of Julie's early decades, *The Princess Diaries* found the Dame acting as Higgins to Anne Hathaway's Eliza. Julie's example continued off screen as well. 'Being a star means acting appropriately,' said Anne, a self-described suburban New Jersey girl. 'Julie is magnificent that way.'

★ ★ ★

Of the many circles Julie Andrews would start to complete in her career, none was more surprising than her return to live television drama. CBS, taking the line that shooting without retakes offered the spirit of adventure, had succeeded in doing what countless producers had imagined for the last three decades: reuniting Georg and Maria von Trapp, when it brought them together in a remake of the much-loved play *On Golden Pond*. Christopher Plummer, who remained prickly towards what he still called 'The Sound of Mucus', relished

511

tackling anew the challenges he had known as a young actor on television: 'There's something to be said about doing it live . . . It has more adrenaline to it.' But when Julie was asked why she should want to revisit the format that most actors of her generation had been so glad to abandon, she replied, 'We're both asking ourselves the same thing . . . '

The broadcast was directed by the play's author Ernest Thompson, in an uphill battle to usurp the memory of the 1981 film, for which Henry Fonda and Katharine Hepburn had won Oscars as Norman and Ethel Thayer — he hating his old age, she bucking him up. 'Yes (Sigh), I'll Watch It' was Anita Gates's weary heading in the *New York Times* on the day of the broadcast, Sunday 29 April 2001: 'The show is clearly a major event, being done live from a soundstage in Los Angeles with a multipart theatrical set, eight cameras and a seven-piece off-screen orchestra. But I feel so manipulated.'

On Golden Pond aired on CBS at nine o'clock that evening. The best report came to me from Sir Ian McKellen, who saw it in New York: 'It was lit as if it were outdoors — the scenery was a bit rocky — and Julie came down the path carrying a garden trug, and as she passed the cameraman, she said, 'How am I doing so far?' It was bliss! I sat through the whole thing, waiting for some other disaster to strike, which it didn't do — she was very good. But we rang friends in California, where it was being shown three hours later, and told them to watch out for the beginning.'

'The most scary thing I've done in thirty years,' was Julie's description. If nothing else, it had reacquainted her with Christopher Plummer, to the delight of millions.

★ ★ ★

Blake Edwards, meanwhile, had completed a script for a Broadway stage musical of *The Pink Panther*. His long-time associate producer Tony Adams had been venturing further into the world of theatre — but Blake, approaching his eightieth birthday, was wary, knowing that their previous show had not paid back its large costs: 'I can't afford to lose the money I did with *Victor/Victoria*.'

At this time, a musical version of Mel Brooks' film *The Producers* was shaping up for Broadway. Julie would later quote her favourite lines from it, bearing in mind her husband's investment on *Victor/Victoria*: 'The first rule is, never put your money in the show. The second is, *Never Put Your Money in the Show!*'

While in the throes of the lawsuit against her surgeons, Julie had spoken to Patrick Pacheco in *TV Guide* about the wear and tear sustained in any long marriage, and whether or not it was worth the effort. 'And in our case, it is worth it . . . Some days I want to kill him, and sometimes I look at him, so handsome, so loving and so amusing, and it's 'Ooohhh' all over again.'

And in 2002, on *Larry King Live* (a show that was very fond of Mr and Mrs Edwards), Blake revealed the sentiment that had helped them at

513

the outset of their life together: 'We didn't think it was going to last, so we might as well have a good time.'

As a vivid snapshot of what Julie had lived alongside for over thirty years — and why she called him Blackie — he described a day when he had climbed the hill of their Malibu estate, looked out at the Pacific and prepared to cut his wrists with a razor blade. His Great Dane had bounded up to him, yelping in the certain knowledge of what his master was about to do. Blake had locked him up, only to have his other dog, a retriever, run around him with a soggy tennis ball. Blake had tossed the ball over the cliff, and had promptly dislocated his shoulder. He had then decided not to kill himself that day — but, walking backwards over the razor blade in the grass, had cut his foot badly enough to end up in hospital in Malibu, shouting, 'Hurry up or I'm going to bleed to death . . .'

Julie had long regarded such stories with equanimity. More disturbing by far was the latest escapade of Blake's eldest grandchild. Twenty-six-year-old Kayti Edwards, it was announced in May 2001, would be seen baring her all in the October edition of porn king Larry Flynt's *Hustler* magazine. But what really hit the headlines was that she would be posing as one of her step-grandmother's most famous characters, Mary Poppins, with carpet bag, flower-sprigged hat, black boots . . . and very little else. A family friend was reported as saying, 'Julie is very upset at Kayti's decision to pose nude, to put it mildly. She has always been a wild girl, but this has pushed the tolerance of the family to breaking point.'

At the end of July, Kayti answered back: 'I'm a single mother. I'm studying to be a trauma nurse and I needed the money to finish university.' She would not have done the shoot, she declared, had her grandparents helped her out of debt: 'If Julie had forbidden me to do the pictures, I'd have replied, 'Give me $10,000 and I won't do them.'' Yet, even as Kayti was about to be displayed in *Hustler*, Julie could be seen on the big screen, grooming her fictional granddaughter to be a young lady.

On Sunday 29 July, *The Princess Diaries* had a gala children's premiere at El Capitan Theatre, Los Angeles. The following Thursday, at ten o'clock in the morning, Disney Studios officially named Soundstage 2 the 'Julie Andrews Stage'. Roy E. Disney, nephew of Walt and vice-chairman of the board, Dick Van Dyke and Mickey Mouse were in attendance at an event which seemed almost to set a seal of royalty on the studio, on the eve of Julie's return to the big screen as Dowager Queen of Genovia. After a summer of big-budget blockbusters aimed at male teenagers — sci-fi remakes and sequels such as *The Mummy Returns*, *Jurassic Park III* and *Planet of the Apes* — the long-ignored little girl market was about to come into its own.

The prediction for the opening on Friday 3 August was that *The Princess Diaries* would be popular, but not outstandingly so. The reviews were mediocre to poor. Susan Wloszczyna in

USA Today prophesied that the film 'will be adored by ten-year-old girls who think they're fourteen going on eighteen'. But Roger Ebert in the *Chicago Sun-Times* dismissed it as 'a march through the swamp of recycled ugly duckling stories, with occasional pauses in the marsh of sit-com clichés and the bog of Idiot Plots'.

Three days later, the cynics were confounded. Trade papers reported a 'major surprise': *The Princess Diaries* had exceeded the wildest hopes of Walt Disney Studios, taking third place in the box-office charts, with an opening weekend haul of $23 million. It proved, said the *Los Angeles Times*, that 'G-rated fare can play in the big leagues.'

'Who knows?' journalist Linda Gross had written of Julie Andrews, as long ago as 1974. 'She may be rediscovered in the future. She could be smashing playing grandmothers.' From a comparatively lowly budget of $26 million, *The Princess Diaries* would storm well above the $100 million mark by the end of September, making Julie's first real film since 1986 (*Relative Values* partially excepted) her most successful in decades — and the Hollywood sleeper hit of the year.

★　★　★

At nine o'clock on the morning of 11 September 2001, Julie received a telephone call on Long Island from Blake, who was in Los Angeles. 'Turn on your television,' he said. She did so

516

— and stood, watching the unfolding carnage in New York.

Just three days before, she had been announced as the only woman among the year's five Kennedy Center Honorees (alongside Jack Nicholson, pianist Van Cliburn, composer and producer Quincy Jones and opera legend Luciano Pavarotti) — evidence, yet again, that America had no intention of relinquishing its love for Julie Andrews. The honour, awarded for lifetime achievement in the performing arts, was the highest of its kind in the United States; bestowed over an entire weekend in Washington DC, the celebrations pushed tolerance for such events to the limit. But this year, they took on a special significance. It was underlined on Saturday 1 December at a State Department dinner, during which Secretary of State Colin Powell contrasted the recent atrocities of 9/11 with the work and spirit of those honoured, toasting Julie as 'an English rose that never withers and never pales'.

The following evening, the award ceremony took place in the Kennedy Center. Both President Bush and Vice-President Dick Cheney attended, appearing in public together for the first time since the horrors of September. Among those who serenaded Julie Andrews were Robert Goulet, Jeremy Irons and Carol Burnett, who ended the tribute with a song that continued to offer hope to audience and star:

My heart will be blessed with the sound of music,
And I'll sing once more.

At the beginning of 2002, tragedy struck Carol, with the death of her daughter Carrie from cancer at the age of thirty-eight. Carrie's godmother Julie Andrews knew more than ever how lucky she was to have Emma, who had always been 'such a trouper with it all', as she had once described her, and with whom her bond had only strengthened since the birth of Sam in 1996.

That March, mother and daughter made a big step forward in their writing ambitions, signing a publishing deal with HarperCollins to form a special imprint, The Julie Andrews Collection. Foremost among the titles would be the *Dumpy* series, sequels to the book that Julie, Emma and Tony had created together in 2000. With the book imprint compounding the huge and somewhat unexpected success of *The Princess Diaries*, Julie's profile in the children's marketplace had reached a new peak. So it was hardly surprising that Disney Studios called again.

Kay Thompson's artful 1950s *Eloise* books were to be made into children's dramas for ABC television's *Wonderful World of Disney*. The role on offer was that of Nanny, delegated to look after clever little six-year-old Eloise, who lives in the Plaza Hotel, Central Park South, while her absent parents dally with the jet set abroad. Julie once again faced the choice that had plagued her for forty years: whether or not to go back into the nursery.

Eloise's nanny had neither the crisp brightness of Mary Poppins nor the joyous abandon of Maria von Trapp. She was elderly, snippety

— and fat. Nevertheless, Julie decided to accept the third childminder role of her career. 'I may get it right this time,' she said, seeing a chance to rework the image. Wearing a straggly salt and pepper wig, frumpy clothes and a big false backside in the name of Art, she told Anita Gates of the *New York Times*, 'It's maybe the one role I've ever done where I actually look better at the end of the day.'

Eloise at the Plaza and *Eloise at Christmas* were shot back-to-back in New York (using the real Plaza Hotel) and Toronto. Filmed in 2002 and broadcast the following year during the Easter and Thanksgiving holidays, they were well received. Ten-year-old Sofia Vassilieva made a remarkably exact Eloise. Julie, nominated for a 2004 Emmy as Outstanding Supporting Actress for *Eloise at Christmas*, was on a roll.

★   ★   ★

Three years earlier, had anyone told Julie Andrews that at the end of 2002 she would be on the road on a concert tour, she would not have believed it. Yet here she was, headlining *A Royal Christmas*, which kicked off a seventeen-day hike on 3 December, bringing Advent cheer to Michigan, Pennsylvania, Ohio, New England, Florida, New York State and Canada. The difference was, this time Julie was not singing. 'I'd like to make that very clear so that I don't fool anybody,' she said in November 2002, mindful of the lawsuit settlement two years earlier.

Instead, she would recite and attempt a degree of Rex Harrison-type delivery, accompanied by Christopher Plummer and Charlotte 'Voice of an Angel' Church. The sixteen-year-old songbird from Wales had sold almost ten million records, and her youthful career and stardom was compared to that of Julie Andrews — by the Dame herself. 'The difference is I did vaudeville and music halls,' said Julie. 'I think Charlotte's career is far more upmarket and certainly much more global.'

But arguably less disciplined, bringing to mind Barbara Andrews's edict: 'Just don't get a big head, because you could be out as quickly as you were in' — words that had always stayed with her daughter.

'I just adore Julie,' Plummer said. 'I've seen her at times over the years, not very much, but whenever we do meet, the years fall away and there's absolutely no strain.'

The stars were joined by 150 dancers, the Westminster Concert Choir and the Royal Philharmonic Orchestra. And, to the audiences' delight and surprise, Julie — very tentatively — began to sing again, in the last week of the tour adding her voice to 'Sunny Banks' and 'I Saw Three Ships' in Nassau, Albany and Boston — and automatically bringing the packed houses to their feet.

Something similar had happened earlier that year, on 20 June at the Samuel Goldwyn Theatre, Beverly Hills, during the *Centennial Tribute to Richard Rodgers*. The non-televised gala performance had been hosted by Julie, together with Rodgers' elder daughter Mary. After various live performances and film clips — including one of Maria on the Austrian hillside — the audience had been taken by complete surprise as Julie softly intoned the words to 'Do-Re-Mi' — in Japanese. She had then joined the massed ranks of cast members in 'Climb Ev'ry Mountain', before embarking on another solo, the first gentle, wistful strains of 'The Sound of Music'. The audience, naturally, had gone crazy.

A few days after the concert, Julie had revealed that — overseen by Dr Steven Zeitels of Harvard Medical School — she was to be a human guinea pig in the field of voice tissue repair. Man-made tissue was to be implanted in her vocal cords in a revolutionary $2.5 million biotechnology project. And, although it had been emphasised that the procedure could take years, Dr Zeitels had said, 'It will give her back the youthful power of her voice.'

★　★　★

At the start of 2003, the sixty-eight-year-old grandmother, who had so recently feared that a once-great career was coming to an end, declared herself 'busier than I have ever been'. The year ahead was practically bursting with commitments. Having returned to nannydom, she was now to resume her royal progress in *The Princess Diaries* 2. In England that summer, Dame Julie would visit Southampton to perform her most quasi-royal duty of all: launching a ship, Crystal Cruises' vessel *Serenity*. She would continue to work with Emma, preparing The Julie Andrews Collection for its print inception that September. And yet, and yet . . .

'I really do miss singing,' she told her old friend Army Archerd for *Variety*. If she was precluded, for now, from exercising her love for musical theatre as a performer, there was another way. 'One director in the family is enough,' she had often quipped, when asked about ambitions in that direction. But, said her daughter and son-in-law, if she were ever to try, 'What better place than Bay Street?'

In January 2003, Steve and Emma Hamilton and Sybil Christopher announced that Julie Andrews would be making her directorial debut at the Bay Street Theatre the following season — with a revival of the very show in which a nineteen-year-old ingénue had first made such an impression forty-nine years earlier: *The Boy Friend*. 'I'm going places I never thought I'd go,' Julie admitted, but added, 'I'm in friendly hands.' She even had the services of Tony Walton as designer — calling her ex-husband 'a lovely human being, and of course, one of the hottest stage and film designers around'. Tony's career had indeed been spectacular. He had won three Tonys, an Emmy and a 1979 Oscar for Bob Fosse's *All That Jazz*, one of the few successful musical films of that period. What with the book imprint and now the show, Emma was seeing her parents together more than at almost any other time in her life.

The author of *The Boy Friend* delayed his trip

from London until the show had settled down after opening in August. 'Julie really was terribly nervous to make sure it had been running for some time,' Sandy Wilson told me. When he arrived, however, there was a crisis that had nothing to do with the show. Emma was being rushed to hospital by Steve, to give birth to her second child, a little girl called Hope, on 17 August.

The following night, when things were a little quieter, Gen Walton — who always referred to Julie as 'our ex' — led Wilson upstairs after the show to a rehearsal room. 'And there she was on her own,' Wilson told me, 'and we fell on each other's neck. I didn't know whether to laugh or cry, so I did both.' And, as of old, 'I noticed her tremendous control; she *notices*, not just herself, but everything.'

'This is lovely,' said Linda Winer in her *Newsday* review of *The Boy Friend*, calling it 'a summer lark with the potential to be considerably more', and crediting Julie with having 'a firm grasp on the sweet foolishness of the show'. But, for the show to move on, the big guns would need to fire a salvo of praise, and this was not forthcoming from the *New York Times*. In words that would have perturbed the original director Vida Hope, critic Alvin Klein considered the company to be 'teetering precariously on the edge of overplaying, at times falling over'. And Meredith Patterson, while boasting the same spring-clear voice and clear-eyed sincerity of her director, bore 'the unreasonable weight of what must be called Ms Andrews' part'.

That summer, Julie had spent a few days in

completing an even older circle, one that had begun its long arc over fifty years earlier. In 1952, she had dubbed the title role in *The Singing Princess*. In 2003, she was doing something similar, albeit moving up a rung. Dream Works Studios had asked her to join the company of *Shrek* 2, the sequel to the massively successful 2001 animated film, providing the voice of Queen Lillian, mother to Princess Fiona (dubbed by Cameron Diaz) who is loved by the shy green ogre Shrek.

There was another parallel with Julie's past. Once again, she was working with some of the finest comedians of the day. The first *Shrek* film had employed the voices of Mike Myers in the title role and Eddie Murphy as his good friend Donkey among the creatures of the kingdom of Duloc. The sequel, once again using Myers and Murphy, now added John Cleese (King Harold), Jennifer Saunders (the wicked Fairy Godmother) and Joan Rivers (Joan Rivers). Julie needed to do little but play the straight man — something she had done so often as a young girl — in her role of anxious consort and mother, upbraiding her spouse with such lines as 'Don't be such a drama king!'

It was a solitary business — far removed from the camaraderie of her usual film sets. Speaking at the Cannes Film Festival, where *Shrek* 2 had its premiere in May 2004, she admitted, 'The worst thing is to be alone, because we normally get to work and bounce off each other.' But the star who had once had a soft spot for the *Monty Python* team had not been totally isolated. 'I had just one day with John Cleese. I was one of the lucky ones as the others were mostly alone. We had a wonderful afternoon — we laughed, talked a lot and drank lots of cups of tea, being British.'

In November, happy to maintain screen queen status a while longer, she started filming *The Princess Diaries 2: Royal Engagement*. The same director and much of the supporting cast were on hand again — to watch and listen as Julie sang once more. 'Your Crowning Glory' was sculpted to what she called her 'five bass notes' and she spoke-sang it with the young rock singer Raven, being very careful not to push her voice to the limit. Nonetheless, the film's musical supervisor Dawn Soler stated that she had seen crew members with tears in their eyes, adding, 'She nailed the song on the first take.'

★ ★ ★

By the end of December 2003, Julie was back on *Larry King Live*, to plug a new book, *Simeon's Gift*, a medieval tale of a wandering minstrel — and the second and third dump truck chronicles (*Dumpy Saves Christmas* and *Dumpy and the Firefighters*), illustrated again by Tony Walton. Quite how Blake Edwards reacted to his wife working so closely with her first husband was politely explored. He did not mind, she averred.

'A little pause there,' said Larry King.

'A little, slight pause,' replied Julie, gently closing the subject down, 'but I think, when all is said and done . . . he doesn't mind.'

She discussed further plans for *The Boy Friend* and the filming of *The Princess Diaries* 2 — calling to mind, as ever, the little girl from Walton-on-Thames who had always known how to 'get on with it', and whose philosophy had long been the same: 'Some people regard discipline as a chore. For me, it is a kind of order that sets me free to fly.'

19

GRANDE DAME

'There's a lot of life in the old girl yet'

— Dame Julie Andrews

In the late 1990s, far from the bright lights of Broadway and the high-rise offices of Hollywood, a Scottish amateur choir would show up one afternoon a week at the Glasgow Film Theatre (not, as urban myth later had it, a retirement home in Inverness). Singing along to the matinee screening of an old musical film, the choir would distribute song sheets, so that other members of the audience might join in some of the numbers. Working with the Glasgow Film Theatre in 1998 was a young man named Robin Baker. And, observing the event, one of the most successful marketing gimmicks of the following decade was born in his mind.

From Glasgow, Baker and his colleague Briony Hanson took the concept of a subtitled musical to the London Lesbian and Gay Film Festival, pitching the idea as a large-scale participatory experience. And, to Baker, there was only one choice of film: *The Sound of Music*. He commissioned a colleague to transcribe the lyrics of all the songs — including the nuns' chants — to be projected on to the

527

screen over the film itself.

On Sunday 18 April 1999, *Sing-a-long-a Sound of Music* had its world premiere at the National Film Theatre, London. 'There were queues of people in dirndls around the block,' Baker told me. But it was the audience reaction, from the moment that Julie Andrews was revealed on screen, which pleased him most. 'They started singing in a beautiful way, investing in the emotion of the piece — it is camp, but it is very emotional — almost in hushed reverence.'

In the interval, there was a fancy-dress competition. 'I had a friend dressed up (in curtains) as the compère, Candy von Floss, and she announced the winner — a *real* nun from south-east London. So many people have said to me, 'It was the most enjoyable evening of my life'.'

Baker then went on holiday to India — and by the time he got back, the idea had been appropriated. The Prince Charles Cinema in the West End of London had started to run the subtitled film as a regular event from August of that year. 'Boo the Baroness! Hiss the Nazis! Cheer Julie!' read the poster, and with the lyrics bouncing along the bottom of the screen, karaoke style, the level of audience participation soon knew no bounds.

By August, *Sing-a-long-a Sound of Music* had become a phenomenon. Film critic Anthony Lane reviewed it, as objectively as he could without missing the point, for the *New Yorker* magazine, calling the subtitling of the Latin chants 'the one work of unquestionable genius that I encountered last year'. And the fancy-dress contestants took his breath away:

There were Nazis, naturally . . . plus a load of people who looked like giant parcels. I didn't get it. 'Who are they?' I said to a nun who was having a quick cigarette before the film. She looked at me with celestial pity and blew smoke. 'Brown Paper Packages Tied Up with Strings,' she replied. I am relieved, on the whole, that I missed the rugby team who piled into one screening as Girls in White Dresses with Blue Satin Sashes; on the other hand, it is a source of infinite sadness to me that I wasn't at the Prince Charles when a guy turned up in a skin-tight, all-over body costume in bright yellow, as Ray, a Drop of Golden Sun.

Its lunatic success was soon duplicated in cities as far apart as New York, San Francisco, Sydney and Amsterdam. At first, the laughter remained affectionate. Dena Hammerstein, the widow of James Hammerstein, Oscar's younger son, watched it with Ian McKellen, who told me: 'We went professionally to see whether the film emerged intact, and we felt it did. It has an extraordinary hold on people's affection. People are not mocking it at the singalong — they are indulging . . . I hope Julie Andrews gets a lot of pleasure out of the fact that she's still *au courant*, really.'
But, as the months drew on, the event

appeared to become rather more cynical, throwing into doubt whether the film as originally made would survive. In London, *Sing-a-long-a Sound of Music* displaced *The Rocky Horror Show* as the biggest cult of its kind, a not altogether comfortable achievement.

Back in Hollywood, the cash flowed in anew, to a surprised and delighted Twentieth Century Fox — but it did not flow to the instigator of the idea. 'I haven't made a cent out of it,' Robin Baker told me. He was in good company. When I asked Julie about the proceedings, she said, with a rather forced laugh: 'I've heard. I'm staggered. I wonder who gets the residuals; that's all I can think of. Certainly not me . . . '

It was doubtful if Julie liked the idea in any case. 'I just didn't get it for a while,' she told the *Irish Times* in December 2001. 'I wondered what it meant. And then I had an X-ray on my ankle a few months ago in New York. The doctor, who was a middle-aged man, very proper, said, 'I went to the *Sing-a-long-a* the other night, and had such a good time.' I said, 'You went to that? Would you mind telling me why? What is it?' He said, 'Julie, I can't tell you; it is such a catharsis to get up and yell and scream and sing.''

She was unlikely ever to see it herself, however. 'It's a little difficult for me to show up at one of those things.' She knew that her presence was liable to start a riot. 'I thought maybe I could go along in my Elizabeth Taylor wig or something. But then if I was spotted I'd really be in trouble.'

In the United States of America, Dame Julie

Andrews now commandeered virtually regal status — compounded by her recent back-to-back monarchs in *The Princess Diaries* and *Shrek 2*. The image was in fact somewhat illusory, given the influence over the years her adopted country had had on her. 'Don't show me how profitable it will be to fall in love with you,' she had once told James Garner on screen. 'Don't Americanize me.' The Americanization of Julie, however, had been a mutually beneficial arrangement, established over decades and now indelible.

She would be forever clear-toned and fresh-faced, 'carrying my country with me', but her diction now told a different story. The letter 'T' had long been elided into a softer 'D', 'delighded' being a favourite word. It was hard to tell if she enjoyed 'writing' or 'riding'. And — horrors! — she was often heard to drop in the odd 'gotten'. In truth, her transatlantic inflection, with touches of Walton-on-Thames, had fallen rather short of the precision for which Professor Higgins (and Madame Stiles-Allen) might have hoped.

If Julie's accent had never been quite as perfect as Americans would have it, they continued to love it regardless, although she modestly put this down, as always, to native generosity: 'They are so fond of anything English: Jane Austen and Shakespeare . . . they were marvellous to us in the war.'

When I asked her if the British had been less appreciative, of both Americans and herself, she answered, 'Well, yes, I didn't want to say that . . . ' Even then, she pulled herself up. 'Perhaps it's not so bad now.' But there was no doubt that, in the land of her birth, there remained a certain ambivalence towards this most ambivalent of stars.

On one hand, in the 2002 initiative by BBC2 to find *The 100 Greatest Britons*, Dame Julie Andrews was voted into fifty-ninth place, sandwiched between Freddie Mercury and Sir Edward Elgar, the only actress in the list. On the other hand, a small British comedy named *Chunky Monkey*, filmed two years earlier by Greg Cruttwell (son of the former principal of the Royal Academy of Dramatic Art), showed how tortuous the legend of *The Sound of Music* could be made to appear.

Costing a mere £160,000, it depicted a sad suburban soul with a 'number one ambition in life': to smear Julie Andrews with Ben & Jerry's Chunky Monkey ice cream and get her to sing 'The Sound of Music', before having sex. 'I wanted to write something that amused me,' said the first-time director, but others failed to share his sense of humour.

Chunky Monkey was, in Cruttwell's words to me, 'stymied for three years' with fivefold threats of litigation: from the creators of the children's television cartoon *Chunky Monkey*, from Unilever over the ice cream brand name, from the Rodgers and Hammerstein Estate over the use of 'The Sound of Music' for what it called a 'depraved film', from the licensors EMI, realising the song catalogue might be withheld from them — and finally from Julie Andrews, through Steve

Sauer, her manager in Los Angeles. 'His client considered this a defamatory act,' Cruttwell told me. 'We did try and point out however that it's really quite the contrary — the character in the film loves Julie Andrews so much that once a month a friend dresses up as Julie, they take the ice cream out of the freezer, she limbers up her vocal cords, and, well . . . it gets a little messy.'

In 2004, *Chunky Monkey* eventually stumbled into the light. Billed as 'The film corporate giants tried to stop you from seeing', it was probably less offensive than its headline-grabbing publicity might have wished it to be, but was nevertheless evidence of Britain's schizophrenia about Julie Andrews. The *Encyclopaedia of British Film*, in its 2005 edition, found it almost as hard to be polite: 'It seems a shame that she, quintessentially English, has wasted herself on many feeble American films, when she could have found feeble films at home, and 'home' needed her more.'

★ ★ ★

The Dame knew where she was wanted. In America, she and her husband continued to live between their Brentwood home in California and their house in North Haven, Long Island, near her daughter and son-in-law Emma and Stephen Hamilton. And they would always have the chalet in Switzerland, where Peter Sellers had once taken photographs on the balcony overlooking the valley, of Mr and Mrs Edwards with their two young adopted daughters.

All their children other than Joanna, the younger of the adopted girls, were now themselves parents. There were seven of the new generation. Jennifer — whose daughter Kayti was herself mother to a girl, Shaely, and a boy, Kaden — had had another daughter, Hannah Schneider. Geoffrey was father to Isabelle and Hank, and Amy had given birth to a baby boy, Max, by her marriage to rock musician Lauren Scheff. Of Emma's two children, Sam and Hope, the former continued to be the sounding board for the *Dumpy* books, which rolled off the press for The Julie Andrews Collection.

Mother and daughter had also written other books, such as *Dragon, Hound of Honour*, which combined Julie's love of animals with her zest for storytelling — in this case, a mystery set in medieval France. Referring to the agonies of her mother's throat operation, Emma had told her: 'Mom, now you have a new voice in which to express yourself.'

'I am well aware that in certain circles I am perceived as a 'celebrity author', especially in my own country, and I have to admit this irritates me,' Julie would later say, in a speech to the Texas Library Association. 'If you think about it, the books I write for children are really an extension of my singing voice.' And, calling to mind her much-loved singing teacher Madame Lilian Stiles-Allen, she would add, 'A beautiful melody is always a thrill . . . but if the words aren't there to sell the song, nothing happens. For me, it has always been about the words.'

Emma was now editorial director of the imprint, which included other authors' work, old and new, that she and her mother felt worthy of notice. One long-lost work, in particular, gave Julie Andrews pleasure in reprinting: *The Little Grey Men* by 'BB'. 'That book probably influenced me as much as anything,' said Julie, remembering her nature-loving father, whom she had so respected, giving it to her as a little girl in Walton-on-Thames.

A fortnight before Christmas 2003, at the Edwards' Brentwood home, Blake picked up the telephone. He listened for a few moments before handing the receiver to his wife, who whooped with delight. It was Frank Pierson, president of the Academy of Motion Picture Arts and Sciences, ringing to say that Blake had been chosen to receive an honorary Oscar 'in recognition of his writing, directing and producing an extraordinary body of work for the screen.'

Julie's award for *Mary Poppins* had stood for almost forty years without a mate. 'Thank God we can now balance the bookcase,' said Blake.

Having slipped on a rug some weeks before, Blake hobbled along on a cane to the Academy Awards ceremony the following February. But when it came to the presentation, he zoomed on stage in an electronic wheelchair during comedian Jim Carrey's introduction, grabbed the award as he zipped past, and crashed through the plasterboard wall on the other side of the stage before rebounding for his speech: 'My mother thanks you, my father thanks you

— and the beautiful English broad with the incomparable soprano and the promiscuous vocabulary thanks you.'

The English broad laughed up at the man to whom she had been married for thirty-four years. Wearing a long white tailored gown, her hair augmented by a chignon, she looked delighted to be there in a purely supportive capacity for once, with the reasonable expectation that her own career was about to consolidate the success of *The Princess Diaries* with the release of two new films that year.

Shrek 2 was to be unveiled at the Cannes Film Festival on 15 May. Flying to the south of France, Julie was joined by most of her voiceover co-stars on the animated picture, including Mike Myers, Cameron Diaz and Eddie Murphy, as well as two non-comedians who gave surprisingly hilarious turns: Antonio Banderas as Puss in Boots and Julie's erstwhile child-fan Rupert Everett as the dastardly Prince Charming

Four days later, the film went on release in America — and was subject to an almost immediate stampede for tickets, adding up to one of the most phenomenal openings in cinema history. In its first week, the film took $130 million; by the end of the month, it had doubled the figure. Three months later, it had earned over $430 million, making it the third highest grossing film of all time in America. Worldwide, it became the seventh biggest film ever — and, overall, the most successful film of 2004.

Its press was ecstatic, particularly for Mike Myers, Cameron Diaz and Antonio Banderas (who credited his characterisation to one of his mother-in-law Tippi Hedren's cats). The *Washington Post* called the film 'a sequel that is better and funnier than the original, which, as you may recall, was pretty darn good and funny to begin with', and complimented the cast behind the cartoons: 'Sure, the animation work is great, but it's the actors and their subtle, complex vocal performances that make us care about these fairy-tale characters.'

USA Today considered that 'John Cleese and Julie Andrews are pitch-perfect as the royal couple who are taken aback when they learn that their princess has married an ogre and become one, too.' And, while few would pay money to see *Shrek 2* for Julie's contribution alone, it was highly gratifying to be part of so successful an enterprise. 'It's done wonders for my standing with my grandchildren,' said Julie.

Her luck was to hold with her second film of the year, *The Princess Diaries 2: Royal Engagement*, in which the press was keen to herald another comeback — that of her voice. The star demurred. 'I do a little speak-singing in *Princess Diaries 2*,' Nancy Mills for the New York *Daily News* reported her as saying, 'but the song was pitched very low for me . . . I wish I could call it singing. I don't want to mislead anyone.'

And, interviewed the following month in London by Michael Parkinson on his ITV chat show, Julie concluded, finally, that any work to restore her throat, such as that suggested by Dr Zeitels two years earlier, was now too late: 'I'm not really going to be singing again, I don't think, sadly . . . I think it was too damaged.'

Despite the legal ramifications of her lawsuit settlement four years earlier, the question remained as to how much more singing could realistically have been expected of Julie Andrews. Seeing and hearing her in *Victor/Victoria* on stage, it was obvious to me that the long, white voice of yesteryear had contracted even before the operation. Her technique remained immaculate — but her instrument could not remain unaffected by the passage of time.

It could be argued that the surgery was intended to repair this. The other issue, however, was more serious for her. On winning so substantial a sum of money for 'the loss of her voice', as her solicitors argued, it was dangerous to see her musical utterances — however limited those might be — referred to in print as 'singing'. She had joined Michael Crawford in a few bars of 'The Rain in Spain' during a PBS *Great Performances* broadcast at City Center, New York in 2000. She had appeared in the Richard Rodgers tribute in 2002. She had been heard to intone during the tour of *A Royal Christmas*. Each time, her efforts had been lauded as tantamount to vocal restoration. And now, the song in *The Princess Diaries* 2.

The sequel received the same tone of reviews as its predecessor. 'Anne Hathaway and Julie Andrews again star,' said the *Boston Globe*; 'the only things missing are a script, a pulse, and a reason why.' But *Premiere* magazine admitted, 'Softies like me would probably be satisfied to watch Julie Andrews change the tires on a Volvo for two hours.'

Variety liked the stars: 'Hathaway once again demonstrates engaging charisma and a flair for physical comedy . . . Andrews radiates class, compassion and worldly wisdom with effortless élan.' But, as to the film: '*The Princess Diaries 2: Royal Engagement* is too blandly insubstantial to expand its appeal beyond its target demographic. Even so, Disney stands a reasonably good chance of generating respectable late-summer B.O.'

Variety was right. Despite the yawns from most major critics, the film opened strongly and ended the year by making just under $100 million, a remarkable feat for a film so heavily geared towards no one but small girls.

'I'm so hugely thrilled that I keep being allowed to play in all these wonderful sandboxes,' Julie told CBS news. 'A little child came up to me the other day with her mother. And her mother said, 'Do you recognise this lady?' And the child looked at me and the mother said, '*Mary Poppins*,' and the child said, 'Yeah.' 'And *The Sound of Music*.' And the little girl said, 'Yeah.' And then she said, '*The Princess Diaries*,' and she went, 'Oh, cool!' And it just struck me so hilarious that I seem to have book-ended my career with all these wonderful family movies.'

As if to emphasise the point, on Tuesday 30 November, she was reunited with Dick Van Dyke and Glynis Johns to celebrate the fortieth anniversary of *Mary Poppins* with a screening of the film at El Capitan Theatre, Hollywood.

'I cannot believe that it's forty years since we

started to make that movie,' was Julie's impression. 'The thing that staggers me is how good all the special effects are . . . You don't see a single chink that doesn't work. There's not a crack in the armour anywhere.'

Very sadly absent was Matthew Garber, Michael Banks in the film, who had died in 1977, aged just twenty-one, of pancreatic disease. But Karen Dotrice, his screen sister, was there, joking of Julie: 'She swore a lot and smoked back then.'

'I never smoked,' said the Oscar-winning star. 'Maybe the occasional four-letter word every once in a while . . . '

Only four months later, she was in London to witness the realisation of a dream of Sir Cameron Mackintosh (producer of her 1993 stage show *Putting It Together*) to bring *Mary Poppins* to the stage. The musical, co-produced by the theatre division of Disney Studios, with a script by Julian Fellowes and extra songs by the British team of George Styles and Anthony Drewe, had received splendid reviews on its premiere the previous December. Dame Julie was assured of a right royal welcome, on 17 March 2005, at a charity performance to benefit, among others, the international relief agency Operation USA (formerly Operation California), for which she continued to work so hard.

From the circle, I could see Julie looking up with pleasure from her box as Mary Poppins, played by Laura Michelle Kelly, drifted over the heads of the audience at the end of the show. Joining the cast on stage at the curtain call, she enthused unreservedly: 'Can you imagine the joy and memories that this has brought back to me? I've been so delighted to see what everybody has done with this lovely piece, and it's a little bit of the old and a lot of the new and I think it's great.'

Back in California, the star was still working for the Mouse House, turning up for the fiftieth anniversary celebrations of Disneyland on 5 May. As the so-called ambassador for the event, Julie was connected by a live video facility to other Magic Kingdoms on three continents, to celebrate the refurbished theme parks, under the heading 'The Happiest Homecoming on Earth'. To Disney, Mary Poppins had never really gone away.

★   ★   ★

In 2004 Julie fulfilled a project dear to her heart, when she hosted a six-part documentary series for PBS television, titled simply *Broadway — The American Musical*. Filmed at the Shubert Theatre on West 44th Street, the series chronicled the century-old history of the musical genre — what might truly be called America's national theatre — beginning with the early vaudeville and minstrel shows, working through such key figures as Florenz Ziegfeld, George Gershwin, Rodgers and Hammerstein, Bob Fosse and Stephen Sondheim, ending with the hightech extravaganzas of the modern day.

Featuring old footage of theatre shows, interviews with artists and commentary from social historians, the mini-series aired from 19 to 21 October 2004. If it was in danger of falling between two stools — of being too esoteric for newcomers, while showing diehard fans little more than they already knew — the passion for the subject felt by its creators made it a moving and compelling piece of work. Somewhere in there was a young girl singing 'I Could Have Danced All Night'. And, for her elder self, the programme had been a labour of love.

At the Emmy Awards in 2005 — more than twenty years after her ABC television series — Julie won her second such trophy, as host of the Outstanding Nonfiction Series, along with her six producers. One of those, Michael Kantor, summed up the endeavour: 'There's no place in the world like Broadway — it's where the American dream is realised eight times a week.' And, in the summer of 2005, Julie returned again to the show that had first brought her to the Great White Way.

Although there had been some talk of her 2003 production of *The Boy Friend* making the journey from Bay Street Theatre to Broadway, it seemed more viable to take it on the road. The revival began with an extended run at the Goodspeed Opera House in East Haddam, Connecticut, where I saw its first performance on 8 July. Many of the Bay Street Theatre cast had been retained, but there was a new Polly in the charming, if slightly metallic, form of Jessica Grové.

Repeating his duties as the show's designer was Tony Walton, smiling broadly as ever. As in

2003, some of his inspiration for the French Riviera backdrops had come from the paintings of Raoul Dufy — Julie's idea. And there was no mistaking the tall, elegant woman in a white trouser suit who slipped into her balcony seat, just before the lights went down, to see how the show would be received away from her home base of Sag Harbor.

The audience lapped it up. A tiny incident, however, stuck in my mind. Towards the end of the show, one of the older actors stumbled on a step — causing the director to shoot out her hand, as if telling her children not to panic, her rictus-tight smile capturing how much she regarded her company as family.

Real-life family took priority, however. During previews, Julie made a round trip to see her brother John, who was very sick, in London. 'If the family is great, then I can embark on anything,' she had told *Vanity Fair*, while preparing for *Victor/Victoria* onstage ten years earlier, 'but if they're not great, then I can't concentrate on anything but trying to put it right.'

She was back in time for the press night on Wednesday 27 July, attended by Christopher Plummer, who lived not far away in Weston, Connecticut. He had also attended a gala in Julie's honour during rehearsals the previous month. There, he had delivered a comic ode to his former co-star, one that recalled Moss Hart seeing him as a possible replacement for Rex Harrison in *My Fair Lady* and then auditioning him for Lancelot in *Camelot*:

Opposite Guenevere and Eliza would have been such fun.
What did I get instead? For God's sake — a nun.

Reaction to the revival of *The Boy Friend* was courteous. 'The production is a delightful confection full of silliness, exuberance and style,' said *Variety*. 'But it remains to be seen if the show translates to larger stages . . . ' The *New York Times* was uncertain. 'As the years pass, spoofs become harder to recreate, at least without divine inspiration, which is not evident here,' wrote Anita Gates, who remarked that 'the production's real star attraction is Ms Andrews', by virtue of her name on the poster alone.

The six-month tour opened in Wilmington, Delaware, where the director celebrated her seventieth birthday on 1 October 2005. Eighty-three-year-old Blake Edwards, his black leather jacket a more accurate indicator of his feisty personality than his walking stick, was there to see his wife cut the giant cake, with the cast of *The Boy Friend* around her; fifty-one years earlier to the day, she had woken up as the newest star on Broadway in the same show, and had cooked bacon and eggs with Dilys Laye.

The tour took in Boston and Chicago (at City Hall, the mayor declared 15 November 'Julie Andrews Day') as well as South Carolina, Pennsylvania, Michigan, Wisconsin, Minnesota, Toronto and Denver, where it ended in early March 2006. In Toronto, reflecting on the show she called 'a lovely piece of lace', Julie spoke of the change in her career: 'I really felt that every instinct I ever had about the theatre was being employed when I was directing . . . Since I'm not singing these days, this is lovely . . . I had my wonderful moment with it and now it's somebody else's chance to do it.'

⋆ ⋆ ⋆

As Julie attained her three score years and ten, so *The Sound of Music* reached the grand old age of forty. Revenue from the *Sing-a-long* continued to gush as merrily as the gratitude of Twentieth Century Fox's new owner. 'Rupert Murdoch keeps thanking Bob,' the director's wife Millicent Wise told me. 'He said, 'If it hadn't been for *The Sound of Music*, we wouldn't have a studio.' ' And she mentioned a recent *Sing-a-long* at the Hollywood Bowl. 'They had almost 18,000 capacity. It has universal appeal; it's an amazing piece of work.'

Julie's explanation for its enduring popularity remained constant: 'It feels like a fresh breeze every time you see it. It's about joy, and I think everybody senses it.' But, she admitted, 'I don't think any of us who were involved in its creation could have ever anticipated its remarkable success.'

In the previous few decades, the film had been dropping down the list of all-time box-office champions. In the late 1970s, it even lost the distinction of being the highest grossing musical to *Grease*. But, when inflation was taken into account, *The Sound of Music* still ranked at the beginning of the new century as one of the most popular entertainments of all time — holding its place in the affections of a worldwide public.

The septet of children (who, long grown, still referred to their director as 'Mr Wise') had, like Julie, enjoyed no further recompense from the film, beyond their original pay and royalties from the album. In April 2003, the screen portrayers of Louisa and Marta von Trapp had joined forces to make a belated entry into *The Sound of Music* money market, by releasing a documentary of behind-the-scenes footage of 'America's favourite movie' for the Arts and Entertainment channel. But, it was alleged, the nun with the switchblade had withheld permission for her likeness to be used in either stills or film — having her own plans for a similar project.

'All of our families shot home movies when we were shooting the film and they're great to see,' Angela Cartwright (Marta) had said. Heather Menzies (Louisa) had been more mutinous: 'We do think we can still do this without Julie's input or approval. There's never really been a dialogue . . . We've just been blocked by the keepers of the moat.'

Two years later, however, all the leading players were joined in actively embracing its legend, any rancour forgotten (or at least stalled). '*The Sound of Music* is our home movie,' said Nicholas Hammond (Friedrich). And Debbie Turner (Brigitte) added: 'We're genuinely friends. We all had our little bumps in the road, maybe.'

Far from trying to escape Maria von Trapp as of yore, Julie Andrews now guarded the image fiercely, introducing the fortieth anniversary DVD by standing in front of a giant picture of her younger self in the Alps, with which Twentieth Century Fox had seen fit to cover one entire side of its high-rise car park. Even Christopher Plummer was reconciled to the film he had been wont to call 'The Sound of Mucus'. 'I was a terrible bore in the beginning,' he admitted, referring to his snobbery about the project, having played the great classical canon before being handed Captain von Trapp. 'But I did make my point, that I wanted the character improved.' Julie reiterated how anxious she had been 'about keeping the astringency in the story', something about which Plummer had worried almost from the point of signing his contract. Yet, while confessing a strong sympathy with W.C. Fields' comment about child actors, he admitted to having grown fond of his screen offspring, 'in the last analysis'. And, interviewed on the Internet by Amazon, Charmian Carr declared, 'I guess you could say that I learned about acting from Julie, and about the art of drinking good liquor from Chris — and am indebted to them both to this day.'

Viewed afresh, without subtitles, the film's unsung heroes turn out to be Ted McCord, the director of photography, and Eleanor Parker as the brittle Baroness. Yet above everything is the luminous truth and clarity of the film's star. '*The Sound of Music* was the actual naked Julie Andrews on the screen,' said Christopher

Plummer. 'If you know her as I do, she's just exactly like that.'

'She's a marvellous lady,' was Robert Wise's last comment to me. 'I love her.'

★   ★   ★

On 14 September 2005, the Oscar-winning director of *The Sound of Music* died at the age of ninety-one. Five weeks later, Julie and Blake suffered another loss, when their long-time business associate and friend Tony Adams died suddenly of a stroke, aged just fifty-two. 'We have known Tony for so many years,' read their statement; 'we felt he was our second son. He was a beloved, dear, trusted and talented friend.'

His widow, Anne Runolfsson, had been Julie's understudy from *Victor/Victoria*, the very show that he had been so instrumental in getting Blake and Julie to bring to Broadway. In many ways, it seemed the end of an era.

The previous year, I had approached the National Film Theatre in London with the idea of mounting a retrospective to the woman who remained Britain's most commercially durable female film star. The response was positive, and I set about choosing a programme of films that reflected the stages of her screen career. At the same time, I was keen to see if opinion, which had so often viewed her askance, had come full circle.

The answer came in the autumn of 2005, in a rush for tickets to the fortieth-anniversary screening of *The Sound of Music* (sans subtitles). Afterwards, the star in person took questions. Her responses were, almost to the word, the same as those I had heard her give many times before. What was different was the level of security that surrounded her, to the extent that the lobbies were completely cleared of people as she left the building (without signing autographs). I wondered why she should put herself through such a schedule, if it required so much mental and physical disassociation.

I noticed the same quality again in November 2006, when I met her for what would be the last time, at the London book signing for her highly successful children's story about a theatrical troupe of mice, *The Great American Mousical*. The seventy-one-year old grandmother had just given a lengthy interview for BBC Radio, but turned up as fresh as a daisy in a well-cut trouser suit, complemented by a long silk scarf. Giving every person in the long queue at least two minutes, she nonetheless gave off the faint impression of an automaton. But I realised that this had nothing to do with her age, and everything to do with the central thrust of her life — to 'get on with it'.

When I enquired about the progress of her long-promised autobiography, she smiled pleasantly and answered: 'It'll be a *little* time coming.'

Two days later, she was asked the same question on BBC Radio. 'I'm about two thirds of the way through it,' she replied. She confirmed that she was only writing about her young life — up to the time she went to Hollywood. 'I really want to write a little bit of theatre history, about the English days of vaudeville, which were really on the tail end of their life when I was touring around England.'

But, asked why it could not extend to the film years, she sounded tired. 'Give me a break — it's hard enough for me to write it to that point.'

Her children's stories seemed virtually to run off her fingertips. But she had been writing her own story for the last six years. Even restricting her canvas to her young stardom was liable to bring back the family spectres of thwarted ambition, alcoholism and poverty — possibly as painful to her now as they ever had been.

Listening to the interview, I pondered why she should be writing it at all if, as I surmised, she were to be so selective. She certainly did not need the money — although her earnings had always been another guarded secret. Julie Andrews had never made the *Sunday Times* Rich List of the wealthiest Britons, its compiler Philip Beresford told me in 2006: 'She's never been in the list. I'm not prepared to make a guesstimate.'

On a more spurious level, she had made several appearances on Richard Blackwell's annual Worst Dressed Women List. Her first entry had been in 1965, in sixth place. The following year, the 'Plain-Jane Pollyanna playing Peter Pan at half-mast' had climbed to second position. Julie finally hit the top spot in 1968, at precisely the point her career was slipping, as 'a Little Bo-Peep illustration for *True Love* magazine'. Her last appearance was in 1972,

Blackwell opining, 'She dresses like the kind of woman every man wants for his . . . maiden uncle.'

As in so many other respects, Julie was never going to be another Audrey Hepburn — but there was no reason why she should have been. And, at seventy-one, she still sported a figure that most women half that age would envy.

Her taste in fashion was always simple — trouser suits tailored plainly to the point of severity, with scarves to break the line. Her jewellery remained almost non-existent. Thankfully, the gold 'J' on a gold halter she wore through the 1970s had gone by the 1990s, but Julie would always retain the good gold watch on her slender wrist. Her earrings would stay large, tending — as with much of her jewellery — to the costume variety rather than rare stones.

Her complexion, always one of her best features, now owed as much to art as nature, but remained none the less impressive, close-pored and soft. 'I drink a great deal of bottled water,' she offered, by way of explanation. 'I have found that travelling as much as I do, my skin would often break out — depending on what the water was like in each place I visited — so I decided to drink only the purest water wherever I went. I do that religiously and I even make my tea with it.' The tea, as always, was good old British PG Tips.

Her eyes, however, were what stayed with me, when I took my last leave of her: blue as ever, true blue, as blue as the cornflowers of her Surrey youth.

Her politics were yet another subject never discussed — but I caught a glimpse of them once, in October 1989, having watched her collect her Lifetime Achievement Award from the British Academy of Film and Television Arts. Afterwards, at a party at the Waldorf Hotel, there was a big cake with the figure of Mary Poppins across it — over the top of which I spoke briefly to the star. Someone else was asking her, of all things, about whether or not she approved of Margaret Thatcher (then experiencing the start of the problems that would lead to her exit from office a year later). 'Yes,' said Julie, cautiously, 'I *think* I do . . . of course, I don't live here . . . '

She was always, from the start, fundamentally conservative, *good* — a word impossible to apply to many stars post-1960. Julie Andrews was the last of a long line of sweet-faced screen heroines, as Sheilah Graham wrote in her book *Scratch an Actor*, in an essay entitled simply 'The Iron Butterfly':

There is always a scrubbed young face that epitomises purity and sweetness on the screen. From Mary Pickford to Rin Tin Tin; Shirley Temple; Lassie; June Allyson; Debbie Reynolds, the eternal Girl Scout; freckled Doris; and now, Julie . . . The nice ladies of the screen are usually the hardest to know, and Miss Andrews is the woman nobody knows. She has worked all her life and never lived. She is cautious. Every action is controlled. Every word carefully weighed. She is encased in an iron sheath of charm that is impossible to penetrate. I have never been able to cut through the metal, and neither has anyone else, to my knowledge.

Picking up my can-opener, I hoped to do my best.

★　★　★

'Move over Julie Andrews, there's a new Maria whirling away on the mountainside.'

Thus declared the *Sun* newspaper on Thursday 16 November 2006. A new production of *The Sound of Music* had just opened at the London Palladium to glowing reviews, particularly for Connie Fisher, plucked from obscurity to don the mantle of Julie Andrews' most famous role.

The sense of déjà vu with which Julie saw, in her words to me, 'the body of work pull into focus,' was nowhere more apparent than in the stage recreations of her films. At the Tony Awards back in June 2002, the Broadway version of Julie's 1967 hit *Thoroughly Modern Millie* had picked up six trophies, including Best Musical and Best Actress in a Musical (newcomer Sutton Foster) for its run at the Marquis Theatre, where Julie had once been the tenant in *Victor/Victoria*. It had been the shape of things to come.

The plans of composer and producer Sir Andrew Lloyd Webber to revive *The Sound of Music* on the West End stage had been long in coming to fruition. In July 2006, he thought he had scored a coup by booking twenty-one year old film star Scarlett Johansson to play Maria. Her Hollywood people, however, were less than keen, allegedly exacting terms that made it impossible for a viable deal to be worked out.

Instead, Lloyd Webber signed up with BBC television to find his leading lady by prime time talent search, calling the programme *How Do You Solve a Problem Like Maria?* At the end of the ten-week contest, the Great British Public voted a twenty-three-year old with a toothy smile, nice voice and fierce ambition to be the new Maria. Connie Fisher from Pembrokeshire, Wales, quit her telesales job to fill not only Dame Julie's shoes as the postulant nun, but also her place on the very stage where she had starred in pantomime: the London Palladium.

Connie was in no doubt about the shadow in which she walked: 'Audiences have always commented on my Julie Andrews-like qualities both on and off stage,' she said, 'and I can't think of a more suitable role.'

Speaking of the workload ahead for his new star, Lloyd Webber commented rather tactlessly, 'We certainly do not want her ending up like Julie Andrews who strained her voice when young and who can no longer sing.' However, his concern seemed groundless, when Connie opened on 15 November to a wildly cheering audience, leading him to remark, 'I've never seen a response from the audience like it in my career.'

By strange coincidence, the very next night,

the Disney/Mackintosh production of *Mary Poppins*, starring Ashley Brown, opened at the New Amsterdam Theatre, Broadway. The reviews were mixed. In the *New York Times*, Ben Brantley headed his opinion with 'Meddler on the Roof': 'The operating philosophy, it would seem, is that a spoonful of spectacle helps the medicine go down.'

Whatever the level of success enjoyed by her successors, it seemed unlikely that any of Dame Julie's great roles would ever have her image erased from them, least of all the role that had so beatified her: Maria von Trapp.

★ ★ ★

Holiday Season, 2006: the age of the Internet, the television shopping channel — and Julie Andrews, whose brand name has rarely held such commercial value.

Down Broadway rolls the eightieth annual Macy's Thanksgiving Day Parade. Riding high, actually and metaphorically, is the star herself on the Mother Goose float. She smiles and waves as regally as ever, miming to her carefully delineated recording of 'The Show Must Go On', which she has intoned to mark the publication of *The Great American Mousical*.

Sitting beside her is Emma, who has seen her mother as the biggest star in the world, a triumphant survivor and — always — as Mum.

★ ★ ★

In late 2006, the Screen Actors' Guild in Los Angeles announced that Julie Andrews was to be honoured with a Lifetime Achievement Award on Sunday 28 January 2007. 'Julie seems genuinely touched and thrilled to be receiving an award from her fellow actors,' said SAG President Alan Rosenberg. 'I have assured her the honour is ours.'

Emphasising her regal aspect in her forthcoming, guaranteed smash hit, *Shrek the Third*, the Queen Mother of Hollywood would continue to accept the tributes that mark out her reign, making her acceptance speeches with the measured skill of an ambassador's wife.

As a little girl, Julie desperately wanted to please her parents and the stepfather whose surname she adopted. 'I've been racing all my life to catch up with myself,' she once said. The consummate professional, she knows now that whatever she does will always be held up as conforming to her image, or trying to break it. She cannot win. Or can she?

Dame Julie Andrews no longer needs to care what anyone thinks.

FILMOGRAPHY

AA: Academy Award **AAN:** Academy Award nomination **GG:** Golden Globe

Credited feature films *(roles played by Julie Andrews in italics)*

The Rose of Baghdad a.k.a. **La Rosa di Bagdad, The Singing Princess** Grand National Pictures, Italy 1949/UK 1952 (US 1967)
Producer and director Anton Gino Domeneghini
Princess Zeila
Co-starring (British voice-overs) Patricia Hayes, Stephen Jack, Howard Marion-Crawford

Mary Poppins Walt Disney, US 1964
Mary Poppins
Producer Walt Disney; director Robert Stevenson; screenplay Bill Walsh, Don DaGradi; song score Robert B. and Richard M. Sherman
Co-starring Dick Van Dyke, David Tomlinson, Glynis Johns
AA: Best Actress (Julie Andrews); Best Original Score (Sherman Brothers); Best Song 'Chim Chim Cher-ee' (Sherman Brothers); Best Editing; Best Special Visual Effects
AAN: Best Picture; Best Director (Robert Stevenson); Best Adapted Screenplay (Bill Walsh, Don DaGradi); Best Music Scoring (Irwin Kostal); Best Colour Cinematography; Best Colour Costume Design

(Tony Walton); Best Colour Art Direction; Best Sound
GG: Best Musical/Comedy Actress (Julie Andrews)

The Americanization of Emily reissued as **Emily** MGM/Filmways, US 1964 (1967)
Emily Barham
Producer Martin Ransohoff; associate producer John Calley; director Arthur Hiller; screenplay Paddy Chayefsky; score Johnny Mandel
Co-starring James Garner, Melvyn Douglas, James Coburn
AAN: Best Black/White Art Direction; Best Black/White Cinematography

The Sound of Music Twentieth Century-Fox, US 1965
Maria von Trapp
Producer and director Robert Wise; screenplay Ernest Lehman; original song score Richard Rodgers, Oscar Hammerstein II (additions Richard Rodgers, Saul Chaplin)
Co-starring Christopher Plummer, Eleanor Parker, Richard Haydn, Peggy Wood
AA: Best Picture; Best Director (Robert Wise); Best Editing (William Reynolds); Best Music Scoring (Irwin Kostal); Best Sound
AAN: Best Actress (Julie Andrews); Best Supporting Actress (Peggy Wood); Best Colour Cinematography (Ted McCord); Best Colour Costume Design (Dorothy Jeakins); Best Colour Art Direction
GG: Best Musical/Comedy Picture; Best Musical/Comedy Actress (Julie Andrews)

558

Torn Curtain Universal, US 1966
Dr Sarah Sherman
Producer and director Alfred Hitchcock; screenplay Brian Moore; additional dialogue Keith Waterhouse, Willis Hall; score John Addison; costumes Edith Head
Co-starring Paul Newman

Hawaii United Artists/Mirisch, US 1966
Jerusha Bromley Hale
Producer Walter Mirisch; director George Roy Hill; screenplay Dalton Trumbo, Daniel Taradash; score Elmer Bernstein
Co-starring Max von Sydow, Richard Harris, Jocelyne LaGarde
AAN: Best Supporting Actress (Jocelyn LaGarde); Best Score (Elmer Bernstein); Best Song 'My Wishing Doll' (Elmer Bernstein, Mack David); Best Colour Cinematography; Best Colour Costume Design (Dorothy Jeakins); Best Special Visual Effects; Best Sound
GG: Best Supporting Actress (Jocelyn LaGarde); Best Score (Elmer Bernstein)

Thoroughly Modern Millie Universal, US 1967
Emily Dillmount
Producer Ross Hunter, director George Roy Hill; screenplay Richard Morris; score Elmer Bernstein; scoring André Previn
Co-starring Carol Channing, James Fox, John Gavin, Beatrice Lillie, Mary Tyler Moore
AA: Best Original Score (Elmer Bernstein)
AAN: Best Supporting Actress (Carol Channing); Best Song 'Thoroughly Modern Millie' (Jimmy

Van Heusen, Sammy Cahn); Best Music Scoring (André Previn, Joseph Gershenson); Best Costume Design (Jean Louis); Best Art Direction; Best Sound
GG: Best Supporting Actress (Carol Channing)

Star! a.k.a. **Loves of a Star** reissued as **Those Were the Happy Times** Twentieth Century Fox, US 1968 (1969)
Gertrude Lawrence
Producer Saul Chaplin; director Robert Wise; screenplay William Fairchild; scoring Lennie Hayton; choreography Michael Kidd
Co-starring Richard Crenna, Michael Craig, Daniel Massey
AAN: Best Supporting Actor (Daniel Massey); Best Song 'Star!' (Jimmy Van Heusen, Sammy Cahn); Best Music Scoring (Lennie Hayton); Best Cinematography (Ernest Laszlo); Best Costume Design (Donald Brooks); Best Art Direction; Best Sound
GG: Best Supporting Actor (Daniel Massey)

Darling Lili Paramount, US 1970
Lili Smith/Lili Schmidt
Producer and director Blake Edwards; screenplay Blake Edwards, William Peter Blatty; song score Henry Mancini, Johnny Mercer; cinematography Russell Harlan
Co-starring Rock Hudson, Jeremy Kemp
AAN: Best Original Score (Henry Mancini, Johnny Mercer); Best Song 'Whistling Away the Dark' (Henry Mancini, Johnny Mercer); Best Costume Design (Donald Brooks, Jack Bear)

GG: Best Song 'Whistling Away the Dark' (Henry Mancini, Johnny Mercer)

The Tamarind Seed Avco Embassy/ITC, UK 1974
Judith Farrow
Producer Ken Wales; director and screenplay Blake Edwards; score John Barry
Co-starring Omar Sharif, Oscar Homolka, Daniel O'Herlihy, Anthony Quayle, Sylvia Syms

10 Warner Brothers/Orion, US 1979
Samantha Taylor
Producers Blake Edwards, Tony Adams; director and screenplay Blake Edwards; score Henry Mancini
Co-starring Dudley Moore, Bo Derek
AAN: Best Original Score (Henry Mancini); Best Song 'It's Easy to Say' (Henry Mancini, Robert Wells)

Little Miss Marker Universal, US 1980
Amanda
Producer Jennings Lang; director and screenplay Walter Bernstein; music Henry Mancini
Co-starring Walter Matthau, Tony Curtis

S.O.B. Paramount/Lorimar, US 1981
Sally Miles
Producers Blake Edwards, Tony Adams; director and screenplay Blake Edwards; music Henry Mancini
Co-starring Larry Hagman, William Holden, Robert Loggia, Richard Mulligan, Robert

Preston, Loretta Swit, Robert Vaughn, Robert Webber, Shelley Winters

Victor/Victoria MGM, UK 1982
Victoria Grant/Count Victor Grazinsky
Producers Blake Edwards, Tony Adams; director and screenplay Blake Edwards; song score Henry Mancini, Leslie Bricusse
Co-starring James Garner, Robert Preston, Lesley Ann Warren
AA: Best Original Song Score (Henry Mancini, Leslie Bricusse)
AAN: Best Actress (Julie Andrews); Best Supporting Actor (Robert Preston); Best Supporting Actress (Lesley Ann Warren); Best Adapted Screenplay (Blake Edwards); Best Costume Design (Patricia Norris); Best Art Direction
GG: Best Musical/Comedy Actress (Julie Andrews)

The Man Who Loved Women Columbia, US 1983
Marianna
Producer and director Blake Edwards; screenplay Blake Edwards, Milton Wexler, François Truffaut
Co-starring Burt Reynolds, Kim Basinger, Marilu Henner, Barry Corbin

That's Life! Columbia, US 1986
Gillian Fairchild
Producer and director Blake Edwards; outline screenplay Blake Edwards and Milton Wexler; score Henry Mancini

Co-starring Jack Lemmon, Chris Lemmon, Jennifer Edwards, Emma Walton
AAN: Best Song 'Life in a Looking Glass' (Henry Mancini, Leslie Bricusse)

Duet for One Cannon, UK 1986
Stephanie Anderson
Producers Yoram Globus and Menahem Golan; director Andrei Konchalovsky; play Tom Kempinski
Co-starring Max von Sydow, Alan Bates, Liam Neeson, Rupert Everett, Cathryn Harrison

A Fine Romance a.k.a. **Cin-Cin, Tchin-Tchin, A Touch of Adultery**
Silvio Berlusconi Communications/Castle Hill, France 1991
Mme Pamela Piquet
Producer Arturo La Pegna; director Gene Saks; screenplay Ronald Harwood
Co-starring Marcello Mastroianni

Relative Values Midsummer Films, UK 2000
Felicity, Countess of Marshwood
Producer Christopher Milburn; director Eric Styles; play Noël Coward
Co-starring Edward Atterton, William Baldwin, Colin Firth, Stephen Fry, Sophie Thompson, Jeanne Tripplehorn

The Princess Diaries Walt Disney, US 2001
Queen Clarisse Renaldi of Genovia
Producers Debra Martin Chase, Whitney Houston; director Garry Marshall; screenplay

Gina Wendkos
Co-starring Anne Hathaway

Shrek 2 Dream Works, US 2004
Queen Lillian
Producers Jeffrey Katzenberg, David Lipman, Aron Warner, John H. Williams; directors Andrew Adamson, Kelly Asbury, Conrad Vernon
Co-starring (voice-overs) Mike Myers, Eddie Murphy, Cameron Diaz, Antonio Banderas, John Cleese, Rupert Everett, Jennifer Saunders, Joan Rivers
AAN: Best Animated Picture; Best Song 'Accidentally in Love'

The Princess Diaries 2: Royal Engagement Walt Disney, US 2004
Queen Clarisse Renaldi of Genovia
Producers Debra Martin Chase, Whitney Houston; director Garry Marshall; screenplay Gina Wendkos
Co-starring Anne Hathaway

Shrek the Third DreamWorks, US 2007
Queen Lillian
Producers Andrew Adamson, Aron Warner, John H. Williams; directors Chris Miller, Raman Hui
Co-starring (voice-overs) Mike Myers, Eddie Murphy, Cameron Diaz, Antonio Banderas, John Cleese, Rupert Everett, Eric Idle, Ian McShane, Justin Timberlake